Understanding Futures Markets

THIRD EDITION

Robert W. Kolb

New York Institute of Finance

New York   London   Toronto   Sydney   Tokyo   Singapore

Library of Congress Cataloging-in-Publication Data

Kolb, Robert W.
  Understanding futures markets / Robert W. Kolb.—3rd ed.
    p.   cm.
  Includes bibliographical references and index.
  ISBN 0-13-928631-4
  1. Futures market—United States.   I. Title.
[HG6024.U6K66   1991]   91-20589
332.64'4—dc20   CIP

This publication is designed to provide accurate and authoritative information in regard to the subject matter covered. It is sold with the understanding that the publisher is not engaged in rendering legal, accounting, or other professional service. If legal advice or other expert assistance is required, the services of a competent professional person should be sought.

From a Declaration of Principles
Jointly Adopted by
A Committee of the American Bar Association
and a Committee of Publishers and Associations

© 1991 by Robert W. Kolb
Simon & Schuster
A Paramount Communications Company

Printed in the United States of America

10   9   8   7   6   5   4   3   2   1

To my mother,

Ruth Register Kolb

Preface

Understanding Futures Markets surveys the broad sweep of futures markets as they exist in the United States. In the last decade, U.S. futures markets have exploded in a flowering that continued through the 1980s and promises to grow to full maturity in the 1990s. New contracts have been introduced, and entirely new possibilities have been explored.

Almost all of this activity began as recently as 1973, with the introduction of futures contracts on foreign exchange. It was followed by the inception of interest rate futures contracts in 1975, stock index futures contracts in 1982, and options on futures contracts shortly thereafter. In many respects, these innovations in futures markets have influenced all financial markets. Stock market practice and the operation of many types of financial institutions have been changed in fundamental ways due to the new activity in futures markets. Even the older futures contracts, those on agricultural and metallurgical commodities, have been revitalized in the process. Today, for example, a strong market for energy futures has emerged.

This book attempts to cover all of these developments in a manner accessible to a wide range of readers. Yet the book offers an unparalleled breadth and depth of coverage. The mathematical demands placed on the reader are modest, yet sufficient mathematical detail is included to ensure a thorough treatment of pricing principles.

Realizing that not every reader will be interested in every aspect of the futures markets, the chapters are organized to facilitate access to specific futures markets. Where the book considers particular aspects of the market in detail, the material is broken into two chapters, one for the basics and a second for refinements. For example, Chapters 1 and 2 both explore the institutional features of futures markets. Chapter 1, *Futures Markets: Introduction*, presents the basic institutional background that is necessary for the development in subsequent chapters. Chapter 2, *Futures Markets: Refinements*, covers some seldom-explored institutional features of the market that are nonetheless critical for someone wishing to trade futures or to understand the markets at a deeper level.

Chapter 3, *Futures Prices*, develops the principles that govern futures prices. The Cost-of-Carry Model provides the framework for understanding the economic factors that govern futures prices. This chapter uses arbitrage arguments to show in detail how cash-and-carry and reverse cash-and-carry trading strategies regulate futures prices. Chapter 4, *Using Futures Markets*, considers how futures markets serve society and the way traders can use the markets. As the chapter explains, futures markets serve society by helping to disseminate information about the likely future direction of price and by providing a means for transferring risk.

Chapter 5, *Agricultural and Metallurgical Futures Contracts*, begins the exploration of specific markets. Because these commodities are so diverse, they illustrate many different principles involved in understanding futures markets. For example, Chapter 5 explains how the Cost-of-Carry Model provides a very good understanding of prices for precious metals, and it explains why adjustments to the model are necessary for other goods, such as grains.

Chapters 6-8 focus on interest rate futures, one of the most vibrant segments of the futures markets. Chapter 6, *A Bond Primer*, provides the background necessary to understand futures pricing and the use of interest rate futures in risk transference. For readers with a good grasp of investment principles, Chapter 6 may be read as a brief review of the most important points. Some readers will be able to skip Chapter 6 altogether. Chapters 7 and 8 focus on interest rate futures directly. Chapter 7, *Interest Rate Futures: Introduction*, covers the most important points about interest rate futures, including pricing and hedging. Chapter 8, *Interest Rate Futures: Refinements*, extends the discussion to consider the specialized issues necessary for a deeper understanding. With this division into two chapters, Chapter 7 gives a comprehensive grasp of interest rate futures and provides the background necessary for Chapter 8.

Chapter 9, *Stock Index Futures: Introduction*, and Chapter 10, *Stock Index Futures: Refinements*, divide the analysis of stock index futures into the general and the detailed. Chapter 9 covers all the basic issues in stock index futures, including pricing, hedging, index arbitrage and program trading. Chapter 10 explores much of the same territory, but with particular attention to the nuances. For example, Chapter 10 considers program trading in detail and explains some of the difficulties that make program trading much more difficult than it might at first appear.

Chapter 11, *Foreign Exchange Futures*, explores futures trading of foreign currencies. In a time when the international scene is becoming ever more important, the foreign exchange markets have been prospering, and they show promise of further development. The chapter begins with a background discussion of the principles of foreign exchange pricing, such as Interest Rate and Purchasing Power Parity. The analysis soon turns to foreign exchange futures themselves, including pricing issues and risk-transference techniques.

Chapters 12 and 13 both focus on options and options on futures. Chapter 12, *An Options Primer*, provides the necessary background for understanding options. The discussion focuses on the no-arbitrage conditions that govern option prices and includes an analysis of the Black-Scholes option pricing model. Relying on the background provided by Chapter 12, Chapter 13, *Options on Futures*, concentrates strictly on options written on futures contracts. The chapter covers a wide range of issues, such as American versus European futures option pricing, using futures options to create synthetic positions, and portfolio insurance with options on futures.

Improvements in the Third Edition

While attempting to maintain the virtues of previous editions, the third edition is greatly expanded and completely rewritten. Particularly important and entirely new features include:

♦   End of chapter questions and problems

♦   Much greater institutional detail on issues such as GLOBEX, dual trading, front running, the Chicago trials, and the struggle between the CFTC and the SEC

♦   Summary boxes to focus attention on key issues

♦   Research literature capsules to provide a highly accessible guide to the academic research on many issues

♦   A bibliography

All of these features are intended to make the book more useful to its diverse audience. First, the summary boxes help to focus the reader's attention on the truly important issues. For example, Chapter 3 on pricing contains many summary boxes to illustrate the arbitrage bounds that result from the Cost-of-Carry Model. Second, the literature summary boxes quickly summarize the research on a particular issue. As an example, the research literature capsule on normal backwardation (Chapter 3, p. 126) captures the key results of 13 different studies. I believe that these research capsules will be very valuable both to readers approaching the futures market for the first time and to readers well acquainted with the market. Finally, Chapter 2 contains almost entirely new institutional material that is extremely current. I hope that exploring the institutional features of the market in detail will bring the market closer to the student and provide a glimpse into the inner workings of futures trading.

Acknowledgments

In writing a book of this type, one must rely on a large set of one's colleagues. As the book appears in successive editions, my debt of thanks becomes ever more extensive. I would like to thank all of the following people for their comments and suggestions for improvement:

Raj Aggarwal	*John Carroll University*
Warren Bailey	*Ohio State University*
Laurence Blose	*Kent State University*
Nusret Cakici	*Rutgers University*
Scott Chambers	*New Mexico State University*
Jack S. K. Chang	*California State University at Los Angeles*
Raymond Chiang	*University of Miami*
Pat Clarke	*University of Massachusetts*
Roger Dahlgran	*University of Arizona*
David Dubofsky	*Texas A&M University*
Paul Fackler	*North Carolina State University*
Dan French	*Texas Christian University*
Hung–Gay Fung	*University of Baltimore*
Gerald Gay	*Commodity Futures Trading Commission and Georgia State University*
Nicholas Gressis	*Wright State University*
G. D. Hancock	*University of Missouri at St. Louis*
Mahamood Hassan	*California State University at Fullerton*
Shantaram Hegde	*University of Connecticut*
Gary D. Koppenhaver	*Iowa State University*
A. G. Malliaris	*Loyola University of Chicago*
Timothy A. Manuel	*University of Wyoming*
James A. Overdahl	*U.S. Securities Exchange Commission*
Ramon Rabinovitch	*University of Houston*
Alan Tucker	*Temple University*
William J. Wilhelm	*Boston College*
Shee Q. Wong	*University of Minnesota at Duluth*

Special thanks are due to a number of other people as well. Andrea Coens and Ginny Guerrant did their usual excellent job of editing the manuscript, and Andrea helped with many of the design elements. Sandi Schroeder prepared the indexes. Linde Barrett oversaw the production of the book, while Kateri Davis, Val Rubler, and Diane Rubler contributed yeoman service with manuscript preparation. Sol Roskin and Robin Hood at the Hallmark Press were instrumental in quality control and ensuring that the production of the book stayed on schedule. Randy Jacques and Sivakumar Venkataramani read the entire manuscript and checked the accuracy of all computations.

I have used the various editions and manuscripts for the book in classes over the years. I would like to thank my students, who allowed me to experiment upon them with different versions of the manuscript. I believe the book is stronger for the comments it has received and from its class testing.

The preceding list of my debts is long. Producing a book is a long and involved process that requires the efforts of many. The contributions of everyone mentioned above helped to make the book possible. To all of the organizations and people who helped product the books I extend my sincerest thanks. Of course, I alone am responsible for any remaining deficiencies.

Contents

3   Futures Prices   76

4   Using Futures Markets   147

8 Interest Rate Futures: Refinements 337

9 Stock Index Futures: Introduction 412

10   Stock Index Futures: Refinements   444

13   Options on Futures   577

1

Futures Markets: Introduction

Introduction

This chapter lays the foundations that are essential to understanding how futures markets function. First, we explore the origins of futures markets. We focus on futures markets in the United States, where they are currently the most complete and provide the widest range of trading opportunities. Futures markets, as they now exist in the United States, are a fairly recent development, but understanding their origins helps us understand both the role these markets play today and likely future changes in that role. Forward contracting, however, has existed for many centuries. The ways in which futures markets differ from forward markets, the chapter's second topic, is important for understanding the techniques that can be applied in futures trading today.

The current organization of active futures markets is more important for the potential user than any historical account. Accordingly, the discussion soon focuses on organized futures exchanges as they exist today, with special emphasis on exchanges in the United States. Before entering the arena of the futures market, a prospective trader must understand the organizational form of the futures exchanges, the types of contracts that are traded, and the ways in which futures exchanges compete with each other for business.

The purposes that futures markets serve and the participants in the markets are then briefly characterized in this chapter. These themes are developed further in Chapter 4. Because regulation is important in determining whether futures markets can serve their social function and the interests of the trading parties, the chapter next discusses the regulatory framework, closing with a description of the taxation of futures markets.

Origins of Forward Contracting

A **forward contract,** as it occurs in both forward and futures markets, always involves a contract initiated at one time; performance in accordance with the terms of the contract occurs at a subsequent time. Further, the type of forward contracting to be considered here always involves an exchange of one asset for another. The price at which the exchange occurs is set at the time of the initial contracting. Actual payment and delivery of the good occur later. So defined, almost everyone has engaged in some kind of forward contract.

The following example illustrates a very simple, yet frequently occurring, type of forward contract. Having heard that a highly prized St. Bernard has just given birth to a litter of pups, a dog fancier rushes to the kennel to see the pups. After inspecting the pedigree of the parents, the dog fancier offers to buy a pup from the breeder. The exchange, however, cannot be completed at this time, since the pup is too young to be weaned. The fancier and breeder thus agree that the dog will be delivered in six weeks and that the fancier will pay the $400 in six weeks upon delivery of the puppy. This contract is not a conditional contract; both parties are obligated to complete it as agreed.[1] The puppy example represents a very basic type of forward contract. The example could have been made more complicated by the breeder requiring a deposit, but that would not change the essential character of the transaction. In this example, there is a buyer and a seller. The buyer is said to have a **long position,** while the seller has a **short position**. The act of buying is also called **going long,** and the act of selling is called **going short**. In order for the contract to trade, there must be a long position and a short position. When one trader buys and another sells a futures contract, the transaction generates one contract of trading **volume**.

Figure 1.1 shows the growth of trading volume on U.S. futures exchanges. From the very nature of the trading, there will always be an equal number of long and short positions outstanding. When a contract is first listed for trading, there has been no volume. Assume that the first trade is for one contract, leaving one trader long one contract and one trader short one contract. At this point, there is one open contract, or one contract is obligated for delivery. The **open interest** is the number of open contracts or the number of contracts obligated for delivery. (As we will see later in this chapter, most contracts do not actually lead to delivery.)

From the simplicity of the contract and its obvious usefulness in resolving uncertainty about the future, it is not surprising that such contracts have had a very long history. The origin of forward contracting is not clear. Some authors trace the practice to Roman and even classical Greek times. Strong evidence suggests that Roman emperors entered forward contracts to provide the masses

Figure 1.1
The Growth of Trading Volume on U.S. Exchanges

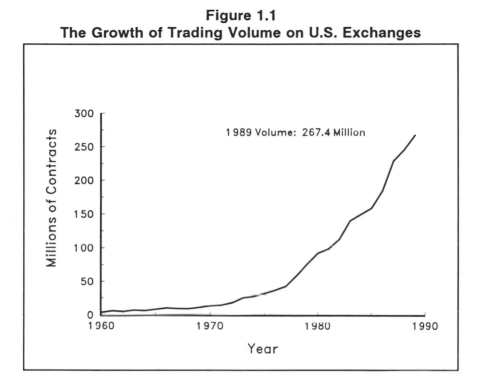

1989 Volume: 267.4 Million

with their supply of Egyptian grain. Others have traced the origin of forward contracting to India.[2]

While there may not be much agreement about the geographical origins of forward contracting, it is clear that trading originated with contracts similar in form to that of the puppy example. In fact, such contracts continue to be important today, not only among dog lovers, but in markets for credit and foreign exchange as well. Billions of dollars of foreign currencies change hands daily in a very sophisticated market that trades contracts for German marks and English pounds. These contracts are very similar in structure to the puppy contract. While these kinds of forward markets are very large and important, and while they resemble futures markets, this book primarily tries to develop an understanding of futures contracts and the organized exchanges where they trade. Comparing the structure of forward and futures contracts helps to illuminate the essential similarities and differences between these two kinds of markets.

Forward versus Futures Markets

While the historical origins of forward contracts are obscure, organized futures markets began in Chicago with the opening of the Chicago Board of Trade in 1848.[3] Despite the loss of records in the great Chicago fire of 1871, it appears that future contracts, as opposed to forward contracts, were being traded on the Board of Trade by the 1860s. Since then, the basic structure of futures contracts has been adopted by a number of other exchanges, both in the United States and abroad. It is important to understand how futures contracts differ from other forms of forward contracts, such as the puppy example. Forward contracts and futures contracts can be distinguished by several important features of futures markets: the existence of an organized futures exchange, the trading of standardized contracts, the role of a clearinghouse, the system of margins and daily settlement, the ability to close contracts easily, and the regulatory structure of the markets.

Main Distinctions Between Futures and Forward Contracts

1. Futures trade on organized exchanges.
2. Futures contracts have standardized contract terms.
3. Futures exchanges have associated clearinghouses to guarantee fulfillment of futures contract obligations.
4. Futures trading requires margin payments and daily settlement.
5. Futures positions can be closed easily.
6. Futures markets are regulated by identifiable agencies, while forward markets are self–regulating.

The Organized Exchange

Futures contracts always trade on an organized exchange. The organization of the Chicago Board of Trade, the oldest and largest futures exchange in the world, is typical. We will use its organizational features to illustrate the institutional characteristics of the other exchanges. The exchange is a voluntary, nonprofit association of its members.[4] **Exchange memberships,** also called **seats,** may be held only by individuals, and these memberships are traded in an active market like other assets. Table 1.1 shows recent membership prices for major futures and security exchanges in the United States. As the prices indicate, these seats are valuable capital assets. Also, the value of these seats fluctuates dramatically.

Table 1.1
Membership Prices of Major U.S. Futures Exchanges

Exchange	Membership Price
Chicago Mercantile Exchange	$380,000
Chicago Board of Trade	305,000
Commodity Exchange of New York	92,500
Coffee, Sugar, and Cocoa Exchange	85,000
New York Cotton Exchange	35,000
New York Mercantile Exchange	300,000

Source: *Futures and Options World*, October 1990. Prices represent last sale.

The prices of these seats depend mainly on recent and anticipated trading volume.[4]

Exchange members have a right to trade on the exchange and to have a voice in the exchange's operation. Members also serve on committees to regulate the exchange's operations, rules, audit functions, public relations, and legal and ethical conduct of members. Often administrative officers of the exchange manage the ordinary operation of the exchange and report to the membership.

According to federal law and the rules of the exchange, trading may take place only during official trading hours in a designated trading area called a **pit**. This is a physical location on the floor of the exchange. Each commodity trades in a designated pit. In contrast to the specialist system used on stock exchanges, futures contracts trade by a system of **open outcry**. In this system, a trader must make any offer to buy or sell to all other traders present in the pit. Traders also use an unofficial, but highly developed, system of hand signals to express their wishes to buy or sell. Officially, however, all offers to buy or sell must be made through open outcry.

Traders in the pit fall into two groups that we can distinguish by their function. First, a trader can trade for his or her own account and bear the losses or enjoy the profits stemming from this trading. Often, these traders are members of the exchange. Second, a trader could be a broker acting on behalf of his or her own firm or on behalf of a client outside the exchange. For example, the brokers trading on the exchange often represent large brokerage houses such as Merrill Lynch or Prudential Bache. Having distinguished between traders who execute trades for their own accounts and those who execute trades for others, we must realize that certain individuals exercise both functions simultaneously.[5]

Members of the exchange who trade in the pits are typically speculators. A **speculator** is a trader who enters the futures market in pursuit of profit, accepting risk in the endeavor. Some of the traders in the pit that trade for their own account may not be full exchange members themselves. It is possible to lease a seat on the exchange from a full member. Also, some exchanges have created special licenses allowing nonmembers to trade in certain contracts in which the exchanges are anxious to build volume. For the most part, a trader in the pit trading for his or her own account is a speculator.

In addition, to speculators, many traders are **hedgers**, traders who trade futures to reduce some pre-existing risk exposure. Hedgers are often producers or major users of a given commodity. For example, hedgers in wheat might include wheat farmers and large baking firms. Notice that these hedgers do not necessarily need to own the wheat when they hedge. A farmer might hedge by selling his anticipated harvest through the futures market. This could occur even before the farmer plants. Similarly, the baker that will eventually bake the farmer's wheat harvest into bread may hedge an expected need for wheat months before the wheat is actually required. Therefore, hedging is the purchase or sale of futures as a temporary substitute for a transaction in the cash market.[7] For the most part, hedgers are not themselves located on the floor of the exchange. Instead, they trade through a brokerage firm. The brokerage firm communicates the order to the pit and has it executed by a broker in the pit.

Thus, there are two different kinds of brokers. An account executive for a brokerage firm is often called a broker. The account executive could be located in any town or city and the account executive deals with his or her customers, conveying their orders to the exchange. A second type of broker is a floor broker, a broker on the floor of the exchange who executes orders for other customers. For a typical transaction entered by a trader off-the-floor of the exchange, the order will be given to the customer's broker (account executive), who will transmit the order to the brokerage firm's representatives at the exchange. There a floor broker, often employed by the brokerage firm, will execute the order on the floor of the exchange.

This organized structure for trading futures contracts differs from the organization of forward markets. Forward markets are loosely organized and have no physical location devoted to the trading.[8] From the puppy example, this difference is clear. Perhaps the best-developed forward market is the market for foreign exchange. It is a worldwide network of participants, largely banks and brokers, who communicate with each other electronically. In the forward market for foreign exchange, there is no organized exchange and no central trading point.[9]

Standardized Contract Terms

As a second major difference between forward and futures contracts, futures contracts always have standardized contract terms. The puppy example is typical of forward contracts in its lack of standardization. The puppy is not a standardized item; the parties agreed on a particular delivery date, but they could have chosen any other date that was mutually agreeable; and there was no mechanism external to the traders to guarantee that the contract would be fulfilled. By contrast, futures contracts are highly uniform and well-specified commitments for a carefully described good to be delivered at a certain time and in a certain manner. Generally, the futures contract specifies the quantity and quality of the good that can be delivered to fulfill the futures contract. The contract also specifies the delivery date and method for closing the contract, and the permissible minimum and maximum price fluctuations permitted in trading.

As an example, consider the Chicago Board of Trade wheat contract. One wheat contract consists of 5,000 bushels of wheat that must be of one of the following types: No. 2 Soft Red, No. 2 Hard Red Winter, No. 2 Dark Northern Spring, or No. 1 Northern Spring. The wheat contract trades for expiration in the following months of each year: July, September, December, March, and May. The Board of Trade also stipulates the delivery terms for completing the contract. To deliver wheat in completion of the contract, the wheat must be in a warehouse approved by the Chicago Board of Trade. These warehouses must be in the Chicago Switching District or the Toledo, Ohio, Switching District.[10] The buyer transmits payment to the seller, and the seller delivers a warehouse receipt to the buyer. The holder of a warehouse receipt has title to the wheat in the warehouse. Delivery can occur on any business day in the delivery month.

The contract also stipulates the minimum price fluctuation, or **tick size**. For wheat, one tick is ¼ cent per bushel. With 5,000 bushels per contract, this gives a tick size of $12.50 per contract. The contract also specifies a **daily price limit**, which restricts the price movement in a single day. For wheat, the trading price on a given day cannot differ from the preceding day's closing price by more than twenty cents per bushel, or $1,000 per contract. When the contract is trading in its delivery month, this price limit is not in effect. Also, when a commodity enters a particularly volatile period, price limits are generally expanded over successive days. For example, when Iraq invaded Kuwait, oil prices skyrocketed for several days. On the first day, the futures price was allowed to rise only by the limit. Because the price rose the limit on one day, the price limit was expanded for the next day. For most commodities, price limits expand over several days until there is no limit on how much the price can change in a day. Also, some commodities do not have price limits.[11] Finally, the exchange also controls the trading times for each futures contract. Wheat trades from 9:30 a.m. to 1:15 p.m. Chicago time on each trading day, except for the last day of trading when trading in the expiring contract ceases at noon. The last trading day for the wheat contract is seven business days before the last business day of the delivery month.

Although these rules may appear highly restrictive, they actually stimulate trading. Because the good being traded is so highly standardized, all the participants in the market know exactly what is being offered for sale, and they know the terms of the transactions. This uniformity helps to promote liquidity. All futures contracts have such a highly developed framework, which specifies all phases of the transaction. As we saw for wheat, these rules regulate all phases of the market, from the amounts the prices can move to the appropriate ways of making delivery. The prospective trader should consult a given contract for these exact details before initiating any trading. Each exchange publishes contract terms.

Features Typically Standardized in a Futures Contract

1. Quantity
2. Quality
3. Expiration months
4. Delivery terms

5. Delivery dates
6. Minimum price fluctuation
7. Daily price limits
8. Trading days and hours

The Clearinghouse

To ensure that futures contracts trade in a smoothly functioning market, each futures exchange has an associated clearinghouse. The clearinghouse may be constituted as a separate corporation or it may be part of the futures exchange, but each exchange is closely associated with a particular clearinghouse. The clearinghouse guarantees that all of the traders in the futures market will honor their obligations.[12] The clearinghouse serves this role by adopting the position of buyer to every seller and seller to every buyer. This means that every trader in the futures markets has obligations only to the clearinghouse and has expectations that the clearinghouse will maintain its side of the bargain as well. Thus, the clearinghouse substitutes its own credibility for the promise of each trader in the market.

The clearinghouse takes no active position in the market, but interposes itself between all parties to every transaction. In the futures market, the number of contracts bought must always equal the number of contracts sold. So, for every party expecting to receive delivery of a commodity, the opposite trading partner must be prepared to make delivery. If we sum all outstanding long and short futures market positions, the total always equals zero.[13]

Table 1.2 shows the typical trading situation. In the table, we assume that all transactions occur on a single day, say May 1. Party 1 trades on the futures exchange to buy one oats contract of 5000 bushels for delivery in September. In order for Party 1 to buy the contract, some other participant must sell. In panel (a) of the table it is apparent that Party 1 and Party 2 have exactly complementary positions in the futures market. One party has bought exactly what the other has sold. Notice that the time of delivery, the amount of oats to be delivered, and

Table 1.2
Futures Market Obligations

The oat contract is traded by the Chicago Board of Trade. Each contract is for 5000 bushels, and prices are quoted in centers per bushel.

(a) Party 1	Party 2
Buys 1 SEP contract for oats at 171 cents per bushel	Sells 1 SEP contract for oats at 171 cents per bushel

(b) Party 1	Clearinghouse
Buys 1 SEP contract for oats at 171 cents per bushel	Agrees to delivery to Party 1 a SEP contract for oats at a price of 171 cents per bushel

(c) Party 2	Clearinghouse
Sells 1 SEP contract for oats at 171 cents per bushel	Agrees to receive from Party 2 1 SEP contract for oats and to pay 171 cents per bushel

the price all match. Without a perfect match in all these respects, there could not have been a transaction. In all probability, the two trading parties will not even know each other. It is perfectly possible that each will have traded through a broker from different parts of the country. In such a situation, problems of trust may arise. How can either party be sure that the other will fulfill the agreement? The clearinghouse exists to solve that problem. As panels (b) and (c) indicate, the clearinghouse guarantees fulfillment of the contract to each of the trading parties. After the initial sale is made, the clearinghouse steps in and acts as the seller to the buyer and acts as the buyer to the seller. In panel (b), the clearinghouse guarantees the buyer of the futures contract, Party 1, that it will deliver at the initially agreed time and price. To the seller, Party 2, the clearinghouse guarantees that it will accept delivery at the agreed time and price, as panel (c) shows. Figure 1.2 illustrates the same idea graphically. Without a clearinghouse, both parties must deal with each other, and they have direct obligations to one another. With a clearinghouse, each party has obligations to the clearinghouse and the clearinghouse will ensure that they perform.

Because of the clearinghouse, the two trading parties do not need to trust each other or even know each other's identity. Instead, the two traders only have to be concerned about the reliability of the clearinghouse. However, the clearinghouse is a large, well–capitalized financial institution. Its failure to perform on its guarantee to the two trading parties would bring the futures market to ruin. In the history of U.S. futures trading, the clearinghouse has always performed as promised, so the risk of a future default by the clearinghouse is very small.[14]

Figure 1.2
The Function of the Clearinghouse in Futures Markets

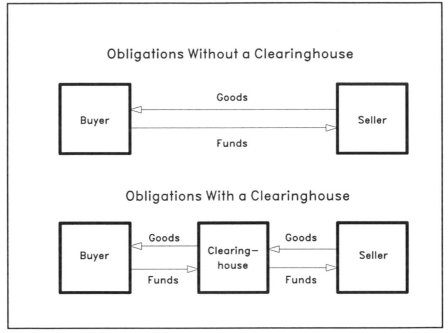

A more careful examination of panels (b) and (c) from Table 1.2 gives further confidence that the clearinghouse will perform as promised. In total, the clearinghouse has no independent position in oats. It is obligated to receive oats and pay 171 cents per bushel, but it is also obligated to deliver oats and receive 171 cents per bushel. These two obligations net out to zero. Since it maintains no futures market position of its own, the riskiness of the clearinghouse is less than it may appear.[15]

Margin and Daily Settlement

In addition to the clearinghouse, there are other safeguards for the futures market. Chief among these is the requirements for margin and daily settlement. Before trading a futures contract, the prospective trader must deposit funds with a broker. These funds serve as a good-faith deposit by the trader and are referred to as **margin**. The main purpose of margin is to provide a financial safeguard to ensure that traders will perform on their contract obligations. The amount of this margin varies from contract to contract and may vary by broker as well. The margin may be posted in cash, a bank letter of credit, or in short-term U.S. Treasury instruments. The trader who posts this margin retains title to it.

Types of Margin.   In this section, we consider the different types of margins and show how margin requirements would affect a trader holding a single futures position. In the next section, we consider margin rules for more complicated positions.

There are three types of margin. The initial deposit just described is the **initial margin**—the amount a trader must deposit before trading any futures. The initial margin approximately equals the maximum daily price fluctuation permitted for the contract being traded. Upon proper completion of all obligations associated with a trader's futures position, the initial margin is returned to the trader. If one has deposited a security as the margin, then the trader earns the interest that accrues while the security has served as the margin.

For most futures contracts, the initial margin may be 5 percent or less of the underlying commodity's value.[16] It may seem strange that the initial margin is so small relative to the value of the commodity underlying the futures contract. The smallness of this amount is reasonable, however, because there is another safeguard built into the system in the form of **daily settlement** or **marking-to-market**. In the futures market, traders are required to realize any losses in cash on the day they occur. In the parlance of the futures market, the contract is marked-to-the-market.

Three Types of Margin

1.   Initial margin
2.   Maintenance margin
3.   Variation margin

To understand the process of daily settlement, consult Table 1.2 again and consider Party 1, who bought one contract for 171 cents per bushel. Assume that the contract closes on May 2 at 168 cents per bushel. This means that Party 1 has sustained a loss of 3 cents per bushel. Since there are 5,000 bushels in the contract, this represents a loss of $150, which is deducted from the margin deposited with the broker. When the value of the funds on deposit with the broker reaches a certain level, called the **maintenance margin**, the trader is required to replenish the margin, bringing it back to its initial level. This demand for more margin is known as a **margin call**. The additional amount the trader must deposit is called the **variation margin**. The maintenance margin is generally about 75 percent of the amount of the initial margin. For example, assume that the initial margin was $1,400, that Party 1 had deposited only this minimum initial margin, and that the maintenance margin is $1,100. Party 1 has already sustained a loss of $150, so the equity in the margin account is $1,250. The next day, assume that the price of oats drops 4 cents per bushel, generating an additional loss for Party 1 of $200. This brings the value of the margin account to $1,050, which is below the level of the required maintenance margin. This means that the broker will require Party 1 to replenish the margin account to $1,400, the level of the initial margin. To restore the margin account, the trader must pay $350 variation margin. Variation margin must always be paid in cash.

Figure 1.3 uses the initial margin level of $1,400 and the maintenance margin level of $1,100 to illustrate this process. At the outset, the value of the margin deposited with the broker is $1,400. First the trader has some small gains, but before too long, losses drop the value of the account below $1,100. As the figure shows, the trader must then restore the value, or equity, in the account to $1,400. This is shown in Figure 1.3 by the large dot. After this first margin call, the trader has some small losses, followed by a large gain and then large losses. These losses generate a second margin call. Figure 1.3 shows only the required cash flows. The trader could have withdrawn cash whenever the value of the equity exceeded $1,400. However, a trader cannot withdraw funds that would leave the account's equity value below the level of the initial margin.

Figure 1.3
Account Equity and Margin Requirements

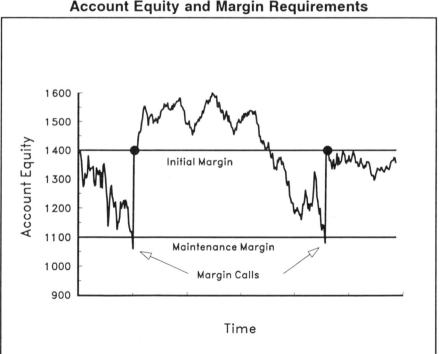

Because futures prices change almost every day, each account will have frequent gains and losses. The losses can require a variation margin payment, and the gains may entitle the trader to withdraw cash. For convenience, traders do not want to face a daily margin call in many cases. There are two basic ways to avoid a margin call. First, a trader can deposit securities with a value well in excess of the initial margin. Second, a trader can deposit funds in excess of the initial margin into an interest-bearing account. In either case, such a deposit provides a liquidity pool that will protect the trader from untimely demands for variation margin payments. Similarly, the trader can instruct the broker to sweep profits from his account into an interest-bearing investment. Those funds can be held ready to meet margin calls as required.

This practice of posting maintenance or variation margin and daily settlement helps make the futures market safer. Assume that Party 1 in Table 1.2 posted only the initial margin, the bare minimum to have the trade executed. Also assume that the trader suffered a loss requiring more margin and that the trader was unable or refused to post the required additional margin. The broker in such a situation is empowered to close the futures position by deducting the loss from the trader's initial margin and returning the balance, less commission costs, to the trader. The broker would also close the trader's entire brokerage account as well. Failure to post the required maintenance margin is a violation of a trader's agreement with the broker. Now it becomes apparent why the initial margin is so small. The initial margin needs to cover only one day's price fluctuation, because any losses will be covered by the posting of additional variation margin. Failure to pay variation margin will lead to the futures position being closed out.[17]

Margin Cash Flows. This section traces the flow of margin funds from the trader to the clearinghouse. The margin system functions through a hierarchy of market participants that links the clearinghouse with the individual trader. The members of an exchange may be classified as clearing members or non clearing members. A **clearing member** is a member of the exchange that is also a member of the clearinghouse. The clearinghouse deals only with clearing members. As a consequence, any non-clearing member must clear his or her trades through a clearing member.

The clearinghouse demands margin deposits from clearing members to cover all futures positions that are carried by that clearing member. For example, a clearing member might be a large broker who executes orders for individual traders and who provides clearing services for some non-clearing members of the exchange. Therefore, the clearing member will impose margin requirements on all of the accounts that it represents to the clearinghouse.

Figure 1.4 shows the margin flows for an individual trader who might trade through a clearing member or a non-clearing member. In the figure, Trader A trades through a broker who is a clearing member. In this case, Trader A

Figure 1.4
Margin Cash Flows

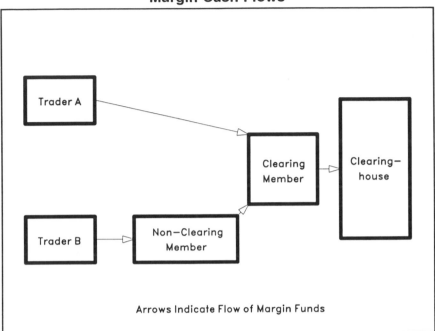

Arrows Indicate Flow of Margin Funds

deposits margin funds with the clearing member, who makes margin deposits with the clearinghouse. As a second alternative in Figure 1.4, Trader B trades through a broker who is a non-clearing member of the exchange. This broker must arrange to clear all trades with a clearing member. In this situation, Trader B deposits margin funds with his or her broker. This broker deposits margin funds with a clearing member, and the clearing member deposits margin funds with the clearinghouse.

It is not very important whether traders A and B trade directly through a clearing member or a non-clearing member. Most large brokerage firms are clearing members, so most individual traders who trade through their local broker will be trading through a clearing member. However, many members of each exchange trade for their own account as speculators. Few of them are clearing members, so they need to clear their trades through a clearing member.

Closing a Futures Position

Initially, we discussed the completion of a futures contract through delivery. However, in the discussion of variation margin we noted that the broker might close the position after trading on May 2. The careful reader might remember that the initial trade shown in Table 1.2 called for a September delivery. In view of that fact, it may not seem that the futures position could be closed in May. There are, however, three ways to close a futures position: delivery, offset, and an exchange-for-physicals (EFP).

Three Ways to Close a Futures Contract

1. Delivery or cash settlement
2. Offset or reversing trade
3. Exchange–for–physicals (EFP) or ex–pit transaction

Delivery. Most futures contracts are written to call for completion of the futures contract through the physical delivery of a particular good. As we have seen in our discussion of the wheat contract, delivery takes place at certain locations and at certain times under rules specified by a futures exchange. In recent years, exchanges have introduced futures contracts that allow completion through **cash settlement**. In cash settlement, traders make payments at the expiration of the contract to settle any gains or losses, instead of making physical delivery. Both physical delivery and cash settlement close the contract in the expiration period. However, few futures contracts are actually closed through either physical delivery or cash settlement. For example, in the fiscal year ending September 30, 1989, only about one-half of one percent of all contracts traded were settled by either physical delivery or cash settlement.[18] Table 1.3 shows the commodity groups and the percentage of contracts completed by delivery or cash settlement within each group. Currencies and metals have the largest portion of deliveries or cash settlements, but these are both less than two percent. In the energy, livestock, and wood groups, delivery is extremely rare. Therefore, the vast majority of all contracts initiated must be completed by some means other than delivery or cash settlement.

Offset. By far, most futures contracts are completed through offset or via a **reversing trade**. To complete a futures contract obligation through offset, the trader transacts in the futures market to bring his or her net position in a particular futures contract back to zero. Consider again the situation depicted in Table 1.2. The first party has an obligation to the clearinghouse to accept 5,000 bushels of oats in September and to pay 171 cents per bushel for them at that time. Perhaps the trader does not wish to actually receive the oats and wants to exit the futures market earlier, say May 10. The trader can fulfill the commitment by entering the futures market again and making the reversing trade depicted in Table 1.4.

Table 1.3
Completion of Futures Contracts
via Delivery or Cash Settlement
October 1, 1988–September 30, 1989

Commodity Group	Volume	Delivered or Settled in Cash	
		Contracts	Percentage
Grains	15,920,321	57,424	0.36
Oilseeds	21,104,497	176,140	0.83
Livestock	8,185,955	12,171	0.15
Other Agricultural	10,749,030	42,251	0.39
Energy/Wood	31,343,764	38,355	0.12
Metals	17,941,194	180,708	1.01
Financial Instruments	136,729,387	854,536	0.62
Currencies	25,684,242	380,455	1.48
All Commodities	267,658,390	1,742,040	0.65

Source: Commodity Futures Trading Commission, *Annual Report*, 1989.

Table 1.4
The Reversing Trade

	Party 1's Initial Position	Party 2
May 1	Bought 1 SEP contract for oats at 171 cents per bushel	Sold 1 SEP contract for oats at 171 cents per bushel
	Party 1's Reversing Trade	Party 3
May 10	Sells 1 SEP contract for oats at 180 cents per bushel	Buys 1 SEP oats contract at 180 cents per bushel

The first line of Table 1.4 merely repeats the initial trade that was made on May 1. On May 10, Party 1 takes exactly the opposite position by selling 1 SEP contract for oats at the current futures price of 180 cents per bushel. This time the trader transacts with a new entrant to the market, Party 3. After this reversing trade, Party 1's net position is zero. The clearinghouse recognizes this, and Party 1 is absolved from any further obligation. In this example, the price of September oats rose 9 cents per bushel during this period, happily yielding Party 1 a profit of $450. Party 2, the original seller, is not affected by Party 1's reversing trade. Party 2 still has the same commitment, because the clearinghouse continues to stand ready to complete this transaction described in Table 1.2. Now the clearinghouse also assumes a complementary obligation to the new market entrant, Party 3. Note that the position of the clearinghouse has not really changed due to the transactions on May 10. Also, Party 2 and Party 3 have complementary obligations after the new trades, just as Party 1 and Party 2 had complementary obligations after the initial transactions on May 1.

In entering the reversing trade, it is crucial that Party 1 sell exactly the same contract that was bought originally. Note in Table 1.4 that the reversing trade matches the original transaction in the good traded, the number of contracts, and the maturity. If it does not, then the trader undertakes a new obligation instead of canceling the old. If Party 1 had sold one DEC contract on May 10 instead of selling the SEP contract, for example, he or she would be obligated to receive oats in September and to deliver oats in December. Such a transaction would result in holding two positions instead of a reversing trade.

Exchange–for–Physicals (EFP). A trader can complete a futures contract by engaging in an EFP. In an EFP, two traders agree to a simultaneous exchange of a cash commodity and futures contracts based on that cash commodity. For example, assume that Trader A is long one wheat contract and genuinely wishes to acquire wheat. Also, assume that Trader B is short one wheat contract and owns wheat. The two traders agree on a price for the physical wheat and agree to cancel their complementary futures positions against each other. Table 1.5 shows this initial position in the first panel. Trader A buys the wheat from Trader B and they report their desire to cancel their futures position to the futures exchange. The exchange notes that their positions match (one short and

---

Table 1.5
An Exchange–for–Physicals Transaction

Before the EFP	
Trader A	**Trader B**
Long 1 wheat futures	Short 1 wheat futures
Wants to acquire actual wheat	Owns wheat and wishes to sell

EFP Transaction	
Trader A	**Trader B**
Agrees with Trader B to purchase wheat and cancel futures	Agrees with Trader A to sell wheat and cancel futures
Receives wheat; pays Trader B	Delivers wheat; receives payment from Trader A
Reports EFP to exchange; Exchange adjusts books to show that Trader A is out of the market	Reports EFP to exchange; Exchange adjusts books to show that Trader B is out of the market

one long) and cancels their futures obligations. The bottom panel of Table 1.5 illustrates the positions of Traders A and B in completing the EFP.

In this example, the result is much like an offsetting trade, because both futures traders have completed their obligations and are now out of the market. However, the EFP differs in certain respects from an offsetting trade. First, the traders actually exchange the physical good. Second, the futures contract was not closed by a transaction on the floor of the exchange. Third, the two traders privately negotiated the price and other terms of the transaction. Because an EFP transaction takes place away from the trading floor of the exchange, it is sometimes known as an **ex–pit** transaction. Federal law and exchange rules generally require all futures trading to take place in the pit. However, the EFP is the one recognized exception to this general rule. EFPs are also known as **against actuals** or **versus cash** transactions.

Exchanges and Types of Futures

Since the founding of the Chicago Board of Trade in 1848, futures markets have flourished. The past decade has been a period of extraordinary growth for futures markets, due largely to the development of entirely new types of contracts in foreign exchange, interest rates, and stock indexes. Within the last few years, several new types of contracts have been developed, including futures on stock indexes and options on futures contracts. The future promises to be a period of continued explosive growth for the industry.

Worldwide Exchanges

Table 1.6 lists the major U.S. futures exchanges, the date they began trading, and the principal types·of contracts they trade. Table 1.7 covers foreign exchanges. The oldest of these is more than 140 years old. Differences in size among these exchanges are striking, ranging from the New York Cotton Exchange, which by state law can trade only cotton futures, to the very large exchanges, such as the Chicago Board of Trade and the Chicago Mercantile Exchange, which have more than 1000 members each and trade a wide variety of futures. The futures markets of Chicago alone directly employ more than 40,000 people.

Types of Futures Contracts

The types of futures contracts that are traded fall into four fundamentally different categories. The underlying good traded may be a physical commodity, a foreign currency, an interest–earning asset, or an index, usually a stock index. Contracts for more than fifty different goods are currently available. While Chapters 5 through 11 deal specifically with each of the different groups of commodities, it is useful to have some appreciation for the range of goods that are traded on the futures market.

Table 1.6
U.S. Futures Exchanges

Exchange and Year Founded	Principal Types of Contracts			
	Physi-cal	Curren-cies	Interest Rates	Index
Chicago Board of Trade (CBT) 1848	◆		◆	◆
Chicago Mercantile Exchange (CME) 1919	◆	◆	◆	◆
Coffee, Sugar and Cocoa Exchange (New York) 1882	◆			◆
Commodity Exchange, Inc. (COMEX) (New York) 1933	◆			
Kansas City Board of Trade (KCBT) 1856	◆			◆
Mid–America Commodity Exchange (Chicago) 1880	◆	◆	◆	
Minneapolis Grain Exchange 1881	◆			
New York Cotton Exchange, Inc. 1870	◆	◆		◆
Citrus Associates of the New York Cotton Exchange 1966	◆			
Petroleum Associates of the New York Cotton Exchange 1971	◆			
New York Futures Exchange (NYFE) 1979				◆
New York Mercantile Exchange 1872	◆			
Chicago Rice and Cotton Exchange 1976	◆			

Sources: *The Wall Street Journal, Futures Magazine, Intermarket Magazine*, various issues, and Chicago Mercantile Exchange, 1985 Annual Report.

Table 1.7
Non–U.S. Futures Exchanges

Exchange	Principal Types of Contracts			
	Physi-cal	Curren-cies	Interest Rates	Stock Index
Bolsa de Mercadorios de Sao Paulo	♦	♦	♦	♦
London International Financial Futures Exchange (LIFFE)		♦	♦	♦
Baltic International Freight Futures Exchange (BIFFEX) (London)				♦
International Petroleum Exchange (London)	♦			
London Futures & Options Exchange (FOX)	♦			
Tokyo International Financial Futures Exchange		♦	♦	♦
Osaka Securities Exchange				♦
Tokyo Commodity Exchange	♦			
Tokyo Stock Exchange			♦	♦
Singapore International Monetary Exchange (SIMEX)	♦	♦	♦	♦
Marche a Terme International de France	♦		♦	♦
Hong Kong Futures Exchange	♦			♦
New Zealand Futures Exchange		♦	♦	♦
Sydney Futures Exchange	♦	♦	♦	♦
Toronto Futures Exchange		♦	♦	♦
Montreal Exchange			♦	
Winnepeg Commodity Exchange	♦			
Kuala Lumpur Commodity Exchange	♦			

Sources: *The Wall Street Journal, Futures Magazine, Intermarket Magazine*, various issues.

Agricultural and Metallurgical Contracts. In the agricultural area, contracts are traded in grains (corn, oats, and wheat), oil and meal (soybeans, soymeal, and soyoil, and sunflower seed and oil), livestock (live hogs, cattle, and pork bellies), forest products (lumber and plywood), textiles (cotton), and foodstuffs (cocoa, coffee, orange juice, rice, and sugar). For many of these commodities, several different contracts are available for different grades or types of the commodity. For most of the goods, there are also a number of months for delivery. The months chosen for delivery of the seasonal crops generally fit their harvest patterns. The number of contract months available for each commodity also depends on the level of trading activity. For some relatively inactive futures contracts, there may be trading in only one or two delivery months in the year.[19] By contrast, an active commodity, such as soybean meal, may have trading in eight delivery months.

The metallurgical category includes the genuine metals, as well as petroleum contracts. These two kinds of goods are really more similar than they appear to be. As will become clear in Chapter 5, they can be treated in a similar way, since both petroleum and metals share an important common characteristic: they are highly storable. Among the metals, contracts are traded on gold, silver, platinum, palladium, and copper. Of the petroleum products, heating oil, crude oil, gasoline, and propane are traded on futures markets.

Interest–Earning Assets. Futures trading on interest-bearing assets started only in 1975, but the growth of this market has been tremendous. Contracts are traded now on Treasury bills, notes, and bonds, on Eurodollar deposits, and on municipal bonds. The existing contracts span almost the entire yield curve, so it is possible to trade instruments with virtually every maturity. The CME trades two contracts with three-month maturities, T-bills and Eurodollar time deposits. This makes possible trading based on anticipated interest rate differentials for the same maturity. In addition, contracts on foreign debt instruments are traded on foreign futures exchanges. For example, the London International Financial Futures Exchange (LIFFE) trades contracts on British government bonds. In September 1990, the CBOT launched a futures contract on Japanese government bonds.

Foreign Currencies. Active futures trading of foreign currencies dates back to the inception of freely floating exchange rates in the early 1970s. Contracts trade on the British pound, the Canadian dollar, the Japanese yen, the Swiss franc, and the West German mark. Contracts are also listed on French francs, Dutch guilders, and the Mexican peso, but these have met with only limited success and are no longer traded. The foreign exchange futures market represents the one case of a futures market existing in the face of a truly active forward market. The forward market for foreign exchange is many times larger than the futures market. Many people believe that the presence of the forward market deterred the introduction and slowed the growth of futures trading in foreign exchange. Contracts on different currencies are also traded on a number of foreign futures exchanges, as Table 1.7 shows.

Indexes. The last major group of futures contracts is for indexes. Most, but not all of these contracts are for stock indexes. Beginning only in 1982, these contracts have been quite successful, with trading on market indexes in full swing. Exchanges trade contracts on four different U.S. stock indexes: the Standard and Poor's 500, a Major Market Index, the New York Stock Exchange Index, and the Value Line Index. Foreign exchanges trade futures on foreign stock indexes, such as the trading of the Japanese Nikkei index on the Tokyo Futures Exchange and on the Singapore International Monetary Exchange (SIMEX) as well.

In September 1990, the Chicago Board of Trade and the Chicago Mercantile Exchange began trading futures contracts based on Japanese financial markets. The Chicago Mercantile Exchange trades a contract based on the Nikkei 225 stock index and the Chicago Board of Trade launched a contract based on the TOPIX index of major firms traded on the Tokyo Stock Exchange.[20] One of the most striking things about these stock index contracts is that they do not admit the possibility of actual delivery. A trader's obligation must be fulfilled by a reversing trade or a cash settlement at the end of trading. Other types of indexes also are traded in futures markets, including a foreign exchange index and an index of municipal bonds.

Figure 1.5
Market Share by Commodity Type

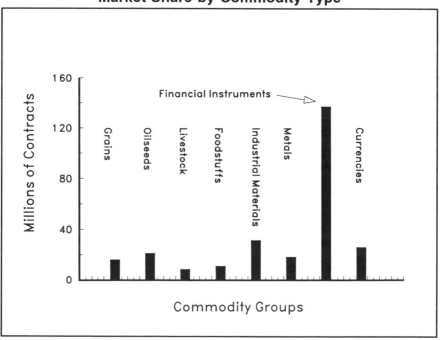

Relative Importance of Commodity Types

Figure 1.5 presents another division of futures contracts into eight categories and shows the relative importance of trading in these different categories in the United States in 1989. As Figure 1.5 shows, over half of the trading volume stems from financial instruments. These include futures contracts based on underlying instruments such as Treasury securities and stock indexes. As we have noted, trading in these contracts began in 1975, so growth in this area has been dramatic. Figure 1.6 shows how the portions of futures trading volume have shifted among these commodity groups over recent years.

Figure 1.6
Changing Commodity Trading Volume

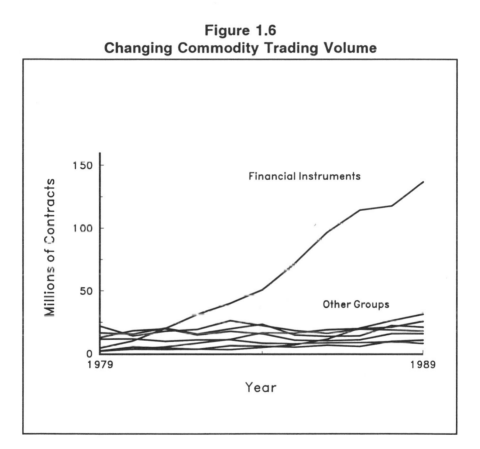

Purposes of Futures Markets

Any industry as old and as large as the futures market must serve some social purpose. If it did not, it would most likely have passed from existence some time ago. Traditionally, futures markets have been recognized as meeting the needs of three groups of futures market users: those who wish to discover information about future prices of commodities, those who wish to speculate, and those who wish to hedge. While Chapter 4 discusses the uses that these three groups make of futures markets in detail, it is important to have some understanding of the social function of futures markets before proceeding. Traditionally, speculation is not regarded as socially useful by itself, although it may have socially useful by-products. Thus, there are two main social functions of futures markets—price discovery and hedging.

Social Functions of Futures Markets

1. Price Discovery
2. Hedging

Price Discovery

Price discovery is the revealing of information about future cash market prices through the futures market. As discussed earlier, in buying or selling a futures contract, a trader agrees to receive or deliver a given commodity at a certain time in the future for a price that is determined now. In such a circumstance, it is not surprising that there is a relationship between the futures price and the price that people expect to prevail for the commodity at the delivery date specified in the futures contract. While the exact nature of that relationship will be considered in detail in Chapter 3, the relationship is predictable to a high degree. By using the information contained in futures prices today, market observers can form estimates of what the price of a given commodity will be at a certain time in the future. The forecasts of future prices that can be drawn from the futures market compare in accuracy quite favorably with other types of forecasts. Futures markets serve a social purpose by helping people make better estimates of future prices, so that they can make their consumption and investment decisions more wisely.

As an example of price discovery and its benefits, consider a mine operator who is trying to decide whether to reopen a marginally profitable silver mine. The silver ore in the mine is not of the best quality, so the yield from the mine will be relatively low. The financial wisdom of operating the mine will depend on the price the miner can obtain for the silver once it is mined and refined. However, the miner must make the decision about the mine today, and the silver will not be ready for market for fifteen months. The crucial element in the miner's decision is the future price of silver.

While the price of silver fifteen months from now cannot be known with certainty, it is possible to use the futures market to estimate that future price. The price quoted in the futures market today for a silver futures that expires in fifteen months can be a very useful estimate of the future price. As we will see in Chapter 3, for some commodities an estimate of the future price of a good drawn from the futures market is one of the best estimates possible. In our example, let us assume that the futures price for silver is high enough to justify starting to operate the mine again. The miner figures that the new mine will be profitable if he can obtain the futures price for the silver when it becomes available in fifteen months. In this situation, the miner has used the futures market as a vehicle of price discovery. Farmers, lumber producers, cattle ranchers, and other economic agents can use futures markets the same way. They all use futures market estimates of future cash prices to guide their production or consumption decisions.

Hedging

Many futures market participants trade futures as a substitute for a cash market transaction. For example, we considered a farmer who sold wheat futures in anticipation of a harvest, and we noted that the farmer used futures as an alternative to the sale of wheat through the cash market. We now consider this classic kind of hedge in more detail. At planting time, the farmer bears a risk associated with the uncertain harvest price his wheat will command. The farmer might use the futures market to hedge by selling a futures contract. If the farmer expects to harvest 100,000 bushels of wheat in nine months, the farmer could establish a price for that harvest by selling 20 wheat futures contracts. (Each wheat contract is for 5,000 bushels.) By selling these futures contracts, the farmer seeks to establish a price today for the wheat that will be harvested in the future. With certain qualifications, this futures transaction protects the farmer from wheat price fluctuations that might occur between the present and the future harvest. The futures transaction served as a substitute for a cash market sale of wheat. A cash market sale was impossible, because the wheat did not actually exist. In this example, the farmer sells wheat in the futures market as a temporary substitute for a future anticipated cash market transaction. Therefore, **anticipatory hedging** is a futures market transaction used as a substitute for an anticipated future cash market transaction.

Hedging transactions can take other forms. For example, consider an oil wholesaler who holds a substantial inventory of gasoline. The wholesaler needs the inventory as a stock from which to service retail customers. If the wholesaler simply holds the stock of gasoline, she must bear the price risk of fluctuating gasoline prices. As an alternative, she can sell crude oil futures as a substitute for selling the gasoline itself. By holding gasoline in her business inventory and selling crude oil futures to offset the risk associated with the gasoline, the wholesaler can reduce her business risk. The wholesaler could have used the cash market directly to reduce risk by simply selling her entire inventory in the cash market. Unfortunately, this method of reducing business risk eliminates the business, because the wholesaler would no longer have the gasoline inventory that is essential to her entire business. Selling futures substitutes for the risk-reducing transaction of selling her entire inventory.

For both of our examples, the hedger uses the futures market as a substitute for a cash market transaction. Both hedgers had a pre-existing risk associated with the commodity being sold. The farmer anticipated harvesting and selling wheat, and he used the futures market as a substitute for a cash market sale of wheat. Even though the farmer did not have wheat on hand when he sold futures, he did have a pre-existing risk in wheat. The risk arose from the anticipated holding of the cash wheat at harvest. For the oil wholesaler, the risk was immediate. As prices of oil fluctuate, the value of her gasoline inventory would fluctuate as well. Thus, the wholesaler had a pre-existing risk associated with the price of oil, and she used the futures market transaction to reduce that risk.

Because hedgers are traders that use futures transactions as substitutes for cash transactions, hedgers are almost always business concerns that deal with a specific commodity. Almost without exception, individual traders are speculators because they enter the futures market in pursuit of profit and increase their risk in the process. By contrast, hedgers have a pre-existing risk exposure of some form that leads them to use futures transactions as a substitute for a cash market transaction. Hedging is the prime social rationale for futures trading, and therefore we will give hedging a great deal of attention throughout the book. Chapter 4 explains the use that the hedger makes of the futures markets, while the techniques and applications of hedging are elaborated for specific markets in Chapters 5 through 11.

Traders in the futures markets are either speculators or hedgers, or the agents of one of these two groups. Yet the benefits provided by the futures market extend to many other sectors of society. The individual interested in forecasts of future prices need not enter the market to benefit. For example, our silver miner did not need to trade any futures to capture the benefits of price discovery. The forecasts are available for the price of the daily newspaper. The chance for hedgers to avoid unacceptable risks by entering the futures market also has wide implications for social welfare. Some individuals would not engage in certain clearly beneficial forms of economic activity if they were forced to bear all of the risk of the activity themselves. Being able to transfer risk to other parties via the futures market enhances economic activity in general. Of course, a general stimulation of economic activity benefits society as a whole.[21]

Regulation of Futures Markets

There are four identifiable tiers of regulation in the futures market: the broker; the exchange and clearinghouse; an industry self-regulatory body, the National Futures Association (NFA); and a federal government agency, the Commodities Futures Trading Commission (CFTC). To a large extent, these tiers overlap, but each regulatory body has its specific duties.

Futures Market Regulators

1. The Broker
2. Exchange and Clearinghouse
3. Industry Self–Regulatory Body—National Futures Association (NFA)
4. Governmental Agency—Commodity Futures Trading Commission (CFTC)

The Broker

As we have seen in our discussion of the margin system, the broker essentially represents his or her customers to the exchange and clearinghouse. In the margin system, the clearinghouse holds the clearing member responsible for all of the accounts that clearing member carries. Because of the representations to the industry that the broker makes on behalf of its client, the broker has a duty to keep informed about the activities of its customer and to ensure that those activities are proper. Among futures market participants, the often repeated rule for brokers is "know your customer." The broker is the industry representative in the best position to know a given customer, because the customer gains access to trading directly through the broker.

As we will see in more detail, some kinds of futures trading are not permitted to any traders. Other traders have restrictions on the kind of trading that they should engage in. As an example, let us consider a **position limit**. For a commodity with a position limit, no single trader is allowed to hold more than a certain number of contracts. This rule limits the influence of a single trader on the market and aims to prevent the trader from controlling the futures price.[22] On occasion, some traders have tried to circumvent this rule by trading through different accounts. Often, the broker can detect such a maneuver and has a duty to report such activity. As this example shows, the broker is often in the best position to detect some abuses, because he or she is closest to the customer. The trading of some customers is restricted due to the nature of the customer's business. For example, some financial institutions are allowed to trade only certain types of futures for hedging purposes. The broker for such an institution should not allow prohibited trading.

In general terms, the broker is responsible for knowing the customer's position and intentions, for ensuring that the customer does not disrupt the market or place the system in jeopardy, and for keeping the customer's trading activity in line with industry regulations and legal restrictions.

Futures Exchanges and Clearinghouses as Regulators

The futures exchanges and clearinghouses have specific regulatory duties. Many of these duties require the exchange and clearinghouse to control the conduct of exchange and clearing members. To do so, the exchanges formulate and enforce rules for their members and rules for trading on the exchange. Generally, the rules of each exchange are designed to create a smoothly functioning market in which traders can feel confident that their orders will be executed properly and at a fair price. Thus, all exchanges prohibit fraud, dishonorable conduct, and defaulting on contract obligations.

More specifically, exchange rules prohibit **fictitious trading**—trading that merely gives the appearance of transacting without actually changing ownership. Exchange rules prohibit circulating rumors to affect price, disclosing a customer's order, trading with oneself, taking the opposite side of a customer's order, making false statements to the exchange, and failing to comply with a legitimate order by the exchange.

The rules also prohibit **pre-arranged trading**. A pre-arranged trade occurs when two futures market participants consult in advance and agree to make a certain trade at a given price. Instead, the rules require that all orders be offered to the entire market through open outcry. The rules prohibit pre-arranged trading because a pre-arranged trade is non-competitive and can be abusive. For example, assume that a floor broker receives an order to buy wheat and that the fair market price for the wheat contract is $4.20 per bushel. In a pre-arranged trade, the floor broker might agree with a friendly floor trader to buy the contract from him or her at $4.21. With the true market value at $4.20, this practice cheats the customer by $.01 per bushel or $50 per contract. Had the order been offered to the market as the rules require, the order would have been filled at the prevailing price of $4.20. Thus, the prohibition of pre-arranged trading aims at ensuring that each order is executed at a fair market price.

The rules also prohibit a broker from trading for his or her own account at the customer's requested price before filling a customer's order. The broker who trades for himself or herself before filling a customer's order engages in the prohibited practice called **front running**. To see why this practice is prohibited, assume that market prices are rising rapidly due to some new information. Assume also that the broker holds a customer order to buy. If the broker executes his or her own order first, the broker's own order will be executed at a more favorable price, because of the quickly rising prices. Thus, front running gives the broker an unfair advantage. As a second example, assume that a broker receives a very large customer order to sell. The broker knows that placing this order will depress the futures price temporarily. The front running broker would enter his or her own order to sell first. The broker's order would be executed at the high price, and the broker would then execute the customer's order. Upon execution of the customer's order, the price falls as the broker anticipated. Now the broker can buy and close his or her position. This gives the broker a profit from front running. In front running, the broker uses his or her special knowledge of order flow or market movement to obtain an unethical and prohibited personal advantage.

Futures exchanges also set daily price limits, position limits, and margin requirements, although the CFTC has a role in each of these types of rules. In addition, each exchange has rules that govern membership on the exchange. For example, exchange rules establish membership requirements and specify how customer complaints are to be resolved. For each of these categories, the rules of the exchange are subject to review by the CFTC. However, the CFTC generally provides broad guidelines within which the exchanges and clearing-houses form their own specific rules.

National Futures Association (NFA)

In 1974, Congress passed a new law for the regulation of futures markets. Part of that law authorized the futures industry to create one or more self-regulatory bodies. The purpose of these bodies according to the act is ". . . to prevent fraudulent and manipulative acts and practices, to promote just and equitable principles of trade, in general, to protect the public interest, and to remove impediments to and perfect the mechanism of free and open futures trading." While the law has contemplated more than a single self-regulatory body, the National Futures Association is the only such body in existence. For many classes of market participants, membership in the NFA is mandatory.

The following parties are required to be members of the NFA: Futures Commission Merchants, Commodity Pool Operators, Introducing Brokers, Commodity Trading Advisors, and Associated Persons. Exchanges, banks, and commodity business firms may join the NFA, but membership is not compulsory. Floor traders and floor brokers are not required to be members, because they are subject to exchange regulation. One must be a member of the NFA in order to do commodity-related business with the public.

The NFA has the responsibility for screening and testing applicants for registration, and it can review personal background information before allowing individuals to register in the various categories of futures professionals. The NFA also requires FCMs and Introducing Brokers to maintain adequate capital and to keep accurate trading records. Finally, the NFA can audit member firms' records and capital adequacy. For serious violations, the NFA can suspend or expel violators from the futures industry. Finally, the NFA operates an arbitration process for resolving trading disputes.

As the NFA states, it seeks to prevent infractions before they occur. By doing so, the NFA helps the futures industry to remain viable by keeping the public trust. However, in assessing the NFA, it is wise to remember that it is an industry self-regulatory body, designed to protect the integrity of the industry and to promote the interests of the industry.

Commodity Futures Trading Commission (CFTC)

The Commodity Futures Trading Commission Act of 1974 established the commission. Before this act, commodity futures markets were regulated solely under the Commodity Exchange Act administered through the Department of Agriculture. The new act supplemented, rather than replaced, the Commodity Exchange Act. The CFTC Act brought currency and metal futures under federal regulation.

The CFTC has specific powers under the CFTC Act. One important area of CFTC jurisdiction concerns the approval of new contracts. Before trading, an exchange must submit the newly designed contract to the CFTC for approval. The CFTC is responsible for determining whether trading in such a contract is contrary to the public interest. To receive approval, the contract must show promise of serving an economic purpose, such as making for fairer pricing of the commodity in some way or in making hedging possible. Providing an arena for speculation is not enough justification to show that a futures contract would serve an economic function.

The CFTC also regulates futures market trading rules, including the daily permitted maximum price fluctuation, certain features of the delivery process, and minimum price fluctuation limits. Generally, the CFTC is not involved in determining membership in the exchanges, but it can review complaints of membership exclusion or other unfair treatment by the exchanges. Perhaps the most striking power of the CFTC is the emergency power to intervene in the conduct of the market itself when the commission believes manipulation is present. Also, the CFTC has the power to require competency tests of brokers and commodity representatives. Figure 1.7 shows the overlapping structure of the regulatory bodies.

Aims of Regulation

Futures market regulations today control both entry into and the operation of futures markets. Before a new contract can be traded, the CFTC must approve the contract for trading, for example.[23] Another dimension of current regulatory

Figure 1.7
Overlapping Futures Market Regulation

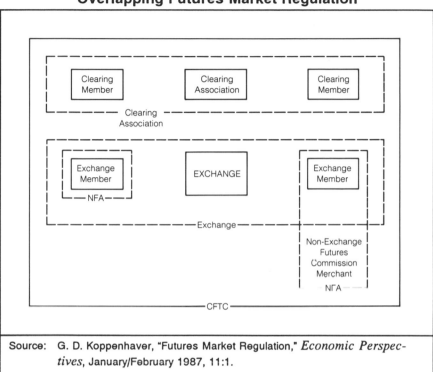

Source: G. D. Koppenhaver, "Futures Market Regulation," *Economic Perspectives*, January/February 1987, 11:1.

practice focuses not on entry but on the operation or performance of futures markets. On the operational side, futures market regulation aims to provide a marketplace in which the social functions of futures markets can be fulfilled. Practices that interfere with the process of price discovery or the efficient transfer of unwanted risk make futures markets perform poorly. For example, practices that make futures prices behave as poor indicators of future spot prices reduce the usefulness of the futures market for price discovery. Also, practices that distort prices can increase the cost of transferring risk. To see more clearly the point of regulation, we consider one of the most feared aspects of future trading abuse, price manipulation.

"It is a felony for a person to manipulate or attempt to manipulate the price of any commodity in commerce or for future delivery."[24] To prove manipulation, the manipulator must be shown to have the ability to set an artificial futures price, must have intended to set an artificial price, and must have succeeded in setting such a price. In essence, an artificial price is a price that does not reflect free demand and supply conditions. By trading in certain ways, it may be possible for a trader or group of traders to move the price in the market from its economically sound or justified price. The basic way of accomplishing this feat is through a market corner or a market squeeze. In a corner or squeeze, a trader or group of traders gains effective control over the pricing mechanism in the futures market. These are discussed in more detail later in Chapter 2.

Given these problems created by price manipulation, it may seem clear that there is a need for government regulation of futures markets. Some observers argue that such governmental regulation is not needed. According to these authors, the exchanges have a strong incentive for self-regulation. Only by attracting the public for trading can the exchange make money as a whole. Therefore, according to this argument, the exchange left to its own devices will be self-regulating, obviating the need for governmental regulation.[25]

In addition to the issue of price manipulation, other areas of concern to regulators include: insider trading, front running, capital formation concerns, and the effect of futures trading on the riskiness of the cash market for commodities. Insider trading is trading on information not available to the public at large. For example, a government clerk working on a forecast of the size of the corn crop has access to information that could be valuable in futures trading. Using such information to guide trading would be a case of insider trading. Recently, insider trading scandals in the stock market have attracted a great deal of public attention. Insider trading in futures markets is not subject to the same limitations as those found in the stock market. Nonetheless, most exchanges have some restrictions on insider trading. Some observers argue that prohibitions against insider futures trading would be actually harmful. Under this view, insider trading contributes to liquidity and to market efficiency.[26]

Taxation of Futures Trading

In 1981, Congress passed a law regarding the taxation of gains and losses in futures trading that had dramatic effects on the ways in which futures contracts could be used. The new law stipulated that all paper gains and losses on futures positions must be treated as though they were realized at the end of the tax year. For tax purposes, this new law meant that the futures positions must be marked-to-market at the end of the year. Forty percent of any gains or losses are to be treated as short-term gains; sixty percent are to be treated as long-term capital gains or losses. Prior to the passage of the Tax Reform Act of 1986, long-term capital gains were taxed at a lower rate than ordinary income or short-term capital gains. The 1986 law stipulates that all income is taxed at one rate. This change removes the protection of the long-term rates, but the new law also reduced overall tax rates. As a net result, the 1986 law seems to have had little effect on profits from futures trading.[27]

Conclusion

As we have seen in this chapter, forward trading has grown out of a need that has been felt for centuries. With the passage of time and the development of a more complex society, futures markets have emerged as a special kind of forward contracting. With their special characteristics of organized exchanges, clearinghouses, financial safeguards, and standardized contracts, futures markets represent a kind of highly specialized forward trading begun in the middle of the nineteenth century and brought into fruition over the last quarter century.

Futures markets depend on well-developed financial markets and on the existence of widely available homogeneous commodities. The availability of standard commodities depends, in turn, on a sophisticated economic infrastructure, with the key element being an integrated transportation system. Futures markets, almost by their very nature, serve a geographically dispersed group of participants. This means that futures markets also depend on the existence of an elaborate communications system.

With these facts in mind, it is clear that futures markets could not really have developed before they did, when telegraphic communication and a suitable financial environment were coming into existence. Their growth, which has recently accelerated, makes futures markets an important economic phenomenon, and one well worth studying.

Questions and Problems

1. In purchasing a house, contracting to buy the house occurs at one time. Typically, closing occurs weeks later. At the closing the buyer pays the seller for the house and the buyer takes possession. Explain how this transaction is like a futures or forward transaction.

2. In the futures market, a widget contract has a standard contract size of 5,000 widgets. What advantage does this have over the well-known forward market practice of negotiating the size of the transaction on a case-by-case basis? What disadvantages does the standardized contract size have?

3. What factors need to be considered in purchasing a commodity futures exchange seat? What are all the possible advantages that could come from owning a seat?

4. Explain the difference between initial and maintenance margin.

5. Explain the difference between maintenance and variation margin.

6. On February 1, a trader is long the JUN wheat contract. On February 10, she sells a SEP wheat futures, and sells a JUN wheat contract on February 20. On February 15, what is her position in wheat futures? On February 25, what is her position? How would you characterize her transaction on February 20?

7. Explain the difference between volume and open interest.

8. Define "tick" and "daily price limit."

9. A trader is long one SEP crude oil contract. On May 15, he contracts with a business associate to receive 1,000 barrels of oil in the spot market. The business associate is short one SEP crude oil contract. How can the two traders close their futures positions without actually transacting in the futures market?

10. Explain how a trader closes a futures market position via cash settlement.

11. Explain "price discovery."

12. Contrast anticipatory hedging with hedging in general.

13. What is "front running?"

14. Explain the difference in the roles of the National Futures Association and the Commodity Futures Trading Commission.

Notes

1. The mutual obligation of both buyer and seller of a futures contract is an important feature of the futures market that helps to distinguish futures contracts from options. If you buy a call option, then you buy the right to obtain a good at a certain price, but the buyer of a call has no obligation. Instead, as the term implies, he has an option to buy something but no obligation to do anything. The buyer of a futures contract, by contrast,

undertakes an obligation to make a payment at a subsequent time and to take delivery of the good that is contracted. The initiation of any futures contract implies a set of future obligations.

2. For a discussion of the historical origins of futures contracting, see A. Loosigian, *Interest Rate Futures*, Princeton, NJ: Dow Jones Books, Inc., 1980. L. Venkataramanan also discusses the origins of forward contracting in his book, *The Theory of Futures Trading*, New York: Asia Publishing House, 1965.

3. For an account of the early days of the Chicago Board of Trade, see *The Commodity Trading Manual*, Chicago: Chicago Board of Trade, 1989.

4. Scott Chambers and Colin Carter, "U.S. Futures Exchanges as Nonprofit Entities," *Journal of Futures Markets*, 10:1, February 1990, pp. 79–88, analyze the difference that their nonprofit status has on the operation of futures exchanges. They argue that this freedom from profit maximizing goals stimulates cross-subsidization of the exchanges' products. In a practical sense, this analysis implies that exchanges use profits from successful contracts to subsidize less profitable contracts.

5. See Raymond Chiang, Gerald D. Gay, and Robert W. Kolb, "Commodity Exchange Seat Prices," *Review of Futures Markets*, 6:1, 1987, pp. 1-12.

6. The practice of trading for one's own account and simultaneously acting as a broker for other parties is known as **dual trading**. In recent months, this practice has come under close scrutiny and some restrictions have been placed on it. We discuss dual trading more fully later in this chapter.

7. This is the classic definition of hedging given by Holbrook Working, "Hedging Reconsidered," *Journal of Farm Economics*, 35, 1953, pp. 544-561.

8. There are some exceptions to this general rule. For example, the London Metals Exchange trades metals forwards, but has a physical trading floor.

9. Chapter 11 discusses the foreign exchange forward market in some detail as a preliminary to the discussion of the foreign exchange futures market.

10. The exchange also controls price differentials for delivery in one location rather than another or the delivery of one grade of the commodity instead

of another. For example, if wheat delivery is to be made in Toledo, the delivery price must be two cents per bushel under the contract price.

11. In general, futures on financial goods tend to have few if any price limits. This means that price limits are restricted mainly to physical commodities. Michael J. Brennan, "A Theory of Price Limits in Futures Markets," *Journal of Financial Economics*, 16:2, June 1986, pp. 213-233, argues that price limits work hand in glove with margins to ensure contract performance. Price limits serve to restrict the flow of information available to traders in the event of dramatic changes in the true economic value of the commodity. If the futures price has moved the limit, the traders' information about the true value of the good is restricted because the trader cannot observe the market price for the good. Therefore, the trader has a stronger incentive to meet his margin call than he or she might have if they knew the true equilibrium price. Price limits do not restrict the trader's information if information is available from sources outside the futures market. For example, in financial markets there are good sources of information beyond the futures markets about the prices of goods. For agricultural markets, the sources of information beyond the futures market are not as valuable, Brennan notes. Thus, we would expect to find few price limits on financial futures, because price limits would not be effective in limiting the trader's information. Correlatively, price limits should be observed on agricultural commodities where the trader's information flow is poorer. Brennan notes that the pattern of price limits on futures is broadly consistent with this observation. Price limits are more popular on agricultural futures than on financial futures.

    Price limits may also provide a cooling-off period when prices are very volatile. For example, C. Ma, R. Rao, and R. Sears, "Volatility, Price Resolution, and the Effectiveness of Price Limits," *Journal of Financial Services Research*, 3:3, December 1989, pp. 165-199, find that volatility the next day is lower and that the price tends to reverse direction after it hit the price limit. This issue remains highly controversial, as the comments on the Ma, Rao, and Sears articles by M. Miller and S. Lehmann indicate.

12. In his article "Market Incompleteness and Divergences Between Forward and Futures Interest Rates," *Journal of Finance*, 35:2, May 1980, pp. 221-234, Edward J. Kane argues that the costliness of the performance guarantees provided by the clearinghouse is sufficient to cause a divergence between the prices of forward and futures contracts. Other justifications for such divergences have emerged, and Chapter 2 considers this topic in greater detail.

13. Notice that this is different from the stock market. Stocks represent title to the real assets of the firms, and these are owned by someone at every point in time. The long and short positions in the stock market, when "netted out," always equal the number of shares actually in existence, not zero, as in the futures market.

14. For more on the clearinghouse and its functions, see Franklin R. Edwards, "The Clearing Association in Futures Markets: Guarantor and Regulator," *The Journal of Futures Markets*, 3:4, Winter 1983, pp. 369-392.

15. We might say that the clearinghouse is "perfectly hedged." No matter whether futures prices rise or fall, the wealth of the clearinghouse will not be affected. This is the case since the clearinghouse holds both long and short positions that perfectly balance each other. Chapter 3 introduces the concept of hedging and it is pursued through all subsequent chapters.

16. One startling example is for the T-bill futures contract. An initial margin deposit of $1,000-2,500 serves as the security for a contract on $1,000,000 face value of Treasury bills.

17. For a more extended discussion of margins, see K. Kahl, R. Rutz, and J. Sinquefield, "The Economics of Performance Margins in Futures Markets," *The Journal of Futures Markets*, Spring 1985, 5:1, pp. 103-112. Some have argued that higher margins impede futures trading in some cases. See R. Fishe and L. Goldberg, "The Effects of Margins on Trading in Futures Markets," *The Journal of Futures Markets*, Summer 1986, 6:2, pp. 261-271. M. Hartzmark, "The Effects of Changing Margin Levels on Futures Market Activity, the Composition of Traders in the Market, and Price Performance," *Journal of Business*, April 1986, 59:2, Pt. 2, pp. S147-S180, argues that changing margin levels may have unpredictable effects on the composition of traders in the market, and he maintains that margin rules are unsuitable as a regulatory tool for controlling excessive speculation. William C. Hunter, "Rational Margins on Futures Contracts: Initial Margins," *Review of Research in Futures Markets*, 1986, 5:2, pp. 160-173, argues that exchanges should set margins to reflect the risk-taking behavior of its members.

18. The Commodity Futures Trading Commission reports that 267,658,390 contracts were traded and that 1,742,040 were settled by delivery or cash settlement during the period October 1, 1988 through September 30, 1989. Commodity Futures Trading Commission, *Annual Report* 1989, p. 101.

19. Often there may be a number of delivery months on which trading is permitted, but contracts with little trading volume will actually have an active market in only one or two delivery months at a time.

20. The CBOT trades its Japanese stock index and its Japanese bond contract in the evening hours as well as during U.S. business hours. The evening session overlaps regular business hours in Japan.

21. In his book, *The Economic Function of Futures Markets*, (Cambridge: Cambridge University Press, 1986), Jeffrey Williams argues that the main purpose of futures markets is to provide means for the borrowing and lending of commodities. In his analogy, the futures market makes the market for commodities behave like the money market, with easy access to borrowing and lending.

22. Position limits do not apply in the same way to hedgers.

23. A strong case can be made for the economic inefficiency of regulating new contract creation. See D. Fischel, "Regulatory Conflict and Entry Regulation of New Futures Contracts," *Journal of Business*, April 1986, 59:2, Part 2, pp. S85-S102.

24. G. D. Koppenhaver, "Futures Market Regulation," *Economic Perspectives*, January/February 1987, 11:1.

25. See F. Easterbrook, "Monopoly, Manipulation, and the Regulation of Futures Markets," *Journal of Business*, 59:2, Part 2, April 1986, pp. S103-S127, who argues against such regulation. By contrast, A. Kyle, in "A Theory of Futures Market Manipulations," in R. Anderson, *The Industrial Organization of Futures Markets*, Lexington, MA: D. C. Heath, 1984, argues that squeezes increase the cost of hedging and should therefore be regulated to make them more difficult.

26. See S. Grossman, "An Analysis of the Role of Insider Trading on Futures Markets," *Journal of Business*, April 1986, 59:2, Part 2, pp. S129-S146.

27. Raymond Chiang and Dennis J. Lasser, "Tax Timing Options on Futures Contracts and the 1981 Economic Recovery Act," *The Financial Review*, 24:1, February 1989, pp. 75-92, examine the impact of the law on the pricing of foreign exchange futures and forward contracts. Upon initial passage, this law applied to futures, but not to forward contracts. (The law was extended to apply to forward contracts effective in 1982.) Chiang and

Lasser examine the differences between futures and forward prices for foreign exchange and conclude that the market responded to the law by widening the differences between forward and futures prices. This response would make sense, because the law temporarily destroyed the tax-timing option on futures contracts, while leaving the option intact on forward contracts. Chiang and Lasser found that the difference between forward and futures prices vanished when the two again became subject to the same tax treatment in 1982.

2

Futures Markets: Refinements

Introduction

In this chapter we explore the structure of the futures markets in more detail than we did in Chapter 1, and we consider some of the organizational issues facing the futures industry today. These issues range from the threat of global competition to turf battles between federal regulatory agencies.

We begin with a more detailed examination of the margin system. In Chapter 1, we considered margins for single futures contracts. Margin rules also apply to combinations of futures positions, and this chapter explores how margins function when traders hold several related futures positions. Today, the exchanges are developing and implementing systems to consider the risk level for a trader's entire position across all futures exchanges.

Exchanges specialize and compete with one another. For example, the Chicago Mercantile Exchange began to trade a Japanese stock index futures contract on September 25, 1990, and the Chicago Board of Trade launched a similar contract on September 27, 1990. Thus, exchanges sometimes compete head to head. However, exchanges also specialize and attempt to develop market niches. In this chapter, we consider how exchange specialization and competition shapes the face of the futures industry and how it leads to new contracts.

The futures industry is large and growing. Such a large industry requires specialization among brokers, trading advisors, and other professionals. In this chapter, we examine some of these specialized functions to show more completely how futures trading functions.

As we noted in Chapter 1, futures were once a virtual U.S. monopoly. In the 1980s, the industry moved toward true international status. Foreign exchanges developed rapidly and exchanges around the world began to trade commodities associated with other countries. This process of internationalization will shape the futures industry for the 1990s and beyond. We consider the impact of internationalization on the futures industry in this chapter.

Internationalization is intimately tied to electronic trading. Today, electronic systems allow traders in New York to trade Japanese markets as if they were sitting in Tokyo. Worldwide electronic trading through a system called GLOBEX is slated to begin in 1991. This chapter considers electronic trading in general and specifically examines GLOBEX, the system that many traders expect to dominate worldwide electronic futures trading.

As financial markets in the United States and around the world become more integrated, regulation becomes more complex and existing regulatory structures show their weaknesses. The stock market Crash of October 1987 has led some observers to question a structure that separates the regulation of stocks and stock index futures. Currently, the U.S. government is prosecuting a number of traders for illegal futures trading. These trials have stimulated criticism of futures markets in general and have led to charges that futures regulation is too lax. This chapter considers these and other regulatory issues and controversies in detail.

Margins: A Closer Look

Chapter 1 introduced the concept of margins for futures markets. There we saw that **initial margin** is a deposit of cash or Treasury securities required before any futures trade. This deposit protects the broker and the market from default by a trader who incurs losses. When the value of that initial deposit is eroded to a level below the **maintenance margin,** the trader must make new payments, called **variation margin,** to restore the value of the trader's account to the level of the initial margin. In this chapter, we extend our discussion of margin to margin practices for combinations of futures positions, and we show how margin rules are being developed to reflect the risk of these combined positions.

Margins for Combinations of Futures Positions

As we will explore in Chapter 4, speculators often hold combinations of related futures positions. Such a combined futures position is called a **spread.** For example, a speculator might hold a long position in a wheat futures contract for July delivery and a short position in a wheat futures contract for September delivery. (The speculator would be attempting to profit on a change in the relationship between the prices on the two futures contracts.) Not surprisingly, the prices of the July and September wheat futures contracts are closely related. In this example, both futures positions are in the same commodity. A spread position with both futures positions in the same commodity is called an **intra-market spread,** a **calendar spread** or a **time spread.**[1] The futures contracts in a spread usually have related price movements, which reduces the risk of a spread relative to a single contract. Because the risk of the spread is less than the risk of holding a single outright contract, the exchange imposes lower margin requirements on such spreads. As an example, the wheat contract might have an initial margin requirement of $2,500 for a single futures contract. If a trader holds an intra-market spread in wheat, the margin could be much lower, say $1,500. This lower spread margin covers both contracts in the spread of our example. Thus, the spread margin per contract is less than half the outright margin. All time spreads receive this favorable margin treatment.

In addition to intra-market spreads, there are also spreads between different, but related, commodities. For example, a trader might hold a long futures position in July wheat and a short position in July oats. A spread in two distinct, but related, commodities is called an **intermarket spread**. Not every pair of commodities is sufficiently related to receive treatment as an intermarket spread. For example, there is a close relationship between wheat and oats, but such a close relationship does not exist between wheat and coffee. The exchanges determine which commodity pairs constitute an intermarket spread for purposes of margins. Table 2.1 shows some pairs of commodities that qualify for spread margins. As the table shows, qualification for intermarket spread margining treatment depends on a close economic relationship between the two commodities. Notice that each of these spread margin pairs is for commodities traded on the same exchange. This system results from the fact that each exchange sets its own margins. With each exchange establishing its margins independently, there is little opportunity for considering spread relationships between related commodities traded on two different exchanges.

Table 2.1
Examples of Intermarket Spreads
Qualifying for Spread Margin Treatment

Exchange	Commodity Pair
Chicago Board of Trade	Treasury bonds vs. Treasury notes
	Any pair of wheat, corn, or oats
	Any pair of soybeans, soyoil, or soymeal
	Gold vs. silver
Chicago Mercantile Exchange	Eurodollars vs. Treasury bills
	Any pair of foreign currencies (British pound, German mark, Swiss franc, French franc, Japanese yen, Canadian dollar, Australian dollar)
	Any pair of cattle, feeder cattle, or hogs
	Pork bellies vs. hogs

Intermarket Cross–Margining

Intermarket cross–margining is a system that establishes a trader's margin requirement by considering the trader's entire portfolio, even if portions of that portfolio are held in different exchanges. In essence, the idea extends the principle of spread margins across exchange boundaries. As an example, Treasury bill and Treasury bond futures prices are clearly related. However, Treasury bill futures trade at the Chicago Mercantile Exchange and Treasury bond futures trade at the Chicago Board of Trade. A margining system that recognizes a spread between bills and bonds would be a system of intermarket cross-margining.

Today there is a limited intermarket cross-margining system. Intermarket cross-margining for futures becomes possible if a trader holds positions on two different exchanges through the same brokerage firm. For example, assume a trader holds a long SEP Treasury bill futures contract and a short SEP Treasury bond contract with her broker, Merrill Lynch. This position would qualify for spread margins, because both sides of the spread are held with the same broker. The broker fulfills the function of identifying the two individual futures positions as two halves of a single spread. However, if the trader held the bill position with Merrill Lynch and the bond position with Salomon Brothers, for example, the position would not qualify for reduced margins.

Recently, some market observers have called for an extension of intermarket cross-margining. Under these proposals, margin rules would consider a trader's full position, not only across different futures exchanges, but across fundamentally different types of instruments. Much of the impetus for such a broad cross-margining system has emerged from studies of the market crash of October 1987. After the crash, the Brady Commission studied the performance of the financial system during that stressful time. As one of their conclusions, the Commission endorsed intermarket cross-margining. Because the Brady Commission focused on equities, we will use stock trading as an example. The principles apply to other kinds of instruments. Individual stocks trade on stock exchanges and through the NASDAQ system. Options on individual stocks and stock indexes trade on various option exchanges. Stock index futures trade on various futures exchanges, as do options on those stock index futures. Considered in total, equity trading spans a large number of exchanges. In total, there are 13 clearinghouses in the United States, all of which impose margin requirements. With some exceptions, one clearinghouse does not recognize the positions that traders hold at other clearinghouses. As a consequence, each position is margined separately.[2]

Full intermarket cross-margining would consider a trader's total equity position of all types in determining the necessary margin position. Because margin requirements are supposed to reflect the trader's risk exposure, such a system of cross-margining would be highly desirable, since it would monitor the trader's total risk. In many instances, a trader's entire portfolio risk can be less than the sum of the risks represented by the individual pieces. For example, a trader holding a large portfolio of individual stocks, who sells a stock index futures contract, is essentially a spread trader. Like spread traders in other goods, this trader's total risk exposure might well be less than the risk exposure represented by either the stock portfolio alone or the futures position alone. Under intermarket cross-margining, the margin requirements would recognize the real extent of the trader's risk.

There are at least five benefits of such a cross-margining system. First, the total amount of initial margin required from traders will be less for a given degree of risk protection. This would free capital for other applications, such as meeting variation margin calls. Second, cross-margining would probably require a central clearinghouse to serve the various markets. Such a central clearinghouse would reduce transfers of money between accounts and increase the operational efficiency of the market. Third, lower margin requirements would help to attract more traders. Having more traders in the system would contribute to making the markets more liquid. Fourth, such a system would help U.S. exchanges compete with the burgeoning foreign financial markets. Finally, in periods of dramatic price changes, cross-margining would reduce the chances of a forced sell-off by some traders. For example, assume there is a large price rise in the stock market and consider a trader who owns stocks and is short a stock index futures contract. Rising stock prices generate a loss for a short stock index futures trader. If the margin system requires margin based only on considering the futures position in isolation, the trader would be required to pay variation margin. However, if the trader owns stock and sells a stock index futures contract against it, the rise in stock prices might generate a gain on the stock itself that would fully offset the losses on stock index futures. The economics of such a situation do not require any increase in the trader's margin payments. Only a system of cross-margining could reflect the true economics of this trader's position.

Cross-margining also may involve certain risks. First, reducing margin might free capital for additional trading, not merely as a reserve against future margin calls. Cross-margining might merely mean that the system as a whole holds less margin money, thereby causing an increase in the overall risk of system-wide default. Second, the offsetting positions might diverge from their normal relationships. In this case, there could be losses on both sides of the position instead of a loss on one side coupled with an offsetting gain on the other.

One impediment to full intermarket cross-margining is the thirteen clearinghouses themselves. Cross-margining means that clearinghouses may be consolidated or eliminated. Therefore, some clearinghouses are reluctant to open a Pandora's box of cross-margining that may lead to their demise.[3]

Table 2.2
Sixteen SPAN Scenarios

1.	Futures unchanged; Volatility up	9.	Futures down 2/3 range; Volatility up
2.	Futures unchanged; Volatility down	10.	Futures down 2/3 range; Volatility down
3.	Futures up 1/3 range; Volatility up	11.	Futures up 3/3 range; Volatility up
4.	Futures up 1/3 range; Volatility down	12.	Futures up 3/3 range; Volatility down
5.	Futures down 1/3 range; Volatility up	13.	Futures down 3/3 range; Volatility up
6.	Futures down 1/3 range; Volatility down	14.	Futures down 3/3 range; Volatility down
7.	Futures up 2/3 range; Volatility up	15.	Futures up extreme move
8.	Futures up 2/3 range; Volatility down	16.	Futures down extreme move

The SPAN Margin System

While full cross-margining remains in the future, a partial cross-margining system is already in widespread use. SPAN stands for *Standard Portfolio Analysis of Risk*. SPAN is in use at most U.S. futures exchanges today. It offers cross-margining between futures and options on futures by considering the entire portfolio in setting margin requirements. The price of an option on a futures contract depends on a number of factors, including the price of the futures, the volatility of price movements on the futures, and the amount of time remaining until the option expires.[4]

The SPAN system considers 16 possible "what if" scenarios to determine the appropriate margin. The 16 scenarios reflect changes in the futures price and changes in the volatility of futures price. Table 2.2 shows the 16 different scenarios. The futures range equals the maintenance margin on a single futures contract and an extreme move is twice the futures range. The SPAN system computes how the value of the portfolio would change under each of the 16 scenarios. The margin requirement equals the largest loss under any of the 16 scenarios.

If a trader holds a combination of futures and option on futures positions, the SPAN system will accurately reflect the risk of the entire position and compute the margin amount commensurate with that level of risk.[5]

Exchange Specialization and Competition

With futures trading on many diverse goods, it is not surprising that we find both specialization among exchanges and contract duplication from exchange to exchange. Often being the first exchange to introduce a contract is a key element of success. For example, among U.S. exchanges, only the International Monetary Market (IMM) of the Chicago Mercantile Exchange trades contracts in foreign exchange.[6] Because the IMM was the first to trade foreign exchange futures, it was able to erect a barrier to entry against the other exchanges. If one exchange begins trading a certain contract, traders will tend to remain with the first exchange, because that contract will have the needed trading volume to provide liquidity. The second exchange that wishes to offer the same contract has a very difficult battle.[7]

In addition to being first with a contract, an exchange may also achieve a certain degree of control by trading contracts in a group of related contracts. The Chicago Board of Trade (CBT or CBOT) trades contracts in the soybean complex, offering contracts on soybeans, soymeal, and soyoil. Trading contracts on all three gives traders the opportunity to trade one contract against the other.[8] With all three contracts trading, there is little opportunity for another exchange to enter the field. If the CBT traded only the soybean contract, then other exchanges might try to enter the market by offering contracts on soymeal or soyoil in an effort to draw away the business from the CBT. To date, the CBT has been successful in maintaining its position in the soybean complex. No other exchange has been successful in this area, although the Mid–America Commodity Exchange tries to compete in soybeans by offering smaller (1,000 versus 5,000 bushel) contracts.[9]

Another example of the grouping phenomenon can be drawn from the interest rate futures market. Successful contracts are traded on interest rate futures at the CBT and the IMM. The IMM trades contracts on only very short maturity instruments, such as 3-month Treasury bills and 3-month Eurodollar time deposits. The CBT, by contrast, trades contracts on instruments of longer maturities, such as Treasury bonds and Treasury notes.

For some commodities, futures contracts trade on a number of exchanges, which gives the appearance of a very heated competition among the exchanges. In such cases, some product differentiation usually makes the competition less direct. A good example of this occurs in the case of wheat. Wheat contracts are traded on the CBT, the Kansas City Board of Trade, the Mid–America Commodity Exchange, and the Minneapolis Grain Exchange. These futures contracts, however, differ in several ways. The standard trading unit is 5,000 bushels for most exchanges, but the Mid–America Exchange trades a contract for

1,000 bushels, thereby appealing to the smaller trader. All four of the contracts specify somewhat different kinds of wheat. However, a different kind of wheat may be substituted for the one actually specified in all of the wheat futures contracts. Such substitutions result in a price differential established by the exchange.

By specifying different deliverable grades of wheat, the exchanges may carve out their own market niches. For example, the Kansas City contract is written for No. 2 Hard Winter wheat with a maximum moisture content of 13.50 percent. The Minneapolis Grain Exchange contract is for U.S. No. 2 Northern Spring wheat, with 13.50 percent protein or higher. The CBT contract calls for delivery of one of the following types of wheat: No. 2 Soft Red, No. 2 Hard Red Winter, No. 2 Dark Northern Spring, or No. 1 Northern Spring. Since the kind of wheat differs slightly in each case, the exchanges avoid direct competition.

For wheat, another important factor in keeping contracts alive on four exchanges is the geographical distance. Each contract must specify how and where delivery can occur. The CBT, Kansas City, and Minneapolis contracts all call for delivery at different places. If we actually consider the cost of taking delivery, the difference between a Kansas City and a Minneapolis delivery is very important, since wheat's bulk makes its transportation quite expensive.

In still other cases, exchanges succeed even though they compete head on. Silver appears to be such a case, with the most active contracts being traded by the CBT and the COMEX. Although the two exchanges are based in Chicago and New York, respectively, geographical distance does not seem sufficient to account for their sustained success. The CBT trades a contract for 1,000 ounces and the COMEX contract is for 5,000 ounces. For both, deliverable silver must be of .999 fineness or higher. The peculiar thing about this market is the apparent dominance by the COMEX in the 5000-ounce contract, and by the CBT in the 1000-ounce contract. The COMEX 5000-ounce contract has a market almost twenty times as large as that for the CBT 1000-ounce contract. Yet both markets appear to be well established.

Contract Innovation and Contract Success

We have seen that exchanges tend to specialize in certain groups of commodities. Yet they compete in fringe areas where their successful contracts overlap. Relatively little is known about what makes a contract succeed or fail. For the exchanges, this is an important question, because introducing a new futures contract requires a substantial expense. The contract must first be designed and then approved by the regulators. Trading must be organized, and the contract must be promoted through advertising. To commit all of these resources and still fail is very frustrating. Yet, by recent estimates, only 30 percent of new futures contracts become profitable. This low success rate for new contracts indicates how much remains to be learned in the areas of contract design and competition.

Table 2.3 lists ten factors that increase the chance of a contract's success.[10] First, there needs to be a large cash market. Usually, futures trading starts only for goods with a well-established market for the cash good. For example, stock index futures trading was attractive because of the active market in stocks. Second, there must be price volatility. If the price does not fluctuate, there can be little interest in trading on the future price of the underlying good. In 1984, a futures contract on the Consumer Price Index (CPI) was launched. It failed in two years, perhaps due to a lack of volatility. Even in periods of high inflation, the CPI may not be particularly volatile. However, the contract launch occurred at an unlucky time of low and stable inflation. Third, there needs to be good information on cash market prices. As we will discuss in Chapter 3, there is an intimate relationship between cash market prices and futures market prices. Traders in both markets look to the other for information about the present and future direction of prices. In essence, traders trade futures contracts against the cash market goods. This makes good information about cash prices essential. Fourth, there must be a lack of close substitutes for the new futures contract. If a successful contract already exists for a particular good, traders will not want to switch to a new and untried similar contract. Traders like to trade in liquid contracts, so they will likely stay with a liquid existing contract rather than try an unproven and illiquid similar futures contract.

Fifth, traders not only trade the futures contract in relation to the cash market, but they also trade one futures against another. Therefore, a contract has an improved chance of success if there is already a similar, but not too similar, existing contract. For example, the Chicago Mercantile Exchange trades Treasury bill and Eurodollar futures. The two are closely related, so the presence of both stimulates spread trading. However, they are sufficiently distinct so that both contracts are valuable. Sixth, the contract must be designed well. In 1975 the Chicago Board of Trade listed a contract on mortgage interest rates, the GNMA

Table 2.3
Commodity Characteristics Desirable for Futures Trading

1.	Large cash market	6.	Good contract design
2.	Substantial price volatility	7.	Strong support from floor traders
3.	Good information on cash prices	8.	Large deliverable supply
4.	Lack of close substitutes	9.	Absence of regulatory barriers
5.	Availability of related contracts for spread trading	10.	Homogeneous cash commodity

contract. The contract suffered from poor design because one set of traders was interested in high coupon GNMAs, while a second group wanted to use the market for low coupon GNMAs. This conflict of trading interest contributed to the demise of the contract.[11] Seventh, there must be strong support from floor traders. When an exchange launches a contract, the exchange members need to support the new contract with active trading. If the members of the exchange are unwilling to trade the contract, the market will lack the liquidity necessary to attract traders from off-the-floor. Other factors on the list, such as price volatility, the potential for spread trading, and an active cash market help to stimulate floor trader interest. Eighth, there should be a large deliverable supply of the cash market good. With a large deliverable supply, no one party can control the cash good and affect price. Ninth, there should be an absence of regulatory barriers. In the early 1980s, the Chicago Board of Trade attempted to list a futures contract based on the Dow-Jones Industrial Index of thirty blue chip stocks. Dow-Jones successfully sued to prevent the listing altogether. Partially as a result of this failure, the Chicago Board of Trade has remained a distant second in stock index futures trading. Finally, the underlying good should be homogenous. This factor is important for ensuring a uniform and large deliverable supply. If the underlying good varies tremendously in quality, for example, the delivery process will be impaired.

In spite of these apparent determinants of futures market success, much is still unknown. Among the exchanges themselves there is considerable consternation about what makes a futures contract succeed. The entire issue of exchange and contract success has been gaining more attention. This issue is essentially an exploration of the industrial organization of futures markets.[12]

Brokers, Advisors, and Commodity Fund Managers

We have already seen that speculators and hedgers are traders who trade for their own accounts. Also, we have mentioned that the market utilizes brokers, an individual who execute trades for a customer, whether a speculator or a hedger. In this section, we consider brokers in more detail, because there are a number of different types of brokers. In addition, this section considers advisors and managers of futures funds, as listed in Table 2.4.

In discussing brokers in Chapter 1, we focused on an individual who executes orders on the floor of the exchange. We mentioned that such a broker is often the employee of a brokerage firm, such as Merrill Lynch. In the futures market, there are special names for the individuals and firms that execute orders on behalf of others.[13]

Table 2.4
Brokers, Advisors, and Fund Managers

1.	Floor Broker (FB)	4.	Associated Person (AP)
2.	Futures Commission Merchant (FCM)	5.	Commodity Trading Advisor (CTA)
3.	Introducing Broker (IB)	6.	Commodity Pool Operator (CPO)

Floor Broker (FB)

When an individual off the floor of the exchange places an order, he or she usually does so through an account executive with a brokerage firm. The order is transmitted to the floor of the exchange where it is executed by a **floor broker**—an individual who executes an order for the purchase or sale of a futures contract for another person. There are about 7,500 floor brokers.

Many floor brokers are members of **broker associations** or **broker groups**. A broker group is an association of floor brokers who band together to fill orders for their customers. The group might be as small as two brokers who cover for each other during vacations or as large as groups of brokers that operate in several markets and who share profits and expenses. These broker groups have become an important force among the trading community. For example, there are more than 200 broker groups at the Chicago Mercantile Exchange and more than 100 at the New York Mercantile Exchange.

Broker groups provide some services to the futures community. First, they provide a training ground for new brokers. Second, they provide a flexible pool of manpower to respond to radical fluctuations in trading volume. Third, they provide an easy way for large brokerage houses to achieve execution in several pits simultaneously. Fourth, the capital of the association stands behind each of the members of the group. Thus, there is less chance of any single broker defaulting.

In recent months, these broker groups have become the object of criticism for several reasons. First, the existence of an association might encourage members to trade with each other preferentially, instead of offering a trade to the entire market as the rules require. Second, broker groups were accused of dishonesty in fulfilling customer orders in some important recent legal actions. (See the discussion of the Chicago Trials later in this chapter.) For example, one member of a broker group might trade for his own account, while another member of the same group might act as a floor broker in executing an order for someone outside the broker group. The temptation exists to give a preferential price to the other member of the broker group at the expense of the outside party.[14]

Futures Commission Merchant (FCM)

A **futures commission merchant** is a firm or individual that accepts orders to trade futures on behalf of another party and who accepts money to support such an order. Thus, a brokerage firm that accepts orders to trade futures is a futures commission merchant or FCM. In many cases, the FCM will be a large firm with offices in many cities that accepts orders from individuals and other firms. The FCM transmits these orders to the floor of the exchange where they are executed by a floor broker. The floor broker may be an employee of the FCM, although this is not always the case. By 1990, there were more than 350 FCMs.

Introducing Broker (IB)

An **introducing broker** is an individual or firm that accepts orders to trade futures, but who does not accept the funds to support such orders. Thus, the FCM accepts money to support the orders (such as margin deposits), but the introducing broker does not. Essentially, the IB finds a customer and solicits that customer's business. However, the IB does not process the trade or hold monies for margin. Instead, the IB works with another broker called a **carrying broker** who processes the trade, holds the margin deposit, and provides accounting and documentation of the trades to the customer. The introducing broker and carrying broker share the commissions earned for executing trades. In 1990, there were more than 1,700 IBs.

Associated Person (AP)

An **associated person** is an individual who solicits orders, customers, or customer funds, or an individual who supervises anyone who makes such solicitations. Thus, a floor broker or an introducing broker is also an associated person, as is the manager of a branch office of an FCM. This broad category includes most of the professional individuals who make their livings in the futures industry. There were more than 55,000 APs in 1990.

Commodity Trading Advisor (CTA)

A **commodity trading advisor** is a person who directly or indirectly advises others regarding their futures trading. This category also applies to individuals who advise the public through written publications or other mass media. Thus, the writer of a futures newsletter that recommends certain positions in the futures market would be a CTA. In 1990, there were more than 2,400 CTAs.

Commodity Pool Operator (CPO)

A **commodity pool operator** is an individual or firm that operates or solicits funds for a commodity pool. A **commodity pool** consists of a collection of funds used to engage in futures trading activities. Typically, a number of individuals contribute funds to form the commodity pool. The pool operator uses those funds to engage in speculative futures trading. The individuals who contributed monies to the pool own a share of the entire pool. Thus, a commodity pool is similar to a mutual fund in which individuals contribute funds for investment in stocks and bonds. In 1990, there were approximately 1,250 commodity pool operators in the United States.

The Internationalization of Futures Markets

For decades, the United States has dominated the futures industry. Until recently, the totality of foreign exchanges generated a relatively insignificant trading volume compared to the United States. That has changed in the last five years, and all indications suggest that foreign futures exchanges will continue to grow much more rapidly than U.S. exchanges.

Growing Foreign Exchanges

Table 2.5 lists the top ten futures exchanges around the world. While U.S. exchanges continue to enjoy a commanding lead, with 73 percent of the top ten exchanges' trading volume, the dominance of the United States has diminished considerably. Japan is the major foreign competitor with 12.5 percent of the top ten exchanges' trading volume.

While the United States clearly dominates worldwide futures trading, other nations and regions continue to obtain a larger share of worldwide volume. In 1989 the United States held 62.21 percent of futures volume, as Table 2.6 shows. However, this was down from a 69.11 percent share in 1988. Most of these foreign exchanges are quite new. In spite of their recent start and relatively small size, the foreign exchanges present new competitive challenges to the dominating Chicago-based exchanges. This competition arises in virtually all types of futures contracts. Table 2.7 lists the most successful contracts traded on foreign exchanges.

Table 2.5
Top Ten Futures Exchanges for 1989

Exchange	1989 Volume	Percentage of Top 10 Volume
Chicago Board of Trade	138,351,317	33.42
Chicago Mercantile Exchange	104,654,463	25.28
New York Mercantile Exchange	38,490,463	9.30
Tokyo Stock Exchange	27,644,506	6.68
Matif–Paris	26,002,003	6.28
London International Financial Futures Exchange	23,859,399	5.76
Commodity Exchange of New York	19,052,952	4.60
Osaka	12,053,413	2.91
Tokyo Commodity Exchange	12,017,889	2.90
Sydney Futures Exchange	11,821,593	2.86
Total Top 10 1989 Volume	413,947,998	100.00

Source: *Futures and Options World Directory and Review*, 1990.

Table 2.6
1989 Futures Trading Volume by Region

Region	Percentage of Volume
United States	62.21
Europe	18.47
Far East	12.20
Other	7.12
(Australia, Brazil, Canada, Kuala Lumpur, New Zealand, Sweden)	

Source: *FIA Review*, May/June 1990.

Around–the–Clock Trading

With the development of foreign futures exchanges, futures trading on some goods continues almost 24 hours a day. In this respect, the three most popular contracts are Treasury bills, Eurodollars, and Treasury bonds. For Treasury bills and Eurodollars, futures contracts trade in Singapore, London, Chicago, and Tokyo. Because these markets trade during local daylight hours, they cover different periods of time. Among them, these futures exchanges offer trading more than 20 hours of each 24 hour period. In many instances, the trading hours overlap. First, Tokyo and Singapore have almost identical trading hours, which one might expect because they are in similar time zones. Before Singapore closes, the London market opens. The Chicago markets open during London's afternoon trading. The only block of time that is not covered is in the late afternoon U.S. time. As recently as 1982, trading on these contracts was only available for 6.5 hours per day.

For U.S. Treasury bonds, similar trading hours are available. Contracts on U.S. bonds trade in London, Chicago, New York, and Tokyo. The Chicago Board of Trade has two sessions per day. One session occurs during regular business hours, while the other covers the evening hours in Chicago. Taken together, these exchanges offer futures trading on Treasury bonds 18.5 hours of each 24 hour period.[15]

Table 2.7
Major Futures Contracts Traded Abroad
Contracts with trading volume greater than 1 million

Contract	Exchange	1989 Volume (millions)
Government Bond	Tokyo Stock Exchange	18.9
Notionnel (Govt. bond)	Matif–Paris	15.0
Short Sterling (Govt. bond)	London International Financial Futures Exchange	7.1
90–Day Bank Bill	Sydney Futures Exchange	5.9
Nikkei 225 (Stock index)	Osaka	5.4
American Soybeans	Tokyo Grain Exchange	4.0
Topix (Stock index)	Tokyo Stock Exchange	3.7
Cotton Yarn	Tokyo Commodity Exchange	3.4
Platinum	Tokyo Commodity Exchange	3.0
Gasoil	International Petroleum Exchange–London	1.7
Cocoa	London Futures and Options Exchange	1.6
Sugar	London Futures and Options Exchange	1.3

Source: *Futures and Options World Directory and Review*, 1990.

U.S. Trading of Foreign Products

While U.S. products dominate around-the-clock trading, a number of foreign products are now available for trading by U.S. participants. (The Commodity Futures Trading Commission [CFTC], a U.S. regulator, must approve contracts before they can trade in the United States.) Currently, the only foreign products available for trading in the U.S. are Japanese government bonds and stock index futures contracts. However, these stock index contracts are based on the stock indexes of England, Canada, and Japan. Further, a number of other goods are under review by the CFTC, and these include interest rate futures from Australia. The next few years will see a rapid expansion of foreign products available for U.S. trading.

International Competition in Trading Costs

With the ability of many traders to choose the country in which they wish to trade, exchange fees become a matter of competitive concern. For example, we have seen that Eurodollars trade in a number of markets worldwide. As a result, exchanges compete for Eurodollar trading volume. One element of this competition is the fee the exchange charges for executing an order. The large exchanges with well-established contracts have the most latitude in setting fees. Traders need those contracts and would likely feel forced to pay even excessively high fees to trade those markets.

Ironically, the largest exchanges, those in the United States, have the lowest fees. These lower fees may reflect economies of scale in operating a futures exchange. European exchanges are somewhat higher, and the highest fees are found in Asian markets. For example, a member of the Chicago Board of Trade can trade a contract for substantially less than $1. By contrast, a member of the Tokyo Commodity Exchange may face a fee as large as $20. Many observers see exchange fees as an important point of future competition among exchanges.[16]

Electronic Futures Trading

From the beginning of organized futures exchanges in the mid-1800s to a few years ago, the system of open outcry has been the only method of futures trading. While open outcry continues to dominate futures trading, we are now seeing the emergence of automated trading systems that promise to change the entire face of the futures markets.

The advent of electronic trading systems also promises to be an important element in global competition among futures exchanges. In futures trading, the

U.S. markets are the oldest and best established. In some ways, the members of the U.S. exchanges are the most conservative and wedded to tradition, particularly the tradition of trading in pits through open outcry. Exchange policies are controlled by exchange members. In the Chicago markets, a high proportion of members are individuals who trade for their own accounts. Their livelihood depends upon the trading acumen that they have developed through their years in the trading pits. Electronic trading systems threaten to make those open outcry skills obsolete. Not surprisingly, these members have resisted any threats to the system of open outcry.

New and smaller exchanges have little tradition to confront. Compared to pit trading with open outcry, electronic trading is definitely cheaper to launch. Many traders also believe that electronic systems are operationally superior to pit trading. Further, there are many different electronic trading systems, all of which have their own features. No matter what one believes about the virtues of open outcry versus electronic trading, it is clear that electronic trading is here to stay. Because electronic trading is largely technologically driven, we can expect accelerating change in this area. This section describes the recent introduction of electronic trading systems.

GLOBEX

Because of initial resistance by U.S. traders, exchanges in the United States have been relatively slow to develop electronic trading systems. However, because the U.S. exchanges dominate world futures markets, any system that prevails in the United States will have an extremely good chance of being the dominant electronic trading system in the world. In 1990, GLOBEX emerged as the dominant electronic trading system in the United States.[17] GLOBEX has been developed by the Chicago Mercantile Exchange and has received the support of the Chicago Board of Trade.[18] As we have seen, these two exchanges generate more than 50 percent of worldwide trading volume. In addition, the Paris exchange, MATIF, will trade through GLOBEX, and GLOBEX has actively been courting other exchanges as potential participants.

To trade futures through GLOBEX, a trader must have access to a GLOBEX terminal. GLOBEX will make these terminals available to traders around the world, and all terminals will be linked electronically to a central computer. The GLOBEX terminal is based on IBM–PC technology and will use an 80386 processor operating under Microsoft Windows.

The GLOBEX screen consists of five windows. First, the Trading Window displays market information on any combination of instruments available for trading through GLOBEX. For example, a trader might want to configure the Trading Window to show information on foreign exchange futures. Second, the Ticker Window shows current market activity. Every trade that occurs on the system is reported to every GLOBEX terminal. Also, the Ticker Window will show each change in the best bid and offer prices. Third, the Host Response Window shows messages from the host or central computer. For instance, a trader will receive order acknowledgments from the central computer in this window. Fourth, information from the cash market appears in the Monitor Window. Futures traders need constant information about the price of the underlying cash market instrument, so the trader will configure the Monitor Window to show the cash instruments that correspond to the futures shown in the Trading Window. Fifth, the Alerts Window alerts the terminal user when prices reach certain pre-set levels.

Transacting on GLOBEX involves seven steps, which are shown in Figure 2.1. First, a trader enters an order through the GLOBEX terminal. Second, the host computer checks the credit of the user to ensure that the trader is entitled to place the order. Third, the computer matches the buy and sell orders. Once the system matches a buy and sell order, a transaction occurs. Fourth, the host computer confirms the transactions to both the buyer's and seller's GLOBEX terminals. Fifth, the host computer reports the transaction to all quote vendors for dissemination to worldwide financial reporting services. Sixth, the host computer routes the transaction to the clearinghouse. Seventh, the accounts are settled for the buyer and seller. The clearing member firm adjusts the buyer's and seller's accounts to show their new position and their new margin requirements that have resulted from the trade.

Initially, GLOBEX will augment open outcry. When it first starts trading, GLOBEX will be restricted to hours when the Chicago Mercantile Exchange is not open. However, when one considers the success of electronic trading systems at other exchanges, it seems clear that GLOBEX has a future that goes far beyond a mere supplement to pit trading. Initially slated to begin trading in 1990, the start of GLOBEX trading was delayed several times, due to the need to test the system further and to consolidate technical links with Reuters. Reuters, a worldwide financial information firm, will disseminate GLOBEX prices.

Electronic Trading Outside the United States

With GLOBEX just beginning to operate in 1991, the United States definitely lags behind some foreign exchanges in electronic trading. For example, some foreign exchanges have been trading futures electronically since 1986. Further, some of these exchanges have only electronic trading for certain contracts. At the London Futures and Options Exchange, administrators believe that electronic trading is the cheapest, best way to list a new contract to see if it will succeed. Table 2.8 lists some of the foreign exchanges that trade options and futures electronically.

Figure 2.1
Order Routing Through GLOBEX

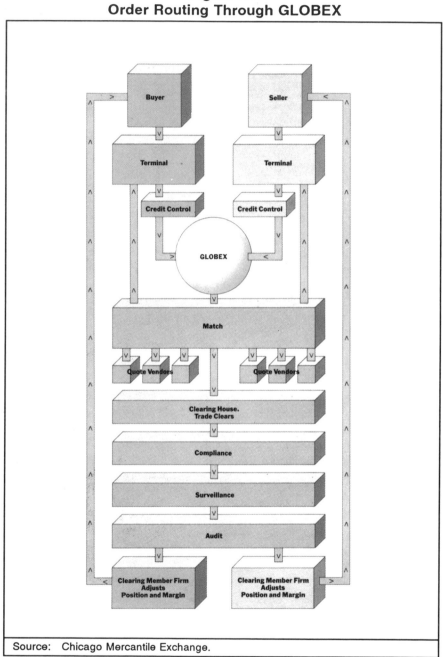

Source: Chicago Mercantile Exchange.

Table 2.8
Electronic Futures Trading

Country/Exchange	Status
Germany—Deutsche Terminboerse	Full automation
Irish Futures and Options Exchange	Full automation
London International Financial Futures Exchange	Full automation
Spain—Mercado de Futuros Financieros	Full automation
Tokyo Stock Exchange	Full automation
New Zealand Futures Exchange	Full automation
Swiss Options and Financial Futures Exchange	Full automation

Source: Amy Rosenbaum, "Scouting Automation: What's the Competition Like?"
Futures, April 1990.

Current Issues in Regulation

In recent years, a number of events have occurred that challenge the integrity of futures markets. In addition, regulatory jurisdictional disputes have arisen that draw the attention of regulatory bodies from the market. Examining these disputes helps to show the regulatory structure of the markets. Finally, this section examines some current regulatory issues that illuminate the operation of the market.

Market Honesty—The Chicago Trials

In January 1989, the federal government revealed that it had been conducting an undercover sting operation designed to uncover fraud and illegal trading at the Chicago Mercantile Exchange and the Chicago Board of Trade. Beginning in early 1987, undercover FBI agents began trading in the Swiss franc and Japanese yen pits at the CME and in the soybean pit at the CBT. After almost two years of gathering evidence through this undercover investigation, the government began indicting traders in 1989. Eventually, the government indicted 47 traders and one clerk.

Indictments charged the traders with fraudulent conduct that allowed them to steal customer funds. Sixteen traders pleaded guilty to some charges. In basic outline, the alleged fraudulent schemes operated as follows: Often the alleged fraudulent activity began after a floor broker made an error in filling an order.

The rules of the exchange require the trader making such an error to pay for the mistake, thereby leaving the customer whole. According to allegations, the broker making the error would induce a friendly floor trader to absorb the loss temporarily. This kept the floor broker from having to make restitution to the customer, but left the broker with an obligation to the accommodating floor trader. Later, when the floor broker held another order, he would trade with the floor trader at a non-competitive price to repay the floor trader for his initial help. In making such a trade, the new customer would unwittingly absorb the loss due to the floor broker's original mistake.

To illustrate this general point more concretely, consider the following constructed example. A floor broker receives an order to buy one Swiss franc futures contract at the current market price of 68.00 cents per franc. By mistake, the broker sells at that price. Before he realizes the error, the price rises to 68.01. Now the broker has an obligation to undo his mistake and absorb the loss from 68.01 to 68.00 for the customer. In other words, the customer is entitled to have his trade filled at the 68.00 purchase price. With a single contract consisting of 125,000 Swiss francs, the total loss is $1,250 per contract. Instead of swallowing the loss, the floor broker of our example induces a friendly floor trader to sell a contract to him at 68.00, and the broker passes this price along to the original customer. At this point, the original customer has no loss, because his or her order is filled at the correct price of 68.00. However, the floor trader has done the floor broker a favor by absorbing the loss of $.01 per contract. Later the floor broker receives an order from a second customer to sell a Swiss franc contract and the market price is 68.40. Instead of selling the contract through open outcry at the fair price of 68.40, the floor broker sells the contract to the cooperative floor trader at 68.39. This repays the floor trader, because the floor trader took a $.01 loss in the first trade and makes up the loss on the second transaction. However, the second customer has been cheated. Instead of receiving the correct price of 68.40, the second customer receives only 68.39. Thus, the fraudulent activity allows the broker to evade responsibility for his or her original error, and the unsuspecting second customer absorbs the loss.[19]

In May 1990, three Swiss franc traders, Mosky, Scheck, and Zatz, went to trial for abuses such as those described in the example. Court documents allege, ". . . brokers regularly solicited accommodating local traders to absorb losses caused by order-filling errors, or outtrades, and repaid such locals through the illegal manipulation of other customer orders in their possession."[20] The three traders were charged with a total of 108 counts. In July 1990, the jury returned a guilty verdict on eight counts, acquitted on 22, and was deadlocked on 78. Zatz was not found guilty on any charge. Scheck was found guilty on a single count of skimming $50 from a customer, and Mosky was found guilty on seven counts in which customers lost a total of $150.[21]

While these verdicts led some to wonder whether the investigation and trial really points to any systematic wrongdoing, other trials remain. Accordingly, it is still early to judge whether these investigations can sustain the claim that the futures markets are generally corrupt. As *Business Week* concluded after the first trial, ". . . sending people to jail for stealing $50 from a customer is something far different from proving pervasive fraud on the commodities floor. Unless [prosecutor] Raphaelson can do that in the upcoming trials, the massive government probe will have proved much ado about little."[22]

In late fall 1990, the government appeared to be having more success. First, six Japanese yen traders, eight soybean traders, and three T-bond traders pleaded guilty and agreed to cooperate with the government. Second, both prosecution and defense appear to agree that evidence is stronger in the trials of soybean and Japanese yen traders.[23]

Audit Trails

Whatever the outcome in the Chicago trials, the indictments have already generated significant change in the futures industry. Most of the abuses alleged in the Chicago indictments turn on falsifying the timing of trades. The exchange is able to track the price of each contract on a minute by minute or even a second by second basis. Assume for a moment that the Swiss franc price remains at 68.00 cents for a full minute. If a trader attempts to record a trade during that minute at a different price, it will be possible to detect the abuse. However, such detection depends upon knowing exactly when a trade occurs. Under the current system, it is possible for traders to misrepresent the timing of a trade. For example, assume a trade takes place during the minute when prices stayed at 68.00. However, in the next minute, the price moves to 68.05. If the trader can record the trade as having taken place in the second minute, he or she has a chance to falsify the trade price as being 68.05 instead of 68.00.

Because the Chicago indictments allege just such abuses, they have stimulated demands for better auditing of trades. Under the current system, traders at the Chicago Board of Trade and the Chicago Mercantile Exchange record the timing of trades only within 30-minute brackets. At most other U.S. exchanges, trades are recorded to the nearest minute. At almost all U.S. exchanges, the trader manually records the time. For a trader bent on fraud, there is ample opportunity for falsifying the timing of a trade.

Exchanges are now working to develop hand-held terminals that will record all trades. Traders in the pit would trade in the normal way, but would immediately enter the result of the trade in the terminal, and the information would be transmitted immediately to the exchange's central computer. Under this system, it would be possible to know exactly when an order was executed. Coupling this information about the timing of the order with knowledge of the futures price at the same time would prevent orders from occurring at fictitious prices. A report from the Government Accounting Office supports this optimistic assessment of hand-held terminals.[24]

Hand-held terminals might help stop abuses such as those alleged in the Chicago trials. However, other forms of automated trading, such as screen trading through GLOBEX or some similar system, would have the same virtues as well. Therefore, the indictments in Chicago have provided an important impetus not only to the development of hand-held terminals, but they have also stimulated a general movement toward automated trading systems to replace open outcry. Table 2.9 lists and defines some of the abuses that increasing automation can help control.

Dual Trading

In **dual trading**, a single individual fulfills the function of a floor trader and a floor broker simultaneously. That is, a single individual trades for his or her own account, while executing orders for traders off-the-floor of the exchange. This practice has been permitted for many decades. However, it does offer potential for abuse. In recent months, the practice has come under fire, partially because

Table 2.9 Abusive Trading Practices	
Pre–arranged trading	agreeing to some aspect of a transaction before it is openly executed on the exchange floor
Accommodation trading	entering transactions to assist another floor participant in accomplishing improper trading objectives
Trading before customers orders, front running	trading for one's personal account or an account in which one has an interest, while having in hand any executable customer order in that contract
Bucketing	failing to introduce an order to the marketplace, traditionally occurring when a broker noncompetitively takes the other side of a customer order to the detriment of the customer or other members
Wash trading	entering transactions to provide the appearance of trading activity without resulting in a change in market position
Curb trading	trading after the official close of trading
Cross–trading	matching customer orders on the floor without offering them competitively
Source: Government Accounting Office, "Automation Can Enhance Detection of Trade Abuses but Introduces New Risks," September 1989.	

it can lead to practices such as those alleged in the Chicago trials. Because dual trading creates a situation in which a single individual has his or her own orders in hand along with orders from an outside customer, dual trading can also facilitate front running, bucketing, or cross-trading.

Dual trading has been a feature of futures markets for decades. Traders maintain that dual trading serves the market in several ways. First, defenders maintain that dual trading helps promote liquidity in the market. If a trader can only execute orders for his or her own account or only execute orders for others, there will be less potential trading volume at any given time. Second, this lack of liquidity may lead to larger spreads between bid and asked prices, thereby making the market less efficient than it would be otherwise. Finally, defenders of dual trading maintain that the practice keeps trading costs low, because a dual trader needs to make only a portion of his or her income by acting as a floor broker.

Dual trading is a pervasive feature of futures trading. In 1989, the CFTC conducted a major study of dual trading. According to this study, over half of all contracts traded were handled by dual traders in the CFTC study period. Further, over 40 percent of the floor participants were dual traders. Also, dual traders executed 46 percent of all personal trading and 82 percent of all customer volume.

Table 2.10 summarizes the major findings of that study. The CFTC found, first, that most dual traders tend to specialize. As a general rule, most dual traders perform mainly as brokers or mainly as floor traders. Few dual traders had a thoroughly mixed collection of orders. Second, dual trading is not concentrated in the less liquid portion of the market, such as low volume contracts or distant expiration months. If dual trading has a primary function of

---

Table 2.10
Major Findings of CFTC Study of Dual Trading

1. Dual traders tend to specialize in acting as floor brokers or floor traders.

2. Dual trading is not more prevalent in low volume markets or more distant trading months.

3. Dual traders do not achieve better execution than non–dual brokers.

4. Dual traders do not perform better than non–dual brokers in providing market liquidity.

Source: Commodity Futures Trading Commission, "Economic Analysis of Dual Trading on Commodity Exchanges," November 1989.

---

providing liquidity to the market, dual trading should be more concentrated in these less liquid trading situations. Third, dual traders and exclusive brokers appear to perform equally well in fulfilling customer orders. Fourth, dual traders do not seem to provide more liquidity to the market than do exclusive traders. Based on its study the CFTC concluded, ". . . dual trading is not critical to providing liquidity and low-cost trade executions on commodity exchanges."[25]

Faced with the conclusions of the CFTC report and a legislative effort in Congress to restrict dual trading, the Chicago Mercantile Exchange imposed restrictions on dual trading in 1990. The CME voted to end dual trading on contracts with daily volume of more than 10,000 contracts. Also in 1990, the CFTC proposed a pilot program in which other exchanges will ban dual trading in one commodity and one financial futures contract. All signs indicate that this CFTC program will be hotly opposed by most other exchanges.

Market Corners and Squeezes

The most dramatic dislocation in a futures market occurs in a corner or squeeze. While various commentators use somewhat different definitions, we will define a **corner** as a successful effort by a trader or group of traders to manipulate the price of a futures contract by gaining effective control over trading in the futures and the supply of the deliverable good. In a market **squeeze**, a trader achieves effective control over the price of a futures contract due to disruptions in the supply of the cash commodity. The manipulative part of a squeeze arises when the trader uses this circumstance to control the price of the good. These disruptions need not be due to actions of the controlling trader, but might originate from other forces, such as the weather.

Manipulating the price of a futures contract is a violation of the Commodity Exchange Act. Such price manipulation not only cheats other traders, but it also impairs the marketplace. First, other traders are cheated because the manipulation forces them to trade at a price that is not economically justified. In general, markets function properly when prices in the market represent the true equilibrium value of the good being traded. By definition, in a corner or squeeze, the price is manipulated, so it cannot be at its equilibrium level. Second, a manipulation also impairs the market because honest traders flee markets in which prices do not correspond to the true economic value of the good being traded. If honest traders abandon the futures market, the market cannot serve its social functions. The market will not serve its price discovery function because the prices in the market are manipulated prices. Also, the market does not provide a means for transferring risk, because honest traders are afraid to participate in the market. For these reasons, the price manipulation associated with a corner or squeeze is the worst fate that can befall a market.

This section discusses one proven manipulation and one alleged manipulation. First, we consider a manipulation in silver by the Hunt brothers of Dallas and their co-conspirators. This manipulation occurred in 1979-1980. Second, we examine an alleged manipulation of soybeans that occurred in 1989. At that time, the large grain-trading firm Ferruzzi Finanziaria held seven million bushels of soybeans, and the exchanges and the CFTC moved to force Ferruzzi to liquidate. In Federal Court, the Hunt brothers were found to have manipulated silver prices. However, Ferruzzi has never been brought to trial, and the manipulation in soybeans has not been proven.

The Hunt Silver Manipulation. With little doubt, the Hunt manipulation of silver in 1979-1980 was the grandest futures manipulation of the twentieth century. At one time, the Hunts and their co-conspirators controlled silver worth more than $14 billion. Figure 2.2 shows the price of silver for 1979 and 1980. At the beginning of 1979, an ounce of silver was worth about $6. In January 1980, the price briefly exceeded $50 during one trading day. In March 1980, the price of silver crashed, and silver fell to the $12 per ounce range. In 1990, silver traded for less than $5 per ounce.

In some ways, the silver manipulation was very simple, while in other ways it was incredibly complex.[26] The manipulative efforts involved many other

Figure 2.2
Silver Prices in 1979–1980

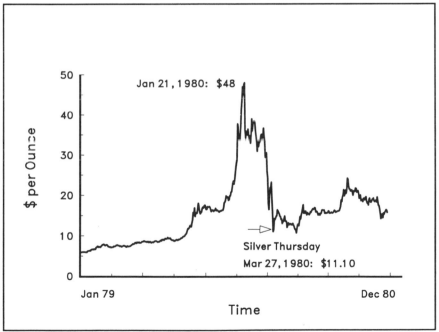

participants besides the flamboyant and well-known Hunts. These other conspirators included a number of very wealthy Saudis. In outline, the Hunts operated a corner on the silver market. They amassed gigantic futures positions and demanded delivery on those contracts as they came due. At the same time, they bought tremendous quantities of physical silver and held the physical silver off the market. Thus, they accelerated demand through the futures market as they restricted supply through the cash market. As a result the price of silver shot up.

As silver approached $50 per ounce in January 1980, the exchanges and the CFTC took effective action by imposing liquidation-only trading. Under **liquidation-only trading**, traders are allowed to trade only to close an existing futures position; they are not allowed to establish any new positions. The next day, the price of silver dropped by $12 per ounce in one day. From January through February and into March, the manipulators struggled to support the price of silver. However, the exchanges also increased margins on silver. On March 19, the Hunts defaulted on their margin obligations. In a final desperate attempt to support the price of silver, the manipulators announced a plan on March 26, 1980 to issue bonds backed by their physical silver holdings. The market interpreted this ploy as an act of desperation and the market crashed again the next day. March 27, 1980 has become known as Silver Thursday because of this famous crash that ended the Hunts' effective domination of silver.

Minpeco, S.A., a Peruvian government-sponsored minerals marketing firm, was a major short trader in the silver market during 1979-1980. They sued the Hunts, their co-conspirators, and their brokers for $90 million of actual losses plus interest, plus trebled punitive damages. Minpeco won about $200 million in settlements and judgments against the defendants. This sum included a pre-judgment settlement payment of $34 million by Merrill Lynch and Bache, two of the conspirators' largest brokers. The jury found that the three Hunt brothers, Bunker, Herbert, and Lamar, had indeed manipulated the silver market. After the verdict, Lamar Hunt, owner of the Kansas City Chiefs NFL team, paid $17 million in settlement. The full settlement was never collected from Bunker and Herbert, who sought protection in bankruptcy. Thus, these two brothers, who began the 1980s among the world's richest men, were bankrupt by 1990.

The Alleged Soybean Manipulation of 1989. The Soybean crisis of 1989 had its origins at least as far back as the preceding year. In 1988, the Midwest suffered a severe drought, which greatly reduced soybean yields. Thus, the market entered the 1989 crop year with greatly diminished supplies. Figure 2.3 shows the price of soybeans for 1989. Through early 1989, Central Soya, a wholly-owned grain subsidiary of the Italian firm Ferruzzi, amassed large holdings of physical soybeans and took large long positions in the May 1989 soybean contract. As late as May 16, Ferruzzi held 16.2 million bushels of May soybean futures. The Chicago Board of Trade revoked Ferruzzi's status as a hedger on May 18. This meant that Ferruzzi was forced to reduce its futures

Figure 2.3
Soybean Prices in 1989

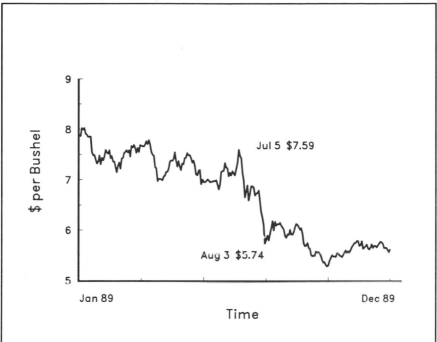

position to the 3 million bushel speculative position limit. As a result, the May contract liquidated in an orderly manner.

However, instead of merely offsetting its May positions, Ferruzzi **rolled its position forward**. That is, Ferruzzi sold May contracts and bought July soybean futures. This action set the stage for a larger problem in July. By early June, Ferruzzi held a long position of 32 million bushels in the July futures contract. In addition, by July 1, Ferruzzi had achieved effective control over the deliverable supply of soybeans. Ferruzzi controlled seven million bushels, while all other traders controlled only 1.6 million. With Ferruzzi holding 32 million bushels in long futures and only 1.6 million bushels available for delivery by other traders, Ferruzzi clearly had a dominant market position.

On July 11, 1989 the Chicago Board of Trade declared that an emergency existed. Effective on July 12, the Board of Trade revoked Ferruzzi's status as a hedger. This meant that Ferruzzi was once again subject to the 3 million bushel position limit. Further, the CBT ordered liquidation of at least 20 percent of futures positions for each of the next several trading days down to an absolute limit of no more than 1 million bushels at the close of trading on July 20. These actions helped avert the crisis, and the July contract traded without further disruptions. On September 15, 1989 Ferruzzi announced that its major grain and oilseed traders in Paris had resigned due to "differences over trading strategies."[27]

Jurisdictional Disputes

As we have seen, the Commodity Futures Trading Commission Act created the CFTC and gave it exclusive powers to regulate futures markets in the United States. In the 1930s, the Securities Act of 1933 brought the stock and bond markets under federal regulation. The Securities Exchange Act of 1934 created the Securities and Exchange Commission (SEC) and gave the SEC broad powers to regulate the market for long-term securities, including the organized stock exchanges.

The law specifically requires that securities exchanges register with the SEC and that they agree to comply with the laws governing them. Further, each exchange must organize its own procedures for the proper conduct of business, consistent with the guidelines prepared by the SEC. These exchange guidelines specify fair and unfair practices and include procedures for disciplining or expelling exchange members who transgress. The SEC has the power to enforce the laws in those cases where exchange self-regulation is lax.

Stock Index Futures.   In the 1930s, there were no futures contracts related to stocks. Futures on stock indexes began to trade only in the early 1980s under the jurisdiction of the CFTC. Later, the SEC came to believe that the proper regulatory body for all instruments related to equities is the SEC. The CFTC resisted giving up jurisdictional authority over the market that it successfully spawned. As a result, the two agencies are locked in a pitched battle to have the right to regulate stock index futures.

Federal regulatory agencies often struggle with each other for importance, and such struggles are not unknown among financial market regulators. However, the current high-stakes battle between the SEC and CFTC stems from the stock market crash of October 1987. On that day, the market lost about 22 percent of its value. As Chapter 10 explains, stock index futures and stock market trading are closely related through the practices of portfolio insurance and program trading. Some market observers believe that the crash was caused, or at least exacerbated, by trading in stock index futures. Others repudiate this conclusion altogether.[28] At any rate, there is no consensus that futures trading is responsible for the crash or even for an overall increase in stock market volatility.

The CFTC and the futures industry are totally opposed to regulation of stock index futures by the SEC. The CFTC clearly does not want to relinquish control of its jurisdiction. Currently, proposals in Congress would shift regulatory jurisdiction of stock index futures to the SEC, and these proposals have the backing of President Bush and Secretary of the Treasury Nicholas Brady. However, the futures industry has a strong Congressional lobby, and the outcome of this dispute is not clear.

Index Participations.　An **index participation** (IP) is an instrument that allows an investor to profit or lose based on the movement of an underlying basket of stocks for a given horizon. At the end of the horizon, the investor can take delivery of the underlying stocks or trade out of the position before delivery becomes required. IPs traded briefly on stock exchanges and at the Chicago Board Options Exchange. These exchanges are regulated by the Securities Exchange Commission.

The CFTC contended that index participations were merely poorly disguised stock index futures. As futures, the CFTC contends that they are subject to regulation by the CFTC, not the SEC. The CFTC sought relief in Federal Court. In August 1989, the court ruled that index participations are stock index futures and, therefore, subject to CFTC regulation. However, the exchanges where index participations were trading were not registered with the CFTC. Therefore, they were forced to stop trading the IPs. The affected exchanges appealed the decision to the Supreme Court, but the Court refused to review the lower court's decision. Thus, judicially at least, IPs are stock index futures, and any exchange wishing to trade them must do so under the regulation of the CFTC.

Conclusion

In this chapter, we have considered some of the organizational features of the futures industry in detail. We began by examining the rules for margins on combinations of futures positions. With greater integration of markets, these futures spreads are becoming more common and presenting a greater challenge to clearinghouses' abilities to assess risk. Currently, efforts to consider the risk of the trader's entire portfolio have led to the SPAN margin system and the development of intermarket cross-margining.

The futures industry today is experiencing dramatic change as markets abroad come to compete with the long-dominant U.S. futures exchanges. To a great extent, this industry development is fueled by the promise or threat of electronic trading. Some industry observers envision a worldwide market with electronic links. In such a world, no exchange is free of competition. In the context of internationalization, we considered GLOBEX, an electronic trading system that may enjoy worldwide use.

We also considered the variety of futures market specialists. The floor broker, futures commission merchant, and introducing broker all play related but specialized roles. The function of the account executive and introducing broker often overlap with the role of the commodity trading advisor. In recent years, managed futures trading has become more important, creating a growing role for the commodity pool operator.

Finally, we considered current issues in regulation. The trials of traders in Chicago and the regulatory struggle between the CFTC and the SEC threaten to change the shape of the entire futures industry. In addition, criticisms of dual trading and the demand for improved audit trails will also change industry practice.

Questions and Problems

1. Explain the difference between an inter-commodity and an intra-commodity spread.

2. A speculator buys a nearby and sells a distant silver futures contract. What must happen for the trader to make a profit from this combined position?

3. A speculator buys a silver futures contract and sells a gold futures contract for the same expiration month. What kind of spread is this? What must happen for the speculator to profit?

4. What is "intermarket cross-margining?" Explain how cross-margining employs the ideas of portfolio theory.

5. If margins are maintained at levels that keep risk constant for individual contracts, but intermarket cross-margining is introduced, what is likely to happen to the overall pool of margin funds across all markets? Explain.

6. Consider a rainfall futures contract that might be written for cash settlement depending on the amount of rainfall by a certain date at a variety of government weather stations. How would such a contract meet the conditions for success outlined in this chapter?

7. Explain the different roles of a floor broker and an account executive.

8. At a party, a man tells you that he is an introducing broker. He goes on to explain that his job is introducing prospective traders such as yourself to futures brokers. He also relates that he holds margin funds as a service to investors. What do you make of this explanation?

9. Assume that you are a floor broker and a friend of yours is a market maker who trades soybeans on the floor of the Chicago Board of Trade. Beans are trading at $6.53 per bushel. You receive an order to buy beans and you buy one contract from your friend at $6.54, one cent above the market. Who wins, who loses and why? Explain the rationale for making such practice illegal.

10. Explain how improving audit trails can help ensure that futures markets operate in greater accordance with the law.

11. Back at the party after several more hours. Your buddy from question 7 buttonholes you again and starts to explain his great success as a dual trader, trading both beans and corn. What do you think?

12. You are having trouble escaping from your friend in question 11. He goes on to explain that liquidation-only trading involves trading soybean against soyoil to profit from the liquidation that occurs when beans are crushed. Explain how your understanding of "liquidation-only trading" differs from your friend's.

13. A trader holds a long position in the MAR T-bond futures contract. She offsets this position and buys a JUN T-bond futures contract. What is the name for this kind of transaction?

Notes

1. The terminology for spreads is quite diverse. The definitions used here are not universal.

2. Virginia Grace France, "The Regulation of Margin Requirements: A Survey," Unpublished working paper, August 1990, University of Illinois, provides a comprehensive survey of margin regulations for futures, options, and options on futures.

3. This discussion of cross-margining draws on three principal sources. John P. Behof, "Intermarket Cross-Margining for Futures and Options," Issue Summary of the Federal Reserve Bank of Chicago, May 1989; Roger D. Rutz, "The Myth and Reality of Intermarket Cross-Margining," *Intermarket*,

August 1988; and Karen Pierog, "Cross-Margining Caught in Clearinghouse Cross Fire," *Futures*, September 1988.

4. Chapter 11 provides an introduction to option pricing and Chapter 12 considers options on futures in detail.

5. For more on the SPAN system, see the following three Chicago Mercantile Exchange booklets, "Standard Portfolio Analysis of Risk," 1989; "SPAN Overview," July 1990; "SPAN Technical Specifications," July 1990; and Terry Mayer, "SPAN-ning the Margin Problem for Commodity Options," *Futures*, December 1989.

6. A subsidiary of the New York Cotton Exchange also trades an index on the value of the U.S. dollar.

7. Da-Hsiang Donald Lien, "Entry-Deterring Contract Specification on Futures Markets," *Journal of Futures Markets*, 10:1, February 1990, pp. 89-95, analyzes exchange motivation in introducing new futures contracts. Consider an exchange that first introduces a contract in a given commodity. Lien argues that this innovative exchange will tend to introduce a conventional cash settlement contract to bar entry from a similar contract by another exchange. Lien argues that, if there were no competitive pressure, the exchange would be more likely to use a different settlement method. Thus, the exchanges and traders of the contract all lose when the innovative exchange chooses a contract specification to deter entry from a competitor.

8. The relationship among soybeans, soymeal, and soyoil is known as the "crush," because beans are crushed to make meal and oil. Chapter 4 examines the pricing of the crush in detail.

9. Recently the Mid-America Commodity Exchange became affiliated with the Chicago Board of Trade.

10. Recently, there have been more formal attempts to explain why some contracts succeed and others fail. Deborah G. Black, *Success and Failure of Futures Contracts: Theory and Empirical Evidence*, Salomon Brothers Monograph Series in Finance and Economics, Monograph 1986-1, argues that the more variable the price of a commodity and the larger the market for the cash good, the better is the chance for a successful futures contract. In addition to these traditional factors, she argued that residual risk and liquidity for cross-hedging were important. The list of ten contract features

stems in part from Black and from Karen Pierog and Jon Stein, "New Contracts: What Makes Them Fly or Fail?" *Futures*, September 1989.

11. Elizabeth Tashjian Johnston and John J. McConnell, "Requiem for a Market: An Analysis of the Rise and Fall of a Financial Futures Contract," *The Review of Financial Studies*, 2:1, 1989, pp. 1-23, conclude that the contract failed due to its poor design. See also Karen Pierog and Jon Stein, "New Contracts: What Makes Them Fly or Fail?" *Futures*, September 1989. Subsequently, the Chicago Board of Trade has tried to introduce improved contracts on mortgage interest rates.

12. See, for example, D. Carlton, "Futures Markets: Their Purpose, Their History, Their Growth, Their Successes and Failures," *The Journal of Futures Markets*, Fall 1984, 4:3, pp. 237-271. See also, Ronald W. Anderson, *The Industrial Organization of Futures Markets*, (Lexington, Mass: D. C. Heath and Company, 1984). Anderson's book contains a number of articles on different aspects of the industrial organization of futures markets.

13. The definitions used in this section are drawn from various publications of the National Futures Association. Statistics regarding the number of firms and individuals of each classification appear in the 1989 *Annual Report* of the Commodity Futures Trading Commission.

14. For more on broker groups, see Ginger Szala and Susan Abbott, "Broker Groups: The Good, the Bad and the Ugly," *Futures*, February 1990.

15. These statistics are drawn from Morton N. Lane, "Round the Clock, Round the World," *FIA Review*, January/February 1990. For more on twenty-four hour trading, see Barbara B. Diamond and Mark P. Kollar, *24-Hour Trading*, New York: John Wiley, 1989.

16. See Amy Rosenbaum, "Are Exchange Fees Worth Scrutiny of Traders?" *Futures*, July 1990.

17. For a comprehensive analysis of GLOBEX, see J. Behof, "GLOBEX: A Global Automated Transaction System for Futures and Options," Federal Reserve Bank of Chicago, Department of Supervision and Regulation, June 1990.

18. At one time, the Chicago Board of Trade sought to develop an independent system, called Aurora. Aurora was intended to be a computer replication of pit trading. However, in Spring 1990, the Chicago Board of Trade and the Chicago Mercantile Exchange agreed to put their full commitment behind GLOBEX, with an unspecified role to be allocated to Aurora.

19. This example is constructed to fit details of the case available in the financial press. It is not based on any facts presented in court documents or on evidence presented at trial. Nor does the example purport to show any guilt on the part of any individual.

20. Scott McMurray, "Futures Pit Trader Goes to Trial," *The Wall Street Journal*, May 8, 1990.

21. David Greising, "Was the Scandal in the Pits Mostly Small Potatoes?" *Business Week*, July 23, 1990 and Scott McMurray, "What Went Wrong in Chicago Pits Case," *The Wall Street Journal*, July 11, 1990.

22. David Greising, "Was the Scandal in the Pits Mostly Small Potatoes?" *Business Week*, July 23, 1990.

23. See D. Greising, "This Time, the Feds' Case May Not Be the Pits," *Business Week*, September 24, 1990.

24. Government Accounting Office, "Automation Can Enhance Detection of Trade Abuses but Introduces New Risks," September 1989. The new risks would arise from typical computer problems: faulty processing, computer breakdown, and lack of computer security. For more on the technology of the hand-held terminals, see Charles Siler, "Fraud Busters," *Forbes*, February 19, 1990.

25. Commodity Futures Trading Commission, "Economic Analysis of Dual Trading on Commodity Exchanges," November 1989.

26. For more on the Hunt manipulation, see Robert W. Kolb and Pablo T. Spiller, *The Hunt Silver Manipulation*, forthcoming from Yale University Press.

27. This account relies on Fred Bailey, "Emergency Action: July 1989 Soybeans," Chicago: Chicago Board of Trade, 1990. See also Keith Schap and Charles Flory, "Ferruzzi vs. CBOT: Who Is Right?" *Futures*, Septem-

ber 1989 and Karen Pierog, "Report Vindicates CBOT Action in July Soybeans," *Futures*, October 1989.

28. Two dispassionate studies reach somewhat similar conclusions. See Lawrence Harris, "S&P 500 Cash Stock Price Volatilities," *Journal of Finance*, 44:5, December 1989, pp. 1155-1175 and G. William Schwert, "Stock Market Volatility," *Financial Analysts Journal*, May/June 1990, pp. 23-34. Harris compares the volatility of the S&P 500 before and after the introduction of stock index futures trading. He finds a small increase in volatility after the introduction of futures trading. However, he acknowledges that other factors besides the beginning of futures trading could be responsible for this increase in volatility. Schwert finds that volatility in the stock market was not particularly high in the 1980s, with the exception of October 1987 and October 1989. (These are the months of the crash and the "little crash" of October 13, 1989.) Schwert concludes that there is little evidence that futures trading of stock indexes has contributed to this volatility. One exception to this conclusion concerns a possible increase in volatility within the trading day. Here the evidence is not clear. One difficulty in assessing the impact of futures trading on intra-day volatility stems from the fact that intra-day prices are only available for fairly recent times. Thus, our historical data are perhaps too weak to draw meaningful comparisons.

3

Futures Prices

Introduction

Having explored the basic institutional features of the futures market in Chapters 1 and 2, we now consider futures prices. In an important sense, the study of the prices in a market provides the essential key to understanding all features of the market. Prices and the factors that determine those prices will ultimately influence every use of the market.

The current excitement about the futures market, and the new types of futures now being traded, mean that futures prices are studied with great diligence. In spite of such concentrated attention, there are many issues about which people disagree. These differences of opinion are reflected in the mode of analysis employed and the kinds of opportunities that different market participants seek in the futures market.

This chapter examines the factors that affect futures prices in general. There is little doubt that the determinants of foreign exchange futures prices and orange juice futures prices, for example, are very different. We must also recognize, however, that a common thread of understanding links futures contracts of all types. This chapter follows that common thread, while subsequent chapters explore the individual factors that affect prices for particular commodities. Perhaps the most basic and most common factor affecting futures prices is the way in which their prices are quoted. Our discussion of futures prices begins with reading the price quotations that are available every day in *The Wall Street Journal*.

Futures market prices bear economically important relationships to other observable prices as well. An important goal of this chapter is to develop an understanding of those relationships. The futures price for delivery of coffee in three months, for example, must be related to the spot price, or the current cash price of coffee at a particular physical location. The **spot price** is the price of a good for immediate delivery. In a restaurant, for example, you buy a cup of coffee at the spot price. The spot price is also called the **cash price** or the **current price**.

This important difference between the cash price and the futures price is called the **basis**. Likewise, the futures price for delivery of coffee in three months must be related in some fashion to the futures price for delivery of coffee in six months. The difference in price for two futures contract expirations on the same commodity is an intra-commodity spread. As we will see, the time spread can also be an economically important variable.

Because futures contracts call for the delivery of some good at a particular time in the future, we can be sure that the expectations of market participants help to determine futures prices. If people believe that gold will sell for $50 per ounce in three months, then the price of the futures contract for delivery of gold in three months cannot be $100. The connection between futures prices and expected future spot prices is so strong, that some market observers believe that they must be, or at least should be, equal.

Similarly, the price for storing the good underlying the futures contract helps determine the relationships among futures prices and the relationship between the futures price and the spot price. By storing goods, it is possible, in effect, to convert corn received in March into corn that can be delivered in June. The difference in price between the March corn futures and the June corn futures must, therefore, be related to the cost of storing corn.

All of these futures pricing issues are interconnected. The basis, the spreads, the expected future spot price and the cost of storage all form a system of related concepts. This chapter describes the linkages among these concepts that are common to all futures contracts. The discussion begins with the futures prices themselves.

Reading Futures Prices

One of the most complete and widely available sources for futures prices is *The Wall Street Journal* (WSJ), which publishes futures prices daily. These prices are reported in a standardized format, as shown in Figure 3.1. A listing in the regular section is a mark of some success for a futures contract. The WSJ also lists some less active contracts.

The date shown near the top of Figure 3.1 is the day for which the prices were recorded. The publication date of the WSJ is the next business day. As the heading states, the open interest, to be discussed later, pertains to the preceding trading day. Figure 3.1 shows quotations for agricultural and metallurgical futures. In later chapters, we present quotations for other kinds of futures. For each contract, the listing shows the commodity, the exchange where it is traded, the amount of the good in one contract, and the units in which prices are quoted. For example, the very first contract is for the corn contract traded by the CBT. One contract is for 5,000 bushels and the prices are quoted in cents per bushel.

Figure 3.1
Futures Price Quotations

COMMODITY FUTURES PRICES

Thursday, October 18, 1990

Open Interest Reflects Previous Trading Day.

–GRAINS AND OILSEEDS–

	Open	High	Low	Settle	Change	Lifetime High	Lifetime Low	Open Interest
CORN (CBT) 5,000 bu.; cents per bu.								
Dec	229½	229¾	227¾	228	– ¾	286½	221½	110,820
Mr91	238½	238½	236½	237	– ¾	302½	230¾	46,591
May	244	244½	242¼	242½	– 1¼	306½	237½	18,632
July	248	248¼	246	246¼	– 1¼	308¼	241½	19,956
Sept	246¾	246¾	245	245	– 1¼	287½	240¼	2,578
Dec	249	249	246½	246¾	– 1¾	275	242½	9,454
Est vol 30,000; vol Wed 24,131; open int 208,115, –360.								
OATS (CBT) 5,000 bu.; cents per bu.								
Dec	124¼	124¼	122	123	– ¼	194¼	110	10,493
Mr91	134	134	132½	133½	....	201	120½	2,904
May	141	141	139½	140½	....	183¾	129	962
July	147	147	145½	146	....	164¾	135½	465
Est vol 1,000; vol Wed 1,345; open int 14,839, +157.								
SOYBEANS (CBT) 5,000 bu.; cents per bu.								
Nov	615½	616½	610	610¼	– 4¼	682	564½	51,894
Ja91	631½	631½	625	625¼	– 4	692	587	26,044
Mar	643	643½	638¼	6438½	– 3¾	703	608	18,170
May	653½	654	649	649	– 3¾	711	614½	10,974
July	662½	663	657½	657¾	– 3	718	625	9,053
Aug	655	656	652½	652½	– 2½	695	628	895
Sept	632	633½	627	627	– 1	670	623	1,024
Nov	621	621	617½	617¾	– 1¾	674	612½	6,681
Est vol 36,000; vol Wed 40,603; open int 124,740, +3,279.								
SOYBEAN MEAL (CBT) 100 tons; $ per ton.								
Oct	181.00	181.00	178.70	179.20	– 1.00	200.00	168.00	560
Dec	185.50	185.50	183.30	183.70	– 1.10	205.50	170.50	35,885
Ja91	187.80	187.80	185.60	186.00	– 1.10	204.00	171.50	12,267
Mar	190.50	190.70	189.20	189.40	– .90	212.00	174.50	8,496
May	192.00	192.00	190.40	190.60	– .80	208.00	175.80	4,881
July	193.50	193.50	191.80	191.80	– 1.20	209.00	177.50	3,782
Aug	193.00	193.00	192.00	192.00	– .50	199.00	176.50	1,397
Sept	191.00	191.00	187.80	187.80	– 1.40	193.50	175.50	1,364
Oct	185.00	185.00	184.00	184.20	– .80	190.00	182.00	514
Dec	185.00	185.00	184.00	184.70	+ .20	189.80	182.00	559
Est vol 18,000; vol Wed 16,015; open int 69,705, +1,155.								

	Open	High	Low	Settle	Change	Lifetime High	Lifetime Low	Open Interest
PORK BELLIES (CME) 40,000 lbs.; cents per lb.								
Feb	67.00	67.15	65.25	66.00	– .70	68.40	49.40	6,053
Mar	66.60	66.87	65.10	65.70	– .72	68.32	49.20	1,105
May	66.70	66.90	65.15	66.10	– .60	68.15	49.50	687
July	65.90	66.00	64.02	64.70	– 1.15	67.05	50.15	228
Est vol 4,840; vol Wed 4,373; open int 8,117, +89.								
–FOOD & FIBER–								
COCOA (CSCE)–10 metric tons; $ per ton.								
Dec	1,180	1,183	1,151	1,163	– 12	1,558	965	17,350
Mr91	1,242	1,243	1,211	1,220	– 17	1,581	985	10,959
May	1,278	1,278	1,250	1,260	– 15	1,572	1,000	5,292
July	1,318	1,319	1,294	1,294	– 21	1,590	1,060	6,919
Sept	....	....	....	1,324	– 21	1,515	1,264	3,926
Dec	1,360	1,370	1,360	1,364	– 21	1,535	1,325	5,618
Mr92	....	....	....	1,399	– 21	....	....	400
Est vol 4,683; vol Wed 4,231; open int 50,464, –597.								
COFFEE (CSCE)–37,500 lbs.; cents per lb.								
Dec	93.10	93.35	92.00	92.60	– .40	109.50	81.00	23,876
Mr91	96.70	96.85	95.55	96.15	– .35	112.00	85.00	11,113
May	98.95	98.95	97.95	98.40	– .30	113.00	91.25	2,703
July	100.50	100.50	100.40	100.50	– .05	111.50	94.00	741
Sept	....	....	....	102.35	– .25	113.50	97.50	648
Est vol 4,824; vol Wed 5,752; open int 39,162, +36.								
SUGAR–WORLD (CSCE)–112,000 lbs.; cents per lb.								
Mar	9.80	10.00	9.58	9.63	+ .14	15.08	9.08	70,095
May	9.82	10.00	9.61	9.62	+ .11	14.91	9.10	21,466
July	9.90	10.05	9.65	9.65	+ .09	14.70	9.17	11,615
Oct	9.92	10.02	9.65	9.67	+ .10	14.40	9.19	9,228
Est vol 24,762; vol Wed 22,367; open int 112,437, –1,056.								
SUGAR–DOMESTIC (CSCE)–112,000 lbs.; cents per lb.								
Jan	23.35	23.37	23.35	23.35	....	23.37	22.50	3,142
Mar	23.33	23.35	23.33	23.33	+ .01	23.35	22.51	1,642
May	23.40	23.41	23.40	23.40	+ .01	23.41	22.76	1,899

	Open	High	Low	Settle	Change	Lifetime High	Lifetime Low	Open Interest
SILVER (CBT)–1,000 troy oz.; cents per troy oz.								
Oct	415.0	417.0	413.0	417.0	– 1.0	632.0	411.0	5
Dec	424.0	425.0	419.0	422.5	– 0.5	645.0	413.0	7,426
Fb91	433.0	433.0	427.0	430.0	....	647.0	420.0	270
Apr	436.0	437.0	436.0	437.0	....	603.0	430.0	187
June	445.0	446.0	440.0	444.0	....	579.0	437.0	2,914
Est vol 500; vol Wed 1,081; open int 10,921, +83.								
CRUDE OIL, Light Sweet (NYM) 1,000 bbls.; $ per bbl.								
Nov	35.00	37.20	34.40	36.80	+ .08	41.15	17.30	42,887
Dec	33.95	35.80	33.95	35.41	– .54	39.90	17.78	67,335
Ja91	32.47	34.30	32.47	33.95	– .52	38.20	17.86	31,686
Feb	31.12	33.00	31.12	32.67	– .45	36.80	18.15	19,812
Mar	29.86	31.25	29.86	31.49	– .37	35.40	18.40	17,656
Apr	28.67	30.30	28.67	30.41	– .26	33.90	18.03	14,183
May	27.58	29.30	27.58	29.43	– .15	32.70	18.03	13,485
June	26.65	28.25	26.65	28.57	– .03	31.50	18.30	10,651
July	26.90	27.40	26.20	27.82	+ .02	30.40	18.31	9,215
Aug	25.60	26.70	25.30	27.17	+ .07	29.50	19.05	8,484
Sept	25.00	26.00	25.00	26.65	+ .13	28.72	19.10	4,546
Oct	24.75	25.30	24.40	26.28	+ .19	28.40	19.63	5,871
Nov	25.10	25.15	24.25	25.96	+ .22	28.10	19.10	5,263
Dec	24.80	25.40	24.30	25.68	+ .24	27.70	19.45	10,136
Ja92	24.50	24.50	23.80	25.42	+ .26	27.60	20.90	6,017
Feb	24.00	24.00	23.50	25.19	+ .28	27.00	21.20	3,552
Mar	24.00	24.00	23.25	24.99	+ .30	26.75	22.40	5,580
Apr	24.00	24.00	23.00	24.81	+ .32	26.50	23.00	9,883
Est vol 116,186; vol Wed 112,138; open int 286,242, +2,134.								
HEATING OIL NO. 2 (NYM) 42,000 gal.; $ per gal.								
Nov	.9325	.9820	.9280	.9651	–.0174	1.0780	.5130	19,270
Dec	.9782	.9900	.9782	.9782	–.0400	1.0850	.5327	23,436
Ja91	.9552	.9770	.9552	.9600	–.0352	1.0725	.5295	15,273
Feb	.9067	.9300	.9067	.9259	–.0208	1.0200	.5260	10,215
Mar	.8527	.8800	.8527	.8759	–.0168	.9650	.5070	6,820
Apr	.8062	.8102	.8062	.8309	–.0153	.9200	.4930	3,025
May	.7737	.8000	.7737	.7959	–.0168	.8850	.4840	2,464
June	.7637	.7750	.7532	.7699	–.0233	.8575	.4840	8,442
July	.7477	.7650	.7477	.7579	–.0263	.8500	.4855	5,269

Source: *The Wall Street Journal*, August 17, 1990.

At this point a word of warning is appropriate. The information about the contracts shown with the prices is useful, but incomplete. For corn, the type of corn that is traded is not mentioned, nor is the delivery procedure. Further, the WSJ does not give information about daily price limits and it does not report the tick size. With so much information omitted, a trader should not trade based just on what the WSJ shows. To have a good insight into the price behavior and the price fluctuations of a contract requires additional information, such as that found in the *Commodity Trading Manual* published by the Chicago Board of Trade.

For each of the delivery months, the price listings have a row of data, with the first line going to the contract that matures next, also called the **nearby contract**. Each succeeding line pertains to another maturity month. Contracts that mature later are called **distant** or **deferred contracts**. The first three columns of prices give the opening, high, and low prices for each contract for the day of trading being reported.

The next price column records the **settlement price**, which is the price at which contracts are settled at the close of trading for the day. The settlement price is not always the last trade price of the day, as it would be with stocks. In Chapter 1, we examined the feature of daily settlement. All margin flows are based on the settlement price. If the settlement price brings a trader's equity below the level required for maintenance margin, then the trader will receive a margin call and will have to pay variation margin.

Typically, the settlement price will equal the last trading price for the day, but they are not always the same. Most exchanges have a settlement committee for each commodity, usually comprised of members of the exchange who trade that commodity. This committee meets immediately at the close of trading to establish the settlement price. The committee is responsible for establishing a settlement price that fairly indicates the value of the futures contract at the close of trading. When trading is active and prices are stable at the end of the day, the settlement committee has an easy job. The prices recorded from trades will be continuous, fluctuating little from trade to trade. In such cases the committee may simply allow the final trading price to be the settlement price. Therefore, in many cases the price for the last trade and the settlement price are the same price, but they are conceptually distinct.

Difficulties arise for the settlement committee, however, when a contract has little trading activity. Imagine that the last trade for a particular maturity of a given commodity occurred three hours before the close of trading and that significant information pertaining to that commodity was discovered after that last trade. In this example, the last actual trade price for the contract does not represent what the true economic price would be at the close of trading. In such a case, the settlement committee performs an important function by establishing a settlement price that differs from the price on the last recorded trade.

To establish a settlement price, the members use information on other maturity months for the same commodity. The difference between prices of contracts for different delivery months is very stable, at least relative to the futures prices themselves. So the settlement committee will use that price difference, or spread, to establish the settlement price on the contract that was not recently traded. Even more drastic situations might arise from time to time, but the settlement committee must establish a settlement price even when there is very little information to go on. Having this function performed by a committee helps rule out the possibility that an inaccurate settlement price might be chosen to generate a windfall gain for the person choosing the settlement price.

The next column, after the settlement price, is denoted as "Change." The value in this column is the change in the settlement price from the preceding day to the current day, the day for which prices are reported. The next two columns show the lifetime high and low prices for each contract. Figure 3.1 indicates how radically prices may differ for some contracts over their life. For the contracts about to mature, the difference between the lifetime highs and lows can be enormous. For the contracts that have just been listed, there has been little time for the lifetime high and low prices to diverge radically.

The final column in Figure 3.1 is headed by the title of "Open Interest," which shows the total number of contracts outstanding for each maturity month. **Open interest** is the number of futures contracts for which delivery is currently obligated. To understand the meaning of this more clearly, assume that the December 1993 widget contract has just been listed for trading, but that the contract has not traded yet. At this point, the open interest in the contract is zero. Trading begins and the first contract is bought. This purchase necessarily means that some other trader sold. This transaction creates one contract of open interest, because there is one contract now in existence for which delivery is obligated.

Subsequent trading can increase or decrease the open interest, as Table 3.1 shows for trading in the incredibly popular widget contract. At t=0, trading opens on the widget contract. The open interest is zero as is volume to date. At t=1, Trader A buys and Trader B sells one widget contract. This transaction creates one contract of volume. After the transaction, the open interest is one contract, because one contract is obligated for delivery, as Table 3.1 shows. At t=2, Trader C buys and Trader D sells three widget contracts. The volume resulting from these trades is three contracts and the open interest is now four contracts. At t=3, Trader A sells and Trader D buys one widget contract, creating one more contract of volume. Notice here that Trader A offsets his one contract through a reversing trade. After this offsetting transaction, Trader A is out of the market. Trader D has reversed one of her three contracts. This reduces the open interest by one contract. At t=4, Trader C sells and Trader E buys one widget contract, for one contract of volume. With this transaction, Trader C reverses one contract,

Table 3.1
How Trading Affects Open Interest

Time	Action	Open Interest
t=0	Trading opens for the popular widget contract.	0
t=1	Trader A buys and Trader B sells 1 widget contract.	1
t=2	Trader C buys and Trader D sells 3 widget contracts.	4
t=3	Trader A sells and Trader D buys 1 widget contract. (Trader A has offset 1 contract and is out of the market. Trader D has offset 1 contract and is now long 2 contracts.)	3
t=4	Trader C sells and Trader E buys 1 widget contract.	3

Ending Positions	Trader	Long Position	Short Position
	B		1
	C	2	
	D		2
	E	1	
	All Traders	3	3

but Trader E enters the market. Because Trader E, in effect, takes the place of Trader C for this one contract, the open interest remains at three. The bottom panel of the table summarizes each trader's position and shows how the open interest remains at three contracts.

When a contract is distant from maturity, it tends to have relatively little open interest. As the contracts approach maturity, the open interest increases. Most often the contract closest to delivery, the nearby contract, has the highest level of open interest. As the nearby contract comes very close to maturity, however, the open interest falls. This is due to the fact that traders close their positions to avoid actual delivery. As we saw in Chapter 1, actual delivery is fairly unusual. When the futures contract matures, all traders with remaining open interest must make or take delivery, and the open interest goes to zero. Recall, also, that the open interest figures reported in the WSJ pertain to the day preceding the day for which prices are reported. Figure 3.2 shows the pattern of open interest for the December 1989 S&P 500 futures contract over its life, and Figure 3.3 shows the pattern of trading volume for the same contract. The open interest and volume of trading follow a predictable pattern, such as the one shown in these two figures. Notice that the peak open interest occurs when the contract has about two to three months remaining until expiration.

In Figure 3.1, beneath the lines for each of the contract maturities, the WSJ reports more trading information. The figure shows the estimated volume for all

Figure 3.2
DEC 1989 S&P 500 Futures Open Interest

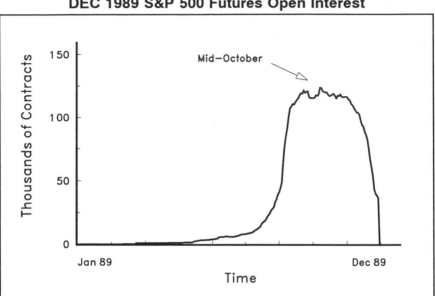

Figure 3.3
DEC 1989 S&P 500 Futures Trading Volume

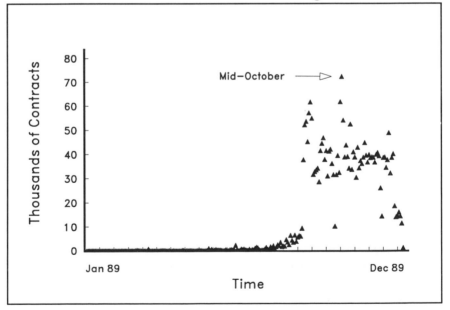

maturities for a given commodity, followed by the actual volume for the preceding day. Next, the open interest for all contract maturities is shown. (This amount should equal the sum of the open interest figures shown for the individual contracts.)[1] Finally, the last number reports the change in the open interest since the preceding day. We may also note that it is possible for the volume of trading to exceed the number of contracts of open interest. This occurs when trading activity is particularly heavy for a given commodity on a certain day. Chapter 4 considers the different trading parties who give rise to the trading volume and open interest.

The Basis and Spreads

In this section, we analyze relationships between two prices. The basis is the relationship between the cash price of a good and the futures price for the same good. We also consider spreads. A **spread** is the difference between two futures prices. If the two prices are for futures contracts on the same underlying good, but with different expiration dates, the spread is an **intra-commodity spread**. If the two futures prices that form a spread are futures prices for two underlying goods, such as a wheat futures and a corn futures, then the spread is an **inter-commodity spread**.

The Basis

The basis receives a great deal of attention in futures trading. The **basis** is the current cash price of a particular commodity at a specified location minus the price of a particular futures contract for the same commodity:

Basis = Current Cash Price − Futures Price

Several features of this definition require explanation. First, the definition of the basis depends upon a cash price of a commodity at a specific location. The cash price of corn, for example, might differ between Kansas City and Chicago, so the basis for those two locations will also differ. Normally, one good cannot sell for different prices in two markets. If such a good had two prices, a trader could buy the commodity in the cheaper market and sell it in the market with the higher price, thereby reaping an **arbitrage profit**—a sure profit with no investment. Prices for corn in Chicago and Kansas City can differ, of course, because of the expense of transporting corn from one location to another. If corn is grown near Chicago, then we might reasonably expect the price of corn in Chicago to be lower than the price of corn in Kansas City. So the basis calculated in considering futures prices may differ, depending upon the geographic location of the spot price that is used to compute the basis.

Usually people speaking of the basis are referring to the difference between the cash price and the nearby futures contract. There is, however, a basis for each outstanding futures contract, and this basis will often differ in systematic ways, depending upon the maturities of the individual futures contracts. Table 3.2 shows spot and futures gold prices for July 11, 1990 and illustrates this phenomenon. The cash, or spot, price is the London A.M. fix, or morning quotation, so the basis pertains to London. The futures prices are from the COMEX. The right column shows the basis for each futures contract. The basis is negative for all delivery months in this example. The chart of the basis shows that it is possible to contract for the future sale or purchase of gold at a price that exceeds the current cash price. The difference between the current cash price of $353.70 per ounce and the price of the more distant futures contracts is striking, as much as $37.80 per ounce for the most distant DEC 1991 contract.

Futures markets can exhibit a pattern of either normal or inverted prices. In a **normal market**, prices for more distant futures are higher than for nearby futures. For example, the gold prices in Table 3.2 represent a normal market. In an **inverted market**, distant futures prices are lower than the prices for contracts nearer to expiration. The interpretation of the basis can be very important, particularly for agricultural commodities. For many commodities, the fact that the harvest comes at a certain time each year introduces seasonal components into the series of cash prices.[2] Many traders believe that understanding these seasonal factors can be very beneficial for speculation and hedging. Also, as will become clear, the basis, such as that shown in Table 3.2, can be used as a valuable information source to predict future spot prices of the commodities that underlie the futures contracts.

Table 3.2
Gold Prices and the Basis
(July 11, 1990)

Contract	Prices	The Basis
CASH	353.70	
JUL 90	354.10	-.40
AUG	355.60	-1.90
OCT	359.80	-6.10
DEC	364.20	-10.50
FEB 91	368.70	-15.00
APR	373.00	-19.30
JUN	377.50	-23.80
AUG	381.90	-28.20
OCT	386.70	-33.00
DEC	391.50	-37.80

A further point about the basis emerges from a consideration of Table 3.2. Notice that the basis for the nearby contract is only - $.40, about one-thousandth of the cash price. There is good reason that it should be so small. The JUL 1990 contract is extremely close to delivery on the date in question, July 11, 1990. At delivery the futures price and the cash price must be equal, except for minor discrepancies due to transportation and other transaction costs. If someone were to trade the JUL 1990 contract on the day in question, the trade would be for the delivery of gold within three weeks. The price of gold for delivery within three weeks must closely approximate the current spot price of gold.

When the futures contract is at expiration, the futures price and the spot price of gold must be the same. The basis must be zero, again subject to the discrepancy due to transaction costs. This behavior of the basis over time is known as **convergence**, as Figures 3.4 and 3.5 illustrate. In Figure 3.4, the cash price lies above the futures price. As time progresses, and the futures contract approaches maturity, the basis narrows. At the maturity of the futures contract, the basis is zero, consistent with the no-arbitrage requirement that the futures price and cash price be equal at the maturity of the futures contract. Figure 3.5 shows the basis itself, corresponding to the prices in Figure 3.4. The basis is positive, but declines to zero as the futures contract approaches maturity.

Figure 3.4
Converging Cash and Futures Prices

Figure 3.5
Convergence of the Basis to Zero

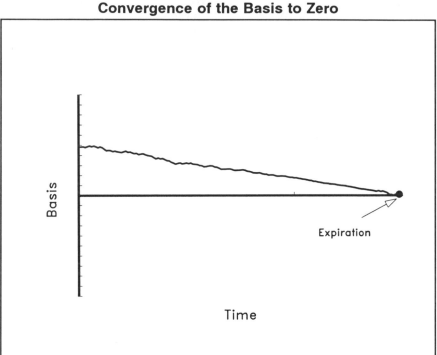

Figure 3.6 illustrates one other feature of the basis that is very important for futures trading. The upper portion of the figure shows prices for the MAR 1990 S&P 500 futures contract. The graph covers the range from 300 to 400, a 100 point range within which the contract traded between July 1989 and its expiration in March 1990. The bottom portion of Figure 3.6 illustrates how the basis for this contract behaved over the same time interval. This bottom panel also covers a 100 point scale to make the two graphs comparable.

As the graph dramatically reveals, the fluctuation in the basis was much less than the range of fluctuation in the futures price itself. This is almost always the case. The basis is almost always much more stable than the futures price or the cash price, when those prices are considered in isolation. The futures price may oscillate and the cash price may swing widely, but the basis (cash - futures price) tends to be relatively steady. The relatively low variability of the basis is very important for hedging and for certain types of speculation, as will be discussed in Chapter 4.

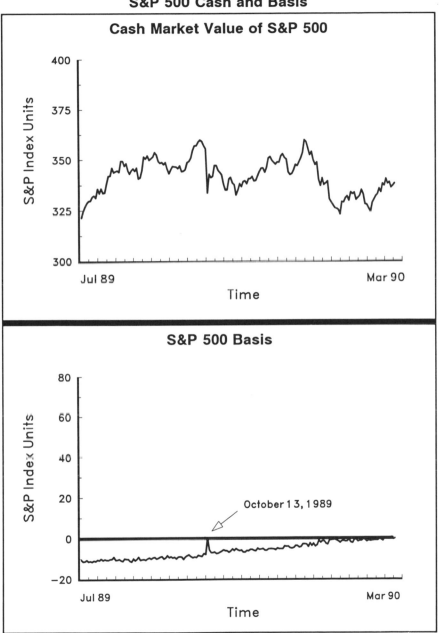

Figure 3.6
S&P 500 Cash and Basis

Cash Market Value of S&P 500

S&P 500 Basis

October 13, 1989

Spreads

Just as there is an important relationship between each futures contract and the cash price of the commodity, the relationships among futures prices on the same good are themselves important. As we discussed in Chapter 1, there are intra-commodity spreads and inter-commodity spreads. An intra-commodity spread is the difference in price between two futures contracts of different maturity dates on the same commodity, and these spreads are important because they indicate the relative price differentials for a commodity to be delivered at two points in time. As we will see, there are strong economic relationships that govern the permissible time spreads that may exist between any two futures contracts.

Spread relationships are important for speculators. Much speculation involves some kind of spread position—the holding of two or more related futures contracts. If a trader hopes to use futures markets to earn speculative profits, an understanding of spread relationships is essential. Since most speculation uses spreads, the search for a profit turns on an ability to identify spread relationships that are economically unjustified. While the understanding of the spread relationships in a particular commodity requires considerable knowledge about the commodity itself, certain general principles apply to all spreads.

Figure 3.7
S&P 500 Spread

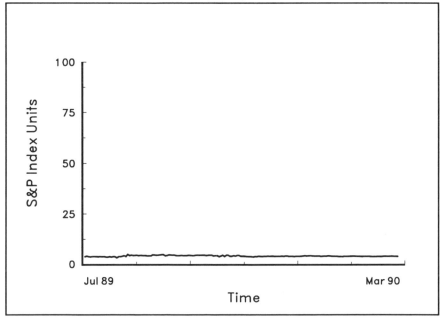

Figure 3.7 shows the spread between the JUN and MAR 1990 S&P 500 futures contracts, computed here as the June price minus the March price. The time period here is the same used in Figure 3.6. Thus, we can see the stability of the spread in Figure 3.7 compared to the price itself in Figure 3.6.[3]

Models of Futures Prices

In this section, we consider two models of futures prices. The first of these is the Cost-of-Carry Model. According to this model, futures prices depend on the cash price of a commodity and the cost of storing the underlying good from the present to the delivery date of the futures contract. The second model is the Expectations Model. According to this view, the futures price today equals the cash price that traders expect to prevail for the underlying good on the delivery date of the futures contract. For example, the futures price in January for the JUL contract is the market's January estimate of what the price of corn will be in July when the futures contract expires.

To explore these models, we employ the concept of arbitrage. We begin by assuming that prices in the market do not allow any arbitrage profits. Under this assumption, we ask what futures pricing relationships are permissible. For the sake of simplicity, we begin by assuming that futures markets are perfect. A **perfect market** is a market with no transaction costs and no restrictions on free contracting between two parties. Thus, the analysis begins under the assumptions of an idealized world—a world that allows no arbitrage and that includes no market frictions. Gradually, we develop a more realistic analysis by relaxing these assumptions. This approach allows us to start the analysis within a fairly simple environment and to add complications after we explore the most essential features of the pricing relationships.

Arbitrage

There are many alternative definitions of "arbitrage." We begin our analysis with a strict conception of arbitrage that we can call "academic arbitrage." In **academic arbitrage** it is possible to trade to generate a riskless profit without investment. An **arbitrageur** is a person who engages in arbitrage. For example, shares of IBM trade on both the New York Stock Exchange and the Pacific Stock Exchange. Suppose shares of IBM trade for $110 on the New York market and for $105 on the Pacific Exchange. A trader could make the following two transactions simultaneously:

Buy 1 share of IBM on the Pacific Exchange for $105.
Sell 1 share of IBM on the New York Exchange for $110.

These two transactions generate a riskless profit of $5. Because both trades are assumed to occur simultaneously, there is no investment. Therefore, such an opportunity qualifies as an academic arbitrage opportunity—it affords riskless profits without investment.

In a well-functioning market, such opportunities cannot exist. If they did exist, they would make all of us fabulously wealthy. The existence of such academic arbitrage opportunities is equivalent to money being left on the street without being claimed. If you have ever been to Wall Street, you know that there is no money lying on that street. To understand futures pricing, we assume that there are no arbitrage opportunities and determine what that assumption implies about prices. In other words, we will determine what we can about futures prices on the assumption that there are no arbitrage opportunities.

In our example of the IBM share, we assumed that there were no transaction costs. For present purposes, we will assume that the futures market is perfect so there are no taxes, no transaction costs, and no frictions of any kind. We will also assume that any commodity can be sold short and that it can be stored. Under these idealized assumptions, we are ready to explore futures pricing relationships. (Later in this chapter, we consider prices in a more realistic setting with transaction costs.)

The Cost–of–Carry Model in Perfect Markets

In this section, we will use the conception of arbitrage that we have just elaborated to explore the Cost-of-Carry Model or carrying charge theory of futures prices. The **cost–of–carry** or **carrying charge** is the total cost to carry a good forward in time. For example, wheat on hand in June can be carried forward to, or stored until, December.

Carrying charges fall into four basic categories: storage costs, insurance costs, transportation costs, and financing costs. Storage costs include the cost of warehousing the commodity in the appropriate facility. While storage seems to apply most clearly to physical goods, such as wheat or lumber, it is also possible to store financial instruments. In many cases, the owner of a financial instrument will leave the instrument in a bank vault. For many goods in storage, insurance is also necessary. For example, stored lumber should be protected against fire, and stored wheat should be insured against water damage.[4]

Types of Carrying Costs

1. Storage Cost
2. Insurance Costs
3. Transportation Costs
4. Financing Costs

The carrying charges also include, in some cases, transportation costs. Wheat in a railroad siding in Kansas must be carried to delivery in two senses. It must be stored until the appropriate delivery time for a given futures contract, but it must also be physically carried to the appropriate place for delivery. As will become obvious, transportation costs between different locations determine price differentials between those locations. Without question, transportation charges play different roles for different commodities. Transporting wheat from Kansas to Chicago could be an important expense. By contrast, delivery of Treasury bills against a futures contract is accomplished by a wire transfer costing only a few dollars. In almost all cases, the most significant carrying charge in the futures market is the financing cost. For most situations, financing the good under storage overwhelms the other costs.

The carrying charge reflects only the charges involved in carrying a commodity from one time or one place to another. The carrying charges do not include the value of the commodity itself. So, if gold costs $400 per ounce and the financing rate is 1 percent per month, the financing charge for carrying the gold forward is $4 per month (1% × $400).

Most participants in the futures markets face a financing charge on a short-term basis that is equal to the repo rate. The **repo rate** is the interest rate on repurchase agreements. In a **repurchase agreement** a person sells securities at one point in time, with the understanding that they will be repurchased at a certain price at a later time. Most repurchase agreements are for one day only and are known, accordingly, as overnight repos. The repo rate is relatively low, exceeding the rate on Treasury bills by only a small amount.[5] The financing cost for such goods is so low because anyone wishing to finance a commodity may offer the commodity itself as collateral for the loan. Further, most of the participants in the market tend to be financial institutions of one type or another who have low financing costs anyway, at least for very short-term obligations.

Cash and Futures Pricing Relationships. The carrying charges just described are important because they play a crucial role in determining pricing relationships between spot and futures prices as well as the relationships among prices of futures contracts of different maturities. For present purposes, we will assume that the only carrying charge is the financing cost at an interest rate of 10 percent per year. As an example, consider the prices and the accompanying transactions shown in Table 3.3.

The transactions in Table 3.3 represent a successful cash–and–carry arbitrage. This is a **cash–and–carry arbitrage** because the trader buys the cash good and carries it to the expiration of the futures contract. The trader traded at t=0 to guarantee a riskless profit without investment. There was no investment, because there was no cash flow at t=0. The trader merely borrowed funds to purchase the gold and to carry it forward. The profit in these transactions was certain once the trader made the transactions at t=0. As these transactions show,

Table 3.3
Cash–and–Carry Gold Arbitrage Transactions

Prices for the Analysis:

Spot price of gold	$400
Future price of gold (for delivery in one year)	$450
Interest rate	10%

Transaction	Cash Flow
t=0 Borrow $400 for one year at 10%.	+$400
Buy 1 ounce of gold in the spot market for $400.	- 400
Sell a futures contract for $450 for delivery of one ounce in one year.	0
Total Cash Flow	$0
t=1 Remove the gold from storage.	$0
Deliver the ounce of gold against the futures contract.	+450
Repay loan, including interest.	-440
Total Cash Flow	+$10

to prevent arbitrage the futures price of the gold should have been $440 or less. With a futures price of $440 for example, the transactions in Table 3.3 would yield a zero profit. From this example, we can infer the following general rule:

Cost–of–Carry Rule 1

The futures price must be less than or equal to the spot price of the commodity plus the carrying charges necessary to carry the spot commodity forward to delivery.

We can express Rule 1 mathematically as follows:

$$F_{0,t} \leq S_0(1 + C) \qquad 3.1$$

where:

$F_{0,t}$ = the futures price at t=0 for delivery at time=t,
S_0 = the spot price at t=0,
C = the cost of carry, expressed as a fraction of the spot price, necessary to carry the good forward from the present to the delivery date on the futures.

As we have seen, if prices do not conform to Cost-of-Carry Rule 1, a trader can borrow funds, buy the spot commodity with the borrowed funds, sell the futures contract, and carry the commodity forward to deliver against the futures contract. These transactions would generate a certain profit without investment, or an arbitrage profit. There would be a certain profit, because it is guaranteed by the sale of the futures contract. Also, there would be no investment, since the funds needed to carry out the strategy were borrowed and the cost of using those funds was included in the calculation of the carrying charge. Such opportunities cannot exist in a rational market. The cash-and-carry arbitrage opportunity arises because the spot price is too low relative to the futures price.

We have seen that an arbitrage opportunity arises if the spot price is too low relative to the futures price. As we now see, the spot price might also be too high relative to the futures price. If the spot price is too high, we have a reverse cash-and-carry arbitrage opportunity. As the name implies, the steps necessary to exploit the arbitrage opportunity are just the opposite of those in the cash-and-carry arbitrage strategy. As an example of the reverse cash-and-carry strategy, consider the prices for gold and the accompanying transactions in Table 3.4.

In these transactions, the arbitrageur sells the gold short. As in the stock market, a short seller borrows the good from another trader and must later repay it. Once the good is borrowed, the short seller sells it and takes the money from

Table 3.4
Reverse Cash-and-Carry Gold Arbitrage Transactions

Prices for the Analysis

Spot price of gold	$420
Future price of gold (for delivery in one year)	$450
Interest rate	10%

Transaction		Cash Flow
t=0	Sell 1 ounce of gold short.	+$420
	Lend the $420 for one year at 10%.	- 420
	Buy 1 ounce of gold futures for delivery in 1 year.	0
	Total Cash Flow	$0
t=1	Collect proceeds from the loan ($420 × 1.1).	+$462
	Accept delivery on the futures contract.	-450
	Use gold from futures delivery to repay short sale.	0
	Total Cash Flow	+$12

the sale. (The transaction is called short selling because one sells a good that he or she does not actually own.) In this example, the short seller has the use of all of the proceeds from the short sale, which are invested at the interest rate of 10 percent. The trader also buys a futures contract to ensure that he or she can acquire the gold needed to repay the lender at the expiration of the futures in one year.

Notice that these transactions guarantee an arbitrage profit. Once the transactions at t=0 are completed, the $12 profit at t=1 year is certain. Also, the trader had no net cash flow at t=0, so the strategy required no investment. To make this arbitrage opportunity impossible, the spot and futures prices must obey Cost-of-Carry Rule 2.

Cost–of–Carry Rule 2

The futures price must be equal to or greater than the spot price plus the cost of carrying the good to the futures delivery date.

Expressing this rule mathematically with the notation we introduced above:

$$F_{0,t} \geq S_0(1 + C) \qquad 3.2$$

If prices do not obey this rule, there will be an arbitrage opportunity. Table 3.5 summarizes the transactions necessary to conduct the cash-and-carry and the reverse cash-and-carry strategies.

To prevent arbitrage, we have seen that the two following rules must hold:

To prevent Cash-and-Carry Arbitrage $F_{0,t} \leq S_0(1 + C)$ 3.1
To prevent Reverse Cash-and-Carry Arbitrage $F_{0,t} \geq S_0(1 + C)$ 3.2

Table 3.5
Transactions for Arbitrage Strategies

Market	Cash–and–Carry	Reverse Cash–and–Carry
Debt	Borrow funds	Lend short sale proceeds
Physical	Buy asset and store; deliver against futures	Sell asset short; secure proceeds from short sale
Futures	Sell futures	Buy futures; accept delivery; return physical asset to honor short sale commitment

---

Together, equations 3.1 and 3.2 imply Cost-of-Carry Rule 3:

Cost–of–Carry Rule 3

The futures price must equal the spot price plus the cost of carrying the spot commodity forward to the delivery date of the futures contract.

Expressing Rule 3 mathematically, we have:

$$F_{0,t} = S_0(1 + C) \qquad 3.3$$

Notice that the relationship of equation 3.3 was derived under the following assumptions: Markets are perfect; that is, they have no transaction costs and no restrictions on the use of proceeds from short sales. It must be acknowledged that this argument explicitly excludes transaction costs. Transaction costs exist on both sides of the market, for purchase or sale of the futures. In many markets, however, transaction costs for short selling are considerably more expensive, which limits the applicability of the Reverse Cash-and-Carry strategy.

Table 3.6
Gold Forward Cash–and–Carry Arbitrage

Prices for the Analysis

Futures price for gold expiring in 1 year	$400
Futures price for gold expiring in 2 years	450
Interest rate (to cover from year 1 to year 2)[9]	10%

Transaction	Cash Flow
t=0 Buy the futures expiring in 1 year.	+$0
Sell the futures expiring in 2 years.	0
Contract to borrow $400 at 10% for year 1 to year 2.	0
Total Cash Flow	$0
t=1 Borrow $400 for 1 year at 10% as contracted at t=0.	+$400
Take delivery on the futures contract.	- 400
Begin to store gold for one year.	0
Total Cash Flow	$0
t=2 Deliver gold to honor futures contract.	+$450
Repay loan ($400 × 1.1)	- 440
Total Cash Flow	+ $10

Spreads and the Cost–of–Carry. These same cost-of-carry relationships also determine the price relationships that can exist between futures contracts on the same good that differ in maturity. As an example, consider the prices and accompanying arbitrage transactions shown in Table 3.6.

As this example shows, the spread between two futures contracts cannot exceed the cost of carrying the good from one delivery date forward to the next, as Cost-of-Carry Rule 4 states:

Cost–of–Carry Rule 4

The distant futures price must be less than or equal to the nearby futures price plus the cost of carrying the commodity from the nearby delivery date to the distant delivery date.

Expressing Rule 4 mathematically, we have:

$$F_{0,d} \leq F_{0,n}(1 + C), \qquad d > n \qquad\qquad 3.4$$

where:

$F_{0,d}$ = the futures price at t=0 for the distant delivery contract maturing at t=d,

$F_{0,n}$ = the futures price at t=0 for the nearby delivery contract maturing at t=n,

C = the percentage cost of carrying the good from t=n to t=d.

As we have seen, if this relationship did not hold, a trader could buy the nearby futures contract and sell the distant contract. The trader would then accept delivery on the nearby contract and carry the good until the delivery of the distant contract, thereby making a profit.

To complete our argument, we analyze what happens if the nearby futures price is too high relative to the distant futures price. To conduct the arbitrage in this case, consider the gold prices and arbitrage transactions shown in Table 3.7. Thus, forward Reverse Cash-and-Carry arbitrage is possible if the nearby futures price is too high relative to the distant futures price. To exclude this arbitrage opportunity, prices must conform to Cost-of-Carry Rule 5:

Cost–of–Carry Rule 5

The nearby futures price plus the cost of carrying the commodity from the nearby delivery date to the distant delivery date cannot exceed the distant futures price.

Expressing Cost-of-Carry Rule 5 mathematically, we have:

$$F_{0,d} \geq F_{0,n}(1 + C), \qquad d > n \qquad\qquad 3.5$$

From our two arbitrage arguments in Tables 3.6 and 3.7, we have derived the rules expressed in equations 3.4 and 3.5. To exclude forward:

Table 3.7
Gold Forward Reverse Cash–and–Carry Arbitrage

Prices for the Analysis:

Futures price for gold expiring in 1 year	$440
Futures price for gold expiring in 2 years	450
Interest rate (to cover from year 1 to year 2)	10%

Transaction	Cash Flow
t=0 Sell the futures expiring in one year.	+$0
Buy the futures expiring in two years.	0
Contract to lend $440 at 10% from year 1 to year 2.	0
Total Cash Flow	$0
t=1 Borrow 1 ounce of gold for one year.	$0
Deliver gold against the expiring futures.	+ 440
Invest proceeds from delivery for one year.	- 440
Total Cash Flow	$0
t=2 Accept delivery on expiring futures.	- $450
Repay 1 ounce of borrowed gold.	0
Collect on loan of $440 made at t=1.	+ 484
Total Cash Flow	+ $34

Cash-and-Carry Arbitrage	$F_{0,d} \leq F_{0,n}(1 + C), \quad d > n$	3.4
Reverse Cash-and-Carry Arbitrage	$F_{0,d} \geq F_{0,n}(1 + C), \quad d > n$	3.5

Following the same pattern of argument we used for spot prices and futures prices, we see that equations 3.4 and 3.5 imply Cost-of-Carry Rule 6.

Cost–of–Carry Rule 6

The distant futures price must equal the nearby futures price plus the cost of carrying the commodity from the nearby to the distant delivery date.

We can express Cost-of-Carry Rule 6 mathematically as follows:

$$F_{0,d} = F_{0,n}(1 + C), \qquad d > n \qquad\qquad 3.6$$

If these relationships were ever violated, profit-hungry traders would immediately recognize the chance and trade until prices adjusted to eliminate all of the arbitrage opportunities.

Summary.   All of the Cost-of-Carry relationships explored to this point assumed that markets are perfect. In particular, we assumed that they allow unrestricted short selling. We made heavy use of these assumptions. For example, we assumed that the borrowing and lending rates were equal, that we could sell gold short and use 100 percent of the proceeds from the short sale, and that it was possible to contract to borrow and lend at forward rates. All of these assumptions require qualifications, which the next section will develop.

The basic rules developed in this section provide a very useful framework for analyzing relationships between cash and futures prices, on the one hand, and spreads between futures prices, on the other. Cost-of-Carry Rule 3 and equation 3.3 express the basic cash-futures relationship:

$$F_{0,t} = S_0(1 + C) \qquad\qquad 3.3$$

Cost-of-Carry Rule 6 and equation 3.6 express the relationship for two futures prices:

$$F_{0,d} = F_{0,n}(1 + C), \qquad d > n \qquad\qquad 3.6$$

Notice that these two equations have the same form. We, therefore, use equation 3.3 to make a final point to summarize the Cost-of-Carry Model in perfect markets. Equation 3.7 says that the cost-of-carry in the perfect market we have been considering equals the ratio of the futures price to the spot price minus 1.

In equation 3.7, the "C" is the **implied repo rate**—the interest rate implied by the difference between the cash and futures prices. Solving equation 3.3 for the cost-of-carry C, we have:

$$C = F_{0,t}/S_0 - 1$$

In a well-functioning market, the implied repo rate must equal the actual repo rate. As we have seen in this section, deviations from this relationship lead to arbitrage opportunities in a perfect market. We now turn to consider the qualifications to the basic conclusion that are required by market imperfections.

The Cost–of–Carry Model in Imperfect Markets

In real markets, four market imperfections operate to complicate and disturb the relationships of equations 3.3 and 3.6. First, traders face transaction costs. Second, restrictions on short-selling frustrate Reverse Cash-and-Carry strategies. Third, borrowing and lending rates are not generally equal as the assumption of perfect markets would imply. Finally, some goods cannot be stored, so they cannot be carried forward to delivery. This section considers each of these in turn.

The main effect of these market imperfections is to require adjustments in the identities expressed by equations 3.3 and 3.6. Market imperfections do not invalidate the basic framework we have been building. Instead of being able to state an equality as we did in the perfect markets framework leading to equations 3.3 and 3.6, we will find that market imperfections introduce a certain indeterminacy to the relationship.

Four Types of Market Imperfections

1. Direct transaction costs.
2. Unequal borrowing and lending rates.
3. Margins and restrictions on short selling.
4. Limitations to storage.

Direct Transaction Costs. In actual markets, traders face a variety of direct transaction costs. First, the trader must pay a fee to have an order executed. For a trader off the floor of the exchange, these fees include brokerage commissions and various exchange fees. Even members of the exchange must pay a fee to the exchange for each trade. Second, in every market, there is a bid-asked spread. A market maker on the floor of the exchange must try to sell at a higher price (the **asked price**) than the price at which he or she is willing to buy (the **bid price**). The difference between the asked price and the bid price is the **bid–asked spread**. In our discussion, we will assume that these transaction costs are some fixed percentage of the transaction amount, T. For simplicity, we assume that the transaction costs apply to the spot market, but not to the futures market.

To illustrate the impact of transaction costs, we use the same prices with which we began our analysis in perfect markets. Now, however, we consider transaction costs of 3 percent. With transaction costs, our previous arbitrage strategy of buying the good and carrying it to delivery will not work. Table 3.8 shows the results of this attempted arbitrage. With transaction costs, the attempted arbitrage results in a certain loss, not an arbitrage profit.

We would have to pay $400 as before to acquire the good, plus transaction costs of 3 percent for a total outlay of $400(1 + T) = $412. We would then have to finance this total until delivery for a cost of $412(1.1) = $453.20. In return, we would only receive $450 upon the delivery of the futures contract. Given these prices, it clearly does not pay to attempt this "cash–and–carry" arbitrage. As Table 3.8 shows, these attempted arbitrage transactions generate a certain loss of $3.20. With transaction costs of 3 percent and the same spot price of $400, the futures price would have to exceed $453.20 to make the arbitrage attractive. To see why this is so, consider the cash outflows and inflows. We pay the spot price plus the transaction costs, $S_0(1 + T)$, to acquire the good. Carrying the good

---

Table 3.8
Attempted Cash–and–Carry Gold Arbitrage Transactions

Prices for the Analysis:

Spot price of gold	$400
Future price of gold (for delivery in one year)	$450
Interest rate	10%
Transaction cost (T)	3%

Transaction	Cash Flow
t=0 Borrow $412 for one year at 10%.	+$412
Buy 1 ounce of gold in the spot market for $400 and pay 3% transaction costs, to total $412.	- 412
Sell a futures contract for $450 for delivery of one ounce in one year.	0
Total Cash Flow	$0
t=1 Remove the gold from storage.	$0
Deliver the ounce of gold to close futures contract.	+450.00
Repay loan, including interest	-453.20
Total Cash Flow	–$3.20

to delivery costs $S_0(1 + T)(1 + C)$. These costs include acquiring the good and carrying it to the delivery date of the futures. In our example, the total cost is:

$$S_0(1 + T)(1 + C) = \$400(1.03)(1.1) = \$453.20$$

Thus, to break even, the futures transaction must yield $453.20. We can write this more formally as:

$$F_{0,t} \leq S_0(1 + T)(1 + C) \qquad\qquad 3.8$$

If prices follow equation 3.8, the cash-and-carry arbitrage opportunity will not be available. Notice that equation 3.8 has the same form as equation 3.1, but equation 3.8 includes transaction costs.

In our discussion of the Cost-of-Carry Model in perfect markets, we saw that futures prices could not be too high relative to spot prices. Otherwise, arbitrage opportunities would be available, as we saw in Table 3.4. We now explore the transactions as shown in Table 3.4, except we include the transaction costs of 3 percent. Table 3.9 shows these transactions.

Table 3.9
Attempted Reverse Cash–and–Carry Gold Arbitrage

Prices for the Analysis:

Spot price of gold	$420
Future price of gold (for delivery in one year)	$450
Interest rate	10%
Transaction costs (T)	3%

Transaction	Cash Flow
t=0 Sell 1 ounce of gold short, paying 3% transaction costs. Receive $420(.97)= $407.40.	+$407.40
Lend the $407.40 for one year at 10%.	- 407.40
Buy 1 ounce of gold futures for delivery in 1 year.	0
Total Cash Flow	$0
t=1 Collect loan proceeds ($407.40 × 1.1).	+$448.14
Accept gold delivery on the futures contract.	-450.00
Use gold from futures delivery to repay short sale.	0
Total Cash Flow	-$1.86

Including transaction costs in the analysis gives a loss on the same transactions that were profitable with no transaction costs. In the original transactions of Table 3.4 with the same prices, the profit was $12. For perfect markets, equation 3.2 gave the no-arbitrage conditions for the reverse cash-and-carry arbitrage strategy.

$$F_{0,t} \geq S_0(1 + C) \qquad\qquad 3.2$$

Including transaction costs, we have:

$$F_{0,t} \geq S_0(1 - T)(1 + C) \qquad\qquad 3.9$$

Combining equations 3.8 and 3.9 gives:

$$S_0(1 - T)(1 + C) \leq F_{0,t} \leq S_0(1 + T)(1 + C) \qquad\qquad 3.10$$

Equation 3.10 defines the **no-arbitrage bounds**—bounds within which the futures price must remain to prevent arbitrage. In general, transaction costs force a loosening of the price relationship in equation 3.3. In perfect markets, equation 3.3 gave an exact equation for the futures price as a function of the spot price and the cost-of-carry. If the futures price deviated from that no-arbitrage price, traders could transact to reap a riskless profit without investment. For a market with transaction costs, equation 3.10 gives bounds for the futures price. If the futures price goes beyond these boundaries, arbitrage is possible. The futures price can wander within the bounds without offering arbitrage opportunities, however. As an example, consider the bounds implied by the transactions in Table 3.8. If there are no transaction costs, the futures price must be exactly $440 to exclude arbitrage. With the 3 percent transaction costs on spot market transactions, the futures price is free to wander within the range $426.80 to $453.20 without creating any arbitrage opportunity, as Table 3.10 shows.

Figure 3.8 illustrates the concept of arbitrage boundaries. The vertical axis graphs futures prices and the horizontal axis shows the time dimension. The solid horizontal line in the graph shows the no-arbitrage condition for a perfect market. In a perfect market, the futures price must exactly equal the spot price times 1 plus the cost of carry, $F_{0,t} = S_0(1 + C)$. With transaction costs, however, we have a lower and an upper bound. If the futures price goes above the upper no-arbitrage bound, there will be a cash-and-carry arbitrage opportunity. This occurs when $F_{0,t} > S_0(1 + T)(1 + C)$. Likewise, if the futures price falls too low, it will be less than the lower no-arbitrage bound. Futures prices that are too low relative to the spot price give rise to a reverse cash-and-carry arbitrage. This opportunity arises when $F_{0,t} < S_0(1 - T)(1 + C)$. Figure 3.8 shows these no-arbitrage boundaries as dotted lines.

Table 3.10
Illustration of No–Arbitrage Bounds

Prices for the Analysis:

Spot price of gold	$400
Interest rate	10%
Transaction costs (T)	3%

No–Arbitrage Futures Price in Perfect Markets

$$F_{0,t} = S_0(1 + C) = \$400(1.1) = \$440$$

Upper No–Arbitrage Bound with Transaction Costs

$$F_{0,t} \leq S_0(1 + T)(1 + C) = \$400(1.03)(1.1) = \$453.20$$

Lower No–Arbitrage Bound with Transaction Costs

$$F_{0,t} \geq S_0(1 - T)(1 + C) = \$400(.97)(1.1) = \$426.80$$

Figure 3.8
No–Arbitrage Bounds

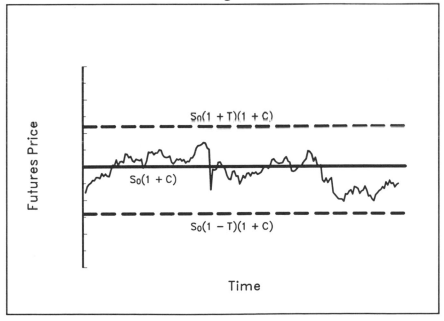

If the futures price stays between the bounds, no arbitrage is possible. If the futures price crosses the boundaries, arbitrageurs will flock to the market to exploit the opportunity. For example, if the futures price is too high, traders will buy the spot commodity and sell the futures. This action will raise the price of the spot good relative to the futures price, thereby driving the futures price back within the no–arbitrage boundaries. If the futures price stays within the boundaries, no arbitrage is possible, and the arbitrageurs will not be able to affect the futures price.

From Figure 3.8, we can note three important points. First, the greater the transaction costs, T, the farther apart will be the bounds. With higher transaction costs, the arbitrage relationships we have been exploring are less binding on possible prices. Second, we have been assuming that all traders in the market face the same percentage transaction costs, T. Clearly, different traders face different transaction costs. For example, a retail trader, who is not an exchange member, can face transaction costs that are much higher than those for a floor trader. It is easily possible for the retail trader to pay as much as 100 times the exchange and brokerage fees paid by a floor trader. Therefore, Figure 3.8 really pertains to a particular trader, not to every trader in the market. Consider a trader facing higher transaction costs of 2T instead of T. For this trader, the no–arbitrage bounds would be twice as wide as those in Figure 3.8. Third, we have seen that market forces exist to keep the futures price within the no–arbitrage bounds, and that each trader faces his or her own particular bounds, depending on that trader's transaction costs.

Differences in transaction costs give rise to the concept of **quasi–arbitrage**. Some traders, such as small retail customers, face full transaction costs. Other traders, such as large financial institutions, have much lower transaction costs. For example, exchange members pay much lower transaction costs than do outside traders. Therefore, the quasi–arbitrageur is a potential cash–and–carry or reverse cash–and–carry trader with relatively lower transaction costs. The futures price should stay within the bounds of the lowest transaction cost trader. Once the futures price drifts beyond the bounds of the lowest transaction cost trader, he or she will exploit the arbitrage opportunity. As we have seen, arbitrage activity will drive the futures price back within the no–arbitrage bounds for that trader.

Thus, in the actual market, we expect to see futures prices within the no–arbitrage bounds of the lowest transaction cost trader. This means that traders with higher transaction costs will not be able to exploit any arbitrage opportunities. If prices start to drift away from the perfect markets equality of equation 3.3, they will be exploited first by the traders with low transaction costs. This exploitation will take place through quasi–arbitrage, because the low transaction cost trader does not face the full transaction costs of an outside trader.

Unequal Borrowing and Lending Rates. In perfect markets, all traders can borrow and lend at the risk-free rate. This is not true in real markets. Generally, traders face a borrowing rate that exceeds the lending rate. In our examples of cash-and-carry and reverse cash-and-carry arbitrage, we have assumed that the two rates were the same. For the cash-and-carry arbitrage, the trader borrows funds, while the trader lends funds in the reverse cash-and-carry arbitrage. Throughout our examples, we assumed that traders could both borrow and lend at a 10 percent rate. If the borrowing and lending rates are not equal, equation 3.10 requires adjustment to reflect that fact. In equation 3.10, the upper bound on the futures price comes from the cash-and-carry arbitrage possibility, as shown in Figure 3.8. In the cash-and-carry arbitrage, the trader borrows funds so the borrowing rate is the appropriate rate in the expression for the upper bound. Analogously, the reverse cash-and-carry trade uses a strategy of lending to fix the lower bound. Thus, the lending rate is appropriate for the expression giving the lower bound. Equation 3.11 reproduces equation 3.10, but reflects the different borrowing and lending rates:

$$S_0(1 - T)(1 + C_L) \leq F_{0,t} \leq S_0(1 + T)(1 + C_B) \qquad 3.11$$

where:

C_L = the lending rate
C_B = the borrowing rate[7]

These differential borrowing and lending rates serve to widen the no-arbitrage boundaries that we have been exploring, because generally $C_L < C_B$. We can illustrate the effect of the differential rates by extending the example of Table 3.10 to include unequal borrowing and lending rates. Table 3.11 illustrates the effect of these unequal rates on the no-arbitrage bounds. As the table shows, including differential borrowing and lending rates widens the no-arbitrage boundaries.

Restrictions on Short Selling. In our analysis, we have so far assumed that traders can sell assets short and use the proceeds from the short sale. In all of our examples, we have also assumed that the short seller has the unrestricted use of all funds arising from the short sale. Consider for a moment, however, the position of the broker who facilitates a short sale. In the stock market, for example, the prospective short seller asks his or her broker to borrow a share from another customer and to sell it on behalf of the short seller. If the short seller received all of the funds from the short sale, the broker would be in a precarious position. The broker has borrowed the share from another customer and must return the share upon demand. If the broker allows the short seller to

Table 3.11
Illustration of No–Arbitrage Bounds
with Differential Borrowing and Lending Rates

Prices for the Analysis:

Spot price of gold	$400
Interest rate (borrowing)	12%
Interest rate (lending)	8%
Transaction costs (T)	3%

Upper No–Arbitrage Bound with Transaction Costs and a Borrowing Rate

$$F_{0,t} \leq S_0(1 + T)(1 + C_B) = \$400(1.03)(1.12) = \$461.44$$

Lower No–Arbitrage Bound with Transaction Costs and a Lending Rate

$$F_{0,t} \geq S_0(1 - T)(1 + C_L) = \$400(.97)(1.08) = \$419.04$$

have all of the proceeds of the short sale, the broker runs a significant risk. The short seller might, for instance, take all of the funds and abscond. Alternatively, the price might move against the short seller and the short seller might not be able to pay to reacquire the stock.

Because of these inherent risks, there are restrictions on short selling in virtually all markets. These restrictions are important, because we found that short selling was a necessary technique for the reverse cash-and-carry arbitrage strategy. If a trader sells the spot good short, expression 3.2 must hold to prevent arbitrage. Further, from 3.1 and 3.2, we were able to derive the no arbitrage condition of 3.3 for a perfect market.

In actual markets, there are serious impediments to short selling. First, for some goods, there is virtually no opportunity for short selling. This is particularly true for many physical goods. Second, even when short selling is permitted, restrictions limit the use of funds from the short sale. Often these restrictions mean that the short seller does not have the use of all of the proceeds from the short sale. A typical percentage for the broker to retain is 50%, meaning that the short seller would have the use of only 50% of the funds.

In the arbitrage relationship of expression 3.2, we concluded that:

$$F_{0,t} \geq S_0 (1 + C)$$

This result assumes unrestricted short selling, so that the short seller had full use of the short sale proceeds, S_0. As we saw, the reverse cash-and-carry transaction employs the short sale and this arbitrage strategy determines the lower bound for the futures price. To reflect the fact that the short seller does not have use of the proceeds, but only some fraction f, we can recast equation 3.2 to say:

$$F_{0,t} \geq fS_0 (1 + C)$$

where:

f = the fraction of usable funds derived from the short sale

This fraction must lie between zero and one. In a perfect market, $f = 1.0$ and it effectively drops out of the equation. With restricted short selling, we can now rewrite our no-arbitrage conditions. First, for a market that is perfect except for restricting short sales, we have a modification of equation 3.3:

$$fS_0(1 + C) \leq F_{0,t} \leq S_0(1 + C) \qquad \qquad 3.12$$

We can also integrate restricted short selling into our imperfect markets framework of equation 3.11. Taking into account transaction costs, differential borrowing and lending rates, and restricted short selling, the no-arbitrage bounds are:

$$fS_0(1 - T)(1 + C_L) \leq F_{0,t} \leq S_0(1 + T)(1 + C_B) \qquad \qquad 3.13$$

The restrictions on short selling widen the no-arbitrage bounds. Notice now, however, that restricted short selling affects only the reverse cash-and-carry strategy, so restricted short selling affects only the lower bound. The effects are substantial, however. Table 3.12 shows the lower no-arbitrage bounds for restrictions on the use of short sale proceeds. When traders face large restrictions on short selling, there is little chance for reverse cash-and-carry arbitrage. If traders can use only half of the short sale proceeds, the lower no-arbitrage bound is so low that it can have little effect on the futures price. We will see, however, that different traders face different restrictions on using proceeds from a short sale. The differential use of these short sale proceeds is related to the concept of quasi-arbitrage. Traders with better access to short sale proceeds have less than full transaction costs to pay when they engage in cash-and-carry or reverse cash-and-carry trading strategies.

Equation 3.13 expresses the final results of our Cost-of-Carry Model analysis and it includes transaction costs, differential borrowing and lending rates, and restrictions on short selling. In complexity, it is a far cry from our

Table 3.12
Illustration of No–Arbitrage Bounds
with Various Short Selling Restrictions

Prices for the Analysis:

Spot price of gold	$400
Interest rate (borrowing)	12%
Interest rate (lending)	8%
Transaction costs (T)	3%

Upper No–Arbitrage Bound with Transaction Costs and a Borrowing Rate

$$F_{0,t} \le S_0(1 + T)(1 + C_B) = \$400(1.03)(1.12) = \$461.44$$

Lower No–Arbitrage Bound with Transaction Costs and a Lending Rate, $f = 1.0$

$$F_{0,t} \ge f S_0(1 - T)(1 + C_L) = (1.0)\$400(.97)(1.08) = \$419.04$$

Lower No–Arbitrage Bound with Transaction Costs and a Lending Rate, $f = 0.75$

$$F_{0,t} \ge f S_0(1 - T)(1 + C_L) = (0.75)\$400(.97)(1.08) = \$314.28$$

Lower No–Arbitrage Bound with Transaction Costs and a Lending Rate, $f = 0.5$

$$F_{0,t} \ge f S_0(1 - T)(1 + C_L) = (0.5)\$400(.97)(1.08) = \$209.52$$

simple perfect markets no–arbitrage relationship of equation 3.3. The two are closely related, however. In terms of equation 3.13, the perfect markets assumptions can be expressed as:

$T = 0$ so there are no transaction costs;

$C_B = C_L = C$ borrowing and lending rates are equal;

$f = 1.0$ traders have full use of short sale proceeds.

If these three conditions hold, we are back to our perfect market assumptions, and equation 3.13 becomes:

$$(1.0)S_0(1 - 0)(1 + C) \le F_{0,t} \le S_0(1 + 0)(1 + C)$$

which reduces to:

$$S_0(1 + C) \leq F_{0,t} \leq S_0(1 + C)$$

$$F_{0,t} = S_0(1 + C)$$

This final expression is simply equation 3.3, the perfect markets version of our Cost-of-Carry Model.

Limitations to Storage.   Of all commodities, gold is perhaps the most storable. It is chemically stable, it has a high value relative to weight and volume, and so on. Some other commodities cannot be stored very well at all, however. The storability of a commodity is important to futures pricing because the arbitrage strategies that we have been considering depend on being able to store the underlying good. For example, the cash-and-carry arbitrage strategy assumes that a trader can buy a commodity today and store it until a later delivery date on a futures contract. If a commodity cannot be stored, some of the arbitrage strategies that we have been considering will not be available. Therefore, the no-arbitrage bounds we have developed will have to be altered to reflect the actual limitations to storage.

In the cash-and-carry arbitrage strategy, the ability to store the commodity limits the futures price relative to the cash price. As we saw in equation 3.1, the futures price cannot exceed the cash price by more than the cost-of-carry. To see the importance of this point, imagine a tasty tropical fruit that can be harvested on only one day per year, and assume that the fruit spoils in one day if it is not eaten. These physical characteristics of the fruit make it impossible to store. This limitation to storage means that a cash-and-carry strategy cannot link futures and cash prices. Because the fruit is not storable, we could say that the storage cost is infinite. Thus, equation 3.1 would merely say that the futures price must be less than infinity. This we already know without a business degree.

While the tropical fruit example is quite fanciful, there are also commodities with very practical limits to storage. The Chicago Mercantile Exchange traded a futures contract on fresh eggs for many years. While eggs can be stored for a while, there are definite limits that cannot be exceeded. Grains and oilseeds play an important role in agricultural futures. While wheat, oats, corn, soybeans, soymeal and soyoil all store well, they cannot be stored indefinitely. Therefore, when storage is limited, the cash-and-carry strategy is also limited. The importance of these limitations to storage varies across commodities. As we noted, they are not important for gold, but they can be important for perishable assets.

How Traders Deal with Market Imperfections.   We have seen that transaction costs, differential borrowing rates, and restrictions on short selling all act to widen the no-arbitrage bounds that link cash and futures prices. It is also important to realize that these factors have vastly different effects on different traders. Also, they differ widely across markets. This section considers these market imperfections in a practical light.

There are two critical points about transaction costs. First, every trader faces transaction costs on every trade. Second, these cost differ widely across traders. Let us consider two extreme cases. In both instances, we are interested in the marginal transaction cost, because the marginal transaction cost determines whether the trade takes place. Imagine a professor in Miami who occasionally dabbles in the futures market. Such a trader will trade through a brokerage firm. The broker will charge a commission, the floor broker who executes the order will face a bid–asked spread, and the trader will have to pay exchange fees as well. Together these costs could be as low as $15-20 or they could be much higher. In addition, the professor incurs substantial search costs to determine how to trade. These are difficult to quantify. In contrast with our dabbling professor, consider a major gold trading firm, such as Handy and Harmon or Engelhard. Such firms refine silver and gold and trade it worldwide. As part of their commercial enterprise, they operate a futures trading desk to hedge their own risk exposure in the gold market. In addition, the traders on the desk actively trade in the market, searching for the arbitrage opportunities that we have been considering. A large trading firm faces a very low marginal transaction cost.

These differences in transaction costs stem from several sources. First, the firm is already in the market for other business purposes. Unlike the professor who studies the market merely looking for a good trading opportunity, these commercial concerns are already in the market in support of their physical metals business. This presence makes their information-gathering cost much lower than that faced by the professor who trades only occasionally. Second, the commercial concern will typically own an exchange membership and have its own people on the floor. If so, the firm faces no brokerage commission, which is a large cost of each trade for the professor.

A third and major factor is the difference in the chance to sell short. Short selling of metals is effectively closed to the professor, but it is virtually wide open for the metals trading firm. For the professor, selling short, if it is possible at all, will involve substantial limitations on the use of the short sale proceeds. The metals trading firm, by contrast, will hold an inventory of gold. Thus, the trading firm can simulate short selling by merely selling some of its inventory. From a trading perspective, the sale of the gold that the firm already owns is identical to selling gold short. As long as the firm has access to a supply of gold it can sell, it can replicate the trading effect of selling short. For firms with substantial gold stocks, there is virtually no limitation to replicating a short sale. In sum, for many markets, large commercial concerns in the business face very low transaction costs. For them, the market imperfections we have examined are of little practical importance. Thus, in some markets, prices closely approximate the perfect markets pricing relationship of equation 3.3.

The Concept of a Full Carry Market

In the price quotations of Figure 3.1, we can readily observe different patterns of prices for different commodities. As we consider more distant corn futures contracts, we see that prices first fall, then rise, then fall again. The peak price is \$2.6375 per bushel for the JUL 1991 contract. For silver, the prices rise in an apparently regular fashion; the more distant the delivery period, the higher the futures price. For crude oil, the SEP 1990 price is highest and all later prices are lower. On any given day, it is possible to observe this same variety of patterns for different commodities.

We can group commodities into different types by the degree to which their prices approximate full carry. In a **full carry market**, futures prices conform to equations 3.3 and 3.6. If prices match the relationships specified in the equation, the market is said to be at full carry. If the futures price is higher than equations 3.3 and 3.6 indicate, then the market is **above full carry**. If the futures price is less than the fully carry price, the market is **below full carry**.

As an example, consider the following data for August 16, 1990.

Gold September 1990	410.20
Gold December 1990	417.90
Banker's Acceptance Rate—90 days[8]	7.80%

Is gold at full carry? In addition to financing, warehousing and insuring gold have a cost. These amounts are negligible for gold in percentage terms, so we ignore them for the present. We begin by annualizing the percentage difference between the two gold prices:[9]

$$\left(\frac{F_{0,d}}{F_{0,n}}\right)^4 = 1.0772$$

Thus, the implied annual percentage difference between the two gold prices is 7.72 percent. This corresponds almost exactly to our interest rate estimate. In fact, this is not surprising because gold is almost always at full carry. From this example, we can see that in a full carry market, prices should be normal. That is, the more distant futures price should exceed the nearby price. Other markets are not at full carry. As we have noted, corn prices in Figure 3.1 are not normal, and crude oil prices in Figure 3.1 are clearly inverted. Some markets are normal at times and near full carry, while they diverge radically from full carry at other times.

We have already seen that a well-developed market for short sales is important in keeping the no-arbitrage bounds tight, so that prices will more closely conform to the full carry relationship. There are five main factors that affect market prices and move them toward or away from full carry: short selling conditions, supply, seasonality of production, seasonality of consumption, and ease of storage.

Market Features that Promote Full Carry

1. Ease of short selling.
2. Large supply.
3. Non–seasonal production.
4. Non–seasonal consumption.
5. Ease of storage.

Ease of Short Selling. We have already seen in our discussion of the Cost-of-Carry Model that short selling restrictions widen the no-arbitrage bounds on futures prices. In the extreme case, where short selling is not permitted, there can be no reverse cash-and-carry arbitrage, so the futures price has no lower no-arbitrage bound. In markets for physical goods, short selling is highly restricted, even though some commercial interests can replicate short selling by reducing their inventories. By contrast, it is very easy to sell financial assets short. For this reason, and for others, financial assets tend to be full carry assets.

Large Supply. If the supply of an asset is large relative to its consumption, the market for the good will more closely approximate a full carry market. On the side of cash-and-carry arbitrage, a large supply makes it easier for traders to acquire the physical good to store for future delivery. Relative to consumption for jewelry or industrial uses, for example, the supply of gold is very large. This factor helps to keep gold near full carry. By contrast, the world supply of copper is low relative to consumption. Typical supplies of copper on hand roughly equal three months of production.[10] Markets for copper and other industrial metals are not full carry markets.

Non–Seasonal Production. Temporary imbalances in supply and demand tend to cause distortions in normal price relationships. If production is highly seasonal, the stock of a good will be subject to large shifts. Many agricultural commodities have highly seasonal production due to their harvest cycles. In these markets, prices tend to be high for periods immediately prior to the harvest and low for the post-harvest months. This principle is reflected in Figure 3.1 to some extent for soybeans. The first futures contract listed is for AUG 1990. Prices rise for each subsequent contract month through JUL 1991, harvest time in the United States. Prices for the two following contract expirations in August and

November are markedly lower. At this time the new crop is in, and soybeans should be abundant.

Non–Seasonal Consumption. Foodstuffs, such as soybeans, may have seasonal production, but consumption is fairly steady. People like to eat all year. For other goods, production is fairly continuous, but consumption is highly seasonal. For example, contract prices for heating oil often show a seasonal pattern of high prices in winter, while gasoline prices are often relatively high for summer months. The prices in Figure 3.1 do not show this pattern for crude oil, however. At least part of the reason stems from the political situation. Figure 3.1 shows prices about two weeks after the Iraqi invasion of Kuwait. The resulting oil shortage and the embargo of Iraqi oil helped to give a premium to cash oil. Thus, this sharp drop in the supply of oil available for immediate consumption raised the price of near–term oil relative to oil for distant delivery. The crude oil prices of Figure 3.1 reflect this pattern of demand and supply with prices that drop steadily for subsequent delivery dates.

For the same date, however, natural gas prices illustrate the seasonal pattern. Table 3.13 shows natural gas futures prices for August 16, 1990. Natural gas is not as highly dominated by Middle Eastern sources relative to oil. The high prices for the winter months correspond to the high seasonal demand for natural gas as a source of heating fuel.

High Storability. In the example of the tropical fruit that must be harvested and eaten in a single day, we have the perfect example of a non-storable commodity. If the good is non-storable, cash-and-carry arbitrage strategies cannot link the cash price with the futures price. Thus, the Cost-of-Carry Model is unlikely to apply to a good with poor storage characteristics. To a great extent,

Table 3.13
Natural Gas Futures Prices
(August 16, 1990)

Expiration Month	Futures Price
SEP 1990	1.430
OCT	1.545
NOV	1.825
DEC	2.175
JAN 1991	2.295
FEB	2.080
MAR	1.800
APR	1.700
MAY	1.700

most physical commodities traded on futures exchanges have good storage characteristics. Some commodities that were less storable—such as fresh eggs and potatoes—have passed from futures trading. To the extent that a commodity has poor storage characteristics, however, the Cost-of-Carry Model is unlikely to apply.

Convenience Yield

We have seen in the preceding section that various factors cause the array of futures prices to vary from full carry for many commodities. In general, the Cost-of-Carry Model fails to apply when an asset has a **convenience yield**—a return on holding the physical asset. When holding an asset has a convenience yield, the futures price will be below full carry. In an extreme case, the market can be so far below full carry that the cash price can exceed the futures price. When the cash price exceeds the futures price, or when the nearby futures price exceeds the distant futures price, the market is in **backwardation**. In Figure 3.1, the crude oil market is in backwardation, expressing the high demand for immediate oil. An asset has a convenience yield when traders are willing to pay a premium to hold the physical asset at a certain time. For example, we have seen that natural gas prices are high in the winter—just when people need heat. Likewise, soybean prices arc high just before harvest—just when supplies are low and people still want to eat.

To explore the concept of the convenience yield more fully, assume that this is October and the cash price of soybeans is $6.00 per bushel. Harvest is one month away and a trader owns 5,000 bushels of soybeans. The futures price of soybeans for November is $5.50. In this example, the market is in backwardation, because the cash price exceeds the futures price. Under these circumstances, the trader will hold the soybeans from October to November only if he or she has some clear need for owning the beans during this period.

If the trader does not need the physical beans for the next month, he or she can sell the beans and buy a NOV futures contract. This strategy will yield a profit of $.50 per bushel, and it will save a month of carrying costs. Clearly, only a person with a need for physical beans will hold them given the price structure. For example, consider a food processor who still wants beans in October. The food processor might derive a convenience yield from owning beans, but only persons with a business need for the beans, such as a food processor, could derive a convenience yield.[11]

If the bean market is below full carry, it might seem that there is an opportunity for a reverse cash-and-carry arbitrage. This strategy requires selling beans short, but it is clear that short selling will not be possible. Short selling involves borrowing beans from someone else. Because the market is below full carry, no one will lend beans costlessly. Anyone who owns the beans holds them because of the convenience yield they derive. If they owned the beans and received no convenience yield, they would sell them outright in the market and buy the cheaper SEP futures to replace their beans in two months. Lending the beans to someone else so that other party can make money is the last application the holder of the physical beans would consider. Thus, if an asset has a convenience yield, the market can be below full carry, or even in backwardation. Such a situation will not provide a field day for reverse cash-and-carry arbitrage strategies, however, because short selling opportunities will not be available.

Summary

In our exploration of the Cost-of-Carry Model, we have seen that cash-and-carry and reverse cash-and-carry strategies place no-arbitrage bounds on futures prices. Transaction costs, differential borrowing and lending rates, restrictions on short selling, and limitations to storage, all act to widen those bounds. Therefore, while the Cost-of-Carry Model reveals much about the determinants of futures prices, it does not provide a complete determination of futures prices.

As we have seen, some commodities have characteristics that promote full carry. These include easy short selling, a large supply of the good, non-seasonal production and consumption, and high storability. Related to these, and also contributing to the applicability of the Cost-of-Carry Model, is the lack of a convenience yield. Because market imperfections and the characteristics of the commodities themselves sometimes combine to force the no-arbitrage bounds apart, other factors help to determine where within the no-arbitrage bounds the futures price will lie. Within the no-arbitrage bounds, the market's expectation plays a large role in futures price determination.

Futures Prices and Expectations

Earlier we considered a tropical fruit that can be harvested on only one day per year, July 4. The fruit is so delicate that it must also be consumed on that day or it will spoil. How would a futures contract on such a fruit be priced? As we explore in this section, the Cost-of-Carry Model breaks down for the pricing of such a futures contract.

Cash-and-carry arbitrage strategies do not apply to this fruit, because it cannot be carried. The fruit spoils in one day. Therefore, the cash price and the futures price are not linked by the opportunity to carry the fruit forward. Another way of making the same point is to say that the cost-of-carry is infinite. Thus, any positive cash price is consistent with any positive futures price, no matter how high.

Reverse cash-and-carry strategies also do not apply. For example, assume that the cash price of the fruit is $2 on July 4, 1991 and the futures price for July

1992 is $1. From our discussion of convenience yield, we know that this backwardation is due to the benefit that holding the cash fruit conveys. Therefore, no one would lend the fruit for short selling. Anyone who does not need the fruit for immediate consumption would merely sell it in the cash market and buy the cheaper futures. In sum, short selling would not be possible, so reverse cash-and-carry strategies will not serve to link the cash and futures prices. Because both the cash-and-carry and reverse cash-and-carry strategies fail for this fruit, they impose no-arbitrage bounds on the futures price.

The Role of Speculation

What does determine the futures price? Assume that market participants expect the price of the fruit in the next harvest to be $10 each. This price is the **expected future spot price**. In this event, the futures price must equal, or at least closely approximate, the expected future spot price. If this were not the case, profitable speculative strategies would arise.

As an example, if the futures price were $15, exceeding the expected future spot price of $10, speculators would sell the futures contract and then plan to buy the fruit for $10 on the harvest date. They would then be able to deliver the fruit and collect $15, for a $5 profit, if all went according to plan. By contrast, if the futures price were below the expected future spot price, say at $7, speculators would buy the futures contract, take delivery on the harvest date paying $7 and plan to sell the fruit at the market price of $10.

In short, the presence of speculators in the market place ensures that the futures price approximately equals the expected future spot price. Too great a divergence between the futures price and the expected future spot price creates attractive speculative opportunities. In response, profit-seeking speculators will trade as long as the futures price is sufficiently far away from the expected future spot price. We can express this basic idea by introducing the following notation.

$$F_{0,t} \approx E_0(S_t) \qquad\qquad 3.14$$

where:

$E_0(S_t)$ = the expectation at t=0 of the spot price to prevail at time t.

Equation 3.14 states that the futures price approximately equals the spot price currently expected to prevail at the delivery date. If this relationship did not hold, there would be attractive speculative opportunities.

Limits to Speculation

With equation 3.14, we have said that the futures price and the expected future spot price should be approximately equal. Why does this relationship hold only approximately? There are two basic answers to this question, one of which is fairly obvious and the second of which is fairly profound. First, the relationship holds only approximately because of transaction costs. Second, if some participants in the market are more risk averse than others, the futures price can diverge sharply from the expected future spot price.

Transaction Costs. Assume that the fruit has a futures price of $9 and an expected future spot price of $10, and assume that the cost of transacting to take advantage of this discrepancy is $2. With these prices, a trader cannot buy the futures for $9 and plan to make a $1 profit by selling the fruit at its expected future spot price. This opportunity is not profitable with the transaction costs, because the total cost of acquiring the fruit would be the $9 delivery on the futures plus the $2 transaction cost. Transaction costs can keep the futures price from exactly equaling the expected future spot price. This parallels our discussion of transaction costs and their effect on the Cost-of-Carry Model.

Risk Aversion. Traders in futures markets can be classified, at least roughly, into hedgers and speculators. Hedgers have a pre-existing risk associated with a commodity and sometimes enter the market to reduce that risk, while speculators trade in the hope of profit. Entering the futures market as a speculator is a risky venture. If people are risk averse, however, they incur risk willingly only if the expected profit from bearing the risk will compensate them for the risk exposure. Without doubt, most participants in financial markets are risk averse, so they seek compensation to warrant their taking a risky position.[12] In the futures markets, speculative profits can come only from a favorable movement in the price of a futures contract.

Assume that the expected future spot price of the fictional fruit is $10.00 and that the corresponding futures price is $10.05. Assume also that there is tremendous uncertainty about what the actual price of the fruit will be. The market expects a cash price of $10 upon harvest, but the fruit is very susceptible to weather conditions and it is also subject to the dread fictional fruit weevil. For a speculator, there appears to be a $.05 profit available from the strategy of selling the futures, buying fruit for $10.00 at harvest, and delivering against the futures contract. This strategy subjects the speculator to considerable risk if the weather is bad or if the weevil strikes, however. Speculators may decide that the expected profit of $.05 is not worth the risk exposure. If the speculators do not pursue the $.05 expected profit, there will be no market forces to drive the futures price into exact equality with the expected future spot price. Thus, the futures price can differ from the expected future spot price if traders are risk averse.

Summary. The strong principles of the Cost-of-Carry Model place no-arbitrage bounds on futures prices in many instances. In some cases those bounds are very wide, or even non-existent, due to transaction costs, restrictions on short selling, or the characteristics of the physical commodity. Within the bounds placed by cash-and-carry and reverse cash-and-carry strategies, expectations play a major role in establishing futures prices. We have seen that speculative strategies are available when the futures price does not equal the expected future spot price. Still, these speculative strategies do not ensure exact equality between the futures price and the expected future spot price. The futures price can diverge from the expected future spot price due to transaction costs or due to risk aversion on the part of traders. Of the two, risk aversion is much more important and deserves extended consideration.

Futures Prices and Risk Aversion

In this section, we explore in detail two theories of how risk aversion can affect futures prices. We have already seen that risk aversion among speculators can allow the futures price to diverge from the expected future spot price. According to the theory of normal backwardation, this divergence occurs in a systematic way. As a second theory, the Capital Asset Pricing Model (CAPM) relates market prices to a measure of systematic risk. Some scholars have applied the CAPM to futures markets to understand the differences that might exist between futures prices and expected future spot prices. We consider the two theories first, and conclude this section by examining the empirical evidence regarding the two theories.

The Theory of Normal Backwardation

Assume for the moment that speculators are rational; that is, they make assessments of expected future prices based on available information. In assessing this information, rational speculators occasionally make mistakes, but on the whole, they process the information efficiently. As a result, their expectations, on average, are realized. This does not imply that they are mistake free. Instead, they make errors of assessment that are not biased.[13] The expectational errors are randomly distributed around the true price that the commodity will have in the future. Assume also that speculators have "homogeneous expectations," that is, they expect the same future spot price.

Such a group of speculators might confront the prices prevailing in a futures market and find that those prices match the expected future spot prices. If the futures price reaches the expected price of the commodity when the futures contract matures, then there is no reason to speculate in futures. If the futures price matches a speculator's expectation of subsequent cash prices for the commodity, then the speculator must expect neither a profit nor a loss by entering the futures market. Yet, by entering the market under such conditions, the speculator would certainly incur additional risk. After all, the trader's expectations might be incorrect. Faced with such a situation, no risk averse speculator would trade, because the speculator would face additional risk without compensation.

Hedgers, taken as a group, need to be either long or short in the futures market to reduce the risk they face in their businesses. For example, a wheat farmer has a long position in cash wheat because he or she grows wheat. The farmer can reduce risk by selling wheat futures. If hedgers are net short, for example, speculators must be net long. For the sake of simplicity, consider a single speculator who is considering whether to take a long position. As just noted above, the rational speculator takes a long futures position only if the expected future spot price exceeds the current futures price. Otherwise, the speculator must expect not to make any profit.

The hedger, we assume, needs to be short to avoid unwanted risk. According to this line of reasoning, he must be willing to sell the futures contract at a price below the expected future spot price of the commodity. Otherwise, the hedger cannot induce the speculator to accept the long side of the contract. From this point of view, he, in effect, buys insurance from the speculator. The hedger transfers his unwanted risk to the speculator and pays an expected profit to the speculator for bearing the risk. The payment to the speculator is the difference between the futures price and the expected future spot price. Even so, the speculator does not receive any sure payment. The speculator must still wait for the expected future spot price to materialize to capture the profit expected for bearing the risk.

Thus far, the discussion has focused on a single hedger and a single speculator. It is necessary, however, to try to do justice to the fact that the marketplace is peopled by many individuals with different needs, different levels of risk aversion, and different expectations (heterogeneous expectations) about future spot prices.

Figure 3.9 depicts the situation that might prevail in the futures market for a commodity. It shows the relevant positions of hedgers and speculators as two groups. As the futures price varies, the number of contracts desired by the two groups will vary as well. We assume that hedgers are net short. At no futures price will hedgers, taken as a group, desire a long position in the futures.[14] This is reasonable given the definition of a hedger as one who enters the futures market to reduce a pre-existing risk. Line WX shows the hedgers' desired position in the futures market for various futures prices. At higher prices, hedgers

Figure 3.9
Hypothetical Net Positions

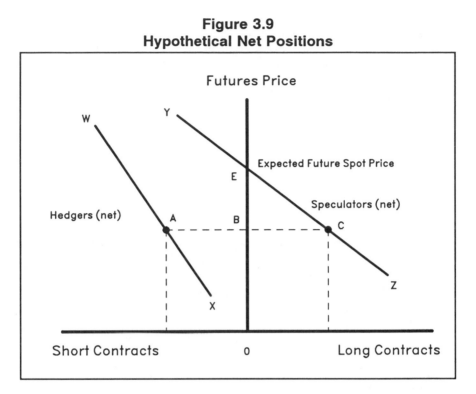

want to sell more futures contracts, as the downward slope for line WX indicates. Lines WX and YZ are drawn as straight lines, but that is only for convenience. Also, note that the hedgers hedge different amounts depending on the futures price. With low prices, they sell fewer contracts, thereby hedging less of their pre-existing risk than they would if futures prices were high.

In Figure 3.9, speculators are willing to hold either long or short net positions as the situation demands. Assuming that the speculators, as a group, correctly assess the appropriate expected future spot price, they will be neither long nor short when the futures price equals the expected future spot price. At that point, speculators hold a zero net position in the futures market. (In such a situation, some speculators would be long, others short, reflecting their divergent opinions. But, in the aggregate, they would hold a net zero position.) Line YZ shows the speculators' desired positions as a function of the futures price. If the futures price exceeds the expected future spot price, the speculators will desire to be net short as well as the hedgers. If the futures price lies below the expected future spot price, speculators will want to be net long, holding some position between E and Z on line YZ.

Not all positions shown on the graph are feasible. If the futures price lies above point E, then both the hedgers and speculators desire to be short. Yet, the number of outstanding short contracts must equal the number of long contracts. As the figure is drawn, there is only one price at which the market can clear: point B. With a price of B, the net short position desired by the hedgers exactly offsets the net long position desired by the speculators. This is reflected graphically by the fact that the distance AB equals the distance BC. Through the typical process by which markets reach equilibrium, the futures market may reach an equilibrium price at B, with the futures price lying below the expected future spot price.

Notice that the slope of WX (the hedgers' line) is steeper than that of YZ (the speculators' line). The more gentle slope of YZ expresses the greater risk tolerance of the speculators. For any drop in the futures price below the expected future spot price, E, the increase in the speculators' demand for long contracts exceeds the drop in the hedgers' desire to hold the short contracts. Indeed, this must be the case. Economically, the speculators must be more risk tolerant than the hedgers. After all, the speculators in this model, accept the risk that the hedgers are unwilling to bear, so the speculators must be more risk tolerant.[15]

This account explains how the futures price can diverge from the expected future spot price, even with no transaction costs. Likewise, if hedgers want to be net long, speculators must be net short. If the speculators are net short, then they can hope to earn a return for their risk-bearing services only if the futures price lies above the expected future spot price. Again the futures price need not equal the expected future spot price. Instead, the relationship between the futures price and the expected future spot price depends in part on whether the hedgers need to be net short or net long.

Clearly, in this model, the futures price will be below the expected future spot price if the hedgers are net short, as in Figure 3.9. The amount of the discrepancy depends upon the risk aversion of the two groups. For example, assume that the speculators are more risk averse than Figure 3.9 depicts. Higher risk aversion is represented in the graph by the steepness of the hedgers' or speculators' line. If the speculators were more risk averse, their line would be steeper. As a result, at price B, the speculators would be willing to hold fewer long contracts and the market would not clear at that price. Instead, the market clearing price would be below B, the exact price depending upon the steepness of the speculators' line. In that case, the market clearing price would be below B and fewer hedgers would be able to hedge.

This approach to determining futures prices originated with John Maynard Keynes and John Hicks. The view that hedgers are net short, as shown in Figure 3.9, is associated with Keynes and Hicks. Over the life of the futures contract, the futures price must move toward the cash price. (This is already clear, since the basis must equal zero at the maturity of the futures contract, as was discussed earlier.) If expectations about the future spot price are correct, and hedgers are net short, then the futures price must lie below the expected future spot price. In such a case, futures prices can be expected to rise over the life of a contract.

The view that futures prices tend to rise over the contract life due to the hedgers' general desire to be net short is known as **normal backwardation**. (Normal backwardation should not be confused with a market that is in backwardation. A market is in backwardation at a given moment if the cash price exceeds the futures price or if a nearby futures price exceeds a distant futures price.) Conversely, if hedgers are net long, then the futures price would lie above the expected future spot price, and the price of the futures contract would fall over its life. This pattern of falling prices is known as a **contango**. Figure 3.10 depicts these price patterns.[16]

Figure 3.10 illustrates the price patterns for futures that we might expect under different scenarios. In considering the figure, assume that market participants correctly assess the future spot price, so that the expected future spot price in the figure turns out to be the actual spot price at the maturity of the futures contract. If the futures price equals the expected future spot price, then the futures price will lie on the dotted line, which equals the expected future spot

Figure 3.10
Patterns of Futures Prices

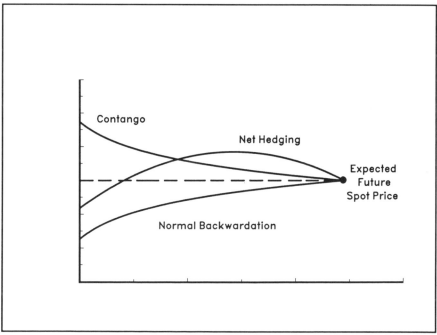

price. With initially correct expectations, and no information causing a revision of expectations, the futures price should remain constant over its entire trading life.

Alternative conceptions certainly exist, such as the theory of normal backwardation and the contango. If speculators are net long, as Keynes and Hicks believed, then futures prices must rise over the life of the contract if the speculators are to receive their compensation for bearing risk. Prices then follow the path that is labeled "Normal Backwardation" in Figure 3.10. With the futures price rising over its life, the speculator earns a return for bearing risk. Notice that the line for normal backwardation terminates at the expected future spot price. This is necessary since the futures price and the spot price must be equal at the maturity of the futures contract, and the figure is drawn assuming that the expected future spot price turns out to be the subsequently observed spot price.

If speculators are net short and are to receive compensation for bearing risk, futures prices must follow a contango, as Figure 3.10 also illustrates. The fall in futures prices, as the contract approaches maturity, gives the short speculators the compensation that induced them to enter the market.

One final possibility is also shown in Figure 3.10, and it is know as the **net hedging hypothesis**. According to this view, the net position of the hedgers might change over the life of the futures contract. When the contract begins trading, the hedgers are net short and the speculators are net long. In such a situation, the futures price lies below the expected future spot price. Over time, the hedgers gradually change their net position. Eventually, the hedgers are net long, requiring the speculators to be net short. For the speculators to receive their compensation in this case, the futures price must lie above the expected future spot price, as it did in the contango.[17]

Perhaps this account of hedgers changing from being net short to net long over the life of the contract appears dubious, but it is certainly conceivable. Consider grain farmers who wish to hedge the crop that they will produce. To hedge the price risk associated with harvest, they need to be short. Cereal producers have a need for the grain, and they hedge their price risk by being long. To show how the price could follow the pattern suggested by the net hedging hypothesis, imagine that the farmers hedge first. This makes the hedgers net short. Later, the cereal producers begin to hedge their future need for the grain, and the net hedging position of the farmers and cereal producers taken together begins to move toward zero. When it reaches zero, the farmers and cereal producers in the aggregate are neither short nor long. Time passes, and still more cereal producers hedge by going long. Eventually, the long hedgers come to predominate and all hedgers taken together are net long. Under such a condition, the futures price must lie above the expected future spot price if the speculators are to receive compensation for bearing risk.

Futures Prices and the Capital Asset Pricing Model

The Capital Asset Pricing Model (CAPM) has been widely applied to all kinds of financial instruments, including futures contracts. Equation 3.15 expresses the basic relationship of the CAPM:

$$E(R_j) = r + \beta_j[E(R_m) - r] \qquad\qquad 3.15$$

where:

r = the risk-free rate
$E(R_j)$ = expected return on asset j
$E(R_m)$ = expected return on the market portfolio
β_j = the "beta" of asset j

The CAPM measures the systematic risk of an asset by β, and β is usually estimated from a regression equation of the following form:

$$r_{j,t} = \alpha_j + \beta_j r_{m,t} + \varepsilon_{j,t} \qquad\qquad 3.16$$

where:

$r_{j,t}$ = the return on asset j in the tth period
$r_{m,t}$ = the return on the market portfolio j in the tth period
α_j = the constant term in the regression
$\varepsilon_{j,t}$ = the residual error for day t

According to the CAPM, only unavoidable risk should be compensated in the marketplace, and traders can avoid much risk through diversification. Even after diversification, risk remains for some assets because the returns of the asset are correlated with the market as a whole. This remaining risk is systematic. In essence, β_j measures the systematic risk of asset j relative to the market portfolio. According to equation 3.15, an asset with $\beta=1$ has the same degree of systematic risk as does the market portfolio and the asset should earn the same return as the market. The risk-free asset has $\beta=0$, and it should earn the risk-free rate of interest.

As we have seen, futures market trading does not require any investment. However, trading futures does require margin payments, but these are not investments. With no funds invested, there is no capital to earn the risk-free interest rate. Therefore, a futures position should have zero return if $\beta=0$. If the beta of a futures position exceeds zero, a long position in the futures contract should earn a positive return. For example, for futures position j, assume the following values hold:

$$E(R_m) = .09$$
$$r = .06$$
$$\beta_j = .7$$

According to equation 3.15, a long position in futures contract j should earn:

$$E(R_j) = \beta_j E(R_m) - r = .7(.09 - .06) = .021$$

Thus, positive betas for futures contracts lead to the expectation of rising futures prices. Zero betas would be consistent with futures prices that neither rise nor fall. A negative beta would imply that futures prices should fall.

Douglas T. Breeden applied a different version of the CAPM to the futures market.[18] In the intertemporal pricing model applied by Breeden, the relevant beta is a consumption beta. The consumption beta uses changes in real consumption rather than a stock index for the beta estimation, so the consumption beta is a linear function of the covariance between returns and aggregate real consumption. While more complex, the consumption-based model has the advantage of being more general.

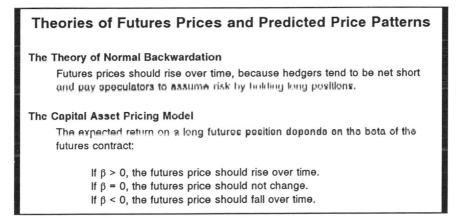

Theories of Futures Prices and Predicted Price Patterns

The Theory of Normal Backwardation

Futures prices should rise over time, because hedgers tend to be net short and pay speculators to assume risk by holding long positions.

The Capital Asset Pricing Model

The expected return on a long futures position depends on the beta of the futures contract:

If $\beta > 0$, the futures price should rise over time.
If $\beta = 0$, the futures price should not change.
If $\beta < 0$, the futures price should fall over time.

Futures Prices and Risk Aversion: Empirical Evidence

We have discussed the theory of normal backwardation and the CAPM separately to this point, yet both theories have strong implications for the behavior of futures prices. First, according to the Theory of Normal Backwardation, we expect futures prices to rise over time, because hedgers are net short and pay speculators to adopt long positions. Second, the CAPM predicts that futures prices should rise if and only if betas for futures are positive. If the beta for a futures contract is zero, the futures price would not be expected to change over its life. Finally, if the beta of a futures contract is negative, the futures price should fall over time.

Evidence on Normal Backwardation.   We begin by considering evidence on the returns for long positions in futures. Evidence on these returns will apply directly to the theory of normal backwardation. Table 3.14 summarizes some of

Table 3.14
Summary of Studies of Normal Backwardation

Study	Key Results
Houthakker (1957)	Found positive returns for cotton, wheat, and corn.
Rockwell (1967)	Found little support for normal backwardation.
Dusak (1973)	Found returns near zero for wheat, corn, and soybeans.
Bodie and Rosansky (1980)	Found positive returns for many commodities.
Carter, Rausser, and Schmitz (1983)	Found positive returns in wheat, corn, and soybeans.
Raynauld and Tessier (1984)	Results for corn, wheat, and oats, did not support normal backwardation.
Chang (1985)	Examined wheat, corn, and soybeans, but results were inconclusive for normal backwardation.
Baxter, Conine, and Tamarkin (1985)	Found no positive returns for wheat, corn, or soybeans.
Park (1985)	No normal backwardation in currencies and plywood, but normal backwardation in metals.
Hazuka (1984)	Evidence from applying the consumption based CAPM to 14 commodities, supported normal backwardation.
Fama and French (1987)	Found positive returns that weakly support normal backwardation.
Ehrhardt, Jordan, and Walkling (1987)	Found no support for normal backwardation in wheat, corn, or soybeans.
Hartzmark (1987)	Found that hedgers made money and speculators lost money, which is inconsistent with normal backwardation.

the many studies of normal backwardation, starting in the 1950s. As the table shows, the results are quite diverse. Consequently, the verdict is not yet in on the theory of normal backwardation. Faced with so many studies, we focus on two of the most often cited studies, one by Katherine Dusak and one by Zvi Bodie and Victor Rosansky. Dusak found that returns for wheat, corn, and soybeans were near zero, and we will discuss aspects of her study in more detail later. Table 3.15 presents the key results of the Bodie and Rosansky study. While Dusak's study focused on just a few commodities (wheat, corn, and soybeans) for the years 1952–1967, Bodie and Rosansky examined futures prices for 23 commodities over the period 1950-1976.[19] Their results are interesting because they stand in almost direct contradiction to Dusak's. Bodie and Rosansky found increasing prices for 22 of 23 commodities. It is important to note, however, that only three of these 22 returns were significantly different from zero. As the summary of other studies in Table 3.14 shows, however, many other researchers do not find any pattern of rising futures prices.

Evidence on the Capital Asset Pricing Model. Katherine Dusak was the first to apply the Capital Asset Pricing Model (CAPM) to futures prices.[20] Dusak modified the CAPM to apply to futures price percentage changes and measured the beta of a futures contract as the covariance of futures price changes with returns on a market index, divided by the variance of the market index. In general, Dusak found that the measured betas for futures contracts were near zero. Table 3.16 shows her key results. As the table indicates, virtually none of the betas differed significantly from zero.

According to the CAPM, an asset with a zero beta should earn the risk free rate of return. As futures markets trading requires no investment, however, there is no commitment of funds to earn the risk free rate. Accordingly, Dusak predicted that futures price changes should be zero on average. In accordance with this CAPM prediction, we noted that Dusak found that the futures prices did not rise. Thus, Dusak found zero systematic risk and zero returns. The zero returns finding opposes normal backwardation. Her combined results of zero systematic risk and zero returns are consistent with the CAPM.

Bodie and Rosansky also computed betas for the commodities in their study. They found that only seven of the 23 commodities examined had positive betas. With negative betas and no investment, the futures prices should have fallen on average, according to the CAPM.[21] Most of the estimated betas, while negative, do not differ significantly from zero. As Bodie and Rosansky explicitly note, their results are inconsistent with the CAPM, but they do support the hypothesis of normal backwardation.

Table 3.15
Returns On Commodity Futures

Annual Returns for 23 Commodity Futures Contracts (percent per year), 1950-76.

Good	Mean Return	Std. Dev.	Std. Error	Highest Annual Return	Lowest Annual Return	Obs.	Beta (std. err.)
Wheat	3.181	30.745	5.917	112.970 (1973)	-37.971 (1976)	27	-0.370 (0.296)
Corn	2.130	26.310	5.063	101.586 (1973)	-26.055 (1955)	27	-0.429 (0.247)
Oats	1.681	19.492	3.751	56.603 (1950)	-27.443 (1955)	27	0.000 (0.194)
Soy-beans	13.576	32.318	6.220	131.590 (1973)	-40.484 (1975)	27	-0.266 (0.317)
Soybean Oil	25.839	57.672	11.099	212.674 (1973)	-27.605 (1975)	27	-0.650 (0.558)
Soybean Meal	11.870	35.599	6.851	101.801 (1973)	-61.686 (1974)	27	0.239 (0.351)
Broilers	13.065	39.202	13.860	75.209 (1974)	-46.239 (1975)	8	-1.692 (0.395)
Plywood	17.968	39.962	16.314	94.595 (1972)	-19.031 (1973)	6	0.660 (0.937)
Potatoes	6.905	42.111	8.104	125.048 (1973)	-73.296 (1953)	27	-0.610 (0.400)
Platinum	0.641	25.185	7.594	47.584 (1967)	-38.524 (1970)	11	0.221 (0.411)
Wool	7.436	36.955	7.12	126.905 (1972)	-45.486 (1974)	27	0.307 (0.362)
Cotton	8.937	36.236	6.974	163.244 (1973)	-41.175 (1974)	27	-0.015 (0.360)
Orange Juice	2.515	31.771	10.047	74.538 (1971)	-32.298 (1976)	10	0.117 (0.557)
Propane	68.260	202.088	71.449	559.206 (1973)	-48.201 (1974)	8	-3.851 (3.788)
Cocoa	15.713	54.630	11.391	197.469 (1976)	-37.538 (1955)	23	-0.291 (0.589)
Silver	3.587	25.622	7.106	48.504 (1967)	-25.614 (1971)	13	-0.272 (0.375)

Table 3.15 continues on the next page.

Table 3.15 (cont.)

Good	Mean Return	Std. Dev.	Std. Error	Highest Annual Return	Lowest Annual Return	Obs.	Beta (std. err.)
Copper	19.785	47.205	9.843	130.135 (1973)	-32.194 (1957)	23	0.005 (0.492)
Cattle	7.362	21.609	6.238	40.991 (1975)	-28.370 (1976)	12	0.365 (0.319)
Hogs	13.280	36.617	11.579	77.564 (1969)	-35.462 (1974)	10	-0.148 (0.641)
Pork Bellies	16.098	39.324	11.352	103.916 (1965)	-28.979 (1976)	12	-0.062 (0.618)
Eggs	-4.741	27.898	5.369	56.425 (1969)	-47.156 (1971)	27	-0.293 (0.271)
Lumber	13.070	34.667	13.101	57.685 (1973)	-28.157 (1970)	7	-0.131 (0.768)
Sugar	25.404	116.215	24.232	492.009 (1974)	-71.799 (1975)	23	-2.403 (1.146)

Source:	Z. Bodie and V. Rosansky, "Risk and Return in Commodity Futures," *Financial Analysts Journal*, May-June 1980, p. 35.

In recent years, the CAPM has come under attack for failing to measure systematic risk appropriately. We have already noted that Breeden sought to develop consumption betas as an alternative to conventionally estimated betas. If true betas are positive, then Bodie and Rosansky's positive returns could be rendered consistent with the CAPM. Breeden found positive betas for many commodities, notably in the livestock category. For grains, generally, betas were still negative. The finding of positive betas is more consistent with the positive price changes noted by Bodie and Rosansky. Nonetheless, we cannot conclude that the behavior of futures prices has been rendered fully consistent with capital market theory.

Summary. It is difficult to interpret the empirical evidence regarding normal backwardation and the CAPM because it is so diverse. In general, it appears clear that no definitive decision on either issue has been reached. Approximately equal numbers of studies support and oppose normal backwardation, and the same is true for the CAPM.

This untidy irresolution may be due to the fact that futures returns are very close to zero. Thus, some studies find average returns significantly different from zero, while others do not. Most studies do seem to find that futures contracts have betas near zero, at least when these betas are measured using conventional

Table 3.16
Key Results from Dusak's Study of Futures Prices

Commodity	Expiration Month	Beta	Std. Err.
Wheat	JUL	.048	.051
	MAR	.098	.049
	MAY	.028	.051
	SEP	.068	.051
	DEC	.059	.048
Corn	JUL	.038	.046
	MAR	-.009	.050
	MAY	-.027	.048
	SEP	.032	.048
	DEC	.007	.047
Soybeans	JAN	.019	.058
	MAR	.100	.065
	MAY	.119	.068
	JUL	.080	.076
	SEP	.077	.065
	NOV	.043	.058

Source: Katherine Dusak, "Futures Trading and Investor Returns: An Investigation of Commodity Market Risk Premiums," *Journal of Political Economy*, 81:6, December 1973.

techniques. Final resolution of these issues will require more comprehensive data sets and analyses than have been employed to date.

Characteristics of Futures Prices

In this section, we consider four characteristics of futures prices and changes in futures prices. First, we consider the relationship between futures prices and forward prices for the same good. Theoretically, these prices could differ even when they depend on the same underlying good. This is possible because of the feature of daily settlement on the futures contract, but not on the forward contract. Second, we consider the forecasting ability of futures prices. If futures prices equal expected future spot prices, the process of price discovery is aided substantially. Third, we consider the distribution of futures price changes. If the distribution of price changes is non-normal, statistical tests become more difficult, because most popular tests assume that the distribution of price changes is normal. As we will see, the distribution is generally not normal. This has important implications in many areas. For example, a test of whether the average change in futures prices is positive depends on the normality of the changes being tested. Fourth, we consider the volatility of futures prices and the effect of futures price volatility on the volatility of cash market prices.

Futures Prices versus Forward Prices

In Chapter 1 we considered the differences between forward and futures markets. Here we analyze the factors that can cause forward and futures prices to diverge, even when the contracts have the same underlying commodities and the same time to expiration. Forward and futures prices can differ because of different tax treatments, different transaction costs, or different margin rules. Also, the chance of a default may be higher on a forward contract, due to the lack of a clearing-house in forward markets. The main conceptual reason for a possible difference in prices stems from the daily settlement that characterizes futures markets, however.

To see the potential difference between forward and futures prices, consider the following example. A gold futures and a gold forward both expire in one year, and the current price of both contracts is $500. We assume that the spot price of gold in one year will also be $500. Thus, there will be no profit or loss on either contract. Also, when the contracts expire, the forward price, the futures price, and the cash price must all be equal. We have explored arbitrage arguments to show that this result must obtain. There are about 250 trading days in a year, so we consider two very simple possible price paths that gold might follow over that year. First, we assume that the futures price rises by $2 each day for 125 days and then falls by $2 per day for 125 days. Second, we assume that the gold price falls by $2 per day for 125 days and then rises by $2 per day for 125 days. Figure 3.11 illustrates the two price paths. Under either scenario, the price will be $500 at expiration in one year. Thus, there is no profit or loss on either contract.

The forward trader is indifferent between the two possible price paths. The forward trader has no cash flow at the beginning and none at the end. Because of daily settlement, however, the futures trader has definite preferences. For example, a long futures trader would much prefer the price to rise first and fall later. Each day the price rises, the long futures trader receives a settlement payment that can be invested. Getting the cash inflows early in the holding period means that the futures trader can earn more interest than otherwise.

Assuming a 10 percent interest rate, the difference in these two price paths is about $25 for the futures trader. If the price rises first, the long futures trader receives payments that can be invested. Later in the year, however, the futures trader must make daily settlement payments. Nonetheless, the trader makes $12.48 in interest by year end if the price rises first in Figure 3.11.[22] Similarly,

Figure 3.11
Possible Futures Price Paths

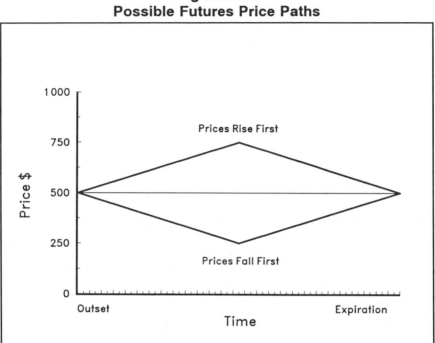

the trader loses $12.48 in interest if prices fall first. Notice that these differences stem strictly from the interest gains or losses on the daily settlement payments. This is clear from the example, because there are no profits or losses on the futures position. Therefore, we can see that the futures trader can be better or worse off than the forward trader.

Of course, traders do not know which will be more attractive until after the event, because no one knows what course prices will take. After all, interest rate movements are subject to chance. This makes it impossible to know at the outset which price path will occur, so the gold trader would not know which contract to take in our example, the forward or the futures.

It is possible to draw a general rule from this analysis. If the futures price is positively correlated with interest rates, then a long trader will prefer a futures position over a forward position. This result has been proven rigorously in a number of studies.[23] While the proof of this proposition is quite mathematical, we can follow the intuition that underlies it.

If the futures price and interest rates rise together, then the long futures trader will receive settlement payments that can be invested at the higher interest rate. If futures prices and interest rates both fall, the futures trader must make settlement payments, but the trader can finance those payments at the new lower interest rate. In this argument, the trader does not need to forecast interest rates to have a preference for futures over forwards. Instead, the preference for a futures over a forward depends only on the correlation between the futures price and the interest rate.

Both the futures and the forward will have the same profit in the end, exclusive of the settlement payments. If the futures position is likely to have more favorable interim cash flows due to its positive correlation with interest rates, the futures price should exceed the forward price. By the same token, if the futures price is negatively correlated with interest rates, then the futures price should be lower than the forward price. This conclusion follows, because the long futures trader will then tend to experience losses just as interest rates rise. Finally, if the price of a commodity is uncorrelated with interest rates, then the forward and futures prices should be equal. Notice that all these conclusions arise strictly from economic reasoning. We now turn to an examination of the evidence.

Theoretical Relationship of Forward and Futures Prices

Correlation of Spot Prices and Interest Rates	Price Relationship
Positive Correlation	Futures Price > Forward Price
Negative Correlation	Futures Price < Forward Price
No Correlation	Futures Price = Forward Price

Table 3.17
Empirical Evidence on Forward versus Futures Prices

Study	Key Results
Cornell and Reinganum (1981)	Found no significant differences between forward and futures prices of foreign exchange.
French (1983)	Found statistically significant differences between forward and futures prices for silver and copper, but the differences were smaller than 1%.
Park and Chen (1985)	Found no significant differences for currencies. For gold, platinum, copper, silver, and silver coins, the differences were significant.

We now consider the practical effect, if any, of a correlation between interest rates and commodity prices on the difference between forward and futures prices. Table 3.17 shows the results from three studies. In general, it appears that foreign exchange futures and forward prices do not differ, although there does seem to be some statistically significant difference for metals. Nonetheless, even when these results were statistically significant, the magnitudes were small and may not have been significant economically. Because of these small magnitudes, it is customary to assume that forward and futures prices are equal for most practical purposes.

Futures Prices and Expected Future Spot Prices

We have stressed that futures markets serve society by providing a mechanism for market agents to form expectations about future spot prices. This is the role of price discovery. Because futures prices change continuously, they clearly cannot always equal the subsequently observed spot price. The futures price could be an estimate of the expected future spot price. If the futures price serves as an unbiased estimate of the future spot price, we would expect futures price changes to average zero in the long run.

We have already seen that the theory of normal backwardation holds that the futures price should rise over time. This theory implies that the average change in the futures price is positive. As a result, normal backwardation implies that the futures price does not, on average, equal the expected future spot price. Rather, normal backwardation holds that the futures price tends to be lower than the expected future spot price. After all, this difference is exactly the expected profit that draws the speculator into the market to provide risk–bearing services.

As we also saw in our discussion of normal backwardation, the empirical evidence is inconclusive. Dusak found approximately zero returns for the commodities she studied. Bodie and Rosansky found positive returns, but they were not significant generally. The results of Fama and French were similar to those of Bodie and Rosansky. Thus, there seem to be some cases in which the futures price does not provide a good estimate of the future spot price. However, results of these studies indicate that rejection of the equality of the futures price and the expected future spot price are not strong. Thus, for practical purposes, the futures price may be the best readily available estimate of the future spot price.

The Distribution of Futures Prices

As we noted earlier, most statistical tests of futures prices rely on the assumption that the underlying price changes are normally distributed. If futures price changes are not normally distributed, then these tests become more difficult to conduct. In this section, we briefly review the evidence on the distribution of futures prices. Table 3.18 summarizes some of the key papers in this area.

Most of these studies address a few similar issues for different commodities and different time periods. First, almost all of the studies examine whether the distribution of futures price changes is normal. Almost universally, they find that the distribution is not normal, because the distribution is leptokurtic. Figure 3.12 illustrates **leptokurtosis**—the tendency for a distribution to have too many extreme observations relative to a normal distribution. In the figure, the solid line shows a normal distribution. The dotted line shows a leptokurtic distribution. The greater frequency of extreme observations makes the tails of a leptokurtic distribution have "fat tails." Almost all of the studies reject the null hypothesis of a normal distribution on the grounds of leptokurtosis. As a second major theme, many of these papers try to determine what distribution futures prices follow if they are not normal. Two candidates dominate. First, the distribution may be stable Paretian. This distribution is symmetrical, like the normal

Table 3.18
Evidence on the Distribution of Futures Prices

Study	Key Results
Stevenson and Bear (1970)	Futures price changes are leptokurtic.
Dusak (1973)	Futures price changes are non–normal, leptokurtic, and seem to be stable Paretian.
Clark (1973)	Cotton futures prices are non–normal, but seem to come from a mixture of normal distributions.
Mann and Heifner (1976)	Futures price changes are non–normal, leptokurtic, and seem to be stable Paretian.
Tauchen and Pitts (1983)	T–bill futures prices appear to come from a mixture of normal distributions.
Cornew, Town, and Crowson (1984)	Futures price changes are leptokurtic, but symmetric.
Helms and Martell (1985)	Futures price changes are non–normal.
Gordon (1985)	Futures price changes are leptokurtic.
Hudson, Leuthold, and Sarassoro (1987)	Futures price changes are leptokurtic.
So (1987)	Currency futures price changes are non–normal and appear to be stable Paretian.
Hall, Brorsen, and Irwin (1989)	Futures price changes are leptokurtic, and appear to be distributed as a mixture of normal distributions.

Figure 3.12
Normality and Leptokurtosis

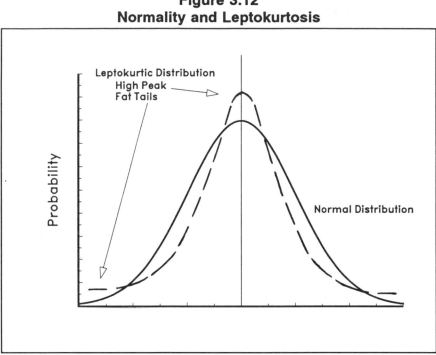

distribution, but it is leptokurtic relative to a normal distribution. Second, some studies find that the distribution of futures price changes seems to be similar to a mixture of two or more normal distributions. Thus, these studies find that the distribution is not normal, but that it can be approximated by a mixture of normal distributions. Both camps agree that this non-normalcy requires extra caution in making statistical inferences about futures prices.

In addition to testing the distribution of futures price changes, several studies have examined whether the times series of futures price changes is autocorrelated. A time series is **autocorrelated** if the value of one observation in the series is statistically related to another. In **first-order autocorrelation,** for example, one observation is related to the immediately preceding observation. This question has considerable practical importance. For example, if futures prices exhibit positive first-order autocorrelation, then positive returns in one period tend to be followed by positive returns in the next period. Similarly, negative returns tend to be followed by subsequent negative returns.

If the correlation were strong enough, it would be possible to devise trading strategies to profit from this follow-on tendency. For example, with positive first-order autocorrelation, one could devise a trading rule to buy the futures

Table 3.19
Evidence on Autocorrelation in Futures Price Changes

Study	Key Results
Stevenson and Bear (1970)	Corn and soybean futures price changes are positively autocorrelated.
Dusak (1973)	Bi–weekly corn, wheat, and soybean futures price changes exhibit some positive autocorrelation.
Cargill and Rausser (1975)	Examining corn, oats, soybeans, wheat, copper, live beef, and pork bellies found positive autocorrelation.
Petzel (1980)	Corn futures price changes are positively autocorrelated.
Helms, Kaen, and Rosenman (1984)	Soy complex futures prices are positively autocorrelated.
Taylor (1985)	Eight agricultural and financial commodities exhibit positive autocorrelation.
Taylor (1986)	Commodity futures prices are positively autocorrelated.

immediately following a price rise. Then, the second price rise would generate a profit.

Almost all studies have found that futures prices exhibit statistically significant first-order autocorrelation. Table 3.19 summarizes some of those studies. While the autocorrelation appears to be significant statistically, it does not appear to be important economically. In other words, the autocorrelation is not strong enough to allow profitable trading strategies after we consider transaction costs.

The Volatility of Futures Prices

In this section, we examine two dimensions of futures price volatility that have received considerable attention from scholars. First, we consider the relationship between futures trading and the volatility of prices for the underlying good. Usually, this issue has been addressed in the following form: "Does the introduction of futures trading make the underlying commodity price more volatile?" Typically, volatility is measured as the variance of price changes. A second issue focuses on patterns in the volatility of futures prices themselves. As we will see, evidence suggests that futures prices become more volatile as they approach the expiration date.

Futures Trading and Cash Market Volatility.   Some market observers allege that futures trading makes prices for the underlying good more volatile. Most recently, this claim has been alleged for equities. These critics of futures markets allege that recent stock market volatility can be traced to the introduction of stock index futures trading.[24] Often these claims are accompanied by proposals for tighter regulation of futures trading. Therefore, the question has important public policy implications.

Most studies of the effect of futures trading on the cash market compare the volatility of the cash market before and after the introduction of futures trading. While not quite unanimous, the weight of evidence seems to suggest that futures trading does not increase the volatility of the cash market. In fact, some studies even find that cash market volatility falls after futures trading starts. Table 3.20 summarizes some of the studies of this issue. As this summary suggests, the evidence is fairly clear that futures trading does not de-stabilize the cash market.

Time to Expiration and Futures Price Volatility.   In a paper now regarded as a classic, Paul Samuelson[25] argued that the volatility of futures prices should increase as the contract approaches expiration. This is the **Samuelson hypothesis.** In his analysis, Samuelson assumed that competitive forces in the futures

---

Table 3.20
Futures Trading and Cash Market Volatility

Study	Key Results
Working (1960)	Futures trading reduces volatility in the onion market.
Gray (1963)	Futures trading reduces volatility in the onion market.
Powers (1970)	Cattle and pork prices were more stable after futures trading began.
Taylor and Leuthold (1974)	For live cattle, prices were more stable after futures trading began.
Froewiss (1978)	Futures trading did not increase mortgage market volatility.
Figlewski (1981)	Futures trading accompanied an increase in mortgage market volatility.
Moriarty and Tosini (1985)	Futures trading did not increase mortgage market volatility.
Bhattacharya, Ramjee, and Ramjee (1986)	Futures trading did not increase mortgage market volatility.

market keep the futures price at a level equal to the expected future spot price at the contract's termination. Under this assumption, futures prices should follow a **martingale**—a price process in which the expected value of the next price equals the current price, so the expected price change is zero. Therefore, this conclusion implies that the futures price equals the expected future spot price.

While the mathematics of Samuelson's model are somewhat complex, the intuition is clear. High price volatility implies big price changes. Price changes are large when more information is being revealed about a commodity. Early in a futures contract's life, little information is known about the future spot price for the underlying commodity. Later, as the contract nears maturity, the rate of information acquisition increases. For example, little is known about a corn harvest a full year before harvest time. As the harvest approaches, the market gets a much better idea of the ultimate price that corn will command. For a futures contract expiring near the harvest, Samuelson's model implies that the futures price should be more volatile as the harvest approaches. Table 3.21 summarizes some of the studies that have examined the Samuelson hypothesis, and most find some support for the hypothesis. Virtually all studies agree that futures prices exhibit **seasonal volatility**—they are more volatile at some periods rather than at others. Thus, the Samuelson hypothesis asserts a particular kind of seasonal volatility, one linked to the maturity of the futures contract.

It is possible that there could be other kinds of seasonal influences on futures prices. In fact, recent research indicates that the seasonality implied by the Samuelson hypothesis may be real, but it is not the main factor driving the seasonality of futures prices. For example, we have already seen how the harvest cycle could influence the variability of cash prices for an agricultural commodity.

Table 3.21
Evidence on the Samuelson Hypothesis

Study	Key Results
Rutledge (1976)	Rejected hypothesis for wheat and soybean oil, but accepted for silver and cocoa.
Grauer (1977)	Found no support for 10 different commodities.
Dusak–Miller (1979)	Found supporting evidence for live beef futures.
Castelino and Francis (1982)	For wheat, corn, and soybean complex, results supported hypothesis.
Anderson (1985)	Supports hypothesis, but finds other more important factors affecting volatility.
Milonas (1986)	Finds support for hypothesis in 10 of 11 commodities.

These recent studies emphasize that the seasonality in futures prices stems from sources other than the time until expiration. For example, R. W. Anderson and J. P. Danthine developed a model in which the variability of futures prices depends on how rapidly supply and demand information for the commodity is being disseminated.[26] In an empirical study of agricultural commodities, Anderson finds that the season of the year has a much greater effect on volatility than does the time to expiration.[27] Other factors besides the time to maturity and the season of the year appear to be important influences on futures price volatility. A study by Kenyon, Kling, Jordan, Seale, and McCabe identified several other factors. For crops under price support, they find that the price support level relative to the futures price has an effect on volatility. They also find that volatility is itself autocorrelated. For example, high volatility in one month is likely to be followed by high volatility the next month.[28] Finally, there also seems to be a day-of-week effect in price volatility; that is, volatility differs depending on the day of the week. Volatility appears to be higher on Mondays than on other days.[29]

Trading Volume and Futures Price Volatility.   In addition to the factors that we have already considered, there appears to be a strong positive relationship between the volume of futures trading and the volatility of futures prices. We noted earlier that futures prices tend to be more volatile when information is coming into the market. Traders who trade based on information are also more likely to trade when information dissemination is rapid. Thus, it is not surprising that information arrival causes prices to be volatile and draws traders to the market, as most studies find. Apparently, the surge in volume and volatility are mainly contemporaneous. There does not seem to be a general tendency for one factor to precede the other.[30]

Conclusion

While futures markets have a reputation for high risk and wild price swings, this chapter has stressed the underlying rationality of futures prices. We cannot deny that prices vary suddenly and sharply in the futures market, but it is quite possible that these price movements accurately reflect the arrival of new information at the market. Further, it is also apparent that futures prices observe the economic laws elaborated above. Both the Cost-of-Carry Model and the expected future price framework provide rational procedures for thinking about the behavior of futures prices. It must also be admitted that futures prices, on the whole, conform to these theories.

If the conclusions reached about futures pricing above are correct, then a picture of the usefulness of the market begins to emerge. If prices react rationally to new information, and if spread relationships are strongly interconnected, and if futures prices are good estimates of expected future spot prices, it is possible to understand the uses that can be made of the market by different elements of society. These different groups in society were identified above as those who wish to discover price information by observing futures markets, as speculators, and as hedgers. If futures prices closely approximate expected future spot prices, then the price discovery function is well served. Speculators, on the other hand, will have a difficult life, because profitable opportunities will not be abundant. Hedgers, for their part, have an apparent opportunity to reduce their risk exposure with relatively little cost.

The next chapter explores how these different groups use the futures market. The difficulties facing speculators are examined more closely, along with the benefits that the futures markets provide to hedgers and to society as a whole.

Questions and Problems

1. Explain the function of the settlement committee. Why is the settlement price important in futures markets in a way that the day's final price in the stock market is not so important?

2. Open interest tends to be low when a new contract expiration is first listed for trading, and it tends to be small after the contract has traded for a long time. Explain.

3. Explain the distinction between a normal and an inverted market.

4. Explain why the futures price converges to the spot price and discuss what would happen if this convergence failed.

5. Is delivery, or the prospect of delivery, necessary to guarantee that the futures price will converge to the spot price? Explain.

6. As we have defined the term, what are the two key elements of "academic arbitrage?"

7. Assume that markets are perfect in the sense of being free from transaction costs and restrictions on short selling. The spot price of gold is $370. Current interest rates are 10 percent, compounded monthly. According to the Cost-of-Carry Model, what should the price of a gold futures contract be if expiration is six months away?

8. Consider the information in question 7. Round trip futures trading cost are $25 per 100 ounce gold contract, and buying **or** selling an ounce of gold incurs transaction costs of $1.25. Gold can be stored for $.15 per month per ounce. (Ignore interest on the storage fee and the transaction costs.) What futures prices are consistent with the Cost-of-Carry Model?

9. Consider the information in questions 7 and 8. Restrictions on short selling effectively mean that the reverse cash-and-carry trader in the gold market receives the use of only 90 percent of the value of the gold that is sold short. Based on this new information, what is the permissible range of futures price?

10. Consider all of the information about gold in questions 7-9. The interest rate in question 7 is 10 percent per annum, with monthly compounding. This is the borrowing rate. Lending brings only 8 percent, compounded monthly. What is the permissible range of futures prices when we consider this imperfection as well?

11. Consider all of the information about gold in questions 7-10. The gold futures expiring in six months trades for $375 per ounce. Explain how you would respond to this price, given all of the market imperfections we have considered. Show your transactions in a table similar to Tables 3.8 or 3.9. Answer the same question, assuming that gold trades for $395.

12. Explain the difference between pure and quasi-arbitrage.

13. Assume that you are a gold merchant with an ample supply of deliverable gold. Explain how you can simulate short selling and compute the price of gold that will bring you into the market for reverse cash-and-carry arbitrage.

14. Assume that silver trades in a full carry market. If the spot price is $5.90 per ounce and the futures that expires in one year trades for $6.55, what is the implied cost-of-carry? Under what conditions would it be appropriate to regard this implied cost-of-carry as an implied repo rate?

15. What is "normal backwardation?" What might give rise to normal backwardation?

16. Assume that the CAPM beta of a futures contract is zero, but that the price of this commodity tends to rise over time very consistently. Interpret the implications of this evidence for normal backwardation and for the CAPM.

17. Explain why futures and forward prices might differ. Assume that platinum prices are positively correlated with interest rates. What should be the relationship between platinum forward and futures prices? Explain.

18. Consider the life of a futures contract from inception to delivery. Explain two fundamental theories on why the futures prices might exhibit different volatility at different times over the life of the contract.

Notes

1. Sometimes the total open interest does not equal the sum of the open interest reported for each contract. This occurs because the WSJ does not report trading in some of the most distant contract maturities, yet these distant contracts are included for the total volume figure.

2. As will be explained in Chapter 4, we expect the price of seasonal goods to be relatively high just before harvest and relatively low just after harvest. It is this kind of consideration that leads futures market observers to expect systematically fluctuating differences in basis over the year.

3. The stability is even more dramatic when we take the difference in scale on the vertical axis into account.

4. In many cases, the owner of these goods will choose to insure these goods for himself or herself. Nonetheless, there is an implicit cost of insurance even when the owner self-insures.

5. For a very informative and readable account of repurchase agreements, see Bowsher, "Repurchase Agreements," *Instruments of the Money Market*, Richmond: Federal Reserve Bank of Richmond, 1981.

6. In the study of the bond market, this rate would be a forward rate of interest. We assume that it is possible to contract at the outset to borrow and lend at the forward rate of interest. This assumption is embraced by the condition of perfect markets.

7. Recall that we are abstracting from all non-interest carrying charges under our assumption of zero transaction costs.

8. Rates on term repurchase agreements are generally not available in the financial press. A banker's acceptance is a negotiable instrument used in international trade that is guaranteed by a bank. Also, the rates quoted in the "Money Rates" section of *The Wall Street Journal* are intended to offer only an indication of the prevailing rates.

9. The ratio of the distant to the nearby futures price defines the interest rate between the two dates t=n and t=d. In this example, d–n is 90 days, so we raise the expression to the 4th power to account for the quarterly compounding.

10. See for example, Table 31-1, Martin J. Pring, *The McGraw–Hill Handbook of Commodities and Futures*, New York: McGraw-Hill, 1985.

11. B. Wright and J. Williams, "A Theory of Negative Prices for Storage," *The Journal of Futures Markets*, 9:1, February 1989, pp. 1-13, explore the convenience yield more rigorously.

12. In his book, *Risk and Risk Bearing*, Chicago: University of Chicago Press, 1940, Charles O. Hardy gives a different interpretation of the behavior of speculators. He likens the futures market to a gambling casino. In Hardy's view, if we ignore transaction costs in the futures market, the expected outcome of any trade is no gain and no loss. If transaction costs are considered, then the expected outcome is slightly negative. This, Hardy suggests, makes the futures market like a gambling casino, since people play, even when they should expect to lose money.

13. An estimator is unbiased if and only if the expected value of the estimator equals the actual value of the parameter being estimated. Rational expectations theory has been applied to the commodities markets in this context. See Thomas J. Sargent, "Commodity Price Expectations and the Interest Rate," *Quarterly Journal of Economics*, 83, February 1969, pp. 126-140, and J. F. Muth, "Rational Expectations and the Theory of Price Movements," *Econometrica*, 29, July 1961, pp. 315-335.

14. By assuming that hedgers will be net short no matter what the futures price, we are merely assuming that their pre-existing risk requires a short position. Some potential hedgers would, of course, abandon their risk-reducing short position if the futures price were low enough. However, in so doing, the potential hedger would have abandoned the intention of hedging and would be speculating. This is clear if we recall that the risk-reducing futures trade is to go short.

15. The idea for Figure 2.9 was suggested by a presentation by Hans Stoll.

16. A normal market gives rise to "normal backwardation" and an inverted market is consistent with prices following a "contango." (In the French futures market, you may sometimes encounter the "Last Contango in Paris." Sorry.)

17. Figure 3.10 was originally adapted from William Sharpe's book, *Investments*, Englewood Cliffs, NJ: Prentice Hall, Inc., 1981.

18. D. Breeden, "Consumption Risk in Futures Markets," *Journal of Finance*, May 1980, 35:2, pp. 503-520.

19. Z. Bodie and V. Rosansky, "Risk and Return in Commodity Futures," *Financial Analysts Journal*, 36:3, May-June 1980, pp. 27-39.

20. See Katherine Dusak, "Futures Trading and Investor Returns: An Investigation of Commodity Market Risk Premiums," *Journal of Political Economy*, December, 1973, 81:6. For an explanation of the CAPM, see R. Kolb, *Investments*, Glenview, IL.: Scott Foresman, Inc., 1989, Chapters 13-15.

21. The prices should have fallen with the negative betas because of the value of using futures contracts to hedge the market risk inherent in a stock portfolio. In the CAPM, an asset with a negative beta has expected returns less than the risk-free rate. With futures, there is no investment, so there are no earnings at the risk-free rate. Because of their hedging usefulness, the negative beta commodity contracts should have had falling prices. Bodie and Rosansky point out that the commodity contracts could have been used over this period as a very effective device for reducing the risk inherent in the S&P 500 without adversely affecting return.

22. This calculation assumes that the interest rate is 10 percent per annum and there are 250 trading periods, for a daily interest factor of 1.000381. Thus, the first day, the price rises by $2 so this gives interest of $2(1.000381)^{250} - $2 = $.20, and so on. Later, when the losses start, the losses must also be compounded out to the horizon.

23. Several papers have appeared to argue against the necessary equality of forward and futures prices. See, for example, George E. Morgan. "Forward and Futures Pricing of Treasury Bills," *Journal of Banking and Finance*, December 1981, pp. 483-496; R. Jarrow and G. Oldfield. "Forward Contracts and Futures Contracts," *Journal of Financial Economics*,

December 1981, pp. 373-382; J. Cox, J. Ingersoll, and S. Ross, "The Relation Between Forward Prices and Futures Prices," *Journal of Financial Economics*, December 1981, pp. 321-346; and S. Richard and M. Sundaresan, "A Continuous Time Equilibrium Model of Forward Prices and Futures Prices in a Multigood Economy," *Journal of Financial Economics*, December 1981, pp. 347-371.

24. We consider the specific evidence for equities in Chapters 8-9.

25. P. Samuelson, "Proof that Properly Anticipated Prices Fluctuate Randomly," *Industrial Management Review*, 6:2, Spring 1965, pp. 41-49.

26. R. W. Anderson and J. P. Danthine, "The Time Pattern of Hedging and the Volatility of Futures Prices," *Review of Economic Studies*, 50:2, April 1983, pp. 249-266.

27. R. W. Anderson, "Some Determinants of the Volatility of Futures Prices," *The Journal of Futures Markets*, 5:3, Fall 1985, pp. 331-348. Anderson analyzed wheat, corn, oats, soybeans, soyoil, live cattle, silver, and cocoa.

28. D. Kenyon, K. Kling, J. Jordan, W. Seale, and N. McCabe, "Factors Affecting Agricultural Futures Price Variance," *The Journal of Futures Markets*, 7:1, February 1987, pp. 73-91.

29. E. Dyl and E. Maberly, "The Daily Distribution of Changes in the Price of Stock Index Futures," *The Journal of Futures Markets*, 6:4, Winter 1986, pp. 513-521; E. Chang and C. Kim, "Day of the Week Effects and Commodity Price Changes," *The Journal of Futures Markets*, 8:2, April 1988, pp. 229-241; G. Gay and T. Kim, "An Investigation into Seasonality in the Futures Market," *The Journal of Futures Markets*, 7:2, April 1987, pp. 169-181.

30. Terrence F. Martell and Avner S. Wolf, "Determinants of Trading Volume in Futures Markets," *The Journal of Futures Markets*, 7:3, June 1987, pp. 233-244; Jonathan M. Karpoff, "The Relation Between Price Changes and Trading Volume: A Survey," *Journal of Financial and Quantitative Analysis*, 22:1, March 1987, pp. 109-126; Philip Garcia, Raymond M. Leuthold, and Hector Zapata, "Lead-Lag Relationships Between Trading Volume and Price Variability: New Evidence," *The Journal of Futures Markets*, 6:1, Spring 1986, pp. 1-10.

4

Using Futures Markets

Introduction

In the two preceding chapters, we discussed the institutional setting of futures markets and the determination of futures prices. This chapter explores three different ways that futures markets serve different elements of society. As we have already noted, futures markets provide a means of price discovery. Second, the futures markets provide an arena for speculation. Third, the futures markets provides a means for transferring risk, or hedging. This chapter explores each of these contributions of futures markets.

The first function of futures markets that we will analyze is the function of **price discovery**—the revelation of information about the prices of commodities in the future. Because prices in the futures markets provide information that is not readily available elsewhere, the markets serve societal needs. We note that price discovery is open to everyone, even non-traders. Futures market price information is available to anyone for the price of a newspaper.

A second major group to benefit from futures markets is comprised of speculators. A **speculator** is a trader who enters the futures market in pursuit of profit, thereby accepting an increase in risk. It may seem strange to list an opportunity for speculation as a service to society, but consider the following examples. Casinos provide speculative opportunities for citizens, and that might be reckoned as a public service. Professional and college sports teams also provide a way for people to speculate by betting, illegally in some states and legally in others.

Clearly, sports teams do not exist so that people can bet on them, but the chance to bet is a side effect, and perhaps a side benefit, of the existence of sports. The situation is similar in the futures markets. Futures markets do not exist in order to provide the chance to speculate, but they do provide speculative opportunities. Less obvious is the way in which speculators themselves contribute to the smooth functioning of the futures market. As we show, the speculator pursues profits. As a side effect, the speculator provides liquidity to the market that helps the market function more effectively.

Hedgers are a third major group of futures market users. A **hedger** is a trader with a pre-existing risk who enters the futures market in order to reduce that risk. For example, a wheat farmer has price risk associated with the future price of wheat at harvest. By trading in the futures market, the farmer may be able to reduce that pre-existing risk. This opportunity to transfer risk is perhaps the greatest contribution of futures markets to society. In many cases, businesses face risks that result from the ordinary conduct of business. Often these risks are undesired, and the futures market provides a way in which risk may be transferred to other individuals willing to bear it. If people know that unwanted risks may be avoided by transacting in the futures market at a reasonable cost, then they will not be afraid to make decisions that will expose them initially to certain risks. They know that they can hedge that risk.

From the point of view of society, hedging has important advantages. Enterprises that are profitable, but that involve more risk than their principals wish to bear, can still be pursued. The unwanted risk can then be transferred in the futures market, and society benefits economically. This is the strongest argument for the existence of futures markets. By providing an efficient way of transferring risk to those individuals in society willing to bear it cheaply, futures markets contribute to the economy.[1]

Price Discovery

In Chapter 3, we explored the connection between futures prices and expected future spot prices in some detail. In particular, we considered evidence on the relationship between futures prices and expected future spot prices. This relationship is crucial for the futures market's ability to fulfill the social function of price discovery. In this section, we consider this issue in more detail.

Students of futures markets admit a close connection between futures prices and expected future spot prices. The question is how the futures market can be used to reveal information about subsequent commodity prices. The usefulness of price forecasts based on futures prices depends on three factors:

1. The need for information about future spot prices;
2. The accuracy of the futures market forecasts of those prices;
3. The performance of futures market forecasts relative to alternative forecasting techniques.

Information

Many individuals and groups in society need information about the future price of various commodities. For example, with information about the price of gold one year from now, it would be relatively simple to make a fortune. Certainly, speculation would be much more rewarding if one had a private and infallible source of information about future spot prices. Aside from such dreams of wealth, information about future spot prices is also needed for more mundane purposes, such as the planning of future investment and consumption by individuals, corporations, and governmental bodies.

Consider an underpaid college professor who wants to buy a house. Interest rates are high, so taking a long-term mortgage in such times would commit him to a lifetime of large payments. On the other hand, if he does not buy a house, then he cannot take advantage of the tax deduction that the interest portion of the house payments would provide. If interest rates were to drop soon, then it would be reasonable to wait to buy the house. By consulting the financial pages of the newspaper, the professor could find out what the market believed about the future level of interest rates. Futures contracts on long-term Treasury bonds are traded on the Chicago Board of Trade. If the interest rate for a bond to be delivered in six months is three percentage points lower than current interest rates, then there is good reason to expect interest rates will fall over the next six months. In such a situation, the college professor might do well to wait a few months to buy his house.

Another example concerns a furniture manufacturer who makes wooden furniture. Assume that she is printing her catalog now for the next year and must include the prices of the different items of furniture. Setting prices in advance is always a very tricky affair. In addition to other problems, the price she charges will depend upon the expected future price of lumber. The cost of lumber varies greatly, depending largely on the health of the construction industry, so it is difficult for her to know how to include that cost factor in her calculations. One way in which she might deal with this is to use the prices from the lumber futures market to estimate the costs of the wood that she will have to purchase later on. In doing so, she uses the futures markets for their **price discovery** benefit.[2]

In both of these examples, individuals used futures prices to estimate the spot price at some future date. The advisability of such a technique depends on the accuracy of the forecasts drawn from the futures market. Futures prices may, of course, differ from subsequently observed spot prices. If there is a large discrepancy, the futures forecasts may not be very useful. Errors could result from two sources: inaccurate but unbiased forecasts and bias in the forecast itself.

Accuracy

A forecasting estimator is unbiased if the average value of the forecast equals the value of the variable to be forecasted.[3] Thus, futures prices might provide unbiased forecasts with very large errors. The situation is reminiscent of the joke about the two economists who predicted the unemployment rate for the next year. The first economist predicted that 12 percent of the work force would be unemployed, while the second put the figure at full employment, or zero percent unemployed. The actual rate turned out to be six percent, from which the economists cheerfully concluded that, on average, they were exactly right. In forecasting the unemployment rate, one could say that the economists had provided an unbiased forecast but one that had large errors.

As is typical for many commodities, the forecasts from the futures market have large errors. Futures prices fluctuate radically, which means that most of the time they provide an inaccurate forecast of the underlying commodity's spot price at the time of delivery. Without question, the large size of the forecast errors from the futures markets limits the forecasts' reliability.[4]

One might reasonably wonder why there should be such large errors. According to the theory of finance, prices in well-developed markets reflect all available information. As new information becomes available, futures prices adjust themselves very swiftly. As a consequence, futures prices tend to exhibit radical fluctuations, which means that the prices will be inaccurate as estimates of subsequent spot prices.

In addition to the large errors that one can observe in futures market forecasts, futures prices may be biased. One possible reason for this was considered in Chapter 3. Futures prices may embody a risk premium that keeps the futures price from equaling the expected future spot price. In general, the possibility of bias is not too great a concern, at least for practical matters. Further, while there is still no real agreement about their existence, there is agreement that, if biases do exist, they are small. In general, the errors in futures forecasts are so large that they tend to drown out any biases that may also be present.

Performance

Since forecasts based on futures prices seem to be so poor, why would anyone care about them? Before discarding the forecasts, consider the alternatives. What other forecast might be more accurate? A considerable amount of study on this topic has failed to lead to any final answer. Nonetheless, evidence suggests that forecasts based on futures prices are not excelled by other forecasting techniques. Futures forecasts have been compared to other techniques and have not been found to be inferior. The current situation in forecasts of the foreign exchange rate is typical. For example, compared to professional foreign exchange forecasting firms, some of which charge large fees, the futures price of foreign currency predicts very well. Many professional firms have recently turned in forecasting records with results worse than those of chance.[5]

In spite of the large errors in forecasts based on futures market prices, the futures market seems better than the alternatives. To summarize, the accuracy of futures forecasts is not that good, but it is certainly better than the alternatives, and futures market forecasts are free. Someone needing a forecast of future spot prices should not rely too heavily on any forecast. When relying on some forecasting technique, however, it should be the forecast freely available in the futures market.

Forecasting Oil Prices: A Case Study

For futures markets to provide a good price discovery mechanism, we want to know the relationship between the forecast derived from the futures market and the actual price of the good that obtains when the futures contract expires. Price discovery depends, it seems, on matching the futures price forecast and the actual spot price that eventually materializes. Every forecasting model must be measured against some alternative model. For example, if we want to forecast the cash price of crude oil, we have several choices. First, we can forecast the future price of oil as equaling the current price of oil. For example, we might forecast that the price of oil in six months will equal the current price of oil. If the futures price cannot beat such a simple forecast, then it has little usefulness. Also, we will want to compare the forecast from the futures market against other more sophisticated models.

For oil-related commodities, Table 4.1 provides a useful example of forecasts from the futures market. This table is drawn from a paper by Cindy W. Ma, in which she tested the forecast accuracy of futures prices against other forecasts. Only a portion of her results are shown in the table. For crude oil, heating oil, and leaded gasoline, Ma composed forecasts of the spot price of each commodity at the expiration of the futures contract. First, she treated the futures market price as the estimate of the future spot price. Second, she took the current cash price as the forecast of the future spot price. Third, she tested four more sophisticated statistical forecasting models against the futures market and the current cash price forecasts. Table 4.1 focuses only on the first two types of forecasts—the futures and cash market forecasts. The errors reported in are approximate percentage errors in the forecast. Thus, for the futures market forecast of the price of crude oil one month before expiration, the error was about 1.5 percent, compared with a forecast error from the cash market of about 2.7 percent. The futures market, on average, offered a better forecast of the spot price of oil in a month. In fact, as Table 4.1 shows, the futures market forecast was better for ten of the twelve forecasts examined. Thus, the futures price today is a better indicator of the future spot price of oil commodities than is the current cash price, at least based on this evidence. In Ma's paper, the futures price also outperformed the complex statistical forecasting techniques.[6]

Ma's paper illustrates the important price discovery benefits that futures markets provide. These benefits are apparent compared to the simple no-change forecast and compared to the more complex statistical forecasts she examined. She concludes that futures-based forecasts are useful based on the following four

Table 4.1
Forecast Errors for Alternative Forecasts

Commodity	Horizon	Futures Error	No–Change Error
Crude Oil	1 Month	.0148	.0268
	2 Month	.0268	.0499
	3 Month	.0456	.0720
	6 Month	.1057	.1469
Heating Oil	1 Month	.0074	.0085
	2 Month	.0182	.0196
	3 Month	.0284	.0305
	6 Month	.0628	.0553
Leaded Gasoline	1 Month	.0129	.0155
	2 Month	.0261	.0281
	3 Month	.0397	.0440
	6 Month	.0956	.0893

Source: Cindy W. Ma, "Forecasting Efficiency of Energy Futures Prices," *The Journal of Futures Markets*, 9:5, October 1989, pp. 393–419.

dimensions: availability, cost, size of forecast error, and performance relative to other methods.

While errors in forecasts drawn from futures markets may be small relative to errors from other methods, they can still be quite large. Thus, futures may provide a forecast that is as good as any available, but it might not be very good in some absolute sense. For example, if we consider Ma's results again, we see that the forecast errors for the futures market forecasts are rather large for the six-month horizon. Here the average errors range from 6 to 10.5 percent, so the futures price forecast does have its limits.

Dimensions of Forecasting Techniques

1. Availability.
2. Cost.
3. Size of forecast error.
4. Performance relative to alternatives.

Forecasting Performance for Different Commodities

We have seen that the forecasts drawn from the futures market may have substantial errors, even if these futures forecasts are better than alternative forecasts. Now we consider how futures forecast performance differs from one commodity to another. This issue has been studied by Eugene F. Fama and Kenneth R. French. They tested the futures forecasting power for 21 different commodities. Table 4.2 is based on Table 5 from their paper and summarizes their results. Applying sophisticated econometric tests, Fama and French find that about half of the commodities they examined had forecast power—the futures price has power to forecast the future spot price. In general, they find the highest forecast power for commodities with the greatest variability in the basis. The basis will be most variable for those commodities to which the Cost-of-Carry Model applies poorly. This leaves the futures price flexible enough to respond to the expected future spot price. The most important lesson to draw from Table 4.2 is that the forecasting ability of futures prices differs from one commodity to the next.

Summary

In discussing price discovery, we have seen that the futures market serves society by providing a means for market observers to form assessments about the future price of commodities. Futures prices are, in essence, a market consensus forecast about the future price of the underlying commodity. Compared to alternatives, the futures price provides a good, perhaps the best, forecast. However, futures price forecasts are subject to two important limitations. First, the errors in futures forecasts can be large, even though they may be smaller than the errors produced by alternative forecasts. The size of the errors in the forecasts of oil prices illustrated this point. Second, the quality of forecasts may differ across

Table 4.2
Forecasting Power of Commodity Futures

Forecasting Power for All Maturities		No Forecasting Power	
Broilers	Hogs	Lumber	Copper
Eggs	Oats	Soyoil	Cotton
Forecasting Power for Most Maturities			
Cattle	Soybeans		
Pork bellies	Soymeal		
Forecasting Power for Some Maturities			
Orange juice	Plywood		

Source: Eugene F. Fama, and Kenneth R. French, "Commodity Futures Prices: Some Evidence on Forecast Power, Premiums, and the Theory of Storage," *Journal of Business*, 60:1, 1987, pp. 55–73.

commodities. From the Fama and French study, we saw that about half of the physical commodities they examined seemed to provide useful futures market forecasts. The other half did not offer good forecasts.

Speculation

Defining speculation or identifying the speculator in the futures market is always difficult. For our purposes, the following definition of a speculator will prove useful. A **speculator** is a trader who enters the futures market in search of profit and, by so doing, willingly accepts increased risk.[7]

Most individuals have no heavy risk exposure in most commodities. Consider an individual who is neither a farmer nor a food processor, but who has an interest in the wheat market. If she trades a wheat futures contract, then she most likely is speculating in the sense defined previously. She enters the futures market, willingly increases her risk, and hopes for profit.

One might object that this individual does not have a pre-existing risk exposure in wheat. In fact, everyone who eats bread does. One's plans for consuming bread may change if wheat prices rise too high. This objection makes a good point. In order to know whether a particular action in the futures market is a speculative trade requires knowledge about the trader's current assets and future consumption plans. For an individual, however, entry into the futures market is most likely to be for speculation. For the woman who traded a wheat futures contract, the size of the wheat contract (5,000 bushels) is so large relative to her needs for wheat that the transaction increases her overall risk. Assuming that she, like most people, is risk averse, she will not expose herself to the additional risk of entering the futures market unless she hopes to profit by doing so. This is what classifies her as a speculator.

Earlier, we also noted that speculators use futures transactions as a substitute for a cash market transaction. For an individual, trading a 5,000 bushel futures contract is unlikely to be a substitute for a cash market transaction, and this criterion also identifies the individual trading wheat as a speculator.

Different types of speculators may be categorized by the length of time they plan to hold a position. Traditionally, there are three kinds of speculators: scalpers, day traders, and position traders.

Scalpers

Of all speculators, scalpers have the shortest horizon over which they plan to hold a futures position. Scalpers aim to foresee the movement of the market over a very short interval, ranging from the next few seconds to the next few minutes. Many scalpers describe themselves as psychologists trying to sense the feel of the trading among the other market participants. In order to do this, they must be in the trading pit; otherwise, they could not hope to see buying or selling pressure building up among the other traders.[8]

Since their planned holding period is so short, scalpers do not expect to make a large profit on each trade. Instead, they hope to make a profit of one or two ticks—the minimum allowable price movement. Many trades by scalpers end in losses or in no profit. If the prices do not move in the scalper's direction within a few minutes of assuming a position, the scalper will likely close the position and begin looking for a new opportunity.

This type of trading strategy means that the scalper will generate an enormous number of transactions. Were he or she to make these transactions through a broker as an off-the-floor participant, the scalper would lose any anticipated profit through high transaction costs. Since scalpers are members of the exchange, or lease a seat from a member, their transaction costs are very low. Scalpers probably pay less than $1 per round-turn in most futures markets, compared to about $25-$80 for an off-the-floor trader who trades through a regular broker.[9] Without these very low transaction costs, the scalper's efforts would be hopeless. To sense the direction of the market and to conserve on transaction costs, a scalper needs to be on the floor of the exchange.

In his book, *The New Gatsbys*, Bob Tamarkin explores the personalities of futures traders based on his own experience. Writing about scalpers, he says:

> Many traded by feel rather than by fundamentals, forgetting about things like leading economic indicators, government policies, and even supplies of commodities. They simply tried to catch the market on the way up and ditch it on the way down. In the trading pits they could do it faster and better than any outside speculators because they were squarely in the heart of the action.

Discussing scalpers in general and describing an individual scalper named Paul, Tamarkin tells us:

> Each trader had a theory about what was happening in the next five minutes. If everyone thought the market was going to open higher, but it opened lower, the psychology in the pit changed immediately. It was a herd mentality fed on raw emotion. It was the easy way. Get the trading feel of the crowd in the pit; then jump on board for the move. By the time the public got in, the market ticked that quarter or half cent, and Paul had his profit. The ultimate price of a commodity may have been determined by supply and demand, Paul thought, but in the interim, emotional factors reigned supreme.[10]

Although it may not be apparent at first glance, scalpers provide a valuable service to the market by their frenzied trading activity. By trading so often, scalpers help supply the market with liquidity. Their trading activity increases the ease with which other market participants may find trading partners. Without high liquidity, some outside traders would avoid the market, which would decrease its usefulness. A high degree of liquidity is necessary for the success of a futures market, and scalpers play an important role in providing this liquidity.[11] We might say that scalpers provide the opportunity for other traders to trade immediately.

To illustrate the role played by scalpers in providing liquidity, consider the following example. An off-the-floor trader might see the most recently quoted price on a ticker machine and desire to trade at that price. If the market is not liquid, then it may be difficult to trade at or near that price for at least two reasons. First, if the market is not liquid, the observed transaction might have occurred some time ago and there may not be anyone willing to trade at that last reported price. Second, without the willing pool of potential traders represented by the scalpers in the pit, the bid-asked spread could be quite wide, making it difficult to trade near the last reported price. The scalpers in the pit are there to seek profit, but they compete with each other to trade. As a result, the presence of the scalpers helps to keep the bid-asked price narrow, to keep the market more active and price quotations more current, and to attract outside traders to the market because they know their orders can be executed near the equilibrium price for the commodity.

Services Provided by Scalpers

1. Provide a party willing to take the opposite side of a trade for an off–the–floor trader.

2. Actively trade, thereby generating price quotations and allowing the market to discover prices more effectively.

3. By competing for trades, help to close the bid–asked spread, thereby reducing execution costs for other traders.

4. Attract hedging activity, because hedgers know their orders can be executed.

In an interesting article, Professor William Silber explores the behavior of scalpers. He arranged to observe all of the transactions of a scalper he identifies only as Mr. X. Mr. X was a trader on the New York Futures Exchange, trading New York Stock Exchange Composite Index futures. For 31 trading days in late 1982 and early 1983, Silber tracked all of Mr. X's trading. Table 4.3 presents some of Silber's results. During this period, Mr. X traded 2,106 times, or about 70 times per day. These transactions involved the purchase and sale (round-turn) of 2,178 contracts.

Table 4.3
Mr. X's Trades Over 31 Trading Days

Total Transactions	2,106
Number of Contracts Traded	2,178
(Round–turns—buy and sell 1 contract)	
Number of Trades	729
(Zero net position to a zero net position)	
Profitable	353 (48%)
Unprofitable	157 (22%)
Scratch	219 (30%)

Source: William L. Silber, "Marketmaker Behavior in an Auction Market: An Analysis of Scalpers in Futures Market," *Journal of Finance*, September 1984, 39:4, pp. 937-953.

Table 4.3 also shows the number of trades, which Silber defines as going from a zero net position and returning to a zero net position. Fewer than half (48 percent) of these trades were profitable, while 22 percent generated losses. Thirty percent were scratch trades—trades with neither a profit nor a loss. The trades generated an average profit of $10.56, or a total trading profit of $7,698.24 over the period. On average a trade took 116 seconds. So the average length of time that Mr. X had a risk exposure was two minutes. The longest trade, hence the longest period of risk exposure, took 547 seconds, or a little over nine minutes. Clearly, Mr. X is reluctant to maintain positions for very long.

Table 4.4 presents one-half hour of Mr. X's trading. During this period, Mr. X made 19 transactions. Notice how Mr. X opens a position, either long or short, and then moves quickly back to a zero position in the market. During this half-hour, Mr. X goes through five trading cycles, beginning and ending the half-hour with a net zero position.

As Silber concludes, the major function that Mr. X provides to the market is liquidity. As a scalper, Mr. X takes the other side of trades coming in from traders off the floor of the exchange. Also, Silber found that Mr. X's trades tended to be more profitable when they were held for a shorter time. For instance, Mr. X's trades taking longer than three minutes were losing trades on average. As Silber concludes: "Scalper earnings compensate for the skill in evaluating market conditions in the very short run and for providing liquidity to the market over the time horizon."[12] This accords with the excerpts from Tamarkin.[13]

Day Traders

Compared to scalpers, day traders take a very farsighted approach to the market. Day traders attempt to profit from the price movements that may take place over the course of one trading day. The day trader closes his or her position before the end of trading each day so that he or she has no position in the futures market overnight. Day traders may trade on or off the floor.

A day trader might follow a strategy such as concentrating activity around announcements from the U.S. government. The Department of Agriculture releases production figures for hogs at intervals that are well known in advance. The day trader may think that the hog figures to be released on a certain day will indicate an unexpectedly high level of production. If so, such an announcement will cause the futures prices for hogs to fall, due to the unexpectedly large future supply of pork. To take advantage of this insight, the day trader would sell the hog contract prior to the announcement and then wait for prices to fall after the announcement. Such a strategy could be implemented without holding a futures market position overnight. Therefore, it is a suitable strategy for a day trader to pursue. (To avoid drastic effects on markets, government announcements are often made late in the day, after the affected market closes.)

The scalper's strategy of holding a position for a very short interval is clearly motivated, but it is not so apparent why day traders limit themselves to price movements that will occur only during the interval of one day's trading. The basic reason is risk. Day traders believe that it is too risky to hold a speculative position overnight; too many disastrous price movements could occur.

To see the danger of maintaining a position overnight, consider a position in orange juice concentrate traded by the Citrus Associates of the New York Cotton Exchange. In late November a trader holds a short position in orange juice futures. The weather in Florida is crucial for orange juice prices, and the trader checks the weather forecast for Florida that day before trading closes. There seems to be no possibility of damaging weather in the next few days, so he maintains his position overnight. Unexpectedly, a strong cold front pushes into Florida and destroys a large portion of the orange crop, which, in November, is still on the trees and not yet mature. Naturally, futures prices soar on the opening of trading the next day, and the trader who held his position overnight suffers a large loss. In fear of such sudden developments, day traders close their positions each day before trading stops.

The overwhelming majority of speculators are either scalpers or day traders, which indicates just how risky it can be to take a position home overnight. As the close of trading approaches each day, the pace of trading increases. Typically, 25 percent of the day's trading volume occurs in the last half hour of trading. The last five minutes are particularly frenetic as traders attempt to close all of their open positions.[14]

Table 4.4
One-Half Hour of Mr. X's Trading

Transaction	Time	Contracts Traded (Buy +/Sell -)	Net Position
1	10:05:29	2	2
2	10:06:47	-2	0
3	10:08:10	5	5
4	10:09:15	-1	4
5	10:09:49	-2	2
6	10:10:25	-1	1
7	10:11:20	-1	0
8	10:12:56	6	6
9	10:13:29	-3	3
10	10:15:38	-1	2
11	10:16:58	-1	1
12	10:17:23	-1	0
13	10:22:25	-5	-5
14	10:23:11	3	-2
15	10:23:23	2	0
16	10:25:26	5	5
17	10:26:12	-1	4
18	10:26:18	-1	3
19	10:28:12	-3	0

Source: William L. Silber, "Marketmaker Behavior in an Auction Market: An Analysis of Scalpers in Futures Market," *Journal of Finance*, September 1984, 39:4, pp. 937-953.

Position Traders

A **position trader** is a speculator who maintains a futures position overnight. On occasion they may hold them for weeks or even months. There are two types of position traders, those holding an **outright position** and those holding a **spread position**. Of the two strategies, the outright position is far riskier.

Outright Positions. An outright position trader might adopt the following strategy if she believed that long-term interest rates were going to rise more than the market expected over the next two months. As interest rates rise, the futures prices, representing the price of bonds, must fall. However, the trader does not really know when during the next two months the rise in rates will occur. To take advantage of her belief about the course of interest rates, she could sell the futures contract on U.S. Treasury bonds traded at the Chicago Board of Trade and hold that position over the next two months. If she is correct, there will be a sharp rise in rates not correctly anticipated by the market, and futures prices will fall. She can then offset and reap her profit.

The danger in this trader's outright position is clear. If she had made a mistake, and interest rates fall unexpectedly, then she will suffer a large loss. The outright position offers a chance for very large gains if she is correct, but it carries with it the risk of very large losses as well. For most speculators, the risks associated with outright positions are too large. The expected trading life of a new trader is about six months, but it is much shorter for outright position traders.

Spread Positions.   More risk-averse position traders may trade spreads. Intra-commodity spreads involve differences between two or more contract maturities for the same underlying deliverable good. In contrast, inter-commodity spreads are price differences between two or more contracts written on different, but related, underlying goods. For example, the difference between the July wheat and corn contracts would be an inter-commodity spread. The spread trader trades two or more contracts with related price movements. The goal is to profit from changes in the relative prices.

Table 4.5
An Inter–Commodity Spread

The wheat and corn contracts are both for 5,000 bushels.

Date	Futures Market
February 1, 1990	Sell 1 JUL wheat contract at 348.50 cents per bushel. Buy 1 JUL corn contract at 247.25 cents per bushel.
May 30, 1990	Buy 1 JUL wheat contract at 332.25 cents per bushel. Sell 1 JUL corn contract at 279.50 cents per bushel.
	Corn Profit: $.3225 per bushel × 5,000 bushels = $1,612.50 Wheat Profit: $.1625 per bushel × 5,000 bushels = $812.50
	Total Profit: $2,425

Consider the case of a spread speculator who believes that the difference between the futures price of wheat and corn is too low. Such a trader believes that the inter-commodity spread between wheat and corn is inconsistent with the justifiable price differential between the two goods. Wheat normally sells at a higher price per bushel than corn, but for this trader the differential in prices is too large. On February 1, 1990, the following closing prices could be observed for the JUL 1990 wheat and corn contracts, quoted in cents per bushel.

| JUL 1990 Wheat | 348.50 |
| JUL 1990 Corn | 247.25 |

The trader believes that this difference of more than one dollar is too large and is willing to speculate that the price of corn will rise relative to the price of wheat. Accordingly, the trader transacts as shown in the top panel of Table 4.5.

Figure 4.1 shows the prices for the JUL 1990 corn and wheat contracts for the relevant period. Prices are expressed in cents per bushel. As the figure shows,

Figure 4.1
July 1990 Wheat and Corn Futures Prices
(February 1—May 30, 1990)

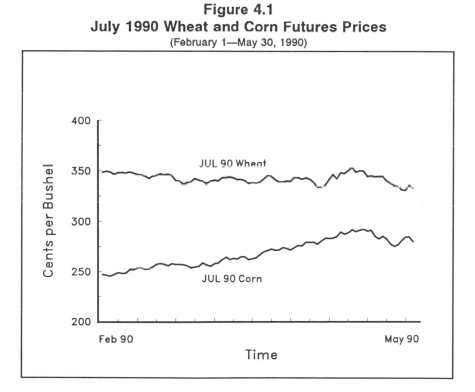

wheat prices began to fall shortly after the trader placed the spread on February 1. Corn prices also started to rise. Therefore, the trader began to make money on both sides of the transaction. Figure 4.2 tracks the profits that the trader enjoyed from February 1 to May 30.

In this example, the trader correctly bet that the price of corn would rise relative to the price of wheat. As it happened, wheat fell and corn rose, giving a gain on both sides of the transaction. However, this result is not necessary for the trader to have a profit. For example, if wheat and corn both rose, but corn rose more, the trade would still be profitable. Similarly, if wheat and corn both fell, but wheat fell more, the trade would also be profitable. In a spread trade, only the relative prices matter, not the absolute prices.

Other types of spread strategies are also possible. In an intra-commodity spread, a trader takes a position in two or more maturity months for the same good. The belief behind this strategy is that the relative prices between delivery dates for the same commodity will change, generating a profit for the trader. Whereas an outright position only requires a belief about the price movement of one commodity, a spread position focuses on the relative price movements between two or more commodities, or contract maturities.

Figure 4.2
Wheat/Corn Spread Profits
(February 1—May 30, 1990)

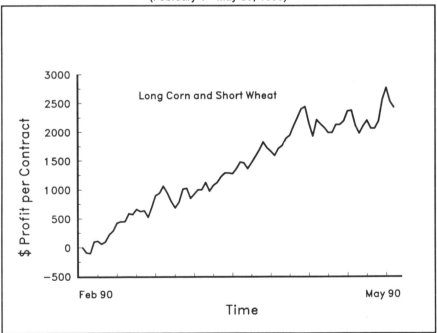

Table 4.6
Copper Futures Prices on November 10

Delivery Month (of following year)	Price (cents per pound)
JUL	67.0
SEP	67.5
DEC	70.5

The spread example considered previously was relatively simple, but spreads can be quite complex. One frequently mentioned complex spread is known as a **butterfly spread**, which is best illustrated by an example. Assume that today is November 10 and the prices for copper are as shown in Table 4.6. In comparing the price for September delivery, 67.5 cents per pound, with the prices on the adjacent delivery months of July and December, it seems that the September price is out of line. To this speculator, it appears that the September price should be about halfway between the July and December prices, but it is seriously below that level. Since the speculator does not really know whether copper prices are going to rise or fall in general, she only wants to attempt to take advantage of this apparent pricing discrepancy between different maturities.

To do this, she initiates a futures transaction known as a butterfly spread, such as the one illustrated in Table 4.7. Since she expects the price of the September contract to rise relative to the July and December contracts, she sells one contract of each of the July and December maturities. To offset the sale of these two contracts, she buys two contracts for the September delivery. By April 15, the prices of all of the contracts have fallen, but their price relationships are much closer to what the speculator believed to be correct. On April 15, the September price has risen, relative to the other contracts, to a point about halfway between them. This is exactly what she expected to happen. The wings of the butterfly spread (the July and December contracts) have flapped, bringing all of the prices into line. As Table 4.7 reveals, this generates a total profit of $750 on the spread.

The classification of speculators into scalpers, day traders, and position traders is useful, but it should not obscure the fact that individuals can have multiple speculative strategies. A particular trader can easily merge his or her activities as a scalper and as a position trader. Those individuals actively trading in the pits would be expected to take advantage of all types of opportunities that might become available.

Table 4.7
A Butterfly Spread in Copper

The copper contract trades on the Commodity Exchange, Inc. Each contract is for 25,000 pounds.

Date	Futures Market
November 10	Sell 1 JUL copper contract at 67 cents per pound. Buy 2 SEP copper contracts at 67.5 cents per pound. Sell 1 DEC copper contract at 70.5 cents per pound.
April 15	Buy 1 JUL copper contract at 65 cents per pound. Sell 2 SEP copper contracts at 67 cents per pound. Buy 1 DEC copper contract at 68.5 cents per pound.

Profits and Losses:

JUL:	+$.02 x 25,000 pounds = +$500	
SEP:	−$.005 x 2 contracts x 25,000 pounds = −$250	
DEC:	+$.02 x 25,000 pounds = +$500	

Total Profit: $750

Speculative Profits

In this section, we review several dimensions of speculative trading. First, we consider the evidence that is available on speculator success and failure for individuals. We have already seen that scalpers seem to make speculative profits. Here, we examine the results of several studies of overall trader performance. Second, we evaluate the practices and profits for some technical trading systems. Third, we consider the aims and performance of commodity pools. Finally, we analyze speculative profits in an efficient markets setting.

Evidence on Speculative Profits

For the most part, speculative profits and losses are difficult to observe. Most traders cherish the privacy of their brokerage accounts. This privacy allows them to enjoy their profits and lick their trading wounds in private and also to tell "fish stories" about their trading prowess. Nonetheless, there are several studies that assess the trading results of speculators. A prime source of this information comes from the CFTC report in which traders with large positions are required to report those positions. This information is made public, although it is

Table 4.8
Evidence on Speculative Profits

Study	Key Results
Stewart (1949)	75% of speculators lost money.
Houthakker (1957)	Small speculators lost in grains, but made profits in cotton.
Rockwell (1967)	Small speculators lose consistently after considering transaction costs.
Ross (1975)	Speculators made money before commissions and lost money including commissions.
Chang and Stevenson (1985)	Small speculators make profits.
Hartzmark (1987)	Large speculators do not earn significant profits; large hedgers do not have significant losses.

presented only in aggregate form. Therefore, it is possible to determine what large (above the reporting requirements) and small (below the reporting requirements) traders are doing in the aggregate. Note that this is not the same as being able to examine a sample of actual trading for particular individuals.

Table 4.8 summarizes some of the studies on speculative profits. These studies do not reach a consensus, and some of the methodologies employed have been criticized. Nonetheless, there appears to be little reason to think that speculators make large profits, particularly after considering transaction costs. Rather, the results of some gains and some losses might be broadly consistent with speculators trading futures contracts that are fairly priced.

Technical Trading Systems

In futures markets, more than any other segment of the financial markets, technical trading systems seem to find favor. This can be verified by browsing through a recent issue of *Futures* and noting the many advertisements for various technical trading systems. **Technical analysis** is a method of analyzing markets that uses only market data (prices, volume, open interest, and similar information) to predict future price movements. For example, technical analysts believe certain price formations suggest that futures prices will rise. Other formations, according to technical analysis, portend a price decline. We do not explore the methods of technical analysis here, but many books cover the subject.[15] Instead, we want to explore the evidence on whether technical analysis can generate speculative profits.

Table 4.9
Evidence on Technical Trading Systems

Study	Key Results
Tomek and Querin (1984)	The chance for a technical trading rule to work is small.
Neftci and Policano (1984)	Some predictive power for T-bills, gold, and soybeans, but none for copper.
Lukac, Brorsen, and Irwin (1988a)	Examination of 12 different technical trading systems found that 7 generate profits, thus providing some support for technical analysis.
Lukac, Brorsen, and Irwin (1988b)	Technical trading systems are similar, and generate trading signals at similar times.
Lukac, Brorsen, and Irwin (1989)	Trading systems require users to specify parameters, but past data do not help choose best parameters.

To have any chance of success, technical analysis depends on the existence of patterns in futures prices. In most markets, scholars find that price patterns do exist, but that these patterns are not sufficiently strong to permit technical trading strategies to generate a profit. To make a trading profit, including covering transaction costs, would require very significant patterns. Stephen J. Taylor finds, for example, that futures prices do exhibit statistically significant patterns, but that these patterns are not strong enough to allow trading profits.[16]

Table 4.9 summarizes the recent evidence on the usefulness of technical trading systems. Many of these studies are based on simulations of trading systems, instead of systems that are in actual use. As the table shows, the studies on the whole seem to suggest that technical analysis may have some merit. However, this is a very controversial area and the final word has not yet been written on this subject. If technical analysis is useful in futures trading, that result would stand in contrast to findings for other financial markets.[17]

Commodity Funds

A **commodity fund** or a **commodity pool** is a financial institution that accepts funds from a variety of participants and uses those funds to speculate in the futures market. As such, its organization is similar to a mutual fund. We have noted that trading futures does not require investment as such. Thus, the commodity funds use their customers' funds for two purposes: margin deposits and earning interest. The interest-earning portion provides a pool of funds for future margin calls. Gains and losses for the funds come from futures trading and from the interest that is being earned. Most funds rely strongly on technical analysis for their trading strategies.

What performance can we expect from commodity funds? To analyze this question, we make two initial assumptions. First, we assume that patterns in futures prices are not sufficient to allow technical analysis to generate profits. Second, we assume that the futures price equals the expected future spot price. Under these two restrictions, we would expect the futures trading portion of the commodity fund to neither lose nor profit. Under our assumptions, the fund might trade, but the expected payoff on each trade would be zero. For the interest-earning portion of their assets, we would expect the invested assets to earn the money market rate of interest. Under these assumptions, we expect a commodity fund to underperform a buy-and-hold money market investment, due to the transaction costs that the fund incurs in its trading strategy. To succeed, the commodity fund must be able to earn speculative profits, presumably through technical trading systems, since most funds rely largely on those systems.

Table 4.10 summarizes the major findings of recent studies of commodity funds. First, pools use only about 20-28 percent of invested funds as margin deposits. Thus, the bulk of the money received sits in a money market

Table 4.10
Studies of Commodity Funds

Study	Key Results
Irwin and Brorsen (1985)	Returns vary widely by year; interest earnings are a large part of total earnings; 65% of funds lost money; including funds in a stock and bond portfolio reduced portfolio risk.
Cornew (1986)	Funds only use 20% of total funds as margin deposits; 80% of funds earn interest.
Murphy (1986)	Performance of technically oriented funds is inferior to stocks and T-bills; adding funds to stock and bond portfolios reduces overall risk; no evidence that funds outperform a buy-and-hold strategy.
Irwin and Brorsen (1987)	Funds place 28% of equity in margins.
Elton, Gruber, and Rentzler (1987)	Overall performance is not attractive alone or as an addition to a stock and bond portfolio; past performance is not a good guide to future performance.
Edwards and Ma (1988)	Pre-public trading results reported in fund prospectuses do not help predict subsequent fund performance and are substantially greater than post-public performance.

investment. Second, returns are often negative. Third, even when funds earn positive returns, they typically do not outperform their inherent level of systematic risk. That is, they do not beat the market. Fourth, even if funds are not attractive as investments in themselves, they might be useful in reducing risk when added to a portfolio of stocks and bonds. Evidence on this point is mixed. Fifth, past performance is not a good guide to future performance. In sum, the evidence seems fairly consistent with an efficient markets perspective. Funds do not seem to be an exciting investment vehicle, but may be a useful tool in some circumstances.

"Normal" Speculative Returns

We have seen several examples of apparently successful speculation. First, we saw that Mr. X in Silber's study earned positive returns by scalping. Second, we considered several studies that reported on speculative profits. Third, we noted that some technical trading systems seem to earn positive returns, while evidence suggests that other systems do not. Finally, we examined commodity pools and found some evidence that some pools make speculative profits. In this section, we want to consider futures market speculation from an efficient markets perspective. To do this, we will review the concept of a "normal profit," and then consider Mr. X's trading in more detail.

An **efficient market** is a market in which prices fully reflect the information contained in a specified information set. To differentiate versions of the efficient markets hypothesis, we can specify different information sets. The traditional versions of the efficient markets hypothesis are known as the weak, semi-strong, and strong versions.[18] The **weak form** of the efficient markets hypothesis claims that prices in a market fully reflect all information contained in the history of volume and price. The **semi-strong** version claims that market prices fully reflect all publicly available information. The **strong** version states that market prices reflect all information, whether public or private. Private information includes information possessed only by corporate insiders and governmental officials.[19] The strong version is almost certainly false, so we will be concerned only with the weak and semi-strong forms.

If the weak-form version is true, then no information about past or present prices or volume is useful for guiding a speculative strategy. If the futures market is weakly efficient, there will be no cash-and-carry arbitrage opportunities of the type we analyzed in Chapter 3. Additionally, technical trading strategies will not work. If the semi-strong version is true, then studying information about the determinants of prices will also not be useful in guiding a trading strategy.

Unlike investing in stocks or bonds, trading futures requires no actual investment, because of the system of margin and daily settlement. This suggests that any steady profits in futures trading would be inconsistent with an efficient market. Thus, the scalping profits of about $10 per contract reviewed earlier seem to fly in the face of the efficient markets hypothesis. We now want to examine some additional costs that the scalper faces.

To trade futures on a major exchange, one must own a seat, or secure the use of a seat from one who does own one. Second, trading on the exchange involves a commitment of time and energy. Since the time and energy is being committed to trading, it cannot be applied elsewhere to earn a return. Third, trading futures necessarily involves risk. Most people are unwilling to risk money unless the expected returns from those risks are high enough to justify the risk. With these ideas in mind, consider Mr. X, who we assume owns a seat on a major exchange. What income does he need to make trading worthwhile from a financial point of view and how does this compare with his actual trading results?

The first consideration is the value of the seat that is required in order to trade. As mentioned in Chapter 1, seats on the exchanges are bought and sold in a market and CBT seats have recently sold in the range of $180,000 to $325,000.[20] Taking a conservative figure of $200,000, it is clear that our trader loses the use of $200,000 by virtue of buying his seat. Assume that an equally risky investment would return a modest 12 percent. To cover the cost of his seat, Mr. X must make $24,000 per year. Second, Mr. X commits his time to trading, and he could hold another job if he were not trading. Most of the traders are people of competence and executive ability, and trading is grueling and nerve-wracking work with long hours that go beyond the limited trading times. Mr. X, having exhibited a willingness to work as hard as a trader must work and with the talents necessary to succeed as a trader, could expect to earn a relatively handsome salary in some other capacity. Perhaps $60,000 per year would be realistic and conservative. As most salaried positions have fringe benefits for medical, dental, and life insurance, this is conservative.

In addition to the foregone opportunities of investing the price of his seat elsewhere and of taking alternative employment, the high risk of trading must also be acknowledged. Relative to trading, a salaried position is very secure. Being risk averse, Mr. X would reasonably expect some compensation for his additional risk exposure. The amount of compensation is very difficult to quantify and clearly depends on his personal risk tolerance. Finally, the character of a trader's work needs to be considered somewhat more fully. Trading is extremely demanding—physically, emotionally, and mentally. A casual survey of the trading pits reveals few elderly participants. From conversations with many traders, it is clear that they do not generally expect to be trading past the age of forty.[21] As another indicator of the level of stress one need only consult *The Wall Street Journal*, which has frequent articles on the problems of traders. They lose their voices from shouting and need voice coaches, they occasionally sustain physical injuries, and they sometimes suffer anxiety as a result of the

Table 4.11
Hypothetical Alternative Income for Mr. X

Resource	Annual Amount
Use of money to secure seat	$24,000
Foregone alternative employment	60,000
Additional risk undertaken	?
Additional stress and strain	?
	Total: $84,000 + ?

stress in their work.[22] While many traders are attracted by the excitement of the pits, many people would demand high compensation for working under such conditions. The extreme physical and psychic demands are difficult to value in terms of dollars, but they are real costs.

Table 4.11 shows that Mr. X should make at least $84,000 per year without there being the slightest hint that super-normal profits are being captured. Many traders make very handsome incomes and live quite well—when they are not on the trading floor. This fact alone does not warrant the conclusions that trading futures contracts is an easy way to get rich quickly. The traders have high costs to cover before they reach the point at which they start to make super-normal profits. The chance to speculate on futures may not be the way to easy street.

The real world data from Silber's study reveals the difficulties traders face. As Silber notes, Mr. X earned relatively little during this period. During the 31 trading days of Silber's sample, Mr. X had average profits of $742 per day. This was before commissions, which averaged $1.22 per contract traded. After commissions, Mr. X had daily profits of $672.00 per day. With approximately 250 trading days per year, Mr. X would earn about $168,000 per year. Silber reports that these results place Mr. X in the upper quartile of scalpers on the NYFE. When we compare these results with the opportunity cost computed in Table 4.11, we can see that Mr. X does well, but not wonderfully. If we consider the risks he takes, the stress and strain he bears, and the out-of-pocket costs he faces, Mr. X will have to do better than he did in this period to convince us that he can beat the market.

Hedging

In contrast to the speculator, the **hedger** is a trader who enters the futures market in order to reduce a pre-existing risk.[23] If a trader trades futures contracts on commodities in which he or she has no initial position, and in which he or she does not contemplate taking a cash position, then the trader cannot be a hedger. The futures transaction cannot serve as a substitute for a cash market transaction. Having a position, in this case, does not mean that the trader must actually own a commodity. An individual or firm who anticipates the need for a certain commodity in the future or a person who plans to acquire a certain commodity later also has a position in that commodity. In many cases, a hedger has a certain **hedging horizon**—the future date when the hedge will terminate. For example, a farmer can anticipate that he or she will want to hedge from planting to the harvest. In other cases, there will be no specific horizon. We begin with two examples in which hedgers have definite hedging horizons.

A Long Hedge

The idea that you may be at risk in a certain commodity without actually owning it may be a confusing idea to some. Yet consider the following example. Silver is an essential input for the production of most types of photographic films and papers, and the price of silver is quite volatile. For a manufacturer of film, there is considerable risk that profits could be dramatically affected by fluctuations in the price of silver. If production schedules are to be maintained, it is absolutely essential that silver be acquired on a regular basis in large quantities. Assume that the film manufacturer needs 50,000 troy ounces of silver in two months and confronts the silver prices shown in Table 4.12 on May 10. The current spot price is 1052.5 cents per ounce, and the price of the JUL futures contract lies above that at 1068.0, with the SEP futures contract trading at 1084.0.

Fearing that silver prices may rise unexpectedly, the film manufacturer decides that the price of 1068.0 is acceptable for the silver that he will need in July. He realizes that it is hopeless to buy the silver on the spot market at 1052.5 and to store the silver for two months. The price differential of 15.5 cents per ounce would not cover his storage costs. Also, the manufacturer will receive an

---

Table 4.12
Silver Futures Prices on May 10

The COMEX trades a silver contract for 5,000 troy ounces.

Contract	Price (cents per troy ounce)
Spot	1052.5
JUL	1068.0
SEP	1084.0

Table 4.13
A Long Hedge in Silver

Date	Cash Market	Futures Market
May 10	Anticipates the need for 50,000 troy ounces in two months and expects to pay 1068 cents per ounce, or a total of $534,000.	Buys ten 5,000 troy ounce JUL futures contracts at 1068 cents per ounce.
July 10	The spot price of silver is now 1071 cents per ounce. The manufacturer buys 50,000 ounces, paying $535,500.	Since the futures contract is at maturity, the futures and spot prices are equal, and the ten contracts are sold at 1071 cents per ounce.
	Opportunity loss: -$1,500	Futures profit: $1,500
	Net Wealth Change = 0	

acceptable level of profits even if he pays 1068.0 for the silver to be delivered in July. To pay a price higher than 1068.0, however, could jeopardize profitability seriously. With these reasons in mind, he decides to enter the futures market to hedge against the possibility of future unexpected increases in prices, and accordingly, he enters the trades shown in Table 4.13.

Taking the futures price as the best estimate of the future spot price, the manufacturer expects to pay 1068.0 cents per ounce for silver in the spot market two months from now in July. At the same time, he buys ten 5,000 ounce JUL futures contracts at 1068.0 cents per ounce. Since he buys a futures contract in order to hedge, this transaction is known as a **long hedge**. The trader is also purchasing a futures contract in anticipation of needing the silver at a future date, so these transactions also represent an **anticipatory hedge**. Time passes and by July, the spot price of silver has risen to 1071.0 cents per ounce, three cents higher than expected. Needing the silver, the manufacturer purchases the silver on the spot market, paying a total of $535,500. This is $1,500 more than expected. Since the futures contract is about to mature, the futures price must equal the spot price, so the film manufacturer is able to sell his ten futures contracts at the same price of 1071.0 cents per ounce, making a three cent profit on each ounce, and a total profit of $1,500 on the futures position. The cash and futures results net to zero. In the cash market, the price was $1,500 more than expected, but there was an offsetting futures profit of $1,500, which generated a net wealth change of zero.

The Reversing Trade and Hedging

One peculiar feature of these transactions is that the manufacturer did not accept delivery on the futures contract but offset the contract instead. Rather than accepting delivery on a contract, it usually is better to reverse the trade because offsetting saves on transaction costs and administrative difficulties. The short trader has the right to choose the delivery destination and the long trader must fear that the short trader will select an unpalatable destination. Instead of taking delivery, the long trader can acquire the physical commodity from normal suppliers. The hedger in this example could have achieved the same result by accepting delivery. If delivery were accepted on the futures contract, the silver would have been secured at a price of 1068.0, which is what happened when the reversing trade was used.

A Short Hedge

Although the long silver hedge involved the purchase of a futures contract, hedges do not necessarily involve long futures positions. A **short hedge** is a hedge in which the hedger sells a futures contract. As an example, we assume the same silver prices and a date of May 10, as shown in Table 4.12. A Nevada silver mine owner is concerned about the price of silver, since she wants to be able to plan for the profitability of her firm. If silver prices fall, she may be forced to suspend production. Given the current level of production, she expects to have about 50,000 ounces of silver ready for shipment in two months. Considering the silver prices shown in Table 4.12, she decides that she would be satisfied to receive 1068.0 cents per ounce for her silver.

To establish the price of 1068.0 cents per ounce, the miner decides to enter the silver futures market. By hedging, she can avoid the risk that silver prices might fall in the next two months. Table 4.14 shows the miner's transactions. Notice that these are exactly the mirror image of the film manufacturer's transactions. Anticipating the need to sell 50,000 ounces of silver in two months, the mine operator sells ten 5,000 ounce futures contracts for July delivery at 1068.0 cents per ounce. On July 10, with silver prices at 1071.0 cents per ounce, the miner sells the silver and receives $535,000. This is $1,500 more than she originally expected. In the futures market, however, the miner suffers an offsetting loss. The futures contracts she sold at 1068.0, she offsets in July at 1071.0 cents per ounce. Once again, the profits and losses in the two markets offset each other, and produce a net wealth change of zero.

Viewing the results from the vantage point of July, it is clear that the miner would have been $1,500 richer if she had not hedged. She would have received $1,500 more than originally expected in the physicals market, and she would have incurred no loss in the futures market. However, it does not follow that she

Table 4.14
A Short Hedge in Silver

Date	Cash Market	Futures Market
May 10	Anticipates the sale of 50,000 troy ounces in two months and expects to receive 1068 cents per ounce, or a total of $534,000.	Sells ten 5,000 troy ounce July futures contracts at 1068 cents per ounce.
July 10	The spot price of silver is now 1071 cents per ounce. The miner sells 50,000 ounces, receiving $535,500.	Buys 10 contracts at 1071.
	Profit $1,500	Futures loss: -$1,500
	Net Wealth Change = 0	

was unwise to hedge. In hedging, the miner and the film manufacturer both decided that the futures price was an acceptable price at which to complete the transaction in July.

Do Hedgers Need Speculators?

Hedging is often viewed as the purchasing of insurance. According to this view, hedgers trade in the futures market and speculators bear the risk that the hedgers try to avoid. Naturally, the speculators demand some compensation for this service. In Chapter 3, the theories of normal backwardation and the contango were considered as explanations of the way in which speculators might receive compensation for bearing risk. In considering the two sides of the silver example, however, no speculators were needed to assume position trades. The long and short hedgers balanced each other out perfectly.

While the example is artificial, it illustrates an important point. Hedgers, as a group, need speculators to take positions and bear risk only for the mismatch in contracts demanded by the long and short hedgers. To the extent that their positions match, position trading speculators are not needed for the job of bearing risk. This helps explain why the risk premiums, if there are any, are not large. In this example, the hedgers do not need speculators to act as position traders. However, even if long and short hedgers were always in balance, the market would still need the liquidity provided by scalpers, such as Mr. X, the scalper we studied earlier.

Cross–Hedging

In the examples of a long and short hedge in silver, the hedgers' needs were perfectly matched with the institutional features of the silver markets. The goods in question were exactly the same goods traded on the futures market, the cash amounts matched the futures contract amounts, and the hedging horizons of the miner and film manufacturer matched the delivery date for the futures contract. In actual hedging applications, it will be rare for all factors to match so well. In most cases the hedged and hedging positions will differ in (1) time span covered, (2) the amount of the commodity, or (3) the particular characteristics of the goods. In such cases, the hedge will be a **cross–hedge**—a hedge in which the characteristics of the spot and futures positions do not match perfectly.

Mismatches that Make a Hedge a Cross–Hedge

1. The hedging horizon may not match the futures expiration date.

2. The quantity to be hedged may not match the futures contract quantity.

3. The physical characteristics of the commodity to be hedged may differ from the futures contract commodity.

As an example, consider the problem faced by a film manufacturer that uses silver, a key ingredient in manufacturing photographic film. Film production is a process industry, with more or less continuous production. However, COMEX silver futures trade for delivery in January, March, May, July, September, and December. The film manufacturer will also need silver in February, April and so on. Thus, the futures expiration dates and the hedging horizon for the film manufacturer do not match perfectly. Second, consider the differences in quantity between the futures contract and the film manufacturer's needs. The COMEX contract is for 5,000 troy ounces of silver. The film manufacturer will likely need many thousands of ounces, so it will be fairly easy for the manufacturer to choose and trade a number of contracts that will bring the quantity of silver futures close to the actual need. However, if a hedger needed to hedge 7,500 ounces, he or she might have a problem choosing between one or two contracts. Finally, consider the differences in the physical characteristics of the silver underlying the futures contract and the silver used in manufacturing film. To produce film, silver needs to be in pellet form and it does not need to be as pure as silver bullion. Also, the pellets contain other metals besides silver. The COMEX silver contract specifies that deliverable silver must be in 1,000 ounce ingots that are 99.9 percent pure. In other words, the silver in the futures contract is extremely pure and refined, not like the adulterated silver products that are typically used in industry. Thus, the film manufacturer will have to hedge his or her industrial silver with pure silver bullion. Cross-hedging is often particularly problematic in the interest rate futures market. Financial instruments are extremely varied in their characteristics, such as risk level, maturity, and coupon rate. By contrast, really active futures contracts are only traded on a few different types of interest-bearing securities.

When the characteristics of the position to be hedged do not perfectly match the characteristics of the futures contract used for the hedging, the hedger must be sure to trade the right number and kind of futures contract to control the risk in the hedged position as much as possible. In general, we cannot expect a cross-hedge to be as effective in reducing risk as a direct hedge. We consider cross-hedging in more detail in later chapters.

Risk–Minimization Hedging

In our first examples, we considered hedges when the hedger had a definite horizon in view. Often, the hedger will not want to hedge for a specific future

Figure 4.3
Soybean Cash Prices
(March 27, 1989—June 4, 1990)

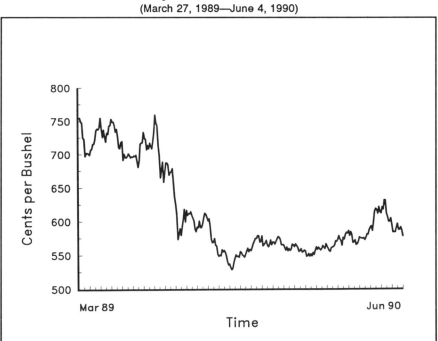

date. Instead, the hedger may want to control a continuing risk on an indefinite basis. Consider, for example, a soy dealer who holds an inventory of soybeans. From this inventory, the dealer meets orders from her customers. As her inventory becomes low, she periodically replenishes her own inventory from cash market sources. The inventory that she holds will fluctuate in value with the price of soybeans. However, she can reduce the fluctuations in the value of her inventory by selling futures contracts, as the following case study shows.

Assume that today is June 19, 1989 and that the dealer's inventory is one million bushels. The cash price of beans has been very volatile in recent months, and is near a high, as Figure 4.3 shows. Therefore, the dealer decides to hedge by selling soybean futures. After she sells futures, she will be long the physical soybeans in her inventory and short soybean futures. If the hedge works, the risk of the combined cash/futures position should be less than the cash position alone.

With an inventory of 1 million bushels, and a soybean contract calling for 5,000 bushels, it might seem wise to sell one bushel in the futures market for each bushel in the cash market. This would call for selling 200 soybean contracts. However, a 1:1 hedge may not be optimal. In our example, the dealer wants to minimize her pre-existing risk that comes from holding her soybean inventory. We assume that she holds a given bean inventory for business reasons, and we treat that inventory decision as fixed. The dealer's problem is to choose the number of futures contracts that will minimize her risk. Thus, we define the **hedge ratio** (HR) as the number of futures contracts to hold for a given position in the commodity:

$$HR = \frac{\text{futures position}}{\text{cash market position}} \qquad 4.1$$

The dealer will trade HR units of the futures to establish the futures market hedge. After establishing the hedge, the trader has a portfolio, P, that consists of the spot position plus the futures position. The profits and losses on the portfolio for one day will be:

$$P_{t+1} - P_t = S_{t+1} - S_t + HR(F_{t+1} - F_t) \qquad 4.2$$

Note that in our initial discussion we considered that the dealer might hedge each bushel in her cash position with one bushel of futures. In that case, the hedge ratio would be -1.0, the negative sign indicating a short position. Generally, if the trader is long the cash commodity, the futures position will be short. Likewise, if the trader is short the cash good, the futures position will be long.

Now, however, the dealer wants to choose the hedge ratio that will minimize the risk of the portfolio of the spot beans and the futures position. The variance of the combined position depends on the variance of the cash price, the variance of the futures price, and the covariance between the two prices. It is a basic statistical rule that the variance of returns on a portfolio, P, of one unit of the spot asset and HR units of a futures contract is given by equation 4.3:

$$\sigma_P^2 = \sigma_S^2 + HR^2 \sigma_F^2 + 2 \, HR \, \rho_{SF} \, \sigma_S \, \sigma_F \qquad 4.3$$

where:

$$\sigma_P^2 = \text{variance of the portfolio, } P_t,$$
$$\sigma_C^2 = \text{variance of } S_t,$$
$$\sigma_F^2 = \text{variance of } F_t,$$
$$\rho_{SF} = \text{correlation between } S_t \text{ and } F_t,$$

The dealer minimizes the variance by choosing a hedge ratio defined as follows:[24]

$$HR = \frac{\rho_{SF} \, \sigma_S \, \sigma_F}{\sigma_F^2} = \frac{COV_{SF}}{\sigma_F^2} \qquad 4.4$$

where:

COV_{SF} = the covariance between S_t and F_t

As a practical matter, the easiest way to find the risk–minimizing hedge ratio is to estimate the following regression:

$$S_t = \alpha + \beta \, F_t + \varepsilon_t \qquad 4.5$$

where:

α = the constant regression parameter,
β = the slope regression parameter,
ε = an error term with zero mean and standard deviation of 1.0.

The estimated β from this regression is the risk-minimizing hedge ratio, because the estimated β equals the sample covariance between the independent (F_t) and dependent (S_t) variables divided by the sample variance of the independent variable. This is exactly the definition we gave of the risk-minimizing hedge ratio in equation 4.4.

From the regression estimation, we also obtain a measure of hedging effectiveness. The coefficient of determination, or R^2, is provided by the regression estimate. Conceptually,

> R^2 = portion of total variance in the cash price changes statistically related to the futures price changes

Thus the R^2 will always be a number between 0 and 1.0. The closer to 1.0, the better the degree of fit in the regression between the cash and the futures and the better chance for our hedge to work well.

There are at least three possible measures of S_t and F_t that we might be tempted to employ in the regression of equation 4.5: price levels, price changes, and percentage price changes. There has been considerable controversy regarding the proper measure.[25] While this controversy is not fully resolved, we recommend using either the change in price or the percentage change in price, not the price level. If the general range of prices over the estimation period is fairly stable, the price change measure will be satisfactory. If the price changes dramatically, using percentage price changes will give better results.[26]

We now apply this regression approach to the problem of our soybean dealer as of June 19, 1989, using 60 days of daily data to estimate the following regression equation:

$$\Delta C_t = \alpha + \beta \Delta F_t + \varepsilon_t$$

where:

$$\Delta C_t = \text{change in cash price on day t}$$
$$\Delta F_t = \text{change in futures price on day t}$$

Estimating the regression gives the following parameter estimates:

$$\hat{\alpha} = .6976$$
$$\hat{\beta} = .8713$$
$$R^2 = .56$$

With the estimated β = .8713, the model suggests selling .8713 bushels in the futures market for each bushel in inventory. With one million bushels in inventory and a futures contract of 5,000 bushels, the model suggests selling 174 contracts, because:

$$.8713 \times (1,000,000/5,000) = 174.26 \text{ contracts}$$

From the estimation of the model, we see that the regression accounts for 56 percent of the variance of the cash price change during our sample period. This is an important point, because the regression chose an estimate of β to maximize the R^2. This provides no certainty that we can expect similar results beyond the estimation period. To this point in our example, we have used the data that would actually be available to a trader on June 19, 1989. We assume that our soybean dealer estimated her hedge ratio and placed the hedge at the close of business on June 19. Next, we want to evaluate the performance of the hedge.

Figure 4.4 shows how soybeans performed from June 20, 1989 through June 4, 1990, when we assume that she offset in the futures market, thereby ending

Figure 4.4
Performance of Hedged and Unhedged Soybean Positions
June 20, 1989—June 4, 1990

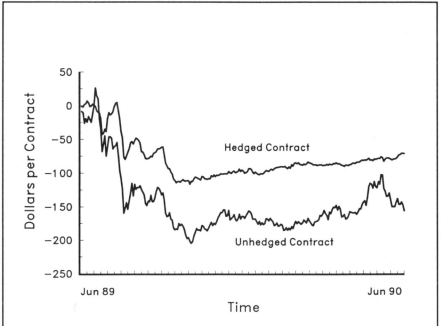

the hedge.[27] The graph in Figure 4.4 shows the wealth change from June 20 forward for one contract of cash soybeans and for a contract (5,000 bushels) of cash soybeans hedged with .8713 futures contracts. As the figure shows, in late summer 1989, soybean prices fell dramatically. From the time the hedge was placed until October 1989, soybean prices fell about $2.00 per bushel. During the same interval, the hedge position lost about $1.00 per bushel. From autumn 1989 through May 1990, prices drifted somewhat higher.

Comparing the unhedged and the hedged strategies, we see that both lost money. However, the hedged strategy avoided about 50 percent of the loss associated with the drop in cash prices. Over the life of the hedge, the unhedged bushel of soybeans lost $1.56 and the hedged bushel lost $.71. On the inventory of one million bushels, this represents a benefit of $850,000 from hedging. From Figure 4.4, we can also see that the hedged position had much less variance than the cash position. For an unhedged bushel, the standard deviation of the price change was $.0815 per day. For the hedged position, the standard deviation was $.0431.

Several special points need to be made about this particular hedge. First, we see that the hedge made money because the short position in the futures gave profits as soybean prices fell. We must realize that bean prices could have risen just as easily. In that event, the futures position in the hedge would have lost money. This brings us to the second point. Hedging aims at reducing risk, not generating profits. In this case, the goal was to reduce variance, which the hedge did. Had bean prices risen, the hedge would also have reduced variance, and would have been successful in attaining its goal. Thus, the hedger must expect an equal chance of monetary gains and losses from placing a hedge. However, with a good hedge, the variance can be reduced substantially.

The period we chose for our analysis was a special time in the bean market. We discussed in Chapter 2 that there may have been an attempted manipulation of the July 1990 soybean futures contract by the Italian grain firm Ferruzzi. Thus, our estimation period consisted of the run-up in prices that culminated in the market crisis of July 1990. The beginning portion of our hedging period includes the price collapse that resulted after Ferruzzi was forced from the market.[28] These events disturbed the normal price relationship between cash and futures prices for soybeans, so this period would be difficult for any hedging model. Nonetheless, the hedge worked fairly well in reducing the volatility of the bean dealer's inventory value. Given the collapsing prices, the hedge also saved her about $850,000.

Costs and Benefits of Hedging

We have defined a hedger as a futures trader with a pre-existing risk who enters the futures market to reduce that risk. We have also seen that this definition implies that hedging activities will be restricted to commercial concerns generally. For most individuals, taking a futures position means that risk increases, because the futures commitment is large relative to the trader's pre-existing risk in that commodity. Therefore, the costs and benefits of hedging will accrue mainly to business firms. In this section, we explore the rationale for hedging by corporations.

Because the analysis is simpler, we begin by considering the incentives for hedging in a perfect market. As we have seen, hedging is essentially a transaction in a financial market. From the point of view of the firm, the decision to hedge is essentially a financing decision. In perfect markets, the financial policy of the corporation is irrelevant, because shareholders can always transact to undo the actions of the firm's managers. For example, as Miller and Modigliani have shown,[29] managerial decisions regarding the mixture of debt and equity can be unwound by the shareholders to create any capital structure the shareholder desires. Thus, if the firm issues no debt, the shareholder can create homemade leverage by issuing debt on his or her personal account.

In futures hedging, the situation is similar. If the firm fails to hedge, the shareholder in a perfect market can effectively hedge his or her stake in the firm by trading a fractional share in the futures market.[30] Similarly, if the firm hedges by selling futures, for instance, the shareholder can create an unhedged personal stake in the firm by buying a fractional futures contract. While hedging in a perfect market cannot increase the value of the firm, it cannot decrease it either, because shareholders can always transact to offset the firm's action. If corporate hedging in a perfect market is pointless, as this argument suggests, then any real benefit to hedging must come from market imperfections.

We consider five market imperfections that can make hedging important and that may impose real costs on firms: taxes, costs of financial distress, transaction costs, principal-agent problems, and the costliness of diversification.

Market Imperfections that Affect Firm Hedging Decisions

1. Taxes.
2. Costs of financial distress.
3. Transaction costs of hedging.

4. Principal–agent problems.
5. Costliness of diversification.

Taxes as an Incentive to Hedge. In a perfect market, there are no taxes. In real markets, when taxes are levied on annual accounting income, they can provide an incentive for a firm to hedge. Consider a firm that will mine 1,000 ounces of gold bullion this year at a cost of $300 per ounce. The futures price for gold, and thus the firm's expected sale price, is $400 per ounce. This price will give a profit of $100,000. However, this is only an expected price, and the actual price may be $300 or $500 per ounce with equal probability, we assume.

We also assume that the tax rate is 20 percent and that the firm has a tax credit of $20,000 that it can apply to offset income taxes. To hedge, the firm would sell futures for its 1,000 ounces of production at the $400 per ounce futures price. Table 4.15 shows the different outcomes depending on the sale price of gold and the firm's decision to hedge or not to hedge.

For both the hedged and the unhedged firm, revenues from selling gold will be either $300,000 or $500,000, depending on whether the gold price is $300 or $500. For the unhedged firm, there is no futures result. If the gold price is $300, the hedged firm has a futures gain of $100,000, because the hedge involved selling 1,000 ounces in the futures market at $400. If the gold price is $500, the hedging firm loses $100,000 in the futures market, because it sold for a futures price of $400 when it could have received $500 by not hedging. Production costs are $300,000 for all scenarios. Pre-tax profits for the unhedged firm will be either zero or $200,000 depending on the price of gold. For the hedged firm, the pre-tax profit will be $100,000 in both cases, due to the hedging.

We can now consider the effect of taxes and the $20,000 tax credit. A tax credit can be used only if the firm owes taxes. For the unhedged firm, the $300 price means that the firm has zero net income and no taxes due. Therefore, the firm cannot use the tax credit, and its after-tax net income is zero. If gold sells for $500, the unhedged firm can use its tax credit fully, and its after-tax net income is $90,000. Thus, the unhedged firm has a 50 percent chance of using its tax credit. For the hedging firm, pre-tax income will be $100,000 no matter what the price of gold may be. This means that its tax obligation will be $20,000 in both cases. Thus, the hedged firm uses its tax credit to honor its taxes. This leaves the hedging firm with $100,000 in after-tax net income, no matter what the price of gold may be.

The difference between the unhedged and hedged firms comes down to the following distinction. By hedging, the firm guarantees that it will be able to use its tax credit. By not hedging, the firm runs a 50 percent chance of not being able to use the $20,000 credit. Notice that the difference in the expected after-tax net income between the two firms exactly equals $10,000, which is exactly the expected loss on being unable to use the tax credit for the unhedged firm ($20,000 × .50). Therefore, in our example, taxes create a legitimate incentive to hedge. With hedging, the firm is able to increase its expected after-tax income. With taxes, hedging can increase the value of the firm.[31]

Costs of Financial Distress as an Incentive to Hedge. In Table 4.15, the expected pre-tax profits are the same for both the no-hedging and the hedging strategies. However, hedging reduces the risk inherent in the pre-tax profits. In perfect markets, reducing risk has no value, as long as expected values remain the same. Under perfect market assumptions, investors can diversify costlessly to create any risk position they desire. If a particular firm follows a high risk strategy and goes bankrupt, assets are immediately deployed in an

Table 4.15
How Taxes Provide an Incentive to Hedge

	Unhedged Firm		Hedged Firm	
Sale Price of Gold	$300	$500	$300	$500
Gold Revenue	$300,000	$500,000	$300,000	$500,000
Futures Result	0	0	+100,000	-100,000
Less Production Cost	-300,000	-300,000	-300,000	-300,000
Pre–Tax Profit	0	$200,000	$100,000	$100,000
Tax Obligation	0	-40,000	-20,000	-20,000
Add Tax Credit (if applicable)	0	+20,000	+20,000	+20,000
Net Income	0	$180,000	$100,000	$100,000
Expected After–Tax Net Income	$90,000		$100,000	

equally useful role. In the real world, by contrast, there are real costs associated with bankruptcy and financial distress. Lawyers and accountants must be paid, for example. In addition, assets cannot be deployed instantly to earn the same return. Therefore, a risk-reducing strategy can help avoid these costs of financial distress, and hedging can consequently increase the value of the firm.

Transaction costs of hedging provide a disincentive for hedging. We have reason to believe that futures prices closely approximate expected future spot prices. If the futures price equals the expected future spot price, the expected profit from trading a futures contract is zero. This holds for both hedging and speculating. Therefore, the expected cost of a hedging transaction is roughly the transaction costs associated with placing and managing the hedge. For any one hedge, the actual result can be wildly favorable or negative, but the expected result is to lose the transaction costs. For the firm that continuously hedges, the law of large numbers comes into play. On some hedges, the firm will win, while it will lose on others. Over many hedges, the law of large numbers assures us that the actual result will more and more closely approximate the theoretical result—no futures gain nor losses, but losses equal to the transaction costs. Therefore, a policy of consistent hedging can be expected to lose the transaction costs in the long run. This high probability of a slightly negative result provides a disincentive for hedging.

Principal–Agent Conflicts as an Incentive to Hedging. In perfect markets, managers of the firm act as pure agents of the shareholders. They operate the firm in the interests of the shareholders, as the shareholders would run the firm for themselves. However, in real firms, managers and shareholders often have conflicting desires. These lead to conflicts between the principals (shareholders) and their agents (managers). For example, managers may like to have sumptuous offices. The shareholders pay for the offices, and the managers use them. In the hedging decision, shareholders may tolerate more risk than managers. Shareholders can hold a portfolio of stocks, so one company may be only a small fraction of the shareholder's portfolio. By contrast, the managers work full-time for the firm and may have a very large portion of their wealth committed to the firm. In this situation, the managers are more anxious than the shareholders to reduce risk. Given the managers' higher risk aversion, they may hedge when shareholders would really prefer that the firm be unhedged.

Lack of Owner Diversification as an Incentive to Hedge. In addition to managers, some shareholders may not be as fully diversified as perfect market conditions would imply. If the shareholders have committed a substantial portion of their wealth to a single firm, they may be highly risk averse like managers. For example, a farmer may have his or her entire wealth committed to a farm. This lack of diversification on the part of the owner can also create an incentive to hedge.

Summary. In this section, we have considered some of the costs and benefits associated with hedging. We began by observing that essentially only firms can hedge, because only firms can reduce their risks by trading futures. In perfect markets, hedging would be pointless, because individual traders can effectively hedge instead of the firm. Therefore, incentives to hedge arise from market imperfections. We saw that taxes and the costs of financial distress can both create a situation in which hedging can increase firm value. We also considered the potential conflicts between owners and managers as principals and agents that can lead the managers to hedge more than the shareholders desire. Finally, we saw that incomplete owner diversification can also create an incentive to hedge.

If futures prices equal expected future spot prices, the expected gain or loss from trading a futures contract is zero, except for the transaction costs that must be paid. This means that the expected monetary payoff from hedging is slightly negative. Persistent hedging is very likely to generate a loss equal to the costs of transacting and the costs of managing the hedge. These costs provide a strong disincentive for the firm to hedge.

Conclusion

In this chapter, we have explored the three major uses that observers and traders make of futures markets. We began by considering the function of price discovery, a service of futures markets that can be enjoyed by traders and non-traders alike. We considered the way in which producers could use information from the futures market to guide their production decisions. If futures prices provide a good guide to future spot prices, then futures markets reveal price information that helps society to allocate capital more efficiently. In our discussion of price discovery, we considered a case study of price discovery in the oil market and we summarized the forecast power that Fama and French found in diverse commodity markets.

The futures market attracts speculators—traders who enter the futures market in pursuit of profit, willingly increasing their risks to do so. We classified speculators according to the length of time they planned to hold a futures position as: scalpers, day traders, and position traders. We noted that spread trading is an important form of speculative trading and considered different spread trading techniques.

We examined the available evidence on the profitability of speculative trading. We found that studies disagree considerably on the magnitude and even the existence of speculative trading profits. We briefly considered the performance of technical trading systems, where we once again found different conclusions in the academic literature. Commodity funds have become important speculative trading vehicles in recent years. We analyzed the evidence on the performance of commodity funds, and again found no evidence of overwhelming trading acumen. Finally, we considered the concept of "normal" speculative profits. This was an effort to take into consideration the investment of funds and time that are necessary to speculate as a scalper or other floor trader. We found that the trader must make a substantial income to justify the investment and loss of other job opportunities.

Hedging is one of the most important social functions of futures markets. A hedger is a trader who enters the futures market in an effort to reduce a pre-existing risk. We saw that traders can hedge by being either long or short in the futures market. Except for providing liquidity, we noted that hedgers needed speculative position traders only to absorb an imbalance between long and short hedgers. Much hedging activity involves an imperfect match between the characteristics of the asset being hedged and the asset underlying a futures contract. Hedging in such a situation is cross-hedging. We gave examples of how traders might use the market to hedge in such a situation. In many instances, hedgers will want to employ risk-minimization techniques for a given position. We showed that it is possible to derive the correct futures position to minimize a given initial risk using a statistical analysis of historical data. Using actual soybean data, we followed a strategy from beginning to end for hedging soybeans over the 1989-1990 period. Finally, we considered the costs and benefits of hedging.

Questions and Problems

1. Explain how futures markets can benefit individuals in society that never trade futures.

2. A "futures price" is a market quoted price today of the best estimate of the value of a commodity at the expiration of the futures contract. What do you think of this definition?

3. Explain the concept of an unbiased predictor.

4. How are errors possible if a predictor is unbiased?

5. Scalpers trade to capture profits from minute fluctuations in futures price. Explain how this avaricious behavior benefits others.

6. Assume that scalping is made illegal. What would the consequences of such an action be for hedging activity in futures markets?

7. A trader anticipates rising corn prices and wants to take advantage of this insight by trading an intra-commodity spread. Would you advise that she trade long nearby/short distant or the other way around? Explain.

8. Assume that daily settlement prices in the futures market exhibit very strong first order serial correlation. How would you trade to exploit this strategy? Explain how your answer would differ if the correlation is statistically significant but, nonetheless, small in magnitude.

9. Assume that you are a rabid efficient markets believer. A commodity fund uses 20 percent of its funds as margin payments. The remaining 80 percent are invested in risk-free securities. What investment performance would you expect from the fund?

10. Consider two traders. The first trader is an individual with his own seat who trades strictly for his own account. The other trader works for a brokerage firm actively engaged in retail futures brokerage. Which trader has a lower effective marginal trading cost? Relate this comparison in marginal trading costs to quasi-arbitrage.

11. Consider the classic hedging problems of the farmer who sells wheat in the futures market in anticipation of a harvest. Would the farmer be likely to deliver his harvested wheat against the futures? Explain. If he is unlikely to deliver, explain how he manages his futures position instead.

12. A cocoa merchant holds a current inventory of cocoa worth $10 million at present prices of $1,250 per metric ton. The standard deviation of returns for the inventory is .27. She is considering a risk-minimization hedge of her inventory using the cocoa contract of the Coffee, Cocoa, and Sugar Exchange. The contract size is 10 metric tons. The volatility of the futures is .33. For the particular grade of cocoa in her inventory, the correlation between the futures and spot cocoa is .85. Compute the risk-minimization hedge ratio and determine how many contracts she should trade.

13. A service station operator read this book. He wants to hedge his risk exposure for gasoline. Every week, he pumps 50,000 gallons of gasoline, and he is confident that this pattern will hold through thick and Hussein. What advice would you offer?

Notes

1. This argument can be expressed more formally by using the theory of complete markets. A market is complete if we can transact for any desired pattern of payoffs. Complete market theory has often been developed by using a state-preference framework of analysis. In the state-preference approach, the objects of choice are defined as payoffs under certain **states of nature**. The states of nature are defined so that each possible occurrence falls under one, and only one, state of nature. In this framework, a market is complete if and only if we can contract for a payoff in any state, or combination of states, of nature. (For a development of the state- preference framework, see S. Myers. "A Time State-Preference Model of Security Valuation," *Journal of Financial and Quantitative Analysis,* March 1968.)

   If markets are complete, then we can freely contract for the set of payoffs that best fits our needs. The more nearly complete markets are, the more society benefits from the ability to fit payoffs to individuals' desired outcomes. With this background, the argument for futures markets is clear: they contribute to the welfare of society by making financial markets more clearly complete. (For a highly mathematical development of complete markets under a state-preference approach, see G. Debreu, *Theory of Value,* New Haven: Yale University Press, 1959.)

2. The furniture manufacturer might also take the step of attempting to "lock-in" these "discovered" prices by buying futures contracts for lumber. Such a step is a small one and emphasizes the intimate connection between price discovery and hedging.

3. For a more formal treatment of the property of unbiasedness in estimators, see J. Kmenta, *Elements of Econometrics,* New York: Macmillan.

4. For an assessment of the accuracy of futures prices as forecasts of expected future spot prices, see R. Kolb, G. Gay, and J. Jordan. "Futures Prices and Expected Future Spot Prices," *Review of Research in Futures Markets,* 1983, 2, pp. 110-123.

5. See Richard Levich. "Currency Forecasters Lose Their Way," *Euromoney,* August 1983, pp. 140-147. Chapter 11 discusses the forecasting accuracy of professional currency forecasters in more detail.

6. What of Ma's tests of four more sophisticated models? We do not present those results. In general, the futures-based forecast dominated the other methods for all horizons and all commodities.

7. Some authors attempt to distinguish speculators from investors. The usual difference between the two definitions seems to lie in their respective attitudes toward risk and the length of time they expect to hold their positions. Speculators are contrasted only with hedgers, so any investor in the futures market, no matter how conservative, would be regarded as a speculator for the purposes of this book.

8. On the floor of the exchanges, different commodities are traded in different pits. A pit is really an area of the floor, surrounded by steps or risers, which are usually about five steps high. The arrangement allows traders to see and communicate with each other. The term "pit" is really synonymous with trading in futures, as indicated by the title of Frank Norris' novel, *The Pit,* which is the story of futures trading in wheat.

9. A round-turn is the initiation and closing of a futures position. For example, a trader buys a futures and sells a futures contract to make one round-turn transaction. The round-turn transaction costs are the costs incurred to complete the entire transaction.

10. Bob Tamarkin, *The New Gatsbys: Fortunes and Misfortunes of Commodity Traders,* New York: William Morrow and Company, Inc., 1985, pp. 26, 43.

11. As discussed in Chapter 2, high liquidity is also crucial in the survival of a particular futures contract. In competing contracts, the one with the initially greater liquidity has a much higher probability of success.

12. William L. Silber, "Marketmaker Behavior in an Auction Market: An Analysis of Scalpers in Futures Markets," *Journal of Finance*, September 1984, 39:4, p. 937-953.

13. B. Wade Brorsen, "Liquidity Costs and Scalping Returns in the Corn Futures Market," *The Journal of Futures Markets*, 9:3, June 1989, pp. 225-236, simulated scalper's behavior using corn data. Using his trading rule, Brorsen estimates scalping profits at about $10.00 per trade. Brorsen comments that his results match those of Silber.

14. In any event, visitors to the exchanges are allowed on the floor only for short periods of time and under the supervision of exchange personnel. Access to the floor near the close of trading is more restricted because as the day's trading nears its close, the level of activity increases dramatically.

15. See, for example, *Commodity Trading Manual*, Chicago: Chicago Board of Trade, 1989, and Martin J. Pring (ed.), *The McGraw-Hill Handbook of Commodities and Futures*, New York: McGraw-Hill, 1985.

16. Stephen J. Taylor, "The Behavior of Futures Prices Over Time," *Applied Economics*, 17:4, August 1985, pp. 713-734.

17. Another recently emerging facet of the debate on patterns in futures prices comes from chaos theory. Some process, whether in nature or in a social process such as a financial market, may appear to consist of purely random behavior. According to chaos theory, this appearance of randomness may be an illusion. With the insights of chaos theory, it may be possible to find patterns in seemingly chaotic data. For an application of this theory to futures markets, see R. Savit, "When Random Is Not Random: An Introduction to Chaos in Market Prices," *The Journal of Futures Markets*, 8:3, June 1988, pp. 271-290.

18. These three versions of the efficient markets hypothesis were first articulated by E. Fama. "Efficient Capital Markets: Theory and Empirical Work," *Journal of Finance,* May 1970, pp. 383-417. For a more recent

survey of the efficient markets literature, see T. Copeland and F. Weston, *Financial Theory and Corporate Policy,* 3rd Ed. Reading, MA: Addison Wesley, 1988.

19. The concept of market efficiency entered the popular culture through the back door with the movie, *Trading Places,* starring Eddie Murphy and Dan Ackroyd. Murphy and Ackroyd acquire some private information about the size of the orange crop by getting early access to a government crop report. Their use of the crop report constitutes the use of private information to earn a supernormal profit trading orange juice futures and is a violation of strong form market efficiency. This information allows them to bankrupt the "bad guys" and to retire to a Pacific island paradise.

20. Traditionally, the most highly valued commodity exchange seats have been those on the Chicago Board of Trade. In late 1982, a seat on the Chicago Mercantile Exchange cost more than a Chicago Board of Trade seat for the first time in history. The prices of these seats are very volatile. The value of the seats responds very directly to the level of trading at the exchange, which is itself quite variable. For a study of commodity exchange seat prices, see R. Chiang, G. Gay, and R. Kolb, "Commodity Exchange Seat Prices," *Review of Futures Markets,* 6:1, 1987, pp. 1-10.

21. The youthfulness of the traders is particularly apparent in the newer markets, such as the interest rate futures market. Relatively, the older, more traditional commodities are traded by older traders. In his book, *The New Gatsbys,* (New York: William Morrow and Co., Inc., 1985), Bob Tamarkin emphasizes the physical strains and the mental stresses that traders endure. For example, see Chapter 20, "Pit Falls."

22. Many traders will not leave the trading pit during the six to seven hour trading session, even to go to the bathroom. It is simply too risky to leave the trading floor for even a short period of time. This indicates the level of stress in the pits.

23. The theory of hedging is still the subject of much debate. For two fairly recent contributions, see C. Smith and R. Stulz, "The Determinants of Firms' Hedging Policies," *Journal of Financial and Quantitative Analysis,* December 1985, 20:4, pp. 391-405 and R. Stulz, "Optimal Hedging Policies," *Journal of Financial and Quantitative Analysis,* 19:2, June 1984, pp. 127-140.

24. To find the risk-minimizing hedge ratio, we take the derivative of the portfolio's risk in equation 3.3 with respect to HR, set the derivative equal to zero, and solve for HR:

$$\frac{d\ \sigma_P^2}{d\ HR} = 2\ HR\ \sigma_F^2 - 2\ \rho_{CF}\ \sigma_C\ \sigma_F = 0$$

$$HR = \rho_{CF}\frac{\sigma_C}{\sigma_F} = \frac{COV_{CF}}{\sigma_F^2}$$

25. See, for example J. Hill and T. Schneeweis, "A Note on the Hedging Effectiveness of Foreign Currency Futures," *The Journal of Futures Markets*, 1:4, Winter 1981, pp. 659-664 and H. Witt, T. Schroeder, and M. Hayenga, "Comparison of Analytical Approaches for Estimating Hedge Ratios for Agricultural Commodities," *The Journal of Futures Markets*, 7:2, April 1987, pp. 135-146.

26. H. Witt, T. Schroeder, and M. Hayenga, "Comparison of Analytical Approaches for Estimating Hedge Ratios for Agricultural Commodities," *The Journal of Futures Markets*, 7:2, April 1987, pp. 135-146, study this issue in detail. They believe that price level regressions can work satisfactorily unless certain adverse conditions prevail. One of these conditions is autocorrelation in the price series—the price level at one time varies systematically with the price level at another time. However, most financial price level series exhibit first-order autocorrelation. For this reason, it is often better to use one of the other approaches.

27. There is nothing special about this ending date. We chose this date, because the July contract is approaching expiration and the open interest in the contract would be falling at this time. Choosing a different date a few weeks one way or the other would not change the results appreciably.

28. Some unbiased observers do not believe that Ferruzzi's departure from the market caused the price collapse. They believe that price effects from Ferruzzi's efforts were very short-lived.

29. M. Miller and F. Modigliani, "The Cost of Capital, Corporate Finance, and the Theory of Investment," *American Economic Review*, 48:3, June 1958, pp. 261-297.

30. Notice that the shareholder can hedge his or her own portion in a perfect market, due to being able to trade a fractional share. In real markets, individuals cannot generally hedge, because futures contracts are large relative to the wealth level and risk exposure of most individuals.

31. The unhedged firm does not necessarily lose its tax credit. Generally, the unhedged firm would be able to retain its tax credit and apply it in a year when it does have positive income and a tax liability.

5

Agricultural and Metallurgical Futures Contracts

Introduction

This chapter explores futures contracts on traditional commodities, those written on agricultural and metallurgical commodities. Much of this chapter develops and applies concepts introduced in Chapters 1-4. We begin with an overview of the basic characteristics of commodities that will affect futures prices. As we have seen in Chapter 3, the Cost-of-Carry Model is the dominant conceptual framework for understanding futures prices. However, we also considered some commodity characteristics that interfere with a smooth application of the Cost-of-Carry Model. These features include storability, seasonal production, and seasonal consumption. We consider each of these in turn.

After reviewing the commodity features that affect futures pricing directly, we turn to an examination of spreads. As we discussed earlier, spreads can be inter-commodity spreads or intra-commodity spreads. This chapter considers both types of spreads in more detail. In this context, we can throw additional light on the Cost-of-Carry Model and the implications of the model's deficiencies for some commodities. As a final major topic, we consider hedging in more detail with some case studies of particular cross-hedging techniques and problems.

Commodity Characteristics

In Chapters 3-4, we developed the Cost-of-Carry Model, which explains futures prices if markets are perfect and if the good underlying the futures is storable. We reviewed the cash-and-carry arbitrage strategy that keeps the futures price from being too high relative to the spot price of a commodity. Similarly, we saw that reverse cash-and-carry strategies kept the futures price from being too low relative to the cash price. In a perfect market, the Cost-of-Carry Model implies an exact value for the price of a futures contract, given information about the spot price and the cost of carrying the good forward in time.

If markets are not perfect, but still allow unrestricted short selling, we found that the Cost-of-Carry Model implies a range of permissible futures prices. This range of permissible prices, or the width between no-arbitrage bounds, centers around the perfect markets price. The width of the no-arbitrage bounds simply reflects the transaction costs due to market imperfections. In both the perfect markets case and the imperfect markets case with unrestricted short selling, the Cost-of-Carry Model implies a very definite permissible price, or range of permissible prices. These prices are defined by the cash-and carry and reverse cash-and-carry arbitrage strategies.

Applying the cash-and-carry arbitrage strategy assumes that the physical good can be stored from one date to the next. If the good cannot be stored, the cash-and-carry strategy is not feasible. If the no-arbitrage link between the cash price and the futures price fails because the physical good cannot be stored, then the futures price is free to rise relative to the cash price. Similarly, the reverse cash-and-carry strategy depends upon short selling. If short selling is not feasible, the reverse cash-and-carry strategy does not apply. Without this link between the cash and futures prices, the cash price is free to rise relative to the futures price. As we have seen, the cash price can even exceed the futures price upon occasion. As we noted in Chapter 3, some goods have a convenience yield, which stems from the usefulness of having them in inventory. For example, during an oil crisis, holding oil in inventory can allow a commercial concern to keep its business open. In this situation, the cash price can rise relative to the futures price to reflect the convenience yield associated with holding the physical good.

In summary, relationships between the cash and futures prices depend upon: transaction costs, the supplies of the commodity, the storage characteristics of the good, the production and consumption cycle for the good, and the ease of short selling the good. Each of these features is usually related to the others. Figure 5.1 attempts to capture some of these relationships for major commodity groups, and it also graphs the supply and storability characteristics of various commodities. We consider the supply issue and storability issues in turn.

If stocks of the good are high relative to consumption, there will be less chance of a shortage. If a commodity is always in good supply, traders will be willing to sell it short. As a result, there will be a lower convenience yield for the good, and it will be more likely to trade in a full carry market. In general, the supply of a good depends upon its production relative to its consumption. If the production of a commodity is smooth, there will be less chance of an

Figure 5.1
Commodity Supply and Storage Characteristics

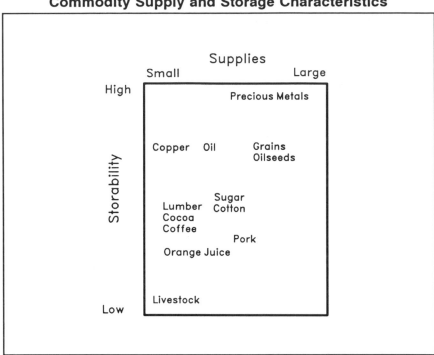

unexpected shortfall in supply. Similarly, if consumption is continuous, there will be less chance of an unexpectedly high demand.

In Figure 5.1, we see that stocks of precious metals are large relative to demand for industrial purposes. In addition to a fairly large stock, precious metals have fairly steady production and consumption. Mine production is generally steady, because it does not depend on weather to any great extent. Similarly, consumption is steady as well, because consumption is mainly for industrial purposes that can be anticipated and the metals are used in a process that continues all year. By contrast, stocks of copper are fairly low, as we noted in Chapter 3. Commodities such as grains and oilseeds have large supplies relative to consumption. However, the supplies of these goods follow the harvest cycle, making the overall level of grain stocks less steady than that of precious metals.

The vertical axis of Figure 5.1 graphs the storability of various commodities. A good is highly storable if it does not spoil and if it can be warehoused cheaply relative to its value. The prime example of a highly storable good is gold. It is cheap to store relative to its value and it will not spoil. In many ways, copper is similar. However, because copper is cheap relative to its bulk, it is not as highly storable as gold. At the other end of the spectrum, livestock is very difficult to store. For example, feeder cattle held in storage continue to grow so that they would not meet the feeder cattle specifications. To be deliverable against the live hog contract, for example, a hog must weigh between 210 and 240 pounds at the time of delivery. Supplies of live animals are also not large relative to annual consumption. Animals too young or too old have diminished value for consumption. With on-hand supplies of livestock being low and storability being poor, livestock lies at the opposite end of the supply/storability spectrum from precious metals.

In the sections that follow, we consider commodities arranged by their storage and supply characteristics. Table 5.1 presents the various features of the commodities and the expected price behavior. If a good has excellent storage characteristics and a large supply relative to consumption, we expect markets for the good to approximate full carry. The prime example of a physical commodity that meets these conditions is gold. Next, we consider commodities that are highly storable, but have supplies that fluctuate due to a production cycle. Here we refer to most agricultural commodities that have a harvest season, such as grains and oilseeds. The harvest may be so large that it drastically increases the availability of the good. This radical change in supply relative to annual consumption can cause important swings in prices. Thus, we expect to observe significant departures from full carry for the futures prices of harvested commodities.[1]

Storability of a commodity can be quite high, but the stocks may fluctuate due to seasonal demand for the good. For example, oil products exhibit strong seasonal demand. Gasoline has its highest demand in summer, while heating oil has its highest demand in winter. These seasonal patterns in demand affect the

Table 5.1
Storage and Stock Characteristics and Price Behavior

Storability	Relative Stocks	Example Commodities
High	High	Precious metals—expect general conformance to full carry.
Good	Production cycle causes fluctuations in stocks	Grains and oilseeds—expect departures from full carry.
Good	Consumption cycle causes fluctuations in stocks	Energy products—expect departures from full carry.
Poor	Low, largely due to poor storability	Livestock—expect frequent departures from full carry.

stocks of oil and can cause departures from full carry. While production of oil is fairly continuous, any disruption in the ordinary production cycle can also cause disruptions in price and departures from full carry. For example, we already discussed in Chapter 3 how the Iraqi invasion of Kuwait helped to throw crude oil prices into backwardation.

If a good has poor storage characteristics, it will probably also have relatively low supplies relative to demand. At the extreme, consider again the tropical fruit example of Chapter 3. There we considered a fruit that is harvested only on a single day. If not eaten, it spoils the same day. In this example, we have a good with very poor storage. This poor storability also affects the supply, because it is impossible to carry the good forward even for one day. While the tropical fruit example is extreme, livestock does exhibit the same characteristics to a considerable degree. Livestock cannot be stored very well because it keeps growing. This poor storability also means that feed lot operators cannot have large supplies relative to consumption, because the stored good cannot be carried forward very well to meet future demand.

Full Carry Markets—Precious Metals

In this section, we consider full carry markets, and we will use precious metals as our prime example of a physical commodity that normally trades in a full carry market. We have seen that a highly storable commodity with a large supply relative to annual consumption should behave according to the Cost-of-Carry Model that we developed in Chapter 3. For precious metals, both the cash-and-carry and reverse cash-and-carry arbitrage strategies are potentially effective because short selling is fairly accessible for precious metals. In particular, quasi-arbitrage strategies are available because large commercial interests hold substantial inventories of gold and other precious metals. As we saw in Chapter 3, these businesses can replicate short selling by selling a portion of their inventory.

A Full Carry Example

Figure 5.2 shows gold prices for the JUN and DEC 1989 COMEX gold futures contracts over the year from March 1988 to March 1989. The graph reveals that the two prices track each other very closely, with the more distant DEC contract lying above the nearby JUN contract. If gold truly is a full carry market, then the difference between these two futures prices must be very closely related to the cost of carrying gold from June 1989 to December 1989. If the DEC price were too high relative to the JUN price, traders would engage in a cash-and-carry strategy of buying the JUN futures and selling the DEC contract. They would arrange to carry the gold from June to December and deliver it against the DEC

Figure 5.2
JUN and DEC 1989 Gold Futures

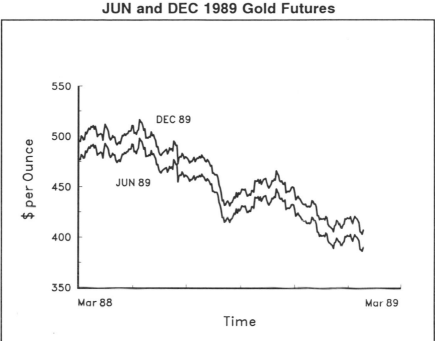

contract. Similarly, if the DEC price were too low, traders would engage in reverse cash-and-carry strategies.

As we know from our more detailed discussion in Chapter 3, the carrying costs consist of storage, insurance, transportation, and financing charges. Generally, the financing cost is so large that it swamps the other costs. Thus, we ignore all but the financing cost in our analysis of the gold market. Accordingly, if gold is a full carry market, we should observe the following relationship, from equation 3.6:

$$F_{0,d} = F_{0,n}(1 + C), \qquad d > n$$

That is, the distant futures price should equal the nearby futures price times 1 plus the cost-of-carry. This is the result we found for a perfect market assuming unrestricted short selling. Applying this equation to our present example implies:

$$DEC \text{ gold futures} = JUN \text{ gold futures } (1 + C) \qquad 5.1$$

Dividing both sides of equation 5.1 by the right-hand side and subtracting 1, we have:

$$\frac{\text{DEC gold futures}}{\text{JUN gold futures } (1 + C)} - 1 = 0 \qquad\qquad 5.2$$

Equation 5.2 should hold in a full carry market, assuming that the market is perfect. Here also, we ignore all carrying costs except for the financing costs. We approximate the financing cost as the T-bill rate for the period June-December 1989.[2] We expect equation 5.2 to hold as an approximation using real data due to slight market imperfections and our imperfect estimate of the financing cost.

To make this computation more concrete, consider the gold data in Table 5.2 for October 13, 1988. Using the data from Table 5.2, the value in equation 5.2 is:

$$\frac{442.60}{426.00 \ (1.038132)} - 1 = .000804$$

While this value is close to zero, it does indicate that a trader with a total carrying cost equal to the estimated T-bill rate could make a profit from a cash-and-carry strategy. For a single ounce, the profit would be $.36:

$$\$442.60 - \$426.00 \ (1.038132) = \$.36$$

For a 100 ounce contract, the profit would be $36.00. This profit calculation ignores transaction costs and all other carrying costs except the estimated T-bill rate. Thus, it seems clear that these prices do not offer a genuine arbitrage opportunity.

We have used an estimate of the T-bill rate for this period of 7.7719%. We can also ask what repo rate these values imply. Once again, ignoring all other transaction costs and carrying costs, the implied repo rate is:

Table 5.2
Data for October 13, 1988

JUN 1989 futures price	$426.00
DEC futures price	442.60
T–bill rate (June–December 1989)	7.7719%
Half–year factor, (1 + C), for June–December 1989	1.038132

$$\frac{\$442.60}{\$426.00} = 1.038967$$

The implied half-year repo rate is 3.8967 percent. To put this in annual terms, we square the right-hand side and find that the implied repo rate is 7.9453 percent. This is 17 basis points (17 hundreths of 1 percent) above the T-bill rate. Therefore, if a trader's financing cost is below 7.9453 percent, he or she can engage in a cash-and-carry arbitrage. However, this financing cost is close to the T-bill rate, so few traders would have such a low borrowing rate. Further, this still does not include any other transaction or carrying costs aside from interest.

From this analysis of October 13, 1988, we can conclude that the gold market was very close to full carry on that day. What of other days? Figure 5.3 graphs the measure of equation 5.2 for March 14, 1988 to March 31, 1989. As the figure shows, all of the values are extremely close to zero, with every value being within one-half of one percent of zero. Also, there does not appear to be any particular bias in the price relationship. Some values lie above zero, while

Figure 5.3
Deviations from Full Carry for Gold

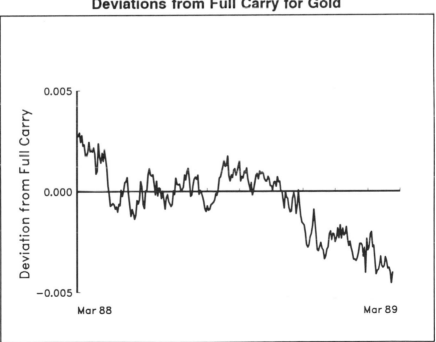

others lie below. For this period, gold behaves almost exactly as a full carry market. Other precious metals behave in a similar fashion, generally conforming to full carry. Thus, the June-December 1989 futures spread very closely conformed to full carry over the year-long period exhibited in Figure 5.3.

Departure from Full Carry—A Silver Example

We have seen that gold is generally a full carry market. The same is true for other precious metals such as silver, platinum, and palladium. However, disruptions can occur to throw the market out of the normal full carry relationship. This section briefly considers one historical example in the silver market.

In Chapter 2, we considered market manipulations and gave the Hunt silver manipulation of 1979-1980 as an example. During this period, the Hunts and their co-conspirators amassed enormous cash and futures positions in silver. When their long futures contracts came to delivery, they accepted delivery on many contracts, forcing the short silver traders to scramble to find physical silver that they could deliver. This urgent and immediate need for physical silver caused the price of nearby silver to rise relative to distant silver.

From our analysis of the gold spread, we can see that such a relative price rise in the nearby contract would cause the measure in equation 5.2 to go below zero. If the measure in equation 5.2 is less than zero, the market is below full carry, because the distant futures price is too low relative to the nearby price. If the market is below full carry, reverse cash-and-carry arbitrage strategies may become attractive. If short selling is possible, traders will borrow the good, sell it in the cash market, and buy futures. Later, they will accept delivery on the futures and use the good to repay the short seller. As we have also seen, the opportunity to sell short means that owners of the good do not derive a convenience value from holding the good. A market can trade below full carry If commercial interests have a need for the physical good as an input to their production processes, then a market can trade below full carry without introducing arbitrage opportunities.

In January 1980, the Hunt manipulation was at its peak and silver hit its all-time record price of $50 per ounce. Figure 5.4 shows our measure from equation 5.2 for the silver market from October 1, 1979 through June 30, 1980. (Data in Figure 5.4 are cash prices and the London Metals Exchange forward price.)[3] As the figure shows, the market fell far below full carry on some days. Most of these days occurred in January 1980, as the price of silver reached its peak and the manipulation was in full flower. These price relationships show that the nearby price of silver was extremely high relative to the more distant price. For most days, the market was below full carry, but still not in backwardation, because the distant price still exceeded the nearby price. On a few days, the cash price actually exceeded the forward price.

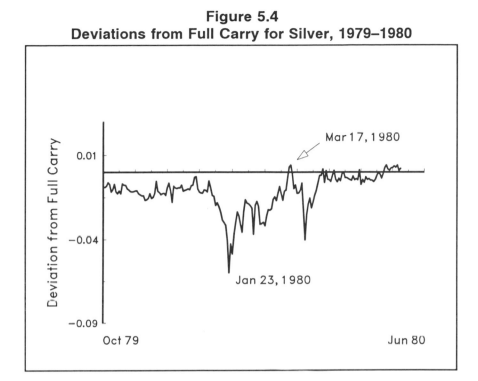

Figure 5.4
Deviations from Full Carry for Silver, 1979–1980

As an example of the disruption, assume that the cash price and the price for delivery in three months are both $40. Also, assume that the three-month cost-of-carry is 4 percent. A trader who owns silver could sell in the cash market and buy in the futures market. This would free $40 per ounce to invest over the next three months and earn 4 percent. For a trader who receives no convenience value from holding silver, this is a very attractive opportunity. In effect, it is a 4 percent quasi-arbitrage profit.

Clearly, any trader who did not derive a convenience value from holding silver should deliver silver to the market and buy the futures with these prices. Any speculator would be sure to do so, because the speculator does not derive a convenience yield; only a trader with a business need for the good can have a convenience yield. In spite of this strong incentive to deliver silver, the Hunt interests continued to hold huge quantities of silver and to acquire more. They took this action even though they had no apparent legitimate commercial use for the silver in the short run.

Other traders, who had no connection with the Hunts, also held silver during this period. What was their motivation? Some commercial firms, such as film manufacturers, needed silver for their production processes. They cannot deliver silver now and buy futures, because they need the silver now to manufacture film. In general, though, all traders who did not derive a convenience value, or who were not attempting to constrict the supply of silver, would be sure to deliver physical silver to the market in order to capture the quasi-arbitrage profit that was available. The fact that the market was so far below full carry indicates the extreme shortage of silver during this period. On Silver Thursday, March 27, 1980, the active phase of the manipulation ended and the market crashed. As Figure 5.4 shows, the silver market quickly returned to approximately full carry.

Commodities with Seasonal Production

In this section, we turn our attention to commodities that are produced seasonally. We also assume that consumption for these goods is fairly steady and that the goods store well. These commodities include those with harvests, such as wheat, corn, oats, barley, and soya products. The fact that new supplies of a commodity become available only periodically, and that the harvest is large relative to existing stocks, has important consequences for the pattern that the cash price of the commodity will follow. As we will see, because the harvest occurs at a certain time, cash prices often exhibit seasonal trends, with important implications for futures prices. In this section, we use several agricultural commodities to illustrate the essential features of pricing.

Inventories and Price Patterns

For commodities with seasonal production, the single most important factor in determining prices is the erratic availability of the commodity. Consider again our tropical fruit that can be harvested only one day a year and spoils in 24 hours. Such a product has bizarre inventory properties. Every day of the year, except for the harvest day, the world inventory is zero. On the harvest day, the fruit is widely available. Such a supply situation would have strong implications for the price of the fruit. On the harvest day, assume that the price is $.10. Although it would not be observable, the price of the fruit on any other day would be infinite; no matter what price is offered, no supply of the fruit would be forthcoming. In such a case, the price would fluctuate between infinity and $.10, the price movement coming on the day of harvest. Although there is no such commodity, this description emphasizes the importance of supply and sudden shifts in inventory for price determination.

Harvestable crops, such as wheat, are similar to the rare fruit, although they can be stored and the harvest is not instantaneous. To see how the harvest patterns of such crops affect their price patterns, we begin by making some simplifying assumptions. First, we assume that the long-term inventory is constant, and that production will equal consumption. This means that the carryover from one harvest to the next is constant. All of these values are assumed to be certain. Figure 5.5 depicts characteristics of such a commodity. In the figure, the top panel shows how the inventory will behave over time. The graph starts at the time of the first harvest, so the inventory is high. Over the crop year, inventory falls due to consumption. This drop continues until the second harvest, and so on. The second panel shows the likely pattern of cash prices. At harvest, cash prices are likely to be low, because there is a glut of the commodity. As the crop year progresses, nothing is added to inventories because the harvest is over. However, continuing consumption causes inventories to drop and cash prices are likely to rise. In the second graph of Figure 5.5, prices rise until the next harvest, when the good is plentiful again.

The third graph in Figure 5.5 shows possible futures prices for two different futures contracts. Both lines are flat, reflecting steady futures prices over the crop year. The top line is a price for a contract that matures just before the fourth harvest. Just before the harvest, the cash price is high, so the futures price should be high as well. The second line is for a futures that matures just after the second harvest. At this time, prices should be low, so the futures price is low over its life. In fact, the two futures prices match the cash price that will prevail when the futures mature.

Figure 5.5 also shows a very important fact about **basis**, the difference between the cash and futures price. Recall that the inventories and price patterns are all presented under conditions of certainty. With certainty, the futures prices must remain constant, with the cash prices fluctuating in accordance with supply. This means that the basis must fluctuate as shown in Figure 5.6. The graph of the basis in Figure 5.6 is consistent with the price patterns of Figure 5.5. Because the cash price is at the same level just prior to each harvest, and because the basis must be zero when the futures contract matures just before the fourth harvest, the basis must be zero or negative over the entire period. A fluctuating basis is often interpreted as a sign of high risk and unstable prices. In this example, there is no risk, since certainty has been assumed. This shows that the basis may fluctuate radically even under conditions of certainty. While a fluctuating basis often signals high risk, this is not always the case. It is important to separate fluctuations in the basis into the expected and unexpected components.[4]

Wheat and Wheat Futures

Wheat is an extremely important crop with a seasonal harvest and good storage characteristics. Of course, wheat does not perfectly meet the simplified conditions of the preceding analysis. Wheat cannot be stored forever, and the harvest is uncertain and extends over time. Examining the characteristics of prices for

Figure 5.5
Inventory and Prices for a Good with Seasonal Production

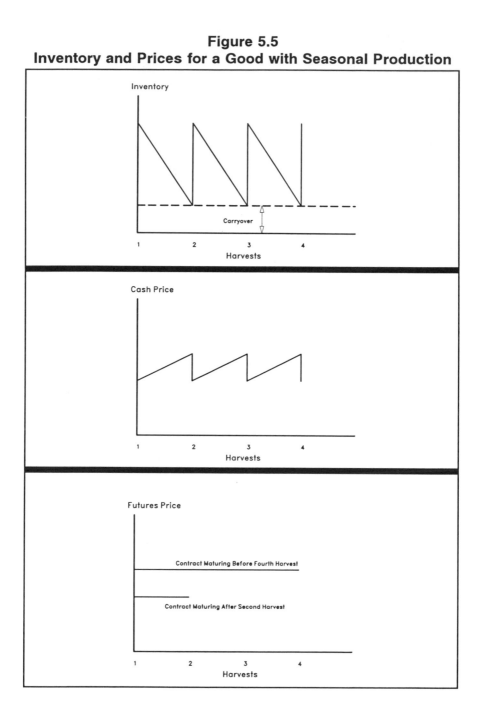

Figure 5.6
The Basis for a Good with Seasonal Production

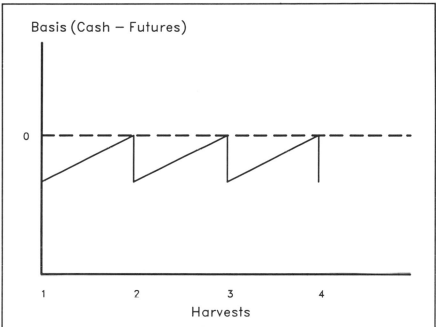

wheat, since it fits our model imperfectly, gives some idea of how sound the preceding way of thinking may be. If the preceding analysis is to be useful for wheat, then wheat should exhibit several important tendencies. First, there should be a seasonal pattern to cash wheat prices. We expect wheat prices to be low in the summer, when wheat is being harvested.

There are numerous varieties of wheat with different growing characteristics and different harvest times.[5] The harvest of winter wheat begins in late May in the southernmost region of the wheat belt and continues through mid-July. Farmers harvest spring wheat in August and September. In addition to the fact that the U.S. wheat harvest covers such an extended period, there are important wheat producers below the equator, such as Argentina, so wheat continually comes to market.

In spite of this continuous worldwide supply of wheat, the seasonal factor in the availability of wheat in the United States is very strong. Figure 5.7 shows the seasonal character of cash wheat prices. This graph presents the average cash price of wheat for each trading day over the 1960–1989 period. As the graph shows, wheat prices tend to be high in winter and low in summer. Table 5.3 presents the average stock of wheat in the United States by month for the crop

Figure 5.7
The Seasonal Character of Cash Wheat Prices

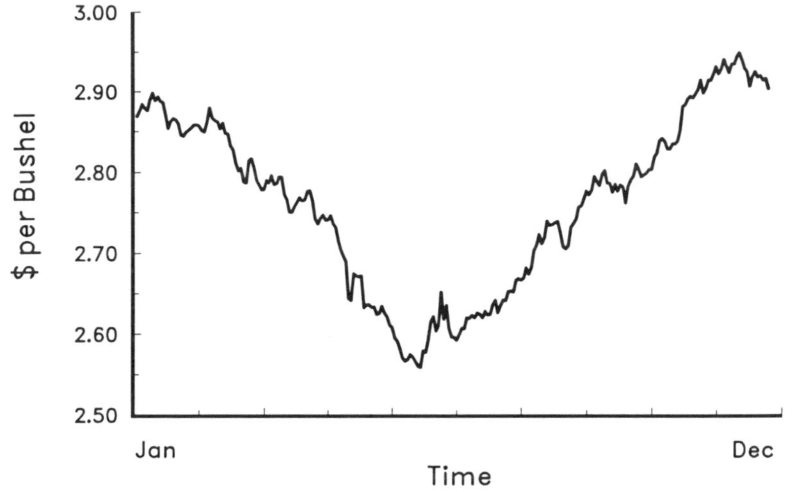

Table 5.3
Average U.S. Wheat Stocks, 1969–1982 Crop Yields

Month	Stock (millions of bushels)	Percentage Change (from preceding month)
June	187.78	−9.40%
July	246.37	31.20
August	338.65	37.46
September	380.19	12.27
October	398.40	4.79
November	379.40	−4.77
December	346.41	−8.70
January	314.28	−9.28
February	284.21	−9.57
March	257.42	−9.43
April	236.14	−8.27
May	205.44	−13.01

years 1969–1982. (The U.S. Department of Agriculture defines the wheat crop year as running from June 1 to May 31.) In June, the carryover from the preceding harvest is nearly depleted, but the new harvest is just becoming available. The stock of wheat continues to grow over the harvest period, reaches its greatest level in October, and then begins to decline again. Notice that the largest surge in the wheat stock occurs in July and August, with an increases of 31 to 38 percent.

According to this reasoning, the increase in supply should cause a drop in price, other factors held constant. Table 5.4 shows the seasonal character of cash wheat prices. Over the period 1892–1990, the table shows the months in which the high and low cash prices for the year occurred. The strongest regularity to be noted is that 43 of the 99 lowest prices occurred in the months of July and August. These months correspond, of course, to the months with the greatest percentage increase in wheat stocks. The highest prices had a similarly strong tendency to occur in December and January, when wheat stocks were low. These results confirm the view that cash prices should be high when inventories are low and that prices should be low when inventories are high.

Table 5.5 shows the distribution of high and low futures prices for the May contract traded at the CBT over the 28 years from 1963–1990. There are several

Table 5.4
Months in Which High and Low Cash Wheat Prices for the Year Occurred, 1892–1990

Data are for calendar years for #2 Winter Wheat.

Month	Number of Highs	Number of Lows
June	3	10
July	3	21
August	1	22
September	7	4
October	4	6
November	9	8
December	19	2
January	18	9
February	9	5
March	8	3
April	9	6
May	10	3

Source: Chicago Board of Trade, *Statistical Annual*, 1981, p. 251; 1985, p. 568; computerized data bank.

Table 5.5
Months in Which High and Low Wheat Futures Prices for the Year Occurred, 1963–1990

Data are for the CBT May contract.

Month	Number of Highs	Number of Lows
June	6	5
July	1	5
August	2	2
September	1	1
October	2	1
November	1	0
December	1	0
January	1	0
February	2	2
March	1	3
April	3	1
May	7	8

Source: Chicago Board of Trade, *Statistical Annual*, 1981, p. 251; 1985, p. 568; computerized data bank.

striking features of these data. First, there is a tendency for many extreme prices, both high and low, to be found in May and June. This is not surprising, because virtually nothing is known about next year's crop, considering that the contract will not be maturing for almost a full year. Therefore, the futures price may be either far above or far below the unknown cash price that will eventually prevail. The large number of highs and lows in these months reflects the large forecasting errors in futures prices when the expiration is distant. In Table 5.5, however, we do not find a tendency for high prices to occur in one month and low prices to cluster in some other time period. Thus, we see that cash prices can be seasonal, while futures prices for the same commodity are not.

Further interesting evidence on the behavior of futures prices is provided by Telser's classic study of wheat and cotton futures. Telser studied the behavior of wheat futures prices over the period 1927-1954, omitting the war years. Table 5.6 presents a portion of his results. As the table shows, Telser segregated these years into groups when the cash price of wheat rose, fell, or remained stable. He then examined the futures prices for these separate periods, noting the number of months when futures prices rose or fell. Over the entire period, futures prices rose about as often as they fell. But in periods of rising cash prices, futures prices tended to rise; when cash prices were falling, so were futures prices.

Table 5.6
Telser's Wheat Futures Results, 1927–1941 and 1946–1954

	Number of Months Futures Rose	Number of Months Futures Fell
Years of Falling Cash Prices	19	42
Years of Stable Cash Prices	45	56
Years of Rising Cash Prices	52	32
Total	116 (47.15%)	130 (52.85%)

Such a phenomenon could be due to two factors. First, there could be seasonal trends in futures prices. Second, new information that caused the cash price to change could have also caused the futures price to change. Of these two explanations, the second is more reasonable. The seasonal pattern of cash wheat prices is well known and should be anticipated by the market. The fact that futures prices moved in the opposite direction from cash prices over one-third of the time (35.17 percent), in conjunction with what has already been observed about the distribution of high and low futures prices, supports a conclusion stated by Telser: "The futures data offer no evidence to contradict the simple . . . hypothesis that the futures price is an unbiased estimate of the expected spot price."[6] As argued in Chapter 3, if futures prices provide unbiased estimates of expected future spot prices and if no new information reaches the market, the futures prices should neither rise nor fall over the life of a contract. On the whole, this is a fair interpretation of the movement of wheat futures prices.

Wheat and the Cost–of–Carry Model

In our analysis of gold as a full carry market, we saw that the spread between the JUN 1989 and DEC 1989 gold futures contracts was almost fully explained by the cost of financing gold from the nearby delivery to the distant futures delivery date. Given the characteristics of wheat, we expect wheat price relationships to differ substantially from the full carry behavior of gold.

First, wheat production is seasonal. Even if the harvest were known well in advance, wheat would still be abundant after harvest and scarce later. Second, the harvest is not known in advance, so shortages or surpluses of wheat can develop. For example, the drought of 1988 caused a general surge in prices as market observers began to anticipate shortages. In general, then, we would not expect wheat to behave as a full carry market in all circumstances. Supply is too variable for that to be a normal event.

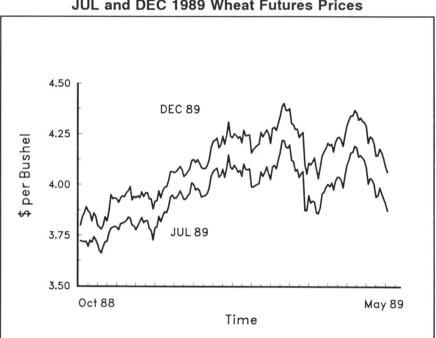

Figure 5.8
JUL and DEC 1989 Wheat Futures Prices

We now examine futures prices for the JUL and DEC 1989 contracts. This will allow a close comparison with our gold analysis which covered almost exactly the same period. Figure 5.8 shows prices for both contracts. In general, they seem to move closely together. However, the spread between the two prices is not as constant as we might expect.

Figure 5.9 shows the deviations from full carry between the two contracts by graphing the value of equation 5.2. Remember that this value considers an estimate of the interest cost as the sole cost of carrying the good forward. In Figure 5.9, we notice two important features. First, compared with the graph for gold, the deviations from full carry are much larger. For wheat, they are about four times as large as the deviations we noted for gold. Second, there is a strong trend in the deviations from full carry for wheat. By contrast, gold was almost always at full carry. The wheat market is first below full carry and then later above full carry.

In the early period, starting with October 1988, the wheat market appears to be below full carry. This implies that the nearby price is high relative to the distant price. As we have seen, when the nearby price is relatively high, the market is expressing an unusual demand for immediate wheat. For late 1988 and

Figure 5.9
Deviations from Full Carry for Wheat

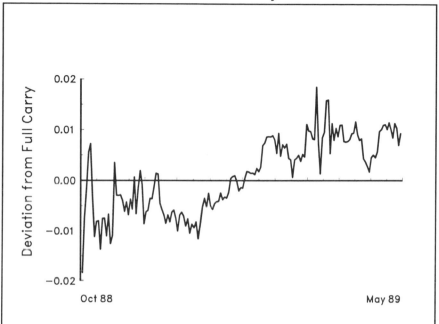

early 1989, the market still reflected the poor 1988 harvest. The shortfall in the harvest probably gave a strong convenience value to wheat.

Later in the period, our computed measure in Figure 5.9 exceeds zero, implying that the DEC price exceeds the JUL price by more than the financing cost of carrying the wheat from July to December. This appears to invite cash-and-carry arbitrage. For gold, the distant futures never exceeded the nearby futures plus the financing cost. For wheat compared to gold, storage, insurance, and transportation are more significant carrying costs. In the gold market, we found that the interest rate alone almost perfectly accounted for the difference between futures prices for two different gold maturities. This is not the case for wheat. In Figure 5.9, the maximum value is about 2 percent. Thus, if storing, transporting, and insuring wheat cost just 0.004 of the wheat's value per month, the market would not be above full carry. For example, if wheat is $4.00 per bushel, and Figure 5.9 shows that the market is 2 percent above full carry, we could engage in a cash-and-carry arbitrage if we could store, insure, and transport wheat for $.016 per bushel per month or less between July and December. This would mean that our cost-of-carry was less than $.16 per month.

From this discussion, we draw three conclusions. First, wheat cash prices are seasonal, due to fluctuating supply and surprises about the harvest. Second, the spread between two futures maturities can vary in a systematic way, due to seasonal factors. Third, in evaluating whether a market is at full carry, we need to include storage, insurance, and transportation costs, as well as the financing cost of the wheat itself.

Commodities with Seasonal Consumption

The seasonal production of many foodstuffs causes commodities to deviate from the strict price patterns of cash-and-carry markets that we found to prevail for gold. The fluctuating stock of these commodities can create shortages and give a convenience value to certain commodities at specific times. In this section, we show that seasonal consumption patterns can produce a similar effect. In general, the convenience value attached to a commodity stems from an imbalance in supply and demand at a given time. This imbalance can result from seasonal production, or from seasonal demand.

Oil and related products provide a clear example of a good with fairly steady production, but highly seasonal demand. We noted in Chapter 3 that demand for gasoline is relatively high in summer and demand for heating oil is relatively high in winter. Because both derive from crude oil, we expect seasonal patterns to emerge for all three oil-related commodities.

Unlike an agricultural crop with a specific harvest time, oil can be produced continuously. At one level, there is little incentive to pump oil unless it can be sold readily. If supply lines are open and functioning freely, there will normally be little incentive to store oil above ground. However, some users of oil will want to store oil against possible disruptions in supply. For such users, holding the physical oil can provide a convenience value.

Until the Iraqi invasion of Kuwait in the summer of 1990, the world oil supply had been in a glut for some time. Thus, there was little incentive to store oil. Seasonal factors might cause a premium for certain types of oil products, but that premium could attach to refining capacity rather than to the need for crude oil itself. Thus, in summer, demand for gasoline might strain refining capacity, even if crude oil is plentiful. The presence of these different factors means that crude oil futures sometimes are at full carry, while at other times, crude oil can have a substantial convenience yield or the market can even be in backwardation. Table 5.7 presents crude oil futures prices for the same date for seven different years.

Table 5.7 shows virtually every possible price pattern. For 1984 and 1985, the price dips and then rises. For these years, the JUN and SEP prices are in

Table 5.7
Crude Oil Futures Prices for March 21 of Various Years

Expiration Month	Contract Expiration Year						
	1984	1985	1986	1987	1988	1989	1990
JUN	30.32	27.76	14.17	18.08	16.19	19.49	19.28
SEP	30.20	27.05	14.60	17.62	16.05	18.45	20.44
DEC	30.28	27.15	15.01	17.57	15.99	17.75	20.44

backwardation and the SEP and DEC prices are below full carry. The 1986 prices approximate full carry, with an implied repo rate between the June and September contracts exceeding 12 percent. For the years 1987–1989, the market was in strict backwardation. From these data, which are fairly representative of price relationships in the crude oil market, we can see that crude oil is very seldom at full carry. Instead of being dominated by storage, varying supply and expectations of future price appear to dominate the price formation process.

Commodities with Poor Storability

In this section, we consider commodities that store poorly. To some extent, we have already examined goods with limited storage. Grains and oilseeds cannot be stored forever, and their high bulk relative to the value of the goods makes it undesirable to store them for long periods in any case. Like foodstuffs, oil is costly to store relative to the value of the product. However, in this section, we want to consider a more extreme case. Our continuing tropical fruit example provides a paradigm case of a good that cannot be stored. Futures contracts do not trade on such goods, which is not surprising. However, futures contracts are written on live animals, and these animals resemble our tropical fruit in some respects.

For example, live cattle must have an average weight between 1,050 and 1,200 pounds at delivery. If cattle are held too long, they cannot be delivered in fulfillment of the contract. The feeder cattle contract specifies cattle that weigh between 600–800 pounds. However, the feeder cattle contract is not settled by actual delivery. Instead, it uses a **cash settlement** technique. At expiration, the final day's settlement price is set equal to the cash price. This forces the futures contract to converge to the cash price and it avoids expensive or cumbersome actual delivery. With cash settlement, it is obviously impossible to engage in actual cash–and–carry strategies, because the physical good cannot be delivered

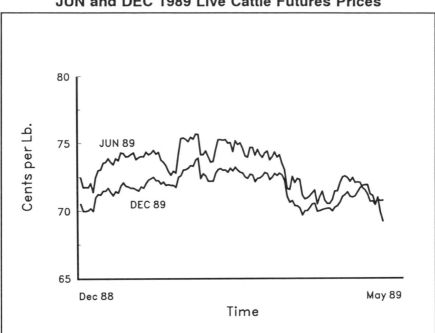

Figure 5.10
JUN and DEC 1989 Live Cattle Futures Prices

to fulfill the futures contract. However, the cash-and-carry trader can simply offset the futures position.

Difficult storage conditions loosen the no-arbitrage connection between futures contracts with different expirations. Figure 5.10 graphs the JUN and DEC 1989 live cattle futures prices. As this graph shows, there is little chance that live cattle adhere to the cash-and-carry strictures. Figure 5.11 presents our familiar measure of full carry. Over the period in Figures 5.10 and 5.11, December 1, 1988-May 25, 1989, the market was below full carry and the price relationship was quite volatile. In markets such as those for cattle, the Cost-of-Carry Model tells us relatively little about what price relationships to actually expect. This is not to say that the prices violate the Cost-of-Carry Model. Instead, the Cost-of-Carry Model does not apply very well. First, the no-arbitrage links that form the heart of the Cost-of-Carry Model break down. If storage is difficult or if short selling is impossible, the Cost-of-Carry Model does not constrain prices to a very considerable degree. As a result, we find prices alternatively at, above, or below full carry.

Figure 5.11
Deviations from Full Carry for Live Cattle

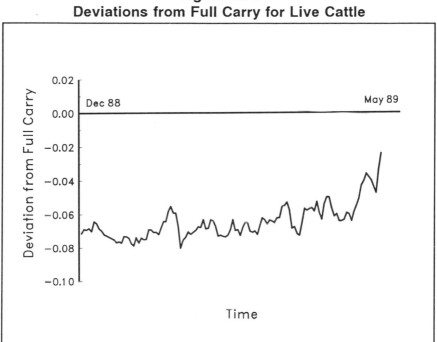

Bull and Bear
Intra-Commodity Spreads

A **bull spread** is an intra-commodity spread designed to profit if the price of the underlying commodity rises. A **bear spread** is an intra-commodity spread designed to profit if the price of the underlying commodity falls. Every intra-commodity spread involves being long one contract maturity and short another. (Of course, even more complicated spreads can have additional contracts, but every intra-commodity spread must have at least two contracts.) In this section, we want to explore some of the conventional rules for determining how to construct bull and bear spreads. To begin, let us consider the basic Cost-of-Carry Model relationship for a full carry market with perfect markets. Under these conditions, the relationship originally given by equation 3.6 is:

$$F_{0,d} = F_{0,n}(1 + C), \qquad d > n$$

Assuming that the carrying cost is constant, an increase in the nearby futures price, $F_{0,n}$, implies that the price of the distant futures, $F_{0,d}$, must rise even more. If it did not, the equation would not hold. Therefore, we can see that the bull spread for a full carry commodity will require the trader to be long the distant contract and short the nearby contract.

As an example, let us consider gold, because we have already seen that the gold market is usually at full carry. We consider the spread between the June and December 1989 contracts. For the time when both contracts were listed, gold was near its peak at the beginning of June 1988. The price of gold fell for the next eight months. Table 5.8 presents the gold futures prices and the gold spread for two dates, June 2, 1988 and February 10, 1989. As the table shows, prices fell substantially over this period. In the last column of the table, we see that the spread also fell. This is a normal relationship for a full carry commodity.

For the same pair of gold contracts, the price of the nearby contract and the spread both changed on a total of 146 days. Of these 146 days, the spread increased when the nearby price rose or the spread narrowed when the nearby price fell on 109 days. These 109 days were in accordance with our expectations. For 37 days the spread widened when the nearby futures price fell or the spread narrowed when the nearby futures price rose.

As a final illustration for these two commodities, we estimated the following regression for daily data on the same two gold contracts:

$$\text{Change in spread} = \alpha + \beta \text{ Change in nearby futures price} + \varepsilon \qquad 5.3$$

The estimated β was .043 with a t-statistic of 11.4 and an $R^2 = .33$. This regression supports the conclusion that the spread should widen as prices rise and narrow as prices fall. Thus the bull spread in gold is to be short the nearby contract and long the distant contract.

For commodities that do not trade in a full carry market, the bull spread need not require a short nearby/long futures position. We have already seen that copper does not trade in a full carry market, due perhaps to higher storage costs and small supplies. Therefore, the bull spread in copper might not be short the nearby and long the distant contract. To illustrate the difference, we examined

Table 5.8
Gold Futures Prices and the Spread

Date	JUN 1989 Futures	DEC 1989 Futures	Spread (DEC–JUN)
June 2, 1988	497.90	516.50	18.6
Feb. 10, 1989	396.60	412.90	16.3

data on the JUL and DEC 1989 copper contract. For these two contracts, there were 248 common days when the spread changed. On 80 of these 248 days, the spread widened when prices rose, or the spread narrowed when prices fell. On 168 days, the spread closed when prices rose, or the spread widened when prices fell. In other words, this is exactly the opposite relationship than the pattern followed by gold.

For copper, we also estimated the regression of equation 5.3. For this estimated equation, $\beta = -.21143$, with a t-statistic of -13.6 and an $R^2 = .35$. Thus, for our copper data, rising copper prices were accompanied by a narrowing spread. This is the opposite of our gold results and exactly opposite of the relationship implied by the Cost-of-Carry Model.

Changes in Spreads and Changes in Prices

Full carry markets	If the commodity price rises, the distant futures price rises more than the nearby futures price.
Non–full carry markets	If the commodity price rises, the nearby futures price rises more than the distant futures price.

Table 5.9 lists commodities that follow each type of relationship. In general, commodities that trade in full carry markets have the bull spread as long distant and short nearby. We have seen why this spread relationship must hold in a full carry market. For a commodity without substantial supplies, such as copper, a futures price rise is likely to result from new information about supply and demand. With stocks being scarce, the nearby contract is likely to change more. With a longer horizon, new stocks can be brought into place, so the price of the distant futures expiration does not change as much as the nearby futures price.

Table 5.9
Bull and Bear Intra–Commodity Spreads

Bull Spread	Bear Spread	Commodities
Short nearby Long distant	Long nearby Short distant	**Full Carry Markets** Gold, silver, platinum, palladium, financials.
Long nearby Short distant	Short nearby Long distant	**Non-Full Carry Markets** Cocoa, copper, wheat, corn, oats, orange juice, plywood, pork bellies, soybeans, soymeal, soyoil, sugar.

Therefore, if the nearby futures price rises substantially and the distant futures price rises only a little, we will have shrinking spreads when prices rise. Thus, in Table 5.9 the difference between full carry and non-full carry markets generates difference in spread price behavior.

Inter–Commodity Spread Relationships

In this chapter, we have been exploring the links between futures contracts on the same underlying commodity. Essentially, we have seen that the Cost-of-Carry Model establishes these links. In this section, we want to consider several important spread relationships between related commodities. Consequently, we examine spread relationships in the soy complex, the energy market, and the livestock market.

Soybeans and the Crush

Soybeans are a major source of protein, and the United States is a major producer. Most years, U.S. production is about 40-50 percent of the world's total. Yet no one eats soybeans, at least not as beans. Soybeans must be crushed to yield edible soymeal and soyoil. A 60-pound bushel of soybeans produces about 48 pounds of soymeal and 11 pounds of soyoil, leaving about one pound of waste hulls. The difference in value between a bushel of soybeans and the resulting meal and oil is the **crush margin**. Falling crush margins often stimulate export of beans, particularly to Western Europe, where the crush margin may be more favorable. While production costs tend to keep the crush margin uniform, demand for final soya products is highly variable and causes the crush margin to fluctuate quite radically. Futures contracts trade on soybeans, soymeal, and soyoil at the Chicago Board of Trade. However, the quantities per contract differ markedly, as Table 5.10 shows.

Table 5.10
Soy Contract Quantities

Contract	Quantity per Contract	Method of Price Quotation
Soybeans	5,000 bushels	$ per bushel
Soymeal	100 tons	$ per ton
Soyoil	60,000 pounds	cents per lb.

Crushing one 5,000 bushel contract of beans yields about 120 tons of soymeal. This is about 1.2 meal contracts. Also, a bushel of beans yields about 11 pounds of oil, so a bean contract generates 55,000 pounds of oil, or about 92 percent of a soyoil contract. As a useful approximation in the trade, crushers figure that crushing 10 contracts of soybeans will produce about 12 contracts of soymeal and 9 contracts of soyoil:

$$10 \text{ contracts} \times 5,000 \text{ bushels} \approx 2,400,000 \text{ lbs. of meal} + 550,000 \text{ lbs. of oil}$$

$$\approx 12 \text{ contracts of meal} + 9 \text{ contracts of oil}$$

In normal conditions, the value of the meal plus the oil must exceed the value of the soybeans. Otherwise, there would be no incentive to grow and crush soybeans. Thus, we expect the crush margin to be positive. However, the margin will fluctuate. Consider the prices for beans, meal, and oil given in Table 5.11. These are prices for three different dates that we will use to give examples of soybean crush spreads.

Crush and Reverse Crush Soybean Spreads

Crush Spread	Long soybeans of one expiration; short soymeal and soyoil for the next expiration.
Reverse Crush Spread	Short soybeans of one expiration; long soymeal and soyoil for the next expiration.

Assuming that today is August 4, 1988, a speculator believes that the crush margin is too small. That is, the speculator believes that by buying beans and selling the combined meal and oil positions, it will be possible to make money.

Table 5.11
Soy Futures Prices

	August 4, 1988	November 14, 1988	December 19, 1988
JUL 89 Beans ($ per bushel)	8.6600	7.8525	8.1700
SEP 89 Meal ($ per ton)	232.5000	232.0000	232.0000
SEP 89 Oil ($ per lb.)	0.2665	0.2442	0.2495

Table 5.12
A Soybean Crush Speculation

Date	Futures Market
August 4, 1988	Buy 10 JUL 89 bean contracts at $8.66 per bushel Sell 12 SEP 89 meal contracts at $232.50 per ton Sell 9 SEP 89 oil contracts at $.2665 per lb.
November 14, 1988	Sell 10 JUL 89 bean contracts at $7.8525 per bushel Buy 12 SEP 89 meal contracts at $232 per ton Buy 9 SEP 89 oil contracts at $.2442 per lb.

Profit/Loss:

Beans: $10 \times 5,000 \times (-\$8.66 + \$7.8525) = -\$40,375$
Meal: $12 \times 100 \times (\$232.50 - \$232) = \$600$
Oil: $9 \times 60,000 \times (\$.2665 - .2442) = \$12,042$

Total Loss: −$27,733

Notice that the soybean contract is for July, while the other contracts are for a September expiration. This two-month interval will allow for crushing the beans. Acting on his belief, the speculator decides to buy ten bean contracts and sell 12 meal contracts along with selling nine oil contracts. Table 5.12 details his transactions.

In Table 5.12 the trader buys JUL beans and sells the corresponding number of SEP meal and oil contracts. Prices quickly move against the trader. By November 14, the trader's speculation is totally under water, as the prices in Table 5.11 reveal. The trader offsets all of the contracts as shown on November 14 in Table 5.12. Total losses exceed $27,000. In this example, the trader was long and bean prices fell. The fall in bean prices need not have been problematic if meal and oil prices had fallen more. However, soymeal fell only $.50 per ton and soyoil fell less than $.03 per pound. These falling prices generated profits of $600 and $12,042, respectively. However, these amounts were insufficient to offset the loss of more than $40,000 on the soybeans.

Not believing his bad luck, the crush trader wants to recoup his losses after exiting the market on November 14. Later that day, the same prices prevail. Perhaps the trend that caused his losses will continue, he reasons. Therefore, he decides to engage in a **reverse crush spread**—selling beans and buying meal and oil. Using the same expirations, the trader sells 10 bean contracts and buys 12 meal and 9 oil contracts. Table 5.11 shows the prices and Table 5.13 details his new transactions. Now the trader is short beans and long meal and oil. Bean prices begin to rise, generating losses on the bean position. If meal and oil rise

Table 5.13
A Soybean Reverse Crush Speculation

Date	Futures Market
November 14, 1988	Sell 10 JUL 89 bean contracts at $7.8525 per bushel Buy 12 SEP 89 meal contracts at $232 per ton Buy 9 SEP 89 oil contracts at $.2442 per lb.
December 12, 1988	Buy 10 JUL 89 bean contracts at $8.17 per bushel Sell 12 SEP 89 meal contracts at $232 per ton Sell 9 SEP 89 oil contracts at $.2495 per lb.

Profit/Loss:

Beans: $10 \times 5,000 \times (\$7.8525 - 8.17) = -\$15,875$
Meal: $12 \times 100 \times (\$232 - \$232) = 0$
Oil: $9 \times 60,000 \times (-\$.2442 + .2495) = \$2,862$

Total Loss: $-\$13,013$

enough, the trader can still have profits. However, over the next month, meal prices do not move at all and soyoil rises only slightly. By December 12, the trader has new losses. The soybean losses are $15,875 and these are not offset by gains on meal and oil. There is absolutely no gain on the meal, and the gain on the oil contracts is only $2,862. This leaves a net loss of $13,013.

Our unfortunate trader first lost on the crush spread from August 4 to November 14. He then lost on the reverse crush spread from November 14 to December 12. The trader was **whipsawed**—losing on both sides of two successive and opposite transactions. While most examples of speculation result in pleasant profits, let this example stand as an example of the losses that can just as easily happen.

Oil and the Crack

Crude oil is like the soybean, not very useful in its natural state, but capable of being transformed into very useful related products. To be useful, crude oil must be refined into other products, such as gasoline, heating oil, or propane. This refining process is known as **cracking**. Thus, as soybeans are crushed, crude oil is cracked. In the distilling process, crude oil is refined at higher temperatures to yield butane and propane. At even higher temperatures the crude yields naphtha, kerosene, and gas oil. Gas oil is then fed to a catalytic cracker or a hydrocracker to produce gasoline. Thus, the same crude oil can produce a variety of products depending on the techniques used to crack it. However, a given barrel of oil can only produce a certain amount of total product. The mix is variable, but the total output is a zero sum game.

Cracking patterns are largely governed by the season of the year. We have already noted that demand for gasoline is higher in summer, and demand for heating oil peaks in winter. Thus, refiners build gasoline inventories in the spring. In late summer and the fall, they change the mix to favor heating oil that will be in demand for winter.

The price relationship between crude oil and its refined products is known as the **crack spread**. There are several kinds of crack spreads. First, there is a crude oil/heating oil crack spread, a crude oil/gasoline crack spread, and other combinations based on multiple units of crude oil. To **buy a crack spread**, a trader buys the refined product and sells the crude. To **sell a crack spread**, the trader sells the refined product and buys the corresponding crude. Selling a crack spread is also known as a **reverse crack spread**. The most popular crack spreads are the 1:1 spreads between crude and heating oil or crude and gasoline.

Four Crack Spreads

Barrels of Crude Oil Input	Barrels of Refined Product Output
1 Crude Oil	1 Gasoline
1 Crude Oil	1 Heating Oil
2 Crude Oil	1 Gasoline and 1 Heating Oil
3 Crude Oil	2 Gasoline and 1 Heating Oil

Energy futures trade on the New York Mercantile Exchange (NYMEX). Well-established contracts include crude oil, heating oil, and gasoline. Table 5.14 summarizes the contract features for these goods. The NYMEX also trades a propane contract, but this contract presently has very low volume and open interest. Unlike many other commodities, the energy complex trades for future delivery in every month. The crude oil contract trades for the next eighteen months. Heating oil and gasoline trade for every month for fifteen consecutive

Table 5.14
Energy Complex Futures Contract Specifications

Commodity	Contract Quantity	Price Quotations	Grade
Crude Oil	1,000 barrels	$ per barrel	West Texas Intermediate
Heating Oil	42,000 gallons	$ per gallon	No. 2
Gasoline	42,000 gallons	$ per gallon	Unleaded

Figure 5.12
JUL 1990 Crude and Heating Oil Futures

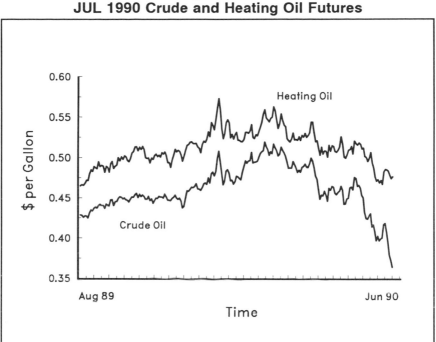

months. As Table 5.14 shows, a crude oil contract consists of 1,000 barrels, and the price is quoted in dollars per barrel. By contrast, the heating oil and gasoline contracts consist of 42,000 gallons, quoted in dollars per gallon. One barrel holds 42 gallons, so the physical quantities of all the contracts are the same. To justify refining, the refined product must be worth more than the crude oil. Figure 5.12 shows the prices of the July 1990 crude oil and heating oil futures, with heating oil lying above the crude oil price. Figure 5.13 shows the spread.

To explore the crack spread, we will consider a 1:1 crude oil/heating oil crack spread and reverse crack spread. Table 5.15 presents prices for crude oil, heating oil, and the crack for three dates. We begin with January 10, 1990. On this date, crude oil trades for about $.48 per gallon and heating oil is at $.5435. This gives a crack spread of $.0602 per gallon. Our trader believes that this differential is not sustainable. She thinks that the justifiable refining spread is only $.04 per gallon. Therefore, she expects the spread to narrow, and she decides to sell heating oil and buy crude oil. This is a reverse crack spread, because she sells the refined product and buys the crude oil. After this transaction, she will profit if the price of crude oil rises relative to the price of heating oil.

Figure 5.13
Spread between JUL 1990 Heating and Crude Oil Futures

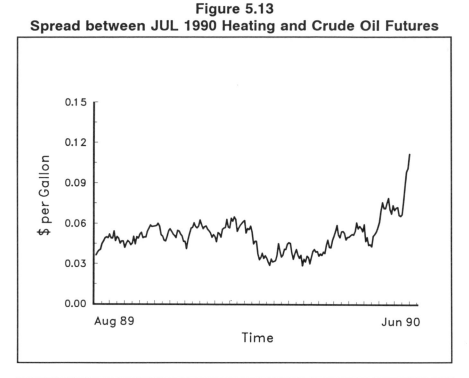

Table 5.15
Energy Complex Futures Prices

Date	Crude Oil ($ per gal.)	Heating Oil ($ per gal.)	Crack Heating Oil – Crude Oil
Jan. 10, 1990	.4833	.5435	.0602
March 13, 1990	.4876	.5193	.0317
May 24, 1990	.4245	.5006	.0761

Table 5.16 shows the transactions of January 10 in the top panel for a single contract. If the spread narrows from $.0602, each $.01 will generate $420, because the spread is for 42,000 gallons. Her view turns out to be correct, and the spread narrows over January and February 1990. By March 13, the spread is at $.0317. She believes this is too narrow. Therefore, she expects the spread to widen. Accordingly, she terminates her reverse crack spread by offsetting her

Table 5.16
A Reverse Crack Speculation

Date	Futures Market
January 10, 1990	Sell 1 JUL 90 heating oil contract at $.5435 per gallon. Buy 1 JUL 90 crude oil contract at $.4833 per gallon.
March 13, 1990	Buy 1 JUL 90 heating oil contract at $.5193 per gallon. Sell 1 JUL 90 crude oil contract at $.4876 per gallon.

Profit/Loss:

Heating Oil: 1 × 42,000 × ($.5435 − .5193) = $1,016.40
Crude Oil: 1 × 42,000 × ($.4876 − .4833) = $180.60

Total Gain: $1,197

two positions. These transactions appear in the bottom panel of Table 5.16. The spread has narrowed, as she anticipated. Crude oil has risen and heating oil has fallen. This gives a gain on both sides of the transaction, because she was long crude oil and short heating oil. As Table 5.16 shows, this gives a total profit of $1,197. This profit can also be calculated directly from the change in the crack spread. As Table 5.15 shows, the spread goes from $.0602 to $.0317. With a position of one contract, she has traded 42,000 gallons. Therefore, her profit is 42,000 × ($.0602 − .0317) = $1,197.

On March 13, 1990, our trader has reason to be satisfied. She believed that the justifiable crack spread was $.04 per gallon. She traded on that belief and profited. Now the crack is at $.0317, which she believes is too low. Proud from her recent success, she decides to increase the size of her position and now place a crack spread. The crack spread consists of buying the refined product and selling crude. Therefore, she enters the transactions shown in Table 5.17. On March 13, she buys 10 contracts of the spread, purchasing heating oil and selling crude. The crack is still .0317. Over the next two months, the spread widens as she had anticipated. By May 24, the crack is $.0761, so she decides to offset. The bottom panel of Table 5.17 shows her transactions on May 24.

With this trade she wins again. Over her holding period, the spread widened from $.0317 to $.0761 per gallon. With 10 contracts, this gave a total profit of 10 × 42,000 × ($.0761−.0317) = $18,648. She lost on one leg of the spread and profited on the other. She was long heating oil, but the price of heating oil fell, so lost $7,854 on that leg. For the crude oil leg, she was long, so the rising price of crude gave a profit. The crude oil profit more than offset the heating oil loss, giving an overall profit on the trade. Notice that her overall profit or loss depended only on the crack spread, not on the direction of oil prices in general.

Table 5.17
A Crack Speculation

Date	Futures Market
March 13, 1990	Buy 10 JUL 90 heating oil contracts at $.5193 per gallon Sell 10 JUL 90 crude oil contracts at $.4876 per gallon
May 24, 1990	Sell 10 JUL 90 heating oil contracts at $.5006 per gallon Buy 10 JUL 90 crude oil contracts at $.4245 per gallon

Profit/Loss:

Crude Oil: $10 \times 42,000 \times (\$.4876 - .4245) = \$26,502$
Heating Oil: $10 \times 42,000 \times (\$.5006 - .5193) = -\$7,854$

Total Gain: $18,648

Feeder Cattle and Live Cattle

We have seen that soybeans are not too useful as beans. If soybeans are not crushed, what can be done with them? Similarly, crude oil must be cracked to achieve maximum usefulness. Other goods, for which futures contracts are traded, can be transformed into some other good at the discretion of the owner. One prime (or choice?) example is the fact that young cattle can be transformed into more mature cattle by keeping and feeding them.

There are three distinct phases of producing fed cattle. First, the cow-calf stage covers the period from conception through weaning. Second, calves are raised for approximately one year on a ranch by a stocker-grower, where they are fed low-cost feeds such as forage crops and roughage. At this point, the cattle are feeder cattle and ready for the third stage. The third stage is a feed lot operation where cattle are confined and fed high cost feed, such as grain and protein concentrates. In the feed lot, the cattle grow and the quality of their meat improves. At the end of this process, the feeder cattle have become live cattle and are ready for slaughter.[7]

The CME trades contracts on both **feeder cattle** and **live cattle,** the younger and the more mature beef, respectively. The feed lot operator takes feeder cattle as inputs and produces live cattle. In effect, the feed lot operator carries feeder cattle forward, transforming them into live cattle by feeding them. This section briefly examines these two futures contracts for cattle as being representative of a commodity that is transformable and non-storable.

The dual contracts traded on cattle raise particularly interesting issues about storage and carrying charges in futures markets. Cattle meeting the feeder cattle contract specifications can be carried forward and delivered against the live cattle contract. Whereas wheat or soybeans might be stored and carried forward to deliver against another contract, they do not gain in value. By contrast, cattle gain in value because they gain weight as they mature. The decision to slaughter feeder cattle, or to carry them forward for delivery as live cattle, depends on the spread between the two futures contracts and the cost of feeding the cattle over the period represented by the spread on the two futures contracts.

Thus, feeder cattle might be held off the market and delivered later against the live cattle contract. The incentive to do so would depend upon the spreads in the prices between the two contracts. If the live steers would bring sufficiently more than the feeder cattle, then one could continue to feed the animals until they reached the weight range of live cattle. (Feeder cattle weigh about 700 pounds and live cattle generally weigh about 1,150 pounds.) Obviously, this possibility restricts the price spread between the two contracts. This kind of relationship is already familiar from the discussion of spreads in Chapters 3 and 4. In those earlier discussions, we noted that the restriction merely limited the amount by which a distant contract could diverge from the price of a nearby contract. The difference could not be sufficiently large to generate an arbitrage opportunity. But this relationship implied no minimum differential between the two contracts. After all, one cannot transform wheat that will be harvested in September into a deliverable commodity for the previous May contract. In other words, in this limited case, reverse cash–and–carry arbitrage is not possible.

This brings up an important difference between contracts, such as wheat and beef contracts. Under some circumstances, steers deliverable on a live cattle futures contract at one time might be deliverable against the feeder contract at an earlier time. If the spread between the feeder contract and the live cattle contract is too small, then it would indicate that a feed lot operator could not profit by continuing to feed the cattle up to the higher weight level. The calf that would be of sufficient weight for delivery against the live cattle contract might better be slaughtered when it has feeder weight. In a certain sense, this means that cattle that would be of live cattle size in the more distant future could be transformed into feeder cattle in the less distant future. Such an opportunity would help keep the spread between the feeder cattle contract and the live cattle contract from getting too small. If the spread is so small that it does not pay to keep feeding cattle, then they will be slaughtered earlier. More and more cattle will be slaughtered earlier, thereby reducing the distant supply of the larger live cattle, until the spread is sufficiently wide to make continued feeding profitable for the most efficient feeders.

In wheat, market forces exist to keep the spread between two contract maturities from getting too large. But with the two cattle contracts, the spread

Figure 5.14
A Time Line for Cattle Production

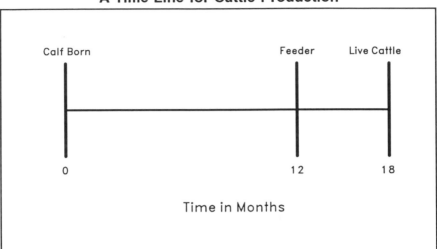

Calf Born   Feeder   Live Cattle

0   12   18

Time in Months

can be neither too large nor too small without calling forth corrective action from feed lot operators, as expressed by their decisions to slaughter or continue feeding younger cattle. Figure 5.14 makes this relationship more explicit by showing a time line for cattle production. If a calf is born at month 0, then it might be deliverable as a feeder at month 12. If kept on feed, then it might be deliverable as live cattle at month 18. Assume that the owner of the newborn calf sold two futures contracts for the calf, one for delivery as a feeder in 12 months, and one for delivery against the live cattle contract in 18 months. For this owner of the calf approaching its twelfth month, there is a basic choice. The owner may deliver the calf against the feeder contract, and offset the live cattle contract. Alternatively, he might offset the feeder contract, maintain the live cattle contract, and plan to deliver the 18 month steer against the live cattle contract when it matures. His decision will be motivated, to a large extent, by the profitability of keeping the cattle on feed from month 12 to month 18. This profitability, in turn, is largely a function of the cost of corn in this interval. As feed prices rise, the profitability of feeding is reduced, other things being equal. In such a case, we would expect the spread between the cash (or nearby futures) price of feeder cattle and the futures price for live cattle (to be delivered six to seven months later) to narrow as corn prices rise. With rising corn prices, holding feeder cattle off the market to mature is less and less attractive.[8] Thus, the cattle futures contract provides another example in which we cannot expect futures prices to be related by a simple application of the Cost-of-Carry Model.

Hedging

In Chapter 4, we considered the motivations for hedging and we explored the basic hedging strategies. In this section, we consider some more complicated strategies that are particular to agricultural and metallurgical markets. Essentially, these involve extensions and refinements of the risk-minimizing hedging approach introduced in Chapter 4. Specifically, we consider three cases: hedging different grades of oil, hedging wheat in multiple markets, and hedging soybeans with soybeans, soymeal, and soyoil futures.

Hedging Worldwide Crude Oil

At first glance, it seems that crude oil is uniformly crude. However, there are different kinds of crude oil originating around the world. We consider six types of oil, ranging from West Texas Intermediate (WTI) to oil from Dubai. While futures now trade on the International Petroleum Exchange for Brent oil and gas oil, the dominant world oil futures market is still the New York Mercantile Exchange, with its focus on West Texas Intermediate (WTI). (This section relies on an article by Gordon Gemmill.[9])

Types of Oil	
Designation	**Description**
WTI	West Texas Intermediate—Midland
Brent	North Sea oil
ANS	Alaskan North Slope oil
Forcados	Nigerian oil
Dubai	Arab light oil
Urals	Soviet oil

In Chapter 4, we saw that we could estimate risk-minimizing hedge ratios by regressing changes in the cash price of a good on changes in the futures price. The resulting β from the regression was the risk-minimizing hedge ratio for the data used in the analysis. The R^2 from the regression served as a measure of hedging effectiveness within the estimation period. The R^2 must fall between 0 and 1.0, and the closer the R^2 is to 1.0, the greater the hedging effectiveness.

Table 5.18 reports the volatility of the weekly price changes for the different oils and the results from two hedging strategies. In the first column of figures, we see that the standard deviation of the change in the price of a barrel of oil varied widely. ANS, WTI, and Brent were all highly volatile, while oil

Table 5.18
Results for Crude Oil Hedging

Oil	Weekly σ ($ per barrel)	R^2 1:1 Hedge	Risk–Minimizing Hedge Ratio	R^2 Risk Min. Hedge
WTI	.8407	.8462	.9991	.8462
Brent	.8238	.5779	.8272	.6042
ANS	.8433	.8284	.9961	.8285
Forcados	.7500	.5010	.7351	.5758
Dubai	.7049	.2959	.6227	.4676
Urals	.6699	.2553	.5956	.4738

Source: Gordon Gemmill, "Hedging Crude Oil: How Many Markets Are Needed in the World?" *The Review of Futures Markets*, 7, 1988, pp. 556–571.

from the Urals had a relatively low volatility. The second column of figures shows the effectiveness of hedging one barrel of spot oil with one barrel of oil in the futures market. The best results were found for hedging WTI spot oil. This is not surprising, because the NYMEX futures contract is based on West Texas Intermediate crude. This illustrates the general rule that hedging works best when the spot and futures instrument are most similar. Results for other types of oil were inferior. In the worst case, hedging oil from the Urals only reduced the price risk of a barrel of oil by about 25 percent.

Gemmill also computed the hedge ratio that would minimize the risk involved in holding a barrel of oil. Table 5.18 presents these hedge ratios as well. We may first notice that the risk-minimizing hedge ratio for WTI oil was almost exactly 1.0, indicating a 1:1 hedge ratio. The hedge ratio for ANS was almost as high. However, for all of the other types of oil, the risk-minimizing hedge ratio was substantially below 1.0. For example, to hedge Urals oil, one needed to trade only .60 barrels of futures for each barrel of spot oil. The final column of Table 5.18 shows the hedging effectiveness for the risk-minimizing hedge. For the WTI oil, the result is the same as a 1:1 hedge. This makes sense because the risk-minimizing hedge is also 1:1 (or at least almost so). By comparing the two columns of R^2s, we see the advantage of going from a naive 1:1 hedge to a risk-minimizing hedge. For WTI, the two hedge ratios were virtually identical, so there was no risk reduction. For other oils, finding the risk-minimizing hedge could increase hedging effectiveness substantially. For Urals oil, the 1:1 hedge eliminated about 26 percent of the risk. With the risk-minimizing hedge, 47 percent of the price risk of Urals oil could be hedged away.

Gemmill's results illustrate several hedging principles. First, finding a futures contract that closely matches the spot commodity is important and will generally improve the hedge considerably. Gemmill's results illustrate this principle, because the WTI hedge worked much better than any other. Second, for cross-hedges, the naive 1:1 hedging approach may be markedly inferior to using a risk-minimizing hedge ratio, although this is not always the case. For Dubai and Urals oil, the increase in hedging performance was the largest in moving from a naive to a risk-minimizing hedge ratio.

Finally, we must be careful in assessing hedging effectiveness. In all of the results in Table 5.18, the measures of hedging effectiveness are for the estimation period. That is, the same data were used to find the hedge ratio and to compute the R^2. Thus, if we estimate the hedge ratio today using historical data, the β and R^2 that we compute will be for our sample period. To hedge into the future, we will use our estimated β. However, we must expect that our hedging effectiveness will be lower on our future hedge than the R^2 we computed. This is almost certain to be the case, because regression analysis chooses the β that will maximize the R^2. Therefore, unless the future relationships are just like those in the past, we can expect the hedging effectiveness to fall as we go from our estimation data into the unknown future.

Hedging Wheat with Multiple Instruments

In Chapter 4, we considered that a risk-minimizing hedging strategy might use more than one type of futures to hedge. In this section, we illustrate such a strategy relying on an article by William W. Wilson.[10] While the Chicago Board of Trade dominates wheat futures trading in the United States, the Minneapolis and Kansas City exchanges also trade wheat futures. Contract terms differ, particularly with respect to the main type of wheat that can be delivered to fulfill the futures contract. The Minneapolis contract calls for Hard Red Spring wheat; the Kansas City contract specifies Hard Red Winter wheat; the Chicago Board of Trade contract focuses on Soft Red Winter wheat.[11] While Wilson considers each of the different kinds of cash wheat, we will focus on the hedging of Soft Red Winter wheat, but we will consider hedging the wheat with futures from three different exchanges.

Table 5.19 summarizes some of Wilson's results. In each case, we consider hedging cash market Soft Red Winter wheat with a futures contract from one or more of the U.S. futures exchanges. In each case, the hedges are estimated over a 26-week life, using a futures contract that expires in 6-10 months from the beginning of the hedging estimation period. In every case, we assume that we are hedging one contract of cash market wheat.

The first three rows of Table 5.19 consider hedging the cash wheat with a single futures contract. For example, using the Minneapolis wheat contract, the hedge ratio is -.69. The negative sign indicates selling, so the recommendation

Table 5.19
Hedging Wheat with Multiple Instruments

	Estimated Risk–Minimizing Hedge Ratio β			R^2 Hedging Effectiveness
	Minneapolis	Kansas City	Chicago	
1 Futures	−.69			.43
1 Futures		−.73		.46
1 Futures			−.67	.52
2 Futures	.69		−1.28	.55
3 Futures	.60	.25	−1.42	.55

Source: William W. Wilson, "Hedging Effectiveness of U.S. Wheat Futures Markets," *Review of Research in Futures Markets*, 3:1, 1984, pp. 64–79.

is to sell .69 futures contracts for each 5,000 bushels of cash market wheat. For Kansas City, the hedge ratio is −.73 and in Chicago the ratio is −.67. The hedging effectiveness is highest for the Chicago market. This is expected, because the cash market wheat is the same as the wheat that underlies the Chicago contract.[12] Notice also that the risk-minimizing hedge ratios all differ from 1.0. This is similar to the result Gemmill found in his crude oil hedging.

The last two rows of Table 5.19 consider hedging cash wheat with a combination of either two or three futures contracts. In the fourth row, cash market wheat is hedged against two markets. For the Soft Red Winter wheat, the best set of two markets is Chicago and Minneapolis. (It is natural for Chicago to be one, because the cash market wheat is the same as the wheat deliverable on the Chicago contract.) Notice that the Chicago hedge ratio now exceeds 1.0 in absolute magnitude. Thus, the risk-minimizing hedge is to sell 1.28 Chicago futures and buy .69 Minneapolis futures. With this strategy, the R^2 is .55. While the R^2 does not appear to have increased very much, from .52 to .55, the difference is statistically significant. This was generally the case in Wilson's study. Using two futures gave a statistically significant improvement in R^2 compared to using a single futures contract.

The final row of Table 5.19 shows the hedge ratios and hedging effectiveness for hedging cash market wheat with three different futures contracts. Now the risk-minimizing strategy is to sell 1.42 Chicago futures and buy .60 Minneapolis and .25 Kansas City contracts. The R^2 is still .55. Thus, for this example, hedging with three contracts rather than two does not materially increase the hedging effectiveness. (In some of Wilson's other results not shown here, hedging with three contracts was statistically superior to hedging with only two.) We note that a statistically significant increase in R^2 is not equivalent to an economically significant improvement.

Out–of–Sample Hedging Effectiveness

In our discussions of risk-minimizing hedging strategies, we have seen that the hedger estimates a hedge ratio on historical data using regression analysis. As we have noted, this technique finds the hedge ratio that would minimize risk, and identically maximize hedging effectiveness, during the estimation period. However, the hedger generally wants to apply the estimated hedge ratio to the future. The period used for the estimation is the in-sample period. A period that is not used for estimating the hedge ratio is an **out–of–sample period**. In this section, we present a simple case study of out-of-sample hedging effectiveness.

For this case study, we use data from 1989 for cash market soybeans and we consider strategies for hedging cash market soybeans with soybean, soymeal, and soyoil futures. Complete data for all variables were available for 194 trading days from March 28, 1989 until December 29, 1989. As we discussed earlier, the soybean contract is written for 5,000 bushels, the soymeal contract for 100 tons, and the soyoil contract for 60,000 pounds. To make these comparable, we express all terms on a dollar per contract basis and assume that we will hedge 5,000 bushels of cash market product. We divide the 194 days of price changes into an in-sample period of the first 100 days and an out-of-sample period of the last 94 days. We estimate our hedge ratios on the first 100 days, and we test hedging effectiveness with those hedge ratios on the final 94 days.

Table 5.20 summarizes the hedge ratios for a variety of hedging combinations within the estimation period. As an example of how to interpret the table, consider the first row. The risk-minimizing hedge ratio for hedging 5,000 bushels of cash soybeans is to sell .96 soybean futures contracts. (A negative

Table 5.20
In–Sample Hedge Ratio Estimates

Hedging Instruments	Beans	Meal	Oil	R^2
Only beans	−.96			.66
Only meal		−1.39		.51
Only oil			−2.17	.48
Beans and meal	−1.20	.45		.67
Beans and oil	−.76		−.73	.69
Meal and oil		−.93	−1.34	.64
Beans, meal, and oil	−.87	.18	−.68	.69

sign indicates a short position.) For hedging the cash product with soymeal alone, the hedge ratio is -1.39. This difference reflects the difference in the value of the contract size. For hedging with a single futures contract, soybean futures perform best. Compared to the R^2 for a hedge with soybean futures, adding a second contract does little. Even using all three commodity futures does not perform much better than soybean futures alone.

While the estimated hedge ratios in Table 5.20 may be important, the real test is the performance of the hedge in the out-of-sample period. We now investigate the performance of these hedge ratios in the latter part of 1989, our out-of-sample period. Table 5.21 summarizes the hedging results by showing the standard deviation and hedging effectiveness for each strategy for both the in-sample and out-of-sample periods. For 5,000 bushels of cash soybeans, we see that the daily standard deviation for the in-sample period was $620. For the second part of the year, our out-of-sample period, the standard deviation was $334. Thus, soybeans were substantially less volatile in the out-of-sample period. We will need to compare hedging strategies in relative terms to take account of the substantial difference in bean volatility between the two sub-periods.

The first column of figures shows the standard deviation for all of the hedging strategies. We see that hedging with soybean futures alone reduced the standard deviation from $620 to $360. This gave a hedging effectiveness of .66, which is shown in the in-sample effectiveness column.[13] For the in-sample strategies, soybean futures worked best among the single futures hedging strategies. For the multiple instrument hedges, a combination of bean and oil

Table 5.21
In–Sample and Out–of–Sample Hedging Effectiveness

Position	Standard Deviation $ per day		Effectiveness	
	In	Out	In	Out
Cash	620	334		
Cash − .96 Beans	360	240	.66	.48
Cash − 1.39 Meal	432	261	.51	.39
Cash − 2.17 Oil	446	302	.48	.18
Cash − 1.20 Bean + .45 Meal	356	246	.67	.46
Cash − .76 Bean − .73 Oil	345	252	.69	.43
Cash − .93 Meal − 1.34 Oil	373	265	.64	.37
Cash − .87 Bean + .18 Meal − .68 Oil	345	253	.69	.43

futures or a combination of bean, meal, and oil futures worked equally well, with a hedging effectiveness of .69.

The most important feature in Table 5.21 is the comparison of the last two columns, which show in-sample and out-of-sample hedging effectiveness. For every hedging strategy, there is a substantial drop in hedging effectiveness for the out-of-sample period. The best performing out-of-sample hedge is the simplest hedge with soybean futures alone. The hedges that work best in the out-of-sample period all include soybean futures. This suggests that simple hedges with a futures contract closely related to the cash market good may be most preferred.

Conclusion

This chapter focused on the relationship between the storage and production characteristics of commodities. We also considered the behavior of their cash and futures prices. The important conclusion of this analysis is that futures prices are rational; they clearly conform to the underlying economic realities specific to the characteristics of the deliverable goods. This is true for goods with quite varied storage and production characteristics, whether they be gold, wheat, soybeans, or cattle.

This rationality of futures prices has two very important implications. First, it indicates that participants in the futures markets for these commodities know the underlying goods and the factors that determine their prices. Second, it implies that potential speculators in futures contracts must be prepared to pit their knowledge of these goods against the collected wisdom of the other futures traders, as represented in the market-determined futures prices. One may still believe, and after all it may be true, that with so many diverse commodities, there must be opportunities for speculative profits for the discerning trader. In the next chapter, we turn our attention to a much more homogeneous commodity—money carried over time. In such a case, the lawlike relationships that have begun to appear here become even more apparent. These relationships have important implications for both speculation and hedging.

Questions and Problems

1. Some futures market experts have proposed a futures contract on computer memory chips. Do you think that prices on such a contract would follow the Cost-of-Carry Model closely? In other words, would the identifiable elements of the cost-of-carry explain most of the difference between spot

and futures prices? What factors would be important in determining whether the contract adhered to the Cost–of–Carry Model?

2. Consider a futures contract on common sand. What are the prospects for success for such a contract? Explain.

3. If there were a futures contract on sand, what would be the likely convenience yield of sand? Explain.

4. The Miami Fictional Futures Exchange contemplates a futures contract on poinciana blossoms, a beautiful but perishable flower found in south Florida. What factors are likely to determine the prices on such a futures and the relationship between spot and futures price?

5. Assume that a research lab announces that palladium can serve as a critical ingredient in nuclear fusion. Thus, palladium can be a key element in creating energy. If palladium futures follow the Cost–of–Carry Model normally, what reaction might you expect for prices of different futures expirations?

6. George Bush believes that high oil prices following the Iraqi invasion were due to speculative fever in the futures market. Assume that you have been retained as an apologist for the futures industry. What answer would you give? In other words, support the argument that such price jumps can be due to rational economic forces.

7. Explain the conditions under which the cash price of a commodity can exhibit seasonal patterns while the futures prices for the same commodity does not.

8. For an intra–commodity spread in a full carry good, explain why the bull spread is to be long the distant expiration and short the nearby expiration.

9. Consider the crack spread. Assume that you believe a major technological breakthrough will be announced soon that will show how to radically reduce the cost of oil refining. How would you trade energy futures to exploit this expectation?

10. Explain how to measure the hedging effectiveness of a risk-minimization hedging strategy. Be sure to contrast in-sample and out-of-sample measures of effectiveness.

Notes

1. We can compare the natural shortages caused by a harvest cycle to the artificial shortages induced by manipulation. Both events can increase the price of the cash commodity relative to the futures price, thereby driving the futures price below full carry.

2. For any given day, we extract the June–December 1989 forward rate from the June and September T-bill futures prices. Chapters 6–8 explain this concept more fully and show how to compute this rate of interest.

3. We use London Metal Exchange (LME) data to illustrate this relationship because the futures markets experienced limit days for almost every trading day in January 1980. The JAN contract did not face position limits, because it was in the delivery month. More distant contracts have price limits, and they hit the limits each day. Thus, a comparison between the unlimited JAN and the limited distant contract prices would not be meaningful. LME prices faced no such limits.

4. The distinction between expected and unexpected changes in the basis is extremely important for interest rate futures, as explained in Chapter 7.

5. For more on the characteristics of the wheat market, see the *Commodity Trading Manual*, Chicago: Chicago Board of Trade, 1989 and D. Morgan. *Merchants of Grain*, New York: Penguin Books, 1982.

6. See the following works, all reprinted in A. Peck, *Selected Writings on Futures Markets*, Chicago: Chicago Board of Trade, 1977; L. Telser, "Futures Trading and the Storage of Cotton and Wheat"; P. Cootner, "Returns to Speculators: Telser vs. Keynes"; R. Gray, "The Search for a Risk Premium"; and H. Working, "Financial Results of Speculative Holding of Wheat."

7. Paul Fackler of North Carolina State University helped clarify the operation of the cattle industry.

8. See R. Leuthold and W. Tomek, "Developments in the Livestock Futures Literature," and W. Purcell, D. Flood, and J. Plaxico, "Cash-Futures Interrelationships in Live Cattle: Causality, Variability, and Pricing

Processes," both in R. Leuthold and P. Dixon, *Livestock Futures Research Symposium,* Chicago: Chicago Mercantile Exchange, 1980; R. Leuthold, "The Price Performance on the Futures Market of a Nonstorable Commodity; Live Beef Cattle," *American Journal of Agricultural Economics,* 56:2, May 1974, pp. 271-279; J. Helmuth, "A Report on the Systematic Downward Bias in Live Cattle Futures Prices," *Journal of Futures Markets,* 1:3, Fall 1981, pp. 347-358; L. Palme and J. Graham, "The Systematic Downward Bias in Live Cattle Futures: An Evaluation," *Journal of Futures Markets,* 1:3, Fall 1981, pp. 359-366; and R. Kolb and G. Gay, "The Performance of Live Cattle Futures as Predictors of Subsequent Spot Prices," *Journal of Futures Markets,* 3:1, Spring 1983, pp. 55-63.

9. Gordon Gemmill, "Hedging Crude Oil: How Many Markets Are Needed in the World?" *The Review of Futures Markets,* 7, October 1988, pp. 556-571. The material has been adapted considerably.

10. William W. Wilson, "Hedging Effectiveness of U.S. Wheat Futures Markets," *Review of Research in Futures Markets,* 3:1, 1984, pp. 64-79.

11. For all of these contracts it is permitted to deliver a grade different than the grade specified in the contract. In addition, some contracts allow delivery of a different type of wheat as well. In each case, the exchange specifies price differentials for the various kinds of wheat that can be delivered.

12. Generally, the best technique is to hedge the specific cash market wheat at the futures market with a contract built around that variety of wheat. For example, to hedge Hard Red Spring wheat, the best futures is probably the Kansas City contract.

13. The measure of effectiveness is the percentage of the original cash market variance that was eliminated. For this first hedge, we compute it as follows:

$$1 - \left(\frac{\sigma_{\text{HEDGED}}}{\sigma_{\text{CASH}}} \right)^2 = 1 - \left(\frac{360}{620} \right)^2 = 0.6629$$

6
A Bond Primer

Introduction

In this chapter, we review some of the basic features of bond pricing and bond portfolio management. For many, the material of this chapter will be strictly review. However, because we make use of the concepts of bond pricing in Chapters 7 and 8, we review them here for convenience.

The chapter begins by considering alternative yield concepts and some of the instruments of the bond market that will be of special importance later. The chapter also reviews principles of bond price movements, duration, the term structure of interest rates, and bond portfolio immunization.

Yield Concepts

A **pure discount bond** is very simple in structure, yet very important in the debt market. For example, many money market instruments are pure discount bonds, such as Treasury bills. A pure discount bond promises to pay a certain amount at a specified time in the future and the instrument is sold for less than this promised future payment. Normally the promised future payment is the **par value** or **face value** of the bond. The difference between the par value and the selling price is the bond discount. For a pure discount bond there is no payment between the original issue of the bond and the maturity of the bond when it pays its face value.

Equation 6.1 gives the price of a pure discount bond:

$$P_i = \frac{C_m}{(1 + r_i)^t} \qquad \qquad 6.1$$

where:

P_i = the price of the bond i
C_m = the cash flow to be paid at the maturity of bond i at time m
r = the annualized yield to maturity on bond i
t = the time in years until the bond matures

As an example, consider a pure discount bond maturing in five years with a face value of $1,000. If the bond yields 12 percent, its price must be $567.43:

$$P = \frac{\$1,000}{(1.12)^5} = \$567.43$$

Even this simplest kind of bond exhibits all of the basic features of bond pricing. The promised cash, the price, and the yield are all related. The yield to maturity is the yield that the bond holder will realize if the promised payment is made. The riskier the promised payment, the higher must be the promised yield or expected return in order to induce investors to hold such bonds.

Most longer term bonds are **coupon bonds**, bonds making regularly scheduled payments between the original date of issue and the maturity date. Coupon bonds also pay the **par value** or **face value** upon maturity. The intervening payments are called **coupons** and are typically paid semi-annually. Equation 6.2 gives the general bond pricing formula for all bonds.

$$P_i = \sum_{t-1}^{M} \frac{C_t}{(1 + r_i)^t} \qquad \text{6.2}$$

where:

C_t = the cash flow from the bond at time t

As an example, consider a coupon bond that has a face value of $1,000, yields thirteen percent, pays a semi-annual coupon of $60, and matures in one year. Normally, the last coupon payment is made at maturity. On the maturity date, the bond will pay the face value amount plus the last coupon payment. With this information, we can apply the bond pricing formula as follows:

$$P = \$\frac{60}{1.065} + \frac{\$1,060}{1.065^2} = 56.34 + 934.56 = \$990.90$$

Notice that we divide the annual yield by 2.0 to reflect the semi-annual compounding.

Accrued Interest

One peculiarity of the bond market awaiting the unwary investor is the unusual way in which bond prices are quoted. For most bonds, the bond price does not reflect the actual price that a purchaser must pay. Instead, the bond costs the quoted price plus the **accrued interest**—the portion of the next coupon payment that has been earned at the time of purchase. As an example, consider a bond paying a $100 semi-annual coupon with a face value of $1,000. At maturity the bond will pay $1,100, consisting of the final coupon payment plus the face value. Immediately prior to maturity, the bond must have a total value just slightly less than the promised payment of $1,100. However, its price will be quoted at $1,000, but it also has $100 of accrued interest. The accrued interest, AI, is calculated using the following formula:

$$AI = \text{Coupon Payment} \left(\frac{\text{days since last coupon payment}}{\text{days between coupon payments}} \right) \qquad 6.3$$

Money Market Yield Calculations

Although the bond pricing formula holds for all bonds, yields on some money market instruments are quoted according to special conventions. Compared to the previous discussion of yields for debt instruments in general, the method of yield calculation and price quotation widely used in the money market is quite different. Many money market securities are quoted in terms of the **discount yield**. The price quotation is expressed in terms of this discount yield, but from this, one must calculate the actual dollar price of the instrument. The formula for the discount yield, d, is:

$$d = \frac{360}{t} \left(\frac{\text{DISC}}{\text{FV}} \right) \qquad 6.4$$

where:

DISC = the dollar discount from the face value
FV   = the face value of the instrument
t   = the number of days until the instrument matures

The actual dollar price, P, depends on the face value and the amount of the dollar discount, DISC:

$$P = FV - DISC = FV \left(1 - \frac{d\,t}{360} \right) \qquad 6.5$$

As an example of the way this system works, consider a 90-day money market instrument with a face value of $1,000,000 with a discount yield of 11 percent. The dollar discount, DISC, for this instrument would be:

$$DISC = \$1,000,000 \left(\frac{.11\,(90)}{360} \right) = \$27,500$$

and the actual dollar price would be:

$$P = FV - DISC = \$1,000,000 - \$27,500 = \$972,500$$

Major Money and Bond Market Instruments

The bond market is divided into the money market and the bond market. The money market trades debt instruments issued with an original maturity of one year or less, while the bond market trades debt instruments issued with longer maturities. In this section, we consider three money market instruments—Treasury bills, Eurodollar deposits, and repurchase agreements, or repos. We also consider Treasury bonds and Treasury notes.

One of the most important kinds of securities in the money market is the **Treasury bill**, or T-bill. T-bills are obligations of the U. S. Treasury, which are issued weekly with a maturity of 91 and 182 days. Bills with a 52 week maturity are offered monthly. In addition there are occasional additional offerings. Normally auctions are held on Mondays, with bids being submitted before 1:30 p.m. Delivery normally takes place on the following Thursday. T–bill yields are expressed on a discount basis. The bills have a minimum denomination of $10,000 and go up from that minimum in increments of $5,000.[1]

A **Eurodollar** is a dollar denominated bank deposit held in a bank outside the United States. A Eurodollar Certificate of Deposit (CD) is a dollar-denominated CD issued by a bank outside the United States.[2] In the Eurodollar market, CDs dominate simple Eurodollar bank deposits. The Eurodollar CD market is about 60 percent as large as the domestic CD market. Many foreign banks issue

Eurodollar CDs to attract dollar denominated funds, and many investors prefer Eurodollar CDs to domestic CDs because Eurodollar CDs pay a somewhat higher rate.

Eurodollar CDs pay a higher rate because they are generally somewhat riskier than domestic CDs. The greater risk arises from the fact that the issuing banks are not as tightly regulated as U.S. banks. Accordingly, these banks must pay more for their funds. Because they escape the cost of tighter regulation, they are also able to pay the higher rate the market demands. To a large extent, the Eurodollar market was created by U.S. banking regulation. Virtually all bank deposits in the U.S. are insured by the Federal Deposit Insurance Corporation (FDIC), an arm of the U.S. government. The charge for this insurance must be paid by the insured bank. For banks outside the United States, the insurance requirements are normally less stringent, so foreign banks can escape some of this cost.

Another feature of U.S. banking regulation that helps to keep the Eurodollar market in business is the imposition of reserve requirements. U.S. banks must keep a certain percentage of their outstanding loans on deposit in the form of non-interest earning assets, such as vault cash. If there were no reserve requirements, banks could create an infinite amount of loans from any deposit base. The higher the reserve requirement as a percentage of loans outstanding, the less a bank can lend with a given deposit base. Reserve requirements for U.S. banks tend to be far more stringent than those imposed on banks abroad. Consequently, the cost of operating many foreign banks is lower than it would be for a U.S. bank.

These regulatory differences create important cost differences between U.S. banks and their foreign competitors, but they also create significant (but usually small) risk differences. Due to the differences in their risk levels and cost structures, banks taking Eurodollar deposits must pay, and are able to pay, a higher interest rate than a domestic U.S. bank.

Repurchase agreements, or **repos,** arise when one party sells a security to another party and agrees to buy it back (repurchase it) at a specified time and at a specified price. The difference between the original sale and repurchase price defines the interest rate. Repos are used mainly for very short-term financing, with the vast majority of repo agreements having a term of just one day. These are called "overnight repos." Many corporations invest excess cash through the repo market. By buying a security with a commitment to resell it the next day at a slightly higher price, a corporation can put its excess cash to work. The desire for this kind of transaction has led to the creation of the repo market, with a current size in excess of $100 billion. Most of the securities used in the repo market are U.S. government securities. One good source for yield quotations on money market instruments is the daily column in *The Wall Street Journal,* entitled "Money Rates," presented in Figure 6.1. Notice particularly that instruments of different maturities have somewhat different yields.

Treasury bonds, and **Treasury notes,** like Treasury-bills, are also issued by the Treasury Department and have the same backing by the government. These notes and bonds have similar payment structures and differ only by the length of time until their maturity. T-bonds are issued with an initial maturity of

Figure 6.1
Money Rates

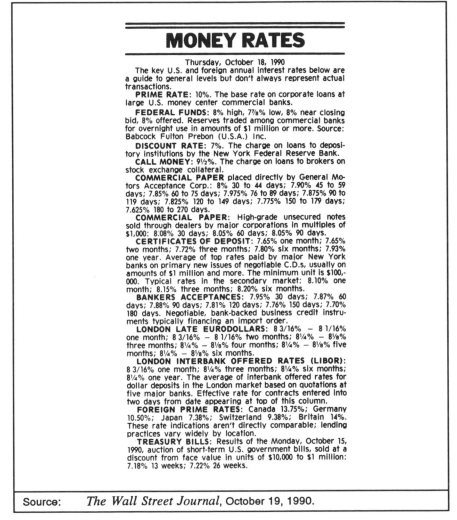

MONEY RATES

Thursday, October 18, 1990

The key U.S. and foreign annual interest rates below are a guide to general levels but don't always represent actual transactions.

PRIME RATE: 10%. The base rate on corporate loans at large U.S. money center commercial banks.

FEDERAL FUNDS: 8% high, 7⅞% low, 8% near closing bid, 8% offered. Reserves traded among commercial banks for overnight use in amounts of $1 million or more. Source: Babcock Fulton Prebon (U.S.A.) Inc.

DISCOUNT RATE: 7%. The charge on loans to depository institutions by the New York Federal Reserve Bank.

CALL MONEY: 9½%. The charge on loans to brokers on stock exchange collateral.

COMMERCIAL PAPER placed directly by General Motors Acceptance Corp.: 8% 30 to 44 days; 7.90% 45 to 59 days; 7.85% 60 to 75 days; 7.975% 76 to 89 days; 7.875% 90 to 119 days; 7.825% 120 to 149 days; 7.775% 150 to 179 days; 7.625% 180 to 270 days.

COMMERCIAL PAPER: High-grade unsecured notes sold through dealers by major corporations in multiples of $1,000: 8.08% 30 days; 8.05% 60 days; 8.05% 90 days.

CERTIFICATES OF DEPOSIT: 7.65% one month; 7.65% two months; 7.72% three months; 7.80% six months; 7.93% one year. Average of top rates paid by major New York banks on primary new issues of negotiable C.D.s, usually on amounts of $1 million and more. The minimum unit is $100,-000. Typical rates in the secondary market: 8.10% one month; 8.15% three months; 8.20% six months.

BANKERS ACCEPTANCES: 7.95% 30 days; 7.87% 60 days; 7.88% 90 days; 7.81% 120 days; 7.76% 150 days; 7.70% 180 days. Negotiable, bank-backed business credit instruments typically financing an import order.

LONDON LATE EURODOLLARS: 8 3/16% − 8 1/16% one month; 8 3/16% − 8 1/16% two months; 8¼% − 8⅛% three months; 8¼% − 8⅛% four months; 8¼% − 8⅛% five months; 8¼% − 8⅛% six months.

LONDON INTERBANK OFFERED RATES (LIBOR): 8 3/16% one month; 8¼% three months; 8¼% six months; 8¼% one year. The average of interbank offered rates for dollar deposits in the London market based on quotations at five major banks. Effective rate for contracts entered into two days from date appearing at top of this column.

FOREIGN PRIME RATES: Canada 13.75%; Germany 10.50%; Japan 7.38%; Switzerland 9.38%; Britain 14%. These rate indications aren't directly comparable; lending practices vary widely by location.

TREASURY BILLS: Results of the Monday, October 15, 1990, auction of short-term U.S. government bills, sold at a discount from face value in units of $10,000 to $1 million: 7.18% 13 weeks; 7.22% 26 weeks.

Source: *The Wall Street Journal*, October 19, 1990.

at least ten years. In practice, the initial time-to-maturity is much greater, usually 25-30 years, with T-notes having an initial maturity of about ten years.

Both T-bonds and T-notes pay semi-annual coupon payments. At the original issuance, the Treasury sets the coupon rate to make the initial price of the bonds close to their par value. Most T-bonds are callable, with the first call date coming five years before the bond matures. Reference to a particular bond might often be made in the form "ten-and-three-eights of 2007 to 2012." This would refer to a bond with a 10-3/8 percent coupon rate that matures in 2012 and is callable beginning in 2007. Most T-bonds and T-notes mature in the months of February, May, August, or November, with the maturity falling on the 15th.

T-bond price quotations show the bid and asked prices as a percent of par, where the digits appearing after the decimal point are expressed in 32nds of one percentage point, as in Figure 6.2. A price quotation of 98.20 reflects a price of 98 plus 20/32 percent of the par value. Quotations also show a yield to maturity. T-bond prices and yields may be calculated according to equation 6.2. Since coupon payments are made semi-annually, application of the formula will yield a semi-annual yield which must be doubled to give the annual yield on the T-bond. To obtain a T-bond one must pay the asked price, which is quoted, and the accrued interest, which is not reflected in the bond price quotation.

Bond Price Changes

Bond prices change for many reasons. First, we explain why a bond must sell at its par value at maturity. This means that the bond price must converge to its par value over its life no matter what other factors are at play. Second, bond prices change when interest rates change. In this section, we show the different ways in which changing interest rates generate changes in bond prices.

Bond Prices and the Passing of Time

Because the price of a bond must equal its par value at maturity, bond prices change due merely to the passage of time. For example, the typical T-bond pays its face value of $1,000 upon maturity. As a result, no matter what the purchase price of the bond, the bond will have a price of $1,000 at maturity. Therefore, the bond's price must converge to $1,000 over its life. This will be true even if interest rates never change.

All bonds can be classified as premium, par, or discount bonds. The price of a **premium bond** exceeds the face value. A **par bond** has a price equal to its face value, and a **discount bond** sells for less than its face value. For a premium bond with time remaining until maturity, an investor must realize that the bond's price will generally fall over its life, even if interest rates do not change. By the

Figure 6.2
T–Bond and T–Note Quotations

TREASURY BONDS, NOTES & BILLS

Thursday, October 18, 1990

Representative Over-the-Counter quotations based on transactions of $1 million or more.

Treasury bond, note and bill quotes are as of mid-afternoon. Colons in bid-and-asked quotes represent 32nds; 101:01 means 101 1/32. Net changes in 32nds. n-Treasury note. Treasury bill quotes in hundredths, quoted on terms of a rate of discount. Days to maturity calculated from trading date. All yields are to maturity and based on the asked quote. For bonds callable prior to maturity, yields are computed to the earliest call date for issues quoted above par and to the maturity date for issues below par. *-When issued.

Source: Federal Reserve Bank of New York.

U.S. Treasury strips as of 3 p.m. Eastern time, also based on transactions of $1 million or more. Colons in bid-and-asked quotes represent 32nds; 101:01 means 101 1/32. Net changes in 32nds. Yields calculated on the bid quotation. ci-stripped coupon interest. bp-Treasury bond, stripped principal. np-Treasury note, stripped principal.

Source: Bear, Stearns & Co. via Street Software Technology Inc.

GOVT. BONDS & NOTES

Rate	Maturity Mo/Yr	Bid	Asked	Chg.	Ask Yld.
$8\frac{1}{4}$	Oct 90n	100:00	100:02	....	5.48
8	Nov 90n	99:31	100:01	− 1	7.27
$9\frac{5}{8}$	Nov 90n	100:03	100:05	− 1	6.93
13	Nov 90n	100:11	100:13	− 1	6.38
$8\frac{7}{8}$	Nov 90n	100:04	100:06	....	6.85
$6\frac{5}{8}$	Dec 90n	99:25	99:27	....	7.31
$9\frac{1}{8}$	Dec 90n	100:08	100:10	....	7.25
$11\frac{3}{4}$	Jan 91n	100:29	100:31	....	7.26
9	Jan 91n	100:11	100:13	....	7.34
$7\frac{3}{8}$	Feb 91n	99:28	99:30	....	7.48
$9\frac{1}{8}$	Feb 91n	100:13	100:15	....	7.48
$9\frac{3}{8}$	Feb 91n	100:19	100:21	....	7.39
$6\frac{3}{4}$	Mar 91n	99:19	99:21	....	7.53
$9\frac{3}{4}$	Mar 91n	100:27	100:29	− 1	7.57
$12\frac{3}{8}$	Apr 91n	102:06	102:08	− 1	7.51
$9\frac{1}{4}$	Apr 91n	100:25	100:27	....	7.58
$8\frac{1}{8}$	May 91n	100:07	100:09	....	7.61
$14\frac{1}{2}$	May 91n	103:27	103:31	....	7.22
$8\frac{3}{4}$	May 91n	100:19	100:21	....	7.63
$7\frac{7}{8}$	Jun 91n	100:02	100:04	....	7.69
$8\frac{1}{4}$	Jun 91n	100:10	100:12	....	7.68
$13\frac{3}{4}$	Jul 91n	104:07	104:09	....	7.64
$7\frac{3}{4}$	Jul 91n	100:00	100:02	....	7.67
$7\frac{1}{2}$	Aug 91n	99:26	99:28	....	7.66
$8\frac{3}{4}$	Aug 91n	100:25	100:27	....	7.67
$14\frac{7}{8}$	Aug 91n	105:24	105:28	....	7.34
$8\frac{1}{4}$	Aug 91n	100:11	100:13	....	7.75
$8\frac{3}{8}$	Sep 91n	100:17	100:19	....	7.71
$9\frac{1}{8}$	Sep 91n	101:07	101:09	....	7.69
$12\frac{1}{4}$	Oct 91n	104:07	104:09	+ 1	7.64
$7\frac{5}{8}$	Oct 91n	99:27	99:29	+ 1	7.72
$6\frac{1}{2}$	Nov 91n	98:22	98:24	....	7.74
$8\frac{1}{2}$	Nov 91n	100:22	100:24	....	7.75
$14\frac{1}{4}$	Nov 91n	106:19	106:23	+ 1	7.57
$7\frac{3}{4}$	Nov 91n	99:27	99:29	....	7.84
$7\frac{5}{8}$	Dec 91n	99:24	99:26	+ 1	7.79
$8\frac{1}{4}$	Dec 91n	100:14	100:16	....	7.80
$11\frac{5}{8}$	Jan 92n	104:11	104:13	....	7.81
$8\frac{1}{8}$	Jan 92n	100:10	100:12	+ 1	7.81
$6\frac{5}{8}$	Feb 92n	98:12	98:14	....	7.90
$9\frac{1}{8}$	Feb 92n	101:15	101:17	+ 1	7.88
$14\frac{5}{8}$	Feb 92n	108:15	108:19	....	7.64
$8\frac{1}{2}$	Feb 92n	100:24	100:26	....	7.86
$7\frac{7}{8}$	Mar 92n	100:00	100:02	+ 1	7.83
$8\frac{1}{2}$	Mar 92n	100:27	100:29	+ 1	7.82
$11\frac{3}{4}$	Apr 92n	105:09	105:11	....	7.86
$8\frac{7}{8}$	Apr 92n	101:13	101:15	+ 1	7.83
$6\frac{5}{8}$	May 92n	98:04	98:06	....	7.88
9	May 92n	101:19	101:21	+ 2	7.86
$13\frac{3}{4}$	May 92n	108:16	108:18	+ 1	7.83
$8\frac{1}{2}$	May 92n	100:27	100:29	+ 1	7.89
$8\frac{1}{4}$	Jun 92n	100:17	100:19	+ 1	7.87
$8\frac{3}{8}$	Jun 92n	100:22	100:24	+ 1	7.89
$10\frac{3}{8}$	Jul 92n	103:27	103:29	....	7.92
8	Jul 92n	100:03	100:05	+ 1	7.90

Rate	Maturity	Bid	Asked	Chg.	Ask Yld.
$7\frac{3}{8}$	May 96n	95:09	95:13	+ 8	8.43
$7\frac{7}{8}$	Jul 96n	97:09	97:13	+ 8	8.46
8	Oct 96n	97:22	97:26	+ 8	8.47
$7\frac{1}{4}$	Nov 96n	94:02	94:06	+ 8	8.50
8	Jan 97n	97:13	97:17	+ 8	8.52
$8\frac{1}{2}$	Apr 97n	99:23	99:27	+ 8	8.53
$8\frac{1}{2}$	May 97n	99:23	99:27	+ 9	8.53
$8\frac{1}{2}$	Jul 97n	99:20	99:22	+ 9	8.56
$8\frac{5}{8}$	Aug 97n	100:08	100:12	+ 9	8.55
$8\frac{3}{4}$	Oct 97n	100:27	100:29	+ 7	8.57
$8\frac{7}{8}$	Nov 97n	101:14	101:18	+ 9	8.58
$8\frac{1}{8}$	Feb 98n	97:12	97:16	+ 8	8.59
7	May 93-98	90:24	91:00	+ 8	8.65
9	May 98n	102:01	102:05	+ 9	8.61
$9\frac{1}{4}$	Aug 98n	103:09	103:13	+ 8	8.64
$3\frac{1}{2}$	Nov 98	93:25	94:25	+ 6	4.27
$8\frac{7}{8}$	Nov 98n	101:05	101:09	+ 9	8.65
$8\frac{7}{8}$	Feb 99n	101:03	101:07	+ 9	8.67
$8\frac{1}{2}$	May 94-99	98:27	99:03	+ 13	8.65
$9\frac{1}{8}$	May 99n	102:16	102:20	+ 10	8.68
8	Aug 99n	95:24	95:28	+ 10	8.68
$7\frac{7}{8}$	Nov 99n	94:26	94:28	+ 9	8.70
$7\frac{7}{8}$	Feb 95-00	94:17	94:21	+ 10	8.72
$8\frac{1}{2}$	Feb 00n	98:23	98:27	+ 11	8.68
$8\frac{7}{8}$	May 00n	100:31	101:01	+ 10	8.71
$8\frac{3}{8}$	Aug 95-00	97:17	97:21	+ 10	8.74
$8\frac{3}{4}$	Aug 00n	100:08	100:10	+ 9	8.70
$11\frac{3}{4}$	Feb 01	119:31	120:07	+ 12	8.74
$13\frac{1}{8}$	May 01	129:20	129:28	+ 12	8.74
8	Aug 96-01	95:00	95:08	+ 10	8.69
$13\frac{3}{8}$	Aug 01	131:25	132:01	+ 15	8.74
$15\frac{3}{4}$	Nov 01	148:21	148:29	+ 22	8.76
$14\frac{1}{4}$	Feb 02	138:14	138:22	+ 17	8.79
$11\frac{5}{8}$	Nov 02	120:10	120:18	+ 12	8.82
$10\frac{3}{4}$	Feb 03	114:00	114:08	+ 14	8.83
$10\frac{3}{4}$	May 03	114:03	114:11	+ 12	8.84
$11\frac{1}{8}$	Aug 03	117:02	117:10	+ 16	8.84
$11\frac{7}{8}$	Nov 03	122:25	123:01	+ 14	8.86
$12\frac{3}{8}$	May 04	127:00	127:08	+ 13	8.88
$13\frac{3}{4}$	Aug 04	138:00	138:08	+ 16	8.89
$11\frac{5}{8}$	Nov 04	121:11	121:15	+ 15	8.92
$8\frac{1}{4}$	May 00-05	95:02	95:06	+ 12	8.84
12	May 05	124:23	124:27	+ 18	8.92
$10\frac{3}{4}$	Aug 05	114:19	114:23	+ 13	8.94
$9\frac{3}{8}$	Feb 06	104:07	104:11	+ 14	8.85
$7\frac{5}{8}$	Feb 02-07	89:17	89:21	+ 13	8.83
$7\frac{7}{8}$	Nov 02-07	91:14	91:18	+ 13	8.84
$8\frac{3}{8}$	Aug 03-08	95:15	95:19	+ 12	8.87
$8\frac{3}{4}$	Nov 03-08	98:21	98:25	+ 12	8.89
$9\frac{1}{8}$	May 04-09	101:18	101:22	+ 11	8.91
$10\frac{3}{8}$	Nov 04-09	110:19	110:23	+ 13	9.02
$11\frac{3}{4}$	Feb 05-10	121:20	121:24	+ 14	9.02
10	May 05-10	107:30	108:02	+ 14	9.00
$12\frac{3}{4}$	Nov 05-10	130:10	130:14	+ 13	9.02
$13\frac{7}{8}$	May 06-11	140:03	140:07	+ 17	9.02

Mat.	Type	Bid	Asked	Chg.	Bid Yld.
May 99	ci	47:13	47:16	+ 8	8.91
May 99	np	47:29	48:01	+ 6	8.78
Aug 99	ci	46:08	46:12	+ 5	8.94
Aug 99	np	46:27	46:31	+ 6	8.79
Nov 99	ci	45:07	45:11	+ 5	8.95
Nov 99	np	45:26	45:30	+ 6	8.80
Feb 00	ci	44:05	44:09	+ 5	8.97
Feb 00	np	44:24	44:28	+ 6	8.82
May 00	ci	43:06	43:10	+ 5	8.97
May 00	bp	43:29	44:01	+ 6	8.79
Aug 00	ci	42:08	42:12	+ 5	8.97
Aug 00	np	43:05	43:09	+ 7	8.75
Nov 00	ci	41:15	41:19	+ 6	8.94
Feb 01	ci	40:09	40:13	+ 5	9.01
May 01	ci	39:11	39:14	+ 5	9.03
Aug 01	ci	38:15	38:19	+ 5	9.03
Nov 01	ci	37:19	37:23	+ 4	9.04
Feb 02	ci	36:21	36:25	+ 5	9.07
May 02	ci	35:25	35:28	+ 5	9.09
Aug 02	ci	34:31	35:03	+ 5	9.09
Nov 02	ci	34:06	34:09	+ 5	9.10
Feb 03	ci	33:11	33:15	+ 5	9.12
May 03	ci	32:19	32:23	+ 5	9.12
Aug 03	ci	31:28	32:00	+ 5	9.12
Nov 03	ci	31:06	31:10	+ 5	9.12
Feb 04	ci	30:12	30:16	+ 5	9.15
May 04	ci	29:23	29:26	+ 5	9.15
Aug 04	ci	29:02	29:05	+ 5	9.15
Nov 04	ci	28:13	28:17	+ 5	9.15
Nov 04	bp	28:13	28:17	+ 5	9.15
Feb 05	ci	27:25	27:29	+ 5	9.15
May 05	ci	27:05	27:09	+ 4	9.15
May 05	bp	27:05	27:09	+ 4	9.15
Aug 05	ci	26:19	26:23	+ 6	9.14
Aug 05	bp	26:22	26:25	+ 5	9.12
Nov 05	ci	26:03	26:07	+ 5	9.12
Feb 06	ci	25:12	25:15	+ 5	9.16
Feb 06	bp	25:27	25:31	+ 4	9.03
May 06	ci	24:26	24:29	+ 5	9.16
Aug 06	ci	24:08	24:12	+ 4	9.16
Nov 06	ci	23:24	23:28	+ 4	9.15
Feb 07	ci	23:06	23:10	+ 4	9.16
May 07	ci	22:22	22:25	+ 5	9.16
Aug 07	ci	22:06	22:09	+ 5	9.16
Nov 07	ci	21:22	21:25	+ 5	9.16
Feb 08	ci	21:07	21:10	+ 5	9.16
May 08	ci	20:24	20:27	+ 5	9.16
Aug 08	ci	20:09	20:12	+ 4	9.16
Nov 08	ci	19:28	19:31	+ 5	9.15
Feb 09	ci	19:12	19:16	+ 4	9.16
May 09	ci	19:00	19:03	+ 4	9.15
Aug 09	ci	18:18	18:22	+ 4	9.15
Nov 09	ci	18:05	18:08	+ 4	9.15
Nov 09	bp	17:25	17:28	+ 4	9.27
Feb 10	ci	17:25	17:29	+ 4	9.14
May 10	ci	17:14	17:17	+ 4	9.13
Aug 10	ci	17:02	17:05	+ 5	9.13
Nov 10	ci	16:23	16:26	+ 5	9.12
Feb 11	ci	16:10	16:13	+ 4	9.13
May 11	ci	15:30	16:01	+ 4	9.13
Aug 11	ci	15:19	15:22	+ 4	9.13
Nov 11	ci	15:08	15:11	+ 4	9.13
Feb 12	ci	14:29	15:00	+ 4	9.13
May 12	ci	14:19	14:22	+ 4	9.13
Aug 12	ci	14:08	14:11	+ 3	9.13
Nov 12	ci	13:31	14:02	+ 4	9.12
Feb 13	ci	13:22	13:25	+ 3	9.11
May 13	ci	13:13	13:15	+ 4	9.11
Aug 13	ci	13:03	13:06	+ 3	9.11
Nov 13	ci	12:27	12:30	+ 4	9.10
Feb 14	ci	12:19	12:21	+ 4	9.09
May 14	ci	12:10	12:13	+ 4	9.09
Aug 14	ci	12:01	12:04	+ 3	9.09
Nov 14	ci	11:26	11:28	+ 4	9.08

Source: *The Wall Street Journal*, October 19, 1990.

same token, the price of a discount bond must rise to reach its par value at maturity. To illustrate the time path of bond prices, assume that interest rates are constant at 10 percent. Figure 6.3 shows the paths that the prices of three bonds must follow over time. Bond 1 is a 20-year 12 percent coupon bond. Bond 2 is a 20-year 10 percent coupon bond and Bond 3 is a 20-year 8 percent coupon bond.

With interest rates constant at 10 percent, Bond 1 is a premium bond. Whenever the coupon rate exceeds the bond's yield the bond must sell at a premium and its price must fall over time. At maturity, the price of Bond 1 equals the par value. The coupon rate of Bond 2 equals the yield of 10 percent. As a consequence, the price of Bond 2 equals its par value over the entire period. Bond 3, with a coupon rate below the yield to maturity, sells at a discount, so its price must rise toward the par value over time, reaching the par value at maturity. The price changes in Figure 6.3 assume constant interest rates. In the real world, with fluctuating interest rates, the price movements become more complex.[3]

Figure 6.3
Bond Price Changes Due to Approaching Maturity

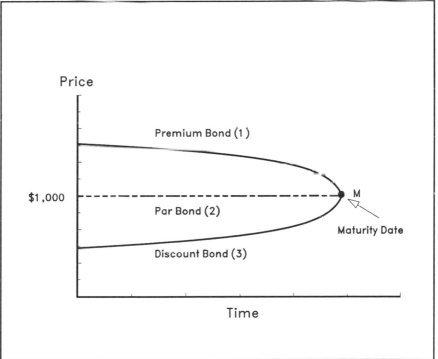

Bond Price Movements and Changing Interest Rates

Bonds with different characteristics respond to changes in the market rates of interest in radically different ways. The effect of a given change in interest rates on the price of a bond depends upon three key variables:

1. the maturity of the bond
2. the coupon rate
3. the level of interest rates at the time of the change in interest rates

This section develops five principles of bond pricing that explain how the price of a bond changes in response to a sudden change in interest rates. These principles reflect the different effects of a change in interest rates as a function of the three key variables: the bond's maturity, the bond's coupon rate, and the prevailing level of interest rates at the time rates change. Throughout this section, we assume that interest rates change instantaneously from one level to another, and we examine how the bond price changes as a result. The starting point is the basic bond valuation equation 6.2.

Bond Pricing Principles

The five bond pricing principles discussed in this section were proven rigorously by Burton Malkiel in a now-famous article.[4] Here the principles are merely stated, rather than proven.

1. Bond prices move inversely with interest rates.
2. Bonds with longer maturities experience greater percentage price changes for a given change in interest rates.
3. As stated in principle 2, the price sensitivity of bonds increases with maturity, but it increases at a decreasing rate.
4. Bonds with lower coupon rates experience greater percentage price changes for a given change in interest rates.
5. For a given bond, the absolute dollar price increase caused by a fall in bond yields will exceed the price decrease caused by an increase in bond yields of the same magnitude.[5]

From these principles we can see that some bonds will be more sensitive to changes in interest rates than others. As an example, consider two bonds with a $1,000 face value. Bonds A and B differ in maturity and coupon rate as the following data show:

	Maturity	Coupon Rate	Price at 10%	Price at 12%
Bond A:	5 years	10%	$1,000.00	$926.40
Bond B:	30 years	6%	$621.41	$515.16

Assume that interest rates on both bonds are initially at 10 percent, so Bond A is priced at its par value of $1,000 and Bond B trades for $621.41. If yields suddenly rise to 12 percent, the price of Bond A will fall to $926.40, while the price of Bond B will be $515.16. According to the principles of bond pricing developed above, we would expect bond B to be more sensitive to a change in interest rates because it has both a longer maturity and a lower coupon rate. In fact, when the yields change, Bond A falls in value by only 7.36 percent. By contrast, Bond B falls by 17.10 percent.

The Need for a Summary Measure

The five principles of bond pricing are all very important for understanding bond investing. However, since each of the principles assumes that all factors are being held constant except for the one under examination, it is still possible to have difficulty comparing the price sensitivity of different bonds. As an example, consider Bonds C and D.

Bond C: 15-year, 8% coupon, yielding 11.94%
Bond D: 20-year, 8% coupon, yielding 13.73%

Although these bonds have the same coupon rate, and the maturity of Bond D is more distant, not all of the other factors are held constant, since the yields on the two securities differ. If the yields were the same, Bond D would clearly have the greater price sensitivity, due to its longer maturity. Perhaps, however, the higher yield of Bond D offsets its longer term-to-maturity. In fact, as Table

Table 6.1
Price Sensitivity of Bonds C and D

	Bond C 15–year, 8% Coupon			Bond D 20–Year 8% Coupon		
Yield Change	Yield (%)	Price ($)	% Price Change	Yield (%)	Price ($)	% Price Change
−2%	9.94	86.68	+16.01	11.73	73.38	+16.01
Before Change	11.94	74.66	0.00	13.73	63.25	0.00
+2%	13.94	65.06	−12.87	15.73	55.15	−12.80

6.1 shows, the two bonds have virtually identical price sensitivity. For both, a drop of 2 percent in yields causes a 16.01 percent price rise, while a 2 percent yield increase causes a price drop of about 12.8 percent.

This example shows two important points. First, holding coupon and maturity constant, a bond with a higher yield has a lower price sensitivity. Second, coupon and maturity are generally not equal across bonds, and it would be very useful to have a summary measure of a bond's price sensitivity to reflect all of the factors that affect a bond's price sensitivity—the maturity, the coupon rate, and the yield-to-maturity. Such a measure is called duration.

Duration

Duration, a concept first developed by Frederick Macaulay, is a single number for a bond that reflects all the factors that affect the bond's price sensitivity to changes in interest rates.[6] Duration depends on three key variables: term-to-maturity, coupon rate, and yield-to-maturity. The duration of bond i, (D_i), is given by equation 6.6:

$$D_i = \frac{\sum_{t=1}^{M} \frac{t\, C_t}{(1 + r_i)^t}}{P_i} \qquad 6.6$$

where:

P_i = the bond's price
C_t = the cash flow from the bond occurring at time t
r_i = the yield-to-maturity on bond i
t = the time measured from the present until a payment is made

The numerator of the duration equation computes the present value of each of the cash flows and weights each by the time until it is received. All of these weighted cash flows are summed, and the sum is divided by the current price of the bond. Thus, duration is a weighted average of the present values of the bond's cash flows, where the weighting factor is the time until the cash flow is to be received. To illustrate the calculation of duration, consider a five-year bond paying an annual coupon of 10 percent. The bond yields 14 percent and has a par value of $1,000. The price of this bond is $862.69. Table 6.2 sets out the cash flows and shows the calculation of this bond's duration, which is 4.10.

There is also another equation for duration, which expresses duration as the negative of elasticity of the bond's price with respect to a change in the discount factor (1 + r).

Table 6.2
The Calculation of Duration

			t		
	1	2	3	4	5
C_t	$100.00	$100.00	$100.00	$100.00	$1,100.00
$C_t/(1 + r)^t$	87.72	76.95	67.50	59.21	571.31
$t[C_t/(1 + r)^t]$	87.72	153.90	202.50	236.84	2,856.55

D_i = (87.72 + 153.90 + 202.50 + 236.84 + 2,856.55)/862.69

= 3,537.51/862.69 = 4.10

$$D = - \frac{\dfrac{dP}{P}}{\dfrac{d\ (1 + r)}{(1 + r)}} \qquad 6.7$$

where dP equals the change in the price and $d(1 + r)$ is the change in the interest rate. Essentially an elasticity measure, duration gives a single measure of the bond price change for a change in the discount factor $(1 + r)$. This is clear when equation 6.7 is re-arranged, as shown in equation 6.8:

$$dP_i = - D_i \left[\frac{d\ (1 + r_i)}{(1 + r_i)} \right] P_i \qquad 6.8$$

Applying equation 6.8 requires knowing the original level of rates, the original price, the change in rates, and the duration of the bond.

To see how this works, consider the bond used to compute duration earlier. That bond was a five-year 10 percent annual coupon bond yielding 14 percent with a duration of 4.10. If yields suddenly fell from 14 to 12 percent, the bond's price would rise, and the amount of the adjustment could be found by using equation 6.8:

$$dP = - 4.10 \left[\frac{-.02}{1.14} \right] \$862.69 = + \$62.05$$

With this change in price, the new price should be the old price plus the price change.

$$\text{New Price} = 862.69 + 62.05 = \$924.74$$

This can be confirmed by applying the bond pricing formula to this bond, using the new yield of 12 percent. According to the bond pricing equation, the new price is $927.90, which is not the same as the new price of $924.74, obtained by using the duration price change equation. There are two reasons for this. First, any such calculation may have some rounding error. Second, the duration price change formula uses concepts derived from calculus, and they will hold exactly only for infinitesimal changes in variables. In this case, the large change in the yield of two percent was responsible for the slight discrepancy between the two methods.

Duration is a very useful tool because it provides such a convenient summary measure of the three key variables that determine bond price movements: the coupon rate, the maturity of the bond, and the level of interest rates. This means that bond investors can compare the price movement sensitivities of different bonds by simply comparing their durations.

The Term Structure of Interest Rates

The term structure of interest rates is the relationship between term-to-maturity and yield-to-maturity for bonds that are similar in all respects except that they differ in their maturities. Because the purpose of yield curve or term structure analysis is to understand the differences in bond yields stemming only from differences in maturity, the bonds used in the analysis must be as similar as possible in other respects except for maturity. For example, all of the bonds used in a yield curve should be similar in their risk level. Also, we should be sure that the bonds have the same call provisions, sinking fund characteristics, and tax status.

These requirements for similarities among bonds used in the yield curve analysis are cumbersome, because it is difficult to find a pool of bonds that meet all of those conditions. For this reason, it is customary to focus on the term structure of Treasury securities. Treasury securities all have the same level of default risk and tend to be alike in their tax status and other features as well. Also, since Treasury securities are lowest in risk, the Treasury yield curve provides the basic yield curve to which the yields of other securities can be related. For these reasons, this section focuses on the Treasury yield curve, such as that shown in Figure 6.4.

Figure 6.4
The Term Structure of Interest Rates

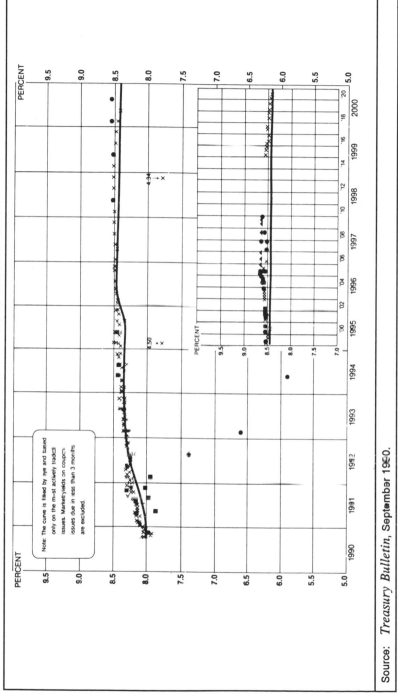

Note: The curve is fitted by eye and based only on the most actively traded issues. Market yields on coupon issues due in less than 3 months are excluded.

Source: *Treasury Bulletin*, September 1990.

At various times, the yield curve can take on a variety of shapes. For example, Figure 6.5 shows dramatically different yield curve shapes for high grade corporate bonds over a century. Even within brief periods, both the level and shape of the yield curve can change violently. The shape of the yield curve contains information about the future course of interest rates. Because the future of interest rates is the most important information that bond investors would like to have, understanding the yield curve is extremely important. Developing this understanding of yield curves first requires a knowledge of forward rates.

Forward Rates

Forward rates of interest are rates to cover future time periods that are implied by currently available spot rates. A spot rate is a yield prevailing at a given moment in time on a security. Given a set of spot rates, it is possible to calculate forward rates for any intervening time period.

For convenience, let us introduce the notation that a bond yield expressed as $r_{x,y}$ is the rate to prevail on a bond for the period beginning at time "x" and maturing at time "y." The present is always time=0, so a bond yield covering any time span beginning at time=0 is a spot rate. For example, $r_{0,5}$ would be the spot rate for an instrument maturing in five years. If the time covered by a particular rate begins after time=0, it is a forward rate. The forward rate to cover a period beginning two years from now and extending three years to time=5 would be $r_{2,5}$ in our notation. Using this notation, we introduce a principle that can be used for the calculation of forward rates: Forward rates are calculated on the assumption that returns over a given period of time are all equal, no matter which maturities of bonds are held over that span of time.

Principle of Calculation for Forward Rates

Forward rates are calculated on the assumption that returns over a given period of time are all equal, no matter which maturities of bonds are held over that span of time.

Taking a five-year period as an example, this principle implies that forward rates can be calculated over the five years on the assumption that all of the following strategies would earn the same returns over the five years:

1. Buy the five-year bond and hold it to maturity.
2. Buy a one-year bond and when it matures, buy another one-year bond, following this procedure for the entire five years.
3. Buy a two-year bond and when it matures, buy a three-year bond and hold it to maturity.

Figure 6.5
Historical Yield Curves

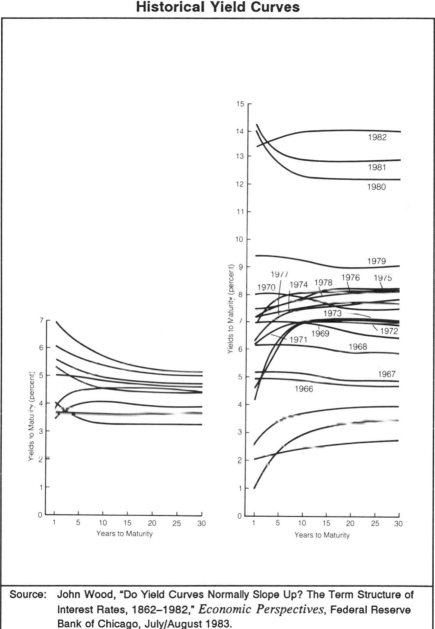

Source: John Wood, "Do Yield Curves Normally Slope Up? The Term Structure of Interest Rates, 1862–1982," *Economic Perspectives*, Federal Reserve Bank of Chicago, July/August 1983.

According to the Principle of Calculation, holding bonds of any maturity over this five-year period would give the same return. Notice that this is not a prediction of returns, but it is an assumption that is used to calculate forward rates.

In terms of the notation being used in this chapter, these three strategies can be expressed as follows:

Hold one five-year bond for five years:

$$\text{Total Return} = (1 + r_{0,5})^5$$

Hold a sequence of one-year bonds:

$$\text{Total Return} = (1 + r_{0,1})(1 + r_{1,2})(1 + r_{2,3})(1 + r_{3,4})(1 + r_{4,5})$$

Hold a two-year bond followed by a three-year bond:

$$\text{Total Return} = (1 + r_{0,2})^2(1 + r_{2,5})^3$$

Further, these forward rates can be calculated by applying the Principle of Calculation, which says that those total returns should all be equal. According to the Principle of Calculation:

$$(1 + r_{0,5})^5 = (1 + r_{0,1})(1 + r_{1,2})(1 + r_{2,3})(1 + r_{3,4})(1 + r_{4,5}) = (1 + r_{0,2})^2(1 + r_{2,5})^3$$

To understand how the Principle of Calculation makes it possible to calculate the forward rates shown here, some values for the spot yields are necessary. For Treasury securities, assume that the following spot yields obtain.

Spot Rate	Yield	Maturity
$r_{0,1}$	.08	1 year
$r_{0,2}$	.088	2 years
$r_{0,3}$	.09	3 years
$r_{0,4}$	.093	4 years
$r_{0,5}$	.095	5 years

These yields are all spot yields and are clearly consistent with an upward sloping yield curve, because the longer the maturity of the bond, the greater the yield. As we will see, this set of spot rates also implies a number of forward rates to cover periods ranging from time=1 to time=5. An investor with a five-year horizon might hold a five year bond, with a yield of 9.5 percent.

However, there are numerous alternative ways of holding a bond investment over the same time period. As an example of how to calculate forward rates, consider the third strategy mentioned above in which the investor might hold a two-year bond followed by holding a three-year bond. Right now, at time=0, it is impossible to know what the yield will be on the three-year bond to cover the time period from time=2 to time=5. This rate cannot be known with certainty until time=2 actually arrives. At time=0, however, it is possible to calculate a forward rate to cover the time span from time=2 to time=5. As shown above, the principle of calculation implies:

$$(1 + r_{0,5})^5 = (1 + r_{0,2})^2 (1 + r_{2,5})^3$$

Using the spot rates given above:

$$(1.095)^5 = (1.088)^2 (1 + r_{2,5})^3$$

Now the only unknown is the forward rate, so the equation can be solved for the forward rate:

$$r_{2,5} = .0997 = 9.97\%$$

The forward rate, implied by this set of spot rates, to cover the period from year 2 to year 5, is 9.97 percent.

Given the relevant spot rates, it is possible to calculate any forward rate. For the five years of this example, all intervening forward rates can be calculated with the data supplied, since the spot rates for all maturities were presented. Notice that nothing has been said so far about how the forward rates are to be interpreted. There are different theories of the term structure that interpret forward rates in somewhat different ways. However, all of the theories that use forward rates to understand the term structure agree that forward rates give important information about the future course of interest rates.

Theories of the Term Structure

Three theories of the term structure have received the greatest attention. They are the Pure Expectations Theory, the Liquidity Premium Theory, and the Market Segmentation Theory. The Pure Expectations Theory and the Liquidity Premium Theory both use forward rates as a key element, and both theories can be stated by their interpretation of forward rates.

The Pure Expectations Theory

The Pure Expectations Theory states that forward rates are unbiased estimators of future interest rates, or that forward rates equal expected future spot rates of interest. An unbiased estimator has an expected value that equals the true value of the parameter being estimated. In somewhat more straightforward language, the Pure Expectations Theory claims that, on average, today's forward rate equals the future spot rate for the period corresponding to the forward rate. In terms of the previous example, where we calculated that the forward rate for a three-period bond to cover from time=2 to time=5 was 9.97 percent, the Pure Expectations Theory would say that 9.97 percent is a good estimate of the spot rate that will prevail on a three-period bond two periods from now. The actual rate may be higher or lower than 9.97 percent, but on average, according to the Pure Expectations Theory, the forward rate will equal the subsequently observed spot rate.

This theory has very strong practical implications. If it is true, the term structure contains predictions of future interest rates. Why should anyone believe this theory? Its defenders explain it this way. The bond market is well developed and populated with many participants having different wealth levels and different preferences. In the bond market there are many people with no particular preference about the maturity of instruments that they hold. In the absence of any strong maturity preference, these investors seek the best rate of return. So, assume for the moment that the expected total return for a five-year investment in Treasury securities is greater from holding a five-year bond for five years, rather than holding a two-year bond followed by a three-year bond. These investors, without strong maturity preferences, would take the higher yielding five-year bond. Anyone holding the two-year bond would sell it in order to invest the funds in the better-performing five-year bond.

As the two-year bonds were sold to switch into five-year bonds, there would be strong price effects on both bonds. The price of the two-year bond would fall and the price of the five-year bond would rise. These investors would stop switching from the two-year to the five-year bond only when the expected returns from the two strategies were equal. Then there would be no further incentive to switch from one to the other. According to the Pure Expectations Theory, there are many bond investors who will switch their funds to any maturity strategy with a higher yield. However, the willingness of these investors to hold whichever maturity strategy has higher expected returns means that all maturity strategies must have the same expected return in equilibrium. In other words, after all of the maturity switching has stopped and an equilibrium has been achieved, there must be an equal expected return for any investment period, no matter what maturities of instruments are held over that period.

Now the stage is set to see how the Pure Expectations Theory ties together forward rates and expected future spot rates. In the previous example, the investor in the five-year bond yielding 9.5 percent is expecting to earn 9.5 percent per year over the five-year period. According to the Pure Expectations Theory, an investor with a five year horizon holding a two-year bond and planning to follow that with holding a three-year bond must be expecting to earn the same 9.5 percent annual return over the entire period. However, the yield-to-maturity on the two-year bond is only 8.8 percent. The investor who earns 8.8 percent for the first two of a five year holding period must earn much more in the last three years to have a 9.5 percent rate of return over the whole period.

One dollar invested for five years at 9.5 percent will be worth $1.57 at the end of the period. If the investor planning to hold the two-year bond at 8.8 percent followed by a three-year bond wants to earn the same rate of return, he or she must expect a higher yield on the three-year bond. In fact, the expected rate of return on the three-year bond must be sufficient so that the returns from the two maturity strategies give the same final wealth for equal investments. It must be that:

$$(1.095)^5 = (1.088)^2 (1 + X)^3$$

where X equals the expected yield on the three-year bond to cover the period from time=2 to time=5. What then is the value of X? Solving this equation for X gives:

$$X = 9.97\%$$

Notice that this expected interest rate for the three year bond exactly equals the forward rate for the same bond calculated above. This is the crux of the argument for the Pure Expectations Theory. If expected returns from all maturity strategies are to be equal, forward rates must necessarily equal expected future spot rates. The equality of forward rates and expected future spot rates follows logically from the view that all maturity strategies have the same expected return over any given holding period. If enough investors do not care about the maturity of the instruments they hold and merely seek the highest expected return, then they will ensure that all different maturity strategies have the same expected return. Also, they will force the major conclusion of the Pure Expectations Theory to be true, namely, that forward rates equal expected future spot rates. Ultimately, the Pure Expectations Theory depends upon the presence of bond investors who are indifferent to the maturities of the bonds they hold and who seek the greatest expected returns.

The Liquidity Premium Theory

In many ways, the Liquidity Premium Theory is similar to the Pure Expectations Theory. At least both theories see the problem in very similar terms. The Liquidity Premium Theory can also be stated by reference to forward rates. The theory holds that forward rates are upwardly biased estimators of expected future spot rates. The theory asserts that the estimates are too high and that forward rates exceed expected future spot rates.

As explained earlier, the Pure Expectations Theory must be true if there are enough bond investors who care only about returns. These investors would ensure that all maturity strategies over a given time span have the same expected return. The Liquidity Premium theorists acknowledge this argument, but they reject the claim that there are numerous investors who are indifferent about the maturities of the bonds that they hold.

The defenders of the Liquidity Premium Theory assert that bondholders prefer to hold short-term bonds rather than long-term bonds. The short-term bonds have less interest rate risk. Clearly, as explained above, the shorter the maturity, the less interest rate risk there will be. The fact that the bonds will not change dramatically in price makes them more attractive than long-term bonds to many investors. According to the Liquidity Premium Theory, short-term bonds are so much more attractive than long-term bonds that investors are willing to pay more for short-term bonds than for long-term bonds. This extra amount that they are willing to pay is the liquidity premium.

The willingness of investors to pay a liquidity premium for the short-term bonds also implies that the yields on short-term bonds will be lower than the yields on long-term bonds, other things being equal. Another way of saying the same thing is to notice that long-term bonds must pay a greater return than short-term bonds to induce investors to commit their funds to the long-term instruments.

If yields on short-term instruments are lower than those on long-term bonds in the normal event, total returns from investing in short maturities will be less than the total return from investing in long maturities, even when the two strategies are pursued over the same time interval. For example, assume that a five-year bond must pay 1/10 of one percent greater yield than a one-year bond, due to investor preferences for short-term securities. Using the values of our continuing example, the five-year bond returns 9.5 percent over its life. With a 1/10 of 1 percent higher yield per annum for the five-year over the one-year instrument, the strategy of holding five one-year bonds in succession must return only 9.4 percent over the five-year period. The one-year spot instrument has a yield of 8 percent. So the yield on the four following one-year bonds must be such that the average annual yield on the strategy of holding the one-year bonds turns out to be 9.4 percent:

$$(1.094)^5 = (1.08) (1 + X)^4$$

$$X = 9.753\%$$

If the total realized return over the five-year period is to be 9.4 percent per year from the strategy of holding one-year bonds, the expected average return per year for years 2-5 must be 9.753 percent.[7] The forward rate $r_{1,5}$ can be calculated as well:

$$(1 + r_{0,5})^5 = (1 + r_{0,1}) (1 + r_{1,5})^4$$

$$r_{1,5} = 9.88\%$$

According to the key claim of the Liquidity Premium Theory, the expected rate of return on a succession of one-year bonds must be less than the expected rate of return on a long-term bond, when the two maturity strategies are pursued over the same period. The returns would differ by the amount of the liquidity premium, other things being equal. In this example, the assumed yield differential between the five-year and the one-year bonds, due to the liquidity premium, was 1/10 of one percent. This implied that the expected rate of return on the one-year bonds covering the last four of the five years was 9.753 percent. However, the forward rate for the same four-year period was 9.88 percent. This result is exactly consistent with the claims of the Liquidity Premium Theory. The forward rate (9.88 percent) exceeds the expected rate (9.753 percent) over this four-year period. If the Liquidity Premium Theory is correct, using forward rates to estimate future spot rates of interest would give estimates that are too high, due to the liquidity premium.

Pure Expectations and Liquidity Premium Theories

Pure Expectations Theory	Forward rates equal expected future spot rates of interest. Therefore, forward rates are unbiased predictors of future spot rates.
Liquidity Premium Theory	Forward rates exceed expected future spot rates of interest by the amount of the liquidity premium. Therefore, forward rates are biased predictors of future spot rates.

Both the Pure Expectations and Liquidity Premium theories are very rigorous and follow logically from their respective beliefs about the preferences and behavior of bond market participants. The basic disagreement between the two theories turns on whether bondholders prefer short-term instruments to long-term instruments. Before examining the evidence about the term structure theories, there is one more theory to consider.

The Market Segmentation Theory

Unlike the Pure Expectations Theory and the Liquidity Premium Theory, the Market Segmentation Theory is not expressly stated in terms of forward rates. According to the Market Segmentation Theory, the yield curve that exists at any one time reflects the actions and preferences of certain major participants in the bond market. To a large extent, the bond market is dominated by large financial institutions, with each kind of institution having strong maturity preferences stemming from the kind of business it pursues. Commercial banks, for example, have relatively short-term liabilities in the form of demand deposits and Certificates of Deposit (CDs). As a consequence, they prefer to invest in relatively short-term bonds.[8] Life insurance companies, by contrast, have their liabilities falling due far in the future upon the death of policyholders. Correspondingly, life insurance companies prefer long-term bonds. Casualty insurers, such as those writing auto and home insurance, have liabilities that fall due in the medium-term and they correspondingly favor medium maturity bonds for their investments.

These preferences of different types of financial institutions stem from the nature of their businesses and a desire to match the maturity of their assets and liabilities in order to control risk. Because of these preferences, the institutions tend to trade bonds only in their respective maturity ranges. For example, to induce a bank to invest in long-term bonds, the long-term bonds must pay an attractively higher yield in comparison to the short-term bonds that banks prefer for business reasons. The desire of these different institutions to participate only in certain maturity segments of the bond markets leads directly to the Segmented Markets Hypothesis: The yield curve is determined by the interplay of supply and demand factors in different segments of the maturity spectrum of the bond market. Financial institutions with strong maturity preferences occupy those different segments and effectively cause the bond market to splinter into different market segments based on maturity.

These preferences for certain maturity ranges are not absolute. If institutions dominated the bond market and never left their preferred maturity habitats, it might even be possible to observe a discontinuous yield curve. However, according to the Market Segmentation Theory, which is also known as the Preferred Habitat Theory, the institutions have preferred maturity ranges, but attractive yields in different maturities lead institutions to accept maturities outside the preferred range. Therefore, a discontinuous yield curve is never observed in practice.

How the Three Theories Explain Different Yield Curves

Any of these three theories of the term structure can explain any observed market yield curve. For example, if the yield curve is upward sloping, the forward rates increase with maturity. According to the Pure Expectations Theory, this implies that short-term interest rates are expected to rise. With a flat yield curve, all forward rates equal the current short-term spot rate, so the Pure Expectations Theory interprets this as the market's belief that interest rates will remain constant. For a downward sloping yield curve, the Pure Expectations Theory stresses the fact that forward rates will be lower the farther they are into the future, and interprets this as the market's belief that short-term interest rates are expected to fall.

The Liquidity Premium Theory can explain any observed yield curve with equal facility, but the explanation is a little more complicated, due to the existence of the liquidity premium. To see the effect of the liquidity premium, assume that the market expects short-term interest rates to be constant forever. Because of the liquidity premium, a long-term bond must pay a higher yield. This means, according to the Liquidity Premium Theory, that the yield curve will be slightly upward sloping even when short-term rates are expected to remain constant. The tendency for the upward slope in the yield curve in such a case would be due strictly to the impact of the liquidity premium. Figure 6.6 depicts this situation. The dotted line in the figure shows the level of the constant expected short-term interest rates. Nonetheless, the yield curve slopes upward due to the impact of the liquidity premium. For this reason, many people believe that an upward sloping yield curve is the normal shape of the yield curve.

If the market yield curve slopes strongly upward, the Liquidity Premium Theory attributes this shape to the presence of two factors, the impact of the liquidity premium and the market's expectation of higher interest rates. Figure 6.7 shows a strongly upward sloping yield curve. The dotted line indicates where the yield curve would be with just a liquidity premium and no expectation of higher rates in the future. The effect of the liquidity premium is always to make the observed yield curve more strongly upward sloping than it would be otherwise. The actual yield curve lies above the dotted line because interest rates are also expected to rise in this example.

For a downward sloping yield curve, the Liquidity Premium Theory says that interest rates are expected to fall by an amount greater than the effect of the liquidity premium. The liquidity premium always has the effect of making the yield curve slope upward more than it otherwise would. With an observed downward slope, the market must be expecting a drop in interest rates sufficiently large to more than compensate for the liquidity premium. The Market Segmentation Hypothesis explains all observed yield curve shapes as being due to the supply and demand factors in each segment of the bond market. According

Figure 6.6
Yield Curve with Equal Expected Future Short–Term Rates

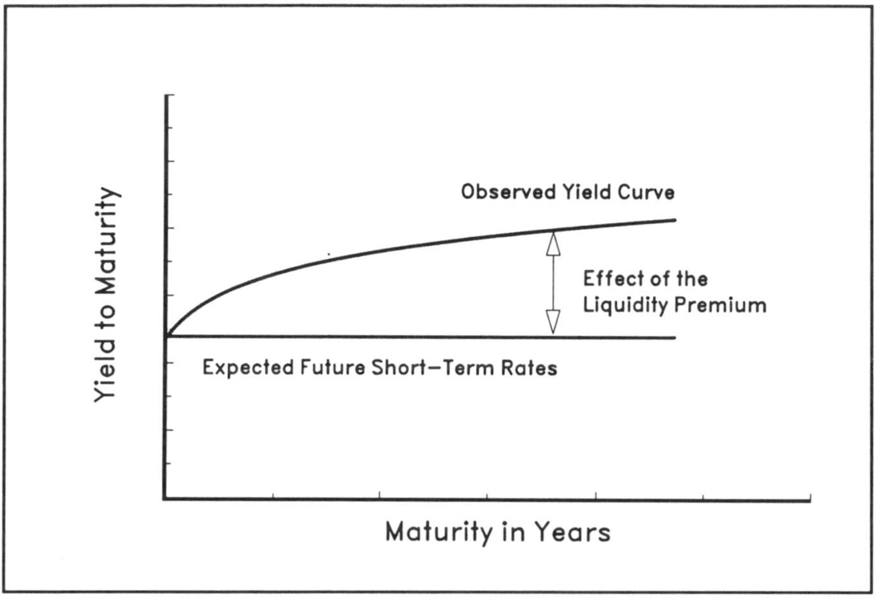

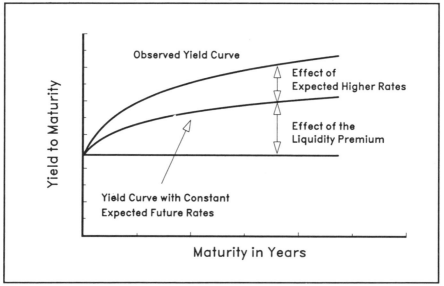

Figure 6.7
Liquidity Premium Theory's Explanation of an
Upward Sloping Yield Curve

to this view, expectations are also important, but the emphasis is on the interests and maturity preferences of the different institutional participants.

Evidence on the Three Theories

Tests of these three theories are numerous, but the evidence is mixed. In spite of some evidence in support of the Market Segmentation Theory, there does seem to be a consensus that it alone cannot explain everything about the yield curve.[9] As a consequence, the real struggle is between the Pure Expectations Theory and the Liquidity Premium Theory.

Meiselman and Santomero both find empirical evidence to support the Pure Expectations Hypothesis.[10] Research by Nelson and McCulloch opposes these results.[11] McCulloch finds a definite, but small, liquidity premium and also finds that virtually all of this premium is confined to very short maturities of about one year or less.

While the different theories of the term structure are sure to survive and also sure to attract more research, it is important not to be misled by minor differences of opinion when there is major agreement. Virtually all of the different theorists would agree on the fundamental proposition that the shape of the yield curve expresses the market's opinion about future interest rates. In general, an upward sloping yield curve implies that rates are expected to rise; a downward sloping yield curve implies that rates are expected to fall. Further, if there does exist a liquidity premium, it is not very large, so forward rates still provide a very good guide to the market's expectation of future interest rates. In fact, the forward rates of interest often provide better forecasts of future interest rates than professional forecasting services.

Bond Portfolio Maturity Strategies

In our discussion of the term structure, we have already seen that the choice of maturities is a very important issue for any bondholder. Where numerous bonds are to be held in a portfolio, there will be some average maturity of the portfolio. Even after the average maturity for the portfolio is chosen, there is still another important investment decision that concerns the maturity structure or the duration structure of the bond portfolio.[12] The maturity structure of the portfolio concerns the way in which funds are allocated to bonds of differing maturity. Depending on the technique chosen, the bond portfolio manager can make the portfolio easy to administer, or the manager can choose maturities to allow dramatic changes in the interest rate sensitivity of the portfolio.

There are two basic approaches, called the Laddered Strategy and the Dumbbell or Barbell Strategy. Each has its own advantages and disadvantages. In the **laddered strategy**, funds in the bond portfolio are distributed approximately evenly over the range of maturities. The name of the laddered strategy comes from the fact that funds are evenly distributed across the maturity range, just as the rungs of a ladder are evenly spaced. The main advantage of the laddered strategy is ease of management. Each year, the short-term bonds mature and the funds provided from this source are committed to long-term bonds. Thus, it is easy to maintain the same kind of maturity distribution with very little transaction cost.

The disadvantage of the laddered approach is the difficulty in changing the maturity composition of the portfolio. Aggressive bond portfolio managers sometimes will wish to change the maturity structure of a bond portfolio to take advantage of anticipated shifts in yields. Recall the bond pricing principles, which noted that a drop in yields would cause an increase in bond prices and that the effect of a given drop in yields would be greater the longer the maturity of a particular bond, other factors being equal. With that principle in mind, if a bond manager believed that interest rates will soon drop by a large amount, he might wish to lengthen the average maturity of the portfolio to get a bigger effect when the drop in yields causes an increase in the price of bonds. With the laddered strategy, it is difficult to have a major effect on the portfolio's maturity without trading many bonds. To lengthen the average maturity of the portfolio, the manager would sell the shortest maturity bonds and invest the funds in the longest maturity bonds. However, with all of the maturities receiving roughly equal investment, there will be too few short-term bonds to sell to have a major effect on the average maturity of the portfolio. After the short maturity bonds are exhausted, the manager would sell medium maturity bonds and use the proceeds to buy long maturity bonds. But shifting funds from medium to long maturity bonds has relatively little effect on the average maturity of the portfolio. As a consequence, the laddered portfolio strategy makes it more difficult to shift the portfolio's maturity structure by large amounts.

With the **dumbbell strategy**, the funds in the bond portfolio are committed just to short maturity and to very long maturity bonds. The concentration of maturities in short and long maturities creates a virtually vacant middle maturity range. Thus, the concentrations on the short and long maturities forms the bells in the dumbbell with the bar being formed by the vacant middle maturity range. The active bond manager using the dumbbell strategy can easily lengthen or shorten the maturity structure of the portfolio, because funds can be shifted between very short and very long maturities.

The dumbbell approach has its own disadvantage, however. In many ways, the dumbbell strategy is like having two portfolios—one with very long maturities and one with very short maturities. Each requires separate management. For the short maturity portion of the portfolio, the manager must reinvest all of the bonds that mature. This necessity to "roll over" the maturing funds requires considerable management attention. For the long maturity portion of the portfolio, the problems are even more acute. With the passing of time, the long maturity bonds will become middle maturity bonds. To maintain the dumbbell shape, the manager must sell middle maturity bonds and reinvest in long maturity bonds. This requires active management as well in selling middle maturity and purchasing long maturity bonds, and the activity incurs substantial transaction costs. In general, then, the dumbbell strategy has the disadvantages of requiring considerably greater management effort and higher transaction costs.

The choice between the laddered or the dumbbell strategy depends on whether one wishes to engage in active management of the bond portfolio. Active management consists essentially of attempting to alter the maturity structure of the bond portfolio to exploit forecasted changes in interest rates. An active manager would prefer the dumbbell strategy. The advisability of active bond management depends on the ability to forecast interest rates. Some portfolio managers believe that it is impossible to forecast interest rates with sufficient accuracy to make active bond portfolio management practical. These managers adopt a passive management strategy, seeking to minimize management expense and to control transaction costs. This approach leads naturally to a preference for the laddered portfolio strategy. The decision to follow an active or passive management strategy depends essentially on the manager's beliefs about his or her interest rate forecasts.

Portfolio Immunization Techniques

Increasingly, bond portfolio managers acknowledge the difficulty in forecasting interest rates. If the bond manager does not know how to alter a portfolio to take advantage of an expected shift in interest rates because he or she has no good reason to expect one shift rather than another, active portfolio management has no useful role.

As bond managers have accepted this perspective, passive strategies have become more popular, particularly **portfolio immunization**. A bond portfolio is immunized if its investment performance is not sensitive to changes in interest rates. In recognition of an inability to predict interest rates, many bond managers find that it makes sense to protect their portfolios from undesirable effects due to changes in interest rates by immunizing their portfolios. These immunization techniques fall into two categories—the **bank immunization case** and the **planning period case**. Both rely on the idea of duration.

The Bank Immunization Case

This form of immunization takes its name form its prominence in commercial banking. In simplest form, a commercial bank borrows money by accepting deposits and uses those funds to make loans. The portfolio of deposits and the portfolio of loans may both be viewed as bond portfolios, with the deposit portfolio constituting the liability portfolio and the loan portfolio constituting the asset portfolio. One of the problems in commercial banking stems from the very short duration of the deposit portfolio, since most deposits can be withdrawn on very short notice. By contrast, the loan portfolio consists of obligations to provide funds for longer periods, because banks make commercial and consumer loans and provide mortgage financing.

The top panel of Table 6.3 shows the position of Simple National Bank, which holds a deposit portfolio and liability portfolio with book and market values of $1,000 each. The duration of the liability portfolio is one year, and for the asset portfolio, the duration is five years. Assume, for the sake of simplicity that the interest rate being earned on both portfolios is 10 percent. With different durations on the two portfolios, the bank has considerable interest rate risk. As we saw earlier, bond prices rise when interest rates fall, so the value of both portfolios will rise. But the asset portfolio is about five times as sensitive to a change in interest rates as the liability portfolio, because its duration is five times as large. If interest rates rise, however, all bond values fall, and the asset portfolio will fall in value much more than the liability portfolio.

To see the effect of this on the bank, assume that interest rates rise from 10 percent to 12 percent on both the deposit and loan portfolios. Applying the duration price change formula for the example of Simple National Bank, the change in the value of the deposit portfolio will be:

$$dP = -1 \ (.02/1.10) \ \$1000 = -\$18.18$$

Table 6.3
Balance Sheet of Simple National Bank

Original Position

Assets		Liabilities	
Loan Portfolio Value	$1,000	Deposit Portfolio Value	$1,000
Portfolio Duration	5 years	Portfolio Duration	1 year
		Owners' Equity	$0
Interest Rate	10 percent	Interest Rate	10 percent

Following Rise in Rates to 12 Percent

Assets		Liabilities	
Loan Portfolio Value	$909	Deposit Portfolio Value	$982
		Owners' Equity	– $72

For the loan portfolio, the same change in rates creates a much larger drop in the portfolio's value:

$$dP = -5 \ (.02/1.10) \ \$1000 = - \$90.91$$

The effects on the bank are shown in the bottom portion of Table 6.3. Because the duration of the asset portfolio was so much greater, the effect of the rise in rates caused its value to drop much more. Starting from a position of no Owners' Equity, the bank moved to a position of negative equity or technical insolvency.

By careful management of the liabilities and the assets, it might have been possible for the bank to achieve the immunized position shown in the original position of Table 6.4, where both the asset and liability portfolios have a duration of three years. Then, with the same shift in rates from 10 to 12 percent, each portfolio would have the same change in value, since the durations are the same.

$$dP = -3 \ (.02/1.10) \ \$1000 = - \$54.55$$

With the value of both portfolios falling by the same amount, the owners' equity would be unchanged, as the bottom portion of Table 6.4 shows. The bank is immunized against a change in interest rates, because the change in rates leaves the equity position of the bank unchanged.

It must be noted that perfect immunization is very difficult for many financial institutions to achieve. Due to the nature of commercial banking, which involves accepting short-term deposits and making long-term loans, it is difficult

Table 6.4
Immunized Balance Sheet of Simple National Bank

Original Position

Assets		Liabilities	
Loan Portfolio Value	$1,000	Deposit Portfolio Value	$1,000
Portfolio Duration	3 years	Portfolio Duration	3 years
		Owners' Equity	$0
Interest Rate	10 percent	Interest Rate	10 percent

Following Rise in Rates to 12 Percent

Assets		Liabilities	
Loan Portfolio Value	$945	Deposit Portfolio Value	$945
		Owners' Equity	$0

to equate the durations of the two portfolios. However, managing the difference in durations of the two portfolios can help to offset the effects of changes in interest rates even if the bank cannot achieve perfect immunization. In fact, virtually every bank in the country has an asset/liability management committee. The committee plays a crucial role in the management of the bank, and the maturity and duration structure of the two sides of the bank's balance sheet is among the most important issues the committee addresses.[13]

The Planning Period Case

The second basic type of immunization for bond portfolios concerns managing a portfolio toward an horizon date. Many bond portfolios have a definite planning period, with the goal being to achieve a target value for the portfolio at the end of the planning period. For example, a wealthy family might establish a trust fund for a child, with instructions that the child have access to the funds on his or her 21st birthday. In such a situation, the bond manager must manage the portfolio with that horizon or planning period in view. A similar problem occurs in pension fund management, with the bond manager managing the bonds in the pension fund toward a horizon date set when pensions become payable.

The problem confronting the bond manager in this case concerns the effect of changing interest rates on the immediate value of the bond portfolio and on the **reinvestment rate,** the rate at which cash thrown off by the bond portfolio can be reinvested. Overall, a manager investing toward a future horizon date tries to maximize the value of the portfolio on that future date, subject to risk constraints. Equivalent to maximizing the future value of a portfolio, a manager might attempt to maximize the **Realized Compound Yield to Maturity (RCYTM).**

$$RCYTM = \sqrt[n]{\frac{Terminal\ Value}{Initial\ Value}} - 1$$

According to this definition, the RCYTM is the compound yield realized on an investment over n periods. For example, for a bond portfolio with an initial value of \$500,000 that is managed for eight years with a resulting terminal value of \$900,000, the RCYTM is:

$$RCYTM = \sqrt[n]{\frac{Terminal\ Value}{Initial\ Value}} - 1 = \sqrt[8]{\frac{\$900,000}{\$500,000}} - 1 = .0762$$

A change in interest rates during the planning period can dramatically affect the Realized Compound Yield to Maturity (RCYTM), as the following example shows. Assume that a bond portfolio consists of one 10 percent annual coupon bond with a face value of $1,000, which matures in five years. If interest rates are currently 10 percent and remain steady for the five-year period, all of the coupon payments may be invested at 10 percent. In this case, the RCYTM will be 10 percent over that five-year period. On the maturity date, the total value of the bond and all re-invested proceeds will be the value of all of the reinvested coupons:

$$\$100(1.10)^4 + \$100(1.10)^3 + \$100(1.10)^2 + \$100(1.10) = \$\ 510.51$$

plus the final coupon payment and the return of principal:

$$\$1,100.00$$

This gives a total future value of $1,610.51. With initial interest rates at 10 percent, the initial value of the bond must have been $1,000, so the RCYTM was:

$$\text{RCYTM} = (\$1,610.51/\$1,000.00)^{.2} - 1 = 10\%$$

If interest rates had suddenly dropped at the beginning of the investment period from 10 to 8 percent, the RCYTM would have been different. The coupon receipts could have been reinvested only at the new rate of 8 percent, so the future value of the coupon payments would be only $486.66, consisting of the value of all of the reinvested coupons:

$$\$100(1.08)^4 + \$100(1.08)^3 + \$100(1.08)^2 + \$100(1.08) = \$\ 486.66$$

plus the final coupon payment and the return of principal:

$$\$1,100.00$$

This gives a total future value of $1,586.66, so the RCYTM on this investment would be:

$$\text{RCYTM} = (\$1,586.66/\$1,000.00)^{.2} - 1 = 9.67\%$$

Planning Period Immunization allows the bond manager to avoid this result. If the duration of the portfolio equals the number of years in the planning period, the portfolio will be immunized. This means that a shift in interest rates will not affect the RCYTM or the terminal wealth achieved over a given planning period.

In this example, the problem arose from the fact that the duration of the bond was less than the planning period. For this particular bond, the duration was 4.17, but the planning period was five years. Assume now that a longer duration bond was also available, one having eight years to maturity, a 10 percent coupon rate, and a yield-to-maturity of 10 percent. With initial yields at 10 percent, this bond would have a price of $1,000 and a duration of 5.87.

For the planning period of five years, and with the availability of these two bonds, it is possible to create a portfolio with a duration of 5.0, to match the five-year horizon. To create the new portfolio, funds must be contributed to both bonds so that the average duration of the portfolio is 5.0. If 51.18 percent of the portfolio's value is committed to the five-year bond, and 48.82 percent is committed to the eight-year bond, the resulting portfolio will have an average duration of 5.0.

$$\text{Portfolio's duration} = .5118 \ (4.17) + .4882 \ (5.87) = 5.0$$

To see how this works in terms of the original example, assume that the bonds are divisible so that $511.80 is invested in the five-year bond and $488.20 is committed to the eight-year bond. In other words, the portfolio is made up of fractions of the two bonds. With these fractions, the cash flows from the portfolio will still be $100 in coupon per year for the first four years. After five years, the five-year bond will mature. Since the portfolio owns 51.18 percent of that bond, it will receive .5118 x $1,100 = $562.98. Also, since the planning horizon is five years, the longer maturity bond will pay its fifth coupon and then be sold at that time, for a price that depends on market conditions.

To see how the immunization works in this case, assume once again that interest rates change from 10 to 8 percent as soon as the portfolio is established. In this case, the future value of the coupons (measured as of year 5) will be $486.66 as before. With interest rates at 8 percent at year 5, the longer maturity bond still has three years to maturity, and its market price will be $1,051.54.

$$P = \$100/1.08 + \$100/(1.08)^2 + \$100/(1.08)^3 = \$1,051.54$$

Because the portfolio owns 48.82 percent of this bond, its value for the portfolio will be $513.36 at year 5. The total future value of the portfolio at year 5 will come from four sources:

1. Future value of reinvested coupons received during years 1–4: $486.66

2. Future value of payoff on five-year bond:
   $562.98 (51.18% of $1100 final payment)

3. The coupon payment at year 5 on the long-term bond:
   (for the portfolio 48.82% of $100) = $48.82

4. Sale at year 5 of long-term bond
   (48.82% of $1051.54 market value): $513.36

The total future value will be $1,611.82 and the RCYTM will be:

$$\text{RCYTM} = (\$1,611.82/\$1,000)^2 - 1 = 10.02\%$$

This is almost exactly identical to the RCYTM had there been no change in rates whatsoever. This result is brought about by the fact that a change in interest rates has two different effects. In this example, the drop in interest rates causes coupons to be reinvested at a lower rate than they would have been had there been no change. Another effect of the drop in interest rates is the capital gain on the two bonds. For the bond maturing in five years, this gain is never realized, but for the eight-year bond, the capital gain is an important part of the immunization. In fact, when duration equals the planning period, a change in interest rates has a reinvestment rate effect that exactly offsets the capital gain or loss caused by the change in interest rates.

This becomes clear by looking at the same example in a slightly different way. At the outset, the portfolio was constituted as follows:

5-year bond:	D=4.17	Investment = $511.80
8-year bond.	D=5.87	Investment = $488.20

Total Investment = $1,000.00

With a drop in interest rates from 10 to 8 percent, the value of the two bonds changes in the following way:

5-year bond:	dP = - 4.17(-.02/1.10)$511.80 = $38.80
8-year bond:	dP = - 5.87(-.02/1.10)$488.20 = $52.10

Total New Value = $1000 + $38.80 + $52.10 = $1,090.90

This amount can only be invested at 8 percent, because interest rates have already changed. Over a five year horizon, they will grow to $1602.89, $(1090.90)(1.08)^5)$ and this gives a RCYTM of almost exactly 10 percent as well.

$$RCYTM = (\$1,602.89/\$1,000)^{.2} - 1 = 9.90\%$$

Here the price increase caused by the drop in rates is almost exactly offset by the drop in the available reinvestment rate over the five-year planning period.[14]

Some Complications with Immunization

Immunization is more complicated than might at first appear. In the examples, we assumed that interest rates changed by the same amount for all different maturities. This is the same as assuming that any change in the yield curve is merely a parallel shift. Such is patently not the case, as the evidence in Figure 6.5 shows. With twisting yield curves, the immunization will not hold exactly. The duration measure introduced in this chapter is known as "Macaulay's duration." There are other more complicated duration measures which can immunize a portfolio when yield curves change in a non-parallel fashion. However, for any particular duration measure, there is some possible yield curve change that will interfere with the immunization.[15]

A second complication arises from the fact that the immunization result holds only for a single change in interest rates, even when rates change by the same amount for all maturities. Duration varies with the interest rate. So if a portfolio is immunized and interest rates change, the portfolio will not be immunized, because the duration of the various bonds can change in different ways. This is not critically important, but it shows that an immunization strategy requires periodic rebalancing to keep the durations of the various bonds where they need to be.

These complications indicate that there is much skill required of bond portfolio managers if they are to be successful. The bond portfolio manager need not expect to make a living by forecasting interest rates and by making dramatic investment decisions. Instead, the task requires a firm understanding of bond pricing principles and their application to the management of complex portfolios.

Conclusion

This bond primer reviewed the basic principles of bond pricing. We considered the bond pricing formulas for pure discount and coupon bonds, taking note of institutional factors such as accrued interest and discount instrument yield calculations. We briefly discussed some of the many types of money market instruments. Five principles govern the way in which the price of a bond will respond to changes in interest rates. We noted that duration provides a single concept that embraces the yield, time to maturity, and coupon rate.

We explored the term structure of interest rates and compared the three major theories of the term structure: the pure expectations theory, the liquidity premium theory, and the market segmentation theory. Finally, we reviewed bond portfolio maturity strategies and techniques for immunizing bond portfolios. These principles will provide a useful background for our discussion of interest rate futures in Chapters 7 and 8.

Questions and Problems

1. Assume that you are a money manager with a large stock of cash that you will be investing in bonds. You anticipate a strong upward movement in interest rates in general. What do your beliefs imply about the kinds of bonds you will select for investment, particularly with respect to maturity and coupon?

2. Again, assume that you expect sharply rising interest rates and you will buy one of the following two bonds: a 20-year 8 percent coupon bond or a 15-year 9¾ percent coupon bond. Does this give you enough information to make a decision? What else might you need to know?

3. As an investor, you are trying to decide between two bonds as investments for a 4-year investment horizon. The first has a 12 percent coupon and matures in 3 years. The other is a zero coupon bond maturing in 5 years. Compare and contrast the risks associated with each bond and their suitability for your investment horizon.

4. Consider a 5-year pure discount bond with a face value of $1000 that yields 10 percent compounded annually. What is its price? What will its price be if interest rates suddenly rise to 11 percent? What will its price be if interest rates suddenly fall to 9 percent? Are the capital gain and loss the same?

5. What is the price of a 3-year 8 percent annual coupon bond yielding 11 percent and having a face value of $1,000? Assume annual compounding. What is the duration of the bond?

6. Consider again the 3-year 8 percent annual coupon bond yielding 11 percent and having a face value of $1,000. Assume that interest rates suddenly rise to 13 percent. Compute the new price of the bond by discounting the cash flows at the new rate and by using the duration price change formula. Are the two answers the same? Why or why not?

7. What is the duration of a pure discount bond yielding 8 percent and maturing in 3 years and having a face value of $1000?

8. What is the duration of a 12 percent annual coupon bond maturing in 5 years and yielding 11 percent? Assume a $1000 face value.

9. Today you purchase a $1000 face value bond paying an 8 percent annual coupon bond and maturing in 5 years for a purchase price of $930. Assuming that you are able to reinvest all coupons at 11 percent, what is your terminal wealth after 5 years? What is your RCYTM?

10. Assume you have an investment horizon of 5 years. You purchase a pure discount bond with a 5 year maturity and a face value of $1000 for a purchase price of $621. Your friend purchases a 10 percent annual coupon bond with a face value of $1000 at par. What is the current interest rate on each bond? Assuming that rates do not change, what will be the terminal wealth and RCYTM for each bond, assuming that your friend reinvests all coupons? Assume that immediately after purchase interest rates drop to 8 percent. What will be the terminal wealth and RCYTM for the two investments?

11. A bank has hired you as a consultant to advise it on its interest rate exposure. The bank has an asset portfolio of $1,000,000 with a duration of 5 years, and the portfolio is currently yielding 12 percent. This asset portfolio is funded by a liability portfolio, also worth $1,000,000, with a duration of 1.5 years and yielding 10.5 percent. Your problem is to advise the bank on its risk exposure in case interest rates change by 1 percent in either direction. Analyze the resulting position of the bank for both of these cases.

12. Assume that you are asked to manage a $1,000,000 immunized portfolio with a horizon date of 3 years. Two bonds are available to you: a 5-year pure discount bond yielding 10 percent and a 2-year 12 percent annual coupon bond yielding 12 percent. How would you make up the immunized portfolio from these two bonds?

13. For the preceding problem, what will be the terminal wealth of the portfolio assuming that interest rates do not change for 3 years? What is the RCYTM over this period? Now assume that interest rates drop by 1 percent on both bonds. Calculate the terminal wealth at the end of 3 years. Do the same assuming a 2 percent rise in rates.

Notes

1. For more details on T-bills and the full range of money market securities, there are two excellent sources: Timothy Q. Cook and Bruce J. Summers, *Instruments of the Money Market*, Richmond, VA: Federal Reserve Bank of Richmond, 1981, 5th edition, and Marcia Stigum, *The Money Market*, Homewood, IL: Dow Jones-Irwin, 1983, Revised Edition, p. 49.

2. In addition to Eurodollars, one sometimes hears mention of Asian dollars and Petro dollars. As defined here, these would be components of the Eurodollar market as well. Asian dollars are dollar denominated deposits held in Asian based banks, while Petro dollars are dollar denominated deposits generated by oil producing countries.

3. Recall that there is also accrued interest to be considered, as explained earlier, and that bond prices are normally quoted ignoring the accrued interest. Thus, in the example of the bond with the coupon rate equal to the yield-to-maturity, the quoted price will always be at par. The accrued interest must be added to the quoted price, however, to determine the actual sales price of the bond.

4. See Burton G. Malkiel, "Expectations, Bond Prices, and the Term Structure of Interest Rates," *Quarterly Journal of Economics*, May 1962, pp. 197-218.

5. These bond pricing principles are discussed in detail and illustrated with examples in R. Kolb, *Investments*, Glenview, IL: Scott Foresman, Inc., Second Edition 1988, Chapter 7.

6. See F. R. Macaulay, *Some Theoretical Problems Suggested by the Movements of Interest Rates, Bond Yields, and Stock Prices in the United States Since 1856*, New York: Columbia University Press, 1938.

7. Here it is not possible to say what the expected rate for each of the one-year bonds would be. But the geometric average of these returns must be 9.753 percent. Fortunately, that is enough for the present purpose.

8. The reasons for this kinds of preference are explained below in the section on Portfolio Immunization Strategies.

9. The Market Segmentation Theory was first advanced by Franco Modigliani and Richard Sutch, "Innovations in Interest Rate Policy," *American Economic Review*, May 1966. Empirical support for the theory can be found in Edward J. Kane and Burton G. Malkiel, "The Term Structure of Interest Rates: An Analysis of a Survey of Interest Rate Expectations," *Review of Economics and Statistics*, August 1967; Wayne Lee, Terry Maness, and Donald Tuttle, "Speculative Behavior and the Term Structure," *Journal of Financial and Quantitative Analysis*, March 1980; and J. W. Elliot and M. E. Echols, "Market Segmentation, Speculative Behavior, and the Term Structure of Interest Rates," *Review of Economics and Statistics*, February 1976.

10. David Meiselman, *The Term Structure of Interest Rates*, Englewood Cliffs, NJ: Prentice Hall Inc. 1962; Anthony M. Santomero, "The Error Learning Hypothesis and the Term Structure of Interest Rates in Eurodollars," *Journal of Finance*, June 1975.

11. Charles Nelson, "Estimation of Term Premiums from Average Yield Differentials in the Term Structure of Interest Rates," *Econometrica*, March 1972; J. Huston McCulloch, "An Estimate of the Liquidity Premium," *Journal of Political Economy*, February 1975.

12. The ideas of this section may be stated with respect to both maturity and duration. For convenience, the focus here is on maturity.

13. For a more thorough discussion of the asset/liability management problem in commercial banks, see Joseph F. Sinkey, Jr., *Commercial Bank Financial Management*, New York: Macmillan Co., 1989, Chapter 17.

14. The slight deviation, from 10.00 percent to 9.90 percent, stems from the fact that the change in interest rates was discrete, changing by a relatively large amount. The immunization result holds exactly only for infinitesimal changes in interest rates. This presents no major difficulties for practical applications.

15. For more on duration, see G. O. Bierwag and G. G. Kaufman, "Coping with the Risk of Interest Rate Fluctuations: A Note," *Journal of Business*, July 1977, pp. 364-370; G. O. Bierwag, "Measures of Duration," *Economic Inquiry*, October 1978, pp. 497-507. For an application of duration and immunization to interest rate futures, see Chapter 8.

7

Interest Rate Futures: Introduction

Introduction

This chapter explores one of the most successful and exciting innovations in the history of futures markets—the emergence of interest rate futures contracts. Since the first contracts were traded on October 20, 1975, the market has expanded rapidly. In spite of a number of relatively unsuccessful contracts that have been introduced, such as commercial paper and Certificate Delivery GNMA contracts, the market has been a huge success.[1] By fall 1990, open interest exceed 800 billion (face value) of underlying financial instruments, up from just $300 billion three years earlier. From inception, the interest rate futures market has come to represent about one-half of the entire futures market, and most industry observers expect the continued growth of the futures market to center around financial instruments.

Almost all of the activity in the U.S. interest rate futures is concentrated in two exchanges, the Chicago Board of Trade and the International Monetary Market of the Chicago Mercantile Exchange. The Board of Trade specializes in contracts at the longer end of the maturity spectrum, with active contracts on long-term Treasury bonds and 10-year, 5-year, and 2-year Treasury notes. In addition, the CBT trades a municipal bond contract. By contrast, the International Monetary Market has successful contracts with very short maturities, trading contracts for three-month Treasury bills and Eurodollar Deposits. While this chapter discusses features of many different contracts, we focus on the seven most important contracts: the T-bond contract, three T-note contracts, and the municipal bond contract traded on the CBT, along with the T-bill and Eurodollar contracts traded on the IMM of the CME. For the most part, these are highly active contracts that differ widely in their contract terms and the maturities of the underlying instruments. Figure 7.1 presents price quotations for these seven contracts.

Figure 7.1
Price Quotations for Major Interest Rate Futures Contracts

FUTURES

```
                                              Yield       Open
                    Open  High  Low Settle  Chg Settle Chg Interest
TREASURY BONDS (CBT)—$100,000; pts. 32nds of 100%
Dec      90-02  90-30  89-31  90-14 +  15  9.042 — .056 241,467
Mr91     89-20  90-17  89-19  90-02 +  16  9.087 — .059  17,317
June     89-15  90-03  89-15  89-21 +  16  9.135 — .060   5,733
Sept     89-18  89-22  89-08  89-09 +  16  9.180 — .060   3,411
Dec      88-22  89-10  88-22  88-30 +  17  9.221 — .065   2,244
Mr92     88-23  88-26  88-20  88-20 +  18  9.259 — .069     475
June     ....   ....   ....   88-10 +  18  9.297 — .069     151
   Est vol 315,000; vol Wed 324,036; op int 270,829, —2,195.

TREASURY NOTES (CBT)—$100,000; pts. 32nds of 100%
Dec      95-01  95-20  95-00  95-11 +  10  8.707 — .049  61,937
Mr91     94-30  95-12  94-30  95-03 +  10  8.746 — .049   4,142
   Est vol 21,000; vol Wed 29,478; open int 66,081, +232.
5 YR TREAS NOTES (CBT)—$100,000; pts. 32nds of 100%
Dec      98-145 98-255 98-14 98-195 + 6.0  8.35  — .04  76,868
Mr91     98-10  98-205 98-10 98-155 + 6.0  8.38  — .04   2,416
   Est vol 8,484; vol Wed 6,241; open int 79,284, +172.
2 YR TREAS NOTES (CBT)—$200,000, pts. 32nds of 100%
Dec      00-027 00-045 00-022 100-03 + ¼  7.948 — .005   6,125
   Est vol 472; vol Wed 940; open int 6,155, —199.

TREASURY BILLS (IMM)—$1 mil.; pts. of 100%
                                            Discount     Open
                    Open  High  Low Settle  Chg Settle Chg Interest
Dec      93.20  93.22  93.16  93.21 — .01  6.79 + .01  36,540
Mr91     93.40  93.43  93.40  93.43  ....  6.57  ....   9,793
June     93.39  93.41  93.38  93.41  ....  6.59  ....     554
Sept     ....   ....   ....   93.32 + .01  6.68 — .01     182
   Est vol 6,657; vol Wed 9,469; open int 47,140, —759.

                                                       Open
                    Open  High  Low Settle  Chg High  Low Interest
MUNI BOND INDEX (CBT)-$1,000; times Bond Buyer MBI
Dec      87-21  88-02  87-15  87-18 —  3  92-21  85-14  8,588
   Est vol 1,200; vol Wed 1,178; open int 8,634, —12.
   The Index: Close 88-14; Yield 7.97.
EURODOLLAR (IMM)—$1 million; pts of 100%
                                              Yield       Open
                    Open  High  Low Settle  Chg Settle Chg Interest
Dec      91.97  92.03  91.94  91.98  ....  8.02  .... 244,022
Mr91     92.13  92.18  92.10  92.14 + .01  7.86 — .01 141,772
June     92.10  92.17  92.06  92.12 + .02  7.88 — .02  83,977
Sept     91.97  92.03  91.96  92.00 + .04  8.00 — .04  53,425
Dec      91.62  91.68  91.61  91.65 + .04  8.35 — .04  42,709
Mr92     91.45  91.52  91.45  91.50 + .05  8.50 — .05  32,581
June     91.28  91.36  91.28  91.34 + .06  8.66 — .06  23,283
Sept     91.15  91.24  91.15  91.21 + .06  8.79 — .06  15,404
Dec      90.93  91.02  90.92  90.99 + .06  9.01 — .06  12,571
Mr93     90.88  90.98  90.88  90.94 + .06  9.06 — .06  10,092
June     90.79  90.88  90.79  90.86 + .07  9.14 — .07   8,560
Sept     90.72  90.81  90.72  90.79 + .07  9.21 — .07   5,320
Dec      90.60  90.70  90.60  90.67 + .07  9.33 — .07   3,422
Mr94     90.61  90.68  90.61  90.66 + .07  9.34 — .07   3,040
June     90.55  90.62  90.55  90.60 + .08  9.40 — .08   2,404
Sept     90.59  90.59  90.58  90.57 + .08  9.43 — .08   1,305
   Est vol 143,092; vol Wed 108,821; open int 683,887,+4,966.
```

Source: *The Wall Street Journal*, October 19, 1990.

Interest Rate Futures Contracts

To understand the interest rate futures market, we need to understand the specifications for the different contracts. Among all the different types of futures contracts, interest rate futures exhibit the most variety, with the characteristics of the futures contracts being tailored to the particular attributes of the underlying instruments. We begin by considering the contract specifications for the major short-maturity contracts.

Treasury–Bill Futures

The T-bill futures contract, traded by the International Monetary Market (IMM) of the Chicago Mercantile Exchange (CME), calls for the delivery of T-bills having a face value of $1,000,000 and a time to maturity of 90 days at the expiration of the futures contract. The contracts trade for delivery in March, June, September, and December. The delivery dates are chosen to make newly issued 13-week T-bills immediately deliverable against the futures contract. Also, a previously issued one-year T-bill will have 13 weeks until maturity, and it can also be delivered against the T-bill futures contract. The IMM permits delivery on the three business days following the last day of trading.

Price quotations for T-bill futures use the IMM-Index, which is a function of the discount yield:

$$IMM \ Index = 100.00 - DY \qquad\qquad 7.1$$

where:

DY = Discount yield, e.g., 7.1 is 7.1 percent

As an example, a discount yield of 8.32 percent implies an IMM-index value of 91.68. The IMM adopted this method of price quotation to ensure that the bid price would be below the asked price, the relationship prevailing in most markets. Price fluctuations may be no smaller than one tick, or one basis point. Given the fact that the instruments are priced by using a discount yield and a contract size of $1,000,000, a one basis point movement in the interest rate generates a price change of $25.00. Equation 7.2 gives the price that must be paid at delivery for the cash market bill:

$$Bill \ Price = \$1,000,000 - \frac{DY \ (\$1,000,000) \ (DTM)}{360} \qquad 7.2$$

where:

DTM = Days until maturity

With a discount yield of 8.32 percent on the futures contract, the price to be paid for the T-bill at delivery would be $979,200:

$$\text{Bill Price} = \$1,000,000 - \frac{.0832 \ (\$1,000,000) \ (90)}{360} = \$979,200$$

If the futures yield rose to 8.35 percent, the delivery price would be $979,125, changing $25 for each basis point. Many futures contracts have a daily price limit, a constraint on how much the futures price is allowed to move in a single day of trading. For example, in former times the limit for the T-bill contract was 60 basis points, or $1,500, in either direction from the previous day's settlement price. The contract specifications have been changed and now there is no limit on the daily price fluctuation.

Figure 7.1 presents price quotations for T-bill futures. These quotations are similar in structure to those for other futures contracts. The first four columns of figures give the open, high, low, and settlement quotations in terms of the IMM Index. The "Chg" column shows the change in the IMM Index from the previous day's settlement. Under the heading "Discount" there is the settlement discount yield and the change in the settlement discount yield. Notice that the settlement discount yield plus the settlement IMM Index always sum to 100.0. Similarly, the change in the IMM Index and the change in the discount yield are always equal in magnitude but opposite in sign. The last column gives the open interest for each contract maturity. The final line of the quotations reports the volume, open interest across all maturities, and the change in the open interest since the previous day.

Although the contract specifications call for the delivery of a T-bill having 90 days to maturity, delivery of 91- or 92-day bills is also permitted with a price adjustment. The price can be adjusted by substituting the correct number of days until maturity in equation 7.2. In any event, all of the delivered T-bills must be of the same maturity. Upon delivery, the short trader must deliver the T-bills and the long trader must pay the Invoice Amount. The Invoice Amount is:

$$\text{Invoice Amount} =$$

$$\$1,000,000 - \frac{\text{T-bill Yield} \ (\$1,000,000) \ (\text{DTM})}{360} \qquad 7.3$$

The actual delivery process extends over two business days. On the first day, the short trader gives notice to the IMM Clearinghouse that he or she will deliver.

The Clearinghouse assigns the delivery to an outstanding long trader. The two traders communicate with their own and the other trader's banks to alert the banks to the impending transactions. To consummate the transaction, the short trader delivers the bills and the long trader pays the short trader. This is accomplished through wire transfers between the banks of the two traders. Figure 7.2 diagrams the delivery process followed by the IMM clearinghouse.

Figure 7.2
Treasury Bill Futures Delivery Procedure

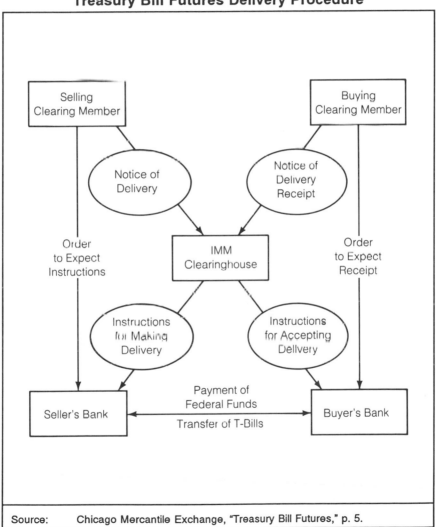

Source: Chicago Mercantile Exchange, "Treasury Bill Futures," p. 5.

Eurodollar Futures

Eurodollar deposits are U.S. dollar deposits held in a commercial bank outside the United States. These banks may be either foreign banks or foreign branches of U.S. banks. The deposits are normally non-transferable and cannot be used as collateral for loans. London dominates the Eurodollar deposit market, so rates in this market are often based on LIBOR, the London Interbank Offer Rate. LIBOR is the rate at which banks are willing to lend funds to other banks in the interbank market. LIBOR is an important rate in international finance. For example, many loans to developing countries have been priced as LIBOR plus some number of percentage points.

Eurodollar futures, like T-bill futures, trade on the IMM of the CME. Eurodollar futures have come to dominate the market for short-term contracts and greatly exceed the T-bill contract in volume and open interest. Like the T-bill contract, the instrument underlying the Eurodollar contract has a three-month maturity. Unlike the T-bill contract, the underlying good is not a bond but a time deposit held in a commercial bank. Also, unlike the T-bill contract, there is no actual delivery on the Eurodollar contract. Instead, the contract is fulfilled by cash settlement.[2]

The Eurodollar futures contract was the first contract to use cash settlement rather than the delivery of an actual good for contract fulfillment. We have already noted that Eurodollar deposits are non-transferable, a feature that by itself precludes delivery. As a result, the IMM requires fulfillment of a contract by a cash payment based on its measure of Eurodollar rates. To establish the settlement rate at the close of trading, the IMM determines the three-month LIBOR rate. It then uses this rate indication to establish the final settlement price. The rules of the exchange are quite explicit:

> The final settlement price shall be determined by the Clearing House as follows. On the last day of trading the Clearing House shall determine the London Interbank Offered rate (LIBOR) for three-month Eurodollar Time Deposit funds both at the time of termination of trading and at a randomly-selected time within the last 90 minutes of trading. The final settlement price shall be 100 minus the arithmetic mean, rounded to the nearest 1/100th of a percentage point, of the LIBOR at these two times.

> To determine the LIBOR at either time the Clearing House shall select at random 12 reference banks from a list of no less than 20 participating banks that are major banks in the London Eurodollar market. Each reference bank shall quote to the Clearing House its perception of the rate at which three-month Eurodollar Time Deposit funds are currently offered by the market to prime banks. These rates

must be confirmed in writing by telex before they are accepted as official; only after confirmation will they be used to determine the final settlement price. The two highest and the two lowest quotes shall be eliminated. The arithmetic mean of the remaining eight quotes shall be the LIBOR at that time. If for any reason there is difficulty in obtaining a quote within a reasonable time interval from one of the banks in the sample, that bank shall be dropped from the sample, and another shall be randomly selected to replace it.[3]

The use of a number of banks with polling at two separate times and confirmation required in writing is designed to thwart any attempted manipulation of the final settlement price. Since its inception in 1981, this procedure has worked very well, with Eurodollar futures having grown very rapidly. Once the final settlement price is determined, traders with open positions settle with cash through the normal marking-to-market procedure. This fulfills their obligation and the contract expires.

Prior to the final trading day, the daily settlement price depends on the quotations in the futures market. In a sense, the futures price appears free to wander from the spot market values except for the final day of trading. This is an illusion, however. Consider, for example, the second to last trading day. Traders know that tomorrow the futures settlement price will be set equal to the average LIBOR actually available from banks. Therefore, the price today cannot be very different from today's cash market LIBOR. If it did differ significantly, traders would enter the market to buy or sell futures and would expect to reap their profit when the futures price is pegged to the cash market LIBOR. This same argument holds for every other day prior to expiration as well, so the Eurodollar futures contract must behave as though there will be an actual delivery at the contract's expiration. We will see evidence of this relationship later.

For the Eurodollar contract, the contract size is for $1,000,000, with the yield being quoted on an add-on basis. The add-on yield is given by:

$$\text{Add-on Yield} = \left(\frac{\text{Discount}}{\text{Price}}\right)\left(\frac{360}{\text{DTM}}\right) \qquad 7.4$$

For example, assume the discount yield is 8.32 percent. We have already seen that this discount yield gives a price of $979,200 for a $1 million face value three-month T-bill. Therefore, the dollar discount is $20,800 and 90 days remain until the bill will mature. With these values we have:

$$\text{Add-on Yield} = \left(\frac{\$20,800}{\$979,200}\right)\left(\frac{360}{90}\right) = .0850$$

Add-on yields exceed corresponding discount yields. In our example, the discount yield is 8.32 percent, and the add-on yield equivalent is 8.5 percent. However, for both measures, a shift of one basis point is worth $25 on a $1,000,000 contract. Note also that these yields and relationships vary with maturity, so the statements made here hold only for three-month maturities.

Figure 7.1 shows price quotations for Eurodollar futures from *The Wall Street Journal*. The quotations have the same structure as the T-bill futures examined in the previous section, but the yields are add-on yields. Like the T-bill contract, the Eurodollar contract uses the IMM Index. Thus, the quoted price is:

$$\text{IMM Index} = 100.00 - \text{LIBOR} \qquad\qquad 7.5$$

Figure 7.3
DEC 1989 T–Bill and Eurodollar Futures Yields

The relationship between the T-bill and Eurodollar futures yields is very stable. For the DEC 1989 contracts, Figure 7.3 shows the settlement yields for both contracts over the lives of the contracts, with Eurodollar yields exceeding T-bill yields. The relationship between the two is very steady. To emphasize this strong correspondence between these yields, we estimated the following regression for the DEC 1989 contracts using daily data:

Change in Eurodollar Yield$_t$ = α + β Change in T-bill Yield$_t$ + e$_t$

The results were:

α = -.00001
β = 1.012   t-statistic = 52.84
R^2 = .8674
Obs. = 429

What the graph strongly indicates, the regression confirms: There is an extremely strong relationship between the level of T-bill and Eurodollar yields. Notice also that the Eurodollar yield lies above the T-bill yield. From the regression we can see that Eurodollar yields move just slightly more than 1:1 for a change in T-bill yields, because the estimated β = 1.012. Later in this chapter, we explore some speculative strategies based on the relationship between these two yields.

Treasury–Bond Futures

Of all futures contracts, the T-bond contract is one of the most complex and most interesting. The complexity of the contract stems from the delivery rules under which it is traded and from the wide variety of bonds that can be delivered to fulfill the contract. For the T-bill contract, delivery takes place within a very narrow span of time, but the Chicago Board of Trade, which trades the T-bond contract, employs a radically different delivery procedure.

In spite of its peculiarities, the T-bond contract is perhaps the single most successful futures contract ever introduced. Starting in August 1977, its success has been amazing. In 1986, for example, more than 52 million T-bond futures contracts were traded, and in 1989 this figure exceeded 70 million. With a face value per contract of $100,000, this represents an underlying value of more than $7.2 trillion. This single contract accounted for more than 50 percent of the CBT's total volume of futures and options contracts.

Figure 7.1 presented quotations for T-bond futures from *The Wall Street Journal*. The structure of these quotations parallels the others we have already examined. The first four columns of figures give the open, high, low, and settlement price for the contract, with the quotations in "points and 32nds of par." For example, a quoted price of 97-26 means that the contract traded for 97 and 26/32nds of par. The decimal equivalent of this value is 97.8125 percent of par. With a par value of $100,000 per contract, the cash price would be $97,812.50. The next column shows the change since the previous settlement in 32nds. The next column shows the bond yield implied by the futures price, followed by the change in the bond yield since the previous settlement. The final column of figures gives the open interest per contract. The final line in the quotations gives the usual volume and open interest information.

For the T-bond contract, the minimum price fluctuation is 1/32nd of one full percentage point of face value. This means that the minimum price fluctuation per contract is $31.25 [(1/32)(.01)($100,000)]. In normal market conditions, the daily price limit is three full points, or 96 32nds, for a daily price limit of $3,000 per contract.[4]

Delivery against the T-bond contract is a several day process that the short trader can trigger to cause delivery on any business day of the delivery month. Like the T-bill and Eurodollar contracts, the T-bond contract trades for delivery in March, June, September, and December. Delivery can be made on any business day of the delivery month, with the short trader choosing the exact delivery day. To effect delivery, the short trader initiates a delivery sequence that extends over three business days. Figure 7.4 shows the delivery procedure for T-bond futures, a procedure that applies to other Board of Trade contracts, such as the T-note futures contracts.

The **First Position Day** is the first permissible day for the short trader to declare his or her intention to make delivery, with the delivery taking place two business days later. The first permissible day for such an announcement falls in the month preceding the delivery month, since delivery can occur as soon as the first business day of the delivery month. If the short declares the intention to deliver on any other day besides the First Position Day, then that day is called **Position Day**. On Position Day, the short trader announces the intention to deliver on the second business day thereafter.

The second day in the delivery sequence is the **Notice of Intention Day**. On this day, the Clearing Corporation matches the short trader with the long trader having the longest outstanding position, and identifies the short and long traders to each other.[5] The short trader is then obligated to make delivery to that particular long trader on the next business day. The third and final day of the delivery sequence is **Delivery Day**, when the actual transaction takes place. On this day the short delivers the financial instrument to the long trader and receives payment. The long trader then has all rights of ownership in the T-bonds that were delivered in fulfillment of the contract.

For the T-bond futures contract, a wide variety of bonds may be delivered against the contract at any one time. The rules of the Board of Trade call for the delivery of $100,000 worth of T-bonds having at least 15 years remaining until maturity or to their first permissible call date.

Figure 7.4
The Delivery Procedure for T–Bond Futures

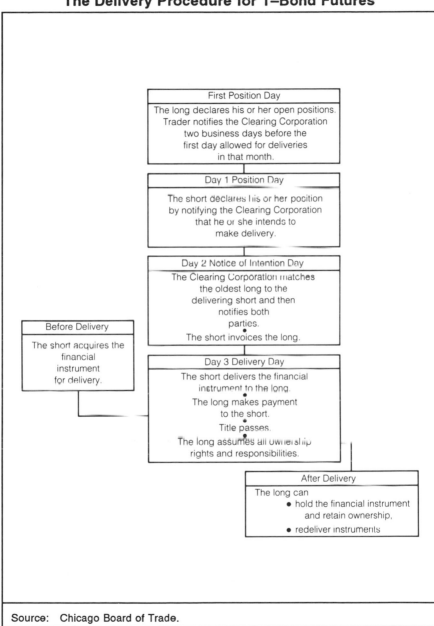

Source: Chicago Board of Trade.

Table 7.1 presents the key dates in the delivery process for both the T–bond and T–note futures contracts for a recent period, and Table 7.2 shows the T–bonds eligible for delivery as of July 20, 1990. The first three columns list the coupon rate, maturity, and market value outstanding. The rest of the table lists conversion factors for each bond and each maturity date. (These conversion factors are explained below.) Where a conversion factor is given for a bond and an expiration date, that bond is deliverable against that futures contract. Notice, however, that the 9–3/8 maturing on February 15, 2006 is not deliverable against the MAR 1991 contract. This bond will not have a full 15 years to maturity in March 1991, so it will not be eligible for delivery. Notice that it still is deliverable, however, against the DEC 90 contract.

As Table 7.2 shows, 23 different bonds could be delivered against the SEP 90 contract. Coupons on these bonds range from 7¼ percent to a full 14 percent and the maturities range from 2006 to 2020. With all of these bonds outstanding, quite a few different bonds will be deliverable against the T–bond contract for years to come.

The fact that some bonds are cheap, and some expensive, suggests that there may be an advantage to delivering one bond rather than another. If there is such an advantage, why did the CBT allow several bonds to be delivered against the contract? These considerations are intimately related and have an important impact on the contract design. The significant differences in maturity and coupon rates among these bonds cause large price differences. Because the short trader chooses whether to make delivery, and which bond to deliver, we might expect that only the cheapest bond would ever be delivered.

To eliminate an incentive to deliver just one particular bond, the CBT initiated a system of conversion factors which alters the delivery values of different bonds as a function of their coupon rate and term-to-maturity. The conversion factors in Table 7.2 are based on a hypothetical bond with 20 years to maturity and an 8 percent coupon rate. A quick glance at Table 7.2 shows that no such bond even existed in August 1990.

Table 7.1
The Delivery Sequence for T–Bond and T–Note Futures

Contract Expiration	First Position	First Notice	First Delivery	Last Trading	Last Delivery
SEP 90	AUG 30	AUG 31	SEP 3	SEP 19	SEP 28
DEC	NOV 29	NOV 30	DEC 3	DEC 19	DEC 31
MAR 91	FEB 27	FEB 28	MAR 1	MAR 20	MAR 29
JUN	MAY 30	MAY 31	JUN 3	JUN 19	JUN 28

Source: Chicago Board of Trade, *CBT Financial Update*, July 29, 1990.

Table 7.2
Deliverable T–bonds and Conversion Factors

Coupon	Maturity	Mkt. Value	MAR 91	JUN 91	SEP 91
7.250	May 15, 2016	18.82	.9194	.9195	.9200
7.500	Nov 15, 2016	18.86	.9460	.9459	.9463
8.125	Aug 15, 2019	20.01	1.0137	1.0139	1.0137
8.500	Feb 15, 2020	10.06	1.0557	1.0558	1.0555
8.750	May 15, 2017	18.19	1.0816	1.0811	1.0811
8.750	May 15, 2020	10.01	1.0841	1.0837	1.0837
8.750	Aug 15, 2020	10.26	1.0841	1.0841	1.0837
8.875	Aug 15, 2017	14.02	1.0952	1.0951	1.0946
8.875	Feb 15, 2019	19.25	1.0968	1.0967	1.0963
9.000	Nov 15, 2018	9.03	1.1105	1.1100	1.1100
9.125	May 15, 2018	8.71	1.1237	1.1232	1.1230
9.250	Feb 15, 2016	7.27	1.1336	1.1334	1.1327
9.375	Feb 15, 2006	4.76	-	-	-
9.875	Nov 15, 2015	6.90	1.2001	1.1992	1.1987
10.375	Nov 15, 2007-12	11.03	1.2155	1.2136	1.2122
10.625	Aug 15, 2015	7.15	1.2789	1.2782	1.2769
11.250	Feb 15, 2015	12.67	1.3429	1.3419	1.3404
11.750	Nov 15, 2009-14	6.01	1.3589	1.3565	1.3545
12.000	Aug 15, 2008-13	14.76	1.3705	1.3682	1.3653
12.500	Aug 15, 2009-14	5.13	1.4278	1.4254	1.4224
12.750	Nov 15, 2005-10	4.74	-	-	-
13.250	May 15, 2009-14	5.01	1.4963	1.4929	1.4899
13.875	May 15, 2006 11	4.61	1.5080	-	-
14.000	Nov 15, 2006-11	4.90	1.5277	1.5229	1.5188

Source: Chicago Board of Trade, *CBT Financial Update*, August 17, 1990.

For purposes of delivery, the CBT adjusts the price of every bond using a conversion factor that is specific to a given bond and a particular futures contract expiration. The invoice amount is calculated according to equation 7.6:

$$\text{Invoice Amount} = \text{DSP} (\$100{,}000) (\text{CF}) + \text{AI} \qquad 7.6$$

where:

DSP = decimal settlement price (e.g., 96–16 = .965)
CF = conversion factor
AI = accrued interest

Each term requires comment. The **Decimal Settlement Price** is simply the decimal equivalent of the quoted price, which is expressed in "points and 32nds of par." The $100,000 reflects the contract amount. The conversion factor attempts to adjust for differences in coupons and maturities among the deliverable bonds.

The conversion factor for any bond can be approximated quite accurately by following two rules:

1. Assume that the face value of the bond to be delivered is $1.
2. Discount the assumed cash flows from the bond at 8 percent using the Bond Pricing Equation.

The result approximates the conversion factor for the bond in question. This will only be an approximation, however, because the official conversion factors reflect quarterly intervals between the present and the delivery date. Exact conversion factors are available in the form shown as Table 7.2 from the Chicago Board of Trade.[6] The conversion factors can also be found from these formulas:

For bonds with an even number of full semi–annual periods until maturity:

$$CF = \sum_{t=1}^{n} \frac{C_t}{1.04^t} + \frac{1}{1.04^n} \qquad 7.7$$

For bonds with an uneven number of full semi-annual periods until maturity:

$$CF = \frac{\displaystyle\sum_{t=1}^{n} \frac{C_t}{1.04^t} + \frac{1}{1.04^n} + C_t}{1.04^{.5}} - .5\,C_t \qquad 7.8$$

where:

CF = conversion factor

C_t = semi-annual coupon payment in dollars assuming a $1 face value bond

n = the number of full semi-annual periods remaining from the bond before maturity (or call if the bond is callable)

As examples, we will compute the conversion factors for the MAR 91 and JUN 91 deliveries of the 7¼ bond maturing on May 15, 2016. On March 1, 1991, there were 50 full semi-annual periods until maturity on this bond, one in May 1991, 48 in the years from November 15, 1991 through November 15, 2015, and one from November 15, 2015 to maturity on May 15, 2016. Assuming a $1 face value, the semi-annual coupon would be $.03625 = .5(.0725). With an even number of periods, we can use the simpler version of the formula:

$$CF = \sum_{t=1}^{50} \frac{.03625}{1.04^t} + \frac{1}{1.04^{50}}$$
$$= .7787 + .1407$$
$$= .9194$$

This matches the conversion factor in the table of .9194.

As a second example, we compute the conversion factor for the same bond for delivery on the JUN 91 contract. On June 1, 1991 this bond has only 49 full semi-annual periods until it matures. Therefore, we use the second version of the conversion factor formula. We have:

$$CF = \frac{\sum_{t=1}^{49} \frac{.03625}{1.04^t} + \frac{1}{1.04^{49}} + .03625}{1.04^{.5}} - .5(.03625)$$

$$= \frac{.7736 + .1463 + .03625}{1.04^{.5}} - .0181$$

$$= .9195$$

This value matches the .9195 of Table 7.2.

Looking closely at the conversion factors in Table 7.2, we can note that the closer the coupon rate is to 8 percent, the closer the conversion factor will be to 1. For a bond with an 8 percent coupon, the conversion factor would equal 1.0. This makes sense, because the conversion factor would be calculated by discounting an 8 percent coupon instrument at 8 percent. For bonds with coupon rates above 8 percent, the shorter the maturity, the closer the conversion factor will be to 1. Just the opposite holds for bonds with coupon rates below 8 percent. In general, if yields are 8 percent across all maturities, the conversion factors will be proportional to the bonds' market prices. This is exactly the desired situation, since the delivery value of a bond should be proportional to its market value.

With a flat term structure and yields at 8 percent, there is no advantage to delivering any bond rather than another. The correlative of this proposition is somewhat disturbing and very important for T-bond futures. If the term structure is not flat, or if yields are not equal to 8 percent, then there is some bond that is better to deliver than the other permissible bonds. This bond is known as the **cheapest-to-deliver**. Among T-bond futures traders, the concept of the cheapest-to-deliver bond is well known. Most brokerage houses have computer systems that show the cheapest-to-deliver T-bonds on a real time basis. Since this feature is well known, futures prices tend to track the cheapest-to-deliver bond, which may change over time.

The interplay of actual bond market prices and the conversion factor biases noted above determine which bond will be the cheapest-to-deliver at any given moment. Prior to actual delivery, some bond will be the cheapest to acquire and to carry to delivery. We have already noted that the cost-of-carry relationship considers the net financing cost of carrying an asset to delivery. In the T-bond futures market, the net financing cost is the price that must be paid for funds less the coupon rate obtained by holding the bond itself. Therefore, at any particular moment, the cheapest-to-deliver bond will be the bond that is most profitable to deliver. In Chapter 8, we explain how to find the cheapest-to-deliver bond in more detail.

Why did the CBT adopt this cumbersome system of conversion factors, particularly since it introduces biases into the market? As we have seen, a substantial deliverable supply of the spot commodity is a necessary condition for a successful futures contract. If the supply of the deliverable commodity is insufficient, then opportunities for market corners and squeezes can arise. To ensure a large deliverable supply, the CBT allowed a wide range of bonds to qualify for delivery. With many bonds eligible for delivery, it is necessary to adjust bond prices to reflect their varying market values.

In futures markets, the short trader usually has choices to make in the delivery process. For example, we have noted that the short trader chooses the exact delivery day in the delivery month and chooses which deliverable bond to deliver. Therefore, the short trader has a number of options imbedded in the futures position. These timing and quality options have a value to the seller, so they effectively reduce the prices that we observe in futures markets. Assessing the value of these options for the seller becomes quite complicated. We consider them briefly later in this chapter, and we focus on them in substantial detail in Chapter 8.

Treasury–Note Futures

As we discussed in Chapter 6, T–bonds and T–notes share a very similar structure, but they differ in the term to maturity at which they are initially offered. Both instruments pay semi-annual coupons. Just as the spot market instruments are very similar, the T–bond and T–note futures contracts are very similar as well.

There are three T–note futures contracts trading at the Chicago Board of Trade. While similar in structure, these contracts are based on notes of varying maturities. Nominally, the contracts are designated as 10–, 5–, and 2–year contracts. However, a range of maturities is deliverable against each contract.

Deliverable T–Note Maturities

2–Year Contract	On the first day of the delivery month, the maturity cannot be less than 1 year 9 months. On the last day of the delivery month, the maturity cannot exceed two years.
5–Year Contract	On the first business day of the delivery month, the bond cannot have a maturity less than 4 years and 3 months nor greater than 5 years and 3 months.
10–Year Contract	From the first day of the delivery month, at least 6 years and 6 months and not more than 10 years to maturity.

T–Note Contract Features

Contract Feature	2–Year	5 Year	10–Year
Contract Face Value	$200,000	$100,000	$100,000
Price Quotation	Points and one quarter 32nds	Points and one half 32nds	Points and 32nds
Tick Size	One quarter of a 32nd	One half 32nd	One 32nd
Price Limits	1 point ($2,000)	3 points ($3,000)	3 points ($3,000)

Notice that the 2–year contract has a face value of $200,000 per contract, while the 5– and 10–year contracts have a face value of $100,000. As we explained in Chapter 6, the shorter the maturity of a bond the less responsive its price will be to changes in interest rates. By having a larger denomination for the 2–year contract, the CBT brings the volatilities of the contracts into the same range. This difference in the volatility of the underlying bonds leads to differences in price quotations. For the 2-year, the tick size is one quarter of a 32nd, while the 5-year contract has a one half of a 32nd tick size. Each contract allows for a range of deliverable maturities, thereby increasing the deliverable supply for each contract.

The T-note and T-bond contracts use the same system of conversion factors as the T-bond contract, and they have the same delivery system. As the quotations of Figure 7.1 show, the 10-year and 5-year contracts have substantial trading volume and open interest. The 2-year contract started trading on June 22, 1990. Therefore, it is still a fledgling contract that must prove itself by building trading volume if it is to succeed.

Price movements of T-bonds and T-notes are closely related. Figure 7.5 shows T-note and T-bond futures prices for contracts expiring in December 1989. Using these prices we estimated the following regression for the T-bond and the 10-year T-note futures contracts:

$$\text{Change in T-bond Futures } P_t = \alpha + \beta \text{ Change in T-note Futures } P_t + e_t$$

Figure 7.5
T-Bond and T-Note Futures Prices

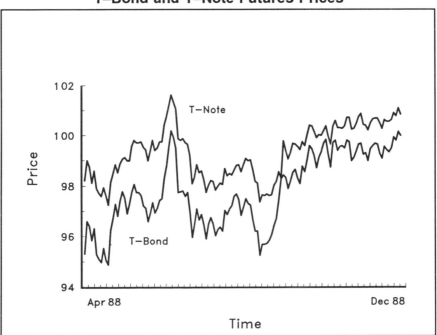

The results were:

$$
\begin{aligned}
\alpha &= -.0148 \\
\beta &= 1.1247 \qquad \text{t-statistic} = 20.40 \\
R^2 &= .7565 \\
\text{Obs.} &= 136
\end{aligned}
$$

This simple exercise emphasizes the close relationship between prices of the two instruments. This correspondence is also clearly visible in Figure 7.5.

Municipal Bond Futures

The Chicago Board of Trade began trading a municipal bond futures contract in June 1985. This contract employs cash settlement similar to that used for Eurodollar futures. Among interest rate futures, it is unique in using a bond index as a basis for pricing the contract.

The futures contract is based on *The Bond Buyer* Municipal Bond Index (MBI) of 40 actively traded tax-exempt bonds issued by municipalities in the United States. The bonds may be general obligation or revenue bonds. The collection of bonds in the Index is quite diverse, including bonds issued by housing authorities, transportation agencies, or pollution control authorities. For example, in summer 1990 the Index included bonds for the Triborough Bridge in New York City, and bonds issued by the Florida Board of Education, the Port Authority of New York and New Jersey, the Atlanta Airport, and the Texas Research Lab. Table 7.3 shows the 40 bonds included in the Index on July 13, 1990. To be included in the Index, a bond must be rated A- or better by Standard & Poor's or A or better by Moody's, with at least $50 million face value outstanding, $75 million for a housing authority bond. The bond must have at least 19 years remaining until maturity and it must be callable within 7 to 16 years. In addition, the bond must pay a fixed semi-annual coupon.

Twice monthly the Index is updated with some bonds being dropped and others added, keeping the total number of bonds at 40. This updating keeps the Index comprised of bonds that meet the conditions outlined above. For example, if a bond's rating drops below the cutoff or if a default occurs, the bond is dropped. Likewise, if a bond is not actively traded, it will be deleted from the Index.

To compute the Index value, five municipal bond brokers are polled for each bond. The brokers state the price at which $100,000 face value of a bond would trade. The highest and lowest prices are discarded, and a simple average of the three remaining quotes is taken as the bond price. Each dollar price is then divided by a conversion factor (CF) to give a **converted price**. As we saw with T-bond and T-note futures, this conversion factor represents the price at which each bond would yield 8 percent. Table 7.3 shows this conversion factor for each

Table 7.3
Bonds in the Municipal Bond Index

Issue	Coupon	Maturity Year	Dollar Price	Conversion Factor	Converted Price
Triborough Bridge	7.125	2019	94.3750	0.9350	100.9358
Ohio Housing Finance	7.650	2029	99.0000	0.9716	101.8938
Puerto Rico Elec Pwr	7.125	2014	96.1250	0.9307	103.2825
Connecticut	6.875	2010	98.0000	0.9152	107.0804
Florida Board of Ed	7.250	2023	99.3125	0.9363	106.0691
Calif Health Fac	7.000	2020	97.6250	0.9257	105.4607
NYS Energy Research Dev	7.250	2024	94.8750	0.9464	100.2483
NY City Muni Water	7.500	2019	98.0000	0.9629	101.7759
Atlanta Airport	7.900	2018	102.1875	0.9904	103.1780
Brazos River Auth Tex	7.200	2018	97.8750	0.9434	103.7471
Matagorda Navigation	7.200	2018	97.8750	0.9434	103.7471
IN Muni PO	7.100	2015	96.5000	0.9357	103.1313
Mass Wtr Resources	7.500	2016	99.2500	0.9619	103.1812
Huntsville AL Waste Disp	7.000	2014	96.2500	0.9238	104.1892
NYS Dorms	7.375	2014	97.7500	0.9536	102.5063
NYS Dorms	7.000	2014	96.7500	0.9238	104.7305
MD Health & Ed	6.750	2023	94.8125	0.9057	104.6842
Port Auth of NY & NJ	7.250	2025	97.8750	0.9434	103.7471
Knox City TN	7.000	2015	97.0000	0.9265	104.6951
MI State Hospital	7.100	2018	98.0000	0.9340	104.9251
No Calif Transmission	7.000	2024	97.7500	0.9246	105.7214
Oklahoma Industries	7.000	2014	96.5000	0.9246	104.3695
Mass Port Authority	7.500	2020	99.0812	0.9622	102.9737
Chicago Pub Bldg Comm	7.125	2015	97.3125	0.9350	104.0775
Hawaii Airports	7.300	2020	97.4375	0.9428	103.3491
Los Angeles Wtr & Pwr	7.125	2030	98.0625	0.9119	107.5365
NYS Energy	7.500	2025	98.3750	0.9642	102.0276
Ohio Housing	7.850	2021	99.6250	0.9905	100.5805
Maricopa Co IDA Ariz	7.000	2013	97.5625	0.9226	105.7573
Wash Pub Pwr #1	7.250	2012	97.7500	0.9428	103.6805
Wash Pub Pwr #3	7.500	2018	98.2500	0.9619	102.1416
Port Auth NY & NJ	7.250	2025	97.7500	0.9434	103.6146
Clark Co Nev IDR	7.800	2020	99.3125	0.9810	101.2360
Frankin Co Convention	7.000	2019	97.8125	0.9226	106.0183
Los Angeles Wastewater	7.150	2020	98.0625	0.9340	104.9920
Martin Co IDA Fla	7.300	2020	99.3750	0.9428	105.4041
LA California	7.000	2021	97.6250	0.9246	105.5862
Palm Beach Co Fla	7.250	2011	99.8750	0.9434	105.8671
Philadelphia Pa Gas Wrks	7.000	2020	97.0625	0.9246	104.9778
NY City Muni Water	7.250	2015	98.7500	0.9443	104.5748

Source: Chicago Board of Trade, *CBT Financial Update,* August 17, 1990.

bond and the bond's converted price. The Index value is the average of the 40 adjusted bond prices, multiplied by a **coefficient** (coeff) that corrects for changes in membership among the 40 bonds.

To see how the coefficient works, let us assume that we are at the beginning of the Index's life, so the coefficient is 1.0 and the average bond price is $101.00, so the Index value will be 101.00. Now one bond is deleted from the index, and a new bond is added. Recomputing the index's value with the substituted bond gives 101.50, we assume. Without adjustment, the Index value will jump from 101.00 to 101.50 just from switching the bonds in the Index. If this were allowed, the replacement of bonds would cause gains and losses without any new information being revealed about interest rates. Therefore, to ensure that the Index value before and after substitution of a bond is the same, the Index must be computed by adjusting the coefficient. The coefficient needs to change so that the Index value is still 101.00 after the substitution. The coefficient (coeff) that keeps the Index value the same is given as follows:

$$\text{New coeff} = \frac{\text{Old coeff}}{\text{New Mean Converted Bond Price}} \qquad 7.9$$

In our example, we would have:

$$\text{New coeff} = \frac{101.00}{101.50} = .9951$$

Multiplying the new average converted price by the new coefficient, .9951, gives the index value before the substitution, 101.00. Taking all of these factors into account, we can express the value of the MBI as follows:

$$\text{MBI} = \text{coeff} \; \frac{1}{40} \sum_{j-1}^{40} \frac{P_j}{CF_j} \qquad 7.10$$

where:

P_j = price of the jth bond, average of three usable price quotations
CF_j = conversion factor for the jth bond
coeff = MBI coefficient

Thus, a futures price of 90-16 indicates 90.50 percent of par. The underlying value of the futures contract is 1,000 times *The Bond Buyer* Index value. Thus a futures price of 90-16 implies a contract size of $90,500. The contract trades for delivery in March, June, September, and December. The tick size is one 32nd or $31.25 per contract. The daily trading limit is three points or $3,000. The contract is settled in cash. Thus, on the final trading day, the settlement price of the futures is set equal to the cash value of the Index. This practice ensures that the futures price and the cash market price will converge when the contract expires.

Pricing Interest Rate Futures Contracts

Introduction

Interest rate futures trade in markets that are virtually always at full carry. In other words, the Cost-of-Carry Model provides a virtually complete understanding of the price structure of interest rate futures contracts. To understand why the Cost-of-Carry Model fits interest rate futures, recall our discussion of Chapter 3. There we identified five features of the underlying good that promote full carry: ease of short selling, large supply of the underlying good, non-seasonal production, non-seasonal consumption, and ease of storage.

The goods that underlie the major interest rate futures contracts meet these conditions very well. First, bonds are created and mature in a non-seasonal way, so the restrictions on seasonality are met virtually perfectly. Second, storage is virtually effortless. Most Treasury securities exist only in computer records, not even being committed to paper. Third, the supply is incredibly ample. For the most important contracts, the underlying instruments are highly liquid debt instruments. For the three T-note contracts, the T-bond contract, and the T-bill contract, the underlying instruments are all issues of the U.S. Treasury. These instruments are available in huge supply and trade in a highly liquid market. The instruments are available in huge supply and trade in a highly liquid market. The Eurodollar and municipal bond contracts both deal with questions of deliverable supply by avoiding delivery completely. They both use cash settlement. Finally, short selling is very well developed in this market. Because these securities are held in such large amounts by futures market participants, these traders can simulate short selling by selling some of their inventory of Treasury securities. Therefore, it appears that interest rate futures prices should behave like the Cost-of-Carry Model in a perfect market. That is, interest rate futures markets should be at full carry.

In Chapter 3 we considered the Cost-of-Carry Model in perfect markets and concluded that the futures price should equal the spot price plus the cost of carrying the spot good forward to delivery on the futures contract:

$$F_{0,t} = S_0(1 + C) \qquad 3.3$$

We also concluded that a similar relationship must hold between a nearby futures price and a distant futures price:

$$F_{0,d} = F_{0,n}(1 + C) \qquad 3.6$$

where:

$F_{0,t}$ = current futures price for a contract that expires at time t
S_0 = current spot price
C = percentage cost-of-carry between two dates
$F_{0,n}$ = nearby futures price
$F_{0,d}$ = distant futures price

Finally, if we assume that the only carrying cost is the financing cost, we also concluded that dividing the futures price by the spot price yielded an **implied repo rate**:

$$\frac{F_{0,t}}{S_0} = 1 + C \qquad 3.7$$

where:

C = the implied repo rate

As we will see, the model applies very well to interest rate futures. However, we must take account of some of the peculiarities of debt instruments.

Cost-of-Carry Model in Perfect Markets

In this section, we apply the Cost-of-Carry Model to interest rate futures under the assumption of perfect markets. In addition, we assume that the only carrying charge is the interest rate to finance the holding of a good, and we assume that we can disregard the special features of a given futures contract. For example, we ignore the options that sellers of futures contracts may hold, such as the option to substitute various grades of the commodity at delivery or the option to choose the exact delivery date within the delivery month, and we ignore the differences between forward and futures prices that may result from the daily resettlement cash flows on the futures contract. In summary, we are assuming:

1. Markets are perfect.
2. The financing cost is the only carrying charge.
3. We can ignore the options that the seller may possess.
4. We can ignore the differences between forward and futures prices.

Later in this chapter, we will relax these assumptions.

Each interest rate futures contract that we have considered specifies the maturity of the deliverable bond. For example, the T-bill futures contract requires that a deliverable T-bill must have a maturity of 90–92 days. This requirement applies on the delivery date. As we saw in Chapter 3, the cash-and-carry strategy involves selling a futures contract, buying the spot commodity, and storing it until the futures delivery date. Then the trader delivers the good against the futures contract. For example, if the futures price of gold is too high relative to the cash market price of gold, a trader could engage in a cash-and-carry arbitrage. Part of this strategy would involve buying gold, storing until the futures expiration, and delivering the gold against the futures contract.

To apply this strategy in the interest rate futures market, we must be very careful. For example, if a T-bill futures contract expires in 77 days, we cannot buy a 90-day T-bill and store it for future delivery. If we attempt to do so, we will find ourselves with a 13-day T-bill on the delivery date. This will not be deliverable against the futures contract. Therefore, to apply a cash-and-carry strategy, a trader must buy a bond that will still have or come to have the correct properties on the delivery date. For our T-bill cash-and-carry strategy, the trader must secure a 167-day T-bill to carry for 77 days. Then, the bill will have the requisite 90 days remaining until expiration on the delivery date.

We illustrate the cash-and-carry strategy with an example. Consider the data in Table 7.4. The yields used in Table 7.4 are not the discount yields of the IMM Index, but the yields calculated according to the Bond Pricing Formula. The example assumes perfect markets, including the assumption that one can either borrow or lend at any of the riskless rates represented by the T-bill yields.

Table 7.4
Interest Rate Futures and Arbitrage

Today's Date: January 5

Futures	Yield According to the Bond Pricing Formula
MAR Contract (Matures in 77 days on March 22)	12.50%
Cash Bills:	
167-day T-bill (Deliverable on MAR futures)	10.00
77-day T-bill	6.00

These restrictive assumptions will be relaxed momentarily. The data presented in Table 7.4, and the assumptions just made, mean that an arbitrage opportunity is present. Since the futures contract matures in 77 days, the spot 77-day rate represents the financing cost to acquire the 167-day T-bill, which can be delivered against the MAR futures contract on March 22. This is possible because the T-bill that has 167 days to maturity on January 5 will have exactly 90 days to maturity on March 22.

As the transactions presented in Table 7.5 indicate, an arbitrage opportunity exists because the prices and interest rates on the three instruments are mutually inconsistent. To implement a cash–and–carry strategy, a trader can sell the MAR futures and acquire the 167-day T-bill on January 5. The trader then holds the bill for delivery against the futures contract. The trader must finance the holding of the bill during the 77-day interval from January 5 to delivery on March 22. To exploit the rate discrepancy, the trader borrows at the short-term rate of 6 percent and uses the proceeds to acquire the long-term T-bill. At the maturity of the futures, the long-term T-bill has the exactly correct maturity and can be delivered against the futures contract. This strategy generates a profit of $2,235 per contract. Relative to the short-term rate, the futures yield and the long-term T-bill yield were too high. In this example, the trader acquires short-term funds at a low rate (6 percent) and reinvests those funds at a higher rate (10 percent). It may appear that this difference generates the arbitrage profit, but that is not completely accurate, as the next example shows.[7]

Consider the same values as shown in Table 7.4, but now assume that the rate on the 77-day T-bill is 8 percent. Now the short-term rate is too high relative to the long-term rate and the futures yield. To take advantage of this situation, we reverse the cash–and–carry procedure of Table 7.5, as Table 7.6 shows. In other words, we now exploit a reverse cash–and–carry strategy. With this new set of rates, the arbitrage is more complicated, since it involves holding

Table 7.5
Cash–and–Carry Arbitrage Transactions

January 5

Borrow $956,750 for 77 days by issuing a 77-day T-bill at 6%.
Buy 167-day T-bill yielding 10% for $956,750.
Sell MAR T-bill futures contract with a yield of 12.50% for $970.984.

March 22

Deliver the originally purchased T-bill against the MAR futures contract and collect $970,984.
Repay debt on 77-day T-bill that matures today for $968,749.

Profit:

$970,984
− 968,749
$ 2,235

Table 7.6
Reverse Cash–and–Carry Arbitrage Transactions

January 5

Borrow $955,131 by issuing a 167-day T-bill at 10%.
Buy a 77-day T-bill yielding 8% for $955,131 that will pay $970,984 on March 22.
Buy one MAR futures contract with a yield of 12.50% for $970,984.

March 22

Collect $970,984 from the maturing 77-day T-bill.
Pay $970,984 and take delivery of a 90-day T-bill from the MAR futures contract.

June

Collect $1,000,000 from the maturing 90-day T-bill that was delivered on the futures contract.
Pay $998,308 debt on the maturing 167-day T-bill.

Profit:

$1,000,000
− 998,308
$ 1,692

---

the T–bill that is delivered on the futures contract. In this situation, the arbitrageur borrows $955,131 for 167 days at 10 percent and invests these funds at 8 percent for the 77 days until the MAR futures matures. The payoff from the 77 day investment of $955,131 will be $970,894, exactly enough to pay for the delivery of the T–bill on the futures contract. This bill is held for 90 days until

June 20 when it matures and pays $1,000,000. On June 20, the arbitrageur's loan on the 167-day T-bill is also due, and equals $998,308. This trader repays this debt from the $1,000,000 received on the maturing bill. The strategy yields a profit of $1,692. Notice in this second example, that the trader borrowed at 10 percent and invested the funds at 8 percent temporarily. This shows that it is the entire set of rates that must be consistent and that arbitrage opportunities need not only involve misalignment between two rates.

From our analyses in Chapter 3, we know that the reverse cash-and-carry strategy involves selling an asset short and investing the proceeds from the short sale. In our example of Table 7.6, the short sale is the issuance of debt. By issuing debt, the arbitrageur literally sells a bond. In Chapter 3, we also noted that a trader could simulate a short sale by selling from inventory. The same is true for interest rate futures. For example, a bank that holds investments in T-bills can simulate a short sale by selling a T-bill from inventory.

To this point, we have considered a cash-and-carry strategy in Table 7.5 and a reverse cash-and-carry strategy in Table 7.6. These two examples show that there must be a very exact relationship among these rates on the different instruments to exclude arbitrage opportunities. If the yield on the MAR futures is 12.50 percent and the 167-day spot yield is 10 percent, there is only one yield for the 77-day T-bill that will not give rise to an arbitrage opportunity, and that rate is 7.15 percent. To see why that is the case, consider two ways of holding a T-bill investment for the full 167-day period of the examples:

1. Hold the 167-day T-bill, or
2. Hold a 77-day T-bill followed by a 90-day T-bill that is delivered on the futures contract.

Since these two ways of holding T-bills cover the same time period and have the same risk level, the two positions must have the same yield to avoid arbitrage. For the examples, the necessary yield on the 77-day T-bill can be found by using the same equation used to find forward rates in Chapter 6. This equation expresses the yield on a long term instrument as being equal to the yield on two short term positions:

$$(1.10)^{167/360} = (1 + x)^{77/360} (1.1250)^{90/360}$$

This equation holds only if the rate, x, on the 77-day T-bill equals 7.1482 percent.

We can also express the same idea in terms of the prices of the bills. To illustrate this point, consider the prices of three securities. The first is a 167-day bill that yields 10.00 percent and pays $1 upon maturity. Second is a T-bill futures with an underlying bill having a $1 face value. With a yield of 12.50

percent, the futures price will be $.970984. Finally, the third instrument matures in 77 days, has a face value of $.970984, and yields 7.1482 percent.

$$P_{167} = \frac{\$1}{(1 + r_{167})^{167/360}} = \frac{\$1}{1.1^{167/360}} = .956750$$

$$P_F = \frac{\$1}{(1 + r_{fut})^{90/360}} = \frac{\$1}{1.1250^{90/360}} = .970984$$

$$P_{77} = \frac{\$.970984}{(1 + r_{77})^{77/360}} = \frac{\$.970984}{1.071482^{77/360}} = .956750$$

The third instrument is peculiar, with its strange face value. However, this is exactly the payoff necessary to pay for delivery on the futures contract in 77 days. Notice also that the 77-day bill and the 167-day bill have the same price. They should, because both prices of $.956750 are the investment now that is necessary to have a $1 payoff in 167 days. The futures yield and the 167-day yield were taken as fixed. The yield on the 77-day bill, 7.1482 percent, is exactly the yield that must prevail if the two strategies are to be equivalent and to prevent arbitrage.

The Financing Cost and the Implied Repo Rate. With these prices, and continuing to assume that the only carrying cost is the financing charge, we can also infer the implied repo rate. We know that the ratio of the futures price divided by the spot price equals 1 plus the implied repo rate. As we have seen, the correct spot instrument for our example is the 167-day bill, because this bill will have the appropriate delivery characteristics when the futures matures. Thus, we have:

$$1 + C = \frac{P_F}{P_{167}} = \frac{.970984}{.956750} = 1.014878$$

Thus the implied repo rate, c, is 1.4878 percent. This covers the cost-of-carry for 77 days from the present to the expiration of the futures. We can annualize this rate as follows:

$$1.014878^{360/77} = 1.071482$$

The annualized repo rate is 7.1482 percent. This exactly matches the interest rate on the 77-day bill that will prevent arbitrage. Therefore, assuming that the interest cost is the only carrying charge, the cost-of-carry equals the implied repo rate.

Cost–of–Carry and the Implied Repo Rate

If markets are perfect and the financing cost is the only carrying charge, then:

$$\text{Cost–of–Carry} = \text{Implied Repo Rate}$$

This equivalence between the cost-of-carry and the implied repo rate also leads to two rules for arbitrage.

Rules for Arbitrage

If the implied repo rate exceeds the financing cost, then exploit a cash–and–carry arbitrage opportunity:

Borrow funds; buy the cash bond; sell futures; hold bond and deliver against futures.

If the implied repo rate is less than the financing cost, then exploit a reverse cash–and–carry arbitrage opportunity:

Buy futures; sell bond short and invest proceeds until futures expires; take delivery on futures; repay short sale obligation.

The Futures Yield and the Forward Rate of Interest. We have seen that the futures price of an interest rate futures contract implies a yield on the instrument that underlies the futures contract. We call this implied yield the futures yield. Now we continue to assume that the financing cost is the only carrying charge, that markets are perfect, that we can ignore the options that the seller of a futures contract may possess, and that the price difference between forward contracts and futures contracts is negligible. Under these conditions, we can show that the futures yield must equal the forward rate of interest.

We continue to use the T-bill futures contract as our example. The T-bill futures, like many other interest rate futures contracts, has an underlying instrument that will be delivered when the contract expires. If we consider the SEP 1991 contract, it calls for the delivery of a 90-day T-bill that will mature in December 1991. The futures yield covers the 90-day span of time from delivery in September to maturity in December 1991. We have seen in Chapter

6 that it is possible to compute forward rates from the term structure. Given the necessary set of spot rates, it is possible to compute a forward rate to cover any given period.

To illustrate the equivalence between futures yields and forward rates under our assumptions, we continue to use our example of a T-bill with a 167-day holding period. Let us assume the following spot yields:

For a 167-day bill	10.0000%
For a 77-day bill	7.1482

Using the equation for forward rates from Chapter 6, these two spot rates imply a forward rate to cover the period from day 77 to day 167:

$$(1 + r_{0,167})^{167/360} = (1 + r_{0,77})^{77/360} (1 + r_{77,167})^{90/360}$$

Substituting values for the spot bills and solving for the forward rate, $r_{77,167}$, gives:

$$(1.10)^{167/360} = (1.071482)^{77/360} (1 + r_{77,167})^{90/360}$$

$$(1 + r_{77,167})^{90/360} = \frac{(1.10)^{167/360}}{(1.071482)^{77/360}} = \frac{1.045205}{1.014877} = 1.029884$$

$$1 + r_{77,167} = 1.1250$$

$$r_{77,167} = .1250$$

Therefore, the forward rate, to cover day 77 to day 167, is 12.50 percent. As we saw above, the futures yield is also 12.50 percent for the T-bill futures that expires on day 77. Therefore, the futures yield equals the forward rate for the same period. In deriving this result, we must bear our assumptions in mind: markets are perfect, the financing cost is the only carrying charge, and we ignore the seller's options and the difference between forward and futures prices.

The Futures Yield and the Forward Rate

If markets are perfect and the non-stochastic financing cost is the only carrying charge, then:

Futures Yield = Forward Rate

The Cost–of–Carry Model for T–Bond Futures

In this section, we apply the Cost-of-Carry Model to the T-bond futures contract. In essence, the same concepts apply, with one difference. The holder of a T-bond receives cash flows from the bond. This affects the cost-of-carry that the holder of the bond actually incurs. For example, assume that the coupon rate on a $100,000 face value T-bond is 8 percent and the trader finances the bond at 8 percent. In this case, the net carrying charge is zero—the earnings offset the financing cost.

To illustrate this idea, let us assume that, on January 5, a T-bond that is deliverable on a futures contract has an 8 percent coupon and costs 100.00. The trader faces a financing rate of 7.1482 percent for the 77 days until the futures contract is deliverable. Because the T-bond has an 8 percent coupon rate, the conversion factor is 1.0 and plays no role. With an 8 percent coupon, the accrued interest from the date of purchase to the delivery date on the futures is:

$$(77/182)(.04)(100,000) = \$1,692$$

Therefore, the invoice amount will be $101,692. If this is the invoice amount in 77 days, the T-bond must cost the present value of that amount, discounted for 77 days at the 77-day rate of 7.1482 percent. This implies a cost for the T-bond of $100,200. If the price is less than $100,200, a cash-and-carry arbitrage strategy will be available. Under these circumstances the cash-and-carry strategy would have the cash flows shown in Table 7.7.

The transactions in Table 7.7 show that the futures price must adjust to reflect the accrual of interest. The bond in Table 7.7 had no coupon payment during the 77-day interval, but the same adjustment must be made to account for cash throwoffs that the bond holder receives during the holding period.

The Cost–of–Carry Model in Imperfect Markets

We now relax our assumption of perfect markets and see how the Cost-of-Carry Model applies to interest rate futures. Specifically, we will focus on the possibility that the borrowing and lending rates may differ. We continue to ignore the seller's options and the price differences between forward and futures contracts. Thus, in this section we analyze the Cost-of-Carry Model for the situation in which:

1. The borrowing rate exceeds the lending rate.
2. The financing cost is the only carrying charge.
3. We can ignore the options that the seller may possess.
4. We can ignore the differences between forward and futures prices.

```
┌─────────────────────────────────────────────────────────────────┐
│                          Table 7.7                              │
│           Cash–and–Carry Transactions for a T–Bond              │
│                                                                 │
│  January 5                                                      │
│  Borrow $100,200 for 77 days at the 77-day rate of 7.1482 percent. │
│  Buy the 8% T-bond for $100,200.                               │
│  Sell 1 T-bond futures contract for $101,692.                  │
│  ─────────────────────────────────────────────────────────     │
│  March 22                                                      │
│  Deliver T-bond; receive invoice amount of $101,692.           │
│  Repay loan of $101,692.                                       │
│  ─────────────────────────────────────────────────────────     │
│                        Profit:  0                              │
└─────────────────────────────────────────────────────────────────┘
```

In Chapter 3 we saw that allowing the borrowing and lending rates to differ leads to an arbitrage band around the futures price. For example, let us assume that the borrowing rate is 25 basis points, or one-fourth of a percentage point, higher than the lending rates. Continuing to use our T-bill example, we have:

Instrument	Lending Rate	Borrowing Rate
77–day bill	7.1482	7.3982
167–day bill	10.0000	10.2500

These assumptions approximate real market conditions. For example, a bank might be able to lend funds to the government by buying a T-bill. To borrow, however, the bank might have to transact at a somewhat higher repo rate.

When it was possible to both borrow and lend at the same rate, our earlier examples showed that the futures yield must be 12.50 percent. Now, with these different borrowing and lending rates, we want to determine how the futures yield can vary from 12.50 percent. To do this we apply the cash–and–carry and reverse cash–and–carry strategies. In both cases, we find the futures price that gives exactly a zero gain or loss on the strategy.

In the cash–and–carry strategy, we sell the futures and borrow in order to buy a good that we can deliver on the futures contract. Table 7.8 details the transactions with unequal borrowing and lending rates. The table illustrates the highest futures yield and lowest futures price that gives a zero profit with the unequal borrowing and lending rates. From this example, we see that the futures yield can be as low as 12.2760 percent without generating an arbitrage opportunity. This futures yield implies that the futures price can be as high as $971,468 and still not generate an arbitrage opportunity.

We now consider the reverse cash–and–carry strategy. Here, we will borrow long–term to finance a short–term investment and we purchase the futures. When

Table 7.8
Cash–and–Carry Transactions
with Unequal Borrowing and Lending Rates

January 5
Borrow $956,750 for 77 days at the 77-day borrowing rate of 7.3982.
Buy 167-day T-bill yielding 10% for $956,750.
Sell 1 T-bill futures contract with a yield of 12.2760% for $971,468.

March 22
Deliver the originally purchased T-bill against the MAR futures contract and collect $971,468.
Repay debt on 77-day T-bill that matures today for $971,468.

Profit: 0

the futures expires, we accept delivery and hold the delivered good until the bond matures. Table 7.9 illustrates the transactions that show how high the futures yield can be and how low the futures price can be without providing an arbitrage opportunity.

From the transactions in Table 7.9, we see that the futures yield can be as high as 12.9751 percent without providing an arbitrage opportunity. Similarly, the corresponding futures price can be as low as $969,961 without creating an arbitrage opportunity.

With equal borrowing and lending rates in our earlier examples, we saw that the futures yield had to be exactly 12.50 percent and the futures price had to be $970,984. The unequal borrowing and lending rates create a no-arbitrage band for the futures. Now the futures yield must fall in the range from 12.2760 to 12.9751 percent, and the futures price must lie in the range $969,961 to $971,468. As long as the futures yield and futures price stay within these respective ranges, arbitrage will not be possible.

A Practical Survey of Interest Rate Futures Pricing. If markets are perfect, if the only carrying charge is the financing cost, if we ignore the seller's options, and if we ignore differences between futures and forward prices, we have seen how the Cost-of-Carry Model specifies an exact futures yield and futures price. If we allow market imperfections in the form of unequal borrowing and lending rates, we have seen that the Cost-of-Carry Model leads to a no-arbitrage band of possible futures prices. Now we provide a practical approach to include other market imperfections in our analysis.

In Chapter 3, we considered transaction costs, a typical market imperfection. There we saw that transaction costs lead to a no-arbitrage band of possible futures prices. In essence, transaction costs increase the no-arbitrage band just as unequal borrowing and lending rates do. In Chapter 3, we also considered

Table 7.9
Reverse Cash–and–Carry Transactions
with Unequal Borrowing and Lending Rates

January 5

Borrow $955,743 at the 167-day borrowing rate of 10.25%.
Buy a 77-day T-bill yielding 7.1482% for $955,743.
Buy one MAR futures contract with a futures yield of 12.9751% for $969,961.

March 22

Collect $969,961 from the maturing 77-day T-bill.
Pay $969,961 and take delivery of a 90-day T-bill on the futures contract.

June

Collect $1,000,000 from the maturing 90-day T-bill that was delivered on the futures contract.
Pay $1,000,000 debt on the maturing 167-day T-bill.

Profit: 0

impediments to short selling as a market imperfection that would frustrate the reverse cash–and–carry arbitrage strategy. From a practical perspective, restrictions on short selling are relatively unimportant in interest rate futures pricing. First, supplies of deliverable Treasury securities are plentiful and government securities have little (or zero) convenience yield. Second, because Treasury securities are so widely held, many traders can simulate short selling by selling T-bills, T-notes, or T-bonds from inventory. Therefore, restrictions on short selling are unlikely to have any pricing effect.[8]

In our analysis of the Cost-of-Carry Model, we found that the futures yield must equal the forward rate of interest, under our assumptions. By assuming that we could ignore the difference between forward and futures prices, we implicitly assumed that we could ignore the effect of daily resettlement cash flows on pricing. However, in Chapter 3, we saw that daily resettlement cash flows could affect pricing of the futures contract if the price of the cash commodity were correlated with interest rates. In the interest rate futures market, the underlying goods are extremely correlated with interest rates. Therefore, we might expect to find differences between futures and forward prices, and between futures and forward yields. In Chapter 3, we saw that a negative correlation between the price of the cash commodity and interest rates would lead to a futures price that is less than the forward price. This is exactly the situation with interest rate futures, because bond prices fall as interest rates rise. Therefore, we would expect the futures price to be less than the forward price for this reason. However, the studies summarized in Table 3.17 indicate that this is not a serious problem in general. From a practical point of view, this difference is unlikely to be critical. We consider the theoretical ramifications of this relationship in more detail in Chapter 8.

In the construction of interest rate futures contracts, we have seen that the seller of a futures contract possesses timing and quality options that may be valuable. For example, the seller of a T-bond futures possesses a timing option because she can decide which day of the delivery month to deliver. Likewise, the seller possesses a quality option, because she can decide which bond to deliver. The buyer of the futures knows that the seller acquires these options by selling the futures. Therefore, the futures price must adjust to account for those options. This means that the futures price with the seller's options must be less than it would be if it had no options attached.

Studies have shown that the seller's options can have significant value. We consider this issue in detail in Chapter 8. Here we note that these options have sufficient value to be of practical importance in using interest rate futures. As we see in Chapter 8, it is even possible that these options can account for 15 percent of the futures price.

Interest Rate Futures Pricing: An Example

We conclude our discussion of interest rate futures pricing in this chapter by applying the Cost-of-Carry Model to actual market data. For this illustration, we consider the difference between the SEP and DEC 1989 T-bond futures prices. Under the simplifying assumptions made above, we would expect these two prices to be closely related by the financing cost of carrying a bond from September to December 1989. We know that market imperfections, the difference between futures and forward prices, and the seller's options might all disturb this relationship. Nonetheless, we expect the main component of this price difference to be tied to the financing cost from September to December.

To apply this idea to actual data, we use the SEP 1989 T-bill futures contract to provide a proxy for the financing rate to hold a T-bond from September to December 1989. To accept delivery on the SEP 1989 T-bond futures and carry the delivered bond forward to the December delivery involves paying the invoice price to acquire the bond, financing the bond for three months at the SEP 1989 T-bill rate, receiving the accrued interest on the bond, which we estimate as having an 8 percent coupon rate, and selling the DEC 1989 futures. In a perfect market, this strategy should yield a zero profit. In other words, we expect the quantity:

$$F_{0,d} + AI - F_{0,n}(1 + C) = 0 \qquad 7.11$$

where:

$F_{0,d}$ = DEC 1989 T-bond futures price
$F_{0,n}$ = SEP 1989 T-bond futures price plus accrued interest due at delivery
C = three month cost-of-carry estimated from SEP 89 T-bill futures
AI = interest accrued from T-bond in December, estimated at $2,000 per contract

Figure 7.6 graphs the value of equation 7.11 for a one contract position. In an absolutely perfect market, we expect the value to be zero. As Figure 7.6 shows, it is extremely close to zero. The minimum value is -$318, and the maximum value is $105. Thus, the graph of the value of equation 7.11 ranges from -3/10 of one percent to +1/10 of one percent. These values are all the closer considering the crude estimate of the accrued interest and the fact that we did not even attempt to find the cheapest-to-deliver bond. Presumably, a more exacting analysis would lead to yet smaller discrepancies.

Figure 7.6
Cost–of–Carry Model for SEP and DEC 1989 T–Bonds

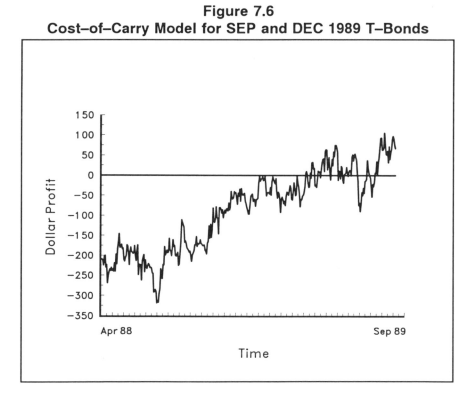

Speculating with Interest Rate Futures

In the interest rate futures market, it is possible to speculate by holding an outright position, or by trading a spread. An outright position, such as buying a T-bill futures, is a simple bet on the direction of interest rates. More sophisticated speculative strategies involve trading spreads. As we discussed in Chapter 4, a spread speculation involves a bet on a change in the relationship between two futures prices. In this section we consider some basic speculative strategies and illustrate them with examples.

The concept of a speculative profit is a very slippery notion, as we discussed in Chapter 4. A speculator might earn accounting profits that constitute a justifiable return to the application of his capital and energies. This is different from economic profit or an economic rent, which would be a profit in excess of return for the use of capital and the bearing of risk. Accounting profits are consistent with market efficiency, but economic profits are not. As the speculative strategies of this section are considered, it is important to keep these different conceptions of profit in mind.

Speculating with Outright Positions

For a speculator with an outright position in futures, the speculation is very simple. The long trader is betting that interest rates will fall so that the price of the futures will rise. The short trader is betting that interest rates will rise so that the futures price will fall.

As an example of an outright speculation, we consider a trader who anticipates rising interest rates on September 20, 1990 following the Iraqi invasion of Kuwait. In particular, the trader believes that short-term rates will rise, so she trades the Eurodollar contract as shown in Table 7.10. To profit from rising rates, the trader must be short in interest rate futures. Accordingly, she

Table 7.10
Speculating with Eurodollar Futures

Date	Futures Market
September 20	Sell 1 DEC 90 Eurodollar futures at 90.30.
September 25	Buy 1 DEC 90 Eurodollar futures at 90.12.
Profit: 90.30 − 90.12 = .18	
Total Gain: 18 basis points × $25 = $450	

sells one DEC 90 Eurodollar contract at 90.30. Five days later, interest rates have risen and the futures contract trades at 90.12. Satisfied with the profit, she sells, for a gain of 18 basis points. Because each basis point is worth $25, her total profit is $450.

Speculating with Spreads

For the most part, speculation with interest rate futures relies on spread trading. An intra-commodity spread is typically a speculation on the term structure of interest rates, for example, a spread between the nearby and distant T-bill futures. An inter-commodity spread can be a speculation on the changing shape of the yield curve, or it can be a speculation on shifting risk levels between different instruments. For example, T-bills and T-bonds have the same default risk, so a bond/bill spread is a yield curve speculation. Often, an inter-commodity spread is a speculation on changing risk levels between different instruments, for example, a spread between T-bills and Eurodollars. Of course, a given spread could combine features of both term structure and risk structure speculations. This section illustrates various different types of spread speculation.

An Intra–Commodity T–Bill Spread.   Table 7.11 presents a series of spot rates and futures rates for T-bills. As the spot rates show, the yield curve slopes upward, with three-month bills yielding 10 percent and 12-month bills yielding 12 percent. The table shows three futures contracts, with the nearby contract maturing in three months. For the futures contracts, the futures yields are consistent with the term structure given by the spot rates, in the sense that the futures yields equal the forward rates from the term structure. Faced with such circumstances, particularly with a very steep upward sloping yield curve, a speculator might believe that the term structure would flatten within six months. Even if one were not sure whether rates were going to rise or fall, the speculator could still profit from a T-bill futures spread by entering the transactions shown in Table 7.12.

Table 7.11
Spot and Futures T–Bill Rates for March 20

Time to Maturity or Futures Expiration	Spot Rates	Futures Contract	Futures Yield	IMM Index
3 months	10.00%	JUN	12.00%	88.00
6	11.00	SEP	12.50	87.50
9	11.50	DEC	13.50	86.50
12	12.00			

Table 7.12
Speculation on T-Bill Futures

Date	Futures Market
March 20	Buy the DEC T-bill futures at 86.50. Sell the SEP T-bill futures at 87.50.
April 30	Sell the DEC T-bill futures at 88.14. Buy the SEP T-bill futures at 89.02.

Profits:

DEC	SEP
88.14	87.50
−86.50	−89.02
1.64	− 1.52

Total Gain: 12 basis points × $25 = $300

If the yield curve flattens, the yield spread between successively maturing futures contracts must narrow. Currently, the yield spread between the DEC and SEP futures contracts is 100 basis points. By buying the more distant DEC contract and selling the SEP contract, the trader bets that the yield differential will narrow. If the yield curve flattens, no matter whether the general level of rates rises or falls, then this spread strategy gives a profit. As Table 7.12 shows, yields have fallen dramatically by April 30. The yield on the DEC contract has fallen from 13.50 percent to 11.86 percent and the SEP yield has moved from 12.50 percent to 10.98 percent. For the profits on this speculative strategy, the important point is that the yield spread has changed from 100 basis points to 88 basis points. This generates a profit on the spread of 12 basis points, or $300 because each basis point change represents $25. The same kind of result could have been obtained in a market with rising rates, as long as the yield curve flattens.

This example shows that all interest rate futures intra-commodity spreads are speculations on the changing shape of the yield curve. No matter what change in the shape of the yield curve is anticipated, there is a way to profit from that change by trading the correct interest rate futures spread.

A T–Bill/T–Bond Spread. To illustrate the use of spreads more completely, consider a flat yield curve, with the rates shown in Table 7.13. Here all rates, spot and futures, are at 12 percent, representing a perfectly flat yield curve. If a trader believes that the yield curve is going to become upward sloping, two strategies could take advantage of this belief. First, the trader could use an intra-commodity spread similar to the spread of Table 7.12. Since the speculator anticipates a positively sloping yield curve, he or she could sell the distant T-bill futures and buy the nearby T-bill futures. This spread would be speculating that the yield curve would become upward sloping for the very low maturity instruments represented by the T-bills.

With an upward sloping yield curve, however, we would expect the greatest difference in yields between short maturity and long maturity instruments, that is, between T-bills and T-bonds. This implies that long-term yields are expected to rise relative to short-term yields. To take advantage of this anticipated change in yields, the trader might use an inter-commodity spread, as shown in Table 7.14.

If long-term yields are expected to rise relative to short-term yields, the best spread strategy calls for selling the futures contract on a long-term instrument while buying a futures on a short-term instrument. This is exactly the course pursued by a speculator who transacts as shown in Table 7.14. With

Table 7.13
Spot and Futures Yields, June 20

Cash Market	Yield	Futures Market	Yield	Price
3-month T-bill	12.00%	SEP T-bill	12.00%	88.00
6-month T-bill	12.00	DEC T-bill	12.00	88.00
10-3/8s 2007–12	12.00	SEP T-bond	12.00	
		DEC T-bond	12.00	

Table 7.14
Inter–Commodity Spread Speculation

Date	Futures Market
June 20	Sell the DEC T-bond futures at 69–29 with a yield of 12%. Buy the DEC T-bill futures at 88.00 with a yield of 12%.
October 24	Buy the DEC T-bond futures at 65–24 with a yield of 12.78%. Sell the DEC T-bill futures at 87.80 with a yield of 12.20%.

Profits:

T-bond	T-bill
69–29	87.80
−65–24	−88.00
4–05	− .20
= $4,156.25	= −$500

Total Profit: $3,656.25

yields at 12 percent, the T-bond instrument has a price of 69-29, and the T-bill futures price is 88.00. By October 14, yields have moved as anticipated, with T-bond futures yields at 12.778 percent and the T-bill futures at 12.20 percent. For the T-bond contract, this gives a price change of 4-05. Since each 32nd of a point of par represents $31.25 on a T-bond futures contract, this gives a total profit on the T-bond contract of $4,156.25. On the T-bill side, rates have not risen as rapidly, only 20 basis points. Since each basis point represents $25, there is a loss on the T-bill futures of $500. When the T-bill loss is offset against the T-bond gain, the net profit from the speculation is $3,656.25.

In this example, we assumed that one T-bond and one T-bill contract were traded. Often such a procedure will not be the best, since different futures contracts have different price volatilities. In this case, the T-bond yield moved almost four times as much as the T-bill yield, but the T-bond price moved more than eight times as much in terms of dollars. This difference in the sensitivity of prices can be very important, both for speculating and for hedging. Notice, also, that both contracts were traded for the same futures delivery month. This shows that a speculative strategy focusing on yield curve changes need not employ different futures maturities. It will be necessary, however, to use either different futures expiration months, or different contracts.

A T–Bill/Eurodollar (TED) Spread. Another basic kind of speculation possible in the interest rate futures market is a speculation on the changing risk structure of interest rates. In these days of a continuing international debt crisis and with the recent invasion of Iraq, it is a time of danger for banks heavily engaged in international lending, with great fear of widespread default on the part of many third world nations. A speculator might view this situation as offering potential opportunity. If the crisis developed, we might expect to find a widening of the yield spread between T-bill deposits and Eurodollar deposits, for example. This widening yield spread would reflect the changing perception of the risk involved in holding Eurodollar deposits in the face of potentially very large loan losses. In February, assume that yields for the DEC T-bill and Eurodollar futures contracts are 8.82 and 9.71 percent, respectively. If the full riskiness of the banks' position has yet to be understood, we might expect the yield spread to widen. This would be the case whether interest rates were rising or falling. To take advantage of this belief, a trader could sell the DEC Eurodollar contract and buy the DEC T-bill contract, as Table 7.15 shows.

Since the trader expects the yield spread to widen, he or she sells the Eurodollar contract and buys the T-bill contract for Index values of 90.29 and 91.18, respectively. Later, on October 14, the yield spread of the example has, in fact, widened, with T-bill yields having moved up slightly so the spread has widened by 27 basis points, which means a profit of $675 on the speculation.

Perhaps the single most important point about speculation can be emphasized using this example. Virtually everyone is aware of the problems being faced by banks involved in international lending, with articles appearing almost daily in *The Wall Street Journal*. Therefore, the futures prices must already have imbedded in them the market's expectation of the future yield spread between T-bills and Eurodollars. By engaging in the speculative strategy discussed here, a trader speculates against the rest of the market. It was not enough to expect yield spreads to widen, but the trader must have expected them to widen more than the market expected. And the trader must have been right to make a profit. This spread relationship is so well known that it has a name—the TED spread (Treasury/EuroDollar).[9]

Notes Over Bonds, the NOB Trade. Like the TED spread, other strategies are sufficiently popular to earn nicknames. The NOB is a speculative strategy for trading T-note futures against T-bond futures. The term "NOB" stands for "Notes over Bonds." As we have seen, prices of bonds and notes are strongly correlated. Because the T-bonds underlying the T-bond futures contract have a longer duration than the T-notes underlying the T-note futures contract, a given change in yields will cause a greater price reaction for the T-bond futures contract. The NOB spread is designed to exploit that fact. Thus, the NOB spread is essentially an attempt to take advantage of either changing levels of yields or a changing yield curve by using an inter-market spread.

If yields rise by the same amount on both instruments, one can expect a greater price change on the T-bond. Assume a trader is long the T-bond futures

Table 7.15
Inter–Commodity Spread in Short Term Rates

Date	Futures Market
February 17	Sell one DEC Eurodollar futures contract with an IMM Index value of 90.29. Buy one DEC T-bill futures contract yielding 8.82% with an IMM Index value of 91.18.
October 14	Buy one DEC Eurodollar futures contract with an IMM Index value of 89.91. Sell one DEC T-bill futures contract yielding 8.93% with an IMM Index value of 91.07.

Profits:	
Eurodollar	T-bill
90.29	91.07
−89.91	−91.18
.38	− .11

Total Profit: 27 basis points × $25 = $675

and short the T-note futures. An equal drop in rates will give a profit on the long T-bond futures that exceeds the loss on the T-note futures, giving a profit on the spread.

Using the NOB to Speculate on Interest Rate Levels

If T–note and T–bond rates are expected to fall by equal amounts:	Buy T–bond futures Sell T–note futures
If T–note and T–bond rates are expected to rise by equal amounts:	Sell T–bond futures Buy T–note futures

---

The NOB can also be used to trade based on expectations of a changing yield curve shape. For example, assume a trader expects the yield curve to become more steeply upward sloping. This implies that yields on the long maturities (T-bonds) would rise relative to yields on shorter maturities (T-notes). To take advantage of this belief, the trader should sell T-bond futures and buy T-note futures. If a trader expects the yield curve to become more downward sloping, the trader would buy T-bond futures and sell T-note futures.[10] Notice that this speculation only concerns the relative yields, not the levels.

Using the NOB to Speculate on Yield Curve Shapes

If the yield curve is expected to become more upward sloping:	Sell T–bond futures Buy T–note futures
If the yield curve is expected to become more downward sloping:	Buy T–bond futures Sell T–note futures

---

Hedging with Interest Rate Futures

In this section, we explore the concept of hedging with interest rate futures. We present a series of examples, progressing from simple cases to more complex situations. In essence, the hedger in interest rate futures attempts to take a futures position that will generate a gain to offset a potential loss in the cash market. This also implies that the hedger takes a futures position that will generate a loss to offset a potential gain in the cash market. Thus, the interest rate futures hedger is attempting to reduce risk, not to make profits.

A Long Hedge Example

A portfolio manager learns on December 15 that he will have $972,000 to invest in 90–day T–bills six months from now. Current yields on T–bills stand at 12 percent and the yield curve is flat, so forward rates are all 12 percent as well. The manager finds the 12 percent rate attractive and decides to lock it in by going long in a T–bill futures contract maturing on June 15, exactly when the funds come available for investment. As Table 7.16 shows, the manager anticipates the cash position on December 15 and buys one T–bill futures contract to hedge the risk that yields might fall before the funds are available for investment on June 15. With the current yield and, more importantly, the forward rate on T–bills of 12 percent, the portfolio manager expects to be able to buy $1,000,000 face value of T–bills because:

$$\$972,065.42 = \$1,000,000/(1.12)^{.25}$$

The hedge is initiated and time passes. On June 15, the 90–day T–bill yield has fallen to 10 percent, confirming the portfolio manager's fears. Consequently, $1,000,000 face value of 90–day T–bills is worth:

$$\$976,454.09 = \$1,000,000/(1.10)^{.25}$$

Table 7.16
A Long Hedge with T–Bill Futures

Date	Cash Market	Futures Market
December 15	A portfolio manager learns he will receive $972,065 in six months to invest in T–bills. Market Yield: 12% Expected face value of bills to purchase $1,000,000.	The manager buys 1 T–bill futures contract to mature in six months. Futures price: $972,065
June 15	Manager receives $972,064 to invest. Market yield: 10% $1,000,000 face value of T–bills now costs $976,454.	The manager sells 1 T–bill futures contract maturing immediately. Futures yield: 10% Futures price: $976,454
	Loss = $4,389	Profit = $4,389
	Net wealth change = 0	

Just before the futures contract matures, the manager sells one June T-bill futures contract, making a profit of $4,388.67. But in the spot market the cost of $1,000,000 face value of 90-day T-bills has risen from $972,065 to $976,454, generating a cash market loss of $4,389. However, the futures profit exactly offsets the cash market loss for a zero change in wealth. With the receipt of the $972,065 that was to be invested, plus the $4,389 futures profit, the original plan may be executed, and the portfolio manager purchases $1,000,000 face value in 90-day T-bills.[11]

By design, this example is extremely artificial in order to illustrate the long hedge. Notice that the yield curve is flat at the outset, and only its level changes. Figure 7.7 portrays the kind of yield curve shift that was assumed. This idealized yield curve shift is unlikely to occur. Also, the assumption of a flat yield curve plays a crucial role in accounting for the simplicity of this example. If the yield curve is flat, spot and forward rates are identical. When one "locks-in" some rate via futures trading, it is necessarily a forward rate that is locked-in, as the next example shows. Also, we assumed the portfolio manager received exactly the right amount of funds at exactly the right time to purchase $1,000,000 of T-bills. These unrealistic assumptions are gradually relaxed in the following examples.

A Short Hedge. A government securities dealer agrees to sell another firm $1,000,000 face value of 90-day T-bills in four months for $967,000, a price that implies a yield of 14.37 percent. The forward rate (for a 90-day T-bill beginning in four months) from the yield curve also equals 14.37 percent, and the yield on the futures contract is also 14.37 percent. Assume also that the current 90-day T-bill spot rate is 13 percent. The difference, measured in yields at the outset, is -1.37 percent (13 percent - 14.37 percent). Table 7.17 shows the security dealer's position in the cash and futures markets. If rates fall below the expected 14.37 percent, the security dealer will have to deliver T-bills worth more than the $967,000 he will receive. To protect against this eventuality, the dealer buys one T-bill futures contract with a futures price of $967,000 and a futures yield of 14.37 percent.

Time passes and the market's expectations are realized. Four months after the hedge is opened, the 90-day T-bill yield is 14.37 percent, as implied by the forward rate. In the cash market, the security dealer delivers T-bills worth the anticipated amount of $967,000 and receives $967,000, generating no profit or loss. In the futures market, the futures yield has been constant at 14.37 percent generating no profit or loss there either.

This example is instructive because of what it reveals about the basis and its role in hedging with interest rate futures. In futures markets for commodities a constant basis helps to insure an effective hedge. Not so with interest rate futures. Figure 7.8 depicts the movement of the basis over time for this example of a short hedge. Measuring the basis as (Spot Yield - Futures Yield), the basis certainly changed dramatically—1.37 percent in four months. But this change in

Figure 7.7
The Idealized Yield Curve Shift for the Long Hedge

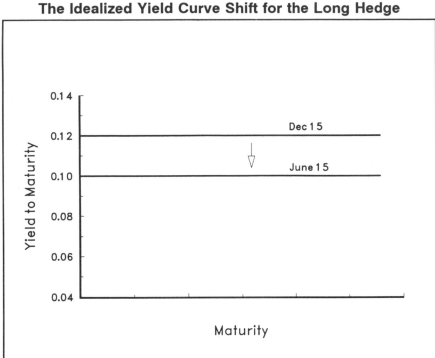

Table 7.17
A Short Hedge Using T–Bill Futures

Date	Cash Market	Futures Market
Time = 0	The security dealer commits to selling $1,000,000 face value of 90-day T-bills in 4 months for $967,000. Implied yield: 14.37% Spot yield: 13.00%	The security dealer buys 1 T-bill futures contract that matures in 4 months. Future price: $967,000 Futures yield: 14.37%
Time = 4 mos.	Spot yield is 14.37%. The security dealer delivers $1,000,000 of T-bills and re-ceives $967.000 as expected.	The security dealer sells 1 T-bill futures contract. With yields at 14.37%, the futures price is $967,000.
	Profit = 0	Loss = 0
	Net wealth change = 0	

the basis did not interfere with the effectiveness of the hedge, because it was completely anticipated by the hedger. The security dealer looked to the forward rate for the time the hedge was to be lifted to determine what price to demand for the T-bills to be sold. Consequently, the hedger using interest rate futures need not be concerned about all changes in the basis, but only unanticipated changes, i.e., changes not consistent with the expectations imbedded in the yield curve at the time the hedge is initiated.

We can make the same point in another way. For the interest rate futures market, we are concerned with the difference between the forward rate and the futures yield. The forward rate is estimated from the term structure at the time the hedge is initiated for the time the hedge is to be terminated. The forward rate of interest is the rate pertaining to the instrument being hedged. For good hedging performance in the interest rate futures market, this difference between the forward rate and the futures yield needs to be constant, as it was in the short hedge example. The next two examples illustrate the importance of changes in this difference between the forward rate and the futures yield.

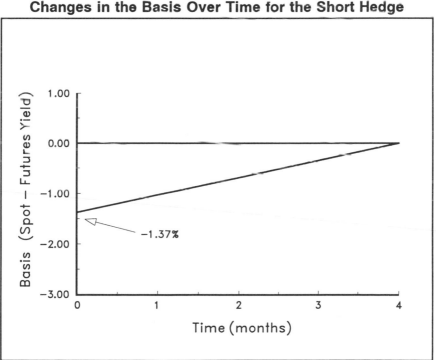

Figure 7.8
Changes in the Basis Over Time for the Short Hedge

The Cross–Hedge

The financial vice-president of a large manufacturing firm has decided to issue $1 billion worth of 90-day commercial paper in three months. The outstanding 90-day commercial paper of the firm yields 17 percent, or 2 percent above the current 90-day T-bill rate of 15 percent. Fearing that rates might rise, the vice-president decides to hedge against the risk of increasing yields by entering the interest rate futures market.

He decides to hedge the firm's commercial paper in the T-bill futures market, since rates on commercial paper and T-bills tend to be highly correlated. Since one type of instrument is being hedged with another, this becomes a "cross-hedge." In general, a cross-hedge occurs when the hedged and hedging instruments differ with respect to: (1) risk level, (2) coupon, (3) maturity, or (4) the time span covered by the instrument being hedged and the instrument deliverable against the futures contract. This means that the vast majority of all hedges in the interest rate futures markets are cross-hedges. The hedge being contemplated by the vice-president is a cross-hedge, because the commercial paper and the T-bill differ in risk. Assuming that the commercial paper is to be issued in 90-days (and that the T-bill futures contract matures at the same time) ensures that the commercial paper and the T-bill delivered on the futures contract cover the same time span.

Therefore, the vice-president decides to sell 1,000 T-bill futures contracts to mature in three months. Table 7.18 shows the transactions. The futures price is $963,575, implying a futures yield of 16 percent. Notice that this differs by 1 percent from the current 90-day T-bill yield of 15 percent. Time passes, and in three months the futures yield has not changed, remaining at 16 percent. However, since the futures contract is about to mature, the spot and futures rates are now equal. Consequently, the trade incurs no gain or loss on the futures contract.

In the cash market the 90-day commercial paper spot rate at the end of the hedging period has become 18 percent, not the 17 percent that was the original 90-day spot rate at the initiation date of the hedge. Since the vice-president **thought** he was "locking-in" the 17 percent spot rate, he expected to receive $961,509,400 for the commercial paper issue. But the commercial paper rate at the time of issue is 18 percent, so the firm receives only $959,465,798. This appears to be a loss in the cash market of $2,043,602. However, this is only appearance. The vice-president may have thought that he was locking in the prevailing spot rate of 17 percent at the time the hedge was initiated, but such a belief was unwarranted. By hedging the issuance of the commercial paper, the vice-president should have expected to lock in the three-month forward rate for 90-day commercial paper.

Table 7.18
A Cross-Hedge Between
T–Bill Futures and Commercial Paper

Date	Cash Market	Futures Market
Time = 0	The Financial V.P. plans to sell 90-day commercial paper in 3 months in the amount of $1 billion, at an expected yield of 17%, which should net the firm $961,509,400.	The V.P. sells 1,000 T-bill futures contracts to mature in 3 months with a futures yield of 16%, a futures price per contract of $963,575, and a total futures price of $963,575,000.
Time = 3 mos.	The spot commercial paper rate is now 18%, the usual 2% above the spot T-bill rate. Consequently, the sale of the $1 billion of commercial paper nets $959,465,798, not the expected $961,509,400.	The T-bill futures contract is about to mature, so the T-bill futures rate = spot rate = 16%. The futures price is still $963,575 per contract, so there is no gain or loss.
	Opportunity loss = ?	Gain/loss = 0
	Net wealth change = ?	

Figure 7.9 clarifies these relationships by presenting yield curves for T–bills and commercial paper. The yield curves are consistent with the data of the preceding discussion. At the outset of the hedge, the 90–day spot T–bill rate is .15, and the commercial paper rate equals .17. The 180–day spot rates are .154989 and .174989 for T–bills and commercial paper, respectively. The shape of the yield curves gives sufficient information to calculate the forward, and hence the futures, rates for the time span covering the period from day 90 to day 180.

Remembering the notation of Chapter 6, that:

$r_{b,e}$ = the rate on a bond to begin at time b and to be held until time e,

it is necessarily the case that:

$$(1 + r_{0,6})^{.5} = (1 + r_{0,3})^{.25} (1 + r_{3,6})^{.25}$$

From Figure 7.9, it is clear that, for T–bills, $r_{0,6}$ = .154989 and $r_{0,3}$ = .15. Therefore:

$$(1.154989)^{.5} = (1.15)^{.25} (1 + r_{3,6})^{.25}$$

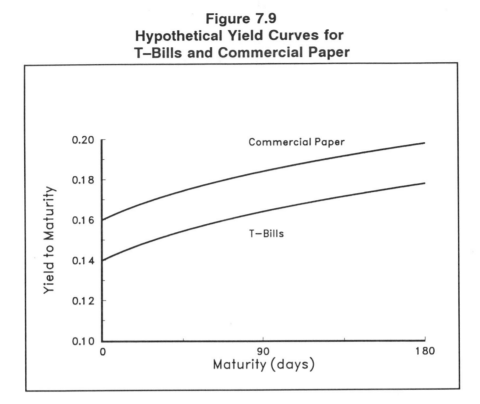

Figure 7.9
Hypothetical Yield Curves for
T–Bills and Commercial Paper

and $r_{3,6} = .16$. That is, the T-bill forward rate for the period to cover from three to six months hence, must be 16 percent. By exactly analogous reasoning, the corresponding commercial paper forward rate must be 18 percent:

$$(1.174989)^5 = (1.17)^{.25} (1 + r_{3,6})^{.25}$$

Therefore, $r_{3,6} = .18$ for commercial paper.

These forward rates, evaluated at time = 0, are the expected future rates to prevail on three-month T-bills and commercial paper beginning in three months. Consequently, the implied yield on the commercial paper of this example is .18, not the .17 that the vice-president attempted to lock in.

Now it is possible to understand exactly why the vice-president was unable to lock in 17 percent, even though it was the spot rate prevailing at the time the hedge was initiated. The reason is simply this: For the time period over which the commercial paper was to be issued (from three to six months in the future), the market believed the 90-day commercial paper rate would be 18 percent in three months. The futures price and yield reflected this belief. Although the vice-president desired a 17 percent rate, the market's expected rate was 18 percent, and by entering the futures contract the vice-president locked in the 18 percent rate. Therefore, the opportunity loss of Table 7.18 is only apparent. The vice-president's expectation of issuing the commercial paper at 17 percent was completely unwarranted. Instead, the vice-president should have expected to issue the commercial paper at the market's expected rate of 18 percent. Then he would have expected to net $959,465,798 for the firm, which is exactly what happened in the example.

A Cross-Hedge with Faulty Expectations

In the preceding example, the vice-president misunderstood the nature of the futures market. If the vice-president had understood everything correctly, Table 7.18 would have shown a zero total wealth change. Thus far, all of the examples have been of perfect hedges—hedges leaving total wealth unchanged. Sometimes, however, even when the hedge is properly initiated with the appropriate expectations, those expectations can turn out to be false. In such cases, the hedge will not be perfect; total wealth will either increase or decrease.

To illustrate this possibility, assume the same basic hedging problem as in the cross-hedge example. In particular, assume that the vice-president wishes to hedge the same issuance of commercial paper and that the yield curves are as shown in Figure 7.9. The actions and expectations of the vice-president, shown in Table 7.19, are exactly correct. The yield curve implies that, in 90 days, the 90-day T-bill and commercial paper rates will stand at 16 and 18 percent, respectively.

However, in this instance, assume that these expectations formed are incorrect. During the 90-day period before the commercial paper was issued, the market came to view the commercial paper as being riskier than was previously thought, and the economy experienced a higher rate of inflation than anticipated. Historically, assume that the yield premium of commercial paper had been 2 percent above the T-bill rate, consistent with Figure 7.9. But now, due to the perception of increased risk for commercial paper, the yield differential widens to 2.25 percent. Then assume that in 3 months the T-bill rate happens to be 16.25 percent, rising due to greater than anticipated inflation. Under these assumptions, the commercial paper rate is 18.5 percent, not the originally expected 18 percent.

As Table 7.19 reveals, the total gain on the futures position is $519,000. Due to the commercial paper rate being 18.5 percent, and not the originally anticipated 18 percent, there is a loss on the commercial paper of $1,013,700. Since the error in expectation was .5 percent on the commercial paper, but only .25 percent on the T-bills, the gain on the futures does not offset the total loss

Table 7.19
A Cross-Hedge With Faulty Expectations

Date	Cash Market	Futures Market
Time = 0	The Financial V.P. decides to sell 90-day commercial paper in 3 months in the amount of $1 billion, at an expected yield of 18%, which should net the firm $959,465,798.	The V.P. sells 1,000 T-bill futures contracts to mature in 3 months, with a futures yield of 16%, a futures price per contract of $963,575, and a total futures price of $963,575,000.
Time = 3 mos.	The spot commercial paper rate was expected to be 18% at this time, but is really 18.5%. Consequently, the sale of the $1 billion of commercial paper nets $958,452,098, not the expected $959,465,798.	The T–bill futures contract is about to mature, so the T–bill futures rate = spot rate = .1625. The futures price is $963,056 per contract, so there is a gain per contract of $519, and a total gain on the 1,000 contracts of $519,000.
	Opportunity loss = $1,013,700	Gain = +$519,000
	Net wealth change = $494,700	

of the commercial paper. This results in a net wealth change of - $494,700. However, the loss would have been -$1,013,700 without the futures hedge.

In general, real world hedges will not be perfect. Rates on both sides of the hedge tend to move in the same direction, but by uncertain amounts. On occasion rates can even move in opposite directions generating enormous gains or losses. In the example just discussed, assume that the commercial paper rate turned out to be 18.5 percent, but that the T-bill rate was 15.75 percent—*below* the expected 16 percent. In this case, the loss on the commercial paper would be -$1,013,700, and the loss on the futures would be -$1,568,000 for a total loss of $2,581,700, because the firm loses on both sides of the hedge. Such an outcome is unlikely, but it is a possible result of which hedgers should be aware.

Conclusion

In this chapter, we have considered the contract specifications of the most important interest rate futures contracts. We have explored the proper pricing of futures contracts using the cost-of-carry framework and have seen how interest rate futures are related to the term structure of interest rates.

We have noted some difficulties in applying the simplest form of the cost-of-carry relationship to interest rate futures, particularly to the T-bond futures contract. The breakdown of the arbitrage conditions gives expectations of future interest rates a role in the determination of interest rate futures prices.

If interest rate futures prices are not determined by strict cost-of-carry relationships, there may be ample reward to various speculative strategies. The chapter concluded by exploring some simple speculative strategies, as well as more complex relationships involving several instruments. In the next chapter, we continue our exploration of interest rate futures by considering the pricing performance and the hedging use of interest rate futures.

Questions and Problems

1. A 90-day T-bill yields 8.75 percent. What is the price of a $1,000,000 face value bill?

2. The IMM Index stands as 88.70. What is the discount yield? If you buy a T-bill futures at that index value and the index becomes 88.90, what is your gain or loss?

3. What is the difference between Position Day and First Position Day?

4. A $100,000 face value T-bond has an annual coupon rate of 9.5 percent and paid its last coupon 48 days ago. What is the accrued interest on the bond?

5. What conditions are necessary for the conversion factors on the CBOT T-bond contract to create favorable conditions for delivering one bond instead of another?

6. The Municipal Bond Index futures does not allow for delivery of bonds. Explain why the futures price must converge to the spot index value nonetheless.

7. The JUN T-bill futures IMM Index value is 92.80, while the SEP has a value of 93.00. What is the implied rate to cover the period from June to September?

8. A spot 180-day T-bill has a discount yield of 9.5 percent. If the implied repo rate for the next three months is 9.2 percent, what is the price of a futures that expires in three months?

9. For the next three futures expirations, you observe the following Eurodollar quotations:

MAR	92.00
JUN	91.80
SEP	91.65

What shape does the yield curve have? Explain.

10. Assume that the prices in the preceding problem pertain to T-bill futures and the MAR contract expires today. What should be the spot price of an 180-day T-bill?

11. The cheapest-to-deliver T-bond is a 12 percent bond that paid its coupon 87 days ago and it is priced at 105-16. The conversion factor of the bond is 1.0900. The nearby T-bond futures expires in 50 days and the current price is 98-00. If you can borrow or lend to finance a T-bond for a total outlay of 2 percent over this period, how would you transact? What if you could borrow or lend at 3 percent? What if you could borrow at 3 percent and lend at 2 percent? Explain.

12. You expect a steepening yield curve over the next few months, but you are not sure whether the level of rates will increase or decrease. Explain two different ways you can trade to profit if you are correct.

13. The Iraqi invasion of Alaska has financial markets in turmoil. You expect the crisis to worsen more than other traders suspect. How could you trade short-term interest rate futures to profit if you are correct? Explain.

14. You believe that the yield curve is strongly upward sloping and that yields are at very high levels. How would you use interest rate futures to hedge a prospective investment of funds that you will receive in nine months? If you faced a major borrowing in nine months, how would you use futures?

15. The spot rate of interest on a corporate bond is 11 percent, and the yield curve is sharply upward sloping. The futures rate on the T-bond futures that is just about to expire is 8 percent, but the yield for the futures contract that expires in six months is 8.75 percent. (You are convinced that this difference is independent of any difference in the cheapest-to-deliver bonds for the two contracts.) In these circumstances, a corporate finance officer wants to lock-in the current spot rate of 11 percent on a corporate bond that her firm plans to offer in six months. What advice would you give her?

Notes

1. A recent spectacular failure was the introduction of a two-year T-note contract in January 1982 that went from its opening to zero volume in nine trading days. See "Two-Year-Notes: A Bungled Opening," *Commodities: The Magazine of Futures Trading*, March 1982, p. 100.

2. For a discussion of the importance of cash settlement, see K. Garbade and W. Silber, "Cash Settlement of Futures Contracts: An Economic Analysis," *The Journal of Futures Markets*, 3:4, Winter 1983, pp. 451-472.

3. Chicago Mercantile Exchange, "Inside Eurodollar Futures," p. 19.

4. In periods of high volatility, this limit can expand.

5. By doing so, the Clearing Corporation fulfills its obligation of being buyer to every seller and seller to every buyer. At the actual delivery, the Clearing Corporation supervises the exchange of T-Bonds and cash, but need not enter the process itself. It should also be noted that fewer than one percent of all futures contracts are satisfied by delivery, the others being completed by reversing trades.

6. The best way to secure a regular source of conversion factors, as well as much other useful information, is to subscribe to the CBT's free monthly publication, *CBT Financial Update*.

7. For studies of this approach to pricing T-Bill futures, see I. Kawaller and T. Koch, "Cash-and-Carry Trading and the Pricing of Treasury Bill Futures," *The Journal of Futures Markets*, 4:2, Fall 1984, pp. 115-123.

8. While restricted short selling is unlikely to be important in interest rate futures pricing, this does not imply that any trader can sell short. Pricing of a security depends on the marginal trader, not every trader and not the average trader. For all practical purposes, the marginal trader in the interest rate futures market may be thought of as a well-capitalized, sophisticated firm active in trading futures. This marginal trader faces the lowest transaction costs, has the lowest price for acquiring information, and has the best access to simulated short selling by selling from an existing inventory.

9.   See the Chicago Mercantile Exchange, "Market Perspectives," February, 1987, 5:1, pp. 1-4. See also the Chicago Mercantile Exchange, "The TED Spread," *Financial Strategy Paper*, 1987.

10. The NOB can also be traded using options on the T-Bond and T-Note futures. See Chicago Board of Trade, "Trading the Option NOB," *Financial Futures Professional*, 9:5, May 1985, p. 2.

11. For simplicity, we use easier price and yield calculations in many of these hedging examples, abstracting from the full complexity of market yield calculations.

8

Interest Rate Futures: Refinements

Introduction

Chapter 8 builds on the foundation of Chapter 7. Having already explored the fundamental features of interest rate futures, we now turn to refining our understanding of these important markets. Thus, Chapter 8 considers more closely some of the same issues addressed in Chapter 7. In addition, we examine some new issues, such as the informational efficiency of the interest rate futures market.

The T-bond contract is perhaps the most important futures contract ever devised. It also happens to be one of the most complicated. We begin this chapter with a detailed analysis of the T-bond contract. This analysis lays the foundation for a richer understanding of how to apply interest rate futures to speculate and to manage risk. Next, we consider the informational efficiency of the interest rate futures markets. A market is efficient with respect to some set of information if prices in the market fully reflect the information contained in that set. There have been many studies of informational efficiency for interest rate futures and we review the results of those studies.

In Chapter 7 we saw that interest rate futures should be full carry markets. However, this conclusion requires some qualifications. Taking the T-bond contract as a model, we analyze the special features of the contract and show how those features can make full carry difficult to measure. For example, seller's options have important implications for the theoretically correct futures price.

Many traders use interest rate futures to manage risk. The techniques for risk management are quite diverse and increasingly sophisticated. Essentially two different sets of techniques apply, depending upon the nature of the risk. Therefore, we consider applications for short-term interest rate futures first and then conclude the chapter by examining the applications of long-term interest rate futures.

The T–Bond Futures Contract in Detail

In Chapter 7 we explored the basic features of the T-bond futures contract. In this section, we first review what we know about the contract from Chapter 7. Then we develop a more complete analysis of the contract. This procedure provides a richer understanding of the contract which helps us to understand how to use interest rate futures for speculation and risk management.

Review of the T–Bond Contract

In our discussion of the T-bond futures contract in Chapter 7, we noted that the contract calls for the delivery of $100,000 principal amount of U.S. Treasury bonds that have at least 15 years to maturity of their first call date at the time of delivery. We noted that the delivery procedure stretched over three business days, with actual delivery occurring on the third day, which could be any business day of the delivery month.

For any particular futures contract expiration, a variety of bonds will be deliverable. These bonds can be of any coupon rate and any maturity above the minimum. In many cases, the bonds that are deliverable will include some recently issued Treasury bonds that may not even have existed when the contract was first listed for trading.

Without some adjustment, one of these bonds is likely to be much better to deliver than the others. For example, if the contract allowed the delivery of any bond without a price adjustment, every trader would want to deliver the cheapest bond. To make the variety of bonds permitted for delivery comparable, the CBT uses a system of conversion factors. Essentially, the conversion factor for a given bond is found by assuming that the bond has a face value of $1 and discounting all of the bond's cash flows at 8 percent. Chapter 7 gives the exact formulas for finding the conversion factors. While the conversion factors eliminate much of the inequalities between various bonds, they do not do a complete job. As a consequence, there is still a particular bond that is cheapest-to-deliver among the bonds permitted for delivery.

As another complication, we noted in Chapter 7 that the seller of the T-bond futures possesses several options. For example, the seller chooses which bond to deliver and which day to make delivery. These and other options have significant value, as we explore next.

The Cheapest–to–Deliver Bond

In this section we show how to determine which bond will be cheapest-to-deliver, and we show how to find the exact invoice amount, including all the nuances in computing accrued interest. First, we analyze the cheapest-to-deliver bond when some time remains before expiration, but there will be no coupon payment. Second, we consider the case when a coupon payment intervenes between the beginning of the holding period and the futures expiration.

The Case of No Intervening Coupons. Assume today is Monday, September 16, 1991 and the SEP 91 T-bond futures settlement price is 93-00. A short trader decides to make today her position day and to deliver against her futures contract. The actual delivery date will be Wednesday, September 18, 1991. She is considering two bonds and wants to know exactly how much she will receive for each and which she should deliver. The two bonds are:

Maturity	Coupon	Price	SEP 91 CF
May 15, 2016	7.25	82-16	.9200
Nov. 15, 2006-11	14.00	140-10	1.5188

We want to determine the exact invoice amount for each bond and which bond is cheapest-to-deliver.

To answer these questions, we first compute the cash price and invoice amounts for $100,000 face value of these bonds. The total price depends upon the stated price plus the accrued interest (AI). In Chapter 7 we saw that a bond accrues interest for each day based on the coupon rate and the principal amount. In the market, the actual calculation also depends upon the number of days in a half-year, as Table 8.1 shows.

Both bonds have the same coupon dates each year, May 15 and November 15, so both are on the May–November cycle. As Table 8.1 shows, for a regular year, there are 184 days in the May–November half-year. From May 15 to September 18 is 126 days. Therefore, the Accrued Interest for each bond is:

7.25% bond: AI = (126/184)(.5)(.0725)($100,000) = $2482
14% bond: AI = (126/184)(.5)(.14)($100,000) = $4793

From Chapter 7:

$$\text{Invoice Amount} = \text{DFP}(\$100,000)(\text{CF}) + \text{AI}$$

where:

DFP = decimal futures price (e.g., 96-16 = .965)
CF = conversion factor
AI = accrued interest

Table 8.1
Days in Half–Years

Interest Period	Days in Half–Year			
	Interest Paid on 1st or 15th		Interest Paid on Last Day	
	Regular Year	Leap Year	Regular Year	Leap Year
January to July	181	182	181	182
February to August	181	182	184	184
March to September	184	184	183	183
April to October	183	183	184	184
May to November	184	184	183	183
June to December	183	183	184	184
July to January	184	184	184	184
August to February	184	184	181	182
September to March	181	182	182	183
October to April	182	183	181	182
November to May	181	182	182	183
December to June	182	183	181	182
1 year (any 2 consecutive half–years)	365	366	365	366
Source: Treasury Circular No. 300, 4th Rev.				

With a September 16 settlement price of 93-00, invoice amounts are:

7.25% bond: .9300($100,000)(.9200) + $2482 = $88,042
14% bond: .9300($100,000)(1.5188) + $4793 = $146,041

Thus, the two bonds have radically different invoice amounts; the 14 percent bond has an invoice amount 66 percent greater than the 7.25 percent bond.

To complete delivery, the short trader must deliver one bond and receive the invoice amount. Which should she deliver? The decision depends upon the difference between the invoice amount and the cash market price, which is the profit from delivery. The bond that is most profitable to deliver is the cheapest-to-deliver bond. In other words, the short trader will select the bond to deliver to maximize profit . For a particular bond i, the profit π_i, is:

$$\pi_i = \text{Invoice Amount} - (P_i + AI_i)$$

$$= (DFP_i)(\$100,000)(CF_i) + AI_i - (P_i + AI_i)$$

Because the accrued interest is included in the invoice amount and subtracted as a payment being made by surrendering the bond, the profit simplifies to:

$$\pi_i = DFP_i(\$100,000)(CF_i) - P_i \qquad 8.1$$

To find the cheapest-to-deliver bond, the short trader will compute the profitability for each deliverable bond. The bond with the maximum profit is the cheapest-to-deliver.[1]

Rules for the Cheapest–to–Deliver Bond

The cheapest–to–deliver bond, among all deliverable bonds, is the bond that is most profitable to deliver, where profit is measured by:

(Decimal Futures Price)($100,000)(Conversion Factor) – Quoted Bond Price

---

For the two bonds, the profit from delivery is:

For the 7.25% bond: $\pi = .9300(\$100,000)(.9200) - \$82,500 = \$3,060$
For the 14% bond: $\pi = .9300(\$100,000)(1.5188) - \$140,313 = \$935.40$

Thus, delivering the 7.25 percent bond is more profitable, so it is cheaper-to-deliver.

Which bond is cheaper-to-deliver depends on the level of interest rates. Figure 8.1 shows the profits from delivery for three bonds:

25 year; 7% coupon
16 year; 14% coupon
20 year; 8% coupon

The 20 year, 8 percent coupon bond is the nominal bond that underlies the futures contract. It has a conversion factor of 1.0, as do all 8 percent coupon bonds. Therefore, the profit from delivery on an 8 percent coupon bond will always be zero if the futures and bond are priced fairly, as Figure 8.1 shows. The practice of using conversion factors does not introduce any biases for an 8 percent coupon bond.

As Figure 8.1 shows, bias is possible for the other two bonds with coupon rates that differ from 8 percent. If interest rates are below 8 percent, Figure 8.1

Figure 8.1
Cheapness for Delivery and Bond Yields

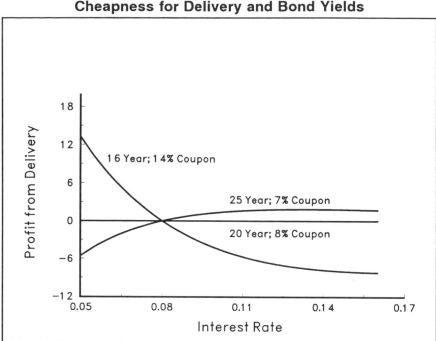

shows that there is an advantage to delivering the 16 year bond. By contrast, if yields exceed 8 percent, it is better to deliver the 25 year bond. At one point in Figure 8.1, a trader can be indifferent about which bond to deliver. Notice that when yields are exactly 8 percent, the profit from delivery for all three bonds is zero.

Cheapest–to–Deliver Bonds

If yields are below 8 percent: Deliver the lowest duration bond (low maturity/ high coupon)

If yields are above 8 percent: Deliver the highest duration bond (long maturity/ low coupon)

We can extract a general rule from this analysis. When interest rates are below 8 percent, there is an incentive to deliver short maturity/high coupon bonds. When interest rates exceed 8 percent, there is an incentive to deliver long maturity/low coupon bonds. Expressing the same idea in terms of duration, a trader should deliver low duration bonds when interest rates are below 8 percent and high duration bonds when interest rates are above 8 percent.

The Case of Intervening Coupons. So far, we have dealt with the cheapest-to-deliver bond when there are no coupon payments to consider. We now consider which bond is cheapest-to-deliver when a bond pays a coupon between the beginning of the cash-and-carry holding period and the futures expiration. To find the cheapest-to-deliver bond before expiration, we apply the cash-and-carry strategy. The bond with the greatest profit at delivery from following the cash-and-carry strategy will be the cheapest-to-deliver.

We assume that a trader buys a bond today and carries the bond to delivery. We compare the cash flows associated with that carry relative to the invoice amount based on today's futures price. Of course, we cannot know the future cash flows with certainty. In particular, the futures price might change. However, we make our computation assuming that interest rates and futures prices remain constant. For this analysis, we must consider the estimated invoice amount plus our estimate of the cash flows associated with carrying the bond to delivery.

The estimated invoice amount depends on three factors:

1. Today's quoted futures price.
2. The conversion factor for the bond we plan to deliver.
3. The accrued interest on the bond at the expiration date.

Acquiring and carrying a bond to delivery involves three cash flows as well:

1. Pay today the quoted price plus accrued interest.
2. Finance the bond from today until expiration.
3. Receive and invest any coupons paid between today and expiration.

We can bring all of these factors together by considering the time line in Figure 8.2.

Today we purchase a bond and finance it until delivery. Between today and delivery, we receive and invest a coupon. At delivery, we surrender the bond and receive the invoice amount. Thus, we have:

Estimated Invoice Amount $= DFP_0(CF) + AI_2$

Estimated Future Value of the Delivered Bond $=$

$$(P_0 + AI_0)(1 + C_{0,2}) - COUP_1(1 + C_{1,2})$$

Figure 8.2
Time Line for Cash–and–Carry Arbitrage

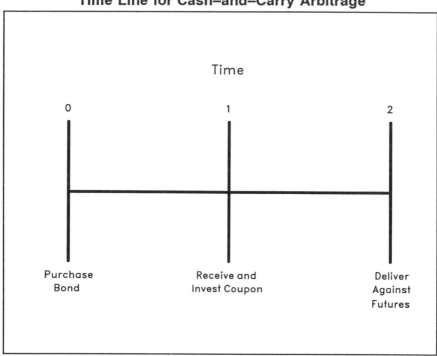

where:

P_0 = quoted price of the bond today, t=0

AI_0 = accrued interest as of today, t=0

$C_{0,2}$ = interest factor for t=0 to expiration at t=2

$COUP_1$ = coupon that will be received before delivery at t=1

$C_{1,2}$ = interest factor from t=1 to t=2

DFP_0 = decimal futures price today, t=0

CF = conversion factor for a particular bond and the specified futures expiration

AI_2 = accrued interest at t=2

The short trader will maximize profit by choosing to deliver the cheapest-to-deliver bond. For bond i, the expected profit from delivery is the estimated invoice amount less the estimated value of what will be delivered:

$$\pi = DFP_0(CF) + AI_2 - \{(P_0 + AI_0)(1 + C_{0,2}) - COUP_1(1 + C_{1,2})\} \quad 8.2$$

As an illustration, assume that today is April 15, 1991 and we want to find the cheapest-to-delivery bond for the SEP 91 futures expiration. We illustrate the computation with the two bonds we have already considered, with different prices for the different date.

Maturity	Coupon	Price	SEP 91 CF
May 15, 2016	7.25	81–24	.9200
Nov. 15, 2006–11	14.00	138–12	1.5188

We assume that the bonds will be financed and the coupons invested at the repo rate of 10 percent and that the settlement price of the SEP 91 T-bond futures on April 15 is 91–10. We assume a $100,000 face value and a target delivery date of September 30, 1991. Figure 8.3 shows all of the dates and the number of days between dates.

Figure 8.3
Dates for Cash–and–Carry Arbitrage

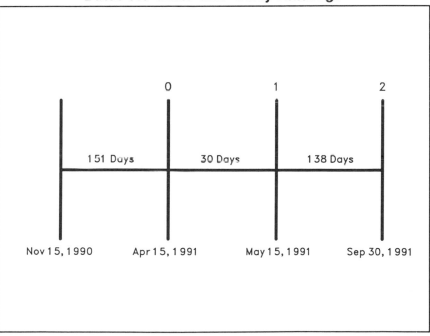

The semi-annual coupons for the two bonds are $3,625 for the 7.25 percent bond and $7,000 for the 14 percent bond. Both bonds paid their last coupon on November 15, 1990, 151 days ago. For a regular year, the November-May half-year has 181 days. Therefore, the accrued interest as of April 15 for the bonds is:

For the 7.25% bond: $AI_0 = \$3,625(151/181) = \$3,024$
For the 14% bond: $AI_0 = \$7,000(151/181) = \$5,840$

The amount to be financed for each bond is:

For the 7.25% bond: $P_0 + AI_0 = \$81,750 + \$3,024 = \$84,774$
For the 14% bond: $P_0 + AI_0 = \$138,375 + \$5,840 = \$144,215$

Next we consider the accrued interest that will accumulate by the delivery date. From May 15, 1991 to September 30, 1991 is 138 days in a half-year of 184 days. Therefore, the bonds have the following accrued interest on September 30, 1991:

For the 7.25% bond: $AI_2 = \$3,625(138/184) = \$2,719$
For the 14% bond: $AI_2 = \$7,000(138/184) = \$5,250$

With a futures price of 91-10 on April 15, 1991, the $DFP_0 = .913125$. The estimated Invoice Amount for the two bonds is:

For the 7.25% bond: $.91325(\$100,000)(.92) + \$2,719 = \$86,738$
For the 14% bond: $.91325(\$100,000)(1.5188) + \$5,250 = \$143,954$

Next, we compute the financing rates. On April 15, 168 days remain until the projected delivery date, so $C_{0,2} = .10(168/360) = .0467$. From May 15, 1991 until September 30, 1991 is 138 days, so $C_{1,2} = .10(138/360) = .0383$. Finally, we are in a position to compute the profits from delivery. Table 8.2 summarizes all of these intermediate calculations.

Table 8.2
Data for Cheapest–to–Deliver Bonds

Bond	P_0	AI_0	$C_{0,2}$	$C_{1,2}$	DFP_0	CF	AI_2
7.25%	81,750	$3,024	.0467	.0383	.91325	.9200	2,719
14.00%	138,375	$5,840	.0467	.0383	.91325	1.5188	5,250

Using the values in Table 8.2, we compute the expected profit from delivering each bond. For the 7.25 percent bond:

$$\pi = (.91325)(100{,}000)(.9200) + 2{,}719$$
$$- [(81{,}750 + 3{,}024)(1.0467) - (3{,}625)(1.0383)]$$

$$= 86{,}738 - 88{,}733 + 3{,}764$$

$$= \$1{,}769$$

For the 14 percent bond:

$$\pi = (.91325)(100{,}000)(1.5188) + 5{,}250$$
$$- [(138{,}375 + 5{,}840)(1.0467) - 7000(1.0383)]$$

$$= \$143{,}954 - \$150{,}950 + \$7{,}268$$

$$= \$272$$

For the 7.25 percent bond, the profit from delivery is $1,769, but delivering the 14 percent bond generates only $272. Therefore, the 7.25 percent bond is cheaper-to-deliver.

The Cheapest–to–Deliver Bond and the Implied Repo Rate. We can also analyze the same situation using the implied repo rate. Here the implied repo rate for the given period equals the net cash flow at delivery divided by the net cash flow when the carry starts:

$$\text{Implied Repo Rate} = \frac{\text{Net Cash Flow Over Horizon}}{\text{Net Cash Flow at Inception}}$$

The numerator consists of cash inflows of the Invoice Amount, plus the future value of the coupons at the time of delivery, less the cost of acquiring the bond initially. The denominator consists of the cost of buying the bond. Therefore, in terms of our notation:

Implied Repo Rate =

$$\frac{DFP_0 \, (100{,}000) \, (CF) + AI_2 + COUP_1 \, (1 + C_{1,2}) - (P_0 + AI_0)}{(P_0 + AI_0)}$$

For the 7.25 percent bond we have:

Implied Repo Rate =

$$\frac{.91325\ (100000)\ (.9200) + 2719 + 3625\ (1.0383) - (81750 + 3024)}{(81750 + 3024)}$$

$$= .0676$$

For the 14 percent bond:

Implied Repo Rate =

$$\frac{.91325\ (100000)\ (1.5188) + 5250 + 7000\ (1.0383) - (138375 + 5840)}{(138375 + 5840)}$$

$$= .0486$$

Annualizing these rates, we have $(.0676)(360/168) = 14.49$ percent and $(.0486)(360/168) = 10.41$ percent. Thus, the low coupon 7.25 percent bond has a higher implied repo rate, suggesting that this bond is better than the 14 percent

---

Table 8.3
Transactions Showing Implied Repo Rates

April 15, 1991
Borrow $144,215 for 168 days at implied repo rate of 10.41 percent.
Buy $100,000 face value of 14% T-bonds maturing on Nov. 15, 2011 for a total price of $144,215, including accrued interest.
Sell one SEP 91 T-bond futures contract at the current price of 91–10.

May 15, 1991
Receive coupon payment of $7,000 and invest for 138 days at 10 percent.

September 30, 1991 (Assuming futures is still at 91–10)
Deliver the bond and receive invoice amount of $143,954.
From the invested coupon receive $7,000 + $7,000(.10)(138/360) = $7,267.
Repay debt: $144,215 + $144,215(.1041)(168/360) = $151,221.

Net Profit = 0

bond to carry to delivery. From this example, we can draw the following rule about the cheapest-to-deliver bond before expiration.

The Cheapest–to–Deliver Bond Before Expiration

The cheapest–to–deliver bond has the highest implied repo rate in a cash–and–carry strategy.

If the implied repo rate equals the borrowing rate, the cash-and-carry arbitrage transaction leaves a zero profit. To illustrate this principle, we focus on the 14 percent bond and the cash-and-carry transactions of Table 8.3. As the example of Table 8.3 shows, financing a cash-and-carry arbitrage at the implied repo rate yields a zero profit.

No–Arbitrage Condition

Cash–and–carry arbitrage nets a zero profit if the actual borrowing cost equals the implied repo rate.

To summarize, we state some general rules about how to conduct arbitrage if the cost of funds varies from the implied repo rate. The transactions we have considered assumed that the futures price did not change and that markets were perfect. In particular, for the reverse cash-and-carry arbitrage, the assumption that the trader has full use of the short sale proceeds was critical. Subject to these restrictions, and the elaboration of the next section, the general rules hold:

1. Cash-and-carry arbitrage nets a zero profit if the actual borrowing cost equals the implied repo rate.
2. If the effective borrowing rate is less than the implied repo rate, one can earn an arbitrage profit by cash-and-carry arbitrage, i.e., buy the cash bond and sell the futures.
3. If the effective borrowing rate exceeds the implied repo rate and if one can sell bonds short, then one can earn an arbitrage profit by reverse cash-and-carry arbitrage, i.e., sell the bond short, buy the futures, and cover the short position at the expiration of the futures.

Why They Call It Risk Arbitrage

In this section, we add more realism to our analysis of arbitrage by considering the peculiarities of the T-bond futures contract in still greater detail. As we will show, market realities add a risk component to both the cash-and-carry and reverse cash-and-carry arbitrage. These complications take our arbitrage framework out of the realm of "academic arbitrage" and show why all arbitrage in the T-bond futures market is really "risk arbitrage." The sources of risk are different for the cash-and-carry and reverse cash-and-carry strategies, and the risks stem from three sources: intervening coupon payments that must face reinvestment, the use of conversion factors, and the options that the seller possesses. In this section, we consider the risks generated by the reinvestment problem and the use of conversion factors. We also treat the seller's options in a general way.

Frustrations to Cash–and–Carry Arbitrage.   A closer examination of Table 8.3 shows some potentially risky elements of the cash-and-carry arbitrage. First, the debt was financed at a constant rate throughout the 168-day carry period. Second, the trader actually was able to invest the coupon at the expected reinvestment rate of 10 percent. Third, the futures price did not change over the horizon. We consider each of these problems in turn.

Assume that the trader in Table 8.3 finances the acquisition of the T-bond with overnight repos. The overnight repo rate changes each day, so the financing cost could drift upward. With an increasing financing cost, the transactions of Table 8.3 will not end in a zero profit. Instead, they will give a loss. Therefore, the transactions in Table 8.3 are potentially risky, depending upon the financing rate for the bond. Second, assume that the bond is financed for the entire period at the implied repo rate of 10.41 percent. Also assume that short-term rates drift lower, so that the coupon can only be invested at 8 percent, not the 10 percent shown in Table 8.3. Now the reinvested coupons will only grow to $7,215, not the $7,267 shown in the table. Therefore, the changing rate will generate a loss. These two examples illustrate the risks that remain inherent in a supposedly riskless cash-and-carry strategy. We now turn to a bigger danger, a change in the futures price can affect the cash flows from the cash-and-carry strategy.

In the transactions of Table 8.3, we assumed that the futures price did not change over the life of the contract. With the financing rates given, the cash-and-carry transactions yielded a zero profit. Now let us assume that the financing of the bond and the investment of the coupon work out exactly as Table 8.3 shows. However, now we consider a drop in the futures price from 91-10 when the contract is initiated to 89-10 at expiration. Such a change in the futures price is entirely feasible, and we need to consider the effect of this changing price on the cash flows from the cash-and-carry strategy.

Table 8.4 presents the same transactions as the zero profit cash-and-carry transactions of Table 8.3. The only difference between the two tables results from a drop in the futures price from 91-10 to 89-10 over the life of the contract. With a futures expiration price of 89-10, the actual invoice amount is:

$$\text{Invoice Amount} = .893125(\$100,000)(1.5188) + \$5,250 = \$140,898$$

The drop in the futures price has generated daily resettlement cash inflows of $2,000 over the life of the contract. With the reduced invoice amount, however, the cash-and-carry transactions generate a loss. As the transactions show, the reason for the loss is that futures price fluctuations generate gains or losses on a $1 for $1 basis. For example, a two point drop in the futures price generates a gain of $2,000 in this case. However, when the futures price changes by one dollar, the delivery value of the bond changes by $1 times the conversion factor, which exceeds 1.0 in our example. This makes it possible for the supposedly riskless transaction to generate a loss. The dropping futures price generates $2,000 in daily resettlement profits, but it reduces the invoice amount from $143,954 to $140,898, a drop of $3,056. Thus, the changing price generates a new profit of $2,000 and a new loss of $3,056, for a net loss of $1,056, as Table 8.4 shows.

Frustrations to Reverse Cash-and-Carry Arbitrage. In reverse cash-and-carry transactions, a trader sells an underlying good short and buys a futures contract. The trader then invests the proceeds from the short sale, planning to take delivery on the futures and return the borrowed commodity. Table 8.5 shows the reverse cash-and-carry transactions that are the exact mirror image of Table 8.3. In Table 8.5, the transactions generate a zero profit. The profit must be zero, because the transactions are exact complements to the transactions in Table 8.3.

We now consider the risk elements inherent in the reverse cash-and-carry transactions. First, all of the same risk elements that plagued the cash-and-carry strategy apply to the reverse cash-and-carry strategy as well. The trader of Table 8.5 could have lost if she had been forced to invest the short sale proceeds at less than the implied repo rate. If she had been forced to pay more than 10 percent on the borrowings to pay the coupon, the transactions would have resulted in a loss also. Finally, if futures prices had risen, she would have had daily resettlement inflows that were less than the rise in the invoice amount, and these would have generated losses as well.

In addition to these sources of risk that plague cash-and-carry and reverse cash-and-carry strategies alike, the reverse cash-and-carry strategy faces other special risks. These stem from the seller's options. In Table 8.5, we made several implicit assumptions. We assumed that the short futures trader delivered on September 30, 1991 and that the short trader delivered exactly the same bond that the trader of Table 8.5 sold short.

From Chapter 7, we know that the short trader of a T-bond futures has several options associated with the delivery. First, the short trader holds a **quality option**—the option to choose which bond to deliver. In Chapter 7, we noted that there are typically more than twenty deliverable bonds. The short trader can

---

Table 8.4
The Risks of Cash–and–Carry Transactions

April 15, 1991

Borrow $144,215 for 168 days at implied repo rate of 10.41 percent.
Buy $100,000 face value of 14% T–bonds maturing on Nov. 15, 2011 for a total price of $144,215, including accrued interest.
Sell one SEP 91 T-bond futures contract at the current price of 91–10.

May 15, 1991

Receive coupon payment of $7,000 and invest for 138 days at 10 percent.

September 30, 1991 (Assuming futures has fallen to 89–10)

Between April and September, the futures price has fallen from 91–10 to 89–10, generating cash inflows of $2,000.
Deliver the bond and receive invoice amount of $140,898.
From the invested coupon receive $7,000 + $7,000(.10)(138/360) = $7,268.
Repay debt: $144,215 + $144,215(.1041)(168/360) = $151,221.

Net Loss = $1,055

Table 8.5
Reverse Cash–and–Carry Transactions
Showing Implied Repo Rates

April 15, 1991

Sell short $100,000 face value of 14% T-bonds maturing on Nov. 15, 2011 for a total price of $144,215, including accrued interest.
Buy one SEP 91 T-bond futures contract at the current price of 91–10.
Lend $144,215 for 168 days at implied repo rate of 10.41 percent.

May 15, 1991

Borrow $7,000 for 138 days at 10 percent and pay coupon payment of $7,000.

September 30, 1991 (Assuming futures is still at 91–10)

Collect investment: $144,215 + $144,215(.1041)(168/360) = $151,221.
Accept delivery on the futures of the same 14% bond that was sold short and pay invoice amount of $143,954.
Return bond to honor short sale.
Pay debt used to finance the coupon payment: $7,000 + $7,000(.10)(138/360) = $7,267.

Net Profit = 0

---

deliver any of these. Therefore, the reverse cash–and–carry trader cannot be sure that she will receive a particular bond in the delivery. If the delivered bond is not the same bond that she sold short, she must go into the market to buy the bond that will allow her to cover the short sale. Of course, this exposes her to the risk that the price of the 14 percent bond could have changed. The seller of a T–bond futures contract also possesses a second important option. The **timing option** is the seller's option to choose the day of delivery. From Chapter 7 we know that delivery can occur on any business day in the delivery month. Therefore, the reverse cash–and–carry trader cannot be sure that delivery will occur on a particular date. This also exposes the trader of Table 8.5 to risk, because she cannot know that the delivery will occur on September 30. In addition to the quality and timing options, the short trader also possesses some other highly specialized options that add to the risk of the reverse cash–and–carry transactions. These options make the reverse cash–and–carry transactions extremely risky. As we discuss in the next section, these options have an important impact on the pricing of T–bond futures.

Seller's Options in T–Bond Futures

The structure of the T–bond futures contract gives the seller timing and quality options. The timing option arises from the seller's right to choose the time of delivery. The quality option stems from the seller's right to select which bond to deliver. Certain features of the T–bond futures contract confer both types of options on the seller. We have already seen that the seller's ability to choose the delivery day impedes the long trader's reverse cash–and–carry trading strategies because the long trader can never know when the short will choose to deliver. However, besides frustrating the long trader, the quality and timing options have specific value for the short trader.

While we may distinguish timing and quality options conceptually, they become entangled in the actual specification of the T–bond futures contract. The two main seller's options in the T–bond futures market are the **wildcard option** and the **end–of–the–month option**. In this section, we discuss these options and analyze their effects on the pricing of the T–bond contract and optimal trading strategies to exploit these options.

The Wildcard Option

In the T–bond futures market, the futures seller chooses the position day by notifying the exchange of an intention to deliver. The actual delivery takes place two business days later. For example, if today is Monday June 13, the trader may notify the exchange of his intention to deliver and June 13 becomes the position day. Actual delivery occurs in two business days on Wednesday June 15. By making June 13 the position day, the short seller determines that the settlement price on June 13 will be the settlement price used to determine the invoice amount.

Under the rules of the exchange, the settlement price is determined at 2 p.m. On position day, the short trader has until 8 p.m. Chicago time to notify the exchange of an intention to deliver. The day of notification becomes the position day, with the invoice amount being based on the settlement price that day. Therefore, the short trader has a window from 2 to 8 p.m. for good luck to strike. If interest rates jump between 2 and 8 p.m., the short trader can notify the exchange of an intention to deliver and secure the 2 p.m. settlement price on the futures. The trader can then deliver the bond that fell in price due to a jump in interest rates.

The **wildcard option** is the option for the seller to lock-in the 2 p.m. price by announcing an intention to deliver anytime before 8 p.m. In fact, the seller possesses a series of wildcard options. For example, on First Position Day, the second-to-last business day of the month preceding expiration, the seller has the wildcard option. If bond prices fall between 2 and 8 p.m. that day, the seller can announce an intention to deliver and capture the 2 p.m. price. If nothing happens between 2 and 8 p.m., the seller need not announce any intention to deliver. Instead, the seller can merely wait until the next day, hoping that something happens between 2 and 8 p.m. to cause a drop in bond prices. The seller can continue to play this game until the third-to-last business day of the month, which is the Last Position Day. In buying a T-bond futures, the long trader has conferred an option to the seller, and the long trader stands at risk each day. The value of the wildcard option depends on the chance that something will happen to cause a drop in bond prices between 2 and 8 p.m. on any possible position day.

Let us explore the effect of changes in interest rates on futures traders by using the data for two bonds in Table 8.6 for June 13. Both bonds, we assume, will pay a coupon on June 15, so we ignore accrued interest. Bond A in the Table has 30 years to maturity, pays a 7 percent coupon, and sells for 88.69 percent of par. It yields 8.00 percent and has a conversion factor for the June

Table 8.6
Bond Data at 2 P.M. on June 13

Bond	Coupon Rate	Price	Conversion Factor	Yield	Profit from Delivery
A: 30–year	.07	88.69	.8869	.0800	0
B: 20–year	.12	139.59	1.3959	.0800	0

T-bond futures of .8869. Bond B has 20 years to maturity, pays a 12 percent coupon, and sells for 139.59 percent of par. It yields 8.00 percent and has a conversion factor of 1.3959. The settlement price on June 13 for the JUN futures is 100-00. For Bond A, the invoice amount is $88,690 and for Bond B it is $139,590. By construction, both bonds have the zero profit from delivery.

Table 8.6 has been constructed so that neither bond is better to deliver than the other. Each gives a delivery profit of zero, because the price is proportional to the conversion factor and there is no accrued interest to consider. The price is proportional to the conversion factor, because we assume that both bonds yield 8 percent. Let us assume that this is the situation when trading ends on June 20. If yields remain unchanged, the trader will be indifferent about delivering one bond or the other.

We want to explore whether a change in interest rates can affect the desirability of delivering and whether changing rates can affect the choice of delivery instrument. Now assume that late in the Chicago afternoon of June 13, interest rates jump by 1 percent due to an invasion of a Middle East principality. Bond A now yields 9.00 percent and its price falls to 79.36 percent of par. Now there is at least one beneficiary of the invasion, because the short trader can deliver this bond against the futures contract.

To buy $100,000 principal amount of Bond A costs, $79,360, and the trader can deliver this bond against the futures contract for the invoice amount of $88,690. This change in rates gives the short trader a profit from delivery of $9,330, the full amount of the bond's price fall. This results from the fact that the invoice amount was set at 2 p.m., but the bond price was free to fall between 2 and 8 p.m. on June 13. The short seller plays his wildcard and announces his intention to deliver. Table 8.7 summarizes this change for Bond A. For Bond B, also shown in Table 8.7, the rise in rates also causes the price to fall from 139.59 to 127.60. This gives a $11,990 profit from delivering Bond B after the rise in rates. Table 8.7 also shows the effect of a fall in rates from 8 to 7

Table 8.7
Wildcard Option Results from Sudden Yield Changes

	Yields Fall to 7%	Yields Rise to 9%
Bond A		
Price	100.00	79.36
Dollar Payoff to Deliver	−$11,310	$9,330
Bond B		
Price	153.39	127.60
Dollar Payoff to Deliver	−$13,800	$11,990

percent. With this fall in rates, the trader shows a loss from delivering, so the trader defers delivery, hoping that rates will rise. In our example of rising rates, the wildcard option paid handsomely. Simply by the good luck of rates rising during the wildcard interval, the short trader was able to secure a delivery profit of $9,330 with Bond A or $11,990 with Bond B.

The chance to wait from 2 to 8 p.m. to play the wildcard is a timing option. However, the wildcard option also involves a quality option. At 2 p.m. on June 10 the trader is indifferent between delivering Bond A and Bond B in Table 8.6, because both have zero delivery profits. When rates rise due to the invasion, the two cash market prices change by different amounts, as Table 8.7 details. With the jump in rates, both bonds are profitable to deliver, but it is clearly better to deliver Bond B for a delivery profit of $11,990, rather than Bond A with a delivery profit of only $9,330. This example illustrates the quality option inherent in the wildcard option.

However, the quality component of the wildcard option is even better than it appears at first. We have seen that the settlement price for computing the invoice amount is fixed at 2 p.m. on position day and that the short trader must announce an intention to deliver by 8 p.m. that same evening. However, the short trader has until 5 p.m. the next business day, Notice of Intention Day, to declare which bond he or she intends to deliver. Thus, the trader has an extra business day to choose the bond that will be best to deliver.

Key Times for the Wildcard Option

Position Day 2:00 p.m.	The settlement price is determined. This settlement price is used to compute the invoice amount for all deliveries announced this day.
Position Day 8:00 p.m.	By 8:00 p.m., the short trader must declare an intention to deliver. The announcement secures the 2:00 p.m. settlement price.
Notice of Intention Day 5:00 p.m.	By this time, the short trader must announce which bond will be delivered.

The change in rates gives a clear preference for delivering one bond rather than another. As Table 8.7 shows for a drop in yields to 7 percent, it is better to deliver Bond A. Of course, the short trader prefers not to deliver if yields fall, but if he must, he prefers to deliver Bond A. This example illustrates how changing interest rates can change the preferred delivery instrument, thereby creating a quality option.

The End–of–the–Month Option

As we have discussed, the seller of a T-bond futures contract may choose to deliver any deliverable bond on any business day of the delivery month. The last trading day for T-bond futures is the eighth to last business day of the delivery month. All contracts open after that time must be satisfied by delivery. The settlement price established on the final trading day is the settlement price used in all invoice calculations for all deliveries in the remainder of the month. The seller must deliver, but he can still make two choices. First, the seller can choose which remaining day to deliver, and the seller can choose which bond to deliver.

Let us assume that interest rates are certain to be stable for those last few days. If so, the seller has a clear means to determine which day to deliver. Each additional day the seller holds the bond, the bond accrues interest. However, for each additional day the seller holds the bond, the seller must finance the bond, presumably at the overnight repo rate. Thus, the seller's choice is clear. If the coupon yield on the bond exceeds the financing rate to hold the bond, the seller should deliver on the last day. If the financing rate exceeds the coupon yield, the seller should deliver immediately. The choice of when to deliver, based on the rate of accruing interest, is a timing option and is known as the **accrued interest option**. It is a component of the end-of-the-month option.

In general, interest rates will not be constant over the last eight business days of the month. As interest rates change during this period, bond prices will change. However, for any given potential delivery day during this period, the invoice amount for a bond will not change. The invoice amount is determined by the settlement price on the last trading day and the amount of accrued interest to the delivery day. From the seller's point of view, the income to be received from delivery is known for each bond. The seller must deliver one of the deliverable bonds, but he still possesses a quality option. The seller can choose which bond to deliver.

Seller's Options in the Real Market

While the seller's options may be interesting and may give a devilish twist to the T-bond and T-note futures contracts, it remains to be seen how important they really are. First, we will examine estimates of the value of the seller's options and their effects on futures prices. Second, we consider the extent to which traders seem to pay attention to these options in guiding their own trading.

The Value of the Seller's Options.   With all perfect market conditions in place, we are accustomed to the conclusion of the Cost-of-Carry Model that the futures price should equal the spot price times one plus the cost-of-carry:

$$F = S(1 + C)$$

In discussing the seller's options, we have seen how they can have value. However, this formulation of the Cost-of-Carry Model leaves no role for the seller's options. If the seller's options have value, then market equilibrium requires that the following equation should hold:

$$F + SO = S(1 + C)$$

where:

$$SO = \text{value of seller's options}$$

This implies that:

$$F = S(1 + C) - SO \qquad\qquad 8.3$$

If this reformulation of the Cost-of-Carry Model did not hold, the market would not be in equilibrium. This reformulation also implies that the futures prices observable in the market should be below the simple cost-of-carry price by the amount of the seller's options.

In other words, the market bids down the futures price because of the seller's options. The futures price must fall until the futures price plus the seller's options, $(F + SO)$, just equals the spot price times one plus the cost-of-carry, $S(1 + C)$. If the futures price were not bid down, then the seller would, in effect, get the options for free, and this would violate the principles of an efficient market.

This approach to the seller's options has been used by a number of scholars to estimate the value of the seller's options inherent in the T-bond futures contract. One difficulty with estimating the value of these options is that options generally have greater value the more time that remains until expiration. In other words, the seller's options should be worth more one year from delivery than they are worth three months from delivery. Table 8.8 summarizes some of the key results about the pricing of the seller's options.

Seller's Options and Trader Behavior. Thus far we have seen that the seller's options appear to have value. Possessing these options suggests that traders should behave in similar ways. Thus, we would expect to find traders delivering the same bonds on the same days and not delivering on the same days. Further, we expect short traders to be aware of, and follow, the optimal policy for delivering to take advantage of their options.

Table 8.9 summarizes aspects of the delivery behavior for recent T-bond expiration months. For the various contracts, the cells show the total number of contracts delivered each day. The number to the right of the slash shows the number of different bond issues delivered that day. An "X" indicates a day not

Table 8.8
Studies of the Seller's Options

Study	Key Results
Gay and Manaster (1984)	Quality option has a significant impact on futures prices. Authors focused on wheat.
Benninga and Smirlock (1985)	Delivery options appear to have significant value.
Gay and Manaster (1986)	Although futures prices partially reflect the value of delivery options, the futures prices are still too high to exclude profitable strategies.
Kane and Marcus (1986a)	At the start of the delivery month, the wildcard option is worth about $200–277 per contract.
Kane and Marcus (1986b)	Delivery option has a noticeable impact on futures prices.
Arak and Goodman (1987)	Market overvalues delivery options. Reverse cash–and–carry positions outperform cash–and–carry strategies.
Hegde (1988)	During the three months before expiration, the average value of the seller's options are worth less than .5% of the futures price.
Barnhill and Seale (1988)	Chance to actively switch cash market bonds before expiration is worth more than the quality option. This switching option is worth more when interest rates are volatile.
Hemler (1988)	Seller's options account for about $1,200 on average during the nine months before expiration. Values are higher the longer until expiration.
Boyle (1989)	In a simulation study, quality option value is significant, but the value of the timing option is small.
Hegde (1989)	Three months before expiration, the delivery options are worth about $464.
Barnhill (1990)	Quality options have less value than previously recognized. The chance to switch cash bonds repeatedly in a cash-and–carry framework is more valuable than the quality option.

available for delivery (weekend, holiday, September 31). As the table shows, relatively few different issues of the many available bonds are delivered. Thus, there seems to be considerable attention paid to the characteristics of the bonds being delivered. Second, deliveries are infrequent in the early part of the month. Traders seem anxious to wait to exploit their end–of–the–month option. On occasion, however, significant deliveries do occur before the last few trading

Table 8.9
T–Bond Delivery Behavior

| | Contracts Delivered Daily/Different Bond Issues Delivered | | | |
Day	DEC 89	MAR 90	JUN 90	SEP 90
1				X
2	X		X	X
3	X	X	X	X
4	3/1	X		
5			1/1	
6				
7				
8				X
9	X		X	X
10	X	X	X	
11	3/1	X	1/1	
12	3/1			
13	3/1		6/1	
14	1/1			
15	2/2			X
16	X		X	X
17	X	X	X	
18		X		
19				
20	998/1		2/1	
21	7/2		2/1	
22	328/4			X
23	X		X	X
24	X	X	X	
25	X	X	10/1	
26			2/2	
27			1/1	
28	12070/5	10/1	425/2	
29	13008/2		16,991/3	X
30	X	8,939/2	X	X
31	X	X	X	X
TOTAL	26,418/7	8949/2	17,441/6	

Source: CBT *Financial Update*, various issues.

days. We might expect all traders to follow the exactly same delivery strategy of delivering the same bond on the same day. In Table 8.9, we see departures from that behavior. Some of the early deliveries of just a few contracts appear to be motivated by other concerns. Also, even when deliveries are heavy, traders deliver different bonds. This suggests that some traders may find it cheaper to deliver a bond from their existing inventory rather than to buy the cheapest-to-deliver bond for the express purpose of making delivery.

Gerald D. Gay and Steven Manaster examined the different strategies open to short T-bond traders to determine whether profits were available from optimal delivery strategies and to determine whether traders followed those optimal strategies.[2] They reach several important conclusions. First, delivery strategies during the 1977-1983 period would have generated profits. This means that futures prices during this period did not fully reflect the value of the options available to the short sellers. Second, they compared an optimal delivery strategy with the actual deliveries during this period. They found that the actual deliveries exploited some, but not all, of the seller's options. In other words, the short traders took advantage of their options to some extent, but they did not fully exploit the options available to them. As Gay and Manaster note, these options may not have been fully understood by traders in this early period. This leaves open the possibility that futures prices will adjust to fully reflect the value of the seller's options as the market moves toward maturity.

Interest Rate Futures Market Efficiency

A market is informationally efficient if prices in that market fully reflect all information in a given information set. If the market is efficient with respect to some information set, then that information cannot be used to direct a trading strategy to beat the market. A trader beats the market by consistently earning a rate of return that exceeds the risk-adjusted market equilibrium rate of return. There are three commonly distinguished forms of the market efficiency hypothesis: the weak form, the semi-strong form, and the strong form. These versions of market efficiency are distinguished by their information sets. The weak form efficiency hypothesis asserts that information contained in the past history of price and volume data cannot be used to beat the market. The semi-strong form asserts that traders cannot rely on public information to beat the market. The strong form asserts that even private information is insufficient to allow a trader to beat the market.

We have seen that cash-and-carry and reverse cash-and-carry arbitrage strategies rely only on observable prices. Thus, successful arbitrage strategies violate weak form efficiency. For example, large divergences between forward and futures rates of interest, for example, would generate important academic arbitrage opportunities. Because the futures market is a zero sum game, in the absence of transaction costs, one participant's profits implies offsetting losses for others.

For these reasons, users of any market should be concerned about market efficiency. This is true whether one is a speculator or hedger. Researchers have long recognized the importance of market efficiency. This section reviews the development of research on interest rate futures market efficiency and draws conclusions about the efficiency based on the state of research to date. In spite of the attention that has been focused on the efficiency question, only T-bill and T-bond futures contracts have been explored well in published works. Almost all of these analyses focus on divergences between forward rates implied by spot market positions and futures market positions. This focus on rate discrepancies means that the tests have sought evidence of academic arbitrage opportunities in the interest rate futures market.[3] Many early tests were based on a less than full understanding of the conditions under which market efficiency could be judged.

Early tests of futures market efficiency focused exclusively on differences between forward rates and futures rates on T-bills. Differences between these rates were sometimes interpreted without further ado as evidence of market inefficiency. Immediate difficulties with this conclusion arose because different researchers arrived at radically different conclusions, some finding efficiency and others finding gross inefficiencies. From preceding chapters, we know that forward and futures rates can differ for at least two basic reasons: market imperfections or the influence of daily resettlement. Many of the earliest researches into efficiency did not take these two factors into adequate consideration, yet both are important.[4]

Attempts to evaluate academic arbitrage opportunities in the T-bill futures market involve taking complementary positions in the futures market and in the spot market. The difference in the futures and forward yields must be sufficiently large to cover considerable transaction costs if there is to be genuine academic arbitrage. While many studies neglected the full magnitude of these transaction charges, more recent studies find potential for arbitrage even after transaction costs.

Depending on the exact way in which the arbitrage attempt is conducted, a trader must incur a variety of transaction costs. To see the full magnitude of these expenses, consider the misaligned futures and cash T-bill prices in Table 8.10. We explored these prices in Chapter 7. The transactions costs incurred to exploit this misalignment depend on the trader's initial position in the spot or futures market. With no position in either market, the trader must pay all transaction costs from the gross trading profits to capture an academic arbitrage profit. If an opportunity is attractive enough to show a profit, even after paying full transactions costs, it can be considered **pure arbitrage**.

Table 8.10
Interest Rate Futures and Arbitrage

Today's Date: January 5

Futures	Yield According to the Bond Pricing Formula
MAR Futures Contract	
(Matures in 77 days on March 22)	12.50%
Cash Bills	
167-Day T-bill	
(Deliverable on MAR Futures)	10.00
77-Day T-bill	6.00

If the trader already holds a portfolio of T-bills, for example, then some transaction costs can be avoided. Some of the costs have already been paid, and they should be considered as sunk costs for the analysis of the arbitrage. If a trader with an initial portfolio can successfully engage in arbitrage, then the profitable transaction is regarded as **quasi-arbitrage**.[5] In discussing pure arbitrage and quasi-arbitrage, we refer to academic arbitrage.

To exploit the rate discrepancies in Table 8.10 via pure arbitrage, the trader must be able to pay a variety of transactions costs:

1. Issuing a 77-day T-bill is equivalent to borrowing. The most creditworthy traders can borrow a T-bill for about 50 basis points above its current yield. For $956,750 for 77 days, the borrowing cost is about $1,023. Consider also that the acquisition of the $956,750 might be through the issuance of a term repo agreement.

2. To buy a 167-day T-bill, a trader must pay the asked price for the bill, even if he or she is a market participant, which could involve an additional cost of about $100. If not a participant in the spot T-bill market, the trader must trade through a broker and pay a commission as well.

3. In selling the MAR futures contract, a trader can receive only the bid price, thereby increasing costs about $25. If he or she is not a trader on the IMM, the trader must pay commission costs as well.

4. Delivering the T-bill also has costs, because the short trader in the futures market bears all costs of delivery. These costs might be about $50.

5. Paying off the due bill also involves transactions costs of the wire transfer and record keeping, which might be $25.

This list of transaction charges is only an indication of the additional expenses that a trader might face in an arbitrage attempt. Many of the charges shown in the list are difficult to gauge, and different market participants face different levels of expense. Nonetheless, the expenses are large and can offset a substantial difference between forward and futures yields. In addition, a trader also faces a cost not shown in the list. To find an arbitrage opportunity, a trader must search for it, and the cost of searching for the opportunity must be included in the calculation of the arbitrage profit.

From the list of transaction costs, we see that some market participants are in a much better position than others. If a participant has a portfolio of spot T-bills, has a very good credit rating, is a trader on the futures exchange, and has a network of computerized information sources already in operation, then the transactions costs incurred in attempting to conduct an arbitrage operation are much smaller. This is the difference between pure arbitrage and quasi-arbitrage. For pure arbitrage, the yield discrepancy must be large enough to cover all transaction costs faced by a market outsider. For quasi-arbitrage, the trader faces less than full transaction costs.

Pure Arbitrage and Quasi–Arbitrage

Pure arbitrage	Arbitrage transactions in which the trader faces full outside transaction costs.
Quasi–arbitrage	Arbitrage transactions in which the trader faces reduced transaction costs, due to an existing initial position in the instruments to be traded.

Rendleman and Carabini conducted one of the most thorough and careful studies of T-bill futures efficiency using daily data for the period from January 6, 1976 to March 31, 1978. The analysis focused on the three futures contracts closest to maturity at any moment. By a careful analysis of the transaction costs faced by a market outsider, Rendleman and Carabini defined a band of difference between the forward rate and the futures rate that would still not support pure arbitrage. In other words, if forward and futures rates diverged only slightly, by 50 basis points or less, the yield difference would not cover transaction costs and pure arbitrage would be impossible. Figure 8.4 shows their results. The divergences between actual and theoretical yields for T-bill futures always fall within the band of 50 basis points, which denotes the no-profit limits. This was true for all 1,606 observations in their sample, supporting their conclusion that the T-bill futures market was efficient—in the sense of excluding opportunities for pure arbitrage.

Regarding quasi-arbitrage opportunities, Rendleman and Carabini found occasions in which a trader could improve the return on a portfolio of spot

Figure 8.4
Pure Arbitrage in T–Bill Futures

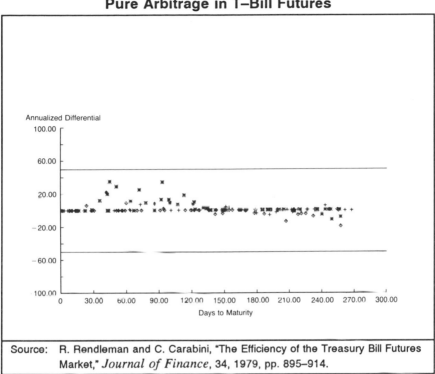

Source: R. Rendleman and C. Carabini, "The Efficiency of the Treasury Bill Futures
Market," *Journal of Finance*, 34, 1979, pp. 895–914.

T-bills. The quasi-arbitrage opportunities were found only infrequently, and no attempt was made to factor in the search costs needed to discover the opportunities. About these quasi-arbitrage opportunities, Rendleman and Carabini conclude: " . . . the inefficiencies in the Treasury bill futures market do not appear to be significant enough to offer attractive investment alternatives to the short-term portfolio manager."

In spite of the care with which the Rendleman and Carabini study was conducted, it is subject to one serious limitation; it relies on daily closing prices. In an evaluation of an arbitrage attempt, the purchase and sale of two related goods must be assumed to occur simultaneously. However, the spot and futures markets for T-bills close at different times. This means that the closing prices for each day will not be prices for the same moment on both markets. In academic jargon, the prices are non-simultaneous or exhibit non-simultaneity.

To improve the test of T-bill futures efficiency, Elton, Gruber, and Rentzler (hereafter EGR) used intra-day prices—prices from throughout the trading day.

With intra-day prices on futures and spot T-bills, they matched the times at which the trades occurred to determine simultaneous prices in both markets. Their data set consisted of a sample of intra-day spot prices spaced approximately an hour apart and every T-bill futures trade during the period from January 6, 1976 through December 22, 1982.

EGR divide the strategies they consider into those that involve immediate and delayed execution. For immediate execution, EGR assume that an arbitrage opportunity is identified from their simultaneous cash/futures price pairs and the trader enters arbitrage transactions at those prices. For delayed execution, EGR assume that an arbitrage opportunity is identified from one cash/futures price pair and the trade is executed at the prices of the next pair. This implies a delay of about one hour between identification and execution. According to EGR's analysis, the immediate execution strategy replicates the situation facing the floor trader, while the delayed execution strategy would be available to a market participant farther removed from the pit.

To analyze pure arbitrage strategies, EGR assume transaction costs on the arbitrage transactions of $175 plus an annual cost of 50 basis points to cover selling a T-bill short. As we have seen, a trader who enters such arbitrage transactions still faces daily resettlement cash flows. Therefore, any planned arbitrage profit can only be an expected profit. The actual profit may differ due to the effect of daily resettlement cash flows. Table 8.11 presents the key results

Table 8.11
Pure Arbitrage Results for T–Bill Futures

	Immediate Execution				Delayed Execution			
Size of Filter	Number of Trades	Expected Profit	Actual Profit	Standard Error	Number of Trades	Expected Profit	Actual Profit	Standard Error
$ 0	2,304	$ 894	$ 889	$15	1,725	$ 893	$ 880	$18
100	2,093	980	975	16	1,569	977	964	19
200	1,902	1,064	1,058	16	1,428	1,059	1,041	19
300	1,738	1,142	1,135	16	1,301	1,137	1,117	20
400	1,595	1,212	1,206	17	1,206	1,199	1,176	20
500	1,469	1,279	1,271	17	1,107	1,267	1,244	21
600	1,332	1,352	1,346	18	1,005	1,339	1,315	22
700	1,190	1,437	1,432	18	890	1,429	1,401	23
800	1,063	1,519	1,516	18	789	1,517	1,490	24

Source: E. Elton, M. Gruber, and J. Rentzler, "Intra–Day Tests of the Efficiency of the Treasury Bill Futures Market," *The Review of Economics and Statistics*, February 1984, Vol. 66, pp. 129–137.

of EGR's study of pure arbitrage for both immediate and delayed execution. EGR assume that these daily resettlement cash flows earn the overnight rate on a certificate of deposit.

The immediate execution results assume that transactions take place immediately upon finding an attractive opportunity, and the expected profit means that the effects of daily resettlement have not yet been considered. However, these results are net of transaction costs. The results are stratified by a filter rule that divides the opportunities by the size of the expected profit. For example, they found a total of 2,304 opportunities with some expected profit. The average expected profit across all of these trades was $894, assuming a transaction of one contract size.

Notice that they found many opportunities with very large discrepancies. For example, they found 1,063 opportunities with expected profits exceeding $800. The actual profit differs from the expected profit due to the interest gain or cost incurred on the daily resettlement cash flows. These differences are very small.[6] If execution of the trades is delayed until the next cash market quotation, the expected profits diminish. Yet overall, EGR's results indicate that these arbitrage opportunities persist. Therefore, EGR conclude that the T-bill futures market is not efficient with respect to pure arbitrage opportunities.[7]

In comparing the Rendleman and Carabini study with the later study by EGR, we must give greater weight to the results of EGR. The data employed by EGR is more complete, and they reduce the problems of non-simultaneous pricing. Recent studies of T-bill futures market efficiency have tended to corroborate the results of EGR.[8]

Having found frequent and significant departures from efficiency in the T-bill futures market, we now turn to the T-bond futures contract. The T-bond futures market has not received nearly the attention devoted to the T-bill futures market. Part of the reason for this difference is the extreme complexity of the T-bond contract, particularly the diversity of deliverable instruments and the seller's options. Since the short trader chooses which bond to deliver in fulfillment of the contract, the long position has no opportunity for arbitrage, as we showed earlier in this chapter. For cash-and-carry arbitrage, the short trader could conduct arbitrage if it were profitable to:

1. buy a bond,
2. sell a futures contract on the bond, and
3. store the bond until delivery.

As we have seen, even such a strategy is limited in its effectiveness. The bond that the short trader might hold will pay a coupon, in most cases, on the 15th of the month preceding delivery. The investment rate for the coupon is uncertain, so the short trader cannot really count on an arbitrage profit if he or she must rely on the cash flow from the reinvested coupons. These conditions drastically restrict the possible arbitrage strategies. Further, we have seen that the futures price is bid down to reflect the seller's options. Capturing profits from the seller's options is risky. As a consequence, the reduction in futures prices to account for the seller's options makes successful arbitrage even less likely.

In their paper on T-bond futures efficiency, Kolb, Gay, and Jordan investigated the possibility of arbitrage for all T-bond futures contracts in existence from December 1977 through June 1981.[9] They analyze just one day for each instrument, the last business day of the month preceding the delivery month. This is the First Position Day. For this date, and for any position day, arbitrage is possible because the trader knows what invoice amount will be received for a particular deliverable bond. The short trader receives the invoice amount upon delivery, with the invoice amount depending on the futures price, the conversion factor, and the accrued interest as discussed earlier in this chapter. From this cash flow, the short trader must pay the cost of acquiring the bond and the financing cost of holding the bond from the time of acquisition until it can be delivered. Since the short trader chooses which bond to deliver, he need find only one deliverable bond that is profitable to secure an arbitrage opportunity. Figure 8.5 shows the profitability of delivery for all deliverable bonds for 15 contract maturities, as calculated for the last business day of the month preceding the delivery month.

Only three contract maturities had a bond that promised a positive cash flow: SEP 78, SEP 80, and MAR 80. For the SEP 78 contract, the positive cash flow was $49.07 and for the SEP 80 contract, the positive cash flow was $27.57. Out of these potential profits, the arbitrageur would have had to pay transaction and search costs, so these two occasions represent no chance for an arbitrage profit.

For the MAR 80 contract, one bond would have yielded a cash flow as large as $591.34. If there is to be hope of arbitrage, it must rest with this contract. This hope, however, appears to be illusory. Prices reported for this date vary widely from source to source, with reported futures prices differing by as much as $1,625. The uncertainty over the actual prices at which one could contract requires that this apparent arbitrage opportunity be regarded as spurious. Kolb, Gay, and Jordan conclude that their results, while limited, are fully consistent with the efficiency of the T-bond futures market.

Because of difficulty with specifying a tight arbitrage link between the cash market and the T-bond futures contract, most subsequent explorations of T-bond futures efficiency have focused on speculative strategies. Successful speculative strategies would constitute evidence against efficiency if they earn a return too great for the level of speculative risk undertaken. However, the difficulty with evaluating such strategies lies in determining a market standard risk/expected return relationship. As a consequence, tests of speculative efficiency are always

Figure 8.5
Potential Arbitrage in T–Bond Futures

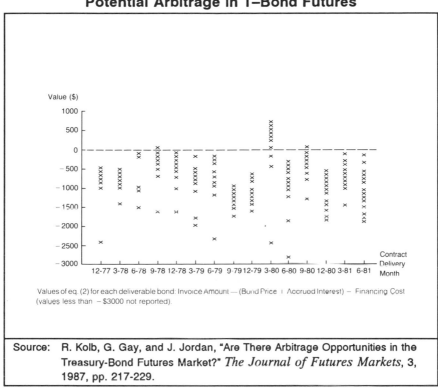

Values of eq. (2) for each deliverable bond: Invoice Amount — (Bond Price + Accrued Interest) — Financing Cost (values less than − $3000 not reported).

Source: R. Kolb, G. Gay, and J. Jordan, "Are There Arbitrage Opportunities in the Treasury-Bond Futures Market?" *The Journal of Futures Markets*, 3, 1987, pp. 217-229.

simultaneous tests of market efficiency and the adequacy of the risk/expected return measure used. Bearing this limitation in mind, we briefly consider some further tests of T-bond futures efficiency.

An important limitation of the Kolb, Gay, and Jordan methodology was the necessary restriction to a period within the delivery month. B. Resnick and E. Hennigar extended a similar analysis to periods outside the delivery month. Their results support the efficiency of the T-bond futures market.[10] In a separate study, Resnick evaluated the pricing relationship between T-bond futures of different maturities, in effect asking if the spread relationships were efficient. Resnick's findings also support a general conclusion of efficiency.[11]

R. Klemkosky and D. Lasser conduct a study similar to Resnick and Hennigar's, but use a different time period and attempt to adjust for taxes. Noting that any kind of cash-and-carry arbitrage evaluation depends on the estimate of borrowing costs, Klemkosky and Lasser find inefficiencies. While they acknowledge that they are unable to fully adjust for risk, Klemkosky and Lasser judge the divergences between the spot and futures prices to be inconsistent with full efficiency. As they conclude: ". . . either the borrowing costs are still being underestimated or the T-bond market was inefficient during periods of high interest rates, possibly because of an extraordinarily large risk premium being placed on the variable coupon reinvestment return."[12]

In a test of speculative efficiency, D. Chance examines speculative strategies based on the response of the futures market to announcements of changes in the Consumer Price Index. Chance found that T-bond futures prices rose following an announcement of lower inflation (measured against past inflation or against "expected" inflation). Chance found that the T-bond futures price adjusted slowly to this information, so that traders could react swiftly to the market and make a speculative profit as the market digested the information over the day following the announcement.[13]

How can we assess the variety of evidence on the efficiency of the interest rate futures market? Several years ago, it appeared the weight of evidence favored efficiency, but today it appears that weight is beginning to shift. The study by Elton, Gruber, and Rentzler is particularly persuasive. The study is extremely rich in observations and every effort seems to have been made to adjust for potential discrepancies. Attempts to assess the efficiency of the T-bond futures markets are much more difficult, and the current state of evidence is inconclusive. In attempting to summarize this evidence in a single sentence, it appears that persistent inefficiencies continue to exist in these markets, but the size of the inefficiencies may not be large enough to reward a change in professions. Remember, none of these studies includes the search cost or the use of human capital required to find and exploit the alleged arbitrage opportunity.

We must also remember that most of these studies have focused on the existence of arbitrage opportunities. Arbitrage, however, is the grossest kind of inefficiency. A market may well have no arbitrage opportunities and still be inefficient. If risky positions can be taken in the futures market, and those risky positions earn returns in excess of a risk-adjusted normal return, then the futures market would still be inefficient. Few tests of such possibilities have been conducted, probably due to the difficulty in defining a risk-adjusted normal return. The ones that have been conducted reach divergent conclusions.

Applications:
Eurodollar and T–Bill Futures

In Chapter 7 we considered speculative strategies and some hedging strategies. In this section we explore alternative risk management strategies using short-term interest rate futures. We proceed by considering a series of examples.

Taken together, these examples provide a handbook of techniques for a variety of risk management strategies. All of these strategies turn on protection against shifting interest rates.

Changing the Maturity of an Investment

Many investors find themselves with an existing portfolio that may have undesirable maturity characteristics. For example, a firm might hold a six-month T-bill and realize that it will have a need for funds in three months. By the same token, another investor might hold the same six-month T-bill and fear that those funds might have to face lower reinvestment rates upon maturity in six-months. This investor might prefer a one-year maturity. Both the firm and the investor could sell the six-month bill and invest for the preferred maturity. However, spot market transactions costs are relatively high, and many investors prefer to alter the maturities of investment by trading futures. The two examples that follow show how to use futures to accomplish both a shortening and lengthening of maturities.

Shortening the Maturity of a T–Bill Investment. Consider a firm that has invested in a T-bill. Now, on March 20, the T-bill has a maturity of 180 days, but the firm learns of a need for cash in 90 days. Therefore, it would like to shorten the maturity so it can have access to its funds in 90 days, around mid-September.

For simplicity, we assume that the short-term yield curve is flat with all rates at 10 percent on March 20. For convenience, we assume a 360-day year to match the pricing conventions for T-bills. The face value of the firm's T-bill is $10 million. With 180 days to maturity and a 10 percent discount yield, the price of the bill is given by:

$$P = FV - [DY(FV)(DTM)]/360$$

where:

P	= bill price
FV	= face value
DY	= discount yield
DTM	= days until maturity

Therefore the 180-day bill is worth $9,500,000. If the yield curve is flat at 10 percent, the futures yield must also be 10 percent, and the T-bill futures price must be $975,000 per contract. Starting from an initial position of a six-month T-bill, the firm of our example can shorten the maturity by selling T-bill futures for expiration in three months, as Table 8.12 shows. On March 20, there was no

Table 8.12
Transactions to Shorten Maturities

Date	Cash Market	Futures Market
March 20	Holds six-month T-bill with a face value of $10,000,000, worth $9,500,000. Wishes a three-month maturity.	Sell 10 JUN T-bill futures contracts at 90.00, reflecting the 10% discount yield.
June 20		Deliver cash market T-bills against futures; receive $9,750,000.

cash flow, because the firm merely sold futures. On June 20, the six-month bill is now a three-month bill and can be delivered against the futures. In Table 8.12, the firm delivers the bills and receives the futures invoice amount of $9,750,000. (Although we have assumed the futures price did not change, this does not limit the applicability of our results. No matter how the futures price changed from March to June, the firm would still receive a total of $9,750,000. We assume that this occurs in June instead of over the period.) The firm has effectively shortened the maturity from six months to three months.

Lengthening the Maturity.   Consider now, on August 21, an investor who holds a $100 million face value T-bill that matures in 30 days on September 20. She plans to reinvest for another three months after the T-bill matures. However, she fears that interest rates might fall unexpectedly. If so, she would be forced to reinvest at a lower rate than is now reflected in the yield curve. The SEP T-bill futures yield is 9.8 percent, as is the rate on the current investment. She finds this rate attractive and would like to lengthen the maturity of the T-bill investment. She knows that she can lengthen the maturity by buying a September futures contract and taking delivery. She will then hold the delivered bills until maturity in December.

With a 9.8 percent discount futures yield, the value of the delivery unit is $975,500. With $100 million coming available on September 20, the investor knows she will have enough funds to take delivery of ($100,000,000/$975,500) = 102.51 futures contracts. Therefore, she initiates the strategy presented in Table 8.13.

On August 21, she held a bill worth $99,183,333, assuming a yield of 9.8 percent. With the transactions of Table 8.13, she had no cash flow on August 21. With the maturity of the T-bill in September, the investor received $100,000,000 and used almost all of it to pay for the futures delivery. She also received $499,000, which we assume she invested at 9.8% for three months. In December, this investment would be worth $499,000 + $499,000(.098)(90/360) = $511,226.

Table 8.13
Transactions to Lengthen Maturities

Date	Cash Market	Futures Market
August 21	Holds 30–day T–bill with a face value of $100,000,000. Wishes to extend the maturity for 90 days.	Buy 102 SEP T–bill futures contracts, with a yield of 9.8%.
September 20	30–day T–bill matures and investor receives $100,000,000. Invest $499,000 in money market fund.	Accept delivery on 102 SEP futures, paying $99,501,000.
December 19	T–bills received on SEP futures mature for $102,000,000.	

With the T bills maturing in December, the total proceeds will be $102,511,226, from an investment that was worth $99,183,333 on August 21. This gives her a discount yield of 9.8 percent over the four-month horizon from August to December.

Notice that this transaction "locked in" the 9.8 percent on the futures contract. In this example, this happens to match the spot rate of interest. However, the important point to recognize is that lengthening the maturity involves locking into the futures yield, no matter what that yield may be. Thus, for the period covered by the T-bill delivered on the futures contract, the investment will earn the futures yield at the time of contracting.

Fixed and Floating Loan Rates

In recent years, interest rates have fluctuated dramatically. These fluctuating rates generate interest rate risk that few economic agents are anxious to bear. For example, in housing finance, home buyers seek fixed rate loans, because the fixed rate protects the borrower against rising rates. By the same token, lenders may be unwilling to offer fixed rate loans, because they fear that their cost of funds might rise. With fixed rate lending, and a rising cost of funds, the lender faces a risk of paying more to acquire funds than it is earning on its fixed rate lending. Therefore, many lenders want to make floating rate loans.

In this section, we show how the borrower who receives a floating rate loan can effectively convert this loan into a fixed rate loan, thereby protecting against rises in interest rates. Similarly, for a lender who feels compelled to offer fixed rate loans, we show how the lender can use the futures markets to make the investment perform like a floating rate loan. Either the borrower or lender can bear the interest rate risk. Whichever party bears the interest rate risk can hedge the risk through the futures market. In a floating rate loan, the borrower bears or hedges the risk. In a fixed rate loan, the lender bears or hedges the risk.

In this section we consider a single transaction from two points of view, the lender's and the borrower's. First, we assume that the loan is a floating rate loan and that the borrower hedges the interest rate risk associated with the loan. Second, we consider a fixed rate loan in which the lender hedges the interest rate risk.

Converting a Floating Rate to a Fixed Rate Loan. A construction firm plans a project that will take six months to complete at a total cost of $100 million. The bank offers to provide the funds for six months at a rate 200 basis points above the 90-day LIBOR rate. However, the bank insists that the loan rate for the second quarter will be 200 basis points above the 90-day LIBOR rate that prevails at that date. Also, the construction company must pay interest after the first quarter. Principal plus interest are due in six months.

Today is September 20 and the current 90-day LIBOR rate is 7.0 percent. The DEC Eurodollar futures yield is 7.3 percent. Based on these rates and the borrowing plan, the construction company will pay 9 percent for the first three months and 9.3 percent for the second three months. These rates give the following cash flows from the loan:

September 20	Receive principal	+$100,000,000
December 20	Pay interest	- 2,250,000
March 20	Pay interest and principal	- 102,325,000

The cash flows for September and December are certain. However, the cash flow in March depends upon the LIBOR rate that prevails in December. The firm expects a 9.3 percent rate, which equals the futures yield for the DEC futures plus 200 basis points. However, between September and December, that rate could rise. For example, if the spot 90-day LIBOR rate in December is 7.8 percent, the firm will pay 9.8 percent and the total interest due in March will be $125,000 higher than expected.

The construction firm decides to lock into the 7.3 futures yield and its expected 9.3 borrowing rate so that it will know its borrowing cost. Starting with a floating rate loan and transacting to fix the interest rate is called a **synthetic fixed rate loan**. Table 8.14 shows how the construction company trades to protect itself from a jump in rates. At the outset, the firm accepts the floating rate scheme for its loan and sells 100 DEC Eurodollar futures. If rates rise, the short futures position will give enough profits to pay the additional interest expense on the second quarter's loan.

As Table 8.14 shows, LIBOR rises by 50 basis points to 7.8 percent. This implies a borrowing rate of 9.8 percent for the second quarter, as the Table shows. However, the rise in rates has created a futures profit of $125,000 = 50

Table 8.14
Synthetic Fixed Rate Borrowing

Date	Cash Market	Futures Market
September 20	Borrow $100,000,000 at 9.00% for three months and commit to extend the loan for three additional months at a rate 200 basis points above the three month LIBOR rate prevailing at that time.	Sell 100 DEC Eurodollar futures contracts at 92.70, reflecting the 7.3% yield.
December 20	Pay interest of $2,250,000. LIBOR is now at 7.8%, so borrow $100,000,000 for three months at 9.8%.	Offset 100 DEC Eurodollar futures at 92.20, reflecting the 7.8% yield. Produces profit of $125,000 = 50 basis points × $25 per point × 100 contracts.
March 20	Pay interest of $2,450,000 and repay principal of $100,000,000.	
	Total Interest Expense: $4,700,000	Futures Profit: $125,000
	Net Interest Expense After Hedging: $4,575,000	

basis points times $25 per basis point times 100 contracts. The table shows that the firm pays $125,000 more interest in the second quarter than anticipated due to the jump in rates. However, this is exactly offset by the futures profit.[14] In September, the firm expected to pay a total of $4,575,000 in interest for the loan. Counting the futures profit, this is exactly the interest that the firm pays because it hedged. By trading in the futures market, the construction firm changed its floating rate loan into a fixed rate loan.

Converting a Floating Rate to a Fixed Rate Loan. We now consider the same transaction from the lender's point of view. If the construction company really wants a fixed rate loan, let them have it, reasons the bank. The bank's cost of funds equals the 90-day LIBOR rate we assume. The bank expects to pay 7.0 percent for funds this quarter and 7.3 percent next quarter, or an average rate of 7.15 percent over the six months of the loan. Therefore, the bank decides to make a fixed rate six-month loan to the construction company at 9.15 percent. The bank's expected profit is the 200 basis point spread between the lending rate and the bank's LIBOR based cost of funds. The bank expects to secure the funds by borrowing:

September 20	Borrow principal	+$100,000,000
December 20	Receive interest	+$2,250,000
	Pay interest	– $1,750,000
March 20	Receive principal and interest	+$102,325,000
	Pay principal and interest	– $101,825,000

If all goes as expected, the bank's gross profit will be $1,000,000. Having made a fixed rate loan, however, the bank is at risk of rising interest rates. For example, if LIBOR rises by 50 basis points to 7.8 percent for the second quarter, the bank will have to pay an additional $125,000 in interest. To avoid this risk, the bank transacts as shown in Table 8.15. Notice how they almost exactly match the transactions of the construction company, except that the bank has a lower borrowing rate. If interest rates rise, the bank's cost of funds rise, just as was the case for the construction company with a floating rate loan. Both the construction company and the bank were able to hedge by selling Eurodollar futures.

With the rise in rates, the bank paid $125,000 more interest than it expected. However, this increased interest was offset by a futures market gain. Originally, the bank wanted to shift the interest rate risk to the construction company. However, as the transactions of Table 8.15 show, the bank is able to give the construction company the fixed rate loan it desires and still avoid the interest rate risk. In essence, the bank creates a **synthetic floating rate loan**. For its customer it offers a fixed rate loan, but the bank transacts in the futures market to make the transaction equivalent to having given a floating rate loan.

Table 8.15
Synthetic Floating Rate Lending

Date	Cash Market	Futures Market
September 20	Borrow $100,000,000 at 7.00% for three months and lend it for six months at 9.15%.	Sell 100 DEC Eurodollar futures contracts at 92.70, reflecting the 7.3% yield.
December 20	Pay interest of $1,750,000. LIBOR is now at 7.8%, so borrow $100,000,000 for three months at 9.8%.	Offset 100 DEC Eurodollar futures at 92.20, reflecting the 7.8% yield. Produces profit of $125,000 = 50 basis points × $25 per point × 100 contracts.
March 20	Pay interest of $1,950,000 and repay principal of $100,000,000.	
	Total Interest Expense: $3,700,000	Futures Profit: $125,000
	Net Interest Expense After Hedging: $3,575,000	

Strip and Stack Hedges

In the example of the synthetic fixed rate loan and synthetic floating rate lending, the interest rate risk focused on a single date. Often, the period of the loan covers a number of different dates at which the rate might be reset. For example, the construction company of our previous example makes a more realistic assessment of how long it will take to complete a project. Instead of six months, the construction firm realizes the project will take a year.

The bank insists on making a floating rate loan for three months at a rate 200 basis points above the LIBOR rate prevailing at the time of the loan. On September 15, the construction company observes the following rates:

Three month LIBOR	7.00%
DEC Eurodollar	7.30
MAR Eurodollar	7.60
JUN Eurodollar	7.90

For these four quarters, the firm expects to finance the $100,000,000 at 9.00, 9.30, 9.60, and 9.90 percent, respectively. Therefore, the construction company expects to borrow $100,000,000 for a year at an average rate of 9.45 percent. This gives a total expected interest cost of $9,450,000.

A Stack Hedge Example. The construction firm decides to lock in this borrowing rate by hedging with Eurodollar futures. To implement the hedge, the firm sells 300 DEC Eurodollar futures. The firm hopes to protect itself against any changes in interest rates between September and December. In December, the futures will expire and the firm will offset the DEC futures and replace them with MAR futures. This is a **stack hedge**, because all of the futures contracts are concentrated, or stacked, in a single futures expiration.

We now consider how the construction firm fairs with a single change in interest rates over the next year. Shortly after the firm enters the hedge, LIBOR rates jump by 50 basis points. Therefore, the firm's borrowing costs for the next three quarters are:

December—March	9.80%
March—June	10.10
June—September	10.40

For simplicity, we consider only one interest rate change, so the firm secures these rates. Table 8.16 shows the construction firm's transactions and the results of the hedge. The firm hedges its $100,000,000 loan with 300 contracts, or $300,000,000 of underlying Eurodollars. After taking the loan, the first quarter's

Table 8.16
Results of a Stack Hedge

Date	Cash Market	Futures Market
September 20	Borrow $100,000,000 at 9.00 for three months and commit to roll over the loan for three quarters at 200 basis points over the prevailing LIBOR rate.	Sell 300 DEC Eurodollar futures contracts at 92.70, reflecting the 7.3% yield.
December 20	Pay interest of $2,250,000. LIBOR is now at 7.8 percent, so borrow $100,000,000 for three months at 9.8 percent.	Offset 300 DEC Eurodollar futures at 92.20, reflecting the 7.8% yield. Produces profit of $375,000 = 50 basis points × $25 per point × 300 contracts.
March 20	Pay interest of $2,450,000 and borrow $100,000,000 for three months at 10.10 percent.	
June 20	Pay interest of $2,525,000 and borrow $100,000,000 for three months at 10.40 percent.	
September 20	Pay interest of $2,600,000 and principal of $100,000,000.	
	Total Interest Expense: $9,825,000	Futures Profit: $375,000
	Interest Expense Net of Hedging: $9,450,000	

rate is fixed at 9.00 percent. Therefore, the firm is at risk for $100,000,000 for three quarters. Because the maturity of the Eurodollars that underlie the futures is only one quarter, it requires three times as much futures value as its spot market exposure.

With the shift in rates, the firm must pay $9,825,000 in interest, which is more than the expected $9,450,000 when the firm took the loan. This difference is due to the across the board interest rate rise of 50 basis points. The same interest rate rise generates a futures trading profit of $375,000. Thus, the futures profit exactly offsets the increase in interests costs and the construction firm has successfully hedged its interest rate risk using a stack hedge.

A Danger in Using Stack Hedges. We now consider a potential danger in using a stack hedge of this type. In the example, the stack hedge worked perfectly because all interest rates changed by the same 50 basis points. As a result, the stack hedge gave a perfect hedge and the construction firm had no changes in its anticipated total borrowing cost. The same stack hedge might have performed very poorly if interest rates had changed in a somewhat different fashion.

For example, after the loan agreement is signed, the funds are received, and the same stack hedge is implemented, assume there is a single change in futures yields as follows. The DEC futures yield rises from 7.3 to 7.4 percent, the MAR futures yield rises from 7.6 to 8.3 percent and the JUN futures yield jumps from 7.9 to 8.6 percent, as Figure 8.6 shows. With this change in rates, the construction firm will have the following borrowing costs and interest expenses:

September–December	9.00%	$2,250,000
December—March	9.40	2,350,000
March—June	10.30	2,575,000
June—September	10.60	2,650,000

This change in rates gives the same increase in borrowing costs from the initially expected level of $9,450,000 to $9,825,000. However, there is one important difference. The DEC futures yield changed by only 10 basis points. Therefore,

Figure 8.6

Yield Curve Shifts

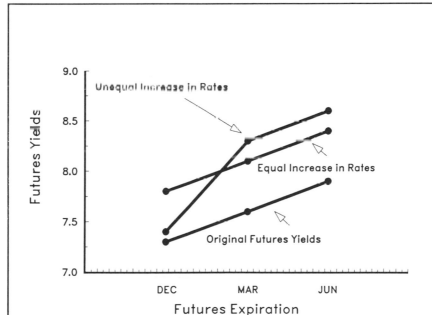

the futures profit on 300 DEC Eurodollar contracts is only $75,000 = 10 basis points times $25 per basis point times 300 contracts. Now the net borrowing cost after hedging is $9,750,000. This is $300,000 more than initially expected.

The graph of Figure 8.6 shows the original position for the DEC, MAR, and JUN Eurodollar futures yields. In our first example of a stack hedge, we assumed that all futures yields rose by 50 basis points. The rates after this equal jump are shown in the graph. We then considered an unequal increase in rates and the effectiveness of the stack hedge. Figure 8.6 shows those unequal rates for which the stack hedge was so ineffective. With the unequal increase in rates, the futures yield curve has steepened considerably. The DEC futures yield increased slightly, but the MAR futures yield increased more, as did the JUN futures yield. The poor performance of the stack hedge was due to this unequal change in rates.

A Strip Hedge.   The stack hedge of the previous example was really hedging against a change in the DEC futures yield, because all of the contracts were stacked on that single futures expiration. Instead of using a concentration of contracts on a single expiration, a **strip hedge** uses an equal number of contracts for each futures expiration over the hedging horizon.

For our example of a $100,000,000 financing requirement at risk for three quarters, we have seen that a Eurodollar hedge requires 300 contracts. In a strip hedge, the construction firm would sell 100 Eurodollar contracts each of the DEC, MAR, and JUN futures. With the strip hedge in place, each quarter of the coming year is hedged against shifts in interest rates for that quarter. To illustrate the effectiveness of this strip hedge for an unequal increase in rates, Table 8.17 shows the results for the construction firm example.

The strip hedge of Table 8.17 works perfectly. The superior performance of the strip hedge results from aligning the futures market hedges with the actual risk exposure of the construction firm. Because the construction firm faced interest rate adjustments each quarter, it needed to hedge the interest rate risk associated with each quarter. This it could do through a strip hedge, but not through a stack hedge.

Strip versus Stack Hedges.   From the example of the strip hedge, it.appears that a strip hedge will always be superior to a stack hedge. While there are many circumstances where a strip hedge will be preferred, it is not always better than a stack hedge. Our earlier example of a firm that had a six month horizon used a stack hedge with great success. Here the stack hedge exactly matched the timing of the firm's interest rate exposure, whereas a strip hedge would not have worked so well. The important point is to use a strip or stack hedge as required to match the timing of the futures hedge to the timing of the cash market risk exposure.

There is also a practical consideration that often leads hedgers to use a stack hedge when theory might favor a strip hedge. To implement a strip hedge

Table 8.17
Results of a Strip Hedge

Date	Cash Market	Futures Market
September 20	Borrow $100,000,000 at 9.00% for three months and commit to roll over the loan for three quarters at 200 basis points over the prevailing LIBOR rate.	Sell 100 Eurodollar futures for each of: DEC at 92.70, MAR at 92.40, and JUN at 91.90.
December 20	Pay interest of $2,250,000. LIBOR is now at 7.8%, so borrow $100,000,000 for three months at 9.8%.	Offset 100 DEC Eurodollar futures at 92.60. Produces profit of $25,000 = 10 basis points × $25 per point × 100 contracts.
March 20	Pay interest of $2,450,000 and borrow $100,000,000 for three months at 10.10%.	Offset 100 MAR Eurodollar futures at 91.70. Produces profit of $175,000 = 70 basis points × $25 per point × 100 contracts.
June 20	Pay interest of $2,525,000 and borrow $100,000,000 for three months at 10.40%.	Offset 100 JUN Eurodollar futures at 91.40. Produces profit of $175,000 = 70 basis points × $25 per point × 100 contracts.
September 20	Pay interest of $2,600,000 and principal of $100,000,000.	
	Total Interest Expense: $9,825,000	Futures Profit: $375,000
	Interest Expense Net of Hedging: $9,450,000	

requires trading more distant contracts. In our example, the construction firm traded the nearby, second, and third contract. There is not always sufficient volume and liquidity in distant contracts to make such a strategy viable. Strips work well with Eurodollar futures because Eurodollar futures now have sufficient volume in distant contracts to make them attractive. This has not always been the case, however. When distant contracts lack liquidity, the hedger must trade off the advantages of a strip hedge with the potential lack of liquidity in the distant contracts. For the dominant interest rate futures contracts, strips work well because of the great liquidity in these markets.[15]

Tailing the Hedge

In Chapter 3 we considered the effect of daily resettlement cash flows on futures pricing and the performance of futures positions. There we concluded that a correlation between the futures price and interest rates could justify a difference between forward and futures prices. A positive correlation between the futures price and interest rates will cause the futures price to exceed the forward price. By contrast, a negative correlation between the futures price and interest rates will cause the futures price to fall below the forward price. In interest rate futures, the futures price is strongly negatively correlated with interest rates, because rising interest rates generate falling interest rate futures prices.

Daily resettlement cash flows also have potential importance for hedging. If a futures hedge generates positive daily resettlement cash flows, those funds will be available for investment once they are received. This means that the futures market hedging gain may unintentionally exceed the cash market loss. While unintentional gains on a futures hedge may not seem to be a problem, it is also possible to have the contrary results. For a hedge that is functioning properly, but the futures position is losing money, the futures position may generate losses that exceed the complementary cash market gain.

In **tailing the hedge** the trader slightly adjusts the hedge to compensate for the interest that can be earned from daily resettlement profits or paid on daily resettlement losses. Thus, the tail of the hedge is the slight reduction in the hedge position to offset the effect of daily resettlement interest. Tailing a hedge can work for any kind of hedging. However, because the daily resettlement cash flows are likely to be more important when the futures price is correlated with interest rates, tailing the hedge is most often observed in interest rate futures hedging.

To illustrate the principle behind tailing the hedge, consider the following idealized example. A large financial institution plans to buy $1 billion in 90-day T-bills 91 days from now. The T-bill futures that expires then has a yield of 10.00 percent, so the expected cost of those T-bills is $975 million. The institution hedges that commitment by buying 1,000 T-bill futures contracts. Overnight, interest rates fall by 10 basis points. With this fall in rates, the expected cost of the T-bills increases to $975,250,000, for a cash market loss of $250,000. The drop in rates, however, generates a futures gain of $250 per contract for a total gain of $250,000. Thus, the futures market gain exactly offsets the cash market loss—at least it does before we consider the interest on the $250,000 daily resettlement.

The $250,000 daily resettlement flow can be invested for the next 90 days over the hedging horizon. (The funds are available for investment for 90 days because we started with a 91-day horizon.) We assume an investment rate of 10 percent with daily compounding and a 360-day year. Therefore, the $250;000 will grow to $256,028 = $250,000(1.1)^{(90/360)}$ by the time the hedge is over. For simplicity, we assume that this is the only change in rates. At the end of the hedging period, the financial institution buys its T-bills and still has $6,028 left over. This is the interest from the daily resettlement cash flow.

Consider now the original hedged position and assume that rates rose by 10 basis points instead of falling. This change in rates generates a $250,000 daily resettlement outflow that the institution would have to finance for the next 90 days. Under this scenario, the financial institution would not be able to buy the T-bills because it would lack $6,028 at the termination of the hedge. The institution had to pay the $6,028 as interest to finance the $250,000 daily resettlement outflow. From this example, it is clear that the financial institution traded too many futures contracts. The total effect on the futures—the daily resettlement cash flow plus interest—exceeded the cash market effect. This was true whether rates rose or fell.

To reduce these errors in hedging, the financial institution could have traded slightly fewer futures contracts. With the 10 percent investment rate on the daily resettlement flow and a 90-day investment horizon, every dollar of daily resettlement flow will grow to $1.0241 = $1(1.1)^{(90/360)}$. Therefore, the financial institution can find the tailed hedge position by multiplying the untailed hedge position by the **tailing factor**. In our example, the tailing factor is $1/1.0241$. Notice, however, that the tailing factor is nothing other than the present value of $1 at the hedging horizon discounted to the present (plus one day) at the investment rate for the resettlement cash flows.[16] Thus, we define the tailing factor as the present value (as of tomorrow) of $1 to be received at the hedging horizon. The tailed hedge position is:

$$\text{Tailed Hedge} = \text{Untailed Hedge(Tailing Factor)} \qquad 8.4$$

In the untailed hedge of 1,000 contracts in our example, the tailed hedge would be 976.45 = 1000/1.0241 contracts. Had the institution traded exactly that number of contracts, the results of the 10 basis point change in rates would have been a daily resettlement cash flow of $244,112.50 = 10 basis points times 25 basis points per contract times 976.45 contracts. This daily resettlement flow would grow to $250,000 = $244,112.50(1.1)^{(90/360)}$ by the time the hedge is lifted. Now the futures market effect at the hedging horizon exactly matches the cash market effect. In summary, to tail the hedge, we discount the untailed hedge position from the hedging horizon date to the present.

Tailing the Hedge

To tail the hedge, find the untailed hedge position. Discount the untailed hedge from the hedging horizon to the present (plus one day) at the discount rate for investing daily resettlement cash flows.

Because the tailed hedge depends on the time from the present to the hedging horizon, the tailed hedge changes constantly even if there is no change in the futures price. For example, in the example of the $1 billion T-bill hedge, assume that the investment rate for daily resettlement cash flows is still 10 percent, but assume that only 31 days remain until the hedge will be terminated. The daily resettlement cash flow will be available for investment over 30 days. The tailing factor in this case is $.9921 = 1/(1.1)^{(30/360)}$. This implies that the tailed hedge position on this date would be 992 contracts. For this example, the tailed hedge grew from 976 to 992 contracts over 60 days. This growth in the tailing factor is just the familiar growth in the present value factor as the discounting period gets smaller. For a hedging horizon of one day, the tailing factor is the present value from the hedging horizon to the present (plus one day). This is no time at all, so the tailing factor one day before the hedging horizon is 1.0.

Because futures can only be traded in whole contracts, tailing the hedge requires a large position, such as the 1,000 contracts of our example, to be useful. Because the tail depends on the interest rate from the present to the hedging horizon, the tail adjustment can only be as good as the hedger's estimate of the term interest rate from the present to the hedging horizon. In most cases the tail adjustment is fairly small in percentage terms. In our original example of a 10 percent interest rate and a 90-day horizon, the tailed hedge was only 2.35 percent smaller than the untailed hedge. The higher the interest rate and the more distant the hedging horizon, the greater will be the tailing factor. However, even in most illustrative examples, the tail is seldom more than 5 percent of the untailed position.[17]

Hedging with T-Bond Futures

This section begins with an example of a cross-hedge of AAA corporate bonds. The example shows that a simple hedging rule of using $1 of futures per $1 of bonds can lead to horrible hedging results. This example leads to a discussion of alternative hedging techniques focusing on hedging with T-bonds.

In all previous hedging examples, the hedged and hedging instruments were very similar. Often, however, the need arises to hedge an instrument very different from those underlying the futures contract. The effectiveness of a hedge depends on the gain or loss on both the spot and futures sides of the transaction. But the change in the price of any bond depends on the shifts in the level of interest rates, changes in the shape of the yield curve, the maturity of the bond, and its coupon rate.

To illustrate the effect of the maturity and coupon rate on hedging performance, consider the following example. A portfolio manager learns on March 1 that he will receive $5 million on June 1 to invest in AAA corporate bonds paying an annual coupon of 5 percent and having ten years to maturity. The yield curve is flat and is assumed to remain so over the period from March 1 to June 1. The current yield on AAA bonds is 9.5 percent. Since the yield curve is flat, the forward rates are also all 9.5 percent, so the portfolio manager expects to acquire the bonds at that yield. However, fearing a drop in rates, he decides to hedge in the futures market to lock-in the forward rate of 9.5 percent.

The next step is to select the appropriate hedging instrument. The manager considers two possibilities: T-bills or T-bonds. However, the AAA bonds have a 5 percent coupon and a 10-year maturity, which do not match the coupon and maturity characteristics of either the T-bills or T-bonds deliverable on the respective futures contracts. The deliverable T-bills have a zero-coupon and a maturity of only 90 days, while the deliverable T-bonds have a maturity of at least 15 years and an assortment of coupons. For this example, assume that the deliverable T-bond is a 20-year, 8 percent coupon bond.

To explore fully the potential difficulties of this situation, we consider hedging the AAA position with T-bill and T-bond futures. We ignore T-notes to dramatize the need to match coupon and maturity characteristics. For the bills and bonds, we assume the yields are 8 and 8.5 percent, respectively. Table 8.18 presents the hedging transactions and results for the T-bill hedge.

Table 8.18
A Cross–Hedge Between Corporate Bonds and T–Bill Futures

Date	Cash Market	Futures Market
March 1	A portfolio manager learns he will receive $5 million to invest in 5%, 10-year AAA bonds in 3 months, with an expected yield of 9.5% and a price of $717.45. The manager expects to buy 6,969 bonds.	The portfolio manager sells $5 million face value of T-bill futures (5 contracts) to mature on June 1 with a futures yield of 8.0% and a futures price, per contract, of $980,944.
June 1	AAA yields have fallen to 9.08%, causing the price of the bonds to be $739.08. This represents a loss, per bond, of $21.63. Since the plan was to buy 6,969 bonds, the total loss is (6,969 × $21.63) = –$150,739.	The T-bill futures yield has fallen to 7.58%, so the futures price = spot price = $981,900 per contract, or a profit of $956 per contract. Since 5 contracts were traded, the total profit is $4,780.
	Loss = –$150,739	Gain = $4,780
	Net wealth change = –$145,959	

Because $5 million is becoming available for investment, assume the manager sells $5 million face value of T-bill futures contracts. Time passes, and by June 1 yields have fallen by 42 basis points on both the AAAs and the T-bills, respectively. The price of the corporate bond is $739.08, or $21.63 higher than the anticipated price of $717.45. Since the manager expected to buy 6,969 bonds, this means that the total additional outlay would be $150,739 (6,969 x $21.63), and this represents the loss in the cash market. In the futures market, rates also fell 42 basis points generating a futures price increase of $956 per contract. Because five contracts were sold, the futures profit is $4,780. However, the loss in the cash market exceeds the gain in the futures market, for a net loss of $145,959. Note that this loss results even though rates changed by the same amount on both investments.

Consider now the same hedging problem, but assume we implement the hedge using $5 million face value of T-bond futures. Table 8.19 presents the transactions and results. Again yields fall by 42 basis points on both instruments. Consequently, the effect on the cash market is the same, but the total futures gain is $193,750, more than offsetting the loss in the cash market and generating a net wealth change = +$43,011.

If the goal of the hedge is to secure a net wealth change of zero, a gain is appropriately viewed as no better than a loss. It is only by accident of rates

Table 8.19
A Cross Hedge Between Corporate Bonds and T–Bond Futures

Date	Cash Market	Futures Market
March 1	A portfolio manager learns he will receive $5 million to invest in 5%, 10-year AAA bonds in 3 months, with an expected yield of 9.5% and a price of $717.45. The manager expects to buy 6,969 bonds.	The portfolio manager sells $5 million face value of T-bond futures (50 contracts) to mature on June 1 with a futures yield of 8.5% and a futures price, per contract, of $96,875.
June 1	AAA yields have fallen to 9.08%, causing the price of the bonds to be $739.08. This represents a loss, per bond, of $21.63. Since the plan was to buy 6,969 bonds, the total loss is (6,969 × $21.63) = –$150,739.	The T-bond futures yield has fallen to 8.08%, so the futures price = spot price = $100,750 per contract, or a profit of $3,875 per contract. Since 50 contracts were traded, the total profit is $193,750.
	Loss = –$150,739	Gain = $193,750
	Net wealth change = +$43,011	

moving in the appropriate direction that the gain was not a loss anyway. Recall that all of the simplifying assumptions were in place—a flat yield curve with rates on both instruments moving in the same direction and by the same amount. However, as noted earlier, the coupon and maturity of the hedged and hedging instruments do not match. From Chapter 6 it is clear that the AAA bond has a different sensitivity to interest rates than either the T-bill or T-bond underlying the futures contract. All three instruments, the bond, the T-bill futures, and the T-bond futures have different durations. Consequently, for a given shift in yields (e.g., 42 basis points), the prices of the three instruments will change by different amounts. Therefore, a simple hedge of $1 in the futures market per $1 in the cash market is unlikely to produce satisfactory results.

Alternative Hedging Strategies

We have seen that simple approaches to hedging interest rate risk often give unsatisfactory results, due to mismatches of coupon and maturity characteristics. For the best possible hedges, we need strategies that take these coupon and maturity mismatches into consideration. This section chronicles some of the major strategies for hedging interest rate risk, starting from simple models and going on to more complex models.

Face Value Naive (FVN) Model. According to the FVN Model, the hedger should hedge $1 of face value of the cash instrument with $1 face value of the futures contract. For example, a hedger wishing to hedge $100,000 face value of bonds would use one T-bond futures contract. The example we just considered used this strategy. The FVN strategy neglects two critically important factors:

1. By focusing on face values, the FVN Model completely neglects potential differences in market values between the cash and futures positions Therefore, keeping face value amounts equal between the cash and futures market can result in poor hedges because the market values of the two positions differ.
2. The FVN Model neglects the coupon and maturity characteristics that affect duration for both the cash market good and the futures contract.

Because of these deficiencies, we will not consider the FVN Model further.

Market Value Naive (MVN) Model. The MVN Model resembles the FVN Model, except it recommends hedging $1 of market value in the cash good with $1 of market value in the futures market. For example, if a $100,000 face value bond has a market value of $90,000 and the $100,000 face value T-bond futures contract is priced at 80-00, the MVN Model would recommend hedging the cash bonds with $1.125 = (90/80)$ futures contracts.

Because it considers the difference between market and face value, the MVN Model escapes the first criticism lodged against the FVN Model. However, the MVN Model still makes no adjustment for the price sensitivity of the two goods. Therefore, we dismiss the MVN Model without further consideration.

Conversion Factor (CF) Model.   The CF Model applies only to futures contracts that use conversion factors to determine the invoice amount, such as T-bond and T-note futures. The intuition of this model is to adjust for differing price sensitivities by using the conversion factor as an index of the sensitivity.

In particular, the CF Model recommends hedging $1 of face value of a cash market security with $1 of face value of the futures good times the conversion factor. As we have seen for T-bond and T-note futures, there are many deliverable instruments with different conversion factors. To apply the CF Model, we must determine which instrument is cheapest-to-deliver and use the conversion factor for that instrument. Assuming we have identified the cheapest-to-deliver security, the hedge ratio (HR) is given by:

$$ HR \; = \; - \left(\frac{\text{Cash Market Principal}}{\text{Futures Market Principal}} \right) (\text{Conversion Factor}) \qquad 8.5 $$

The negative sign indicates that one must take a futures market position opposite to the cash market position. For example, if the hedger is long in the cash market, the hedger should sell futures.

As an example, assume that a bond manager wishes to hedge a long position of $500,000 face value of bonds with T-bond futures. We assume the cheapest-to-deliver bond has a conversion factor of 1.2. In this situation, the manager should sell $600,000 worth of T-bond futures [$500,000(1.2)] or six contracts. The CF Model attempts to secure the same amount of principal value of bonds on both the cash and futures sides of the hedge. This method is useful principally when one contemplates delivering a cash market bond against a futures contract.

Basis Point (BP) Model.   The BP Model focuses on the price effect of a one basis point change in yields. For example, we have seen that a change of one basis point causes a $25 change in the futures price of a T-bill or Eurodollar contract. Assume that today is April 2 and that a firm plans to issue $50 million of 180-day commercial paper in six weeks. For a one basis point yield change, the price of 180-day commercial paper will change twice as much as the 90-day T-bill futures contract, assuming equal face value amounts. In other words, on $1 million of 180-day commercial paper, a one basis point yield change causes a $50 price change. In an important sense, the commercial paper will be twice as sensitive to a change in yields.

To reflect this greater sensitivity, we can use the BP Model to compute the following hedge ratio:

$$HR = -\frac{BPC_C}{BPC_F} \qquad\qquad 8.6$$

where:

BPC_C = dollar price change for a 1 basis point change in the cash instrument,

BPC_F = dollar price change for a 1 basis point change in the futures instrument.

The ratio BPC_C/BPC_F indicates the relative number of contracts to trade. In our commercial paper example, the cash basis price change (BPC_C) is twice as great as the futures basis price change (BPC_F), so the hedge ratio is -2.0.

To explore the effect of this weighting consider the following BP Model hedge of the commercial paper. Planning to issue commercial paper, the firm will lose if rates rise, because the firm will receive less cash for its commercial paper. As it needs to sell the commercial paper, it is now long commercial paper and must hedge by selling futures. With a -2.0 hedge ratio and a $50 million face value commitment in the cash market, the firm should sell 100 T-bill futures contracts.

Table 8.20 presents the BP Model transactions. After rates on both sides of the contract move by 45 basis points, we have the following result. In the cash market, the firm receives $112,500 less than anticipated for its commercial paper. This loss, however, is exactly offset by the price movement on the $100 million of T-bills underlying the futures position. The BP Model helped identify the correct number of futures to trade for each unit in the cash market. By contrast, the FVN Model would have suggested trading only 50 futures, which would have hedged only half of the loss.

Sometimes the yields may not change by the same amount as they did in Table 8.20. In that case, the hedger may wish to incorporate the relative volatility of the yields into the hedge ratio. For example, assume that the commercial paper rate is 25 percent more volatile than the T-bill futures rate. In other words, a 100 basis point rise in the T-bill futures rate normally might be accompanied by a 125 basis point rise in the commercial paper rate. To give the same total price change in the futures market as in the cash position, we would need to consider that difference in volatility in determining the hedge ratio. In that case, the hedge ratio becomes:

Table 8.20
Hedging Results with the BP Model
for the Commercial Paper Issuance

April 2

Cash Market	Futures Market
Firm anticipates issuing $50 million in 180-day commercial paper in 45 days at a yield of 11%.	Firm sells 100 T-bill June futures contracts yielding 10% with an index value of 90.00

May 15
Spot market and futures market rates have both risen 45 basis points. The spot rate is now 11.45% and the futures market yield is 10.45%.

Cash Market Effect	Futures Market Effect
Each basis point move causes a price change of $50 per million-dollar face value. Firm will receive $112,500 less for the commercial paper, due to the change in rates. (45 basis points × –$50 × 50 contracts = –$112,500)	Each basis point increase gives a futures market profit of $25 per contract. Futures Profit = 45 basis points × +$25 × 100 contracts = +$112,500

Net wealth change = 0

$$HR = -\left(\frac{BPC_C}{BPC_F}\right) RV \qquad 8.7$$

where:

RV = volatility of cash market yield relative to futures yield, normally found by regressing the yield of the cash market instrument on the futures market yield.

If we incorporate RV, assumed to be 1.25, into our commercial paper hedge, the transactions would appear as shown in the top portion of Table 8.21. Now the hedge ratio is:

Table 8.21
Hedging Results with the BP Model Adjusted for Relative Yield Variances for the Commercial Paper Issuance

April 2

Cash Market	Futures Market
Firm anticipates issuing $50 million in 180–day commercial paper in 45 days at a yield of 11%.	Firm sells 125 T-bill June futures contracts yielding 10% with an index value of 90.00.

May 15

Spot market rates have risen 56 basis points to 11.56% and futures rates have risen 45 basis points to 10.45%

Cash Market Effect	Futures Market Effect
Each basis point move causes a price change of $50 per million-dollar face value. Firm will receive $140,000 less for the commercial paper, due to the change in rates. 56 basis points × –$50 × 50 contracts = –$140,000	Each basis point increase gives a futures market profit of $25 per contract. Futures Profit = 45 basis points × +$25 × 125 contracts = +$140,625

Net wealth change = $625

$$\text{HR} = -\left(\frac{\$50}{\$25}\right) 1.25 = -2.5$$

Consequently, the hedger sells 125 T-bill futures contracts. Assume again that the T-bill yields rise by 45 basis points. Also, true to its greater relative volatility, the commercial paper yield moves 56 basis points, 1.25 times as much. Because more T-bill futures were sold, the T-bill futures profit still almost exactly offsets the commercial paper loss.

Regression (RGR) Model. One way of calculating a hedge ratio for interest rate futures is the regression technique we considered in Chapter 5. The hedge ratio found by regression minimizes the variance of the combined futures–cash position during the estimation period. This estimated ratio is applied to the hedging period.

For the RGR Model the hedge ratio is:

$$HR = \frac{COV_{C,F}}{\sigma_F^2} \qquad\qquad 8.8$$

where:

$COV_{C,F}$ = covariance between cash and futures,
σ_F^2 = variance of cash and futures.

As noted in Chapter 4, this hedge ratio is the regression coefficient found by regressing the change in the cash position on the change in the futures position. These changes can be measured as dollar price changes or as percentage price changes.

$$\Delta C_t = \alpha + \beta \Delta F_t + \varepsilon_t$$

The RGR Model uses the hedge ratio that gives the lowest sum of squared errors for the data used in the estimation. Using the estimated hedge ratio for an actual hedge assumes that the relationship between the price changes on the futures and cash instruments does not change dramatically between the sample period and the actual hedging period.[18]

This is a practical assumption. If the relationship is basically unchanged, then the estimated hedge ratio will perform well in the actual hedging situation. Fundamental shifts in the relationship between the price of the futures contract and the cash market good can lead to serious hedging errors. This danger is present in all hedging situations, but may be exacerbated in interest rate hedging. Without doubt, the RGR Model has proven its usefulness in the market for the traditional futures contracts, and it has been adapted for use in the interest rate futures market by Louis Ederington, Charles Franckle, Joanne Hill, and Thomas Schneeweis.[19]

However, there are some problems in applying the RGR Model to interest rate hedging. First, since the technique involves statistical estimation, the technique requires a data set for both cash and futures prices. This data may sometimes be difficult to acquire, particularly for an attempt to hedge a new security. In such a case, no cash market data would even exist, and a proxy would have to be used. Second, the RGR Model does not explicitly consider the differences in the sensitivity of different bond prices to changes in interest rates. As the examples of Tables 8.18 and 8.19 indicate, this can be a very important factor. The regression approach does include the different price sensitivities indirectly, however, since their differential sensitivities will be reflected in the estimation of the hedge ratio. Third, any cash bond will have a predictable price movement over time. As we saw in Chapter 6, the price of any instrument will equal its par value at maturity. The RGR Model does not consider this change in the cash bond's price explicitly, but the sample data should reflect this price movement tendency. Fourth, the hedge ratio is chosen to minimize the variability in the combined futures–cash position over the life of the hedge. Since the RGR hedge ratio depends crucially on the planned hedge length, one might reasonably prefer a hedging technique focusing on the wealth position of the hedge when the hedge ends.[20] After all, the wealth change from the hedge depends on the gain or loss when the hedge is terminated, not on the variability of the cash-futures position over the life of the hedge. In spite of these difficulties, the RGR Model is a useful way to estimate hedge ratios, both for traditional commodities and, to a lesser extent, for interest rate hedging.

Price Sensitivity (PS) Model. The PS Model has been designed explicitly for interest rate hedging.[21] The PS Model assumes that the goal of hedging is to eliminate unexpected wealth changes at the hedging horizon, as defined in equation 8.9:

$$dP_i + dP_F(N) - 0 \qquad\qquad 8.9$$

where:

  dP_i = unexpected change in the price of the cash market instrument
  dP_F = unexpected change in the price of the futures instrument
  N = number of futures to hedge a single unit of the cash market asset

Equation 8.9 expresses the goal that the unexpected change in the value of the spot instrument, denoted by i, and the futures position, denoted by F, should together equal zero. If this is achieved, the wealth change, or hedging error, is zero. Instead of focusing on the variance over the period of the hedge, the PS Model uses a hedge ratio to achieve a zero net wealth change at the end of the hedge.

The problem for the hedger is to choose the correct number of contracts, denoted by N in equation 8.9, to achieve a zero hedging error. Equation 8.10 gives the correct number of contracts to trade (N), per spot market bond:

$$N = -\left(\frac{R_F\, P_i\, D_i}{R_i\, FP_F\, D_F} \right) RV \qquad\qquad 8.10$$

where:

R_F = 1 + the expected futures yield
R_i = 1 + the expected yield to maturity on asset i
FP_F = the futures contract price
P_i = the price of asset i expected to prevail at the hedging horizon
D_i = the duration of asset i expected to prevail at the hedging horizon
D_F = the duration of the asset underlying futures contract F expected to prevail at the hedging horizon
RV = the volatility of the cash market asset's yield relative to the volatility of the futures instrument's yield

In non-technical terms, equation 8.10 says that the number of futures contracts to trade for each cash market instrument to be hedged is the number that should give a perfect hedge, assuming that yields on the cash and futures instrument change by the same amount. To explore the meaning and application of this technique, consider again the AAA bond hedges of Tables 8.18 and 8.19. The large hedging errors resulted from the different price sensitivities of the futures instruments and the AAA bonds.

Table 8.22 presents the data needed to calculate the hedge ratios for hedging the AAA bonds with T-bill or T-bond futures. Here we assume that the cash and futures market assets have the same volatilities, so RV = 1.0. For the T-bill hedge:

$$N = - \frac{(1.08) \ (-\$717.45) \ (7.709)}{(1.095) \ (\$980,944) \ (.25)} = .022244$$

Table 8.22
Data for the Price Sensitivity Hedge

Cash Instrument		T–Bill Futures		T–Bond Futures	
P_i	$717.45	FP_i	$980,944	FP_F	$96,875
D_i	7.709	D_F	.25	D_F	10.143
R_i	1.095	R_F	1.08	R_F	1.085
		N	.022244	N	.005577
		Number of Contracts to Trade	155	Number of Contracts to Trade	39

The hedger should buy .022244 T-bill futures per AAA bond to be hedged. Because the portfolio managers plans to buy 6,969 bonds, he should hedge this commitment by trading 155 (actually, 155.02) T-bill futures. For the T-bond hedge:

$$N = -\frac{(1.085)\ (-\$717.45)\ (7.709)}{(1.095)\ (\$96,875)\ (10.143)} = .005577$$

With 6,969 bonds to hedge, the portfolio manager should buy 39 (actually, 38.8667) T-bond futures.

With either of these hedges, the same shift in yields on the AAA bonds and the futures instrument should give a perfect hedge. Table 8.23 presents the performance of these two hedges for the same 42 basis point drop in rates used above in Tables 8.18 and 8.19.

With the given hedges and the same drop in yields, the T-bill hedge gave a futures gain of $148,203 to offset the loss on the AAA bonds of $150,742. The futures gain on the T-bond hedge is $150,608. The next row of Table 8.23 shows the size of the hedging error for the T-bill and T-bond hedges, while the final row gives the percentage of the cash market loss that was hedged. The T-bill hedge was 98.32 percent effective, while the T-bond hedge was 99.91 percent effective. Both hedges were almost perfect. The slight errors were due to rounding error and to the large change in interest rates. In these examples, the PS Model worked very effectively. In actual hedging situations, one could not hope for such nearly perfect results, since yields need not change by the same amount on all instruments all of the time.

Conclusion. It is difficult to compare all of the hedging models reviewed in this section, because they differ so much in aim and complexity. The naive hedges, FVN and MVN, are probably appropriate only for hedging short-term instruments with short-term futures contracts. The Conversion Factor Model is

Table 8.23
Performance Analysis of Price Sensitivity Future Hedge

	Cash Market	T–Bill Hedge	T–Bond Hedge
Gain/Loss	−$150,742	+$148,203	+$150,608
Hedging Error	−	$2,539	$134
Percentage of Cash Market Loss Hedged		98.32%	99.91%

essentially a naive model applicable to futures contracts with the structure of T-note or T-bond futures contracts.[22]

The most widely used technique is some version of the PS Model, although the Regression Model also is often employed. In fact, it has been shown that the PS and RGR Models are equivalent when the hedging horizon is instantaneous.[23] Because of problems in acquiring data for the RGR Model, the PS Model appears to be preferred. As one observer notes:

> We find that the duration hedge is more conveniently constructed than any regression-based hedge, because neither historical data series nor regression analyses need be used, and price sensitivity/duration-based hedge ratios can be altered in numerous ways to increase hedging effectiveness, such as estimating relative yield volatilities, modeling the basis, and accounting for the influences of call provisions on interest rate sensitivities. . . . In practice we find that simple price-sensitivity duration hedges perform as well as any currently available technique. Thus, simply constructed duration-based hedges appear to dominate the more elaborately constructed regression-based hedges.[24]

A number of studies of hedging effectiveness have been conducted. However, their results are not conclusive in deciding which hedging technique is best. Differences in data sets, time periods, and other factors conspire to make the results difficult to compare across studies.

In a number of papers J. Hill and T. Schneeweis find that the RGR Model is an effective hedging tool.[25] However, D. Lasser finds the RGR Model to perform no better than various naive models.[26] Chiang, Gay, and Kolb find that the PS Model is more effective than naive models in hedging the risk of corporate bonds.[27] Similarly, D. Chance, M. Marr, and G. Thompson find the PS Model to be useful in hedging shelf registrations.[28] Finally, A. Toevs and D. Jacob offer a useful comparison of a number of hedging strategies, including the naive models and the RGR Model, in which they find the PS Model to be the most effective.[29] Table 8.24 summarizes the various approaches to hedging.

Immunization with Interest Rate Futures

Chapter 6 considered the risk associated with duration mismatches. In the Bank Immunization case, we saw how a financial institution might immunize itself from interest rate risk by adjusting the durations of its asset and liability portfolios. In the Planning Period case, we saw that immunization could be achieved by setting the duration of a bond portfolio equal to the length of the planning period. Often such immunization is very difficult to achieve. For example, banks cannot simply turn away depositors because they wish to lengthen the duration of their liabilities. With the development of interest rate futures markets, financial managers have a valuable new tool to use in immunization strategies. This section presents two examples of immunizing with interest rate futures, one for the Planning Period Case and one for the Bank Immunization Case. Table 8.25 presents data on three bonds we will use in the immunization examples, along with data for T-bill and T-bond futures contracts. The table reflects the assumption of a flat yield curve and instruments of the same risk level.

The Planning Period Case. Consider a $100 million bond portfolio of Bond C with a duration of 9.285 years. Assume now that a manager wants to shorten the portfolio duration to six years to match a given planning period. The shortening could be accomplished by selling Bond C and buying Bond A until the following conditions are met:

$$W_A \, D_A + W_C \, D_C = 6 \text{ years}$$
$$W_A + W_C = 1$$

where W_I = percent of portfolio funds committed to asset I. This means that the manager must put 56.54 percent of the $100 million in Bond A, the funds coming from the sale of Bond C. Call this Portfolio 1.

Alternatively, the manager could adjust the portfolio's duration to match the six year planning period by trading interest rate futures. In Portfolio 2, the manager will keep $100,000,000 in Bond C and trade futures to adjust the duration of the combined portfolio of Bond C and futures. If Portfolio 2 is to be comprised of Bond C and T-bill futures, the T-bill futures position must satisfy the condition:

$$P_P = P_C N_C + FP_{T\text{-bill}} N_{T\text{-bill}}$$

where:

$$
\begin{aligned}
P_P &= \text{value of the portfolio} \\
P_C &= \text{price of Bond C} \\
FP_{T\text{-bill}} &= \text{T-bill futures price} \\
N_C &= \text{number of C bonds} \\
N_{T\text{-bill}} &= \text{number of T-bills}
\end{aligned}
$$

In Chapter 6 we studied equation 6.8, which expresses the change in the price of a bond as a function of duration and the yield on the asset:

Table 8.24
Summary of Alternative Hedging Strategies

Hedging Model	Basic Intuition
Face Value Naive (FVN)	Hedge $1 of cash instrument face value with $1 of futures instrument face value.
Market Value Naive (MVN)	Hedge $1 of cash instrument market value with $1 of futures instrument market value.
Conversion Factor (CF)	Find ratio of cash market principal to futures market principal. Multiply this ratio by the conversion factor for the cheapest–to–deliver instrument.
Basis Point (BP)	For a 1 basis point yield change, find the ratio of the cash market price change to the futures market price change. (Sometimes weighted by the relative volatility of interest rates on the cash market instrument compared to the futures instrument interest rate.)
Regression (RGR)	For a given cash market position, use regression analysis to find the futures position that minimizes the variance of the combined cash/futures position.
Price Sensitivity (PS)	Using duration analysis, find the futures market position designed to give a zero wealth change at the hedging horizon. (Sometimes weighted by the relative volatility of interest rates on the cash market instrument compared to the futures instrument interest rate.)

$$dP = -D\{d(1 + r)/(1 + r)\}P \qquad\qquad 5.8$$

Applying equation 6.8 to the portfolio value, Bond C, and the T–bill futures we have the following immunization condition:

$$-D_p \left[\frac{d(1 + r)}{1 + r} \right] P_p =$$

$$-D_c \left[\frac{d(1 + r)}{(1 + r)} \right] P_c\ N_c + -D_{T\text{-bill}} \left[\frac{d(1 + r)}{(1 + r)} \right] FP_{T\text{-bill}}\ N_{T\text{-bill}}$$

This can be simplified to:

$$D_P P_P = D_C P_C N_C + D_{T\text{-bill}} FP_{T\text{-bill}} N_{T\text{-bill}}$$

Table 8.25
Instruments for the Immunization Analysis

	Coupon	Maturity	Yield	Price	Duration
Bond A:	8%	4 yrs.	12%	885.59	3.475
Bond B:	10%	10 yrs.	12%	903.47	6.265
Bond C:	4%	15 yrs.	12%	463.05	9.285
T–Bond Futures*	8%	20 yrs.	12%	718.75	8.674
T–Bill Futures*	–	¼ yr.	12%	972.07	.25

*For comparability, face values of $1,000 are assumed for these instruments.

Because immunization requires mimicking Portfolio 1, which has a total value of $100,000,000 and a duration of six years, it must be that:

$$P_P = \$100,000,000$$
$$D_P = 6$$
$$D_C = 9.285$$
$$P_C = \$463.05$$
$$N_C = 215,959$$
$$D_{T\text{-bill}} = .25$$
$$FP_{T\text{-bill}} = \$972.07$$

Solving for $N_{T\text{-bill}} = -1,351,747$ indicates that this many T–bills (assuming $1,000 par value) must be sold short in the futures market. Because a T–bill futures contract has a $1,000,000 face value, this technique requires selling 1,352 contracts. The same technique used to create Portfolio 2 can be applied using a T–bond futures contract, giving rise to Portfolio 3. Solving:

$$D_P P_P = D_C P_C N_C + D_{T\text{-bond}} FP_{T\text{-bond}} N_{T\text{-bond}}$$

for $N_{T\text{ bond}}$ gives $N_{T\text{-bond}} = -52,691$. Since T–bond futures contracts have a face value denomination of $100,000, the trader must sell 527 T–bond futures contracts. For each of the three portfolios, Table 8.26 summarizes the relevant data.

To see how the immunized portfolio performs, assume that rates drop from 12 to 11 percent for all maturities. Assume also that all coupon receipts during the six-year planning period can be reinvested at 11 percent until the end of the planning period. With the shift in interest rates the new prices are:

Table 8.26
Portfolio Characteristics for the Planning Period Case

		Portfolio 1 (Bonds Only)	Portfolio 2 (Short T-Bill Fut.)	Portfolio 3 (Short T-Bond Fut.)
Portfolio	W_A	56.54%	–	–
	W_C	43.46%	100%	100%
	W_{Cash}	~0	~0	~0
Number	N_A	63,844	0	–
	N_C	93,856	215,959	215,959
	$N_{T\text{-}bill}$	–	(1,351,747)	–
	$N_{T\text{-}bond}$	–	–	(52,691)
Value	$N_A P_A$	56,539,608	–	–
	$N_C P_C$	43,460,021	99,999,815	99,999,815
	$N_{T\text{-}bill} FP_{T\text{-}bill}$	–	1,313,992,706	–
	$N_{T\text{-}bond} FP_{T\text{-}bill}$	–	–	37,871,656
	Cash	371	185	185
Portfolio Value	$N_A P_A +$ $N_C P_C +$ Cash	100,000,000	100,000,000	100,000,000

Source: R. Kolb and G. Gay, "Immunizing Bond Portfolios with Interest Rate Futures," *Financial Management*, Summer 1982, pp. 81-89.

Table 8.27
Effect of a 1% Drop in Yields
on Realized Portfolio Returns

	Portfolio 1	Portfolio 2	Portfolio 3
Original Portfolio Value	100,000,000	100,000,000	100,000,000
New Portfolio Value	105,660,731	108,914,787	108,914,787
Gain/Loss on Futures	–0–	(2,946,808)	(3,128,792)
Total Wealth Change	5,660,731	5,967,979	5,785,995
Terminal Value of all Funds at t=6	197,629,369	198,204,050	197,863,664
Annualized Holding Period Return over 6 years	1.120234	1.120776	1.120455

Source: R. Kolb and G. Gay, "Immunizing Bond Portfolios with Interest Rate Futures," *Financial Management*, Summer 1982, pp. 81-89.

$$P_A = \$913.57$$
$$P_C = \$504.33$$
$$FP_{T\text{-}bill} = \$974.25$$
$$FP_{T\text{-}bond} = \$778.13$$

Table 8.27 shows the effect of the interest rate shift on portfolio values, terminal wealth at the horizon (year 6), and on the total wealth position of the portfolio holder. As Table 8.27 reveals, each portfolio responds similarly to the shift in yields. The slight differences are due to either rounding errors or the fact that the duration price change formula holds exactly only for infinitesimal changes in yields. The largest difference (between terminal values for Portfolios 1 and 2) is only .29 percent, which reveals the effectiveness of the alternative strategies.

The Bank Immunization Case.   Assume that a bank holds a $100,000,000 liability portfolio in Bond B, the composition of which is fixed. The bank wishes to hold an asset portfolio of Bonds A and C that will protect the wealth position of the bank from any change as a result of a change in yields.

Five different portfolio combinations illustrate different means to achieve the desired result:

Portfolio 1: Hold Bond A and Bond C (the traditional approach)
Portfolio 2: Hold Bond C; SELL T-bill futures
Portfolio 3: Hold Bond A; BUY T-bond futures
Portfolio 4: Hold Bond A; BUY T-bill futures
Portfolio 5: Hold Bond C; SELL T-bond futures

For each portfolio in Table 8.28, the full $100,000,000 is put in a bond portfolio (and is balanced out by cash). Portfolio 1 exemplifies the traditional approach of immunizing by holding only bonds. Portfolios 2 and 5 are composed of Bond C and a short futures position. By contrast, the low volatility Bond A is held in Portfolios 3 and 4. In conjunction with Bond A, the overall interest rate sensitivity is increased by buying interest rate futures.

Now assume an instantaneous drop in rates from 12 to 11 percent for all maturities. Table 8.29 shows the effect on the portfolios. As the rows reporting wealth change reveal, all five methods perform similarly. The small differences stem from rounding errors and the discrete change in interest rates.

One important concern in the implementation of immunization strategies is the transaction cost involved. In immunizing, commission charges, marketability, and liquidity of the instruments involved become increasingly important. These considerations highlight the practical usefulness of interest rate futures in bond

Table 8.28
Liability Portfolio and Five Alternative Immunizing Portfolios

		Liability Portfolio	Portfolio 1 (Bonds Only)	Portfolio 2 (Short T-Bill Futures)	Portfolio 3 (Long T-Bond Futures)	Portfolio 4 (Long T-Bill Futures)	Portfolio 5 (Short T-Bond Futures)
Portfolio	W_A	0	51.98%	0	100%	0	0
	W_B	100%	0	0	0	0	0
	W_C	0	48.02%	100%	0	0	0
	W_{Cash}	~0	~0	~0	~0	~0	~0
Number of	N_A	0	58,695	0	112,919	112,919	0
	N_B	110,684	0	0	0	0	0
	N_C	0	103,704	215,959	0	0	215,959
	N_{T-bill}	0	0	(1,242,710)	0	0	0
	N_{T-bond}	0	0	0	44,751	1,148,058	(48,441)
	$N_A P_A$	0	51,979,705	0	99,999,937	99,999,937	0
	$N_B P_B$	99,999,673	0	0	0	0	0
	$N_C P_C$	0	48,020,137	99,999,815	0	0	99,999,815
	Cash	327	158	185	63	63	185
	$N_{T-bill}P_{T-bill}$	0	0	(1,208,001,110)	0	0	0
	$N_{T-bill}P_{T-bill}$	0	0	0	0	1,115,992,740	0
	$N_{T-bond}P_{T-bond}$	0	0	0	32,164,781	0	(34,816,969)
Portfolio Value		100,000,000	100,000,000	100,000,000	100,000,000	100,000,000	100,000,000

Source: R. Kolb and G. Gay, "Immunizing Bond Portfolios with Interest Rate Futures," *Financial Management*, Summer 1982, pp. 81-89.

Table 8.29
Effect of a 1% Drop in Yields on Total Wealth

	Liability	Port. 1	Port. 2	Port. 3	Port. 4	Port. 5
Original Port. Value	100,000,000	100,000,000	100,000,000	100,000,000	100,000,000	100,000,000
New Port. Value	105,910,526	105,923,188	108,914,788	103,159,474	103,159,474	108,914,788
Profit on Futures	0	–	(2,709,108)	2,657,314	2,502,766	(2,876,427)
Total Wealth Change (Port. and Futures)	5,910,526	5,923,188	6,205,680	5,816,788	5,662,240	6,038,361
Total Wealth Change (Asset–Liability Port.)	–	12,622	295,154	(93,738)	(248,286)	127,835
% Wealth Change	–	.00013	.00295	(.00094)	(.00248)	.00128

Source: R. Kolb and G. Gay, "Immunizing Bond Portfolios with Interest Rate Futures, *Financial Management*, Summer 1982, pp. 81-89.

portfolio management. Consider as an example the transaction costs associated with the different immunization portfolios for the Planning Period Case. Starting from the initial position of $100,000,000 in Bond C, and wishing to shorten the duration to six years, Table 8.30 shows the trades necessary and the estimated costs involved. To implement the "bonds only" traditional approach of Portfolio 1, one must sell 122,103 bonds of type C and buy 63,844 bonds of type A. Assuming a commission charge of $5 per bond, the total commission is $929,735. By contrast one could sell 1,352 T-bill futures contracts to immunize Portfolio 2, or sell 527 T-bond futures contracts for Portfolio 3, at total costs of $27,040 and $10,540, respectively. (Additionally one would have to deposit approximately $2,000,000 margin for the T-bill strategy or $800,000 for the T-bond strategy. But this margin deposit can be in the form of interest earning assets.) Table 8.30 presents these transaction costs calculations.

Clearly there is a tremendous difference in transaction costs between trading the cash and futures instruments. In an extreme example of this type, the transaction costs for the "bonds only" case is prohibitive, amounting to almost 1 percent of the total portfolio value. It is practically impossible for another reason: the volume of bonds to be traded is enormous, exceeding any reasonable volume for bonds of even the largest issue. The superior marketability and liquidity of the futures market is clearly evident. The 1,352 T-bill futures

Table 8.30
Transaction Costs for the Planning Period Case

	Portfolio 1	Portfolio 2	Portfolio 3
Number of Instruments Traded			
Bond A	63,844	–	–
Bond C	(122,103)	–	–
T–Bill Futures Contracts	–	1,352	–
T–Bond Futures Contracts	–	–	527
One Way Transaction Cost			
Bond A @ $5	319,220	–	–
Bond C @ $5	610,515	–	–
T–Bill Futures $20	–	27,040	–
T–Bond Futures @ $20	–	–	10,540
Total Cost of Becoming Immunized	$929,735	$27,040	$10,540

Source: R. Kolb and G. Gay, "Immunizing Bond Portfolios with Interest Rate Futures," *Financial Management*, Summer 1982, pp. 81-89.

contracts are a small percentage of the daily volume or recent open interest. Likewise, the 527 T-bond futures constitute only a trivial fraction of the volume and open interest in that market. The evident ability of the futures market to absorb the kind of activity involved in this example demonstrates the practical usefulness of interest rate futures in managing bond portfolios.[30]

Until recently, immunization strategies for bond portfolios have focused on all bond portfolios. Here it has been shown that interest rate futures can be used in conjunction with bond portfolios to provide the same kind of immunization. The method advocated here works equally well for the Planning Period Case and the Bank Immunization Case. Note that all of the examples assumed parallel shifting yield curves. If the change in interest rates brings about non-parallel shifts in the yield curve, then the "bonds only" and "bonds-with-futures" approaches will give different results. Which method turns out to be superior would depend upon the pattern of interest rate changes that actually occurred.[31]

Conclusion

Interest rate futures constitute one of the most exciting and complex financial markets. Only in recent years have the uses of the market begun to mature and there remain many potential users who could benefit from the market. As we have seen, interest rate futures have many applications, including bond portfolio management. Interest rate futures can also be used to control foreign interest rate risk, to manage public utilities and insurance companies, to hedge mortgage financing risk, and to reduce risk in creative financing arrangements. Other uses abound and are just starting to be explored.

Questions and Problems

Assume today is January 30, 1992. You are considering two bonds as potential bonds for delivery against the JUN 92 T-bond futures contract, which settled at 102-08. First is the 7¼ bond that matures on May 15, 2016. Second, you might deliver the 13¼ bond that matures on May 15, 2014 but is callable on May 15, 2009. Use this information for questions 1-8.

1. Using the facts outlined above, find the conversion factors for the two bonds for the JUN 92 futures contract.

2. On January 30, 1992, what is the accrued interest on each bond?

3. Consider a position day of June 15, 1992. What is the accrued interest on each bond?

4. Assuming the settlement price on position day (June 15, 1992) is 114-00, find the invoice amounts for both bonds.

5. The 7¼ bond trades for 85-00 and the 13¼ is at 137-00. Which bond do you expect to be cheaper to deliver? (Assume a financing rate of 8 percent.)

6. Assume that between now (January 30, 1992) and delivery on June 15, 1992 that you can finance a cash and-carry transaction at 8 percent. This is your borrowing and lending rate. Further assume that you have full use of all short sale proceeds. Find all possible arbitrage strategies.

7. Find the implied repo rates for both bonds.

8. Continue to assume that you can borrow and lend at 8 percent. However, now you can use only 90 percent of any short sale proceeds on a reverse cash-and-carry strategy. How does this change your trading strategy, if at all?

9. Explain the risks inherent in a reverse cash-and-carry strategy in the T-bond futures market.

10. Explain how the concepts of quasi-arbitrage help to overcome the risks inherent in reverse cash-and-carry trading in T-bond futures.

11. Assume economic and political conditions are extremely turbulent. How would this affect the value of the seller's options on the T-bond futures contract? If they have any effect on price, would they cause the futures price to be higher or lower than it otherwise would be?

12. Explain the difference between the wildcard option and the end-of-the-month option.

13. Some studies find that interest rate futures markets were not very efficient when they first began but that they became efficient after a few years. How can you explain this transition?

14. Assume you hold a T-bill that matures in 90 days, when the T-bill futures expires. Explain how you could transact to effectively lengthen the maturity of the bill.

15. Assume that you will borrow on a short-term loan in six months, but you do not know whether you will be offered a fixed rate or a floating rate loan. Explain how you can use futures to convert a fixed to a floating rate loan and to convert a floating rate to a fixed rate loan.

16. You fear that the yield curve may change shape. Explain how this belief would affect your preference for a strip or a stack hedge.

17. A futures guru says that tailing a hedge is extremely important because it can change the desired number of contracts by 30 percent. Explain why the guru is nuts. How much can the tailing factor reasonably change the hedge ratio?

18. We have seen in Chapters 4 and 5 that regression-based hedging strategies are extremely popular. Explain their weaknesses for interest rate futures hedging.

19. You estimate that the cheapest-to-deliver bond on the T-bond futures contract has a duration of 6.5 years. You want to hedge your medium term Treasury portfolio that has a duration of 4.0 years. Yields are 9.5 percent

on the futures and on your portfolio. The value of your portfolio is $120,000,000, and the futures price is 98-04. Using the PS Model, how would you hedge?

20. Explain the relationship between the bank immunization case and hedging with the PS Model.

21. Compare and contrast the BP Model and the RGR Model for immunizing a bond portfolio.

Notes

1. We ignore the differences between the three day settlement process in futures markets and the one day settlement procedures common in the cash market.

2. G. Gay and S. Manaster, "Implicit Delivery Options and Optimal Delivery Strategies for Financial Futures Contracts," *Journal of Financial Economics*, 16:1, May 1986, pp. 41-72.

3. Some of the more important studies of interest rate futures markets, other than those to be discussed specifically, include: W. Poole, "Using T-Bill Futures to Gauge Interest-Rate Expectations"; D. Puglisi, "Is the Futures Market for Treasury Bills Efficient?"; A. Vignola and C Dale, "Is the Futures Market for Treasury Bills Efficient?"; R. Lang and R. Rasche, "A Comparison of Yields on Futures Contracts and Implied Forward Rates"; B. Branch, "Testing the Unbiased Expectations Theory of Interest Rates"; D Capozza and B. Cornell, "Treasury Bill Pricing in the Spot and Futures Markets"; and "The Efficiency of the Treasury Bill Futures Market. An Analysis of Alternative Specifications." All of these articles are reprinted in G. Gay and R. Kolb, *Interest Rate Futures: Concepts and Issues*, Richmond, VA: Robert F. Dame, Inc., 1982.

4. The importance of various institutional factors was brought to attention by E. Kane, "Market Incompleteness and Divergences Between Forward and Futures Interest Rates," *Journal of Finance*, 35:2, May 1980, pp. 221-234.

5. See R. Rendleman and C. Carabini, "The Efficiency of the Treasury Bill Futures Market," *Journal of Finance*, 34:4, 1979, pp. 895-914. In this article, they develop the idea of quasi-arbitrage.

6. Because these differences are so small, EGR's results imply that the difference between forward and futures prices should be small. Their expected profit results would be actual profit results except for daily resettlement interest flows. Because the difference between actual and expected profits is trivial, we may conclude that the difference between a forward and futures price will usually be trivial as well.

7. EGR consider other efficiency tests and find that the T-bill futures market fails those tests as well. For example, when prices vary from the cash-and-carry arbitrage relationship, just taking a position in the underpriced side of the transaction yields significant profits.

8. For other studies of T-bill futures market efficiency, see S. Hegde and B. Branch, "An Empirical Analysis of Arbitrage Opportunities in the Treasury Bill Futures Market," *The Journal of Futures Markets*, Fall 1985, 5:3, pp. 407-424; M. Monroe and R. Cohn, "The Relative Efficiency of the Gold and Treasury Bill Futures Markets," *The Journal of Futures Markets*, Fall 1986, 6:3, pp. 477-493. This same discrepancy between forward and futures rates is substantiated by L. Allen and T. Thurston, "Cash-Futures Arbitrage and Forward-Futures Spreads in the Treasury Bill Market," *The Journal of Futures Markets*, 8:5, October 1988, pp. 563-573. I. Kawaller and T. Koch, "Cash-and-Carry Trading and the Pricing of Treasury Bill Futures," *The Journal of Futures Markets*, 4:2, Summer 1984, pp. 115-123, find that the nearby futures market is efficient and conclude that the Cost-of-Carry Model provides a good description of pricing in T-bill futures. S. Hegde and B. McDonald, "On the Informational Role of Treasury Bill Futures," *The Journal of Futures Markets*, 6:4, Winter 1986, pp. 629-643. D. Lasser, "Influence of Treasury Bill Futures Trading on the Primary Sale of the Deliverable Treasury Bill," *The Journal of Futures Markets*, 22:4, November 1987, pp. 391-402 examines the initial sale prices of T-bills that will be deliverable on the futures versus T-bills that are not deliverable. Lasser concludes that there may be a slight premium for T-bills that will be deliverable. However, he acknowledges some uncertainties about this conclusion.

9. See R. Kolb, G. Gay, and J. Jordan, "Are There Arbitrage Opportunities in the Treasury-Bond Futures Market?" *Journal of Futures Markets*, 2:3, Fall 1982, pp. 217-230.

10. B. Resnick and E. Hennigar, "The Relationship Between Futures and Cash Prices for U.S. Treasury Bonds," *Review of Research in Futures Markets*, 2:3, 1983, pp. 282-299.

11. B. Resnick, "The Relationship Between Futures Prices for U. S. Treasury Bonds," *Review of Research in Futures Markets*, 3:1, 1984, pp. 88-104.

12. R. Klemkosky and D. Lasser, "An Efficiency Analysis of the T-Bond Futures Market," *The Journal of Futures Markets*, 5:4, Winter 1985, pp. 607-620. Quoted material is from page 620.

13. D. Chance, "A Semi-Strong Form Test of the Efficiency of the Treasury Bond Futures Market," *The Journal of Futures Markets*, Fall 1985, 5:3, pp. 385-405. M. Rzepczynski, "Risk Premiums in Financial Futures Markets: The Case of Treasury Bond Futures," *The Journal of Futures Markets*, 7:6, December 1987, pp. 653-662, tests whether there is a risk premium in T-bond futures. He finds that T-bond futures prices are biased estimators of the final futures price when the contract is distant from delivery. However, for contracts relatively close to expiration, the T-bond futures price provides a good estimate of the terminal futures price.

14. We ignore the daily resettlement feature and the interest that could have been earned on the $125,000 futures profit in the second quarter.

15. Liquidity is important, because the bid-asked spread will be larger for illiquid contracts. This increases the transaction costs the hedger faces. However, trading nearby contracts and rolling them over as time progresses generates a higher volume of trading, and this higher volume is also costly. Therefore, there is a tradeoff between the higher bid-asked spread of distant contracts and having to roll a hedge repeatedly. Also, available liquidity has developed in some futures and been lost in others. In 1991, Eurodollar and T-bond futures certainly have ample liquidity for fairly long strips. Strips are also feasible in other interest rate futures contracts.

16. Strictly speaking, it is the discount factor from the hedging horizon to the present plus one day. For example, the hedge was initiated with 91 days to the horizon, the cash flow was generated on that day and became available for investment with 90 days to run until the hedging horizon.

17. For more on tailing, see I. Kawaller, "Hedging with Futures Contracts: Going the Extra Mile," *Journal of Cash Management*, July-August 1986, pp. 34-36 and I. Kawaller and T. Koch, "Managing Cash Flow Risk in Stock Index Futures: The Tail Hedge," *The Journal of Portfolio Management*, 15:1, Fall 1988, pp. 41-44.

18. The same would be assumed if percentage price changes or price levels were used.

19. See L. Ederington, "The Hedging Performance of the New Futures Market," *Journal of Finance*, 34:1, March 1979, pp. 157-170; C. Franckle, "The Hedging Performance of the New Futures Market: Comment," *Journal of Finance*, 35:5, December 1980, pp. 1272-1279; and J. Hill and T. Schneeweis, "Risk Reduction Potential of Financial Futures," in G. Gay and R. Kolb, *Interest Rate Futures: A Comprehensive Introduction*, Richmond, VA: Robert F. Dame, Inc., 1982, pp. 307-324.

20. The dependence of the RGR hedge ratio on the planned length of the hedging period was proven by C. Franckle, "The Hedging Performance of the New Futures Market: Comment," *Journal of Finance*, 35:5, December 1980, pp. 1272-1279.

21. See R. Kolb and R. Chiang, "Improving Hedging Performance Using Interest Rate Futures," *Financial Management*, 10:4, 1981, pp. 72-79 and "Duration, Immunization, and Hedging with Interest Rate Futures," *Journal of Financial Research*, 10:4, Autumn 1982, pp. 161-170.

22. G. Gay and R. Kolb, "Removing Bias in Duration Based Hedging Models: A Note," *The Journal of Futures Markets*, 4:2, Summer 1984, pp. 225-228, show that the price sensitivity model performs better when the hedge ratio is adjusted to reflect the cheapest-to-deliver bond. W. Landes, J. Stoffels, and J. Seifert, "An Empirical Test of a Duration-Based Hedge: The Case of Corporate Bonds," *The Journal of Futures Markets*, 5:2, Summer 1985, pp. 173-182, provide a test of the price sensitivity model for hedging corporate bonds with T-bond futures. They find that this hedging technique provides substantial protection of principal in fixed-income portfolios.

23. A. Toevs and D. Jacob, "Futures and Alternative Hedge Ratio Methodologies," *Journal of Portfolio Management*, 12:3, Spring 1986, pp. 60-70.

24. A. Toevs and D. Jacob, "Futures and Alternative Hedge Ratio Methodologies," *Journal of Portfolio Management*, 12:3, Spring 1986, p. 68.

25. For an example, see J. Hill and T. Schneeweis, "Risk Reduction Potential of Financial Futures," in G. Gay and R. Kolb, *Interest Rate Futures: Concepts and Issues*, Englewood Cliffs, NJ: Prentice Hall, 1982, pp. 307-324.

26. D. Lasser, "A Measure of Ex-Ante Hedging Effectiveness for the Treasury-Bill and Treasury-Bond Futures Markets," working paper.

27. R. Chiang, G. Gay, and R. Kolb, "Interest Rate Hedging: An Empirical Test of Alternative Strategies," *Journal of Financial Research*, 6:3, Fall 1983, pp. 187-197.

28. D. Chance, M. Marr, and G. Thompson, "Hedging Shelf Registrations," *The Journal of Futures Markets*, 6:1, Spring 1986, pp. 11-27.

29. A. Toevs and D. Jacob, "Futures and Alternative Hedge Ratio Methodologies," *Journal of Portfolio Management*, 12:3, Spring 1986, pp. 60-70.

30. This discussion of immunization with futures draws upon G. Gay and R. Kolb, "Immunizing Bond Portfolios with Interest Rate Futures," *Financial Management*, 11:2, Summer 1982, pp. 81-89.

31. P. Little, "Financial Futures and Immunization," *Journal of Financial Research*, 9:1, Spring 1986, pp. 1-12, and D. Chance, "Futures Contract and Immunization," *Review of Research in Futures Markets*, 5:2, 1986, pp. 124-141 develop the application of immunization with interest rate futures. D. Chambers, "An Immunization Strategy for Futures Contracts on Government Securities," *The Journal of Futures Markets*, 4:2, Summer 1984, pp. 173-187, extends immunization strategies by using a number of duration measures instead of a single duration. He calls this series of durations a duration vector.

9

Stock Index Futures: Introduction

Introduction

Everyone who follows the financial news hears predictions about the future of the stock market. Usually these predictions refer to the future movement of some stock market index. With the advent of stock index futures trading in 1982, these pundits can now trade to take advantage of their insights. (Perhaps they should be required to do so.) In addition to providing a chance to speculate, stock index futures also have a role in hedging various kinds of portfolio risk.

This chapter begins our exploration of stock index futures and the indexes upon which they are based. Currently, futures trade actively on three broad market indexes: the Major Market Index (MMI), the Standard and Poor's 500 (S&P 500), and the New York Stock Exchange (NYSE) Index. Several other contracts trade inactively, so this chapter considers only the three main indexes.[1]

At first glance, it might seem that the three indexes are very similar, because each is a broad market index. Important differences exist among the indexes, however. Successful trading of the index contracts requires a thorough understanding of the construction of the indexes. When the differences and inter-relationships among the indexes are understood, it is easier to understand the differences among the futures contracts that are based on those indexes. The differences among the indexes should not be exaggerated, however. The kinds of risk and the expected changes in the levels of the indexes are predicted by the **Capital Asset Pricing Model** (CAPM). The CAPM expresses the relationship between the returns of individual stocks and partially diversified portfolios, on the one hand, and the broad indexes on the other.

As is the case with all futures contracts, the exact construction of the contracts is very important for the trader. No-arbitrage conditions constrain the possible deviations between the price of the futures contract and the level of the underlying index. Cash-and-carry strategies keep the futures price from being too high relative to the price of the stock market index. Similarly, reverse cash-and-carry strategies keep the futures price from being too low relative to stock prices. In other words, potential arbitrage strategies constrain the basis for stock index futures as these strategies do for other types of futures contracts.

The Three Indexes

The three indexes, the Major Market Index, the Standard and Poor's 500, and the New York Stock Exchange Composite Index, are all familiar, but few people are actually acquainted with their calculation and method of composition. For an understanding of stock index futures, however, a thorough knowledge of the indexes is indispensable. In general, stock market indexes can either be equally weighted or value weighted. In an **equally weighted index**, each stock in the index has an equal impact on the value of the index, without regard to the size of the firm that has issued the stock. In a **value weighted index**, each stock in the index affects the index value in proportion to the market value of all shares outstanding. Thus, in an equally weighted index, IBM and Apple Computer would both have the same role in the index, even though the market value of IBM shares is many times that of Apple Computer. By contrast, in a value weighted index, IBM would have a much more dominant role, proportional to its market value. Of the indexes we will consider, the MMI index is an equally weighted index, while the S&P 500 and NYSE indexes are value weighted.

All three indexes exclude dividends, which means that the indexes do not reflect the full appreciation that the market has enjoyed over any given period. The omission of dividends is very important for understanding the pricing of the futures contracts as well. As we will see in our discussion of pricing, the presence of dividends is a major factor.

The Major Market Index

In the early 1980s, the Chicago Board of Trade attempted to launch a futures contract based on the most famous of all stock market indexes—the Dow Jones Industrial Average (DJIA). After prolonged legal maneuvering, Dow Jones succeeded in preventing the futures contract from trading. In response, the CBT created the Major Market Index (MMI). The MMI consists of 20 stocks chosen so that the MMI behaves as much as possible like the DJIA, which consists of 30 stocks. In fact, 17 of the 20 MMI stocks are also included in the DJIA.

The MMI is computed by adding the share prices of the 20 stocks comprising the index and dividing by the MMI divisor. Similarly, the DJIA is computed by adding the prices of the 30 represented shares and dividing by the Dow Jones divisor. For both indexes, the divisor is used to adjust for stock splits, mergers, stock dividends, and changes in the stocks included in the index. The MMI is constructed so that the MMI value is about one-fifth of the DJIA.

For both the MMI and the DJIA, the index can be computed according to the following formula:

$$Index = \frac{\sum_{i=1}^{N} P_i}{Divisor} \qquad 9.1$$

where:

P_i = price of stock i

Table 9.1 presents the composition of the MMI and the DJIA, with illustrative prices. Given the extreme similarity in the stocks included, it is not surprising that the MMI behaves much like the DJIA. In fact, the CBT boasts a 98.6 percent correlation between the MMI and the DJIA. Figure 9.1 highlights that close relationship by graphing the two indexes over the 1982-1989 period.

Figure 9.1
Major Market Index vs. Dow Jones Industrials
January 4, 1982—January 29, 1989

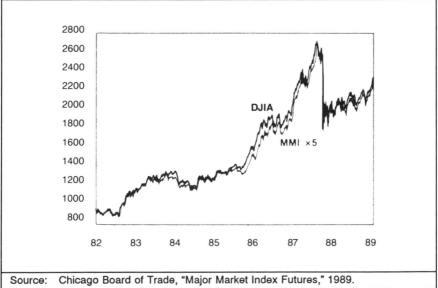

Source: Chicago Board of Trade, "Major Market Index Futures," 1989.

Table 9.1
Comparison of the Major Market Index
and the Dow Jones Industrial Average

Major Market Index 20 Companies		Dow Jones Industrial Average 30 Companies	
Firm	Price	Firm	Price
American Express	59.000	American Express	59.000
AT&T	25.500	AT&T	25.500
Chevron	44.625	Chevron	44.625
DuPont	87.500	DuPont	87.500
Eastman Kodak	63.625	Eastman Kodak	63.625
Exxon	69.375	Exxon	69.375
General Electric	79.000	General Electric	79.000
General Motors	74.500	General Motors	74.500
IBM	123.125	IBM	123.125
International Paper	74.125	International Paper	74.125
Merck	109.500	Merck	109.50
3M	109.250	3M	109.250
Philip Morris	71.250	Philip Morris	71.250
Procter & Gamble	76.750	Procter & Gamble	76.750
Sears Roebuck	43.500	Sears Roebuck	43.500
USX	25.000	USX	25.000
Coca–Cola	36.750	Coca–Cola	36.750
Dow Chemical	55.875	Allied–Signal	41.500
Johnson & Johnson	70.500	American Can	88.000
Mobil	38.500	Bethlehem Steel	6.250
		Goodyear	49.250
		Inco	12.750
		McDonald's	61.500
		Navistar Int'l	6.000
		Owens–Illinois	42.000
		Texaco	36.000
		Union Carbide	23.000
		United Technologies	45.250
		Westinghouse Electric	58.500
		Woolworth	43.750
TOTAL	1337.250	TOTAL	1689.375
Divisor	3.70681	Divisor	0.889
Index Value	360.75	Index Value	1900.31

Notice that the MMI value is multiplied by 5.0 to bring it into closer conformity with the magnitude of the DJIA.

For the MMI and the DJIA, each stock has the same weight in computing the index, even though some firms have much greater market value than others. A one dollar change in IBM (the largest market value firm) has the same effect as a one dollar change in a firm with a small market value. Stocks with a greater market value have the same role as stocks with a smaller market value. Therefore, the MMI and DJIA are both equally weighted indexes.

Because the indexes depend on the number of dollars from summing all the prices, the MMI and DJIA do not reflect the percentage change in the price of a share. For example, consider a stock that doubles from $1 to $2, and contrast this price change with a stock that moves from $100 to $101. In the first case, a stock has increased 100 percent, while in the latter case, a stock has increased just 1 percent. For the MMI and the DJIA, both stock price changes have the same effect on the index, because the index depends on the sum of the prices, not the percentage price changes of the individual stocks.

As Table 9.1 shows, both the MMI and DJIA use a divisor to compute the index value. The divisors used in computing the indexes are designed to keep the index value from changing due to stock splits or stock dividends or due to a substitution of one stock for another in the index. To see how the divisor functions, assume that Dow Jones decides to delete Navistar International from the index and replace it with Dow Chemical. In Table 9.1, Navistar is priced at 6.00, and we assume that Dow Chemical trades at 47.00. If the substitution is made, the new total of prices is 1730.375. If the divisor is not changed, the new index value will be 1946.43. Thus, the substitution of one stock for another, with no change in the divisor, manufactures a jump in the DJIA of 46 points. Obviously, this cannot be permitted or the index will become meaningless as a barometer of stock prices.

For the index to reflect the level of prices in the market accurately, simply substituting one stock for another should not change the index. The same principle holds for stock dividends and stock splits. Therefore, the divisor must change to accommodate the change in stocks or the stock dividend or the stock split. In our example of substituting Dow Chemical for Navistar, the divisor must change to maintain a constant index value of 1900.31 with the new total of prices of 1730.375. Therefore, the new divisor must satisfy the following equation:

$$1900.31 = \frac{1730.375}{\text{New Divisor}}$$

$$\text{New Divisor} = \frac{1730.375}{1900.31} = .9106$$

Thus, to keep the index value unchanged, the new divisor must be .9106. Generalizing from this example, we see that equation 9.2 gives the value for the new divisor:

$$\text{New Divisor} = \frac{\text{New Sum of Prices}}{\text{Index Value}} \qquad 9.2$$

To find the new divisor, compute the new sum of prices that results from substituting one firm for another. Then divide this sum by the original index value.

The S&P 500

Of the three indexes, the S&P 500 index is the most widely used in the finance industry. For example, many managers are judged by comparing the performance of their portfolios to the performance of the S&P 500. The index is based on 500 firms which come from various industries and most of which are listed on the New York Stock Exchange.[2] Together, these 500 firms comprise approximately 80 percent of the total value of the stocks listed on the New York Stock Exchange.

Each of the stocks in the index has a different weight in the calculation of the index, and the weight is proportional to the total market value of the stock (the price per share times the number of shares outstanding). Therefore, the S&P 500 Index is a value weighted index. This contrasts with the composition of the MMI and the DJIA, which assign equal weight to each firm. The value of the S&P 500 Index is reported relative to the average value during the period of 1941–1943, which was assigned an index value of 10. As a simplified example of the way the index is computed, assume that the index consists of only three

---

Table 9.2
Calculation of S&P 500

	Outstanding Shares		Price		Value
Company ABC	100	×	$50	=	$ 5,000
Company DEF	300	×	40	=	12,000
Company GHI	200	×	10	=	2,000
		Current Market Valuation		=	$19,000

If the 1941–43 value were $2,000, then $19,000 is to $2,000 as X is to 10.

$$\frac{\text{Current Market Valuation}}{\text{1941–43 Market Valuation}} = \frac{\$19,000}{\$2,000} = \frac{X}{10}$$

$$\$190,000 = \$2,000X$$
$$95.00 = X$$

Source: CME, "Inside S&P 500 Stock Index Futures."

securities, ABC, DEF, and GHI. Table 9.2 shows how the value of the three firms would be weighted to calculate the index. For each stock, the total market value of the outstanding shares is computed. In the Table, the three firms' shares have a total value of $19,000. If the value in the 1941–1943 period had been $2000, the current level of the index would be calculated as shown in the Table, where "X" is the current index level with a value of 95.00. Mathematically, the calculation of the index is given by:

$$\text{S \& P Index}_t = \left(\frac{\sum_{i=1}^{500} N_{i,t} \, P_{i,t}}{O.V.} \right) 10 \qquad \qquad 9.3$$

where:

O.V. = original valuation in 1941–43
$N_{i,t}$ = number of shares outstanding for firm i
$P_{i,t}$ = price of shares in firm i

Figure 9.2
Recent History of the S&P 500 Index

The weights of each firm change as their prices rise and fall relative to other firms represented in the index. Firms such as Exxon, AT&T, and IBM represent large shares of the index, while other firms have only a minuscule impact. The index is computed on a continuous basis during the trading day and reported to the public.

Figure 9.2 shows the recent levels of the index. There is considerable variability in the performance of the index over time, even though it is a large portfolio of the very largest and most stable firms. As we will see in the next chapter, recent developments in the stock index futures market have given new importance to the volatility of stock market indexes.

The New York Stock Exchange Composite

The New York Stock Exchange Composite Index is broader than the S&P 500, since it includes all stocks listed on the New York Stock Exchange. As of year-end 1989 there were 1,720 issues traded on the NYSE and, therefore, included in the index. Four firms, IBM, Exxon, General Electric, and AT&T make up about 8 percent of the total value of the NYSE listed securities. The largest 50 companies account for about 39 percent of the value of the NYSE capitalization, with the smallest 1,670 making up the remaining 61 percent.

The weight of each stock in the index is proportional to its value, just as is the case with the S&P 500 Index. Therefore, the NYSE index is a value weighted index. The NYSE and S&P 500 indexes use a similar method to calculate the indexes. However, the NYSE Composite Index takes its base date as December 31, 1965. At any subsequent point in time, the value of the NYSE Index is given by:

$$
\text{NYSE Index}_t = \left(\frac{\sum_{t-1}^{1720} N_{i,t} \, P_{i,t}}{O.V.} \right) 50.0 \qquad 9.4
$$

where:

O.V. = original value of all shares on the NYSE as of December 31, 1965

Equation 9.4 says that the value of the NYSE Index equals the current value of all shares listed on the NYSE divided by the December 1965 base value, with the result being multiplied by 50 as a simple scaling device. This gives an initial value of 50.00 for the index. By late 1974, the index stood at 32.89, was as high as 81.02 in 1980, and exceeded 170.00 in early 1987.

Comparison of the Indexes

Because we will consider three futures contracts, it is important to understand the relationships among the three underlying indexes, since such knowledge is important in choosing the most appropriate contract for speculation or hedging. For hedging, the choice of an index depends on the relationship between the good being hedged and the characteristics of the index. For speculation, the volatility of the index is particularly important.

As we know from portfolio theory, the more fully diversified a portfolio is, the less unsystematic risk it should contain. With less unsystematic risk, the total risk should be lower. For 1989, the standard deviation of the daily percentage changes in the indexes was as follows:

MMI	.009114
S&P 500	.008193
NYSE	.007415

As we might expect, the more stocks in the index, the less volatile the percentage price change. Also, because big firms tend to be more stable than small firms, we would expect a value weighted index to be less volatile than an equally weighted index.

In spite of differences in volatility, the correlations among all of these indexes are high, typically exceeding 95 percent. We might expect these results, because each index is based on a diversified portfolio. As the S&P 500 index represents about 80 percent of the value of NYSE stocks, there is an extremely high correlation between the S&P 500 and NYSE Composite indexes. The correlation between the MMI and the other two indexes is somewhat lower, reflecting the less diversified character of the MMI. Table 9.3 presents a correlation matrix for the three indexes during 1989. The correlations are based on daily percentage changes in the index values over the 250 trading days in 1989. In every case, the correlation is greater than 95 percent. The S&P 500 and

Table 9.3
Correlation of Daily Percentage Changes in Index Values

	MMI	S&P 500	NYSE
MMI	1.0000	.9595	.9550
S&P 500		1.0000	.9974
NYSE			1.0000

NYSE are the most closely correlated. This is due to the large number of identical stocks and the great diversification represented by these portfolios, in addition to the fact that both of these indexes are value weighted indexes. The great similarity in these indexes suggests that one index might be a good substitute for either of the other two for hedging or risk management purposes.

Stock Index Futures Contracts

All three futures contracts share certain basic similarities in terms of the calculation of their value and the method by which they are settled. Table 9.4 summarizes these features. Each futures contract has its respective index's current value multiplied by some dollar amount as the underlying contract value. For the S&P 500 and the NYSE Composite, $500 is the multiplier. For the MMI, the multiplier is $250. These values are set arbitrarily by the exchange but are important because they determine the contract size. On August 29, 1990, the indexes and the futures contracts had the following values:

Futures	Index	Futures Contract Value
MMI	536.70	$134,175.00
S&P 500	324.19	162,095.00
NYSE	177.78	88,890.00

Therefore, the MMI and S&P 500 futures have similar values, with the S&P 500 being almost twice the size of the NYSE contract.

All three contracts are settled in cash, so there is no delivery in the stock index futures market. For the S&P 500 contract, the final settlement price

Table 9.4
Summary of Stock Index Futures Contracts

Contract	Contract Size	Trading Months	Index Composition	Index Weighting
MMI	$250 × Index	Monthly	20 blue–chip stocks, mostly in the DJIA	Equal
S&P 500	$500 × Index	Quarterly	500 mostly NYSE stocks	Market Value
NYSE	$500 × Index	Quarterly	All NYSE common stocks	Market Value

depends upon the opening value of the index on the third Friday of the delivery month, with the delivery months being March, June, September, and December. For the NYSE Index contract, the final settlement value depends on the opening prices on the third Friday of the delivery month. Again, contract maturities fall in March, June, September, and December. In contrast to these contracts with quarterly maturities, the MMI contract has maturities available for every month.[3]

With the futures contracts being stated in terms of so many dollars times the value of the index, the dollar change in the futures contracts can be quite different. The relative dollar change in the different futures will depend on some factors that we have already considered, such as the different volatilities of the indexes and the correlations among the indexes. Table 9.5 presents data based on the indexes to illustrate comparative volatilities. The data in Table 9.5 are based on daily absolute changes in the indexes for 1989. The first row of data shows the average absolute daily change in the index values for the three indexes. The MMI index typically changes more than the S&P 500 or the NYSE index in terms of the index units. This is also substantiated by the greater standard deviation for the MMI. However, the greater volatility of the MMI in index units does not necessarily translate into greater volatility in terms of dollars. As we have seen in Table 9.4, the MMI futures contract is based on a multiplier of $250 times the index, while the other two contracts use a multiplier of $500. To compare the dollar volatility of the futures contracts, the last two rows of Table 9.5 present the dollar changes implied for the futures. For example, the average daily change in the MMI index times the futures contract multiplier of $250 is $790. But the equivalent measure for the S&P 500 index is $940, based on its multiplier of $500. For the NYSE index, the corresponding absolute dollar change would be $470. In dollar terms, it appears that the most volatile futures contract is the S&P 500, closely followed by the MMI. The NYSE is considerably less volatile. This comparative dollar volatility is not a point in favor of any contract. However, it does show that the MMI and S&P

Table 9.5 Daily Absolute Changes in the Indexes—1989			
	MMI	S&P 500	NYSE
Mean Change	3.16	1.88	0.94
Standard Deviation	3.38	1.98	1.01
Implied Mean Change for Futures	$790	$940	$470
Implied Mean Standard Deviation for Futures	$845	$990	$505

Figure 9.3
Quotations for Stock Index Futures

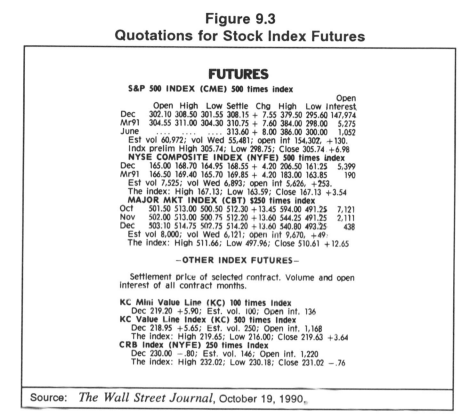

FUTURES

S&P 500 INDEX (CME) 500 times index

	Open	High	Low	Settle	Chg	High	Low	Open Interest
Dec	302.10	308.50	301.55	308.15	+ 7.55	379.50	295.60	147,974
Mr91	304.55	311.00	304.30	310.75	+ 7.60	384.00	298.00	5,275
June	....	....	....	313.60	+ 8.00	386.00	300.00	1,052

Est vol 60,972; vol Wed 55,481; open int 154,302, +130.
Indx prelim High 305.74; Low 298.75; Close 305.74 +6.98

NYSE COMPOSITE INDEX (NYFE) 500 times index

	Open	High	Low	Settle	Chg	High	Low	Open Interest
Dec	165.00	168.70	164.95	168.55	+ 4.20	206.50	161.25	5,399
Mr91	166.50	169.40	165.70	169.85	+ 4.20	183.00	163.85	190

Est vol 7,525; vol Wed 6,893; open int 5,626, +253.
The index: High 167.13; Low 163.59; Close 167.13 +3.54

MAJOR MKT INDEX (CBT) $250 times index

	Open	High	Low	Settle	Chg	High	Low	Open Interest
Oct	501.50	513.00	500.50	512.30	+13.45	594.00	491.25	7,121
Nov	502.00	513.00	500.75	512.20	+13.60	544.25	491.25	2,111
Dec	503.10	514.75	502.75	514.20	+13.60	540.80	493.25	438

Est vol 8,000; vol Wed 6,121; open int 9,670, +49.
The index: High 511.66; Low 497.96; Close 510.61 +12.65

—OTHER INDEX FUTURES—

Settlement price of selected contract. Volume and open
interest of all contract months.

KC Mini Value Line (KC) 100 times Index
Dec 219.20 +5.90; Est. vol. 100; Open int. 136
KC Value Line Index (KC) 500 times Index
Dec 218.95 +5.65; Est. vol. 250; Open int. 1,168
The index: High 219.65; Low 216.00; Close 219.63 +3.64
CRB Index (NYFE) 250 times Index
Dec 230.00 −.80; Est. vol. 146; Open int. 1,220
The index: High 232.02; Low 230.18; Close 231.02 −.76

Source: *The Wall Street Journal*, October 19, 1990.

500 contracts have an effective contract size that is much larger than that of the NYSE.

Figure 9.3 presents price quotations for stock index futures. The organization of the quotations is similar to those of other commodities. Particularly interesting is the relative success of each of the contracts, with the clearly dominating contract being the S&P 500. The NYSE Index contract occupies a middle ground, while the MMI contract has relatively high volume and relatively low open interest. Since the stock market crash of 1987, stock index futures trading has slowed considerably. Before the crash, daily volume typically exceeded 150,000 contracts, with open interest at levels above 100,000 contracts. By 1990, volume was off markedly, although open interest remained relatively high. In 1986, total volume for stock index futures was about 25 million contracts, while 1989 volume was about half that amount.

Stock Index Futures Prices

Like most financial futures, stock index futures essentially trade in a full carry market. Therefore, the Cost-of-Carry Model provides a virtually complete understanding of stock index futures pricing. When the conditions of the Cost-of-Carry Model are violated, arbitrage opportunities arise. For a cash-and-carry strategy, a trader would buy the stocks that underlie the futures contract and sell the futures. The trader would then carry these stocks until the futures expiration. The cash-and-carry strategy is attractive when stocks are priced too low relative to the futures. In a reverse cash-and-carry strategy, the trader would sell the stocks short and invest the proceeds, in addition to buying the futures. The reverse cash-and-carry strategy is attractive when stocks are priced too high relative to the futures. Thus, any discrepancy between the justified futures and cash market prices would lead to a profit at the expiration of the futures, simply by exploiting the appropriate strategy. From Chapter 3, the basic Cost-of-Carry Model for a perfect market with unrestricted short selling was given by equation 3.3:

$$F_{0,t} = S_0(1 + C) \qquad 3.3$$

where:

$F_{0,t}$ = futures price at t=0 for delivery at time t
S_0 = spot price at t=0
C = the percentage cost of carrying the good from t=0 to time t

The Cost–of–Carry Model for Stock Index Futures

Applying equation 3.3 to stock index futures faces one complication—dividends. Holding the stocks gives the owner dividends; however, each of the indexes is simply a price index. The value of the index at any time depends solely on the prices of the stocks, not the dividends that the underlying stocks might pay. Because the futures prices are tied directly to the index values, the futures prices do not include dividends.

To fit stock index futures, equation 3.3 must be adjusted to include the dividends that would be received between the present and the expiration of the futures. In essence, the chance to receive dividends lowers the cost of carrying the stocks. Carrying stocks requires that a trader finance the purchase price of the stock from the present until the futures expiration. However, the trader will receive dividends from the stock, which will reduce the value of the stocks. This contrasts directly with the cost-of-carry for holding a commodity like gold. As we have seen, gold generates no cash flows, so the cost-of-carry for gold is essentially the financing cost. For stocks, the cost-of-carry is the financing cost for the stock, less the dividends received while the stock is being carried.

As an example, assume the present is time zero and a trader decides to engage in a self-financing cash-and-carry transaction. The trader decides to buy and hold one share of Widget, Inc., currently trading for $100. Therefore, the trader borrows $100 and buys the stock. We assume that the stock will pay a $2 dividend in six months and the trader will invest the proceeds for the remaining six months at a rate of 10 percent. Table 9.6 shows the trader's cash flows. In Table 9.6, a trader borrows funds, buys and holds a stock, receives and invests a dividend, and liquidates the portfolio after one year. At the outset, the stock costs $100, but its value in a year, P_1, is unknown. From Table 9.6, the trader's cash inflow after one year is the future value of the dividend, $2.10, plus the current value of the stock, P_1, less the repayment of the loan, $110.

From this example, we can generalize to understand the total cash inflows from a cash-and-carry strategy. First, the cash-and-carry strategy will return the future value of the stock, P_1, at the horizon of the carrying period. Second, at the end of the carrying period, the cash-and-carry strategy will return the future value of the dividends—the dividend plus interest from the time of receipt to the horizon. Against these inflows, the cash-and-carry trader must pay the financing cost for the stock purchase.

We are now in a position to determine the futures price that is consistent with the cash-and-carry strategy. From the arguments of Chapter 3, we know that equation 3.3 holds as an equality with perfect markets and unrestricted short selling. The cash-and-carry trading opportunity requires that the futures price

---

Table 9.6
Cash Flows from Carrying Stock

t=0	
Borrow $100 for 1 year at 10%	+ 100
Buy 1 share of Widget, Inc.	− 100
t=6 months	
Receive dividend of $2	+$2
Invest $2 for 6 months at 10%	−$2
t=1 year	
Collect proceeds of $2.10 from dividend investment	+2.10
Sell Widget, Inc. for P_1.	+ P_1
Repay debt	− 110.00
Total Profit: P_1 + $2.10 − $110.00	

must be less than or equal to the cash inflows at the futures expiration. Similarly, the reverse cash-and-carry trading opportunity requires that the futures price must equal or exceed the cash inflows at the futures expiration. Therefore, the stock index futures price must equal the cost of the stocks underlying the stock index, plus the cost of carrying those stocks to expiration, $S_0(1 + C)$, minus the future value of all dividends to be received, $D_i(1 + r_i)$. The future value of dividends is measured at the time the futures contract expires. More formally:

$$F_{0,t} = S_0(1 + C) - \sum_{i-1}^{N} D_i(1 + r_i) \qquad 9.5$$

where:

$F_{0,t}$ = stock index futures price at t=0 for a futures contract that expires at time t

S_0 = the value of the stocks underlying the stock index at t=0

C = the percentage cost of carrying the stocks from t=0 to the expiration at time t

D_i = the ith dividend

r_i = the interest earned on carrying the ith dividend from its time of receipt until the futures expiration at time t

---

Cost–of–Carry Model for Stock Index Futures

The futures price must equal the price of the shares underlying the stock index plus the cost of carrying the stock to the futures expiration, minus the future value of the dividends the stocks will pay before expiration.

$$F_{0,t} = S_0(1 + C) - \sum_{i-1}^{N} D_i(1 + r_i)$$

Fair Value for Stock Index Futures

A stock index futures price has its **fair value** when the futures price fits the Cost-of-Carry Model. In this section we consider a simplified example of determining the fair value of a stock index futures contract. We consider a futures contract on an equally weighted index, and for simplicity we assume that there are only two stocks. Table 9.7 provides the information that we will need.

Table 9.7
Information for Computing Fair Value

Today's date:	July 6
Futures expiration:	September 20
Days until expiration:	76
Index:	Equally weighted index of two stocks
Index divisor:	1.80
Interest rates:	All interest rates are 10 percent

Stock A

Today's price	$115
Projected dividends	$1.50 on July 23
Days dividend will be invested	59
r_A	.10(59/360) = .0164

Stock B

Today's price	$84
Projected dividends	$1.00 on August 12
Days dividend will be invested	39
r_B	.10(39/360) = .0108

Based on the data in Table 9.7, the index value is 110.56, as given by:

$$\frac{P_A + P_B}{\text{Index Divisor}} = \frac{115 + 84}{1.8} = 110.56$$

The cost of buying the stocks underlying the portfolio is simply the sum of the prices of stocks A and B, or $199. For carrying the stocks to expiration, the interest cost will be 10 percent for 76 days or 2.11 percent. Thus, the cost of buying and carrying the stocks to expiration is $199(1.0211) = $203.20. Offsetting this cost will be the dividends received and the interest earned on the dividends. For the stocks, the future value of the dividends at expiration will be:

For Stock A:	$1.50(1.0164) = $1.52
For Stock B:	$1.00(1.0108) = $1.01

Therefore, the entire cost of buying the stocks and carrying them to expiration is the purchase price of the stocks plus interest, less the future value of the dividends measured at expiration:

$203.20 - $1.52 - $1.01 = $200.67

In the Cost-of-Carry Model, we know that the futures price must equal this entire cost-of-carry. However, the futures price is expressed in index units, not the dollars of the actual stock prices. To find the fair value for the futures price, this cash value of $200.67 must be converted into index units by dividing by the index divisor, 200.67/1.8 = 111.48. Thus, the fair value for the futures contract is 111.48. Because it conforms to the Cost-of-Carry Model, this fair value for the futures price is the price that precludes arbitrage profits from both the cash–and–carry and reverse cash–and–carry strategies.

Index Arbitrage and Program Trading

In the preceding section we saw how to derive the fair value futures price from the Cost-of-Carry Model. From Chapter 3 we know that deviations from the theoretical price of the Cost-of-Carry Model gives rise to arbitrage opportunities. If the futures price exceeds its fair value, traders will engage in cash–and–carry arbitrage. If the futures price falls below its fair value, traders can exploit the pricing discrepancy through a reverse cash–and–carry trading strategy. These cash–and–carry strategies in stock index futures are called **index arbitrage**. This section presents an example of index arbitrage using a simplified index with only two stocks. Because index arbitrage can require the trading of many stocks, index arbitrage is often implemented by using computer program to automate the trading. Computer directed index arbitrage is called **program trading**. We introduce program trading later in this section, but we reserve the fullest discussion for Chapter 10.

Index Arbitrage

Table 9.7 gave values for stocks A and B, and we saw how to compute the fair value of a stock index futures contract based on an index composed of those two stocks. With the values in Table 9.7, the cash market index value is 110.56, and the fair value for the futures contract is 111.48, where both values are expressed in index points. If the futures price exceeds the fair value, cash–and–carry index arbitrage is possible. A futures price below its fair value creates an opportunity for reverse cash–and–carry index arbitrage.

To illustrate cash–and–carry index arbitrage, assume that the data of Table 9.7 hold, but that the futures price is 115.00. Because this price exceeds the fair value, an index arbitrageur would trade as shown in Table 9.8. At the outset on July 6, the trader borrows the money necessary to purchase the stocks in the index, buys the stocks, and sells the futures. On July 23 and August 12, the trader receives dividends from the two stocks and invests the dividends to the

Table 9.8
Cash–and–Carry Index Arbitrage

Date	Cash Market	Futures Market
July 6	Borrow $199 for 76 days at 10%. Buy stock A and stock B for a total outlay of $199.	Sell 1 SEP index futures contract for 115.00.
July 23	Receive dividend of $1.50 from stock A and invest for 59 days at 10%.	
August 12	Receive dividend of $1.00 from stock B and invest for 39 days at 10%.	
September 20	For illustrative purposes, assume any values for stock prices at expiration. We assume that stock prices did not change. Therefore, the index value is still 110.56.	
	Receive proceeds from invested dividends of $1.52 and $1.01. Sell stock A for $115 and stock B for $84. Total proceeds are $201.53. Repay debt of $203.20.	At expiration, the futures price is set equal to the spot index value of 110.56. This gives a profit of 4.44 index units. In dollar terms, this is 4.44 index units times the index divisor of 1.8.
	Loss: $1.67	Profit: $7.99
Total Profit: $7.99 – $1.67 = $6.32		

expiration date at 10 percent. Like all stock index futures, our simple example uses cash settlement. Therefore, at expiration on September 20, the final futures settlement price is set equal to the cash market index value. This ensures that the futures and cash prices converge and that the basis goes to zero.[4]

The profits or losses from the transactions in Table 9.8 do not depend on the prices that prevail at expiration on September 20. Instead, the profits come from a discrepancy between the futures price and its fair value. To illustrate the profits, we assume that the stock prices do not change. Therefore, the cash market index is at 110.56 at expiration. As Table 9.8 shows, these transactions give a profit of $6.32.

This will be the profit no matter what happens to stock prices between July 6 and September 20. For example, assume the prices of stocks A and B both rose by $5, to $120 and $89, respectively. The cash market cash flows will then come from the sale of the shares, the future value of the dividends, and the debt repayment:

Sale of stock A	+120.00
Sale of stock B	+89.00
Future value of dividends on stock A	+1.52
Future value of dividends on stock B	+1.01
Debt repayment	-203.20
Futures profit/loss	-2.01

On the futures transaction, the index value at expiration will then equal 116.11 = (120 + 89)/1.8. This gives a futures loss of 1.11 index points, or $2.01. Taking all of these cash flows together, the profit is still $6.32. The profit will be the same no matter what happens to stock prices.

If the futures price is too low relative to the fair value, arbitrageurs can engage in reverse cash-and-carry transactions. For example, assume that the futures price is 105.00, well below its fair value of 111.48. Now the arbitrageur will trade as shown in Table 9.9. Essentially, the transactions in Table 9.9 are just the opposite of those in Table 9.8. The most important difference is that the

Table 9.9
Reverse Cash–and–Carry Index Arbitrage

Date	Cash Market	Futures Market
July 6	Sell stock A and stock B for a total of $199. Lend $199 for 76 days at 10%.	Buy 1 SEP index futures contract for 105.00.
July 23	Borrow $1.50 for 59 days at 10% and pay dividend of $1.50 on stock A.	
August 12	Borrow $1.00 for 39 days at 10% and pay dividend of $1.00 on stock B.	
September 20	For illustrative purposes, assume any values for stock prices at expiration. We assume that stock prices did not change. Therefore, the index value is still 110.56.	
	Receive proceeds from investment of $203.20. Repay $1.52 and $1.01 on money borrowed to pay dividends on stocks A and B. Buy stock A for $115 and stock B for $84. Return stocks to repay short sale.	At expiration, the futures price is set equal to the spot index value of 110.56. This gives a profit of 5.56 index units. In dollar terms, this is 5.56 index units times the index divisor of 1.8.
	Profit: $1.67	Profit: $10.01
	Total Profit: $1.67 + $10.01 = $11.68	

trader sells stock short. Having sold the stock short, the trader must pay the dividends on the stocks as they come due.

The transactions give the trader a net profit of $11.68. Again, this profit does not depend upon the actual stock prices that prevail at expiration. Instead, the profit comes from the discrepancy between the actual futures price of 105.00 and the fair value of 111.48. Once the trader initiates the transactions in Table 9.9, the profit will depend only on the discrepancy between the fair value and the prevailing futures price. The profit will equal the error in the futures price times the index divisor: (111.48 - 105.00)1.8 = $11.68.[5]

Program Trading

While we have illustrated the cash-and-carry and reverse cash-and-carry transactions with a hypothetical two stock index futures contract, real stock index futures trading involves many more stocks. The MMI is smallest with 20 stocks, while the S&P 500 contains (of course) 500 stocks, and the NYSE index has about 1,700 underlying stocks. To exploit index arbitrage opportunities with actual stock index futures requires trading the futures and simultaneously buying or selling the entire collection of stocks that underlie the index.

If we focus on the S&P 500 futures contract, we can see that the transactions of Tables 9.8 and 9.9 call for the buying or selling of 500 stocks. The success of the arbitrage depends upon identifying the misalignment between the futures price and the fair futures price. However, at a given moment the fair futures price depends upon the current price of 500 different stocks. Identifying an index arbitrage opportunity requires the ability to instantly find pricing discrepancies between the futures price and the fair futures price reflecting 500 different stocks. In addition, exploiting the arbitrage opportunity requires trading 500 stocks at the prices that created the arbitrage opportunity. Enter the computer!

Large financial institutions can communicate orders to trade stock via their computer for very rapid execution. Faced with a cash-and-carry arbitrage opportunity, one of these large traders could execute a computer order to buy each and every stock represented in the S&P 500. Simultaneously, the institution would sell the S&P 500 futures contract. The use of computers to execute large and complicated stock market orders is called **program trading**. While computers are used for other kinds of stock market transactions, index arbitrage is the main application of program trading. Often "index arbitrage" and "program trading" are used interchangeably. Program trading has been blamed for much of the recent volatility in the stock market, including the crash of October 1987. Chapter 10 presents a real-world example of program trading and analyzes the hidden risks in this kind of index arbitrage. Chapter 10 also discusses the evidence on program trading and stock market volatility.

Predicting Dividend Payments and Investment Rates

In the example of computing fair value from Table 9.7, we assumed certainty about the amount, timing, and investment rates for the dividends on stocks A and B. In the actual market, these quantities are highly predictable, but they are not certain. Dividend amounts and payment dates can be predicted based on the past policy of the firm. However, these quantities are far from certain until the dividend announcement date when the firm announces the amount and payment date of the dividend. In practice, there is quite a bit of variability in the payment of dividends depending on the time of year. Figure 9.4 shows a typical distribution of dividend payments through the year. Notice how dividends tend to cluster at certain days in early March, June, September, and December.[6]

Figure 9.4
Typical Distribution of Dividend Payments

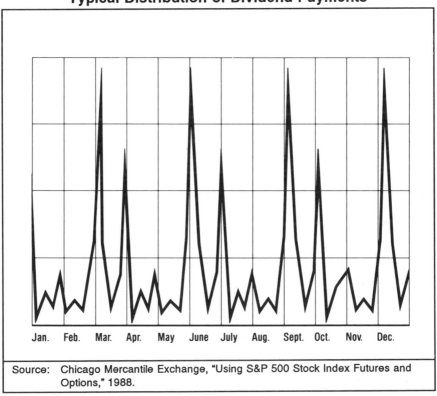

Source: Chicago Mercantile Exchange, "Using S&P 500 Stock Index Futures and Options," 1988.

In actual practice, traders follow the dividend practices of firms to project the dividends that the stocks underlying an index will pay each day. This problem varies in difficulty from one index to the next. The MMI has only 20 very large firms with relatively stable dividend policies. By contrast, the NYSE index has about 1,700 firms. Many of these firms are small and may have irregular dividend payment patterns. Therefore, it is more difficult to predict the exact dividend stream for the NYSE or the S&P 500 index. While the difficulties in predicting dividends may introduce some uncertainties into the cost-of-carry calculations, projections of dividends prove to be quite accurate in practice.

In our example of computing the fair value of a stock index futures contract and in our arbitrage examples, we also assumed that dividends could be invested at a known rate. In practice, it is difficult to know the exact rate that will be received on invested dividends. While knowing the exact rate to be received on invested dividends is difficult, good predictions are possible. For the most part, the futures expiration date is not very distant, so the current short-term interest rate can provide a good estimate of the investment rate for dividends.

Market Imperfections and Stock Index Futures Prices

In Chapter 3 we saw that four different types of market imperfections could affect the pricing of futures contracts. Those market imperfections are: direct transaction costs, unequal borrowing and lending rates, margins and restrictions on short selling, and limitations to storage. As we also saw in Chapter 3, the effect of these market imperfections is to create a band of no-arbitrage prices within which the futures price must fall. In this section we consider these imperfections briefly in the context of stock index futures.

Direct transaction costs affect stock index futures trading to a considerable extent. Relative to many goods, transaction costs for stocks are low in percentage terms. Nonetheless, stock traders face commissions, exchange fees, and a bid-asked spread. In general, these costs may be about one-half of 1 percent for stock market transactions. Even with such modest transaction costs, we cannot expect the Cost-of-Carry Model to hold as an exact equality. Instead, these transactions costs will lead to a no-arbitrage band of permissible stock index futures prices.

Unequal borrowing and lending costs, margins, and restrictions on short selling all play a role in stock index futures pricing. In the stock market, the restrictions on short selling are quite explicit. The Federal Reserve Board will not allow a trader to use more than 50 percent of the proceeds from a short sale. The short seller's broker may restrict that usage to an even smaller percentage. As we have seen in Chapter 3, these factors all force slight discrepancies in the Cost-of-Carry Model. The pricing relationship of equation 9.5 holds as an approximation, not with exactitude. Thus, these market imperfections create a no-arbitrage band of permissible futures prices. However, a highly competitive trading environment and low transaction costs keep this no-arbitrage band quite tight around the perfect markets theoretical fair value of equation 9.5.

Because the stocks of the MMI, S&P 500, and NYSE indexes are so widely held by financial institutions with low transaction costs, quasi-arbitrage is a dominant feature of stock index futures trading. As an example of the importance of quasi-arbitrage, consider the differential use of short sale proceeds for a retail customer and a pension fund with a large stock portfolio. Assume that the retail customer must sell a stock short through her broker. This customer will be able to use only half of the proceeds of the short sale. By contrast, we will assume that the pension fund already owns the stocks necessary to sell short for the reverse cash-and-carry transaction. In this situation, the pension fund can simulate a short sale by selling a portion of its stock portfolio. Because the pension fund is actually selling stocks, not technically selling short, it receives the full use of its proceeds. However, selling stocks from a portfolio is a perfect substitute for an actual short sale. Thus, the pension fund faces substantially lower transaction costs than the retail customer for engaging in reverse cash-and-carry arbitrage. A similar conclusion emerges from considering program trading. A small retail trader faces enormous transaction costs in attempting to engage in index arbitrage. The quasi-arbitrage opportunities enjoyed by financial institutions ensure that no individual could ever engage in index arbitrage. In Chapter 10 we review the evidence on stock index futures pricing and show that these markets approximate full carry markets. This suggests that quasi-arbitrage is a dominant feature of stock index futures pricing.

Speculating with Stock Index Futures

Speculating with stock index futures is exciting. Futures contracts allow the speculator to make the most straightforward speculation on the direction of the market or to enter very sophisticated spread transactions to tailor the futures position to more precise opinions about the direction of stock prices. Further, the low transactions costs in the futures market make the speculation much easier to undertake than similar speculation in the stock market itself. With three different broad market indexes, the speculative opportunities are virtually endless.

One of the simplest speculative positions arises from a belief about impending market movements. If a trader anticipates a major market rally, he could simply buy a futures contract and hope for a price rise on the futures contract when the rally actually occurs. While this course of action is very simple, it does not do full justice to the complexity of the speculative opportunity. The trader might also consider which contract maturity is desirable as a trading vehicle and which of the three contracts to trade.

In major market moves, stocks of small firms tend to move more dramatically than the stocks of large well-capitalized firms. If the trader believes that a major advance is impending, then he or she has a definite reason to prefer the NYSE Index to the S&P 500 Index and to prefer the S&P 500 Index to the MMI. Comparing the MMI and the S&P 500 Index, we would expect the MMI to be more sluggish because it is more completely dominated by large firms.

With these differential responses in mind, one conservative speculation position strategy could use a spread between two indexes. If the trader anticipates a major market increase, but wishes to closely control her risk exposure, she might use a spread between the MMI and the S&P 500 indexes. Assume that she anticipates a market rise in April. Consistent with this outlook, the transactions of Table 9.10 show how to initiate a spread to speculate on an anticipated market rally. The prescient speculator buys two SEP MMI futures contracts at 534.50 on April 22 and sells one SEP S&P 500 futures contract at 333.00. She has bought two MMI futures and sold only one S&P 500 futures contract because she is aware of the differential price volatilities between the two contracts, such as the difference reported in Table 9.5.

A few weeks later, prices have risen, with the MMI futures trading at 556.30 and the S&P 500 futures at 342.15. The wisdom in her plan is soon validated by a market rally. Not wishing to be greedy, she elects to close her position on May 6. She sells the two MMI contracts at 556.30 and buys the S&P 500 contract at 342.15. Her spread has worked perfectly. The MMI futures has gained 4.08 percent while the S&P 500 Index contract gained only 2.75 percent. Therefore, the gain on the MMI of 21.80 index points times $250 per point times

Table 9.10
A Conservative Inter–Commodity Spread

Date	Futures Market	
April 22	Buy 2 SEP MMI futures contracts at 534.50. Sell 1 SEP S&P 500 futures contract at 333.00.	
May 6	Sell 2 SEP MMI futures contracts at 556.30. Buy 1 SEP S&P 500 futures contract at 342.15.	
		MMI	**S&P 500**
	Sell	556.30	333.00
	Buy	534.50	342.15
	Profit (points)	21.80	− 9.15
	× $500	$10,900.00	− $4,575.00
Total Profit: $6,325		
Note:	Each MMI index point is worth $250 on the futures contract, while each S&P 500 index point is worth $500. However, the trader bought 2 MMI contracts.	

two contracts is $10,900. This gain more than offsets the loss on the S&P 500 contract of $4,575, the product of 9.15 points times $500 per point. The total gain is $6,325.

Contracts farther from expiration often respond to a given market move more than the nearby contracts and the index itself. The speculator could have initiated an intra-commodity spread to take advantage of this same market rally. Table 9.11 shows one possible set of transactions using the S&P contract and the same dates. The speculator believes that the more distant contracts will be more responsive to a market move than the nearby contracts. Believing that the market will rise, she buys the more distant DEC contract at 361.90 on April 22, while simultaneously selling the nearby JUN contract at 359.80. By May 6, the rally has occurred, so she reverses her position by buying the JUN contract at 367.50 and selling the DEC contract at 369.75. As the table shows, the JUN contract has moved 7.70 points and the more sensitive DEC contract has moved 7.85 points. The strategy has worked, in a certain sense, because the more distant contract was more sensitive. However, the difference in the price changes was not very large. In fact, the gross profit on the spread was only $75, hardly enough to cover the transaction costs.

In an important sense, both spreads were too conservative. In the example of Table 9.11, the trader correctly anticipated the market move. An outright long position in any contract would have worked well, but the conservative trader managed to protect herself completely out of the benefits that could have been obtained, given the major character of the market advance. For the speculator committed to spread trading, the stock index futures market presents a problem, because the different contracts tend to be so highly correlated.

Table 9.11
A Conservative Intra–Commodity Spread

Date	Futures Market		
April 22	Buy 1 DEC S&P 500 contract at 361.90. Sell 1 JUN S&P 500 contract at 359.80.		
May 6	Sell 1 DEC S&P 500 contract at 369.75. Buy 1 JUN S&P 500 contract at 367.50.		
		June	December
	Sell	359.80	369.75
	Buy	367.50	361.90
	Profit (points)	– 7.70	7.85
	× $500	– $3,850.00	$3,925.00
	Total Profit: $75		

To trade spreads in stock index futures, it is often desirable to use a ratio spread. In a **ratio spread**, the trader trades more contracts on one side of the spread than on the other. The example of Table 9.10 is a ratio spread, because the trader used two MMI contracts and one S&P 500 contract. Thus, the ratio in this spread was 2:1. However, a more aggressive trader might have used an even higher ratio.

Risk Management with Stock Index Futures

Hedging with stock index futures applies directly to the management of stock portfolios.[7] The usefulness of stock index futures in portfolio management stems from the fact that they directly represent the market portfolio. Before stock index futures began trading, there was no comparable way of trading an instrument that gave the price performance so directly tied to a broad market index. Further, stock index futures have great potential in portfolio management due to their very low transaction costs. In this section we consider some hedging applications of stock index futures.

A Short Hedge and Hedge Ratio Calculation

As a first case, consider the manager of a well-diversified stock portfolio with a value of $40,000,000, and assume that the portfolio has a beta of 1.22 measured relative to the S&P 500. This implies that a movement of 1 percent in the S&P 500 index would be expected to induce a change of 1.22 percent in the value of the stock portfolio. The portfolio manager fears that a bear market is imminent and wishes to hedge his portfolio's value against that possibility. One strategy would be to liquidate the portfolio and place the proceeds in short-term debt instruments and then, after the bear market, return the funds to the stock market. Such a plan is infeasible. First, the transaction costs from such a strategy are quite high. Second, if the fund is large, liquidating the portfolio could drive down stock prices. This would prevent the portfolio manager from liquidating the portfolio at the prices currently quoted for the individual stocks.

As an obvious alternative to liquidating the portfolio, the manager could use the S&P 500 stock index futures contract. By selling futures, the manager should be able to offset the effect of the bear market on the portfolio by generating gains in the futures market. One kind of naive strategy might involve trading one dollar of the value underlying the index futures contract for each dollar of the portfolio's value. Assuming that the S&P Index futures contract stands at 212.00, the advocated number of futures contracts would be given by:

$$\frac{V_P}{V_F} = \frac{\$40,000,000}{(212)\ (\$500)} = 377 \text{ contracts}$$

where:

V_P = value of the portfolio
V_F = value of the futures contract

One problem with this approach is that it ignores the higher volatility of the stock portfolio relative to that of the S&P 500 Index. As noted above, the beta of the stock portfolio, as measured against the index, was 1.22. Table 9.12 shows the potential results of a hedge consistent with these facts. The portfolio manager initiates the hedge on March 14, selling 377 DEC futures contracts against the $40,000,000 stock portfolio. By August 16, his fears have been realized and the market has fallen. The S&P index, and the futures, have both fallen by 4.43 percent to 203. The stock portfolio, with its greater volatility, has fallen exactly 1.22 times as much, generating a loss of $2,161,840. This leaves a net loss on the hedge of $465,340. The failure to consider the differential volatility between the stock portfolio and the index futures contract leads to sub-optimal hedging results.

The manager might be able to avoid this result by weighting the hedge ratio by the beta of the stock portfolio. According to this scenario, the manager could use equation 9.6 to find the number of contracts to trade:

$$\left(\frac{V_P}{V_F}\right) \beta_P = \text{\# of contracts} \qquad\qquad 9.6$$

Table 9.12
A Short Hedge

	Stock Market	Futures Market
March 14	Hold $40,000,000 in a stock portfolio.	Sell 377 S&P 500 December futures contracts at 212.00.
April 16	Stock portfolio falls by 5.40% to $37,838,160.	S&P futures contract falls by 4.43% to 203.00.
	Loss: –$2,161,840	Gain: $1,696,500
	Net Loss: –$465,340	

where:

β_P = beta of the portfolio that is being hedged

Using this approach for our example, the manager would trade 460 contracts:

$$\left(\frac{\$40,000,000}{(\$212)\ (500)} \right) 1.22 = 460 \text{ contracts}$$

Had the manager traded 460 contracts, the futures gain reported in Table 9.12 would have been $2,070,000 instead of $1,696,500. This higher gain would have almost exactly offset the loss on the spot position of $2,161,840. Note, however, that these excellent results depend on two crucial assumptions. First, such results could be achieved only if the movement of the stock portfolio during the hedge period exactly corresponded to the volatility implied by its beta. Second, the technique of equation 9.6 uses the beta of the stock portfolio as measured against the S&P 500 Index itself. This assumes that the futures contracts moves exactly in tandem with the spot index. This assumption is clearly violated by recent market experience, because the futures contracts for all of the indexes are more volatile than the indexes themselves. This is reflected by the fact that the futures contracts generally have betas above 1.0 when they are measured relative to the stock index itself. The methodology of equation 9.6 does not take this into account, since it implicitly assumes the index and the futures contracts to have the same price movements, which would imply equal betas. We consider more sophisticated approaches to this type of hedging problem in Chapter 10.

A Long Hedge

As with all other futures contracts, both long and short hedges are possible in stock index futures. Imagine a pension fund manager convinced that she stands at the beginning of an extended bull market. She anticipates that $6,000,000 in new funds will become available in three months for investment. Waiting three months for the funds to invest in the stock market could mean that the bull market would be missed altogether. An alternative to missing the market move would be to use the stock index futures market. The pension manager could simply buy an amount of a stock index futures contract that would be equivalent in dollar commitments to the anticipated inflow of investable funds. On May 19, with the SEP NYSE Index futures contract standing at 174.40, the futures contract represents an underlying cash value of $87,200. The pension manager can secure her position in the market by buying $6,000,000 worth of futures. Since she expects the funds in three months, the SEP contract is a natural

Table 9.13
A Long Hedge with Stock Index Futures

	Stock Market	Futures Market
May 19	A pension fund manager antici- pates having $6,000,000 to invest in three months.	Buys 69 SEP NYSE futures at 174.40.
August 15	$6,000,000 becomes available for investment.	The market has risen and the NYSE futures stands at 178.50.
	Stock prices have risen, so the $6,000,000 will not buy the same shares that it would have on May 19.	Futures profit: $141,450

expiration to use, so she buys 69 SEP contracts, as shown in Table 9.13. By August 15, the market has risen, so the $6,000,000 could not buy the same shares that would have been possible on May 19. To offset this fact, the pension manager has earned a futures profit of $141,450. This gain in the futures market helps offset the new higher prices that would be incurred in the stock purchase.

Conclusion

In this chapter we have explored the major stock indexes on which futures contracts are traded. In addition, we have considered the structure of the futures contracts based upon them and the differences among the various futures contracts. We applied familiar cash-and-carry and reverse cash-and-carry arbitrage strategies to show that stock index futures prices should conform to the Cost-of-Carry Model. However, we noted that the Cost-of-Carry Model must be adjusted to reflect the dividends that stocks pay. In the context of the Cost-of-Carry Model, we saw that index arbitrage and program trading are just applications of cash-and-carry approaches to futures pricing.

The chapter considered some speculative trading strategies that use intra-commodity and inter-commodity spreads. We also considered an example of a ratio spread. In addition to speculative applications, stock index futures are useful for managing risk. We considered some examples of short and long hedges. In the short hedge example, we showed how a portfolio manager could protect against a potential bear market. With a long hedge example, we showed how a trader could capture a potential bull market by using futures as a substitute for actually buying shares.

Questions and Problems

1. Distinguish between the MMI and the Dow Jones Industrial Averages.

2. Assume that the MMI Index stands at 340.00 and the current divisor is 0.8. One of the stocks in the index is priced at $100.00 and it splits 2:1. Based on this information, answer the following questions:

   a. What is the sum of the prices of all the shares in the index before the stock split?
   b. What is the value of the index after the split? Explain.
   c. What is the sum of the prices of all the shares in the index after the split?
   d. What is the divisor after the split?

3. What is the main difference in the calculation of the MMI and the S&P 500 indexes? Explain.

4. For the S&P 500 Index, assume that the company with the highest market value has a 1 percent increase in stock prices. Also, assume that the company with the smallest market value has a 1 percent decrease in the price of its shares. Does the index change? If so, in what direction?

5. Table 9.3 shows the correlations among the three indexes. Explain why the correlation between the NYSE Composite and the S&P 500 should be the highest of all correlations.

6. The S&P 500 futures is scheduled to expire in half a year, and the interest rate for carrying stocks over that period is 11 percent. The expected dividend rate on the underlying stocks for the same period is 2 percent of the value of the stocks. (The 2 percent is the half-year rate, not an annual rate.) Ignoring the interest that it might be possible to earn on the dividend payments, find the fair value for the futures if the current value of the index is 315.00.

7. Consider a very simple index like the MMI, except assume that it has only two shares, A and B. The price of A is $100.00, and share B trades for $75.00. The current index value is 175.00. The futures contract based on this index expires in three months, and the cost of carrying the stocks

forward is .75 percent per month. This is also the interest rate that you can earn on invested funds. You expect stock A to pay a $3 dividend in one month and stock B to pay a $1 dividend in two months. Find the fair value of the futures. Assume monthly compounding.

8. Using the same data in problem 7, now assume that the futures trades at 176.00. Explain how you would trade with this set of information. Show your transactions.

9. Using the same data in problem 7, now assume that the futures trades at 174.00. Explain how you would trade with this set of information. Show your transactions.

10. For a stock index and a stock index futures constructed like the MMI, assume that the dividend rate expected to be earned on the stocks in the index is the same as the cost of carrying the stocks forward. What should be the relationship between the cash and futures market prices? Explain.

11 Your portfolio is worth $100 million and has a beta of 1.08 measured against the S&P futures, which is priced at 350.00. Explain how you would hedge this portfolio, assuming that you wish to be fully hedged.

12. You have inherited $50 million, but the estate will not settle for six months and you will not actually receive the cash until that time. You find current stock values attractive and you plan to invest in the S&P 500 cash portfolio. Explain how you would hedge this anticipated investment using S&P 500 futures.

Notes

1. Prominent among these inactive contracts is the Value Line Contract on the Kansas City Board of Trade. Formerly, this contract was actively traded, but its construction was very complicated, being a geometric average of 1700 stocks. Partially for this reason, its popularity faded during the late 1980s. A change in the composition of the index did little to restore its faded luster. By 1990, daily volume had fallen to a few hundred contracts and open interest in all contracts was below 2,000.

2. In earlier times, the S&P 500 consisted of 400 industrial firms, 40 financial institutions, 40 utilities, and 20 transportation firms.

3. At any time, contracts on the MMI trade for the first three consecutive months and the next three months in the March, June, September, December delivery cycle.

4. As we will see in Chapter 10, trading for the S&P 500 and the NYSE futures contracts ends on one day, and the final settlement price is set at the next day's opening price.

5. These calculations are sometimes off by a penny or two due to rounding.

6. G. Gastineau and A. Madansky, "S&P 500 Stock Index Futures Evaluation Tables," *Financial Analysts Journal*, 39:6, November-December 1983, pp. 68-76, were among the first to recognize the importance of the daily dividend flows for stock index futures pricing.

7. The hedging potential of stock index futures has been widely recognized even in the early stage of trading. See: N. Weiner, "The Hedging Rationale for a Stock Index Futures Contract," *Journal of Futures Markets*, 1:1, Spring 1981, pp. 59-76; S. Figlewski, "Hedging with Stock Index Futures: Theory and Application in a New Market," Finance Working Paper No. 139, University of California at Berkeley; S. Figlewski and S. Kon, "Portfolio Management with Stock Index Futures," *Financial Analysts Journal*, 38:1, January-February 1982, pp. 52-60; D. Grant, "How to Optimize with Stock Index Futures," *Journal of Portfolio Management*, 8:3, Spring 1982, pp. 32-36; and D. Grant, "A Market Index Futures Contract and Portfolio Selection," *Journal of Economics and Business*, 34:4, 1982, pp. 387-390.

10

Stock Index Futures: Refinements

Introduction

In Chapter 9 we saw that stock index futures prices are governed by the Cost-of-Carry Model. Because stocks often pay dividends, we saw how to tailor the Cost-of-Carry Model to reflect the dividends on the stocks that underlie the stock index futures. In this chapter, we explore some of the empirical evidence on the relationship between theoretical and observed market prices. As in any violation of cost-of-carry principles, arbitrage opportunities should be possible if stock index futures prices do not correspond to theoretically determined prices.

Index arbitrage is the specific name given to attempts to exploit discrepancies between theoretical and actual stock index futures prices. As we also discussed in Chapter 9, index arbitrage usually proceeds through program trading. With the advent of program trading, there has been some evidence of a link between high index price variability and the style of trading used by program traders. This chapter considers some of the evidence on volatility and explores the market concern about volatility.

Because of the perception that futures trading is responsible for stock market volatility, new concern has focused on trading practices in the futures market, leading to some changes in trading rules. This chapter also considers some of the new trading practices rules recently implemented in the S&P 500 futures pit.

Chapter 9 considered some speculative and hedging applications of stock index futures. This chapter explores some more sophisticated techniques for using stock index futures that are becoming an important tool in portfolio management. By trading stock index futures in conjunction with a stock portfolio, a portfolio manager can tailor the risk characteristics of the entire portfolio. These strategies have aspects of both speculation and hedging. Two of the most notable of these are asset allocation and portfolio insurance, which we consider in some detail.

Stock Index Futures Prices

In this section we consider a variety of issues related to stock index futures pricing. First, we examine the empirical evidence on stock index futures efficiency. Namely, do stock index futures prices conform to the Cost-of-Carry Model? Evidence suggests that the market was not efficient when trading began, but that it is now efficient. Second, we consider the effect of taxes on stock index futures prices. A tax-timing option available to traders of stocks, but denied to stock index futures traders, might explain the discrepancy between theoretical and actual prices for stock index futures. Third, we consider the timing relationship between stock index futures prices and the cash market index. Does the futures price lead the cash market index, or does the cash market index lead the futures? Finally, we consider seasonal impacts on stock index futures pricing. Here "seasonal" refers not only to the time of year, but also to the time of month, time of week, and even time of day.

Stock Index Futures Efficiency

In Chapter 9, we saw that cost-of-carry principles apply directly to the pricing of stock index futures. In particular, if the spot stock index price and the futures price are misaligned, cash-and-carry or reverse cash-and-carry arbitrage opportunities will become available. We considered examples of these kinds of transactions in Chapter 9. In this section, we consider whether the stock index futures market is informationally efficient. If it is efficient, then stock index futures prices should conform to the Cost-of-Carry Model that we developed in Chapter 9. As we will see, the general conclusion suggests that the market was inefficient in the early days of trading but that it now conforms well to the Cost-of-Carry Model.

Exploring actual market data, Modest and Sundaresan apply the carrying charges model to form permissible bounds for futures prices and try to take into account the actual transaction costs that would be incurred in trading the futures and the stocks in the indexes.[1] The bounds depend critically on the assumptions of a $25 round trip transaction cost for the futures contract and $.10 per share transaction costs for the stock itself. We must also assume that the T-bill rate is the appropriate interest rate for all calculations of carrying charges.

Modest and Sundaresan's analysis makes two additional assumptions. The first concerns the assumption that we make regarding the use of proceeds from short selling stocks. If a trader does not have full use of the proceeds from short sales due to margin requirements, then the interest on the proceeds that cannot be used has a marked impact on the analysis. We have already encountered this issue in our discussion of T-bill futures efficiency. Essentially, an arbitrage opportunity might require the short sale of the stock index, which means that the individual stocks comprising the index are sold short in the stock market. In this situation, the short seller may not receive full use of the proceeds from the short sale, because the broker will hold a significant fraction of those proceeds as protection against default by the short seller. Therefore, the success of any such arbitrage depends critically upon assumptions regarding the use of short sale proceeds. Modest and Sundaresan examine alternative assumptions about the use of short sale proceeds.

A second critical assumption concerns dividends. We have already seen in Chapter 9 that dividends are important to the pricing of stock index futures. In addition, the extreme inter-temporal variation in dividends shown in Figure 9.4 means that their effect will vary dramatically from one time period to the next. For accuracy in pricing stock index futures, taking account of dividends is very important.

We begin our discussion of this issue by focusing on a paper that examined the early history of trading, "The Relationship Between Spot and Futures Prices in Stock Index Futures Markets: Some Preliminary Evidence." This article by David Modest and Mahadevan Sundaresan addresses most of the issues that are necessary to determine the efficiency of prices in a market. For instance, we have seen that every real market has a range of permissible no-arbitrage prices. This no-arbitrage band arises because of transaction costs and restrictions on short selling. Therefore, tests of market efficiency depend critically on careful estimations of these transaction costs.

Modest and Sundaresan computed the no-arbitrage boundaries for the DEC 1982 futures contract under the assumptions outlined above and present those results in Figure 10.1. The graph tracks the futures prices from April 21 through September 15, 1982. The dotted lines on the graph show the bounds, which are adjusted for dividends and the assumption that half the proceeds from short sales are available. The solid line represents the actual futures price. Clearly, the futures price lies within the bounds except for near misses on two occasions. On the whole, these results are consistent with the rationality of futures pricing. In another part of their study, the bounds were also adjusted for dividends, but with the assumption that one has use of 100 percent of the proceeds from short sales. In this situation, arbitrage opportunities were consistently available.

In their study, Modest and Sundaresan did not attempt to include an estimate of the daily dividend payment from the S&P 500 index. Instead, they estimated the dividend rate on the index using quarterly dividend data and then interpolated that into monthly dividend data. As a result, their study does not reflect the high variability in dividends on a daily basis. The graph of Figure 10.1 applies to the DEC 1982 contract for April 21 to September 15, 1982. Over

Figure 10.1
No-Arbitrage Bounds and Futures Prices

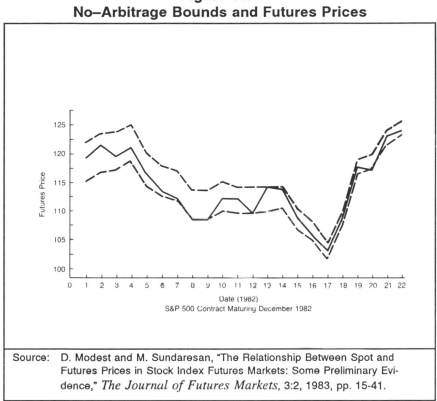

Source: D. Modest and M. Sundaresan, "The Relationship Between Spot and Futures Prices in Stock Index Futures Markets: Some Preliminary Evidence," *The Journal of Futures Markets*, 3:2, 1983, pp. 15-41.

that time, dividends had very sharp quarterly peaks. Had Modest and Sundaresan been able to take these daily fluctuations into account more accurately, we would expect observed prices to lie more consistently within the no-arbitrage bounds, and their paper would be even more valuable.

Perhaps of equal importance to the exact treatment of dividends is the assumption made about the use of proceeds from short sales. In addition, we have seen that some traders face full transaction costs. By contrast, other traders face much lower transaction costs. For example, large institutions with significant portfolios can simulate short selling by selling part of their existing portfolio. In this simulated short selling, they retain full use of the proceeds. Throughout our discussion, we have referred to arbitrage activities by these low transaction cost traders as **quasi-arbitrage**.

Modest and Sundaresan's results clearly point to quasi-arbitrage opportunities. In the early days of stock index futures trading, it appears that significant

Table 10.1
Studies of the Efficiency of Stock Index Futures

Modest and Sundaresan (1983)	For quasi–arbitrageurs, profits are available.
Modest (1984)	Arbitrage profits are available, but only to traders with full use of short sale proceeds.
Figlewski (1984)	Arbitrage opportunities were available in early trading, but these are disappearing.
Figlewski (1984)	By 1984, the stock index futures market was fairly efficient and moving toward higher efficiency.
Peters (1985)	In early trading, the market was inefficient, but it has been growing more efficient.
Billingsly and Chance (1988)	Stock index futures spreads have been efficiently priced since the inception of trading, but a few arbitrage opportunities were found.
Saunders and Mahajan (1988)	Early trading exhibited inefficiencies, but these disappeared as the market matured.
Brenner, Subrahmanyam and Uno (1990)	In the Japanese market, early trading exhibited inefficiencies, but these have disappeared as the market matured.

quasi–arbitrage opportunities were available. However, after the seasoning of the market, prices tended to remain within the no–arbitrage bounds. While such conclusions depend upon estimates of transaction costs, other studies substantiate the conclusion reached by Modest and Sundaresan. Table 10.1 summarizes some of these studies.

Taxes and Stock Index Futures Pricing

The studies of the Cost-of-Carry Model for stock index futures prices in Table 10.1 generally do not consider taxes. A difference in tax treatment between futures and the stocks themselves might justify a discrepancy from the Cost-of-Carry Model. In such a case, the market might be efficient.

Comparing a long position in the stocks underlying an index and a long position in the stock index futures contract shows that there is a difference in tax treatment. The owner of a stock may have a paper gain or loss on the stock as the end of the year approaches. For example, assume that a share was purchased for $100 and that the trader pays taxes at the rate of 30 percent. If the stock sells for $90 as the end of the year approaches, the trader has the option to sell the stock for $90, realizing a $10 loss. If he or she sells the stock, taxable income will be reduced by $10. With a 30 percent tax rate, selling the stock generates a tax saving of $3. By contrast, assume that the stock price is $110 instead of

$90 as the end of the year approaches. In this situation, the tax saving strategy is to wait until after the turn of the year to take the gain, thereby deferring the taxes for a full year by just waiting a few days to make the trade.

Because futures prices are marked to market at year-end for tax purposes, the futures contract possesses no tax-timing option. In the futures markets, tax rules require all paper gains or losses to be recognized as cash gains or losses each year. The tax-timing option included with the stock, but lacking with the futures contract, implies that rational pricing must reflect the value of the tax-timing option in the relationship between the cash and futures prices of the stock index.

This possibility was first noted by Bradford Cornell and Kenneth French. They showed how this tax-timing option could give extra value to the stocks relative to the futures. Cornell and French compute the value of the tax option as the difference between the observed market price and the price implied by the carrying charges model. While the tax option clearly has a value, the technique adopted by Cornell and French assumes that the stock index futures contract is priced rationally, and they compute the value of the option in accordance with that fundamental belief. For the purpose of trying to evaluate the price performance characteristics of the stock index futures contract, note that the tax timing option would have a value, but that a trader cannot immediately assume that its value is equal to the discrepancy between the observed market price and the theoretically justified price assuming no tax-timing option. However, in an empirical study of the effect of the tax-timing option on futures prices, Cornell concludes that the tax-timing option does not appear to affect prices.[2] Cornell suggests that trading may be dominated by tax-free investors, or that other tax rules may prevent the tax timing option from significantly affecting prices.

The Day of the Week Effect in Stock Index Futures

It has been well documented that returns on many securities vary by the day of the week. There is nothing in the financial theory to explain why returns on Thursday should be different from returns on Tuesday or Wednesday.[3] Nonetheless, a great deal of evidence shows that returns differ depending on the day of the week. In particular, Friday returns are generally high and Monday returns (the return from Friday close to Monday close) are even negative. These return differences are substantial and it may be possible for investors to earn a return that beats the market by timing their purchases to take advantage of these persistent differences. If so, the day of the week effect would show either that the semi-strong efficient market hypothesis (EMH) was not true or that the CAPM was not true, or both. If the CAPM is the correct pricing relationship in the market, then the EMH must be false, because it appears that prices do not adjust correctly to reflect all available information. If the EMH is true, it seems that the CAPM must be false, because there must be additional risk factors not

Table 10.2
Day of the Week Effect in Stock Index Futures

Cornell (1985)	No effect in S&P 500 futures.
Dyl and Maberly (1986a)	Prices fall from close on Fridays to open on Mondays.
Dyl and Maberly (1986b)	Authors cannot replicate Cornell's 1985 results.
Junkus (1986)	Prices fall from close on Fridays to open on Mondays.
Phillips–Patrick and Schneeweis (1988)	Stock dividend payment patterns may explain part of the weekend effect.

recognized by the CAPM to explain the different returns depending on the day of the week.

The day of the week effect has also been explored in the stock index futures market. One early study found no evidence of the day of the week effect in the futures market.[4] However, subsequent studies have found a statistically significant effect in the S&P 500 futures contract.[5] Given the strong relationship that must hold between stock index futures and the stock index itself, we would expect to find an effect in the futures market if there is one in the stock market itself. Table 10.2 summarizes some of the studies of the day of the week effect in stock index futures. Most studies find a weekend effect—price changes from the Friday close to the Monday open are low or negative.[6]

Leads and Lags in Stock Index Prices

We have seen that arbitrage seekers force stock index cash market and futures market prices to conform to the Cost-of-Carry Model. Thus, a movement in one price must generate a movement in the other price to keep prices in conformance with the Cost-of-Carry Model.

At first blush, it might seem that the index should lead the futures. For example, if new information arrives in the market about a particular stock, the price of that stock will change. The index value changes to reflect the new price of the constituent stock. To keep prices in conformance with the Cost-of-Carry Model, the index futures price must change. Under this scenario, the cash market index changes first and the futures index price changes later. Thus, the cash index leads the futures price.

However, the dominant information affecting the stock market might be more general information. If the most important information affects the general level of stock prices, rather than the price of a single firm, there may be a different transmission of stock price changes. For an example too strange to believe, assume that Iraq invades Kuwait and that this is bad news for stock prices. Traders may react to this information by trading in either the stock market or the stock index futures market. The choice of market will be affected by both the relative liquidity and the transaction costs in the two markets. If liquidity and transaction costs are most important, futures trading will be more attractive. Thus, with the invasion news, traders might first sell index futures, driving down the futures price. The cash market index must then adjust to exclude arbitrage opportunities. Under this scenario, the futures price will lead the cash market index.

These leads and lags are most likely to occur on a minute to minute basis. If the leads or lags persisted over days, for example, they could well lead to arbitrage opportunities. Whether the cash market index leads the futures, or vice versa, is essentially an empirical question. The question of leads and lags has been explored in several studies of stock index futures. Joseph Finnerty and Hun Park examine leads and lags for the MMI futures and the cash market index for 24 contracts between August 1984 and August 1986. Finnerty and Park find that the MMI futures price tends to change before the MMI cash market index. Specifically, they found that 16 of these 24 contracts exhibited a significant tendency for the futures price to change before the cash price.[7]

Ira Kawaller, Paul Koch, and Timothy Koch examine leads and lags in S&P 500 index futures and cash trading.[8] Their data consist of minute to minute prices of the S&P 500 cash and futures for all trading days in 1984 and 1985. They find that the cash and futures move almost in lock step, but that there are significant leads and lags. Most notably, the cash market index lags the futures market index price. On many occasions, the stock index lagged the futures index price by 20–45 minutes. Sometimes the futures lagged the stock market index, but the lag seldom extended beyond one minute. As Kawaller, Koch, and Koch conclude, "The length of the lead from futures to the index reflects, in part, inertia in the stock market. Stocks are not traded as readily as futures contracts." These general results are confirmed in another study by Anthony Herbst, Joseph McCormack and Elizabeth West.[9] They conclude that the futures price reacts in less than one minute to a change in the spot market index, but that the spot market index can take much longer to react to the futures market price change.

While stock index futures prices may lead the stock index, this differential movement does not necessarily create arbitrage opportunities. First, movements in the two prices are generally almost simultaneous. Quickly responding prices may not allow any arbitrage opportunities. Second, both prices vary constantly by small amounts as new information reaches the market. Even substantial lags would not create an arbitrage opportunity if the difference in prices is small. In other words, the futures price could always lead the cash market index. However, if the price difference is small, the difference in prices could always remain within the no-arbitrage bounds of the Cost-of-Carry Model.

Real World Program Trading

Chapter 9 explained the basic idea of index arbitrage through program trading. There we considered an imaginary two stock index and showed how to engage in cash-and-carry and reverse cash-and-carry strategies to exploit mispricing of the index versus the index futures. To provide a more realistic feel for real world program trade in stock index futures, this section begins with an historical example of an actual program trade. We then consider the risks inherent in program trading that make the enterprise much more perilous than our historical example would seem to indicate. Finally, we conclude with some statistics on the extent of program trading in today's markets.

Real World Program Trading: An Example

This section discusses an historical example of a cash-and-carry program trading transaction.[10] The trader buys the stocks and carries them forward while selling the futures to profit from the spot being underpriced relative to the futures. Table 10.3 shows the actual prices for the MMI stocks on February 26, 1986, when the trade began. The table also shows the MMI stock prices at the end of the trade on March 21, 1986 and the dividends that the various stocks paid between the two dates.

Faced with the prices shown for February 26, 1986 in Table 10.3, the trader bought 2,000 shares of each of 20 stocks, with a total purchase price of $2,749,000. The trader used $1,374,500, or 50 percent, of his own funds and borrowed the same amount at 8.5 percent. At the same time, he sold 35 MAR 1986 MMI futures at 313.55. This value implies an underlying stock value of $2,743,563 (313.55 index value × $250 multiplier × 35 contracts). Trading this number of contracts gives the spot and futures positions very similar dollar values, which is exactly the desired relationship to profit on the relative mispricing.

Risks in Index Arbitrage and Program Trading

The index arbitrage transactions on February 26 in Table 10.4 ensure a profit, subject to a few minor risks. Because the stock index contracts are settled in cash, the spot and futures values at the close of trading for the contract must converge. For the MAR 1986 MMI, trading ended on March 21. Table 10.4 shows the transactions involved in this arbitrage. All of the values in Table 10.4 are actual market prices. Notice that the purchase of shares in Table 10.4 used 50 percent debt and 50 percent investable funds. This is necessary because of Federal Reserve Board requirements that no more than 50 percent of the

Table 10.3
Data for Index Arbitrage

Firm	Price Feb. 26	Price Mar. 21	Dividends $/Share
American Express	64.000	65.625	
AT&T	22.500	22.875	
Chevron	37.875	37.375	
Coca–Cola	92.000	100.375	.78
Dow Chemical	48.750	52.375	
DuPont	70.500	72.500	
Kodak	55.000	59.750	
Exxon	54.875	54.750	
General Electric	75.500	75.750	.58
General Motors	78.250	83.250	
IBM	158.125	148.500	
International Paper	57.000	60.000	
Johnson & Johnson	48.375	54.000	
Merck	150.750	161.250	.90
3M	97.25	104.000	
Mobil Oil	30.125	29.500	
Philip Morris	101.125	119.250	1.15
Procter & Gamble	67.000	73.500	
Sears	42.875	46.125	
U.S. Steel	22.675	22.750	
MMI Index	311.740	328.070	
MAR 86 MMI Futures	313.550	328.070	

purchase price of stocks can be borrowed. Table 10.4 reflects the opportunity cost of those invested funds by assuming that they could have earned the 8.5 percent interest rate that was paid to borrow money.

In computing the cash flows in Table 10.4, we consider all interest, dividends, and out of pocket transaction costs. The dividends totaled $3.41 from Table 10.3. With 2,000 shares of each firm, the total dividends received were $8,820. Total transaction costs were $1,100. This is about $.014 per share to buy and the same amount to sell, including the futures contracts. Notice, however, that the analysis does not reflect the daily resettlement cash flows that may have been incurred between February 26 and March 21, nor do we consider interest that might have been earned on the dividends received. In addition, the cash flow

```
┌─────────────────────────────────────────────────────────────────────┐
│                           Table 10.4                                 │
│                  Program Trading Transactions                        │
│                                                                       │
│ February 26, 1986                                                     │
│ ┌───────────────────────────────────────────────────────────────────┤
│ │ Sell 35 MMI MAR 1986 futures at 313.55.                            │
│ │                                                                     │
│ │ Use $1,374,500 of investable funds; borrow another $1,374,500 at    │
│ │ 8.5% and use these funds to buy 2,000 shares of each of the 20      │
│ │ stocks comprising the MMI at a total cost of $2,749,000.            │
│ └───────────────────────────────────────────────────────────────────┤
```

Table 10.4
Program Trading Transactions

February 26, 1986

Sell 35 MMI MAR 1986 futures at 313.55.

Use $1,374,500 of investable funds; borrow another $1,374,500 at 8.5% and use these funds to buy 2,000 shares of each of the 20 stocks comprising the MMI at a total cost of $2,749,000.

March 21, 1986

Buy 35 MMI MAR 1986 futures at 328.07.

Sell all stocks purchased on February 26, receiving $2,893,000.

Pay interest of $8,438 on borrowed $1,374,500.

Charge opportunity cost of own $1,374,500 that was invested at appropriate cost of funds of 8.5% for a total of $8,438.

Pay transaction costs: – $1,100.

Dividends received while stocks were owned: +$6,820.

Net Cash Flows:

February 26	None, because we will charge an opportunity cost for the portion of funds that were invested.	
March 21	Futures	–$127,050
	Stocks	144,000
	Transaction Costs	– 1,100
	Dividends	6,820
	Interest on Actual Loan	– 8,438
	Opportunity Cost on Invested Funds	– 8,438
	Arbitrage Profit	$ 5,794

computation does not reflect the cost of searching for this opportunity.[11]

This kind of transaction has certain elements of risk stemming from three sources. First, there is execution risk, because the trader must successfully enter and close the entire position. To establish the position, the trader must buy 2,000 shares of 20 stocks and sell 35 futures contracts. Imagine that the trader finds the opportunity and sells futures. Then the trader starts buying shares of the 20 stocks. During this time, assume that three of the stocks increase in price by $1.00 each. Because the trader has sold the futures contracts, the price of that side of the position is fixed. With three stocks increasing in price by $1.00, the long position in the stocks will cost a total of $6,000 more than anticipated. If this happens, the trader pays $6,000 more than anticipated for the stocks, and the arbitrage profit turns to an arbitrage loss.[12]

The second part of the execution risk exposure occurs on March 21 when the position must be closed. The profit or loss on the futures contract depends on the index value at the close of trading on March 21. However, the risk arbitrage strategy calls for the stocks to be sold at the end of trading on the same day. If the stocks are held until the next day, there will be considerable risk, because any kind of news could be received after the close of trading on March 21. Because of this risk, it is customary to close out such stock positions at the close of trading on the futures expiration day. To close the position, the trader enters a market on close order to sell these stocks. A **market on close order** instructs the broker to sell these shares for the market price at the close of trading. The obvious goal is to sell the shares at the settlement price of the day's trading, because that will be the share price that figures into the index, and the index value on that day determines the futures profit or loss. If the trader could be certain that the shares would be sold at the day's closing price, this element of risk would be eliminated. However, it is difficult to trade in the last 15–30 seconds to get execution at the day's final price. Therefore, there is risk involved in closing the position as well as opening the position.

In addition to execution risk, there is some risk that the dividends will not be paid as the trader anticipates. In this example, if the firms cancel their dividend payments, the trader does not receive $6,820 and the transactions will generate a loss. Such a rash of dividend cancellations is unlikely, but at least remotely possible. The final source of risk is financing risk. The trader might not be able to secure financing for the entire period at the same rate. If the stocks are financed with overnight obligations and interest rates suddenly jump, financing costs could be higher than anticipated. In summary, the index arbitrage transaction faces execution risk, dividend risk, and interest rate risk. Of these, execution risk is the most important. Nonetheless, once the transactions of February 26 are put in place, there is very little real danger of a loss.[13]

Recent Program Trading Activity

To illustrate the extent of program trading, we focus on recent program trading activity on the New York Stock Exchange (NYSE).[14] During 1988–1990, program trading accounted for about 10 percent of all trades on the NYSE. Because program trades involve more shares than the average trade, program trading accounted for about 16 percent of all volume during this period. Buy programs and sell programs occurred with almost equal frequency over this period.

Of program trades, slightly less than half were used for index arbitrage. Program trading is also used for other purposes such as portfolio insurance trading, which is discussed later. Program trades can be initiated by a brokerage firm as a principal or as an agent for another party. Roughly 30-35 percent of program trades in 1988-1990 were executed by brokerage firms as principals, with about 65-70 percent being executed for customers. Morgan Stanley is a frequent leader in both categories. In August 1990, the top three firms in executing program trades for customers were Morgan Stanley, PaineWebber, and Kidder Peabody. For January-August 1990, the leading firms in program trading for customers were Morgan Stanley, PaineWebber, and First Boston.

Hedging with Stock Index Futures

In Chapter 9 we considered the basic techniques for hedging with stock index futures. We presented examples of short and long hedges and discussed a hedging strategy for hedging a portfolio with stock index futures that reflected the beta of the portfolio being hedged. The hedge position from Chapter 9 was:

$$\left(\frac{V_P}{V_F}\right) \beta_P = \text{\# of contracts} \qquad 9.6$$

where:

V_P = value of the portfolio
V_F = value of the futures contract
β_P = beta of the portfolio that is being hedged

In this section we analyze stock index futures hedging. We begin by showing that the hedge equation 9.6 gives the futures position to establish a combined stock and futures portfolio with the lowest possible risk. We illustrate this hedging technique with actual market data. It is also possible to use futures to alter the beta of an existing portfolio. For example, if a stock portfolio has a beta of 0.8 and the desired beta is 0.9, it is possible to trade stock index futures to make the combined stock and futures portfolio behave like a stock portfolio with a beta of 0.9. Finally, we consider techniques for tailing the hedge.

The Minimum Risk Hedge Ratio

In Chapter 9 we studied the problem of combining a cash market position with futures to minimize risk. There we took the cash market position as fixed and sought to find the futures hedge ratio, HR, that would minimize risk. From equation 4.3 we saw that the risk of a combined cash and futures position equals:

$$\sigma_P^2 = \sigma_C^2 + HR^2 \sigma_F^2 - 2\,HR\,\rho_{CF}\,\sigma_C\,\sigma_F \qquad 4.3$$

where:

$$\sigma_P^2 = \text{variance of the portfolio}$$
$$\sigma_C^2 = \text{variance of asset C}$$
$$\sigma_F^2 = \text{variance of asset F}$$
$$\rho_{CF} = \text{correlation between assets C and F}$$
$$\sigma_C = \text{standard deviation of asset C}$$
$$\sigma_F = \text{standard deviation of asset F}$$

From equation 4.3, the risk-minimizing hedge ratio, HR, is:

$$HR = \frac{\rho_{CF}\,\sigma_C\,\sigma_F}{\sigma_F^2} = \frac{COV_{CF}}{\sigma_F^2} \qquad 4.4$$

where:

COV_{CF} = the covariance between C and F

As a practical matter, the easiest way to find the risk-minimizing hedge ratio is to estimate the following regression:

$$C_t = \alpha + \beta_{RM} F_t + \varepsilon_t \qquad 10.1$$

where:

C_t = the returns on the cash market position in period t
F_t = the returns on the futures contract in period t[15]
α = the constant regression parameter
β_{RM} = the slope regression parameter for the risk-minimizing hedge
ε = an error term with zero mean and standard deviation of 1.0

The estimated beta from this regression is the risk-minimizing hedge ratio, because the estimated β_{RM} equals the sample covariance between the independent (F) and dependent (C) variables divided by the sample variance of the independent variable. The R^2 from this regression shows the percentage of risk in the cash position that is eliminated by holding the futures position.

At this point, it is important to distinguish the beta in equation 10.1 and the beta of the portfolio in the sense of the Capital Asset Pricing Model. The CAPM beta is the beta from regressing the returns of a given asset on the returns from the "true" market portfolio. However, the returns on the true market portfolio are unobservable. Therefore, as a practical measure, proxies are used for the market portfolio and the betas of assets are estimated by regressing the returns of a particular asset on the returns from the proxy of the market portfolio. The potential confusion becomes more dangerous because the S&P 500 spot index is one of the best-known proxies for the true market portfolio.

In equation 9.6 we computed a hedge ratio using the beta for the portfolio. This beta is the estimated CAPM beta, because it is estimated by regressing the returns from a portfolio on the proxy for the market portfolio. By contrast, the beta in equation 10.1 is the beta for a risk-minimizing hedge ratio and is not the same as the estimated CAPM beta. The beta in equation 10.1 is found by regressing the returns of the portfolio on the returns from the futures contract. The estimated CAPM beta is found by regressing the returns of the portfolio on the returns of the spot market index being used as a proxy for the unobservable true market portfolio. Thus, the hedging position in equation 9.6 is not a risk-minimizing hedge. Nonetheless, such hedges can be very useful. We might think of the hedge ratio in equation 9.6 as a rough-and-ready approximation to risk-minimizing hedging.

Betas	
CAPM Beta	The beta estimated by regressing the returns of an asset on the returns of the true market portfolio.
Estimated CAPM Beta	The beta estimated by regressing the returns of an asset on the returns of a proxy for the true market portfolio. The proxy is usually a stock index such as the S&P 500.
Beta for a Risk-Minimizing Hedge Ratio	The beta from regressing the returns of a cash market position to be hedged on the returns of the futures contract to be used for hedging.

Having found the risk-minimizing hedge ratio, β_{RM}, we need to compute the number of contracts to trade. The solution to this problem almost exactly matches the hedging position in equation 9.6, but we use the risk-minimizing hedge ratio, β_{RM}, instead of the CAPM beta for the portfolio, β_P. Thus, the risk-minimizing futures position is:

$$\left(\frac{V_P}{V_F}\right) \beta_{RM} = \text{\# of contracts}$$

A Minimum Risk Hedging Example

In this section we consider an example of a minimum risk hedge in stock index futures using actual market data. Let us assume a trader has a portfolio worth $10 million on November 28, 1989. The portfolio is invested in the 20 stocks in the MMI. The portfolio manager will hedge this cash market portfolio using the S&P 500 JUN 90 futures contract. We consider each step that the portfolio manager follows to compute the hedge ratio and to implement the hedge.

Organize Data and Compute Returns. The manager plans to hedge according to equation 9.6. Therefore, she needs to find the beta for the hedge ratio. Accordingly, she collects data for her portfolio value for 101 days from July 6, 1989 through yesterday, November 27, 1989. She also finds the price of the S&P 500 JUN 90 futures for each day. There is nothing magic about using 101 days, but these data are available and she believes that this procedure will provide a sufficient sample to estimate the hedging beta. From the 101 days of prices, she computes the daily percentage change in the value of the cash market portfolio and the futures price. This gives 100 paired observations of daily returns data.

Estimate Hedging Beta. With the data in place, the portfolio manager regresses the cash market returns on the returns from the futures contract as shown in equation 10.1. From this regression the estimated beta is .8801, so β_{RM} = .8801. This indicates that each dollar of the cash market position should be hedged with $.8801 dollars in the futures position. The R^2 from the regression is .9263, and this high R^2 encourages the belief that the hedge is likely to perform well. Again, for emphasis the estimated beta from regressing the portfolio's returns on the stock index futures returns is not the same as the portfolio's CAPM beta; β_P does not equal β_{RM}.[16]

Compute Futures Position. The portfolio manager wants to hedge a $10 million cash portfolio with the S&P JUN 90 futures contract. Having found the risk-minimizing hedge ratio, she needs to translate the hedge ratio into the correct futures position that takes account of the size of the futures contract. On

November 27, the S&P futures closed at 354.75. The futures contract value is for the index times $500. Therefore, applying equation 9.6, she computes the number of contracts as:

$$\left(\frac{V_P}{V_F}\right)\beta_{RM} = \left(\frac{\$10,000,000}{(354.75)(\$500)}\right).8801 = 49.6180$$

The estimated risk-minimizing futures position is 49.62 contracts, so the portfolio manager decides to sell 50 contracts.

Evaluate Hedging Results.   Figure 10.2 shows the value of the unhedged and hedged portfolio for the next 60 days until February 22, 1990, when our trader decides to terminate the hedge. The unhedged portfolio's ending value is $9,656,090. The settlement price for the futures on February 22 is 330.60.

Figure 10.2
Hedged and Unhedged Portfolio Values

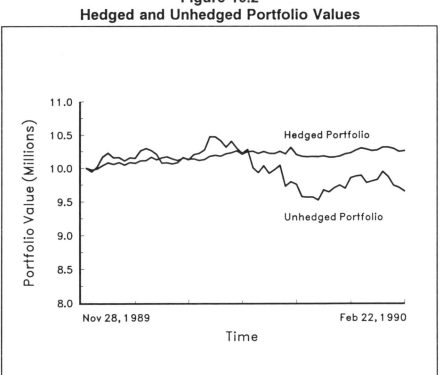

Therefore, the futures profit is 50($500)(354.75 - 330.60) = $603,750. The futures profit results from trading 50 contracts with each index point being worth $500 and the index having fallen 24.15 points. The value of the hedged portfolio consists of the cash market portfolio plus the futures profit, so the hedged portfolio's terminal value is $10,259,840. In this example, the hedge protected the portfolio against a substantial loss.

Ex–Ante versus Ex–Post Hedge Ratios

In our risk-minimizing hedging example, we computed β_{RM} = .8801 using historical data and applied the hedge ratio to a future period. It is highly unlikely that the estimated hedge ratio would equal the hedge ratio that we would have used if we had perfect foresight about the behavior of the cash market position and the futures price. This is the difference between an ex–ante and an ex–post hedge ratio. **Ex–ante**, or **before the fact**, the best hedge ratio we could find was .8801. **Ex–post**, or **after the fact**, some other hedge ratio would be likely to perform better than the ex–ante hedge ratio of .8801. In this section we consider the difference between ex–ante and ex–post hedge ratios in the context of our example.

The portfolio manager used historical returns from July 7 to November 27, 1989 to estimate the hedge ratio of .8801. She applied this hedge ratio on November 28, 1989 and maintained the hedged position until February 22, 1990. The ex–post risk-minimizing hedge ratio was not available to her when she made her hedging decision on November 28, 1989. What would have been the ideal risk-minimizing hedge ratio, if she had complete knowledge about how prices would move from November 28, 1989 to February 22, 1990? To find this ex–post hedge ratio, we estimated equation 10.1 using data from November to February and found an ex-post hedge ratio of .9154. This implies a futures position of 51.61 contracts. We round this to 52 contracts. Figure 10.3 shows the results from hedging with the ex–ante and ex post hedge ratios.

In a world with perfect foresight, the ex-post hedge ratio is the risk-minimizing hedge ratio we would like to use. However, the ex–ante hedge ratio is the best estimate we can make at the time the decision must be implemented. As Figure 10.3 shows, the ex–ante hedge ratio performs quite well. The terminal value of the hedge with the ex–ante hedge ratio is $10,259,840. With the ex–post hedge ratio, the terminal value is $10,283,990. While the ex–ante hedge ratio performed well, the ex–post hedge ratio would have been even better. This is exactly the result that we would expect.

Altering the Beta of a Portfolio

Portfolio managers often adjust the CAPM betas of their portfolios in anticipation of bull and bear markets. If a manager expects a bull market, she

Figure 10.3
Ex–Ante versus Ex–Post Hedging Results

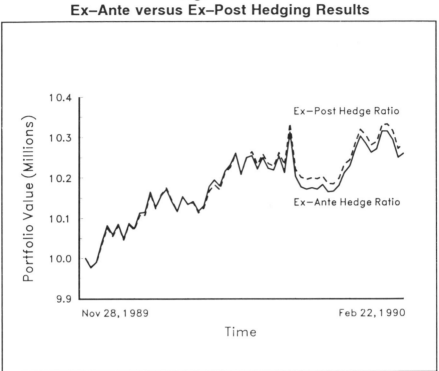

might increase the beta of the portfolio to take advantage of the expected rise in stock prices. Similarly, if a bear market seems imminent, the manager might reduce the beta of a stock portfolio as a defensive maneuver. If the manager trades only in the stock market itself, changing the beta of the portfolio involves selling some stocks and buying others. For example, to reduce the beta of the portfolio, the manager would sell high beta stocks and use the funds to buy low beta stocks. With transaction costs in the stock market being relatively high, this procedure can be expensive.

The portfolio manager has an alternative. She can use stock index futures to create a combined stock/futures portfolio with the desired response to market condition. In this section we consider techniques for changing the risk of a portfolio using stock index futures.

In the Capital Asset Pricing Model all risk is either systematic or unsystematic. **Systematic risk** is associated with general movements in the market and affects all investments. By contrast, **unsystematic risk** is particular to a certain investment or a certain range of investments. Diversification can almost completely eliminate unsystematic risk from a portfolio. The remaining systematic risk is unavoidable. Studies show that a random selection of 20 stocks will create a portfolio with very little unsystematic risk. Therefore, in this section we restrict our attention to portfolios that are well diversified and consequently have no unsystematic risk.

Starting with a stock portfolio that has systematic risk only and combining it with a risk-minimizing short position in stock index futures creates a combined stock/futures portfolio with zero systematic risk. According to the Capital Asset Pricing Model, a portfolio with zero systematic risk should earn the risk-free rate of interest. Instead of eliminating all systematic risk by hedging, it is possible to hedge only a portion of the systematic risk to reduce, but not eliminate, the systematic risk inherent in the portfolio. Similarly, a portfolio manager can use stock index futures to increase the systematic risk of a portfolio.

A risk-minimizing hedge matches a long position in stock with a short position in stock index futures in an attempt to create a portfolio whose value will not change with fluctuations in the stock market. To reduce, but not eliminate the systematic risk, a portfolio manager could sell some futures, but fewer than the risk-minimizing amount. For example, to eliminate half of the systematic risk, the portfolio manager could sell half of the number of contracts stipulated by the risk-minimizing hedge. The combined stock/futures position would then have a level of systematic risk equal to half of the stock portfolio's systematic risk.

It is also possible to trade stock index futures to increase the systematic risk of a stock portfolio. If a trader buys stock index futures, he increases his systematic risk. Therefore, if a portfolio manager holds a stock portfolio and buys stock index futures, the resulting stock/futures position has more systematic risk than the stock portfolio alone. For example, assume a portfolio manager buys, instead of sells, the risk-minimizing number of stock index futures. Instead of eliminating the systematic risk, the resulting stock/long futures position should have twice the systematic risk of the original portfolio.

We can illustrate this principle by considering the same data we used to illustrate the risk-minimizing hedge. In that example, the risk-minimizing futures position was to sell 50 contracts. Selling 50 contracts created a stock/futures position with zero systematic risk. By selling just 25 contracts, the portfolio manager could cut the systematic risk of the original portfolio in half. Similarly, by buying 50 contracts, the resulting stock/futures position would have twice the systematic risk of the original futures position.

Figure 10.4 shows the price paths of two portfolios over the 60 day hedging period from November 28, 1989 to February 22, 1990. First, the graph shows the unhedged portfolio. Its value begins at $10 million and terminates at $9,656,090, as we have seen. Over this period, the unhedged portfolio lost about $350,000. The graph also shows the portfolio created by holding the stocks and buying 50

Figure 10.4
Price Paths for Hedged and Unhedged Portfolios

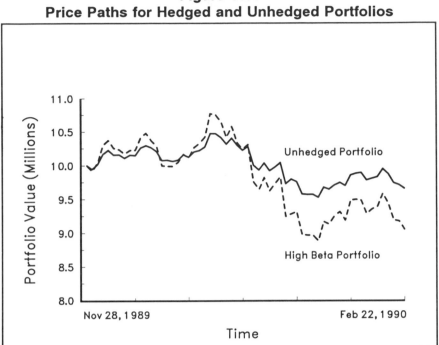

futures contracts. In our analysis of the risk-minimizing hedge, we found that the trader could minimize risk by selling 50 futures contracts. Buying 50 contracts doubles the systematic risk. The new portfolio of stock plus a long position of 50 contracts increases the sensitivity of the portfolio to swings in the stock market. In effect, holding the stock portfolio and buying stock index futures simulates more than 100 percent investment in the stock index. Stock prices in general fell during this 60-day period. For example, the all stock portfolio lost 3.44 percent of its value over this period.

By buying stock index futures, the portfolio manager would increase the overall sensitivity of the portfolio to changes in the stock market. Not surprisingly, then, the stock/long futures portfolio lost more than the pure stock portfolio. As Figure 10.4 shows, every move of the stock/long futures portfolio exaggerates the movement of the all stock portfolio. For the portfolio of stock plus a long position of 50 index futures, the terminal value is $9,052,340. This portfolio lost 9.48 percent of its value. However, as Figure 10.4 shows, for periods when the stock prices advanced from their initial level, the stock/long futures position rose even more. This is just what we expect, because buying futures increases the systematic risk of the existing stock portfolio.

Asset Allocation

In **asset allocation**, an investor decides how to divide funds among broad asset classes. For example, the decision to invest 60 percent in equities and 40 percent in T-bills is an asset allocation decision. The choice between investing in General Motors and Ford Motors is not an asset allocation decision. Thus, asset allocation focuses on the macro level commitment of funds to various asset classes and the shifting of funds among these major asset classes. In this section, we use the basic Cost-of-Carry Model to show how a trader can radically adjust an initial portfolio to move from equities to T-bills or from T-bills to equities by using stock index futures. Because these portfolio maneuvers radically change the type of asset the trader holds, the maneuvers implement asset allocation decisions.[17]

The basic Cost-of-Carry Model we have used since Chapter 3 asserts that the futures price equals the spot price times one plus the cost-of-carry under suitable market conditions:

$$F_0 = S_0(1 + C) \qquad\qquad 3.3$$

where:

F_0 = the futures price at t=0
S_0 = the spot price at t=0
C = the percentage cost of carrying the spot good from t=0 to the futures expiration

The cost-of-carry includes the financing cost of purchasing the asset, plus storage, insurance, and transportation. As we have seen in Chapter 3, for financial futures the cost-of-carry essentially equals the financing cost, because storage, insurance, and transportation are negligible. Therefore, in a full carry market, a cash-and-carry strategy of selling a futures and buying and holding the spot good until the futures expires should earn the financing rate, which essentially equals the risk-free rate of interest. We can express this relationship as:

$$\text{Short-Term Riskless Debt} = \text{Stock - Stock Index Futures} \qquad 10.2$$

Creating a Synthetic T–Bill

From the analysis in the preceding section, we see that the basic cash–and–carry strategy of holding the stock and selling futures gives a resulting stock/futures portfolio that mimics a T–bill. Of course, it does not create a real T–bill. Instead, the stock/futures portfolio behaves like a T–bill. We might say that the trader creates a synthetic T–bill by holding stock and selling futures.

Synthetic T–bill = Stock - Stock Index Futures

This synthetic T–bill is related to risk-minimizing hedging. In a minimum risk hedge, a trader sells futures against a stock portfolio to create a combined stock/futures portfolio that has no systematic risk. A portfolio with no systematic risk has an expected return that equals the risk-free rate. Thus, the position created by risk-minimizing hedging is essentially the creation of a synthetic T–bill.

Thus, consider the asset allocation decision of a trader with a stock portfolio. Assume the trader believes that a bear market is imminent and that the proper asset allocation decision is to hold no equities and to invest all funds in T–bills. The trader can sell all of the equities and invest the funds in T–bills. However, selling an entire portfolio can incur substantial transaction costs. Instead, the manager can implement the asset allocation decision by selling stock index futures against the portfolio. By implementing a risk-minimizing hedge, the manager creates a synthetic T–bill.

Creating a Synthetic Equity Position

It is also possible to use stock index futures to create a synthetic stock market position. Consider now a trader who holds all assets in T–bills. We assume that this trader expects a stock market surge, and she would like to take advantage of the rising stock prices. However, she is reluctant to incur all of the transaction costs associated with buying stocks. She too can implement her asset allocation decision by using stock index futures. Rearranging equation 10.2 shows how to create the risky stock position:

Synthetic Stock Portfolio = T–bills + Stock Index Futures

The trader can buy stock index futures and hold the futures in conjunction with T–bills to mimic a stock portfolio. Thus, she implements her asset allocation decision by trading stock index futures.

In our discussion of asset allocation, we have considered examples of using stock index futures to change from 100 percent stock investment to 100 percent

T-bill investment, and vice versa. Of course, the change in the portfolio does not need to be so radical. When we considered hedging, we saw that a trader can implement a risk-minimizing hedge or a transaction that shapes the risk of the portfolio. For example, by trading half of the risk-minimizing futures position, a trader could cut the systematic risk of the stock position in half. Similarly, by holding stock and buying stock index futures, the trader can increase the systematic risk of the position. The same principles apply to asset allocation decisions. For the trader with an initial stock position, selling half of the risk-minimizing number of futures results in a portfolio that behaves like a portfolio that is invested half in stock and half in T-bills. Similarly, a trader with a long position in stock who buys stock index futures creates a combined stock/futures portfolio that behaves like a leveraged stock portfolio.

Portfolio Insurance

As we have seen, traders can tailor the risk of a stock portfolio by trading stock index futures. For a given well-diversified portfolio, selling stock index futures can create a combined stock/futures portfolio with reduced risk. Holding a stock portfolio and buying stock index futures results in a portfolio with greater risk and expected return than the initial portfolio.

Portfolio insurance refers to a collection of techniques for managing the risk of an underlying portfolio. With most portfolio insurance strategies, the goal is to manage the risk of a portfolio to ensure that the value of the portfolio does not drop below a specified level, while at the same time allowing for the portfolio's value to increase. Portfolio insurance strategies are often implemented using options, as we will discuss in Chapter 13. However, stock index futures are equally important tools for portfolio insurance. Implementing portfolio insurance strategies using futures is called **dynamic hedging**. Although the mathematics of dynamic hedging are too complex for full treatment here, we can understand the basic idea behind portfolio insurance with stock index futures.

A Portfolio Insurance Example

Consider a fully diversified stock portfolio worth $100 million. The value of this portfolio can range from zero to infinity. Many investors would like to put a floor beneath the value of the portfolio. For example, it would be very desirable to ensure that the portfolio's value never falls below $90 million. Portfolio insurance offers a way to control the downside risk of a portfolio. However, in a financial market there is no free lunch, so it is only possible to limit the risk of a large price fall by sacrificing some of the potential for a gain. Portfolio insurance, like life insurance, is not free, but it may be desirable for some traders.

We have seen that a risk-minimizing hedge converts a stock portfolio to a synthetic T-bill. By fully hedging our example stock portfolio, we can keep the portfolio's value above $100 million. A fully hedged portfolio will increase in value at the risk-free rate, although full hedging eliminates all of the potential gain in the portfolio beyond the risk-free rate. In dynamic hedging, however, the trader holds the stock portfolio and sells some futures contracts. The more insurance the trader wants, the more futures he or she will sell.

Let us assume that a stock index futures contract has an underlying value of $100 million and a trader sells futures contracts to cover $50 million of the value of the portfolio. Thus, in the initial position, the trader is long $100 million in stock and short $50 million in futures, so 50 percent of the portfolio is hedged. Table 10.5 shows this initial position in the time zero row. At t=0, there has been no gain or loss on either the stock or futures. In the first period, we assume that the value of the stock portfolio falls by $2 million. The 50 futures contracts cover half of that loss with a gain of $1 million. Therefore, at t=1, the combined stock/futures portfolio is worth $99 million. Now the manager increases the coverage in the futures market by selling 5 more contracts. This gives a total of 55 short positions and coverage for 56 percent (55/99) of the total portfolio. In the second period, the stock portfolio loses another $2 million, but with 55 futures contracts, the futures gain is (55/99)$2 million = $1.11 million. This gives a total portfolio value of $98.11 million.

By t=4, the stock portfolio has fallen $10 million, but the futures profits have been $6.21 million. This gives a total portfolio value of $96.21 million. Also, the manager has increased the futures position in response to each drop in stock prices. At t=4, the trader is short 80 contracts, hedging 83 percent of the stock market portfolio. At t=5, the stock price drops dramatically, losing $35.86 million. The futures profit covers $30.65 million. This leaves a total portfolio

Table 10.5
Portfolio Insurance Transactions and Results

Time	Gain/Loss $ millions		Total Value	Futures Position	Portion Hedged
	Stocks	Futures			
0	0.00	0.00	100.00	−50	.50
1	−2.00	1.00	99.00	−55	.56
2	−2.00	1.11	98.11	−60	.61
3	−2.00	1.22	97.33	−70	.72
4	−4.00	2.88	96.21	−80	.83
5	−36.86	30.65	90.00	−90	1.00
6	−10.00	10.00	90.00	−90	1.00

value of $90 million. However, this is the floor amount of the portfolio, so the trader must now move to a fully hedged position. If the stock portfolio is only partially hedged, the next drop in prices can take the value of the entire portfolio below the floor amount of $90 million. At t=6, the price of the stocks drops $10 million, but the futures position fully covers the loss. Therefore, the combined portfolio maintains its floor value of $90 million.

Table 10.5 shows the basic strategy of portfolio insurance with dynamic hedging. Initially, the portfolio is partially hedged. If stock prices fall, the trader increases the portion of the portfolio that is insured. Had the stock portfolio risen in value, the futures position would have lost money. However, the loss on the futures position would have been less than the gain on the stocks, because the portfolio was only partially hedged. As the stock prices rose, the manager would have bought futures, thereby hedging less and less of the portfolio. Less hedging would be needed if the stock price rose, because there would be little chance of the portfolio's total value falling below $90 million.

Implementing Portfolio Insurance

By design, Table 10.5 is highly simplistic. First, it does not show how the starting futures position was determined. Second, it does not show how the adjustments in the futures position were determined. Third, it considers only large changes in the value of the stock portfolio. For instance, the smallest change in the Table is 2 percent of the stock portfolio's value. The exact answer to these questions is highly mathematical. However, we can explore these issues in an intuitive way.

Choosing the initial futures position depends on several factors. First, it depends on the floor that is chosen relative to the initial value of the portfolio. For example, if the lowest acceptable value of the portfolio is $100 million, then the manager must hedge 100 percent at t=0. Thus, the lower the floor relative to the portfolio value, the lower the percentage of the portfolio the manager will need to hedge. Second, the purpose of the insurance strategy is to guarantee a minimum terminal portfolio value while allowing for more favorable results. As a consequence, the futures position must take into account the volatility of the stock portfolio. The higher the estimated volatility of the stock portfolio, the greater the chance of a large drop in value that will send the total portfolio value below the floor. Therefore, the portion of the portfolio that is to be hedged depends critically on the estimated volatility of the stock portfolio. Of course, this will differ both across time and for portfolios of different risk.

Adjustments in the futures position depend upon the same kinds of considerations that determine the initial position. First, the value of the portfolio relative to the floor is critical. Second, new information about the volatility of the stock portfolio also affects the futures position. In Table 10.5, the volatility of the stock portfolio accelerates. Each percentage drop is larger than the previous. Therefore, this increasing volatility will lead to a larger short futures position than would otherwise be necessary.

In Table 10.5, the drops in the stock portfolio's values are large. In actual practice, dynamic hedging works by continually monitoring the value of the portfolio. Small changes in the portfolio can trigger small adjustments in the futures position. For many portfolios, monitoring and updating can occur many times a month. This is the reason it is called dynamic hedging—the hedge is monitored and updated continuously, often with computerized trading programs. Table 10.5 does not show that continual monitoring. Instead, we might take the different rows in the table as snapshots of the portfolio's value at different times.

Table 10.5 abstracts from some of the cash flow issues that dynamic hedging will raise. For example, it does not explicitly consider the cash flows that come from daily settlement of the futures position. There are a host of technical issues such as these that actual dynamic hedging must face.[18]

Index Futures
and Stock Market Volatility

The link between stock market volatility and stock index futures trading has become important in public policy debates. Some critics of index futures have already sought limitations of index trading on the principal grounds that index trading contributes to increased stock market volatility. As we will see, the evidence supporting this proposition is far from conclusive. However, even if it were proven that stock index futures trading did increase stock market volatility, is that bad? To most economists, price volatility results from the arrival of new information in the market. Traders receive new information that causes them to reassess the true value of the good being traded. In an efficient market, the price quickly adjusts to reflect this new information. One result of this process is volatility. Thus, economists often interpret volatile prices as evidence of a properly functioning and informationally efficient market. Under this view, volatility is good, not bad. Nonetheless, if stock index futures trading contributed to volatility in a way that was not tied to information or a properly functioning market, the futures trading could be deleterious to the market.

In this section we consider the links between stock index trading and stock market volatility. Even before the Crash of October 1987, critics of index futures trading claimed that the stock index futures market was responsible for an increase in the volatility of the stock market. In essence, the argument asserts that strategies such as program trading and portfolio insurance disrupt the stock market and cause stock prices to swing wildly as they are forced into alignment with stock index futures prices. We begin by considering the evidence on stock market volatility itself. While there may be a general perception of greater stock market volatility, the evidence on this issue is mixed. Next, we consider possible links between stock market volatility and stock index futures trading, particularly index arbitrage and portfolio insurance. Finally, we analyze the Crash of 1987 and the mini-crash of October 1989 to consider the impact of stock index futures on the stock market itself.

Has Stock Market Volatility Increased?

Here we consider whether there has been an increase in stock market volatility. While this may seem to be a fairly straightforward question, the evidence is mixed. These diverse conclusions stem in part from differences in the time periods examined. For instance, some studies compare volatility across the decades, while others focus on changes in volatility within the 1980s. Also, some studies consider volatility from month to month, others focus on day to day volatility, while still other articles examine volatility within a single day and ask whether this intra-day volatility is increasing.

Stock Volatility: The Long View.   Several studies have examined stock market volatility for periods of many decades, some even going into the last century. Table 10.6 summarizes the results of several recent studies. For the most

Table 10.6
Studies of Long–Run Stock Market Volatility

Study	Key Results
Becketti and Sellon (1989)	For monthly data from 1918–1988, 1930s were most volatile, and 1900s were not unusual. Frequency of large daily jumps in 1980s was higher than the 1960s and 1970s.
Jones and Wilson (1909)	For daily and monthly data for 1885–1989, no long–run tendency for volatility to increase over the decades. 1930s were most volatile. Volatility in 1980s was only somewhat higher than recent decades.
Fortune (1989)	For monthly data from 1926–1987, no long–term increase in volatility. Since WW II, perhaps a mild increase in volatility.
Schwert (1990)	For monthly data from 1834–1989, no tendency for stock market volatility to increase. The most volatile decade was the 1930s, by far.
Gerety and Mulherin (1990)	For the 1933–1989 period, found no tendency for volatility to increase. The 1930s was the most volatile decade, and October 1987 the most volatile single month.

part, these studies focus on monthly stock portfolio returns. The general conclusion is clear: there has been no tendency for stock market volatility to increase from decade to decade. The 1930s had the highest volatility in this century, but there is weak evidence that the 1980s were more volatile than other decades since World War II. Figure 10.5 depicts this long-run pattern of volatility.

Stock Volatility in the 1980s. Even if the 1980s were not more volatile than other decades, it is still possible that volatility increased within the decade. With the 1980s, we consider conclusions using daily data and intra-day data. Within the 1980s, October–December 1987 show high volatility. (The Crash occurred on October 19, 1987.) However, there appears to be no general tendency for volatility to have increased over the 1980s.

Figure 10.5
Index of Stock Market Volatility: 1927–1987

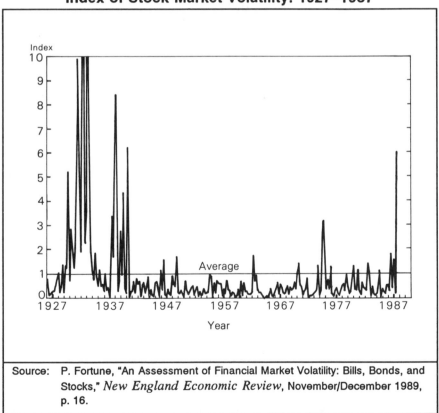

Source: P. Fortune, "An Assessment of Financial Market Volatility: Bills, Bonds, and Stocks," *New England Economic Review*, November/December 1989, p. 16.

Becketti and Sellon suggest that we distinguish normal volatility and jump volatility. The ordinary variability of stock returns, perhaps measured best by the standard deviation, is **normal volatility**. By contrast, **jump volatility** is the occasional extreme jump in prices. Figure 10.6 shows the frequency of large jumps in stock returns from 1962-1988.[19] Sellon and Becketti conclude that 1986-1988 exhibit high jump volatility, but they are quick to point out that this evidence does not suggest a permanent shift to a market with higher jump volatility. More data are needed to answer that question. Further, even in terms of jump volatility, the 1980s were not high compared to other decades before the 1960s. For example, only 4 of the 34 largest daily drops in 105 years occurred in the 1980s.[20] This is approximately the number of observations one would expect to find by chance.

Figure 10.6
Frequency of Jumps in Stock Returns, 1962–1988

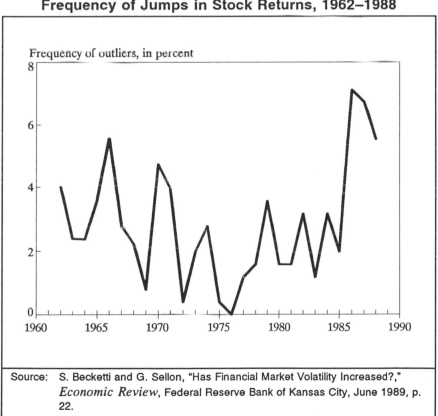

Source: S. Becketti and G. Sellon, "Has Financial Market Volatility Increased?," *Economic Review*, Federal Reserve Bank of Kansas City, June 1989, p. 22.

Schwert also considered intra-day data in his analysis of stock market volatility. He examined returns over 15-minute intervals for February 1, 1983–October 19, 1989. He found that October 19-31, 1987 and October 13, 1989 stood out. (Friday, October 13, 1989 was the date of the "mini-crash.") However, volatility quickly returned to normal levels after these episodes of high volatility. From this review of a century of stock prices, we can conclude that there has been no increase in long-term volatility. Jump volatility seems to have been high in 1986-1988 compared to the 1960-1988 period. However, jump volatility for the 1980s appears to be about normal compared to the rest of the century.

Do Stock Index Futures Cause Market Volatility?

There are two main practices in stock index futures trading that are alleged to cause stock market volatility. These are index arbitrage (particularly program trading) and portfolio insurance. Both practices contribute to volatility, critics say, because they quickly dump large orders on the market at critical times. These large orders can reinforce existing trends in prices, thereby contributing to stock market volatility. We consider each in turn.

Index Arbitrage and Stock Market Volatility. In index arbitrage, traders search for discrepancies between stock prices and futures prices. When the two prices differ from the Cost-of-Carry Model enough to cover transaction costs, index arbitrageurs sell the overpriced side of the pair and buy the underpriced. Typically, the arbitrageur holds the combined stock/futures position until expiration. At expiration, the cash settlement procedures for index futures guarantee that the stock and futures prices will converge. This convergence is guaranteed to hold at the open of trading on the expiration day, because the last futures settlement price is set equal to the opening cash market index value on that day. Some stock index futures also use the closing price as the final settlement price. In that case, to take advantage of convergence, index arbitrageurs often unwind their positions by entering market-on-close orders for the last trading day of the futures. A market-on-close order sells or buys a stock at the market price prevailing at the close of trading.

Consider now an index arbitrageur who is long stock and short futures. We assume that the futures settles based on the closing price and that the trader enters a market-on-close order to sell the stocks. Assume also that other arbitrageurs are also long stock and short futures and seek to unwind their positions in a similar manner. All of these stocks will come to market at the same time, so there could be an extremely large number of stocks to be sold all at once at the close of trading. Critics fear that this practice can lead to dramatic volatility in the market in a way that disrupts trading. Particularly, they fear that such high jump volatility might scare away some investors.

Notice that this effect occurs only if there is a substantial order imbalance among index arbitrageurs. There may be a very high level of index arbitrage with no serious order imbalance. Assume for a moment that, over the life of the futures, the stock and futures prices vary in being high or low relative to the Cost-of-Carry Model. Some traders will initiate their index arbitrage transactions by buying stocks, while others will arbitrage by selling stocks. At the expiration of the futures, the unwinding could result in roughly equal numbers of buy and sell orders for stocks. In such a situation, we would not expect index arbitrage to have any effect on prices, and it could not contribute to volatility.

Portfolio Insurance and Stock Market Volatility. Portfolio insurance can also contribute to potential order imbalances that might affect stock prices. From our example of a portfolio insurance trade in Table 10.5, we see that a drop in stock prices requires the portfolio insurer to sell additional stock index futures. Similarly, when prices rise, the insurer buys stock index futures. A potential problem for market volatility arises because portfolio insurance generates trading in the same direction that the market happens to be moving. Thus, portfolio insurance can contribute to the existing momentum of the market.

To see the potential effects of portfolio insurance in exacerbating an existing trend, assume that the stock and futures prices are tightly linked by the Cost-of-Carry Model. Due to this linkage, a drop in stock prices will quickly stimulate a drop in futures. The same transmission will occur from a drop in futures to a drop in stock prices. Now assume that there is a large drop in stock prices.

In response to the drop in stock prices, the futures price will have to fall. The Cost-of-Carry Model requires this adjustment. However, the drop in stock prices also stimulates a large number of orders from portfolio insurers to sell index futures. This is clear from our example in Table 10.5. Critics fear that the sell orders from portfolio insurers might temporarily depress the futures price below the price justified by the Cost-of Carry Model. Assuming this happens, stock prices must again fall to match the depressed futures price. Now, with this next drop in stock prices, the portfolio insurers must again sell futures. Critics of portfolio insurance fear that this selling-price fall-selling scenario could create a spiral of falling prices and more sell orders, putting the entire market into a tailspin that could be disastrous.

Summary. According to critics, unrestricted stock index futures trading can contribute to stock market volatility, or even panics, by creating order imbalances that force stock prices below the prices justified by economic fundamentals. For index arbitrage, the feared order imbalance is most likely to occur at the expiration of the futures. Critics fear that portfolio insurers will respond to a sudden drop in stock prices by dumping sell orders onto the stock index futures market, thereby depressing prices. These depressed prices will feed into the stock market causing another drop in prices. The portfolio insurer will again sell stock index futures, and perhaps help to create a downward price spiral. (On the other hand, if prices fall too much, the stocks will be cheap, and value-oriented investors will be attracted to buy. This buying would help to restore prices to their rational levels.)[21]

Volatility and Stock Index Futures Before the Crash

Long before the Crash of October 1987 and the mini-crash of October 1989, critics charged that stock index futures increased volatility. Here we consider the empirical evidence on this issue that is not related to the Crash or mini-crash. The Crash and crashlet we discuss later. We begin by considering the pre- and post-futures trading periods in general. Later, we consider the expiration days for the futures.

Volatility and the Introduction of Stock Index Futures. To determine whether stock index futures increase stock market volatility, some studies have compared the volatility of the stock market before and after the introduction of stock index futures in 1982. Santoni computed the means and standard deviations of percentage changes in the S&P 500 index before and after the introduction of S&P 500 futures in April 1982. Table 10.7 presents his key results. Focusing on the standard deviations, we see that weekly and daily standard deviations changed little. The weekly standard deviations rose slightly, while the daily standard deviations fell just a little. Neither difference is statistically significant. Santoni also considered intra-day variability and concluded that it fell slightly, but statistically significantly, after the introduction of the S&P 500 futures. Other studies have examined the issue using a similar approach. Table 10.8 summarizes some of these studies. Most of these studies find no increase in overall volatility after the introduction of futures trading. However, some do find increases in volatility for intra-day data.

Table 10.7
S&P 500 Index Statistics:
Before and After Futures Trading

	Before April 1982		After April 1982	
	Mean	Std. Dev.	Mean	Std. Dev.
Weekly	.130	1.68	.306	1.74
Daily	.004	0.95	.069	0.88

Source: G. Santoni, "Has Programmed Trading Made Stock Prices More Volatile?" *Review*, Federal Reserve Bank of St. Louis, May 1987, pp. 18–29.

Table 10.8
Studies of Volatility and the Start of Index Futures Trading

Study	Key Results
Santoni (1987)	No significant increase in daily or weekly S&P 500 volatility after futures trading began.
Edwards(1988a)	No significant increase in daily or intra–day S&P 500 volatility after futures trading began.
Edwards (1988b)	No significant increase in daily or intra–day S&P 500 or NYSE volatility after futures trading began.
Harris (1989)	Forms a control group of non–S&P 500 stocks to simulate S&P 500 stocks. Groups had same volatility before S&P 500 futures trading. After trading began, S&P 500 stocks were slightly more volatile.
Lockwood and Linn (1990)	For hourly returns on Dow Jones stocks, found increasing volatility after index futures began to trade.

This table does not report results for expiration days.

One study mentioned in Table 10.8 requires more explanation. The Harris study created a sample of stocks with the same volatility as the S&P 500 before futures trading began. After trading began, the S&P 500 stocks increased in relative volatility. This is an interesting approach, because it suggests that being in the index can make stocks riskier. This might be due to the futures trading on the index.[22]

While comparing pre–and post–index futures trading may shed some light on the volatility effect of futures trading, the technique has some dangers. For example, if volatility increases, might there be some other factor that explains the increase, such as inflation or deficits? Also, even if volatility does not change, it is still possible that stock index futures stimulated volatility and some other factors offset the increase in volatility caused by futures.[23]

Stock Volatility on Expiration Days. Even if index futures trading cannot be charged with a general increase in stock market volatility, it might still be associated with episodic increases in volatility—the jump volatility that Santoni considered. In particular, the unwinding of index arbitrage programs at the futures expiration might cause an order imbalance that could increase volatility. Accordingly, this section focuses on stock index futures and expiration day volatility.

In 1985–86, stock index futures, options on the stock index, and options on the stock index futures had common expiration dates four times per year and generally settled based on closing prices. (Now some instruments settle based on opening prices.) The convergence of these three expirations gave them the name

Table 10.9
Evidence on Expiration Day Volatility

Study	Key Results
Stoll and Whaley (1986)	Expiration day volume and volatility is greater, particularly in the last hour of trading.
Stoll and Whaley (1987)	Expiration day volume and volatility is greater, particularly in the last hour of trading.
Santoni (1987)	Expiration day volatility is not greater
Edwards (1988a)	Expiration day volatility is greater.
Edwards (1988b)	Expiration day volatility is greater.
Feinstein and Goetzmann (1988)	Expiration day volatility is greater.

of the **triple witching hour**—witching because of the fear of high volatility. For these expiration days, most studies find higher volatility than on other days. Table 10.9 summarizes some of the studies of expiration day volatility. For the most part, the higher volatility is concentrated in the last hour of trading. (Recall that this study covered a period when the final settlement price was determined at the close of trading. Now there is a trend for the opening price to be used as the final settlement price for the futures.)

Table 10.10 summarizes some key results from the Stoll and Whaley 1986 study of expiration day volatility. The Table shows the mean and standard deviation of returns computed from minute by minute price data. As the Table shows, the standard deviation was higher when the futures expired than when

Table 10.10
Expiration Day Stock Price Volatility
(Final Hour of Trading)

S&P 500	Expiring Instrument		
	Futures	CBOE S&P Options	Nothing
Mean	-.352	.026	.061
Std. Dev.	.641	.261	.211
Observ.	10	16	97

Source: H. Stoll and R. Whaley, "Expiration Day Effects of Index Options and Futures," New York University: Monograph Series in Finance and Economics, 1986.

nothing expired. However, when the CBOE S&P 100 Option expired, but the futures did not, the volatility is not significantly higher than days on which nothing expired. Also, stock prices tend to fall on expiration days. If we compare the behavior of the S&P 500 Index on expiration days with its behavior on non-expiration days, the price effect and the volatility effect are both statistically significant.

Figure 10.7, also drawn from the Stoll and Whaley study, illustrates the dramatic price movements that can occur as the futures expires. Figure 10.7 traces the minute by minute level of the S&P 500 index for the last 30 minutes of trading on December 20, 1985 and for the first 30 minutes on the next trading day. This figure gives a visual impression of the kinds of swings the index can take in a very short period of trading time. Stoll and Whaley found also that stock prices tend to rise in the first 30 minutes of trading on the first trading day after expiration. In summary, higher volatility does appear to be associated with futures expirations, particularly in the final hour of trading when many index arbitrage positions are being closed.[24]

Figure 10.7
Minute–By–Minute S&P 500 Index Values
(December 1985 Expiration)

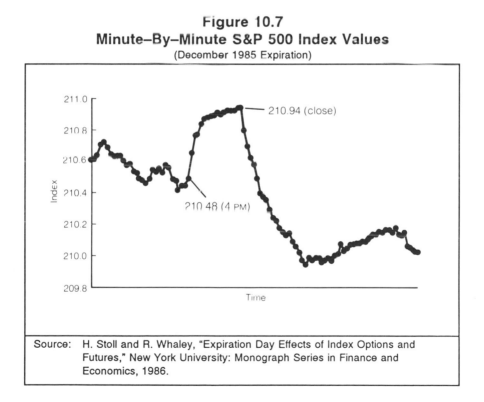

Source: H. Stoll and R. Whaley, "Expiration Day Effects of Index Options and Futures," New York University: Monograph Series in Finance and Economics, 1986.

Index Futures
and Stock Market Crashes

Even if futures expirations cause higher volatility for an hour once per quarter, the effect cannot be very serious. However, if futures are somehow responsible for market crashes, the matter has a completely different and more ominous character. In October 1987, the Crash led some to believe that the entire financial system was threatened. The events of October 19, 1987, touched off a series of debates and policy discussions that still continues. This section analyzes the relationship between stock index futures and stock prices during October 1987. Later we consider the mini-crash of October 13, 1989.

The Crash of October 19, 1987, is as controversial as it is dramatic. The Dow Jones Industrial Average lost 22.61 percent of its value that day. Trading volume was so heavy that it brought the trade processing divisions of brokerage houses to a virtual halt. During the day, it was often impossible to trade or even obtain accurate price quotations. In many respects, there was no stock market on that Black Monday. No sooner did trading cease than finger pointing started. Some fingers pointed at the trade deficit, while others pointed at the budget deficit. Still others pointed to the futures market as the cause of the crash. Here are a few choice quotations. Anis C. Wallace: "Investors knew that stocks were overpriced by any traditional valuation measure such as price/earnings ratios and price to book value. They also knew that the combination of program trading and portfolio insurance could send prices plummeting." David E. Sanger: "On Monday, October 19, Wall Street's legendary herd instinct, now embedded in digital code and amplified by hundreds of computers, helped turn a sell-off into a panic." Donald Regan: "In my mind, we should start by banning index option arbitrage and then proceed with other reforms which will restore public confidence in the financial markets." Marshall Front: "Futures and options are like barnacles on a ship. They take their life from the pricing of stocks and bonds. When the barnacles start steering the ship, you get into trouble, as we saw last week."[25]

In the aftermath of the crash, the government formed a presidential task force under Nicholas Brady, now Secretary of the Treasury, to study the crash and its causes. The report of the task force is widely known as the Brady Report. While most observers agree that the inability of cash markets to handle the incredible order flow contributed to the market turmoil, the Brady Report attributed the fall in prices to index arbitrage and portfolio insurance. This view of the Crash has become known as the **cascade theory**. According to the Brady Report, portfolio insurers sought to liquidate their equity exposure by selling stock index futures. This selling action drove futures prices below their equilibrium price. In terms of the Cost-of-Carry Model, the selling by portfolio insurers created a reverse cash-and-carry arbitrage. Seeing a profit opportunity, index arbitrageurs implemented reverse cash-and-carry strategies by buying futures and selling stocks. This action depressed prices further, and with new lower equity prices, portfolio insurers dumped more stock index futures, depressing prices still further. The vicious cycle was started. The repeated action of index arbitrageurs and portfolio insurers caused a downward "cascade" in prices. Thus, the Brady Report maintains that "mechanical, price-insensitive selling" by institutions was a key cause of the crash.[26]

The Stock/Futures Basis on October 19

The cascade theory, and thus the conclusions of the Brady Report, rest on the view that the stock/futures basis on October 19 was disrupted by the actions of "mechanical, price-insensitive" trading systems. Specifically, the Brady Report alleges that futures prices that day were too low relative to stock values. Therefore, the stock/futures basis becomes a critical empirical issue. The price relationships between stocks and stock index futures have been studied on a minute-to-minute basis for both the S&P 500 and the MMI.[27] Both markets reveal a similar story. At first glance, the usually tight relationship of the Cost-of-Carry Model apparently failed completely. However, in large part, this appearance was due to the inability to trade or even to know the current value of individual shares. For instance, even though the market opened at 9:30 New York time, some stocks did not trade for more than an hour. Among the MMI stocks, Exxon was the last one to start trading at 11:23. With stocks failing to trade in New York, traders were forced to use Friday prices as guides to Monday values. Such an estimate was, to say the least, imprecise.

Figure 10.8 shows the spread between the cash and futures using Chicago time. The extremely large difference at the open was due largely to the late opening of the individual stocks in New York. Until the stocks began to trade, there was no cash market for the traders in Chicago to use as a guide to proper values for the futures. However, it appears that the futures and stock did track each other with some accuracy during the middle of the day when prices were somewhat more available. The situation in the S&P 500 was similar. L. Harris summarizes: "Nonsynchronous trading explains part of the large absolute futures-cash basis observed during the crash. The remainder may be due to disintegration of the two markets."[28] Thus, even in the madness, the Cost-of-Carry Model was functioning with the available information. There was simply very little information flow. However, the stock/futures basis did seem to respond to the information that was available.

Figure 10.8
The MMI Spread, October 19, 1987

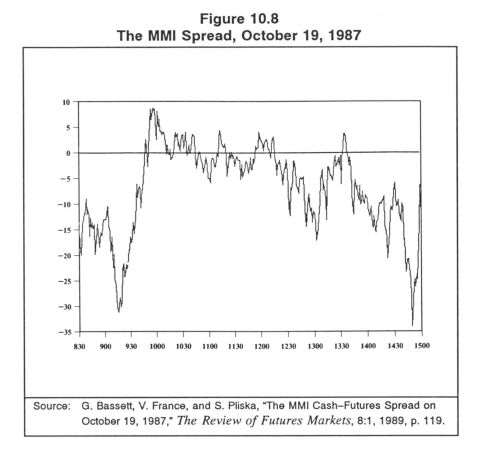

Source: G. Bassett, V. France, and S. Pliska, "The MMI Cash–Futures Spread on
October 19, 1987," *The Review of Futures Markets*, 8:1, 1989, p. 119.

Order Imbalance, Index Arbitrage, and Portfolio Insurance on October 19

Even if the basis held to the Cost-of-Carry Model as well as one could expect
given the dramatic events on October 19, there is still a residual concern about
the role of index arbitrage and portfolio insurance. That day, 16 firms accounted
for almost all stock index arbitrage and portfolio insurance trading. Twelve firms
concentrated on index arbitrage, while four focused on portfolio insurance. About
9 percent of NYSE volume was generated by index arbitrage trading. For stock
index futures, 12 to 24 percent of selling originated through portfolio insurance
activity.[29] As a percentage of activity, these numbers suggest the possibility that
futures related activity was large enough to significantly affect the day's trading.

One interesting piece of evidence comes from comparing S&P 500 stocks
with non–S&P 500 stocks. Blume, MacKinlay, and Terker found that S&P stocks

fell about seven percentage points farther than non-S&P 500 stocks on October 19. By mid-morning during the recovery on October 20, the difference had been almost eliminated. In other words, stocks in the S&P 500 fell more during the crash, but bounced back to parity with other stocks very quickly.[30] Also, Blume, MacKinlay, and Terker found that the fall in S&P 500 stock prices was positively correlated with order imbalances on October 19. With heavy sell orders awaiting execution, stock prices fell more than at other times. If this order imbalance was related to futures trading, then the futures market could share some responsibility for the drop in the market.

Some evidence appears to show that futures trading is not necessary to start a panic in a given market, but this theory does not really absolve futures of all responsibility. The Crash was a worldwide phenomenon, as Richard Roll points out.[31] Of 23 markets worldwide, 19 fell by more than 20 percent. Further, the Crash seems to have begun in non-Japanese Asian markets, spread to European markets, then North American, then Japanese. This progression took place around the clock as trading developed on October 19 and 20. Comparing market performance and the presence of computer-directed trading in isolation, Roll found that, if computer trading had any impact at all, it actually helped reduce the market decline.

The fact that the Crash started in markets with limited futures trading does appear to show that other factors were at work besides futures trading. This opens the possibility of a **contagion theory** of the Crash. A crash develops in one country's market for some unknown reason. News arrives in other markets carrying the disease of the crash, which helps a crash develop in the second market. This kind of contagion theory was developed by King and Wadhwani.[32]

Assume that the U.S. market is infected and a crash starts to develop. The U.S. crash is then intensified by order imbalance resulting from futures trading. Now other countries could catch the crash disease from the US in its more heightened and virulent form. Yet this does not seem to fit the facts for October 1987. First, the U.S. lost less than most other markets, both those that had crashed before and those that crashed later. Based on the version of the contagion theory just explained, we would expect the U.S. Crash to be deeper than that of countries that crashed earlier.

Summarizing the portion of evidence related to futures, the Crash did not start in the U.S., so the futures markets could not have been the original source of the problem. The Crash in the U.S. was not relatively more severe, even though futures markets are more developed in the U.S. than elsewhere. There was no tendency for the crashes in markets trading after the U.S. Crash to be more severe than crashes in markets trading before the U.S. Nonetheless, if futures contributed to the U.S. Crash and if the contagion theory has merit, then the U.S. Crash could have contributed to crashes that occurred later.

Thus, residual suspicion about the role of futures remains, even though, to date, there is no compelling evidence to show that futures trading, whether index arbitrage or portfolio insurance, caused the Crash.[33] Study continues and the issue remains controversial. However, there does seem to be fairly widespread rejection of the Brady Report's main conclusion that the Crash was caused by index arbitrage and portfolio insurance leading to a cascade in stock prices.[34]

Policy Recommendations and Changing Trading Rules

In proposals for reform, the Brady Report recommended that the regulatory system be modified to have a single agency, that there be a unified clearing system for all financial markets, that margins be consistent between cash and futures markets, and that information systems across markets be improved. The Report also recommended that exchanges implement **circuit breakers**—systems of planned trading halts—in times of volatility. There is continuing action on all of these fronts and much has already been implemented.[35]

In Chapter 2 we reviewed the struggle between the CFTC and the SEC for regulatory control over stock index futures. The Brady Report gave strong impetus to the SEC in this battle which continues without resolution. Chapter 2 also considered the issue of unified clearing. There we discussed intermarket cross-margining. Efforts to unify the margin system have been stimulated by the Crash and the Brady Report.

Since the Crash, circuit breakers have been put in place and refinements to the system continue. In essence, a circuit breaker is a planned de-coupling of the stock index futures market and the stock market through price limits and trading halts. The system also permits delaying program trades. The idea is to halt trading when prices fall below their fundamental values. During the pause in trading, the effect of mob psychology will dissipate, and when trading resumes, prices will return to rational levels. These circuit breakers are controversial and their value is unknown.

However, even if trading is halted, prices can continue to fall and traders will be stuck with additional losses. According to market lore, the worst fear of many traders is to be stuck in a position. Some scholars believe that trading halts may create more panic than calm and consequently assert that trading halts are unwise.[36] Nonetheless, futures markets already embody something like circuit breakers in the form of daily price limits. Also, defenders of circuit breakers believed they performed well in the mini-crash of October 13, 1989.

Probably the most controversial recommendation of the Brady Report is that there be "consistent margins" between stock and futures markets. This has been interpreted as calling for a large increase in futures margins. Such a policy would destroy the futures market as it now exists. According to defenders of futures, this policy recommendation betrays a complete lack of understanding of futures margins.[37] Futures margins are not a partial payment for a good as they are in the stock market. Instead, futures margins serve as a security bond for the changes in the futures price that day. The bond is payable daily and renewable daily. In the ensuing debate, margin levels have become a political football in the struggle between the CFTC and the SEC. Also, stock index margins have been raised by the futures exchanges in an apparent effort to deter any move for even higher margins. In defense of the futures margining system, it is important to realize that no customer funds were lost due to failure to meet margin calls and no clearinghouse failed because of the Crash.

The Mini–Crash of October 13, 1989

Almost exactly two years after the Crash, it seemed that history would repeat itself. On October 13, 1989, a Friday the thirteenth, stock prices began a sickening slide. That day, the Dow dropped 190 points, with a 135 point drop in the final hour of trading. This mini-crash provided an opportunity to test some of the procedures instituted after the Crash.

Falling prices triggered a circuit breaker at 2:15 p.m. for the MMI futures and at 3:07 p.m. on the S&P 500 futures. For both contracts, trading could resume only at prices above the price that triggered the circuit breaker. Trading resumed and the circuit breaker was hit again for the S&P 500. In assessing the performance of the circuit breakers, both the CFTC and the exchanges seem to feel that they performed well.[38] Further efforts to refine the system continue and the market awaits further, perhaps more severe, tests of the system.

Conclusion

This chapter reviewed a wide range of issues related to stock index futures. We began by examining stock index futures pricing. We considered the efficiency of the stock index futures markets, the effect of taxes on stock index futures prices, the influence of seasonal factors on prices, and leads and lags between the futures market and the stock market. Next, we considered a real-world example of program trading, focusing on an index arbitrage example. This example showed the hidden risks in the apparently riskless strategy of index arbitrage. We also reviewed the level of program trading in recent years.

To extend the introduction to hedging in Chapter 9, we worked through an example of minimum risk hedging in detail, and we considered the difference between ex-ante and ex-post hedge ratios. We also saw how to use a hedging approach to adjust the beta of a portfolio. Adjusting the beta by a small amount may be a hedging activity, but we also explored asset allocation using stock index futures. Using stock index futures, traders holding riskless bonds can simulate full investment in equities. Similarly, a trader fully invested in equities can use stock index futures to make the combined stock/futures portfolio behave like a riskless bond.

This chapter also focused on the connection between stock index futures and stock market volatility. As we saw, the main arguments for a connection rely on order imbalances that might be caused by index arbitrage or portfolio insurance. We saw some evidence of these order imbalances and increased volatilities on expiration days. Finally, we considered the Crash of 1987 and the mini-crash of 1989. Although futures do not appear to be responsible for the price changes observed on these days, the events have been important in changing the institutional arrangements in the futures market.

Questions and Problems

1. Explain the market conditions that cause deviations from a computed fair value price and that give rise to no-arbitrage bounds.

2. The No-Dividend Index consists only of stocks that pay no dividends. Assume that the two stocks in the index are priced at $100 and $48, and assume that the corresponding cash index value is 74.00. The cost of carrying stocks is 1 percent per month. What is the fair value of a futures contract on the index that expires in one year?

3. Using the same facts in problem 2, assume that the round-trip transaction cost on a futures is $30. The contract size, we now assume, is for 1,000 shares of each stock. Trading stocks costs $.05 per share to buy and the same amount to sell. Based on this additional information, compute the no-arbitrage bounds for the futures price.

4. Using the facts in problems 2 and 3, we now consider differential borrowing and lending costs. Assume that the 1 percent per month is the lending rate and assume that the borrowing rate is 1.5 percent per month. What are the no-arbitrage bounds on the futures price now?

5. Using the facts in problems 2-4, assume now that the short seller receives the use of only half of the funds in the short sale. Find the no-arbitrage bounds.

6. Consider the trading of stocks in an index and trading futures based on the index. Explain how different transaction costs in the two markets might cause one market to reflect information more rapidly than the other.

7. For index arbitrage, explain how implementing the arbitrage through program trading helps to reduce execution risk.

8. Index arbitrageurs must consider the dividends that will be paid between the present and the futures expiration. Explain how overestimating the dividends that will be received could affect a cash-and-carry arbitrage strategy.

9. Explain the difference between the beta in the Capital Asset Pricing Model and the beta one finds by regressing stock returns against returns on a stock index.

10. Explain the difference between an ex-ante and an ex-post minimum risk hedge ratio.

11. Assume you hold a well-diversified portfolio with a beta of 0.85. How would you trade futures to raise the beta of the portfolio?

12. An index fund is a mutual fund that attempts to replicate the returns on a stock index, such as the S&P 500. Assume you are the manager of such a fund and that you are fully invested in stocks. Measured against the S&P 500 index, your portfolio has a beta of 1.0. How could you transform this portfolio into one with a zero beta without trading stocks?

13. You hold a portfolio consisting of only T-bills. Explain how to trade futures to create a portfolio that behaves like the S&P 500 stock index.

14. In portfolio insurance using stock index futures, we noted that a trader sells additional futures as the value of the stocks falls. Explain why traders follow this practice.

Notes

1. D. Modest and M. Sundaresan, "The Relationship Between Spot and Futures Prices in Stock Index Futures Markets: Some Preliminary Evidence," *Journal of Futures Markets*, 3:1, Spring 1983, pp. 15-41.

2. B. Cornell and K. French, "Taxes and the Pricing of Stock Index Futures," *Journal of Finance*, 38:3, June 1983, pp. 675-694. B. Cornell, "Taxes and

the Pricing of Stock Index Futures: Empirical Results," *The Journal of Futures Markets*, 5:1, 1985, pp. 89-101.

3. Returns from Friday to Monday should be three times as great as the returns from one trading day to the next because funds are committed for three days instead of one.

4. B. Cornell, "The Weekly Pattern in Stock Returns: Cash Versus Futures: A Note," *Journal of Finance*, 40:2, June 1985, pp. 583-588.

5. E. Dyl and E. Maberly, "The Daily Distribution of Changes in the Price of Stock Index Futures," *The Journal of Futures Markets*, 6:4, Winter 1986 and E. Dyl and E. Maberly, "The Weekly Pattern in Stock Index Futures: A Further Note," *Journal of Finance*, 41:5, December 1986, pp. 1149-1152.

6. There is also a turn of the year effect. Stock returns tend to be higher in January than in any other month. In January, much of the returns are concentrated in the first few business days. R. Clark and W. Ziemba, "Playing the Turn-of-the-Year Effect with Index Futures," *Operations Research*, 35:6, November-December 1987, pp. 799-813, corroborates this effect in stock index futures. Clark and Ziemba argue that it is possible to exploit this opportunity by trading stock index futures spreads.

7. Joseph E. Finnerty and Hun Y. Park, "Stock Index Futures: Does the Tail Wag the Dog?" *Financial Analysts Journal*, 43:2, March-April 1987, pp. 57-61.

8. I. Kawaller, P. Koch, and T. Koch, "The Temporal Relationship between S&P 500 Futures and the S&P 500 Index," *Journal of Finance*, 42:5, December 1987, pp. 1309-1329 and "The Relationship Between the S&P 500 Index and S&P 500 Index Futures Prices," Federal Reserve Bank of Atlanta, *Economic Review*, May/June 1988, pp. 2-9.

9. A. Herbst, J. McCormack, and E. West, "Investigation of a Lead-Lag Relationship Between Spot Stock Indices and Their Futures Contracts," *The Journal of Futures Markets*, 7:4, 1987, pp. 373-381.

10. This example was the focus of a *Business Week* article, "A Real Life Strategy for Making 14% Risk-Free," April 7, 1986.

11. I. Kawaller, "A Note: Debunking the Myth of the Risk-Free Return," *The Journal of Futures Markets*, 7:3, 1987, pp. 327-331, analyzes some of the risk associated with index arbitrage. As the title of the article implies, the process of index arbitrage does not necessarily guarantee a totally risk-free return.

12. Stephen Bodurtha and Thomas Quinn consider a patient program trading strategy designed to minimize execution costs. They conclude that such a strategy can reduce execution costs and provide superior results. See S. Bodurtha and T. Quinn, "Does Patient Program Trading Really Pay?" *Financial Analysts Journal*, 46:3, May-June 1990, pp. 35-42.

13. I. Kawaller, "A Note: Debunking the Myth of the Risk-Free Return," *The Journal of Futures Markets*, 7:3, June 1987, pp. 327-331, provides an excellent discussion of these risk elements in index arbitrage. J. Merrick, Jr., "Early Unwindings and Rollovers of Stock Index Futures Arbitrage Programs: Analysis and Implications for Predicting Expiration Day Effects," *The Journal of Futures Markets*, 9:2, 1989, pp. 101-111, studies the possibility of terminating index arbitrage transactions before the contract expires. He finds that early termination can often provide even higher returns than holding the arbitrage position until expiration.

14. Data in this section are drawn from PaineWebber's, "Index Derivatives Monitor," various issues.

15. Strictly speaking, there is no return on a futures contract because a position in a futures contract requires no investment. By the futures return we mean the percentage change in the futures price.

16. For the same period, estimating the CAPM beta by regressing the portfolio's returns against the S&P 500 cash market returns gave $\beta_p = 1.0762$.

17. Asset allocation certainly has its critics. For instance, some critics charge that asset allocation is really nothing other than market timing in disguise. Asset allocation presumes that the trader can guess the next hot market sector. According to this view, the cost of this market timing is the loss of precious diversification plus the squandering of transaction costs. See P. Samuelson, "Asset Allocation Could Be Dangerous to Your Health," *Journal of Portfolio Management*, 16:3, Spring 1990, pp. 5-8.

18. The following articles introduce various aspects of portfolio insurance. For the most part, they are not highly mathematical. M. Rubinstein, "Alternative Paths to Portfolio Insurance," *Financial Analysts Journal*, 41:4, July–August 1985, pp. 42–52; F. Black and R. Jones, "Simplifying Portfolio Insurance," *Journal of Portfolio Management*, 14:1, Fall 1987, pp. 48–51; T. O'Brien, "The Mechanics of Portfolio Insurance," *Journal of Portfolio Management*, 14:3, Spring 1988, pp. 40–47; P. Abken, "An Introduction to Portfolio Insurance," *Economic Review*, Federal Reserve Bank of Atlanta 72:6, November/December 1987, pp. 2–25; H. Bierman, "Defining and Evaluating Portfolio Insurance Strategies," *Financial Analysts Journal*, 44:3, May–June 1988, pp. 84–87. The following articles are somewhat more technical or specialized, but of considerable interest. F. Gould, "Stock Index Futures: The Arbitrage Cycle and Portfolio Insurance," *Financial Analysts Journal*, 44:1, January–February 1988, pp. 48–62; J. Merrick, "Portfolio Insurance with Stock Index Futures," *The Journal of Futures Markets*, 8:4, 1988, pp. 441–455; R. Bookstaber and J. Langsam, "Portfolio Insurance Trading Rules," *The Journal of Futures Markets*, 8:1, 1988, pp. 15–31; Y. Zhu and R. Kavee, "Performance of Portfolio Insurance Strategies," *Journal of Portfolio Management*, 14:3, Spring 1988, pp. 48–54; J. Singleton and R. Grieves, "Synthetic Puts and Portfolio Insurance Strategies," *Journal of Portfolio Management*, 10:3, Spring 1984, pp. 63–69; M. Kritzman, "What's Wrong with Portfolio Insurance?" *Journal of Portfolio Management*, 13:1, Fall 1986, pp. 13–17. Finally, Donald L. Luskin, *Portfolio Insurance: A Guide to Dynamic Hedging*, New York: J. Wiley, 1988, contains a collection of interesting articles on portfolio insurance.

19. The definition used for large jumps is somewhat complex, but essentially a large jump is a daily return that is substantially larger than the typical change in prices.

20. C. Jones and J. Wilson, "Is Stock Price Volatility Increasing?" *Financial Analysts Journal*, 45:6, November–December 1989, pp. 20–26.

21. J. Hill and F. Jones, "Equity Trading, Program Trading, Portfolio Insurance, Computer Trading and All That," *Financial Analysts Journal*, 44:4, July–August 1988, pp. 29–38, provide a good discussion of the variants of these techniques. The paper provides a good taxonomy of the different mechanisms by which stock index futures trading might affect stock prices.

22. In a related study, S. Thosar and S. Trigeorgis examined changes in stock volatility as the stocks entered or left the S&P 500. They find a significant increase in volatility after stocks enter the S&P 500. This might be due to

the effects of program trading. See S. Thosar and S. Trigeorgis, "Stock Volatility and Program Trading: Theory and Evidence," *Journal of Applied Corporate Finance*, Winter 1990, pp. 91-96.

23. A. MacKinlay and K. Ramaswamy, "Index-Futures Arbitrage and the Behavior of Stock Index Futures Prices," *The Review of Financial Studies*, 1:2, Summer 1988, pp. 137-158, studied the relative volatility of futures and the index itself. They found that the futures is more volatile than the Cost-of-Carry Model implies and that this excess volatility increases for longer maturity futures.

24. To combat the volatility associated with the triple witching hour, the exchanges altered the expiration rules, beginning with the June 1987 expiration. Currently, S&P 500 stock index futures have their expiration value set in the morning on expiration day to give more time for index arbitrageurs to unwind their stock positions in an orderly manner. The NYSE is struggling to have the CBOE, the American Stock Exchange, and the Chicago Board of Trade change the expiration of their equity instruments to a morning expiration as well. H. Stoll, "Index Futures, Program Trading and Stock Market Procedures," *The Journal of Futures Markets*, 8:4, 1988, pp. 391-412 analyzes the decision to use the opening price as the settlement price. On balance, he finds it desirable because it allows the specialist to delay the opening until he or she finds traders to offset any temporary order imbalance. A. Herbst and E. Maberly, "Stock Index Futures, Expiration Day Volatility, and the Special Friday Opening: A Note," *The Journal of Futures Markets*, 10:3, 1990, 323-325, find that the new expiration procedures substantially reduce volume at expiration, but that it has not affected daily volatility.

25. All quoted in G. Santoni, "The October Crash: Some Evidence on the Cascade Theory," *Review*, Federal Reserve Bank of St. Louis, May/June 1988, pp. 18-33.

26. *Report of the Presidential Task Force on Market Mechanisms*, 1988, p. v. See also G. Santoni, "The October Crash: Some Evidence on the Cascade Theory," *Review*, Federal Reserve Bank of St. Louis, May/June 1988, pp. 18-33 for a thoughtful critique of the Brady Report. P. Tosini, "Stock Index Futures and Stock Market Activity in October 1987," *Financial Analysts Journal*, 44:1, January/February 1988, pp. 28-37 also discusses the cascade theory.

27. See L. Harris, "The October 1987 S&P 500 Stock-Futures Basis," *Journal of Finance*, 44:1, March 1989, pp. 77-99; G. Bassett, V. France, and S. Pliska, "The MMI Cash-Futures Spread on October 19, 1987," *The Review of Futures Markets*, 8:1, 1989, pp. 118-138; G. Wang, E. Moriarty, R. Michalski, and J. Jordan, "Empirical Analysis of the Liquidity of the S&P 500 Index Futures Market During the October 1987 Market Break," Commodity Futures Trading Commission Staff Working Paper #88-6, February 1989; G. Santoni, "The October Crash: Some Evidence on the Cascade Theory," *Review*, Federal Reserve Bank of St. Louis, May/June 1988, pp. 18-33.

28. L. Harris, "The October 1987 S&P 500 Stock-Futures Basis," *Journal of Finance*, 44:1, March 1989, p. 77.

29. These values are drawn from P. Tosini, "Stock Index Futures and Stock Market Activity in October 1987," *Financial Analysts Journal*, 44:1, January-February 1988, pp. 28-37.

30. M. Blume, A. MacKinlay, and B. Terker, "Order Imbalances and Stock Price Movements on October 19 and 20, 1987," *Journal of Finance*, 44:4, September 1989, pp. 827-848.

31. R. Roll, "The International Crash of October 1987," *Financial Analysts Journal*, 44:5, September-October 1988, pp. 19-35.

32. M. King and S. Wadhwani, "Transmission of Volatility Between Stock Markets," *The Review of Financial Studies*, 3:1, 1990, pp. 5-33.

33. The Office of Technology Assessment, U.S. Congress, studied the Crash and reported on it in its study, "Electron Bulls & Bears: U.S. Securities Markets & Information Technology," September 1990. The study concluded that the responsibility of futures for the Crash could not be resolved by statistical analysis.

34. Among those who reject the Brady Report conclusions of a futures induced cascade are: G. Santoni, "The October Crash: Some Evidence on the Cascade Theory," *Review*, Federal Reserve Bank of St. Louis, May/June 1988, pp. 18-33; J. Hill, "Program Trading, Portfolio Insurance, and the Stock Market Crash: Concepts, Applications and an Assessment," Kidder Peabody, January 1988; R. Roll, "The International Crash of October 1987," *Financial Analysts Journal*, 44:5, September-October 1988, pp. 19-35; D. Harrington, F. Fabozzi, and H. Fogler, *The New Stock Market*, Chicago:

Probus Publishing Co., 1990; M. Miller, B. Malkiel, M. Scholes and J. Hawke, "Stock Index Futures and the Crash of '87," *Journal of Applied Corporate Finance*, 1:4, Winter 1989, pp. 6-17.

35. James T. Moser, "Circuit Breakers," *Economic Perspectives*, Federal Reserve Bank of Chicago, September/October 1990, pp. 2-13, explains the role of circuit breakers and distinguishes volume-triggered, order-imbalance, and price-limit circuit breakers. Merton H. Miller, "Volatility, Episodic Volatility and Coordinated Circuit-Breakers," keynote address 2nd Annual Pacific-Basin Finance Conference, Bangkok, Thailand, June 1990, reviews the role of circuit breakers and finds that they are likely to be ineffective in reducing market volatility.

36. E. Fama, "Perspectives on October 1987, or, What Did We Learn from the Crash?" and R. Roll, "The International Crash of October 1987," *Financial Analysts Journal*, September-October, 1988, pp. 19-35. See also G. Schwert, "Stock Market Volatility," *Financial Analysts Journal*, 46:3, May-June 1990, pp. 23-34.

37. See, for example, M. Miller, B. Malkiel, M. Scholes, and J. Hawke, "Stock Index Futures and the Crash of '87," *Journal of Applied Corporate Finance*, 1:4, Winter 1989, pp. 6-17.

38. See "CFTC Reviews Friday the 13th," *Futures Industry Association Review*, November/December 1989, pp. 10-11.

11

Foreign Exchange Futures

Introduction

Foreign currencies are traded in both a highly active forward market and a futures market. The foreign exchange market is the only one in which a successful futures market has grown up in the face of a robust forward market. The forward market for foreign exchange has existed for a long time, but the foreign exchange futures market developed only in the early 1970s, with trading beginning on May 16, 1972 on the International Monetary Market (IMM) of the Chicago Mercantile Exchange (CME). Without doubt, the presence of such a strong and successful forward market retarded the development of a futures market for foreign exchange. This dual market system means that the futures market cannot be understood in isolation from the forward market. The conceptual bond arises both from the similarity of the two markets and from the fact that the forward market continues to be much larger than the futures market. Because many traders are active in both markets, familiar cash-and-carry and reverse cash-and-carry strategies ensure that the proper price relationships between the two markets are maintained.

As discussed in Chapter 3, forward and futures markets for a given commodity are similar in many respects. Because of this similarity, specific price relationships must hold between the two markets to prevent arbitrage opportunities. While any observer might be more impressed by the similarities in the two markets, the forward and futures markets differ in several key respects. Particularly important are the differences in the cash flow patterns (due to daily resettlement in the futures market) and the different structures of the contracts with respect to their maturities.

To understand foreign exchange futures trading, this chapter begins with a brief discussion of the markets for foreign exchange: the spot, forward, and futures markets. Next, we review the most important factors in determining exchange rates between two currencies, including the exchange rate regimes of fixed versus floating rates, the question of devaluation, and the influence of balance-of-payments. Against this institutional background, we analyze no-arbitrage pricing relationships, such as the Interest Rate Parity Theorem (IRP) and the Purchasing Power Parity Theorem (PPP). These theorems essentially express the pricing relationship of the Cost-of-Carry Model. We also examine the relationship between forward and futures prices and the accuracy of foreign exchange forecasting. As always in the futures market, the twin issues of speculation and hedging play an important role, and we consider them in detail.

Price Quotations

In the foreign exchange market, every price, or exchange rate, is a relative price. To say that one dollar is worth 2.5 Deutschemarks (DM 2.5) also implies that DM 2.5 will buy $1.00, or that DM 1 is worth $.40. All foreign exchange rates are related to each other as reciprocals, a relationship that is quite apparent in Figure 11.1, which shows the foreign exchange quotations as they appear daily in *The Wall Street Journal*. The quotations consist of two double columns of rates, one for the U.S. Dollar Equivalent of the foreign currency and one set of two columns for the amount of foreign currency per U.S. dollar. Each set of quotations shows the rates for the current and the preceding business day. We focus only on the two columns of current quotations. The rate in one column has its reciprocal in the other column. (Sometimes these are not exact due to transaction costs.) The value of $/DM($ per DM) is just the reciprocal of the value of DM/$(DM per $). For some countries, such as Australia, the quotations show only the spot rate, the rate at which Australian and U.S. dollars may be exchanged at the moment.

For many major currencies, such as those of Germany, England, Japan, and Canada, the quotations show forward rates for periods of 30, 90, and 180 days into the future. The 30-day forward rate, for example, indicates the rate at which a trader can contract today for the delivery of some foreign currency 30 days hence. If the trader buys the foreign currency, then he or she agrees to pay the 30-day forward rate in 30 days for the currency in question, with the actual transaction taking place in 30 days. This kind of transaction exactly fits the description of forward markets in Chapter 1.

The quotations shown in Figure 11.1 are provided by Bankers' Trust Company, a major participant in the foreign exchange market. The market from which these quotations are drawn is made up of large banks in the U.S. and abroad. This market is known as the **interbank market**. As Figure 11.1 notes, the quotations pertain to transactions in amounts of $1 million or more. As is typical of forward markets, there is no physical location where trading takes place. Instead, banks around the world are linked electronically with each other.

Figure 11.1
Foreign Exchange Quotations

EXCHANGE RATES

Thursday, October 18, 1990

The New York foreign exchange selling rates below apply to trading among banks in amounts of $1 million and more, as quoted at 3 p.m. Eastern time by Bankers Trust Co. Retail transactions provide fewer units of foreign currency per dollar.

Country	U.S. $ equiv. Thurs.	U.S. $ equiv. Wed.	Currency per U.S. $ Thurs.	Currency per U.S. $ Wed.
Argentina (Austral) ...	.0001859	.0001842	5380.00	5429.00
Australia (Dollar)	.7705	.7763	1.2979	1.2882
Austria (Schilling)	.09483	.09385	10.55	10.66
Bahrain (Dinar)	2.6532	2.6532	.3769	.3769
Belgium (Franc)				
Commercial rate	.03240	.03210	30.86	31.15
Brazil (Cruzeiro)	.01097	.01107	91.18	90.31
Britain (Pound)	1.9701	1.9605	.5076	.5101
30-Day Forward	1.9602	1.9510	.5102	.5126
90-Day Forward	1.9438	1.9334	.5145	.5172
180-Day Forward	1.9214	1.9120	.5205	.5230
Canada (Dollar)	.8540	.8558	1.1710	1.1685
30-Day Forward	.8508	.8526	1.1754	1.1729
90-Day Forward	.8450	.8471	1.1835	1.1805
180-Day Forward	.8375	.8395	1.1940	1.1912
Chile (Official rate)	.003046	.003046	328.35	328.35
China (Renmimbi)	.211864	.211864	4.7200	4.7200
Colombia (Peso)	.001912	.001912	523.00	523.00
Denmark (Krone)	.1750	.1732	5.7156	5.7736
Ecuador (Sucre)				
Floating rate	.001168	.001168	856.00	856.00
Finland (Markka)	.28149	.27952	3.5525	3.5775
France (Franc)	.19906	.19726	5.0235	5.0695
30-Day Forward	.19877	.19697	5.0309	5.0769
90-Day Forward	.19818	.19639	5.0459	5.0919
180-Day Forward	.19723	.19543	5.0703	5.1168
Germany (Mark)	.6671	.6611	1.4990	1.5127
30-Day Forward	.6670	.6610	1.4992	1.5129
90-Day Forward	.6665	.6604	1.5003	1.5142
180-Day Forward	.6653	.6592	1.5031	1.5170
Greece (Drachma)	.006623	.006555	151.00	152.55
Hong Kong (Dollar) ...	.12858	.12866	7.7770	7.7725
India (Rupee)	.05556	.05556	18.00	18.00

Source: *The Wall Street Journal*, October 19, 1990.

The large banks in the market have trading rooms elaborately equipped with electronic communications devices. A trader in such a room may have access to 60 telephone lines and five or more video quotation screens.[1] The market has no regular trading hours and is open somewhere in the world 24 hours per day. In addition to banks, some large corporations have access to the market through their own trading rooms.

Regional banks are unlikely to have their own trading rooms. Instead, they clear their foreign exchange transactions through correspondent banks with whom they have the appropriate arrangements. Corporations that are too small to have their own trading room, as well as individuals, make foreign exchange transactions through their own banks. As Figure 11.1 notes, the rates quoted are not available to small retail traders. Instead, retail transactions will be subject to a larger bid-asked spread that allows the bank providing the foreign exchange service to make a profit.

Geographical and Cross-Rate Arbitrage

A number of pricing relationships exist in the foreign exchange market, the violation of which would imply the existence of arbitrage opportunities. The first two to be considered involve **geographical arbitrage** and **cross-rate arbitrage**. One of the best ways to learn about the relationships that must exist among currency prices is to explore the potential arbitrage opportunities that arise if the pricing relationships were violated.

Geographical arbitrage occurs when one currency sells for two prices in two different markets. Such pricing would be a simple violation of the law of one price. As an example, consider the following exchange rates between German marks and U.S. dollars as quoted in New York and Frankfurt. These are 90-day forward rates.

New York	$/DM	.42
Frankfurt	DM/$	2.35

The New York price, quoted as $ per DM, implies a DM/$ price equal to the inverse of the $/DM price:

$$\frac{1}{.42} = DM/\$ = 2.381$$

In New York, the DM/$ rate is 2.381, but in Frankfurt, it is 2.35. Since these are not equal, an arbitrage opportunity exists. To test for a geographical arbitrage opportunity, simply take the inverse of the price prevailing in one market and compare it with the price quoted in another market.

To conduct the arbitrage, the trader purchases the currency where it is cheap and sells it where it is expensive. In New York, a trader receives 2.381 DM per dollar, but only 2.35 DM per dollar in Frankfurt. Therefore, the DM is cheaper in New York. To exploit this pricing discrepancy, the trader transacts as shown in Table 11.1. These transactions represent the exploitation of an arbitrage opportunity since they ensure a profit with no investment. At the outset, there is no cash flow. The only cash flow involved in the transactions occurs simultaneously when the commitments initiated at t=0 are completed at t=90. The profit, however, was certain from the time of the initial transactions.

Table 11.1
Geographical Arbitrage

This is an arbitrage transaction since it has a certain profit with no investment. Notice that the arbitrage is not complete until the transactions at t = 90 are completed.

t = 0 (the present)
Buy DM 1 in New York 90 days forward for $.42
Sell DM 1 in Frankfurt 90 days forward for $.4255.

t = 90
Deliver DM 1 in Frankfurt; collect $.4255.
Pay $.42; collect DM 1.

	Profit	$.4255
		− .4200
		$.0055

Arbitrage is also possible to exploit misalignments in cross-rates. To understand a cross-rate, consider the following example. In New York, an exchange rate is quoted for the dollar versus the German mark. There is also a rate quoted for the dollar versus the British pound. Together, these two rates imply an equilibrium exchange rate between the German mark and the British pound. This implied exchange rate is a **cross-rate**. Therefore, the exchange rates in New York involving the dollar imply an exchange rate between the mark and pound that do not involve the dollar. Figure 11.2 shows quotations for cross-rates from *The Wall Street Journal*.

If the direct rate quoted elsewhere for the mark versus the pound does not match the cross-rate in New York, an arbitrage opportunity exists. As an example, assume that the following rates are observed, where SF indicates the Swiss franc, and all of the rates are 90-day forward rates:

New York	$/DM	.42
	$/SF	.49
Frankfurt	DM/SF	1.2

The exchange rates quoted in New York imply the following cross-rate in New York for the DM/SF:

$$DM/SF = \left(\frac{1}{\$/DM}\right)\$/SF = \left(\frac{1}{.42}\right).49 = 1.167$$

Figure 11.2
Cross Rates

Key Currency Cross Rates Late New York Trading Oct. 18, 1990

	Dollar	Pound	SFranc	Guilder	Yen	Lira	D-Mark	FFranc	CdnDlr
Canada	1.1693	2.3041	.92838	.69312	.00940	.00104	.78083	.23309	......
France	5.0165	9.885	3.9829	2.9736	.04035	.00447	3.3499		4.2902
Germany	1.4975	2.9508	1.1890	.88767	.01204	.00133		.29851	1.2807
Italy	1121.8	2210.4	890.63	664.94	9.022		749.08	223.61	959.3
Japan	124.33	244.99	98.714	73.699		.11084	83.025	24.784	106.33
Netherlands ..	1.6870	3.3242	1.3394		.01357	.00150	1.1265	.33629	1.4427
Switzerland ...	1.2595	2.4818		.74659	.01013	.00112	.84107	.25107	1.0771
U.K.	.50749		.40293	.30082	.00408	.00045	.33889	.10116	.43401
U.S.		1.9705	.79397	.59277	.00804	.00089	.66778	.19934	.85521

Source: Telerate

Source: *The Wall Street Journal*, October 19, 1990.

Because the rate for the directly quoted DM/SF in Frankfurt differs from the cross-rate quoted in New York, an arbitrage opportunity exists. To exploit the arbitrage opportunity, one can trade only the exchange rates actually shown. For example, in New York there may not be a market for DM in terms of the Swiss franc.[2] To exchange DM to SF in the New York market involves two transactions. First, a trader sells DM for $ and then buys SF with $.

To know how to trade, one must know which currency is relatively cheaper in a given market. In New York one receives DM 1.167 per SF, but in Frankfurt SF 1 is worth DM 1.2. The DM, therefore, is cheaper in Frankfurt than in New York. Table 11.2 shows the transactions required to conduct the arbitrage.

Forward and Futures Market Characteristics

The institutional structure of the foreign exchange futures market resembles that of the forward market, with a number of notable exceptions. While the forward market is a worldwide market with no particular geographical location, the principal futures market is the International Monetary Market (IMM) of the Chicago Mercantile Exchange (CME).[3] In the futures market, contracts trade on the most important currencies, such as the German mark, the British pound, the Canadian dollar, the Swiss franc, and the Japanese yen. All of the contracts trade

---

Table 11.2
Cross–Rate Arbitrage Transactions

t = 0 (the present)

    Sell SF 1 90 days forward in Frankfurt for DM 1.2.
    Sell DM 1.2 90 days forward in New York for $.504.
    Sell $.504 90 days forward in New York for SF 1.0286.

t = 90 (delivery)

    Deliver SF 1 in Frankfurt; Collect DM 1.2.
    Deliver DM 1.2 in New York; Collect $.504.
    Deliver $.504 in New York; Collect SF 1.0286.

Profit:
SF 1.0286
− 1.0000
SF .0286

---

on the MAR, JUN, SEP, DEC cycle with expiration on the third Wednesday of the expiration month. By contrast, forward market quotations are stated for a given number of days into the future.[4] In the futures market, the exchange determines the maturity date of each contract. With each passing day, the futures expiration comes one day closer. In the forward market, contracts for expiration 30, 90, and 180 days into the future are available each trading day. In the futures market, contracts mature on only four days of the year; in the forward market, contracts mature every day. In the forward market, contract size is negotiated. In the futures market, the rules of the exchange determine the contract size. Table 11.3 summarizes the differences between forward and futures markets for foreign exchange. The most important differences are the standardized contract, the standardized delivery dates, the differences in daily cash flows, and the differences in the ways contracts are closed. It is particularly interesting to note that less than 1 percent of all foreign exchange futures are completed by delivery, but delivery occurs on more than 90 percent of all forward contracts.

    The forward market for foreign exchange dates back to beyond the reaches of history, while the futures market began only in the 1970s. The major center for the forward market continues to be London, but New York has been gaining in importance as the market for foreign exchange in the U.S. has grown rapidly. While foreign currency futures trading has grown dramatically, the forward market still dwarfs the futures market by a factor of about 20 to one, as measured by the U.S. dollar volume of trading. Since banks are the major participants in the forward market, it is not too surprising that their level of activity in the futures market is rather limited.

Table 11.3
Futures vs. Forward Markets

	Forward	Futures
Size of Contract	Tailored to individual needs.	Standardized.
Delivery Date	Tailored to individual needs.	Standardized.
Method of Transaction	Established by the bank or broker via telephone contract with limited number of buyers and sellers.	Determined by open auction among many buyers and sellers on the exchange floor.
Participants	Banks, brokers and multi–national companies. Public speculation not encouraged.	Banks, brokers and multinational companies. Qualified public speculation encourag-ed.
Commissions	Set by "spread" between bank's buy and sell price. Not easily determined by customer.	Published small brokerage fee and negotiated rates on block trades.
Security Deposit	None as such, but compen-sating bank balances re-quired.	Published small security deposit required.
Clearing Operation (Financial Integrity)	Varies across individual banks and brokers. No sepa-rate clearinghouse function.	Handled by exchange clear-inghouse. Daily settlements to the market.
Marketplace	Over the telephone world-wide.	Central exchange floor with worldwide communications.
Economic Justification	Facilitate world trade by pro-viding hedge mechanism.	Same as forward market. In addition, it provides a broader market and an alternative hedging mechanism via pub-lic participation.
Accessibility	Limited to very large custom-ers who deal in foreign trade.	Open to anyone who needs hedge facilities, or has risk capital with which to specu-late.
Regulation	Self–regulating.	April 1975—Regulated under the Commodity Futures Trading Commission.
Frequency of Delivery	More than 90% settled by actual delivery.	Less than 1% settled by actual delivery.
Price Fluctuations	No daily limit.	No daily limit.
Market Liquidity	Offsetting with other banks.	Public offset. Arbitrage offset.

Source: IMM, "Understanding Futures in Foreign Exchange Futures," pp. 6–7.

Figure 11.3 shows foreign exchange futures price quotations. The columns of quotations follow the pattern set for other types of contracts, showing the open, high, low, and settlement prices, and the change in the settlement price since the preceding day. The next two columns present the high and low lifetime prices for each contract, while the final column shows the open interest in each contract. The final line of data for each contract shows the estimated volume of the current day, the actual volume of the preceding day, the current open interest across all contract maturities for each contract, and the change in the open interest since the preceding day.

While the price quotations for each currency are similar, there are some differences. First, different contracts trade a different number of units of the foreign currency. For instance, one contract is for 12.5 million yen but only

Figure 11.3
Foreign Exchange Futures Quotations

FUTURES

	Open	High	Low	Settle	Change	Lifetime High	Low	Open Interest
JAPANESE YEN (IMM) 12.5 million yen; $ per yen (.00)								
Dec	.8007	.8046	.7957	.8030	+ .0066	.8046	.6290	70,923
Mr91	.8005	.8040	.7961	.8027	+ .0066	.8040	.6315	5,028
June	.8010	.8010	.8010	.8022	+ .0066	.8010	.6641	126

Est vol 44,347; vol Wed 44,321; open-int 76,077, −1,675.

	Open	High	Low	Settle	Change	Lifetime High	Low	Open Interest
DEUTSCHEMARK (IMM)−125,000 marks; $ per mark								
Dec	.6620	.6685	.6600	.6678	+ .0076	.6685	.5764	60,631
Mr91	.6605	.6675	.6595	.6667	+ .0076	.6675	.5820	2,121

Est vol 42,033; vol Wed 37,760; open int 62,810, −1,390.

	Open	High	Low	Settle	Change	Lifetime High	Low	Open Interest
CANADIAN DOLLAR (IMM)−100,000 dlrs.; $ per Can $								
Dec	.8468	.8492	.8411	.8478	− .0013	.8734	.8050	19,635
Mr91	.8388	.8410	.8325	.8397	− .0013	.8665	.7990	4,572
June	.8300	.8315	.8290	.8324	− .0013	.8576	.7995	1,750
Sept	.8260	.8260	.8215	.8266	− .0013	.8530	.7985	1,285

Est vol 14,868; vol Wed 11,591; open int 27,245, +298.

	Open	High	Low	Settle	Change	Lifetime High	Low	Open Interest
BRITISH POUND (IMM)−62,500 pds.; $ per pound								
Dec	1.9408	1.9560	1.9330	1.9542	+.0128	1.9638	1.5640	29,080
Mr91	1.9200	1.9320	1.9094	1.9300	+.0126	1.9400	1.6580	1,933

Est vol 22,168; vol Wed 15,717; open int 31,019, +176.

	Open	High	Low	Settle	Change	Lifetime High	Low	Open Interest
SWISS FRANC (IMM)−125,000 francs-$ per franc								
Dec	.7868	.7950	.7833	.7945	+ .0089	.7965	.6300	35,173
Mr91	.7869	.7945	.7830	.7942	+ .0091	.7950	.6500	1,565
June	....	....		.7938	+ .0092	.7930	.7065	122

Est vol 36,668; vol Wed 28,641; open int 36,910, −419.

	Open	High	Low	Settle	Change	Lifetime High	Low	Open Interest
AUSTRALIAN DOLLAR (IMM)−100,000 dlrs.; $ per A.$								
Dec	.7630	.7662	.7629	.7655	− .0046	.8300	.7570	1,928

Est vol 635; vol Wed 881; open int 1,955, +17.

	Open	High	Low	Settle	Change	Lifetime High	Low	Open Interest
U.S. DOLLAR INDEX (FINEX) 500 times USDX								
Dec	82.90	83.20	82.20	82.26	− .76	96.46	82.20	3,259

Est vol 3,708; vol Wed 1,438; open int 3,468, +23.
The index: High 82.78; Low 81.97; Close 81.98 −.67

Source: *The Wall Street Journal*, October 19, 1990.

125,000 marks. The difference in quantity reflects the vast difference in the value between a single mark and a single yen. In 1990, one U.S. dollar was worth more than 100 yen but less than two marks. Notice also that the quotations for the yen have two zeroes suppressed.

The foreign exchange futures market has grown rapidly, as depicted by Figure 11.4. From a level of only 199,920 contracts in 1975, the total trading volume on foreign exchange futures climbed to just over 26 million by 1989. Figure 11.5 shows the share of volume for each currency in 1989.[5]

Determinants of Foreign Exchange Rates

As with almost any good, fundamental factors shape the exchange rate that prevails between the currencies of two countries. These factors are numerous and quite complex, with entire books being written on the subject. Consequently, the brief discussion that follows merely indicates some of the most important

Figure 11.4
Growth in Trading in Foreign Exchange Futures

Figure 11.5
Market Share for Foreign Currencies Futures in 1989

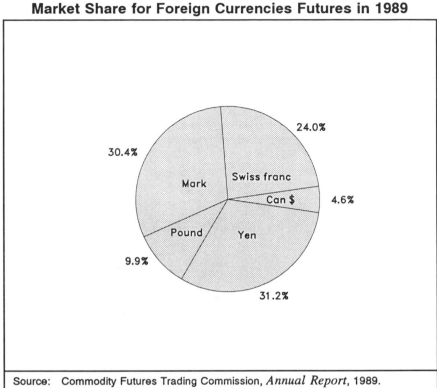

24.0%

30.4%

Swiss franc

Mark

Can $ 4.6%

Pound   Yen

9.9%

31.2%

Source: Commodity Futures Trading Commission, *Annual Report*, 1989.

influences on exchange rates. One way of thinking about currencies is to regard them as essentially similar to other assets, subject to the same basic laws of supply and demand. When a particular currency is unusually plentiful, its price might be expected to fall. Of course, the price of a given currency, in terms of some other currency, is merely the exchange rate between the two currencies. In foreign exchange, the flow of payments between residents of one country and the rest of the world gives rise to the concept of a balance of payments.[6] The balance of payments is generally calculated on a yearly basis. If expenditures by a particular country exceed receipts, then that country has a deficit in its balance of payments; if receipts exceed expenditures, then the country has a surplus. The balance of payments encompasses all kinds of flows of goods and services among nations, including the movement of real goods, services, international investment, and all types of financial flows.

To illustrate how the balance of payments influences exchange rates, consider the following example. A country, Importeria, trades with other countries and always imports more goods than it exports. This means that there is always a net flow of real goods into Importeria. Importeria must pay for these goods in some way, so we assume that the government of Importeria simply prints additional currency to pay for the excess goods that it imports. Such a practice must eventually cause a change in the exchange rates between Importeria and its trading partners. As the trading partners continue to send more and more goods to Importeria, they collectively have fewer and fewer real goods themselves, but a growing supply of the currency of Importeria.

As the world's supply of Importeria's currency swells, it becomes apparent that it has only a few uses. It can be used to acquire other currencies, or it can be used to purchase goods from Importeria. However, the accumulation of Importeria's currency continues until there is an excess supply at the prevailing exchange rate, so the value of Importeria's currency must fall. Just as Importeria cannot continually import more than it exports without causing the value of its currency to fall, no country can continually consume more than it creates without eventually causing a fall in the value of its currency.

Fixed Exchange Rates

The currency adjustment that Importeria might have to suffer depends on the international exchange rate system. For most of the history of the United States, there has been a system of **fixed exchange rates**. A fixed exchange rate is a stated exchange rate between two currencies at which anyone may transact. A country, such as Importeria, might import more than it exports for quite some time without causing a change in the fixed exchange rate. However, even fixed exchange rates are only fixed in the short run, and they are subject to periodic adjustments. For Importeria, the continual excess of imports over exports puts pressure on the value of Importeria's currency as the world supply of Importeria's currency continues to grow. Eventually, the fixed exchange rate between Importeria's currency and that of other nations will be adjusted. For Importeria, the value of the currency will have to fall or be **devalued**. The value of other currencies will increase relative to Importeria's, so these currencies are said to have been **revalued**. Devaluations and revaluations, when they occur, are usually large in size. It is not uncommon for the value to change by 25 to 50 percent, or even more.

It may seem perplexing that the value of the currencies would not adjust smoothly over time, as Importeria continued its program of excess imports. A fixed exchange rate system, however, prevents gradual adjustment. Rates are fixed through the intervention of the central banks of Importeria and other countries. As excess supplies of Importeria's currency accumulate, central banks may use their reserves of other currencies to buy Importeria's, thereby easing the imbalance between supply and demand that would arise at the fixed level of rates. In effect, central banks would be absorbing the excess supply of

Importeria's currency which would otherwise exist at the fixed level of exchange rates. If the pressures against the currency of Importeria are not too severe, purchases by central banks may succeed in maintaining the fixed level of exchange rates. Often, however, the excess supply of a currency may become excessive. Then central banks become unable, or unwilling, to purchase all of the currency that is supplied. When this happens, a country like Importeria would be forced to devalue its currency and set a new rate of exchange as the official rate. If the value of the Importeria unit of currency was one-tenth of a U.S. dollar before the devaluation, it might be reset at one-twelfth of a dollar after the devaluation. After the devaluation, Importeria would try to maintain the new exchange rate. If Importeria continues to import much more than it exports, it would soon face another devaluation.

One obvious and apparently disadvantageous feature of a fixed exchange rate system is that changes in the exchange rates occur infrequently, but when they do, the changes are rather large. There are, however, considerable advantages to a fixed exchange rate system. First, fixed exchange rates make planning exchange transactions considerably easier. If businesses can depend on a fixed exchange rate for the next year, they would not face **exchange risk**—the risk that the value of a currency will change relative to other currencies. Freedom from exchange risk facilitates business planning and promotes international trade. Second, for firms engaged in international commerce, fixed exchange rates mean that accounting income is not sensitive to exchange rate fluctuations. Third, a fixed exchange rate may provide a form of discipline for economic policies by the participating countries. According to this argument, governments would realize that pursuing certain policies would be likely to lead to devaluation.

Perhaps for these reasons, and also as a signal of financial probity, the industrialized West pursued a fixed exchange rate policy from the end of World War II until 1971. During this period, the dollar was even convertible into gold at a rate of $35 per ounce, according to the Bretton Woods Agreement. Other major currencies fixed their value in terms of the U.S. dollar. In August 1971, faced with a weakening dollar and a soaring balance of payments deficit, the United States abandoned the gold standard. In spite of attempts to re-establish some semblance of a fixed rate system, notably the Smithsonian Agreement of 1971, March 1973 witnessed a new era in international foreign exchange. The fixed rate system was abandoned, with daily fluctuations in exchange rates becoming the norm.

Other Exchange Rate Systems

This free market system of exchange rates prevails today, but there are a number of important exceptions and variations that the foreign exchange trader must consider. With the breakdown of the Bretton Woods system and the failure of the Smithsonian Agreement, countries were free to adopt a variety of strategies where their exchange rates were concerned. This freedom has led to such strategies as free floats, managed or dirty floats, pegs, and joint floats. A currency is **freely floating** if it has no system of fixed exchange rates and if the country's central bank does not attempt to influence the value of the currency by trading in the foreign exchange market. Few countries have truly freely floating exchange rates, because central banks seem unable to resist the temptation to intervene. When the central bank of a country engages in market transactions to influence the exchange value of its currency, but the rate is basically a floating rate, the country is following a policy of a **managed float** or a **dirty float**. Opposed to this floating system, a number of countries use a **pegged** exchange rate system. The value of one currency might be pegged to the value of another currency, that itself floats. For example, Importeria might try to maintain a fixed exchange rate with the dollar, but the dollar itself floats against most of the world's currencies. In such a situation, the currency of Importeria is pegged to the dollar. Pegged currencies may be pegged to a single currency, while others could be pegged to a basket, or portfolio, of currencies.

One other policy for exchange rate management is particularly important for the foreign exchange futures market—the policy of a joint float. In a **joint float**, currencies participating in the joint float have fixed exchange values relative to other currencies in the joint float, but the *group* of currencies floats relative to other currencies that do not participate in the joint float. The prime example of the joint float technique comes from the European Economic Community (EEC), or the common market. The member nations formed the European Monetary System (EMS) in 1979 and created the European Currency Unit (ECU). The basic strategy of the EMS agreement is to maintain very narrowly fluctuating exchange rates among the currencies of the participating countries.[7]

In theory, a joint float system means that the values of the currencies of the participating countries will be fixed relative to one another but will float relative to external countries. This has important implications for speculation and hedging in all of these currencies, particularly where the futures market is concerned. Recent experience has shown that some countries may be forced to devalue their currency relative to those of the group. Italy has faced the problem several times since the inception of the EMS. More recently, France has devalued several times. In such cases, it is apparent that a trader may have difficulty using the German mark as a cross-hedge against the Italian lire or the French franc.

Forward and Futures Prices for Foreign Exchange

As we discussed in Chapter 3, a distinction between forward and futures prices emerges from the daily resettlement feature of futures contracts. Consider a forward and futures contract on foreign exchange that have the same expiration. Both the futures and the forward will have the same profit in the end, exclusive of interest earned on the resettlement payments. If the futures position is likely to have more favorable interim cash flows due to its positive correlation with interest rates, the futures price should exceed the forward price. By the same token, if the futures price is negatively correlated with interest rates, then the futures price should be lower than the forward price. This conclusion follows, because the futures trader will then tend to experience losses just as interest rates rise. Finally, if the price of a commodity is uncorrelated with interest rates, then the forward and futures prices should be equal. Notice that all these conclusions arise strictly from economic reasoning and hold if investors are risk-neutral. We now consider the evidence on this issue from the foreign exchange market.

Theoretical Relationship of Forward and Futures Prices

Correlation of Spot Prices and Interest Rates	Price Relationship
Positive Correlation	Futures Price > Forward Price
Negative Correlation	Futures Price < Forward Price
No Correlation	Futures Price = Forward Price

Table 11.4 summarizes the results of studies that have examined the relationship between forward and futures prices for foreign exchange. In essence, these studies find very little difference. As one study concluded, "The foreign

Table 11.4
Studies of Foreign Exchange Futures and Forward Prices

Study	Key Results
Cornell and Reinganum (1981)	Futures and forward prices are statistically and economically indistinguishable.
Park and Chen (1985)	Futures and forward prices are statistically and economically indistinguishable.
Fieleke (1985)	Differences between futures and forward prices are negligible.
Chang and Chang (1990)	Correcting for the timing of delivery dates in Cornell and Reinganum does not change the conclusion. Futures and forward prices for foreign exchange are statistically indistinguishable.

exchange data reveal that mean differences between forward and futures prices are insignificantly different from zero, both in a statistical and economic sense."[8] In view of these findings, results based on research in the forward market will be regarded as holding for the futures market as well. Such a procedure is justifiable, but we must still interpret these cross market results with caution. Nonetheless, understanding of the foreign exchange futures market can be greatly enhanced, particularly in regard to questions of market efficiency and forecasting accuracy, by using research conducted with forward market data.

More Futures Price Parity Relationships

Earlier in this chapter, we noted the geographical or cross-rate arbitrage opportunities that occur when foreign exchange rates are improperly aligned among single contracts. The arbitrage examples of Tables 11.1 and 11.2 arose from a pricing discrepancy in the foreign exchange rates for a single maturity of 90 days forward. Other price relationships are equally important and determine the permissible price differences that may exist between foreign exchange rates for delivery at different times. These relationships are expressed as the **Interest Rate Parity Theorem** (IRP) and the **Purchasing Power Parity Theorem** (PPP). As we will see, the IRP is simply the Cost-of-Carry Model in a very thin disguise.[9]

Interest Rate Parity Theorem

The Interest Rate Parity Theorem asserts that interest rates and exchange rates form one system. According to IRP, foreign exchange rates will adjust to ensure that a trader earns the same return by investing in risk-free instruments of any currency, assuming that the proceeds from investment are repatriated into the home currency by a forward contract initiated at the outset of the holding period. We can use the rates of Table 11.5 to illustrate interest rate parity. Faced with the rates in Table 11.5 and assuming interest rate parity holds, a trader must earn the same return by following either of two strategies:

Strategy 1:   Invest in the U.S. for 180 days.

Strategy 2:   (a)   Sell $ for DM at the spot rate.
               (b)   Invest DM proceeds for 180 days in Germany.
               (c)   Sell the proceeds of the German investment for dollars through a forward contract initiated at the outset of the investment horizon.

Table 11.5
Interest Rates and Exchange Rates to
Illustrate Interest Rate Parity

| Exchange Rates | $/DM | Interest Rates | |
		U.S.	Germany
Spot	.42	–	–
30–day	.41	.18	.576
90–day	.405	.19	.33
180–day	.40	.20	.323

With our sample data, the following equation expresses the same equivalence:

$$\$1(1.20)^{.5} = [(\$1/.42)(1.323)^{.5}](.40)$$

In the equation, Strategy 1 is on the left-hand side. There one dollar is invested at the 20 percent U.S. rate for one-half year. For Strategy 2 on the right hand side, the dollar is first converted into marks at the spot rate of $.42 per DM. The trader invests these proceeds at the German mark rate for one-half year. This 180-day rate is 32.3 percent. Investment of the German funds will pay DM 2.7386 in 180 days. The investment proceeds are sold for dollars using the 180-day forward rate of .40. For this 180-day horizon, the equivalence between the two strategies holds, so no arbitrage opportunity is available. In this example, the Interest Rate Parity Theorem holds.

Interest Rate Parity and the Cost–of–Carry Model

In essence, the Interest Rate Parity Theorem is simply the exchange rate equivalent of the Cost-of-Carry Model. To see this equivalence, consider the cash-and-carry strategy for the interest rate market. In a cash-and-carry transaction a trader follows these steps: Borrow funds and buy a bond, carry the bond to the futures/forward expiration, and sell the good through a futures/forward contract arranged at the initial date. The cost-of-carry is the difference between the rate paid on the borrowed funds and the rate earned by holding the bond. Our familiar cash-and-carry strategy is known as **covered interest arbitrage** in the foreign exchange market. In covered interest arbitrage, a trader borrows domestic funds and buys foreign funds at the spot rate. The trader then invests these funds at the foreign interest rate until expiration of the forward/futures contract. The trader also initiates a futures/forward contract to convert the proceeds from the foreign investment back into the domestic currency. The cost-of-carry is the difference between the interest rate paid to borrow funds and the interest earned on the investment in foreign funds.

Thus, a trader borrows the domestic currency, DC, at the domestic rate of interest, r_{DC}, and exchanges these funds for foreign currency, FC, at the spot exchange rate. The trader receives DC/FC units of the foreign currency and invests at the foreign interest rate, r_{FC}. This rate, r_{FC}, is the interest rate applicable to the time from the present to the expiration of the forward or futures. At the outset of these transactions, t=0, the trader also sells the forward or futures contract at price $F_{0,t}$ for the amount of funds $(DC/FC)(1 + r_{FC})$. With these transactions, the trader has no net cash flow at t=0. At expiration the trader receives $(DC/FC)(1 + r_{FC})$ units of the foreign currency from the investment of foreign funds. The trader delivers this foreign currency against the forward or futures contract and receives $F_{0,t}$ in the domestic currency. The trader then must pay the debt on the original borrowing, which is $DC(1 + r_{DC})$. If IRP, or equivalently, the Cost-of-Carry Model, holds, the trader must be left with zero funds. Otherwise an arbitrage opportunity exists.

Applying this notation to our previous example of the cost-of-carry transactions for the 180-day horizon, we can generalize this example to write an equation for IRP or the Cost-of-Carry Model as it applies to foreign exchange. For convenience, we begin with $1 as the amount of the domestic currency, DC. Before, for our example, we wrote:

$$\$1(1.20)^{.5} = [(\$1/.42)(1.323)^{.5}](.40)$$

In the new notation this translates as:

$$DC(1 + r_{DC}) = (DC/FC)(1 + r_{FC})F_{0,t}$$

Remember that r_{DC} and r_{FC} are the interest rates for the specific period between the present, t=0, and the expiration of the futures at time t.

Isolating the futures price on the left-hand side gives:

$$F_{0,t} = \frac{DC\,(1 + r_{DC})}{\left[\dfrac{DC}{FC}\right](1 + r_{FC})} = FC\left(\frac{1 + r_{DC}}{1 + r_{FC}}\right) \qquad 11.1$$

Equation 11.1 says that, for a unit of foreign currency, the futures price equals the spot price of the foreign currency times the quantity:

$$\left(\frac{1 + r_{DC}}{1 + r_{FC}} \right) \qquad\qquad 11.2$$

This quantity is the ratio of the interest factor for the domestic currency to the interest factor for the foreign currency. We can compare this to our familiar equation 3.3 for the Cost-of-Carry Model in perfect markets with unrestricted short selling:

$$F_{0,t} = S_0(1 + C) \qquad\qquad 3.3$$

where:

$F_{0,t}$ = the futures or forward price at t=0 for a foreign exchange contract to expire at time t

S_0 = the spot price of the good at t=0

C = the percentage cost of carrying the good from t=0 to time t

Equations 3.3 and 11.1 have the same form. Therefore, the quantity in 11.2 equals one plus the cost of carry, $(1 + C)$. The cash-and-carry strategy requires borrowing at the domestic rate, r_{DC}, so this is an element of the carrying cost. However, the borrowed domestic funds are converted to foreign currency and earn at the foreign interest rate r_{FC}. Therefore, the foreign earnings offset the cost being incurred through the domestic interest rate. The net result is that quantity 11.2 gives the value for one plus the carrying cost. As a simpler approximation, we note that:

$$1 + \text{Cost-of-Carry} = \left(\frac{1 + r_{DC}}{1 + r_{FC}} \right) \approx 1 + (r_{DC} - r_{FC}) \qquad 11.3$$

Therefore, the cost-of-carry approximately equals the difference between the domestic and foreign interest rates for the period from t=0 to the futures expiration. To complete this discussion, let us apply this equation for the 180-day horizon using the rates in Table 11.5. We have already seen that there is no arbitrage possible for this horizon. For this example data we have:

$F_{0,t}$ = .40

S_0 = .42

r_{DC} = .095445 for the half-year

r_{FC} = .150217 for the half-year

Applying equation 11.1 to this data, we have:

$$.40 = .42 \left(\frac{1.095445}{1.150217} \right)$$

This equation holds exactly. The cost-of-carry is -0.047619. For this example, the approximate cost-of-carry for the half-year is:

$$r_{DC} - r_{FC} = .095445 - .150217 = -0.054772$$

Thus, the cost-of-carry for the half-year is approximately -.05. The cost-of-carry is negative because the cash-and-carry trader pays at the domestic rate but earns interest at the higher foreign rate. For the same reason, the futures price of the foreign currency must exceed the spot price. If the foreign rate of interest had been lower, the futures price of the foreign currency would have to be lower than the spot price to avoid arbitrage.

Exploiting Deviations from Interest Rate Parity

The analysis of the values in Table 11.5 shows that there is not an arbitrage opportunity in the 180-day contract. If the Interest Rate Parity Theorem is to hold in general, there cannot be an arbitrage opportunity for any investment horizon. In Table 11.5, the rates allow an arbitrage opportunity in the 90-day contract. This is apparent when one realizes that the strategy of holding the U.S. dollar and DM investment does not yield the same 90-day terminal wealth in U.S. dollars when the marks are converted into dollars by issuing a forward contract. The following computation illustrates the different terminal dollar values earned by the two strategies:

Strategy 1: (hold in U.S.)
$$\$1(1.19)^{.25} = \$1.0444$$

Strategy 2: (convert to DM, invest, and use forward contract)
$$(\$1/.42)(1.33)^{.25} \, (.405) = \$1.0355$$

Strategy 1, investing in the U.S., gives a higher payoff than converting dollars to marks and investing in Germany. This difference implies that an arbitrage opportunity exists.

This is also evident by applying the Cost-of-Carry Model for foreign exchange to the 90-day values in Table 11.5. For this horizon, the values in Table 11.5 imply:

$F_{0,t} = .405$
$S_0 = .42$
$r_{DC} = .044448$ for the quarter-year
$r_{FC} = .073898$ for the quarter-year

With these values, the futures price should be 0.408482:

$$FC \left(\frac{1 + r_{DC}}{1 + r_{FC}} \right) = .42 \left(\frac{1.044448}{1.073898} \right) = .408482$$

Because the futures price is less than this amount, an arbitrage opportunity exists. With our example data, it is clearly better to invest funds in the U.S. rather than Germany. Table 11.6 shows the transactions that will exploit this discrepancy, assuming that the transactions begin with $1.00.

```
┌─────────────────────────────────────────────────────────────┐
│                       Table 11.6                            │
│                Covered Interest Arbitrage                    │
│                                                             │
│ t = 0 (present)                                             │
│                                                             │
│     Borrow DM 2.3810 in Germany for 90 days at 33%.        │
│     Sell DM 2.3810 spot for $1.00.                         │
│     Invest $1.00 in the U.S. for 90 days at 19%.           │
│     Sell $1.0355 90 days forward for DM 2.5570.            │
├─────────────────────────────────────────────────────────────┤
│ t = 90 (delivery)                                           │
│                                                             │
│     Collect $1.0444 on investment in U.S.                  │
│     Deliver $1.0355 on forward contract; Collect DM 2.5570.│
│     Pay DM 2.5570 on DM 2.3810 that was borrowed.          │
├─────────────────────────────────────────────────────────────┤
│                     Profit:                                 │
│                         $1.0444                             │
│                       − 1.0355                              │
│                         .0089                               │
└─────────────────────────────────────────────────────────────┘
```

This kind of arbitrage in foreign exchange is covered interest arbitrage. With these transactions, the trader uses a forward contract to cover the proceeds from the DM investment. The proceeds are covered, because the trader arranges through the forward contract to convert the DM proceeds into dollars as soon as the proceeds are received. The IRP Theorem asserts that such opportunities should not exist. The section on market efficiency explores whether the Interest Rate Parity Theorem actually holds.

Purchasing Power Parity Theorem

The Purchasing Power Parity Theorem (PPP) asserts that the exchange rates between two currencies must be proportional to the price level of traded goods in the two currencies. Purchasing power parity is intimately tied to interest rate parity, as we discuss later. Violations of PPP can lead to arbitrage opportunities, such as the following example of "Croissant Arbitrage."

For croissant arbitrage we assume that transportation and transaction costs are zero and that there are no trade barriers, such as quotas or tariffs. These assumptions are essentially equivalent to our usual assumptions of perfect markets. The spot value of the French franc is $.10 and the cost of a croissant in Paris is FF 1, as Table 11.7 shows. In New York a croissant sells for $.15, so this price creates an arbitrage opportunity. A trader can exploit this opportunity by transacting as shown in the bottom portion of Table 11.7. Given the other values, the price of a croissant in New York must be $.10 to exclude arbitrage.

Table 11.7
Croissant Arbitrage

	FF/$	Cost of One Croissant
Paris	10	FF 1
New York	10	$.15

Arbitrage Transactions:
  Sell $1 for FF 10 in the spot market.
  Buy 10 croissants in Paris.
  Ship the croissants to New York.
  Sell 10 croissants in New York at .15 for $1.50.

Profit:
$1.50
− 1.00
.50

Over time, exchange rates must also conform to PPP. The left column of Table 11.8 presents prices and exchange rates consistent with PPP at t=0. The right column shows values one year later at t=1, after a year of inflation in France and the United States. During this year, French inflation was 20 percent, so a croissant now sells for FF 1.2. In the U.S. inflation was 10 percent, so a croissant is now $.11. To be consistent with PPP, the exchange rates must also have adjusted to keep the relative value of the franc and dollar consistent with the relative purchasing power of the two currencies. As a consequence, the dollar must now be worth FF 10.91. Any other exchange rate would create an arbitrage opportunity. The requirement that PPP holds at all times means that the exchange rate must change proportionately to the relative price levels in the two currencies.

Table 11.8
Purchasing Power Parity over Time

Expected Inflation Rates from t= 0 to t=1:	$	.10
	FF	.20

	t=0	t=1
Exchange Rates FF/$	10.00	10.91
Croissant Prices		
Paris	FF 1.00	FF 1.20
New York	$ .10	$ .11

Purchasing Power and Interest Rate Parity

The intimate relationship that exists between the Purchasing Power Parity Theorem and the Interest Rate Parity Theorem originates from the link between interest rates and inflation rates. According to the analysis of Irving Fisher, the nominal, or market, rate of interest consists of two elements, the **real** rate of interest and the **expected** inflation rate. This relationship can be expressed mathematically as follows:

$$(1 + r_n) = (1 + r^*) [1 + E(I)] \qquad 11.4$$

where, r_n is the nominal interest rate, r^* is the real rate of interest, and $E(I)$ is the expected inflation rate over the period in question. Since the expected inflation is the expected change in purchasing power, the Purchasing Power Parity Theorem expresses the linkage between exchange rates and relative inflation rates. A difference in nominal interest rates between two countries is most likely due to differences in expected inflation. This means that interest rates, exchange rates, price levels, and foreign exchange rates form an integrated system.[10]

Foreign Exchange Futures Prices and Expected Future Exchange Rates

Throughout this book, and particularly in Chapter 3, we have stressed the relationship between futures prices and expected future spot prices. If risk–neutral speculators are available in sufficient quantity, their profit seeking activity will drive the futures price toward equality with the expected future spot price. The same process occurs in the foreign exchange market. The linkages among interest rates, price levels, expected inflation, and exchange rates merely emphasize the fundamental relationship that exists between forward and futures foreign exchange prices, on the one hand, and the expected future value of the currencies, on the other.

To investigate these relationships, consider the exchange rates and price levels of Table 11.9. In the left panel, a set of consistent exchange rates, interest rates, expected inflation rates, and croissant prices are presented for March 20, 1991. The right panel presents the expected spot exchange rate for March 20, 1992, along with expected croissant prices, consistent with the expected levels of inflation in France and the United States.

Assume that all of these values hold and that the expected spot exchange rate in one year is FF 11 per dollar. With the MAR 1992 futures price of 10.45 FF/$, a speculative opportunity exists as follows. A speculator might buy a futures contract for the delivery of dollars in one year for FF 10.45 per dollar. If the expectation that the dollar will be worth FF 11 in one year is correct, the

Table 11.9
Price Levels, Interest Rates,
Expected Inflation and Exchange Rates

March 20, 1991		March 20, 1992	
Exchange Rates FF/$		Expected Spot Exchange Rate	
Spot	10.00	10.45	
MAR 1992 Futures	10.45		
Interest Rates (1–year maturities)			
U.S.	.12		
France	.17		
Expected Inflation Rates (for the next year)			
U.S.	.10		
France	.15		
Croissant Prices		Expected Croissant Prices	
U.S.	$ .10	U.S.	$ .11
France	FF 1	France	FF 1.15

speculator will earn a profit that results from acquiring a dollar via the futures market for FF 10.45 and selling it for the price of FF 11. If we assume that avaricious risk-neutral speculators are present in the foreign exchange market, the discrepancy between the futures price of 10.45 FF/$ and an expected spot exchange rate of 11 FF/$ (at the time the futures contract matures) cannot exist. In fact, given a profusion of risk-neutral speculators, the only expected spot exchange rate to prevail on March 20, 1992, which would eliminate the incentive to speculate, would be 10.45 FF/$. Of course, different market participants have different expectations regarding inflation rates and expected future spot exchange rates, and this difference in expectations is the necessary requirement for speculation.

Foreign Exchange
Forecasting Accuracy

In this section we examine the evidence on the accuracy of foreign exchange futures and forward prices as forecasts of future spot exchange rates. As we have just argued in the preceding section, the presence of risk-neutral speculators should drive the futures and forward prices into equality with the expected future spot rate of exchange. If today's expectation of future exchange rates is unbiased, and if the forward and futures prices equal that expectation, we would find that today's forward or futures exchange rate should, on average and in the long run, equal the subsequently observed spot exchange rate. Thus, there are two parts to this equivalence. First, does the forward or futures price equal the market's expectation of the future spot exchange rate? Second, is today's expectation of the future spot exchange rate unbiased? That is, does today's expectation of the future spot exchange rate, on average and in the long run, equal the actual subsequently observed spot rate?

Methodology for Tests of Forecasting Accuracy

Unfortunately, there is no truly accurate way to observe today's market expectation of future exchange rates. Therefore, most tests assume that the market expectation is an unbiased estimate of the future spot exchange rate. Under this assumption, scholars test the relationship between the forward and futures price today and the subsequently observed spot rate. In our notation, they test the following equivalence:

$$F_{0,t} = S_t \qquad\qquad 11.5$$

where:

$F_{0,t}$ = the forward or futures price at t=0 for a contract expiring at time t
S_t = the spot exchange rate observed at time t

Testing the equivalence in equation 11.5 determines whether the forward or futures price is a good estimate of the future spot rate of exchange. Even if there are large deviations between the two prices in 11.5, it is still possible that the forward or futures price could provide an unbiased prediction of the future spot rate. An **unbiased predictor** is a predictor whose expected value equals the variable being predicted. In other words, if the quantity $F_{0,t} - S_t$ equals zero, on average, the forward or futures price would provide an unbiased estimate of the future spot rate of exchange.

No predictor is perfect. Therefore, it is possible that the forward or futures price may seem to be error ridden. However, the most relevant test of any predictor comes from testing the accuracy of the predictor against alternative predictors. As we will see, forward and futures prices do not provide very good predictions of future spot rates—unless we compare them to alternative forecasting schemes.

Earlier in this chapter, we reviewed the evidence on the relationship between futures and forward prices of foreign exchange. There we saw that the evidence strongly suggests that the two are equal. We rely on that equivalence in this section. In the discussion that follows, we speak of futures and forward prices in general, without distinguishing the two.

Tests of Market–Based Forecasts

A **market–based forecast** is a forecast of a future economic value derived from an examination of current market prices. In the context of foreign exchange, we ask whether the current futures price provides a good market-based forecast of the future foreign exchange rate. As we have seen, this essentially amounts to testing the equivalence of futures prices and subsequently observed spot exchange rates.

Table 11.10 summarizes some of the many tests of the forecasting accuracy of futures and forward prices. While earlier studies generally found that futures prices were unbiased predictors of future spot rates, later studies clearly find bias. This change in results may be due to the development of more refined statistical tools. Therefore, we must conclude foreign exchange futures prices do not provide unbiased forecasts of the subsequently observed spot exchange rate. Further, the errors in the forecasts appear to be quite large as well. Some studies summarized in Table 11.10 also find that the current spot rate outperforms the futures rate as a predictor of subsequent spot prices.

Table 11.10
Tests of Futures Forecasts of Foreign Exchange Rates

Study	Key Results
Levich (1979)	Futures exchange rates appear to provide unbiased forecasts.
Kohlhagen (1979)	In the long run, the forward exchange rate serves as an unbiased predictor, but biases are found in the short run.
Hansen and Hodrick (1980)	Reject hypothesis that forward exchange rates are an unbiased estimate of future spot exchange rates.
Meese and Rogoff (1983)	Current spot rate provides a better prediction of future exchange rates than does the forward rate.
Chiang (1986)	Current spot rate provides a better prediction of future exchange rates than does the forward rate.
Hodrick and Srivastava (1987)	Today's futures price is a biased forecast of tomorrow's futures price.
McCurdy and Morgan (1987)	Rejects hypothesis of unbiasedness.
Kodres (1988)	Previous tests of futures based forecasts do not address the problem of price limits. Taking price limits into account, the forecasts are still biased.

With biased forecasts, it appears that profit opportunities would abound. If the futures price tends to be low relative to the future spot price, a trader could buy futures, plan to take delivery on the futures, and plan to sell the foreign currency for a profit. However, even if the forecasts are biased, it does not mean that profit opportunities abound. However, these studies do not find biases that are sufficiently large or consistent to allow profitable trading strategies. In summary, the errors in forecasts of future exchange rates appear to be large, and biases do seem to exist in these forecasts, although the biases appear to be too small to allow profitable exploitation.

Competitors of Market–Based Forecasts

If we consider the futures price as a forecast of the future spot rate of exchange, we must conclude that the forecast is likely to have large errors, and we must acknowledge that the forecast may be biased. These two features do not appear to recommend market-based forecasts of future spot exchange rates. Perhaps some other type of forecast is better. The usefulness of market-based forecasts of future exchange rates depends, however, on a whole range of factors, including availability, cost, extent of bias, size of the forecast error, and performance of the forecast relative to other methods. In this section, we compare market-based forecasts with the performance of commercial forecasting firms. As will become apparent, in spite of their limitations, the futures forecasts have important advantages.

Clearly, the futures forecast has an advantage in availability and cost. Both are readily available every day for the price of *The Wall Street Journal*. If forward and futures prices provide the best forecast of the future spot rate that is available, the biases in the forecasts are probably not too serious. Even if the biases are substantial, the futures forecast may still be the best forecast available. Perhaps the most severe challenge to the market-based forecasts comes from the forecasting services that prepare and disseminate forecasts of exchange rates. However, market-based forecasts appear to have smaller errors than forecasts from commercial firms.[11]

The Efficiency of Foreign Exchange Futures Markets

The efficiency of the foreign exchange market has been explored by numerous researchers over an extended time. In spite of this attention, the efficiency of the market remains an open question. This situation is not unusual when a complex empirical issue in finance is at stake. If arbitrage opportunities such as geographical, cross-rate, or covered interest arbitrage exist, then the foreign exchange market is inefficient. Reflection on the structure of the market helps support the case for efficiency. With a worldwide network of active traders, all linked by sophisticated information systems and all aware of the profits implied by arbitrage opportunities, we might expect any incipient arbitrage opportunities to be detected very early. As quasi-arbitrage opportunities appear, we would expect traders to adjust their trading patterns to exploit even the slightest opportunity. This activity, we expect, should eliminate any observable arbitrage opportunities.

On the other hand, the foreign exchange market is unique in attracting central bank intervention from a variety of countries. If central banks cannot leave their hands off the market and insist on managing floating rates, the character of the market could be affected. If the market is subject to the actions of well-capitalized governmental agencies with agendas that are not profit-determined, then we might expect profit opportunities to arise from betting against central banks. In this section, we explore the evidence on market efficiency, beginning with an example of interest rate parity.

We have seen that deviations from interest rate parity create opportunities for cash-and-carry and reverse cash-and-carry trading strategies. With transaction costs, slight deviations from interest rate parity are possible, because transaction costs make it unprofitable for traders to exploit minor discrepancies. The arbitrage opportunity depends upon finding deviations from interest rate parity large enough to cover all transaction costs and still leave a profit. As a result, one way of searching for the existence of violations of the Interest Rate Parity Theorem is to look for the occurrence of large deviations from interest rate parity. Table 11.11 shows deviations from interest rate parity for some major currencies on which futures contracts trade. Richard M. Levich selected .25 percent as a permissible deviation from interest rate parity, which would still be consistent with the absence of arbitrage opportunities. He believed that this fourth of one percent would be a reasonable bound for transaction costs to form a no-arbitrage band around the price exactly consistent with IRP. As Table 11.11 shows, a high percentage of Levich's observations fall within that band. From this, Levich concludes, "Therefore, the Eurocurrency market is efficient in that there are few unexploited opportunities for risk-free profit through covered interest arbitrage."[12]

To what extent do deviations outside the band of .25 percent represent arbitrage opportunities? If we find only few opportunities, it may still be worthwhile to look for them. Based on Table 11.11, it seems potentially worthwhile to follow the Swiss franc, since over 20 percent of the observations appear to lie outside the stated boundaries. The critical question here is the selection of the no-arbitrage boundaries. If transactions costs exceed .25 percent, then the bounds are too narrow. By the same token, perhaps transactions costs are really less than .25 percent, and the no-arbitrage boundaries are too lax.

Table 11.11
Percentage of Deviations from
Interest Parity Within +/–.25%
(All assets are for 3–month maturities.)

Country	Percentage within Bounds
Canada	93.43
United Kingdom	96.68
Germany	98.82
Switzerland	78.59

Source: Richard M. Levich, "The Efficiency of Markets for Foreign Exchange: A Review and Extension." Reprinted in Kolb and Gay, *International Finance: Concepts and Issues*, Richmond, VA: Robert F. Dame, Inc., 1982.

These questions are not easy to answer, since it is virtually impossible to know what measure of transaction costs to use. The most striking feature of Table 11.11, however, appears to be the prevalent tendency for so many opportunities to fall within .25 percent of exact interest rate parity. While it may not be possible to say that no arbitrage opportunities are to be found in the foreign

Table 11.12
Evidence on the Efficiency of Foreign Exchange Futures

Study	Key Results
Levich (1979)	Deviations from IRP appear to fall within no–arbitrage bounds, consistent with market efficiency.
Cornell and Dietrich (1978)	The market for foreign exchange is weakly efficient.
Thomas (1986)	Simple speculative strategies appear to earn significant profits.
Glassman (1987)	Futures markets were inefficient, particularly during early history of trading.
Cavanaugh (1987)	Serial correlation is sufficiently strong to allow speculative profits to traders with low transaction costs.
Levine (1989)	Rejects the PPP version of the efficient markets hypothesis.
Harpaz, Krull, and Yagil (1990)	The U.S. Dollar Index futures contract is inefficient.

exchange market, it is much more impressive to note how closely the observations tended to correspond to interest rate parity.[13]

Levich's study characterizes the earlier evidence on the efficiency of foreign exchange markets. Nonetheless, more recent evidence on forward and futures markets for foreign exchange suggests that the markets are not efficient. Table 11.12 summarizes some studies of market efficiency. These studies suggest that foreign exchange significantly departs from theoretical pricing relationships. Further, some studies find that speculative strategies can earn significant profits. Part of the findings seem to be due to intervention in the foreign exchange markets by central banks. As a tentative explanation, it seems possible that central banks intervene to stabilize currencies. In the process, they provide profits to savvy speculators. However, most of these opportunities appear to be quite small.

Speculation in Foreign Exchange Futures

We have seen that the market for foreign exchange has some significant inefficiencies. This inefficiency appears to open the door to speculative strategies. Nonetheless, we should not expect gross inefficiencies in the market. For example, it still appears that market-based forecasts outperform professional forecasts. This suggests that attempts to "beat the market" may still be hazardous. In this section, we illustrate strategies to speculate with foreign exchange. These strategies presume that the trader has well-developed expectations about the value of foreign exchange rates.

Speculating with an Outright Position

In speculation, the most important single point to remember is that the trader opposes his or her wisdom to the opinion of the entire market, since prices available in the market reflect the consensus opinion of all participating parties. The dependence of speculative profits on superior estimation of future exchange rates is demonstrated in Tables 11.13 and 11.14. Imagine a speculator who confronts the exchange rates of Table 11.13 between the U.S. dollar and the German mark on April 7. As an expression of the market's beliefs, these exchange rates imply that the mark will rise relative to the dollar. The speculator, however, strongly disagrees. She believes that the price of the mark, in terms of dollars, will actually fall over the rest of the year. Table 11.14 shows the speculative transactions she enters to take advantage of her belief.

Since the speculator expects the mark to fall, she sells the DEC futures contract for .4286. If the subsequent spot price is less, she makes a profit. The

Table 11.13
Foreign Exchange Prices—Spot and Futures, April 7

	$/DM
Spot	.4140
JUN Futures	.4183
SEP Futures	.4211
DEC Futures	.4286

Table 11.14
Speculation in Foreign Exchange

	Cash Market	Futures Market
April 7	Anticipates a fall in the value of the DM over the next 8 months.	Sell one DEC DM futures contract at .4286.
December 10	Spot Price $/DM = .4211	Buy one DEC DM futures contract at .4218.
	Profit:	
		$ .4286
		− .4218
	Profit per DM	$ .0068
	Times DM per contract	× 125,000
	Total Profit	$ 850

speculator does not need to actually be correct in the stated belief that the spot exchange value of the mark will fall over the next eight months. A profit is assured if the mark is worth less than the DEC futures price. On December 10, as Table 11.14 shows, the DEC futures is .4218 and the spot exchange rate is 0.4211. Notice that the belief that the mark would fall in value was incorrect. The December 10 spot price still exceeds the original spot price, as does the price of the DEC futures contract. Nonetheless, the drop in the futures price from .4286 to .4218 generates a profit of $.0068 per mark. Since the DM contract calls for delivery of 125,000 marks, the total profit is $850.

Speculating with Spreads

In addition to outright positions, such as the position in the previous example, various spread strategies are also possible. These include intra-commodity and inter-commodity spreads. Some inter-commodity spreads are important, because they allow positions that might not be attainable easily in other markets. The only U.S. futures market for individual foreign exchange contracts is the IMM. In the IMM all prices are stated in terms of dollars. A speculator might believe that the Swiss franc will gain in value relative to the German mark but might also be uncertain about the future value of the dollar relative to either of these currencies. It is possible to speculate on the SF/DM exchange rate by trading on the IMM futures market.

Table 11.15 presents market prices on the IMM for June 24 for the $/DM and $/SF spot and future exchange rates. The futures prices imply cross-rates between the mark and franc as well, as shown in the right column. The structure of rates is peculiar, with the DM/SF rate dipping first and then rising. In particular, a speculator finds the implied cross-rate for December to be too low. The speculator believes that the Swiss franc will tend to appreciate against the mark over the coming year. Even though it is impossible to trade the mark against the Swiss franc directly on the IMM, given the available rate quotations, the speculator can use a spread to achieve the desired speculative position.

Since the speculator believes that the value of the mark will fall relative to the Swiss franc, he must also believe that the value of the mark relative to the dollar will perform worse than the value of the Swiss franc relative to the dollar. In other words, even if the mark appreciates against the dollar, his belief about the relative value of the Swiss franc implies that the Swiss franc would appreciate even more against the dollar. Likewise, if the mark falls against the dollar, the speculator would believe that the Swiss franc would either gain or not fall as much as the mark. It is important to realize that the speculator need not have any belief regarding the performance of the dollar relative to either of the European currencies. He is merely going to trade through the dollar to establish a position in the DM/SF exchange rate.

Table 11.16 shows the transactions necessary to exploit the belief that the December cross-rate is too low. If the speculator is correct, the mark will fall relative to the Swiss franc. Therefore, he sells one DEC mark contract at .4115

Table 11.15
Spot and Futures Exchange Rates, June 24

	$/DM	$/SF	Implied DM/SF Cross–Rate
Spot	.3853	.4580	1.1887
SEP	.3915	.4616	1.1791
DEC	.4115	.4635	1.1264
MAR	.4163	.4815	1.1566
JUN	.4180	.5100	1.2201

Table 11.16
A Speculative Cross–Rate Futures Spread

Date	Futures Market
June 24	Sell one DEC DM futures contract at .4115. Buy one DEC SF futures contract at .4635.
December 11	Buy one DEC DM futures contract at .3907. Sell one DEC SF futures contract at .4475.

Futures Trading Results:

	DM	SF
Sold	.4115	.4475
Bought	− .3907	− .4635
	$.0208	−$.0160
× 125,000	= $2,600	− $2,000

Total Profit: $600

and buys one DEC Swiss franc contract at .4635. This spread is equivalent to speculating that the implied cross-rate of 1.1264 is too low, or that it will require more than 1.1264 DM to buy 1 SF by December. By December 11, the two contracts are approaching expiration, and the speculator offsets both contracts. He buys the DEC DM contract at .3907 and sells the SF contract at .4475. This generates a profit of $.0208 per DM and a loss of $.0160 per SF. Both contracts are written for 125,000 units of the foreign currency, so the net profit on the spread transaction is $600.

As a final example of currency speculation, consider the spot and futures prices for the British pound in Table 11.17. A speculator observes these relatively constant prices, but believes that the British economy is even worse

Table 11.17
Spot and Futures Prices, August 12

	$/British Pound
Spot	1.4485
SEP	1.4480
DEC	1.4460
MAR	1.4460
JUN	1.4470

Table 11.18
Time Spread Speculation in the British Pound

Date	Futures Market
August 12	Buy one DEC BP futures contract at 1.4460. Sell one MAR BP futures contract at 1.4460.
December 5	Sell one DEC BP futures contract at 1.4313. Buy one MAR BP futures contract at 1.4253.

		December	March
	Sold	1.4313	1.4460
	Bought	– 1.4460	– 1.4253
		– $.0147	$.0207
× 25,000	=	- $367.50	+ $517.50

Total Profit: $150

than generally appreciated. Specifically, she anticipates that the British inflation rate will exceed the U.S. rate. Therefore, the trader expects the pound to fall relative to the dollar. One easy way to act on this belief is to sell a distant futures contract, but this position trader is very risk averse, and she decides to trade a spread instead of an outright position. She believes that the equal prices for the DEC and MAR contracts will not be sustained, so she trades as shown in Table 11.18, selling what she believes to be the relatively overpriced MAR contract and buying the relatively underpriced DEC contract. By December, the speculator's expectations have been realized and the pound has fallen relative to the dollar, with the more distant futures contract falling even more. The speculator then closes her position on December 5 and realizes a total profit of $150, as Table 11.18 shows. As a result of her conservatism, the profit is only $150. Had the trader taken an outright position by selling the MAR contract, the profit would have been $517.50. In these examples of successful speculations it must be recognized that the speculator pits his or her knowledge against the collective opinion of the entire market, as that opinion is expressed in market prices.

Hedging with Foreign Exchange Futures

Many firms, and some individuals, find themselves exposed to foreign exchange risk. Importers and exporters, for example, often need to make commitments to buy or sell goods for delivery at some future time, with the payment to be made in a foreign currency. Likewise, multinational firms operating foreign subsidiaries receive payments from their subsidiaries that may be denominated in a foreign currency. A wealthy individual may plan an extended trip abroad and may be concerned about the chance that the price of a particular foreign currency might rise unexpectedly. All of these different parties are potential candidates for hedging unwanted currency risk by using the foreign exchange futures market.

If a trader faces the actual exchange of one currency for another, the risk is called **transaction exposure,** because the trader will transact in the market to exchange one currency for another. Firms often face **translation exposure,** the need to restate one currency in terms of another currency. For example, a firm may have a foreign subsidiary that earns profits in a foreign currency. However, the parent company prepares its accounting statements in the domestic currency. For accounting purposes, the firm must translate the foreign earnings into the domestic currency. While this procedure does not involve an actual transaction in the foreign exchange market, the reported earnings of the firm expressed in the domestic currency can be volatile due to the uncertain exchange rate at which the subsidiary's foreign earnings will be translated into the domestic currency. In the examples that follow, we consider hedges of both transaction and translation exposure.

Transaction versus Translation Exposure

Transaction exposure	Foreign exchange risk associated with exchanging one currency for another.
Translation exposure	Foreign exchange risk associated with expressing the value of one currency in terms of another for accounting purposes without actually exchanging currency

---

Hedging Transaction Exposure

The simplest kind of example arises in the case of someone like Moncrief Snobbody, who is planning a six-month trip to Switzerland. Moncrief plans to spend a considerable sum during this trip, enough to make it worthwhile to attend to exchange rates, shown in Table 11.19. With the more distant rates lying above nearby rates, Moncrief fears that spot rates may rise even higher, so he decides to lock-in the existing rates by buying Swiss franc futures. Because he plans to depart for Switzerland in June, he buys two JUN SF futures contracts at the current price of .5134. He anticipates that SF 250,000 will be enough to cover his six-month stay, as Table 11.20 shows. By June 6, Moncrief's fears

Table 11.19
Swiss Exchange Rates, January 12

Spot	.4935
MAR	.5034
JUN	.5134
SEP	.5237
DEC	.5342

Table 11.20
Moncrief Snobbody's Swiss Franc Hedge

	Cash Market	Futures Market
January 12	Moncrief plans to take a six–month vacation in Switzerland, to begin in June; the trip will cost about SF 250,000.	Moncrief buys 2 JUN SF futures contracts at .5134 for a total cost of $128,350.
June 16	The $/SF spot rate is now .5211, giving a dollar cost of $130,275 for SF 250,000.	Moncrief delivers $128,350 and collects SF 250,000.
	Savings on the Hedge = $130,275 – 128,350 = $1,925	

have been realized, and the spot rate for the SF is .5211. Moncrief, consequently, delivers $128,350 and collects SF 250,000. Had he waited and transacted in the spot market on June 6, the SF 250,000 would have cost $130,275. Hedging his foreign exchange risk, Moncrief has saved $1,925, which is enough to finance a few extra days in Switzerland.

In this example, Moncrief had a pre-existing risk in the foreign exchange market, since it was already determined that he would acquire the Swiss francs. By trading futures, he guaranteed a price of $.5134 per franc. Of course, the futures market can be used for purposes even more serious than reducing the risk surrounding Moncrief Snobbody's Swiss vacation.

Hedging Import/Export Transactions

Consider a small import/export firm that is negotiating a large purchase of Japanese watches from a firm in Japan. The Japanese firm, being a very tough negotiator, has demanded that payment be made in yen upon delivery of the watches. (If the contract had called for payment in dollars, rather than yen, the Japanese firm would bear the exchange risk.) Delivery will take place in seven

Table 11.21
$/Yen Foreign Exchange Rates, April 11

Spot	.004173
JUN Futures	.004200
SEP Futures	.004237
DEC Futures	.004265

months, but the price of the watches is agreed today to be Yen 2850 per watch for 15,000 watches. This means that the purchaser will have to pay Yen 42,750,000 in about seven months. Table 11.21 shows the current exchange rates on April 11. With the current spot rate of .004173 dollars per yen, the purchase price for the 15,000 watches would be $178,396. If the futures prices on April 11 are treated as a forecast of future exchange rates, it seems that the dollar is expected to lose ground against the yen. With the DEC futures trading at .004265, the actual dollar cost might be closer to $182,329. If delivery and payment are to occur in December, the importer might reasonably estimate the actual dollar outlay to be about $182,000 instead of $178,000.

To avoid any worsening of his exchange position, the importer decides to hedge the transaction by trading foreign exchange futures. Delivery is expected in November, so the importer decides to trade the DEC futures. By selecting this expiration, the hedger avoids having to roll over a nearby contract, thereby reducing transaction costs. Also, the DEC contract has the advantage of being the first contract to mature after the hedge horizon, so the DEC futures exchange rate should be close to the spot exchange rate prevailing in November when the yen are needed.

The importer's next difficulty stems from the fact that the futures contract is written for Yen 12.5 million. If he trades three contracts, his transaction will be for 37.5 million. If he trades four contracts, however, he would be trading 50 million, when he really only needs coverage for 42.75 million. No matter which way he trades, the importer will be left with some unhedged exchange risk. Finally, he decides to trade three contracts. Table 11.22 shows his transactions. On April 11 he anticipates that he will need Yen 42.75 million, with a current dollar value of $178,396 and an expected future value of $182,329, where the expected future worth of the yen is measured by the DEC futures price. This expected future price is the most relevant price for measuring the success of the hedge. In the futures market, the importer buys three DEC yen contracts at .004265 dollars per yen.

On November 18, the watches arrive, and the importer purchases the yen on the spot market at .004273. Relative to his anticipated cost of yen, he pays

Table 11.22
The Importer's Hedge

	Cash Market	Futures Market
April 11	The importer anticipates a need for yen 42,750,000 in November, the current value of which is $178,396, and which have an expected value in November of $182,329.	The importer buys 3 DEC yen futures contracts at .004265 for a total commitment of $159,938.
November 1	Receives watches; buys yen 42,750,000 at the spot market rate of .004273 for a total of $182.671.	Sells 3 DEC yen futures contracts at .004270 for a total value of $160,125.

Spot Market Results:	Futures Market Results:
Anticipated Cost $182,329 – Actual Cost – 182,671 –$ 342 Net Loss: – $155	Profit = $187

$342 more than expected. Having acquired the yen, the importer offsets his futures position. Since the futures has moved only .000005, the futures profit is only $187. This gives a total loss on the entire transaction of $155. Had there been no hedge, the loss would have been the full change of the price in the cash market, or $342. This hedge was only partially effective for two reasons. First, the futures price did not move as much as the cash price. The cash price changed by .000008 dollars per yen, but the futures price changed by only .000005 dollars per yen. Second, the importer was not able to fully hedge his position, due to the fact that his needs fell between two contract amounts. Since he needed Yen 42.75 million and only traded futures for Yen 37.5 million, he was left with an unhedged exposure of Yen 5.25 million.

Hedging Translation Exposure

Many corporations in international business have subsidiaries that earn revenue in foreign currencies and remit their profits to a U.S. parent company. The U.S. parent reports its income in dollars, so the parent's reported earnings fluctuate with the exchange rate between the dollar and the currency of the foreign country in which the subsidiary operates. This necessity to restate foreign currency earnings in the domestic currency is translation exposure. For many firms, fluctuating earnings are anathema. To avoid variability in earnings stemming from exchange rate fluctuations, firms can hedge with foreign exchange futures.

Table 11.23
Exchange Rates for the German Mark

	January 2	December 15
Spot	.4233	.4017
DEC Futures	.4211	.4017

Table 11.23 shows DM exchange rates for January 2 and December 15. Faced with these exchange rates is the Schropp Trading Company of Neckarsulm, a subsidiary of an American firm. Schropp Trading expects to earn DM 4.3 million this year and plans to remit those funds to its American parent. With the DEC futures trading at .4211 dollars per DM on January 2, the expected dollar value of those earnings is $1,810,730. If the mark falls, however, the actual dollar contribution to the earnings of the parent will be lower.

The firm can either hedge or leave unhedged the value of the earnings in marks, as Table 11.24 shows. With the rates in Table 11.23, the 4.3 million marks will be worth only $1,727,310 on December 15. This shortfall could have been avoided by selling the expected earnings in marks in the futures market in January at the DEC futures price of .4211. Table 11.24 shows this possibility.

Table 11.24
Schropp Trading Company of Neckarsulm

January 2

	DM 4.3 million
Expected earnings in Germany for the year:	DM 4.3 million
Anticipated value in U.S. dollars:	$1,810,730
(computed @ .4211 $/DM)	

Schropp Trading Company's Contribution to its Parent's Income:

	Unhedged	Hedged
Contribution to Parent's Income in U.S. Dollars from DM 4.3 million earnings (Assumes spot rate of .4017)	$1,727,310	$1,727,310
Futures profit or loss (Closed at the spot rate of .4017)	0	$ 84,875
Total	$1,727,310	$1,812,185

With a contract size of DM 125,000, the firm could have sold 35 contracts at the January 2 price. This strategy would have generated a futures profit of $84,875 (35 contracts × 125,000 marks × $.0194 profit per mark). This futures profit would have almost exactly offset the loss in the value of the mark, and Schropp Trading could successfully make its needed contribution to the American parent, by remitting $1,812,185.[14]

Recent Studies of Hedging Strategies

Scholars continue to develop new techniques for hedging foreign exchange risk and they continue to appraise existing methods. Table 11.25 summarizes some studies of hedging techniques.

First, minimum variance hedging is directly relevant to foreign exchange hedging. Chapters 4 and 10 elaborated examples of how these hedges work. The same techniques apply to foreign exchange futures hedging. Grammatikos and Saunders, for example, find that minimum risk hedge ratios tend to be quite stable. Lypny confirms this result for efforts to hedge currency portfolios. However, Swanson and Caples warn that mis-estimation can lead to an overstatement of minimum risk hedge ratios.

Table 11.25
Studies of Hedging with Foreign Currency Futures

Study	Key Results
Grammatikos and Saunders (1983)	Minimum variance hedge ratios are fairly stable.
Chang and Shanker (1986)	Foreign exchange futures are more useful as a hedging vehicle than foreign currency options.
Swanson and Caples (1987)	Autocorrelation in foreign exchange prices can lead to overstatement of minimum variance hedge ratios.
Eaker and Grant (1987)	Cross–hedging with foreign currency futures is less effective than same–asset hedges, but cross–hedging is still useful.
Lypny (1988)	For a portfolio of currencies, naive hedging works well. Minimum variance hedge ratios can sometimes increase risk.
Braga, Martin, and Meilke (1989)	DM currency futures can be used as an effective cross–hedge for $/Italian lira foreign exchange exposure.

We gave an example of speculating on a cross-rate by trading foreign exchange futures. Some studies suggest that futures can be used to effectively cross-hedge exchange risk. For example, Braga, Martin, and Meilke illustrate how to hedge exchange risk between the dollar and Italian lira by using German mark futures. As Eaker and Grant warn, however, cross-hedging is less effective than direct hedging. Finally, Chang and Shanker find that futures are a superior hedging vehicle compared to foreign currency options.

Conclusion

This chapter began by exploring the foreign exchange spot and forward markets. Of all goods with futures markets, the foreign exchange market is unique in the strength of the forward market. In fact, the forward market is much larger than the futures market. Nonetheless, as we discussed, forward prices and futures prices for foreign exchange are virtually identical.

Because foreign exchange rates represent the price of one unit of money in terms of another unit of money, every foreign exchange rate is clearly a relative price. Because of this unique character of foreign exchange markets, we considered the determinants of foreign exchange rates, such as the balance of payments. With modern money being a creation of governments, government intervention in the foreign exchange market is more dominant than in most other markets. Governments attempt to establish exchange rate systems that either fix the value of a currency in terms of another currency, or allow the value of currencies to float. Even when the value of a currency is allowed to float, governments often intervene to manage the value of their currency.

As we have seen for all markets, no-arbitrage conditions constrain foreign exchange rates. One of the most famous of these relationships is the Interest Rate Parity Theorem. As we discuss in detail, the IRP Theorem is just the Cost-of-Carry Model for foreign exchange. Thus, foreign exchange pricing principles match the concepts we have developed for other markets.

Compared to many other markets, there have been a number of studies of the forecasting accuracy of futures and forward exchange rates. These studies ask whether the futures price is a good forecast of the spot price that will prevail at the futures expiration. In general, most of these studies find significant errors or biases in the futures-based forecast. However, compared with most professional forecasting services, the futures price still provides a superior forecast of future spot prices.

The evidence on the efficiency of the foreign exchange market is probably more negative than the evidence for any of the other markets we have considered. Most studies seem to agree in finding significant departures from efficiency. These range from violations of parity conditions to finding successful speculative strategies. The reason for this apparent inefficiency is unclear, but several studies point to central bank intervention as a possible explanation: Central banks enter the market to pursue policy objectives, thereby providing speculators with profit opportunities. Whether this tentative explanation can be sustained is not totally clear.

As with all futures markets, the foreign currency futures market has numerous hedging applications. We showed how to use foreign currency futures to hedge risk for importers and exporters. Also, we considered the problems of transaction and translation exposure. In transaction exposure, a trader actually faces the exchange of one currency for another and wishes to hedge the future commitment of funds. In translation exposure, funds received in one currency will be restated for accounting purposes in another currency. Because it concerns only accounting, translation exposure need not require the actual exchange of one currency for another. Nonetheless, firms can hedge translation exposure to avoid the volatility of reported earnings in the home currency.

Questions and Problems

1. The current spot exchange rate for the dollar against the Japanese yen is 146 yen per dollar. What is the corresponding U.S. dollar value of one yen?

2. You hold the current editions of *The Wall Street Journal* and *The Financial Times*, the British answer to the WSJ. In the WSJ, you see that the dollar/pound 90-day forward exchange rate is $2.00 per pound. In *The Financial Times*, the pound 90-day dollar/pound rate is £.45 per U.S. dollar. Explain how you would trade to take advantage of these rates, assuming perfect markets.

3. In problem 2, we assumed that markets are perfect. What are some practical impediments that might frustrate your arbitrage transactions in problem 2?

4. In the WSJ, you see that the spot value of the German mark is $.63 and the Swiss franc is worth $.72. What rate of exchange do these values imply for the Swiss franc and German mark? Express the value in terms of marks per franc.

5. Explain the difference between a pegged exchange rate system and a managed float.

6. Explain why covered interest arbitrage is just like our familiar cash-and-carry transactions from Chapter 3.

7. For covered interest arbitrage, what is the cost-of-carry? Explain carefully.

8. The spot value of the German mark is $.65, and the 90-day forward rate is $.64. If the U.S. dollar interest factor to cover this period is 2 percent, what is the German rate? What is the cost of carrying a German mark forward for this period?

9. The French franc is worth $.21 in the spot market. The French franc futures that expires in one year trades for $.22. The U.S. dollar interest rate for this period is 10 percent. What should the French franc interest rate be?

10. Using the data in problem 9, explain which country is expected to experience the higher inflation over the next year. If the expected inflation rate in the U.S. is 7 percent, what inflation rate for the French franc does this imply?

11. Using the data of problem 9, assume that the French franc interest rate for the year is also 10 percent. Explain how you might transact faced with these values.

12. Many travelers say that shoes in Italy are a big bargain. How can this be, given the Purchasing Power Parity Theorem?

13. For the most part, the price of oil is denominated in dollars. Assume that you are a French firm that expects to import 120,000 barrels of crude oil in six months. What risks do you face in this transaction? Explain how you could transact to hedge the currency portion of those risks.

14. A financial comptroller for a U.S. firm is reviewing the earnings from a German subsidiary. This sub earns DM 1 million every year with exactitude, and it reinvests those earnings in its own German operations. This plan will continue. The earnings, however, are translated into U.S. dollars to prepare the U.S. parent's financial statements. Explain the nature of the foreign exchange risk from the point of view of the U.S. parent. Explain what steps you think the parent should take to hedge the risk that you have identified.

Notes

1. One such trading room was featured in the film, *Rollover*, starring Kris Kristofferson and Jane Fonda. In this story of international financial intrigue and panic, Kristofferson played the brilliant hard-nosed manager of the trading room, who saves the world from financial collapse.

2. Actually, in major foreign exchange centers, such as New York, some traders will make markets in the major cross-rates. For many currencies in many markets, however, a separate quotation for cross-rates is not available.

3. The Financial Instrument Exchange (FINEX) is an arm of the New York Cotton Exchange. FINEX trades a contract based on a U.S. dollar index as well, but it is not very active. See T. Eytan, G. Harpaz, and S. Krull, "The Pricing of Dollar Index Futures Contracts," *The Journal of Futures Markets*, 8:2, April 1988, pp. 127-139, for a summary of the contract terms and an analysis of pricing the futures contract.

4. Although maturities of 30, 90, and 180 days are normally listed, forward market transactions may be arranged with different maturities to suit the needs of the customer.

5. Figure 11.5 does not reflect trading in the French franc and the Australian dollar, which together account for less than one-half of one percent of the trading in 1989.

6. For more on the balance of payments, see the International Monetary Fund's *Balance of Payments Statistics*.

7. The origins and structure of the European Monetary System are discussed by N. Pinsky and J. Kvasnicka. "The European Monetary System," G. Gay and R. Kolb, *International Finance: Concepts and Issues*, Richmond, VA: Robert F. Dame, Inc., 1982.

8. See B. Cornell and M. Reinganum, "Forward and Futures Prices: Evidence from the Forward Exchange Markets," *Journal of Finance*, 36:5, December 1981, pp. 1035-1045.

9. R. Roll and B. Solnik, "On Some Parity Conditions Encountered Frequently in International Economics," *Journal of Macroeconomics*, 1:3, Summer 1979, pp. 267–283, review the parity conditions that we consider in this chapter.

10. For a more formal discussion of the Interest Rate Parity and Purchasing Power Parity Theorems, and the linkages between the two theorems, see I. Giddy. "An Integrated Theory of Exchange Rate Equilibrium," R. Kolb and G. Gay, *International Finance: Concepts and Issues*, Richmond, VA: Robert F. Dame, Inc., 1982.

11. See, for example, R. Levich, "Evaluating the Performance of the Forecasters," in R. Ensor (ed.) *The Management of Foreign Exchange Risk*, Second Edition, Euromoney Publications, 1982, pp. 121–134.

]12. See R. Levich, "The Efficiency of Markets for Foreign Exchange: A Review and Extension," G. Gay and R. Kolb, *International Finance: Concepts and Issues*, Richmond, VA: Robert F. Dame, Inc., 1982, p. 406.

13. Many other empirical tests tend to confirm the conclusion of efficiency reached by Levich, and a number of these are included in the bibliography to his article.

14. For more on hedging foreign exchange risk see J. Westerfield, "How U.S. Multinationals Manage Currency Risk"; L. Jacque, "Management of Foreign Exchange Risk: A Review Article"; and I. Giddy, "Why It Doesn't Pay to Make a Habit of Forward Hedging," all of which appear in R. Kolb and G. Gay, *International Finance: Concepts and Issues*, Richmond, VA: Robert F. Dame, Inc., 1982. Giddy argues that frequent small risks should not be hedged. His argument first assumes that there are no transaction costs. Since the futures exchange rate is equal to the expected future spot rate, a trader expects neither a gain nor a loss on a given hedge. If the trader makes many hedges, then he is almost certain to have a result very close to a zero gain or loss. In such an event, there is no benefit or detriment, except, perhaps, a reduction in variance. If transaction costs are considered, however, he would expect to lose the amount of the transaction costs on a given hedge. With many hedges, the net expected result is to lose the amount of the transaction costs, so the trader would be well advised not to make a habit of forward hedging. When the risk is large or will occur only infrequently, then he may reasonably hedge. Giddy intends his argument to apply only to the hedging of numerous small transactions.

12

An Options Primer

Introduction

As the name implies, an **option** is the right to buy or sell for a limited time a particular good at a specified price. Such options have obvious value. For example, if IBM trades at $120 and an investor has the option to buy a share at $100, this option must be worth at least $20, the difference between the price at which you can buy IBM by exercising the option ($100) and the price at which you could sell it in the open market ($120).

This chapter explores the options market of the United States. Prior to 1973, options of various kinds were traded over the counter. But in 1973, the Chicago Board Options Exchange (CBOE) began trading options on individual stocks. Since that time the options markets have experienced rapid growth, with the creation of new exchanges and many different kinds of new option contracts.

Options markets are very diverse, and they have their own particular jargon. As a consequence, understanding options requires a grasp of the institutional details and terminology employed in the market. The chapter begins with a discussion of the institutional background of options markets, including the kinds of contracts traded and the price quotations for various options.

The successful option trader must also understand the pricing relationships that prevail in the options market. For example, how much should an option to buy IBM at $100 be worth if IBM is selling at $120? With IBM trading at $120, how much more would an option be worth if it required a payment of only $90 instead of $100? Similarly, how much would an option to sell IBM for $115 be worth if IBM is trading at $120? These are the kinds of questions that prospective option investors need to have answered. Fortunately, the pricing principles for options are well developed. While the particular answers to these questions may sometimes be surprising, they are very logical upon reflection.

For a potential speculator in options, these pricing relationships are of the greatest importance. As in the futures market, much option speculation relies on techniques of spreading. This chapter examines some of the speculative strategies that investors might utilize. However, options are also important for hedging, and the use of options for risk control is a well-defined area of study that is also very important for an understanding options markets. For example, the new options contracts on stock indexes have gained wide acceptance among portfolio managers as a potential tool for controlling the risk of their equity portfolios.

Options and Options Markets

There are two major classes of options, call options and put options. Ownership of a **call option** gives the owner the right to buy a particular good at a certain price, with that right lasting until a particular date. Ownership of a **put option** gives the owner the right to sell a particular good at a specified price, with that right lasting until a particular date. For every option, there is both a buyer and a seller. In the case of a call option, the seller receives a payment from the buyer and gives to the buyer the option of buying a particular good from the seller at a certain price, with that right lasting until a particular date. Similarly, the seller of a put option receives a payment from the buyer. The buyer then has the right to sell a particular good to the seller at a certain price for a specified period of time.

In all cases, ownership of an option involves the right, but not the obligation, to make a certain transaction. The owner of a call option may, for example, buy a good at the contracted price during the life of the option, but there is no obligation to do so. Likewise, the owner of a put option may sell a good under the terms of the option contract, but there is no obligation to do so. Selling an option does commit the seller to specific obligations. The seller of a call option receives a payment from the buyer and in exchange for this payment, the seller of the call option must be ready to sell a given good to the owner of the call, if the owner of the call wishes. The discretion to engage in further transactions always lies with the owner of an option. Option sellers have no such discretion. They have obligated themselves to perform in certain ways if the owners of the options so desire. Later in this chapter we will see the conditions under which buyers and sellers find it reasonable to act differently.

Option Terminology

There is great deal of special terminology associated with the options market. The seller of an option is also known as the **writer** of an option, and the act of selling an option is called **writing an option**. As mentioned above, the buyer of an option may require certain performances by the writer of an option. In the case of a call option, the owner has the right to buy a given good under certain circumstances. If the owner of the call takes advantage of the option, he or she is said to "exercise the option." An owner exercises a call option by buying a good under the terms of an option contract. Each option contract stipulates a price that will be paid if the option is exercised, and this price is known as the **exercise price** or the **striking price**. In our first example of the call option to buy IBM at $100 (when it is selling at $120) the exercise price would be $100, because this is the amount that must be paid to exercise the option.

Every option involves a payment from the buyer to the seller. This payment is the price of the option, but it is also called the option **premium**. Also, every option traded on an exchange is valid for only a limited period of time. For example, an option on IBM might be valid only through August of the present year. The option has no validity after its "expiration date" or its "maturity." This special terminology is used widely in the options market and throughout the rest of this chapter.

Option Exchanges

As Table 12.1 shows, there are quite a few options exchanges in the United States trading a variety of goods. This list can be expected to expand in the future. However, some of the goods shown in Table 12.1 are struggling with low volume and may be expected to cease trading. The present is a time of expansion

---

Table 12.1
U.S. Options Exchanges and Goods Traded

Chicago Board Options Exchange
Individual Stocks
Stock Market Indexes

American Exchange
Individual Stocks
Stock Market Indexes
Computer Technology Index
Institutional Index

Philadelphia Exchange
Individual Stocks
Foreign Currencies
Gold and Silver Index
Stock Market Indexes

Pacific Exchange
Individual Stocks
Technology Index

New York Stock Exchange
General Stock Market Indexes

Note: This listing does not include options on futures contracts.

---

and experimentation in the options market, and there will be a continuing process of maturation.

In many respects, options exchanges and futures exchanges are organized similarly. In the options market, as in the futures market, there is a seller for every buyer and both markets allow offsetting trades. To buy an option, a trader simply needs to have an account with a brokerage firm holding a membership on the options exchange. The trade can be executed through the broker with the same ease as executing a trade to buy a stock itself. The buyer of an option will pay for the option at the time of the trade, so there is no more worry about cash flows associated with the purchase. For the seller of an option, the matter is somewhat more complicated. In selling a call option, the seller is agreeing to deliver the stock for a set price if the owner of the call so chooses. This means that the seller may need large financial resources to fulfil his or her obligations. Because the broker is representing the trader to the exchange, the broker is also obligated to be sure that the trader has the necessary financial resources to fulfil all obligations. For the seller, these obligations are not known at the time the option is sold. Accordingly, the broker needs financial guarantees from option writers. In the case of a call, the writer of an option may already own the shares of stock and deposit these with the broker. Writing call options against stock that the writer owns is called writing a **covered call**. This gives the broker complete protection, because the shares that are obligated for delivery are in the possession of the broker. If the writer of the call does not own the underlying stocks, he or she has written a **naked option**. In such cases, the broker may require substantial margin deposits of cash or securities to ensure that the trader has the financial resources necessary to fulfil all obligations.

The Option Clearing Corporation (OCC) oversees the conduct of the market and helps to make the market orderly. As in futures markets, the option buyer and seller have no obligations to a specific individual, but obligations to the OCC. If an option is exercised, the OCC matches buyers and sellers, and manages the completion of the exercise process.

This management of the exercise process and the standardization of contract terms are the largest contributions of the OCC. With standardized contract terms, traders can focus on their trading strategies without having to learn the intricacies of many different option contracts. The benefits of the OCC in the marketplace are perhaps clearest in considering option quotations.

Option Quotations

No matter what the exchange or the good underlying the option, the quotations are similar. Because the market for individual stocks is the oldest and has the most overall trading activity, we will use the quotations for IBM to illustrate the basic features of the prices. Figure 12.1 shows quotations for call and put options on individual stocks from *The Wall Street Journal*.

Figure 12.1
Quotations for Options on Individual Stocks

CHICAGO BOARD

Option & NY Close	Strike Price	Calls—Last Oct	Calls—Last Nov	Calls—Last Dec	Puts—Last Oct	Puts—Last Nov	Puts—Last Dec
Baybks	12½	1¼	r	r	r	r	r
13⅞	17½	r	r	r	r	4½	r
BergBr	25	r	r	1	r	r	r
Blkbst	15	4⅜	r	5¼	r	5/16	⅝
19⅜	17½	r	2⅝	r	r	13/16	1¼
19⅜	20	⅛	1¼	1¾	¾	2 1/16	2¼
19⅜	22½	r	7/16	¾	r	r	3⅝
BrMySq	50	s	s	r	s	s	⅜
60⅜	55	5¾	6	7	r	r	⅞
60⅜	60	⅝	2	3⅛	⅜	1⅝	2¼
60⅜	65	r	r	1	r	r	4⅞
60⅜	70	s	s	¼	s	s	r
Bruns	7½	1/16	r	r	r	r	r
Chamln	25	r	1	r	r	1	r
24¾	30	r	r	⅜	r	r	5⅜
CompSc	35	4¼	4¼	r	r	r	r
38⅞	45	r	r	r	r	r	5⅞
ContBk	7½	r	r	r	⅛	r	13/16
7⅞	10	r	r	r	r	r	2¾
CypSem	10	r	r	1	r	r	r
Dow Ch	35	r	r	r	r	¼	¾
40⅞	40	1	2¼	3⅛	¼	1⅜	2
40⅞	45	r	½	1	4⅛	4⅜	4¾
FFB	15	r	r	r	r	2⅛	r
13⅝	17½	r	s	r	r	s	4⅞
Ford	25	s	r	r	s	r	½
30⅞	30	⅞	1½	2 1/16	¼	1⅜	1¾
30⅞	35	r	¼	½	4	5	5
30⅞	40	r	r	⅛	r	r	r
Gap	40	r	r	r	r	1	1⅞
45¼	45	¾	3¼	r	9/16	2⅞	r
45¼	50	r	r	2	r	6⅛	r
45¼	55	r	r	⅞	r	r	r
Gen El	45	r	8⅞	r	r	⅜	⅝
53⅝	50	3¾	4¾	5⅛	1/16	1¼	1⅞
53⅝	55	⅛	1½	2 5/16	1⅜	2⅞	3⅝
53⅝	60	r	5/16	¾	7⅜	r	7¼
53⅝	70	r	s	3/16	r	s	17¼
53⅝	75	s	s	⅛	s	s	r
G M	30	s	r	r	s	¼	½
35⅞	35	1¼	2⅛	2¾	⅛	1⅝	1⅝
35⅞	40	r	¼	⅝	4⅛	r	4¾
Hanson	20	r	r	½	r	r	r

Option & NY Close	Strike Price	Calls—Last Oct	Calls—Last Nov	Calls—Last Jan	Puts—Last Oct	Puts—Last Nov	Puts—Last Jan
5¾	7½	r	r	¾	⅞	r	2
5¾	10	r	r	r	r	r	4
5¾	20	r	s	r	r	s	14⅜
Hornstk	15	2½	r	r	r	r	r
17⅝	17½	5/16	1⅜	2 3/16	5/16	1¼	1⅞
17⅝	20	r	⅜	1¼	2⅜	r	r
17⅝	22½	1/16	3/16	¾	r	r	r
Imcera	45	r	r	r	r	r	5/16
56¾	50	r	7⅜	r	r	r	r
56¾	55	1½	2⅝	r	r	1⅜	r
Intrmc	12½	1¼	r	r	¼	r	r
13⅝	15	1/16	r	1 9/16	r	r	r
I B M	95	8¾	9¾	11	1/16	1 1/16	2 13/16
103¾	100	2½	5⅜	8¼	3/16	2⅜	4⅛
103¾	105	⅜	r	5¼	1⅞	4½	6¼
103¾	110	1/16	⅞	3⅛	6⅞	8¼	9½
103¾	115	r	5/16	1⅝	r	r	r
103¾	120	1/16	s	11/16	r	s	r
103¾	125	r	s	5/16	r	s	r
In Pap	45	r	2⅜	r	⅛	1½	r
46⅛	50	1/16	r	1¼	4¼	4⅝	5
Itel	10	r	¼	7/16	r	1⅞	r
8¼	15	r	1/16	⅛	r	r	r
JanBel	7½	⅜	1	r	r	r	r
8⅛	10	r	r	r	2½	r	r
John J	50	16¼	s	s	r	s	s
66½	55	r	s	12⅝	r	s	¾
66½	60	6¼	r	8½	r	r	r
66½	65	1 9/16	3	5	⅛	1 9/16	2¾
66½	70	1/16	⅝	2¼	3¾	r	5¼
66½	75	r	s	¾	r	s	r
66½	80	r	s	r	13⅝	s	r
Kerr M	45	r	r	r	1/16	1¼	r
LAGear	10	1⅞	2¼	2⅞	r	r	1 7/16
11¾	12½	1/16	¾	1⅞	¾	1⅞	2⅞
11¾	15	r	3/16	⅞	3¼	3⅞	4⅜
11¾	17½	r	1/16	r	6	r	r
11¾	20	r	s	3/16	r	s	r
11¾	22½	r	s	r	11	s	r
11¾	25	r	s	r	13½	s	r
11¾	35	r	s	r	23¼	s	r
LAC	10	r	r	⅜	r	r	r
LizCla	22½	¾	r	3¼	r	r	r
23¾	25	1/16	1	r	1	r	r
23¾	30	1/16	r	r	7	r	r
23¾	35	r	s	r	11	s	r

Option & NY Close	Strike Price	Calls—Last Oct	Calls—Last Nov	Calls—Last Feb	Puts—Last Oct	Puts—Last Nov	Puts—Last Feb
Ogden	15	r	r	r	r	r	⅞
OshK A	20	r	r	r	⅝	r	r
Pansph	10	r	r	r	r	1⅝	r
Pegsus	10	r	1¼	2	r	r	r
11	12½	r	¼	⅞	r	r	r
Promus	10	r	r	1¾	r	r	r
10¼	12½	r	r	r	r	2¾	r
Raythn	65	r	r	r	3/16	r	r
Reuter	45	r	1 5/16	r	r	r	r
Slumb	55	r	2½	r	⅝	r	r
55⅜	60	r	r	3	4½	r	r
Shawln	17½	r	⅝	r	r	r	r
16½	20	r	r	13/16	r	r	r
Shell	55	r	r	r	r	3	r
SestBk	5	r	r	1	r	r	1 3/16
Southn	25	r	⅞	r	r	r	r
Tribune	30	s	3⅛	3⅞	s	1½	2¼
33	35	r	⅞	r	r	3⅞	4⅝
33	40	r	r	r	r	r	8⅛
UAL	80	13	12½	r	1/16	15/16	r
93	85	8½	r	r	1/16	1¾	r
93	90	4	7½	12½	⅜	3½	6¾
93	95	1	3	9½	4¾	5½	9
93	100	½	3	7⅝	7½	8½	11¼
93	105	⅛	1⅞	6⅜	11½	12½	15
93	110	⅛	1⅜	4½	17½	16½	18½
93	115	⅛	1½	4¼	22⅛	r	22½
93	120	1/16	1	3	28½	r	r
93	125	r	11/16	3¼	r	r	r
93	130	r	½	3	r	r	r
93	135	r	r	r	r	41	r
93	140	s	3/16	1¾	s	r	44½
93	145	s	r	r	s	r	55
93	150	s	r	1⅛	s	r	r
93	160	s	r	1⅛	s	r	r
93	165	s	⅛	r	s	r	r
UST	30	1⅝	r	3	r	⅜	r
U Tech	40	r	r	r	r	r	⅝
47	45	r	3¼	4¾	r	⅞	r
47	50	r	¾	2⅛	r	r	r
47	55	r	⅛	r	r	r	r

Total call vol 70,090 **Call open int** 3,544,060
Total put vol 48,152 **Put open int** 1,910,411

r-Not Traded. s-No Option.

Source: *The Wall Street Journal*, October 19, 1990.

Beneath the identifier for each stock, the quotations list the closing price of the stock for the day. The second column lists the various striking prices or exercise prices that are available. The striking prices are kept fairly near the prevailing price of the stock. As the stock price fluctuates, new striking prices are opened for trading, typically at intervals of $5. As a consequence, volatile stocks are likely to have a greater range of striking prices available for trading at any one time. Each contract is written on 100 shares, but the prices quoted are on a per share basis. Typically, several different maturities are available for both the call and the put options. These options expire on particular days of the expiration month, shown at the top of the column of quotations. The exact expiration date is determined by the rules of each exchange and differ from exchange to exchange. Also, different stocks trade on different expiration cycles. Instead of prices for some specific options, the quotations show an "r" for an option that was not traded that day, or an "s" for an option that is not listed for trading.

The quotations in Figure 12.1 illustrate several important features about options. First, for any given expiration, the lower the striking price for a call, the greater will be the price. Second, for the same stock and the same exercise price, a call option with a longer expiration has a higher value. Third, for call options on the same stock with the same expiration, the lower the exercise price, the higher the value of the option. As we will see below in the section on option pricing, there are very clear reasons why these kinds of pricing relationships must prevail in the marketplace.

Option Pricing

Option pricing affords one of the showcase results of research in modern finance. The pricing models developed for options perform very well, and a study of these models is very useful for the trader. In fact, as we will see, traders on the options exchanges have immediate access to the information provided by option pricing models through machines located on the floors of the exchanges. Prices of options on stocks without cash dividends depend on five factors:

S Stock price
E Exercise price
t Time until expiration
σ The volatility of the underlying stock
r The risk-free interest rate

Initially, it will be very useful to consider the effects of just the first three factors, the stock price, the exercise price, and the time until expiration. Later we will consider the more complicated situations that arise from taking into account different interest rate environments and different risk levels. For a call option, we can express the call price as a function of the stock price, the exercise price, and the time until expiration using this compact notation:

C(S,E,t)

For example, the equation

$$C(\$120, \$100, .25) = \$22.75$$

says that a call option on a share trading at $120, with an exercise price of $100, and one-fourth of a year to expiration has a price of $22.75.

Pricing Call Options at Expiration

By the term **at expiration** we refer to the moment just prior to expiration. If the option is not exercised at this time, it will expire immediately and the option will have no value. The value of options at expiration is an important topic because many of the complications that ordinarily affect option prices disappear when the option is about to expire. With this terminology in mind, let us consider the value of a call option at expiration, where $t = 0$. In this case, only two possibilities may arise, regarding the relationship between the exercise price (E) and the stock price (S). Either $S > E$ or $S \leq E$. If the stock price is less than or equal to the exercise price ($S \leq E$) the call option has no value. To see why this is the case, consider a call option with an exercise price of $80 on a stock trading at $70. Since the option is about to expire, the owner of the option has only two alternatives. The option may be exercised, or it may be allowed to expire. If the option is exercised in this situation, the holder of the option must pay the exercise price of $80 and receive a stock trading in the market for only $70. In this situation, it does not pay to exercise the option and the owner allows it to expire worthless. Accordingly, this option has no value and its market price will be zero. Employing our notation, we can say:

If $S \leq E$, $C(S,E,0) = 0$

If an option is at expiration and the stock price is less than or equal to the exercise price, the call option has no value.

This equation simply summarizes the conclusion we have already reached.

The second possible relationship that could hold between the stock price and the exercise price at expiration is for the stock price to exceed the exercise price ($S > E$). Again, in our notation,

If $S > E$, $C(S,E,0) = S - E$

If the stock price is greater than the exercise price, the call option must have a price equal to the difference between the stock price and the exercise price.

If this relationship did not hold, there would be arbitrage opportunities. Assume for the moment that the stock price is $50 and the exercise price is $40. If the option were selling for $5, an arbitrageur would make the following trades:

Transaction	Cash Flow
Buy a call option	$ -5
Exercise the option	-40
Sell the stock	50
Net Cash Flow	$ 5

As these transactions indicate, if the call price is less than the difference between the stock price and the exercise price, there will be an arbitrage opportunity.

What if the price of the call option exceeds the difference between the stock price and the exercise price? Continuing to use our example of a stock priced at $50 and the exercise price of the option being $40, assume now that the call price is $15. Faced with these prices, an arbitrageur would make the following transactions:

Transaction	Cash Flow
Write a call option	$ 15
Buy the stock	- 50
Initial Cash Flow	-$35

The owner of this call option must then immediately exercise the option or allow it to expire. If the option is exercised, there are these additional transactions:

Transaction	Cash Flow
Initial cash flow	-$35
Deliver stock	0
Collect exercise price	+$40
Net Cash Flow	$ 5

In this case, there is still a profit of $5. Alternatively, the owner of the option may allow the option to expire. In that event, the arbitrageur would simply sell the stock as soon as the option expires and receive $50. In this case the profit would be $15, since the arbitrageur simply keeps the option premium. In this second situation, in which the call price is greater than the stock price minus the exercise price, the holder of the call option would exercise the option. But the important point is to see that the arbitrageur would make a profit no matter what the holder of the call might do.

At expiration, if the stock price exceeds the exercise price, we have seen that the price of the call must equal the difference between the stock price and the exercise price. From reflection on the situation in which the stock price is less than or equal to the exercise price and the situation in which the stock price exceeds the exercise price, we can state the first basic principle of option pricing:

$$C(S,E,0) = \max(0, S - E)$$

At expiration, a call option must have a value that is equal to zero or to the difference between the stock price and the exercise price, whichever is greater.

This condition must hold, otherwise there will be arbitrage opportunities awaiting exploitation.[1]

Option Values and Profits at Expiration

In this discussion, it is important to distinguish the option's value or price and the profit or loss that a trader might experience. The value of options at expiration can be shown very easily by considering a concrete example. Consider a call and a put option, both with a striking price of $100. Figure 12.2 shows the value of these options at expiration for various stock prices. The graph shows the value of the options on the vertical axis and the stock price on the horizontal

Figure 12.2
Values of Call and Put Options at
Expiration when the Striking Price Equals $100

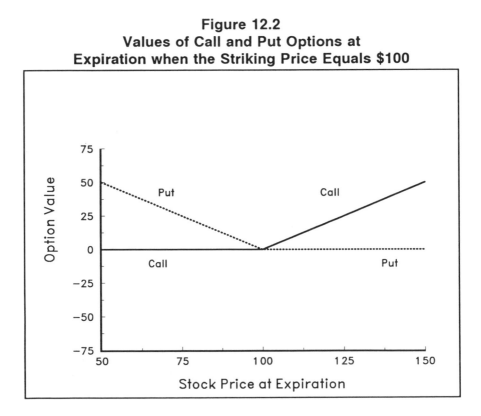

axis. If the stock price is less than or equal to the exercise price of $100, the value of the call option must be zero, as the graph shows with a solid line. For stock prices above the exercise price, the call price equals the difference between the stock price and the exercise price. This is reflected by the fact that the graph of the call option's value rises one dollar for each dollar the stock prices is above $100. Figure 12.2 also shows the value for a put option as a dotted line. Although we have not discussed the pricing of put options in any detail, the reader can reach the conclusion that this is the correct graph by the same kind of argument given above for call options.

Consider now the same situation, with two put and call options, each having an exercise price of $100, but now assume that trades had taken place for the options with premiums of $5 on each of the put and call options. Knowing the price paid for the options allows us to calculate the profits and losses at expiration for the sellers and buyers of both the put and call options. Figure 12.3 presents alternative outcomes for all of these trading parties. The first panel shows the profit and loss positions for the call option. The solid line pertains to the buyer of the call, and the dashed line to the seller. (Throughout this chapter and the next, solid lines are used to indicate long positions and dashed lines are used to indicate short positions.) For any stock price less than or equal to the exercise price of $100, the option will expire worthless and the purchaser of the call will lose everything that was paid for the call. If the stock price exceeds $100, reaching say, $105, the owner of the call will exercise the call, paying $100 for the share and receiving a share worth $105. With a share price of $105, the call owner breaks even exactly. His or her entire cash flow has been the $5 for the option plus the $100 exercise price. This total outflow of $105 is exactly matched by the receipt of the share that is worth $105. For the call owner, any stock price less than $100 results in the loss of the total amount paid for the option. For stock prices greater than the exercise price, the call owner will exercise the option. The call owner may still lose money even with exercise. In this example, the stock price must be greater than $105 to generate any net profit for the call owner.

For the writer of the call, notice that the profit picture is exactly opposite from that of the call owner's. The best situation for the writer of the call is for the stock price to stay at $100 or below. In this situation, the call writer keeps the entire option premium and the call option will not be exercised. If the stock price is $105, the option will be exercised and the writer of the call must deliver shares now worth $105 and receive only $100 for them. At this point, the loss on the exercise exactly equals the premium already received, so the call writer breaks even. If the stock price exceeds $105, the call writer has a net loss. Notice that the buyer's profits exactly mirror the seller's losses and vice versa. This emphasizes that the options market is a **zero sum game**. That is, the buyer's gains are the seller's losses and vice versa. If we sum all of the gains

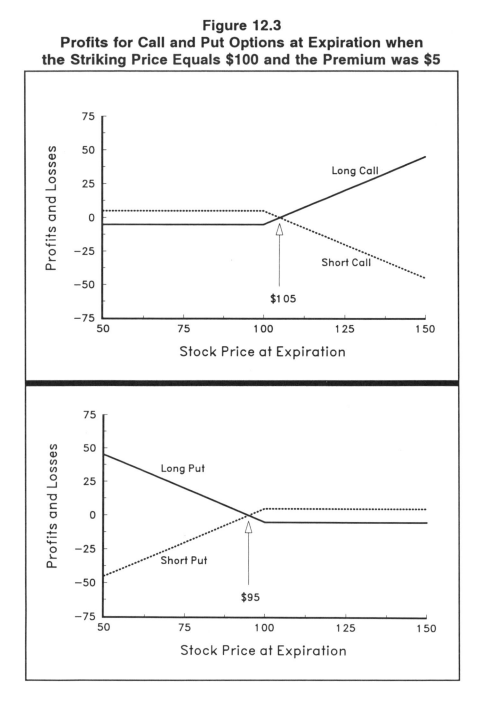

Figure 12.3
Profits for Call and Put Options at Expiration when
the Striking Price Equals $100 and the Premium was $5

and losses in the options market, ignoring transaction costs, the total will equal zero.

The second panel of Figure 12.3 shows the profit and loss positions for the put traders. If the put buyer pays $5 for a put with an exercise price of $100, he or she breaks even at $95. The writer of a put also breaks even at $95. These graphs indicate the wide variety of possible profit and loss patterns traders may create by using the options market. As we will see, this kind of graph is useful for analyzing a wide variety of market strategies.

A Call Option with a Zero Exercise Price and an Infinite Time until Expiration

It may appear unimportant to consider an option with a zero exercise price and an infinite time until expiration, because such options are not traded in the options market. However, this kind of option represents an extreme situation, and as such it can be used to set boundaries on possible option prices. An option on a stock with a zero exercise price and an infinite time to maturity can be surrendered at any time, without any cost, for the stock itself. Since such an option can be transformed into the stock costlessly, it must have a value as great as the stock itself. Similarly, an option on a good can never be worth more than the good itself. This allows us to state a second principle of option pricing:

$$C(S,0,\infty) = S$$

A call option with a zero exercise price and an infinite time to maturity must sell for the same price as the stock.

Together, these first two principles allow us to specify the upper and lower possible bounds for the price of a call option as a function of the stock price, the exercise price, and the time to expiration. Figure 12.4 presents these boundaries. If the call has a zero exercise price and an infinite maturity, the call price equals the stock price, as shown by the 45 degree line from the origin. This represents the upper bound for an option's price. Alternatively, if the option is at expiration, the price of the option must lie along the heavy line running from the origin to the point at which the stock price equals the exercise price (S = E), and then upward at an angle. If the stock price is less than or equal to the exercise price, the call price must be zero as shown in the graph. If the stock price exceeds the exercise price, the option must trade for a price equal to the difference between the stock price and the exercise price. Other options, such as those with time remaining until expiration and with positive exercise prices would have to lie in the shaded region between these two extremes. To understand option pricing, we need to consider other factors that more tightly restrict permissible option prices.

Figure 12.4
Bounds for Call Option Prices

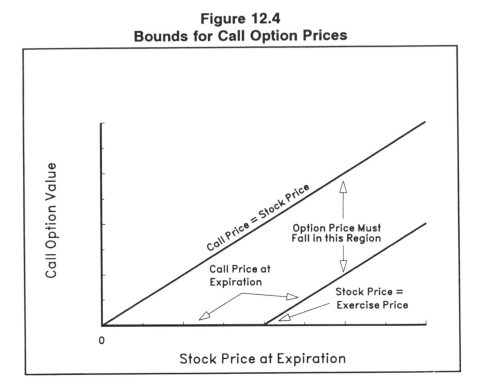

Relationships Between Option Prices

As noted above, there are numerous striking prices and expiration dates available for options on the same stock. Not surprisingly, definite relationships must be maintained between these different kinds of options, if there are not to be arbitrage opportunities. The relationship can be defined as follows:

If $E_1 < E_2$, $C(S,E_1,t) \geq C(S,E_2,t)$

If two call options are alike, except the exercise price of the first is less than that of the second, then the option with the lower exercise price must have a price that is equal to or greater than the price of the option with the higher exercise price.

In this situation, both options allow the owner of the option to acquire the same share of stock for the same period of time. However, the option with the lower exercise price allows the owner of that option to acquire the stock for a lower price. Therefore, the option with the lower exercise price should have a greater

552   *Chapter 12*

value. To see why this rule must hold, imagine a situation in which there are two options that are just alike, except the first has an exercise price of $100 and sells for $10. The second option has an exercise price of $90 and sells for $5. The profit and loss graphs for both options are shown in Figure 12.5. The option with the $90 exercise price has a much better profit and loss profile than the option with the $100 exercise price. No matter what the stock price might be at expiration, the option with the $90 exercise price will perform better.

This is already an impossible pricing situation, because it represents a disequilibrium result. With these prices, all participants in the market would want the option with the $90 exercise price. This would cause the price of the option with the $100 exercise price to fall until investors were willing to hold it too. But such a situation could only occur if it were not inferior to the option with the $90 exercise price.

The same point can be made in the following context, because the profit and loss opportunities shown in the first panel of Figure 12.5 create an arbitrage

Figure 12.5
Why Options with Lower Striking Prices Cannot Have Lower Prices Than Options with Higher Exercise Prices

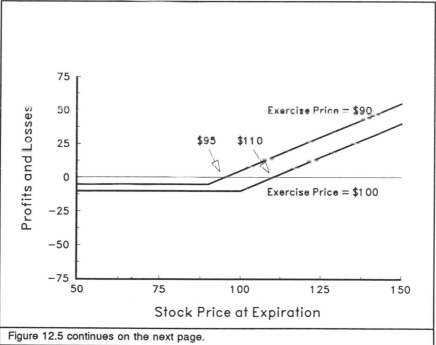

Figure 12.5 continues on the next page.

Figure 12.5 Continued

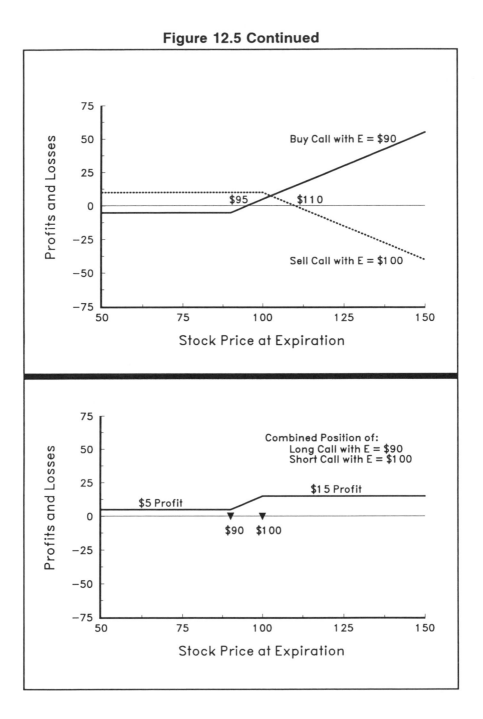

opportunity. Faced with these prices, the arbitrageur would simply transact as follows:

Transaction	Cash Flow
Sell the option with the $100 exercise price	$10
Buy the option with the $90 exercise price	- 5
Net Cash Flow	$ 5

This gives a combined position that is graphed in the second panel of Figure 12.5. Here the sale of the option with the $100 striking price is shown as the dashed line. To see why this is a good transaction to make, consider the profit and loss position on each option and the overall position for alternative stock prices that might prevail at expiration.

	Profit or Loss on the Option Position		
Stock Price at Expiration	For E = $90	For E = $100	For Both
80	- $5	+$10	+ $5
90	- $5	+$10	+ $5
95	0	+$10	+$10
100	+ $5	+$10	+$15
105	+$10	+ $5	+$15
110	+$15	0	+$15
120	+$20	- $5	+$15

For any stock price, there will be some profit. If the stock price is $90 or less, the profit will be $5 from the options position, plus the net cash inflow of $5 received when the position was initiated. As the stock price at expiration goes from $90 to $100, the profit goes up, until the maximum profit of $15 on the options position is achieved at a stock price of $100. For stock prices at expiration greater than $100, the profit on the options position remains at $15. This result is graphed in the third panel of Figure 12.5. This does not show the $5 inflow that was received when the position was initiated.

With the prices in the example, it is possible to trade to guarantee a total profit of at least $10 and perhaps as much as $20, without risk or investment, so it is an example of arbitrage. If option prices are to be rational, they cannot allow arbitrage. In order to eliminate the arbitrage opportunity, the price of the option with a striking price of $90 must be at least as large as the price of the option with the striking price of $100.[2]

A similar principle refers to the expiration date:

If $t_1 > t_2$, $C(S,t_1,E) \geq C(S,t_2,E)$

If there are two options that are otherwise alike, the option with the longer time to expiration must sell for an amount equal to or greater than the option that expires earlier.

Intuitively, this principle must hold, because the option with the longer time until expiration gives the investor all of the advantages that the one with a shorter time to expiration offers. But the option with the longer time to expiration also gives the investor the chance to wait longer before exercising the option or before the option expires. In some circumstances, the extra time for the option to run will have positive value.[3]

If the option with the longer period to expiration sold for less than the option with the shorter time to expiration, there would also be an arbitrage opportunity. To see how to conduct the arbitrage, assume that two options are written on the same stock with a striking price of $100. Let the first option have a time to expiration of six months and assume it trades for $8, while the second option has three months to expiration and trades for $10. In this situation, the arbitrageur would make the following transactions.

Transaction	Cash Flow
Buy the 6-month option for $8.	-$8
Sell the 3-month option for $10.	+$10
Net Cash Flow	+$2

By selling the longer maturity option and buying the shorter maturity option, the option trader receives a net cash flow of $2. However, there might appear to be some risk, because the option that was sold might be exercised. To see that the trader's position is secure, consider that if the option that is sold is exercised against the arbitrageur, he or she can simply exercise the 6-month option that was purchased and used the stock that is received to deliver on the 3-month option. This will guarantee that the $2 can be kept, so there will be a $2 profit no matter what happens to the stock price. Since this profit is certain and was earned without investment, it is an arbitrage profit. This result requires that the 6-month option be an American option so that it could be exercised at will prior to expiration. The option with the longer time to expiration cannot be worth less than the option with the shorter time to expiration. Otherwise, there will be arbitrage opportunities.

Generally, the option with the longer time to expiration will actually be worth more than the option with the shorter time to expiration, as Figure 12.6 shows. We have already seen that any option must be worth at least the difference between the stock price and the exercise price (S - E) at expiration. If the stock price is greater than the exercise price (S > E), a call option is said to be **in the money,** but if the stock price is less than the exercise price (S < E),

Figure 12.6
Bounds on Option Prices and Permissible
Relationships Between Pairs of Option Prices

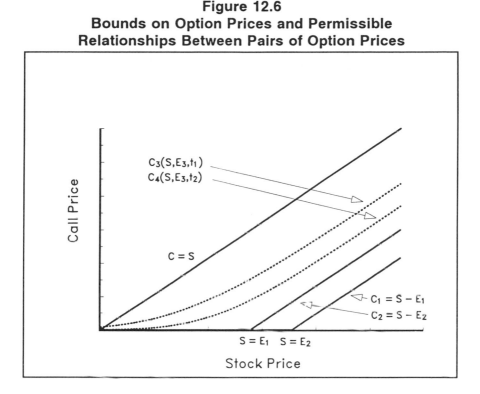

the option is **out of the money**. If the stock price equals the exercise price (S = E), the option is **at the money**. Prior to expiration, the value of an in the money call option normally exceeds the difference between the stock price and the exercise price, S - E. This difference, S - E, is known as the **intrinsic value** of the option— the value of the option if it were exercised immediately. We can expect an in the money option prior to expiration to be worth more than S - E, because the value of being able to wait to exercise normally has value. If the option is exercised prior to expiration, the trader receives only the amount S - E for the option. By selling the option in the market, the trader receives the market price, which normally exceeds S - E. Therefore, it generally will not pay to exercise an option early. In the case of a dividend paying stock, this will not always be true.

Thus far we have set bounds for option prices and we have established relationships between pairs of options, as shown in Figure 12.6. In Figure 12.6, the two options, C_1 and C_2, are alike except that option C_1 has a lower exercise price. Accordingly, the figure shows that its price is more tightly bounded than that of option C_2. The two options in the second pair, C_3 and C_4, differ only by the time to expiration. Consistent with this fact, the price of the option with the longer time to expiration, C_3, has a higher price. While we can now put bounds on the overall price of options and can establish which of two options should have the higher price, we need to be able to put further restrictions on the price of a call option. To do this, we need to consider the impact of interest rates.

Call Option Prices and Interest Rates

By considering the following example, we can gain a greater understanding of the relationship between call option prices and interest rates and place tighter restrictions on the price of a call option. Assume that a stock now sells for $100 in the marketplace and that over the next year its value can change by 10 percent in either direction. For a round lot of 100 shares, the value one year from now will be either $9,000 or $11,000. Assume also that the risk-free rate of interest is 12 percent and that a call option exists on this stock with a striking price of $100 per share and an expiration date one year from now. With these facts in mind, imagine two portfolios constructed in the following way:

Portfolio A   100 shares of stock, current value $10,000.

Portfolio B   A $10,000 pure discount bond maturing in one year, with a current value of $8,929, which is consistent with the 12 percent interest rate.
One option contract, with an exercise price of $100 per share, or $10,000 for the entire contract.

Which portfolio is more valuable, and what does this tell us about the price of the call option? In one year, the stock price for the round lot will be either $11,000 if the price goes up by 10 percent, or $9,000 if the price goes down by 10 percent. This result is shown for Portfolio A in Table 12.2. For Portfolio B, there are both bonds and the call option to consider. As also shown in Table 12.2, the bonds will mature in one year and will be worth $10,000, no matter what happens to the stock price. The stock price will have a strong effect on the value of the call option, however. If the stock price goes up by 10 percent, the call option will be worth exactly $1,000, the difference between the stock price and the exercise price (S - E). If the stock price goes down by 10 percent, the option expires worthless. So if the stock price goes down, Portfolio B will be worth $10,000, while if the stock price goes up, Portfolio B will be worth $11,000.

In this situation, Portfolio B is clearly the better portfolio to hold. If the stock price goes down, Portfolio B is worth $1,000 more than Portfolio A. But if the stock price goes up, Portfolios A and B have the same value. An investor

Table 12.2
Portfolio Values in One Year

	Stock Price Change	
	+10%	−10%
Portfolio A		
Stock	$11,000	$9,000
Portfolio B		
Maturing Bond	$10,000	$10,000
Call Option	$1,000	0

could never do worse by holding Portfolio B, and there is some chance that he or she could do better. Therefore, the value of Portfolio B must be at least as great as the value of Portfolio A.

This tells us something very important about the price of the option. Since Portfolio B is sure to perform at least as well as Portfolio A, it must cost at least as much. Further, we know that the value of Portfolio A is $10,000, so the price of Portfolio B must be at least $10,000. The bonds in Portfolio B cost $8,929, so the option must cost at least $1,071. This means that the value of the call must be worth at least as much as the stock price minus the present value of the exercise price, or in the notation, it must be the case that:

$$C \geq S - \text{Present Value}(E)$$

If the call did not meet this condition, any investor would prefer to purchase Portfolio B rather than Portfolio A. Further, there would be an arbitrage opportunity.[4]

Previously, we were able to say only that the price of the call must be either zero or S - E at expiration. Based on the reasoning from the example, we can now say the following:

$$C \geq S - \text{Present Value}(E)$$

The call price must be greater than or equal to the stock price minus the present value of the exercise price.

This substantially tightens the bounds that we can put on the value of a call option.

As the next example indicates, it must also be true that the higher the interest rate, the higher the value of call option, if everything else is held constant. In the previous example, the interest rate was 12 percent, and we were able to conclude that the price of the call option must be at least $1,071, because:

$$C \geq \$10,000 - \frac{\$10,000}{(1.12)} = \$1,071$$

For the same portfolio, imagine that the interest rate had been 20 percent rather than 12 percent. In that case, the value of the call option must have been at least $1,667, as shown by the following equation:

$$C \geq \$10,000 - \frac{\$10,000}{(1.20)} = \$1,667$$

From this line or reasoning, we can assert the following principle:

If $r_1 > r_2$, $C(S,E,t,r_1) \geq C(S,E,t,r_2)$

Other things being equal, the higher the risk-free rate of interest, the greater must be the price of a call option.

Prices of Call Options and the Riskiness of Stocks

Surprisingly enough, the riskier the stock on which an option is written, the greater will be the value of a call option. This principle can also be illustrated by an example. Consider a stock worth $10,000 that will experience either a 10 percent price rise or a 10 percent price decline over the next year. As we have seen in our earlier example of Table 12.2, a call option on such a stock with an exercise price of $10,000 and a risk-free interest rate of 12 percent, would be worth at least $1,071. Now consider a new stock, which trades at $10,000, but that will experience either a 20 percent price increase or a 20 percent price decrease over the next year. If we hold the other factors constant, by assuming that interest rates are 12 percent per year, and focus on an option with a striking price of $10,000, what can we say about the value of the call option?

As Table 12.3 shows, the call option on the stock that will go up or down by 10 percent must be worth at least $1,071. If the stock price falls, the call will be worth zero. If the stock price rises, the call will be worth $1,000. In the bottom panel of Table 12.3, the stock will rise or fall by 20 percent. If the stock price falls, the call in this case will be worth zero. This is the same result as the call in the top panel. If prices go up, the call in the bottom panel will be worth $2,000, which is the difference between the exercise price and the stock price.

Table 12.3
Portfolio Values in One Year

	Stock Price Change	
	+10%	−10%
Portfolio B		
Maturing Bond	$10,000	$10,000
Call Option	$1,000	0
In Portfolio B, the call option must be worth at least $1,071.		

	Stock Price Change	
	+20%	−20%
Portfolio A		
Stock	$12,000	$8,000
Portfolio B		
Maturing Bond	$10,000	$10,000
Call Option	$2,000	0

In this scenario, any investor would prefer the option in the bottom panel, because it cannot perform worse than the call in the top panel, and it might perform better if the stock prices go up. Therefore, the call in the bottom panel must be worth at least as much as the call in the top panel, but it will probably be worth more. But the only difference between the two cases is the risk level of the stock. In the top panel, the stock will move up or down by 10 percent, but the stock in the bottom panel is riskier, because it will move up or down 20 percent. Notice that the expected payoff for both stocks is the same; only the risk differs. By reflecting on this example, we can derive the following principle:

If $\sigma_1 > \sigma_2$, $C(S,E,t,r,\sigma_1) \geq C(S,E,t,r,\sigma_2)$

Other things being equal, a call option on a riskier good will be worth at least as much as a call option on a less risky good.

Call Options as Insurance Policies

In Table 12.3, the call option will be worth either $1000 or zero in one year, and the value of that option must be at least $1,071. At first glance, it is a terrible investment to pay $1,071 or more for something that will be worth either zero or $1,000 in a year. However, the option offers more than a simple investment opportunity, because it also involves an insurance policy. The insurance character of the option can be seen by comparing the payoffs from Portfolio A and

Portfolio B. If the stock price goes down by 10 percent, portfolio A will be worth $9,000 and Portfolio B will be worth $10,000. If the stock price goes up by 10 percent, both portfolios will be worth $11,000. Holding the option insures that the worst outcome from the investment will be $10,000. This is considerably safer than holding the stock alone. Under these circumstances it can make good sense to pay $1,071 or more for an option that has a maximum payoff of $1,000, because part of the benefit from holding the option portfolio is the insurance that the total payoff from the portfolio will be at least $10,000. This also clarifies why the value of an option is higher for a riskier underlying stock. The riskier the stock, the more valuable will be an insurance policy against awful outcomes.

Previously, we said that the price of the option must be at least as great as the stock price minus the present value of the exercise price. However, this formulation neglects the value of the insurance policy inherent in the option. If we take that into account, we can say that the value of the option must be equal to the stock price minus the present value of the exercise price, plus the value of the insurance policy inherent in the option. Or, where the value of the insurance policy is denoted by I, the value of the call option is given by:

$$C(S,E,t,r,\sigma) = S - \text{Present Value}(E) + I$$

However, we have no way, thus far, of putting a numerical value on the insurance policy denoted by I. That task requires an examination of the option pricing model.

The Option Pricing Model

To this point, by a process of reasoning about option prices and finding the boundaries for option prices that rule out arbitrage opportunities, we have learned a great deal about call option prices and the relationship of these prices to other variables. In the preceding discussion we identified five variables that affect the value of a call option. In the following list, a plus sign by a variable indicates that the price of a call option is larger the larger the value of the associated variable.

+	S	Stock Price
−	E	Exercise Price
+	t	Time to Expiration
+	r	Risk-Free Interest Rate
+	σ	Variability of the Stock

While we now know the basic factors that affect the prices of call options and the direction of their influence, there is still a great deal to learn. For example, in exploring the bounds of option pricing, we considered an example in which the stock price could move by 10 percent up or down in a year. This is obviously a great simplification of reality. In a given period of time, stock prices can take on a virtually infinite number of values. Also, stock prices change continuously for all practical purposes. To be able to put an exact price on a call option requires a much more realistic model of stock price behavior.

This is exactly the approach that was taken by Fischer Black and Myron Scholes as they developed the Option Pricing Model (OPM).[5] Strictly speaking, their model applies to European options on non-dividend paying stocks. But adjustments can be made to the model to deal with other cases.[6] The mathematics of their model are extremely complex, but they were able to derive their model by assuming that stock prices follow a certain kind of path through time called a **stochastic process**. A stochastic process is simply a mathematical description of the change in the value of some variable through time. The particular stochastic process used by Black and Scholes is known as a **Wiener**

Figure 12.7
One Possible Realization of a Wiener Process

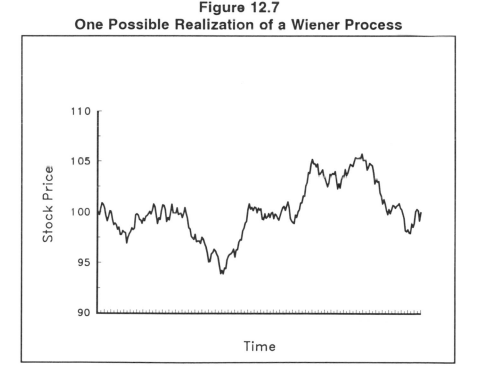

process. The key features of the Wiener process is that the variable changes continuously through time and that the changes that it might make over any given time interval are distributed normally. Figure 12.7 shows a graph of the path that stock prices might follow if they followed a Wiener process.

Essentially, the difference between our discussion to this point and the achievement of the OPM is that the OPM gives a mathematical expression to the value of call option. Whereas we were unable to say what the call price should equal, Black and Scholes present a theoretical formula for the price of a call option. If we know the values of the five variables listed earlier, we can use the OPM to calculate the theoretical price of an option. Further, while we cannot consider the mathematics that Black and Scholes used, we can understand how to calculate option values according to their model, and we can understand the relationship between the OPM and the conclusions we have reached in previous sections. The formula for the Black-Scholes OPM is given by:

$$C = S\,N(d_1) - E\,e^{-rt}\,N(d_2)$$

where:

$$d_1 = \frac{\ln(S/E) = [r + .5\,\sigma^2]t}{\sigma\sqrt{t}}$$

$$d_2 = d_1 - \sigma\sqrt{t}$$

$N(d_1)$, $N(d_2)$ = cumulative normal probabilty values of d_1 and d_2, respectively
S = stock price
E = exercise price
r = the risk-free rate of interest
σ = the instantaneous standard deviation of the stock's return
t = time to expiration of the option

The most difficult part of this formula to understand is the use of the normal cumulative probability function, but this is exactly the part of the OPM that reflects risk and allows the model to give such good results for option prices. The best way to understand the model is with an example, so we assume values for the five parameters and calculate the Black-Scholes option price:

S = $100
E = $100
t = 1 year
r = 12%
σ = 10%

With these values it is possible to calculate the Black-Scholes theoretical option value, and the first task is to calculate values for d_1 and d_2.

$$d_1 = \frac{\ln(S/E) + [r + .5\ \sigma^2]t}{\sigma\sqrt{t}}$$

$$= \frac{\ln(100/100) = [.12 + .5\ (.01)]1}{(.1)\ (1)} = \frac{0 + .1250}{.1}$$

$$= 1.25$$

$$d_2 = d_1 - \sigma\sqrt{t}$$

$$= 1.25 - (.1)\ (1) = 1.15$$

Having calculated the values of d_1 and d_2, the next step is to calculate the cumulative normal probability values of these two results. Essentially, these two values are simply z-scores from the normal probability function, such as the one shown in Figure 12.8. This graph highlights the two values of interest, 1.15 and 1.25. In calculating the cumulative normal probability values of $d_1 = 1.25$ and $d_2 = 1.15$, we simply need to determine the proportion of the area under the curve that lies to the left of the value in question. For example, if we were interested in a z-score of 0.00, we would know that 50 percent of the area under the curve lies to the left of a z score of 0.00, because the normal probability distribution is symmetrical about its mean, and we know that the z-scores are standardized so that they have a mean of 0.00.

Because the standardized normal probability distribution is so important and so widely used, tables of its values are included in virtually every statistics textbook. A typical table is shown in Appendix A to this book. As the table shows, the probability of drawing a value from this distribution less than or equal to $d_1 = 1.25$ is .8944. So the two values we seek are:

$$N(d_1) = N(1.25) = .8944$$
$$N(d_2) = N(1.15) = .8749$$

Returning to the OPM, we can now make the final calculation:

$$C = S\ N(d_1) - E\ e^{-rt}\ N(d_2)$$
$$= \$100\ (.8944) - \$100\ e^{-(.12)(1)}\ (.8749)$$
$$= \$89.44 - \$100\ (.8869)\ (.8749)$$
$$= \$89.44 - \$77.60$$
$$= \$11.84$$

Figure 12.8
The Normal Probability Function

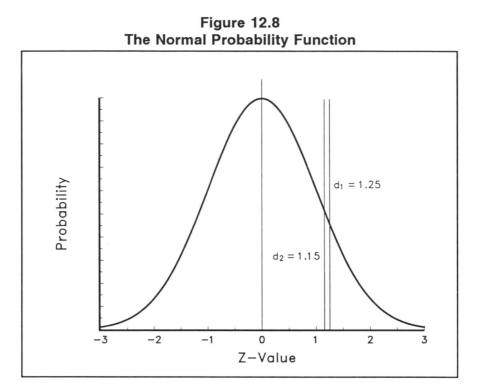

In this calculation, the term e^{-rt} = .8869 is simply the discounting factor for continuous time with an interest rate of 12 percent and a period of one year.[7] So, according to the OPM, the call option in this case should be worth $11.84.

This calculation of the value of this option by the OPM corresponds very closely to our earlier example from Table 12.2. There, for an option with similar characteristics, we concluded that the option must be worth at least $10.71. The result from the OPM is consistent with our earlier analysis, but it is much more exact. The difference between the OPM value of $11.84 and the minimum value of $10.71 is due to the value of the insurance policy that we were unable to capture without the sophisticated approach of the OPM.[8]

Also, it should be clear that the OPM is very close to the result that we reached by just a process of reasoning. We were able to conclude that:

$$C = S - \text{Present Value}(E) + I$$

and the OPM says that:

$$C = S\ N(d_1) - E\ e^{-rt}\ N(d_2)$$

The term $E\,e^{-rt}$ is simply the present value of the exercise price when continuous discounting is used. This means that the OPM asserts:

$$C = S\ N(d_1) - \text{Present Value(E)}\ N(d_2)$$

The terms involving the cumulative probability function are the terms that take account of risk. Coupled with the rest of the formula, they capture the value of the insurance policy. If the stock involved no risk, the calculated values for d_1 and d_2 would be very large and then the calculated cumulative functions would both approach a value of 1. If $N(d_1)$ and $N(d_2)$ both equal 1, the OPM could be simplified to:

$$C = S - \text{Present Value(E)}$$

which is the result we were able to reach without the OPM. This expression simply does not reflect the value of the option as an insurance policy, a value we know it has and that we can measure by using the OPM.

Upon first acquaintance with the OPM, many people think that it is too complicated to be useful. Nothing could be further from the truth. Of all of the models in finance, the OPM is among those that have received the widest acceptance by actual investors. For example, there are machines on the floor of the CBOE that give traders OPM prices for all options using instantaneously updated information on all of the parameters in the model. Further, most investment banking houses have staffs that specialize in options and which use the OPM on a daily basis. Finally, the OPM has achieved such widespread acceptance that some calculator manufacturers have even made special modules to allow their calculators to automatically calculate OPM values.

This widespread acceptance is due in large part to the very good results of the OPM. The Black-Scholes theoretical model price is usually very close to the market price of the option. Without doubt, the OPM has contributed greatly to our understanding of option pricing and many traders find it sufficiently valuable to use it as a key tool in their trading strategies.

The Valuation of Put Options

Although the OPM pertains specifically to call options, it can also be used to price put options, through the principle of "put-call parity."[9] Assume that an investor makes the following transactions, where the put and call have the same expirations and are on the same stock:

Buy one share of stock S = $100
Buy one put option with price P = ?, E = $100, and t = 1 year
Sell one call option with price C = $11.84, E = $100, and t = 1 year

Table 12.4
Possible Outcomes for Put–Call Parity Portfolio

Stock Price	Call Value	Put Value	Portfolio Value
$80	$0	$20	$100
$90	$0	$10	$100
$100	$0	$0	$100
$110	–$10	$0	$100
$120	–$20	$0	$100

At expiration, the stock price could have many different values, some of which are shown in Table 12.4. The interesting feature about this portfolio is that its value will be the same, $100 = E, no matter what the stock price is at expiration. Holding these three instruments in the way indicated gives a risk free investment that will pay $100 = E at expiration, so the value of the whole portfolio must equal the present value of the riskless payoff at expiration. This means that we can write the following:

$$S - C + P = \frac{E}{(1 + r)^t}$$

The value of the put-call portfolio equals the present value of the exercise price discounted at the risk-free rate.

Since it is possible to know all of the other values, except for the price of the put P, we can use this put-call parity relationship to calculate P. To see how this is done, let us assume as before that r = .12 and that the call value is $11.84, as was calculated according to the OPM. Rearranging the put-call parity formula gives the following:

$$P = \frac{E}{(1 + r)^t} - S + C$$

$$P = \frac{\$100}{(1.12)} - \$100 + \$11.84 = \$1.13$$

Under these circumstances, the put should be worth $1.13.

Speculating with Options

Many option traders are attracted to the market by the exciting speculative opportunities that options offer. Relative to stocks, options offer a great deal of leverage. A given percentage change in the stock price will cause a much greater percentage change in the price of the option.

In our example of the option worth $11.84 above, consider the effect of a sudden 10 percent change in the price of the stock. If the stock price changes by 1 percent, the option price will change by 7.52 percent in the same direction. The call values shown below were calculated from the Black-Scholes formula, assuming only that the stock price had changed as indicated.

Original Values	1% Stock Price Increase	1% Stock Price Decrease
S = $100	S = $101	S = $99
C = $11.84	C = $12.73	C = $10.95

This leverage means that trading options can give investors much more price action for a given investment than simply holding the stock. It also means that options can be much riskier than holding stock.

While options can be risky as investments, they need not be. In fact, options can be used to take very low risk speculative positions by using options in combinations. The combinations are virtually endless, including "strips," "straps," "spreads," and "straddles." To give an idea of the possibilities, we will consider only one of the possibilities, a straddle.

Option Speculating with Straddles

A straddle is a position involving a put and a call option on the same stock. To buy a straddle, an investor purchases both the put and the call. Consider a put and a call option and assume that both have an exercise price of $100. Assume further that the call sells for $10 and that the put trades at $7. Table 12.5 shows the profits and losses for the call, the put, and the straddle, as a function of the stock price at expiration. If the stock price equals the exercise price at expiration, both the put and the call expire worthless, and the loss on the straddle is $17, the entire premium paid for the position.

Any movement in the stock price away from $100 at expiration gives a better result. In fact, the value of the straddle increases $1 for every $1 movement in the stock price at expiration away from $100. The straddle position breaks even if the stock price either rises to $117 or falls to $83. In other words, a $17 price movement away from the exercise price at expiration will cover the

Table 12.5
Payoffs for Calls, Puts, and a Straddle at Expiration

Stock Price at Expiration	Call Profit/Loss	Put Profit/Loss	Straddle Profit/Loss
$50	−$10	+$43	+$33
$80	−$10	+$13	+$ 3
$83	−$10	+$10	0
$85	−$10	+$ 8	−$ 2
$90	−$10	+$ 3	−$ 7
$95	−$10	−$ 2	−$12
$100	−$10	−$ 7	−$17
$105	−$ 5	−$ 7	−$12
$110	0	−$ 7	−$ 7
$115	+$ 5	−$ 7	−$ 2
$117	+$ 7	−$ 7	0
$120	+$10	−$ 7	+$ 3
$150	+$40	−$ 7	+$33

Note: Profit/Loss figures reflect the amounts paid for the instruments:
Call = $10
Put = $7
Straddle = Call + Put = $17

initial investment of $17. If the price of the stock differs greatly from the exercise price, there is an opportunity for substantial profit. These possible results are shown graphically in Figure 12.9. The top panel shows the profit and losses for the long positions in the call and put options.

The lower panel shows the profits and losses for buying the straddle position with a solid line. As this graph makes clear, the purchaser of a straddle is betting that the price of the stock will move dramatically away from the exercise price of $100. The owner of the straddle will profit if the stock price goes above $117 or below $83. The lower panel also shows the profit and loss position for the seller of a straddle with the dotted lines. The seller of the straddle will profit if the stock price at expiration lies between $83 and $117. Obviously, the purchaser of this straddle would be making a bet on a large movement in the stock price in some direction, while the seller of a straddle would be betting that the stock price remains reasonably close to the exercise price of $100. By using different combinations of long and short positions in call and put options, it is possible to construct an option portfolio with almost any imaginable set of payoffs. This straddle presents just one of those possibilities.

Figure 12.9
Put, Call, and Straddle Profit and Losses

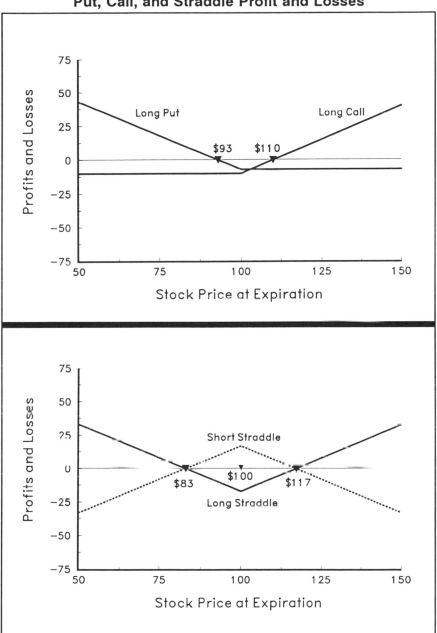

Hedging with Options

As we have already seen with futures, very risky financial instruments can be used to control risk. One of the most important applications of options is their use as a hedging vehicle. Once again, the OPM gives important insights into this process.

To illustrate the idea of hedging with options, let us use our original example of a stock selling at $100 and having a standard deviation of 10 percent. We saw earlier that a call option with an exercise price of $100 and a time to expiration of one year would sell for $11.84. We also saw that a sudden 1 percent price rise in the stock from $100 to $101 would drive the option price to $12.73. If the stock price and the option price are so intimately related, it should be possible to use options to offset risk inherent in the stock.

This possibility is shown in Table 12.6. Consider an original portfolio comprised of 8944 shares of stock selling at $100 per share and assume that a trader sells 100 option contracts, or options on 10,000 shares, at $11.84. In the Table, this short position in the option is indicated by a minus sign. That entire portfolio would have a value of $776,000. Now consider the effect of a 1 percent change in the price of the stock. If the stock price increases by 1 percent to $101, the shares will be worth $903,344 for a gain of $8,944. The option price will increase from $11.84 to $12.73. But this portfolio involves a short position in 10,000 options, so this creates a loss of $8,900. After these two effects are taken into account, the value of the whole portfolio will be $776,044. This is virtually identical to the original value.

Table 12.6
A Hedged Portfolio

Original Portfolio: S = $100 C = $11.84

8,944 shares of stock	$894,400
A short position for options on 10,000 shares (100 contracts)	−$118,400
Total Value	$776,000

Stock Price Rises by 1%: S = $101 C = $12.73

8,944 shares of stock	$903,344
A short position for options on 10,000 shares (100 contracts)	−$127,300
Total Value	$776,044

Stock Price Falls by 1%: S = $99 C = $10.95

8,944 shares of stock	$885,456
A short position for options on 10,000 shares (100 contracts)	−$109,500
Total Value	$775,956

On the other hand, if the stock price falls by 1 percent, there will be a loss on the stock of $8,944. The price of the option will fall from $11.84 to $10.95, and this means that the entire drop in price for the 10,000 options will be $8,900. Taking both of these effects into account, the portfolio will then be worth $775,956. As this example indicates, the overall value of the portfolio will not change no matter what happens to the stock price. If the stock price increases, there is an offsetting loss on the option. Likewise, if the stock price falls, there will be an offsetting gain on the option.

In this example, holding .8944 shares of stock for each option sold short will give a perfect hedge. The value of the entire portfolio will be insensitive to any change in the stock price. How can we know exactly the right number of options to trade to give this result? The careful reader might recall the number .8944. When the value of this call option was calculated, we saw that $N(d_1) = .8944$. This value gives the appropriate hedge ratio to construct a perfect hedge, and the principle can be summarized by the following rule:

A portfolio comprised of a short position of one option and a long position of $N(d_1)$ shares of the stock will have a total value that will not fluctuate as the share price fluctuates.

Alternatively, to hedge a long position of one share in a stock, sell a number of options equal to $1/N(d_1)$.

This hedge will hold for infinitesimal changes in the stock price. In the preceding example, the hedge was not quite perfect because the change in the stock price was discrete. Actually, the value of the portfolio fluctuates by only .00057. Also, a change in the stock price will change the value of $N(d_1)$, because the value of d_1 will change. This means that the hedge must be adjusted periodically as the stock price changes if it is to be kept perfect.

Conclusion

This chapter introduced options and has explored the basic pricing principles of both call and put options. Starting merely from the assumption that options should be priced in a way that allows no arbitrage opportunities, it is possible to bound option prices very closely. Essentially, it can be shown using the no-arbitrage condition that call option prices are a function of the stock price, the exercise price of the option, the time to expiration, the interest rate, and the risk level of the good underlying the option. Additionally, Black and Scholes have developed an option pricing model that gives an exact price for a call option as a function of the same five variables. While their model is a theoretical model, it has been shown to accord very well with actual option prices.

Options are useful financial instruments for both speculation and hedging. For example, an investor expecting a stock price to increase can profit from being correct by buying a call option or selling a put option on that stock. Further, by speculating with options, it is possible to achieve more leverage than by merely trading the stock itself. Options are useful for controlling risk as well, because the careful combination of options and positions in the underlying good can give virtually any degree of risk that is desired. Further, combinations of options themselves widen the range of payoff possibilities available to the investor. This chapter paves the way for a consideration of options on futures contracts in the next chapter.

Questions and Problems

1. Respond to the following claim: "Buying a call option is very dangerous because it commits the owner to purchasing a stock at a later date. At that time the stock may be undesirable. Therefore, owning a call option is a risky position."

2. "I bought a call option with an exercise price of $110 on IBM when IBM was at $108 and I paid $6 per share for the option. Now the option is about to expire and IBM is trading at $112. There's no point in exercising the option, because I will wind up paying a total of $116 for the shares—$6 I already spent for the option plus the $110 exercise price." Is this line of reasoning correct? Explain.

3. What is the value of a call option on a share of stock if the exercise price of the call is $0 and its expiration date is infinite? Explain.

4. Why is the value of a call option at expiration equal to the maximum of zero or the stock price minus the exercise price?

5. Two call options on the same stock have the following features. The first has an exercise price of $60, a time to expiration of three months, and a premium of $5. The second has an exercise price of $60, a time to expiration of six months, and a premium of $4. What should you do in this situation? Explain exactly, assuming that you transact for just one option. What is your profit or loss at the expiration of the nearby option if the stock is at $55, $60, or $65?

6. Two call options are identical except that they are written on two different stocks with different risk levels. Which will be worth more? Why?

7. Assume the following: a stock is selling for $100, a call option with an exercise price of $90 is trading for $6 and matures in one month, and the interest rate is 1% per month. What should you do? Explain your transactions.

8. Two call options on the same stock expire in two months. One has an exercise price of $55 and a price of $5. The other has an exercise price of $50 and a price of $4. What transactions would you make to exploit this situation?

Notes

1. Most of the principles indicated here were originally proven rigorously by Robert C. Merton, "Theory of Rational Option Pricing," *Bell Journal of Economics and Management Science*, 4:1, 1973, pp. 141-183.

2. There is still an interesting result to be noted here. If the prices are equal, a trader could buy the option with the lower striking price and sell the one with the higher striking price. This strategy would not guarantee a profit, but it could not lose. Further, there would be some situations in which it would pay off. For this reason, options with lower exercise prices almost always sell for higher, not just equal, prices, as the quotations from *The Wall Street Journal* make clear.

3. Strictly speaking, this argument holds for "American options." An "American option" allows exercise at any time until maturity. By contrast, a "European option" allows exercise only at maturity. Thus, an American option gives all the advantages of the European option, plus it allows the possibility of early exercise. For this reason, an American option must always have a value at least as great as a European option, other factors being equal.

4. The arbitrage transactions would involve buying Portfolio B and selling Portfolio A short. Assume that the price of the call option is $1,000 and try to work out the transactions and the arbitrage profit that must result.

5. Fischer Black and Myron Scholes, "The Pricing of Options and Corporate Liabilities," *Journal of Political Economy*, 81:3, Part 1, 1973, pp. 637–654.

6. These adjustments and further developments of the OPM are beyond the scope of this text. The interested student should see R. Jarrow and A. Rudd, *Option Pricing*, Homewood, IL: Richard D. Irwin, 1983, for a complete exposition of these other developments. Another excellent resource on options is P. Ritchken, *Options: Theory Strategy, and Applications*, Glenview, IL: Scott Foresman and Co., 1987. See also, R. Kolb, *Options: An Introduction*, Miami: Kolb Publishing Co., 1991.

7. Compare this continuously compounded rate to the simple rate of $1/1.12 = .8929$. The continuously compounded value will always be smaller than the result for any other compounding interval.

8. Actually, part of the difference is due to the discounting method. Had our example used continuous discounting at 12 percent, we would have found that the value of the option had to be at least as great as $100 - $100 (.8869) = 11.31. This is much closer to the OPM value of $11.84.

9. The put–call parity relationship was first derived by H. Stoll, "The Relationship Between Put and Call Option Prices," *Journal of Finance*, 24:5, December 1969, pp. 801–824.

13

Options on Futures

Introduction

Both financial futures and exchange traded options were introduced in 1973. This double introduction signaled the beginning of a wave of rapid innovation in financial markets. Innovation may have slowed after the financial tumult of the 1980s, but the period of innovation is not yet over. Participants in the financial markets must learn to deal with yet another fundamentally different kind of instrument—an option written on a futures contract. To further complicate matters, for many instruments there are options on the instruments themselves as well as options on the futures on the same instruments.

The pricing principles for options contracts are quite complex and a number of books have been devoted just to options.[1] In Chapter 12 we provided an introduction to the options market and pricing principles for options. There we considered only **options on physicals**, options on the underlying goods themselves. This chapter extends the principles of Chapter 12 to options on futures.

We first describe the institutional character of the market for options on futures. Next, we consider pricing principles. As we will see, prices of options on futures are closely related to prices of options on the underlying good. We discuss some of the problems in determining theoretical prices for options on futures, and we analyze the efficiency of the market for options on futures. The remainder of the chapter focuses on speculation and hedging. We consider the speculative opportunities that options on futures provide, contrasting these speculative positions with positions using futures. Trading options against an existing position allows subtle shifts of the risk character of the underlying position. Options on futures are also valuable for hedging. We show how to create a synthetic futures position with options on futures. This innovation opens all the possibilities of futures–style hedging to the hedger who trades options on futures.

Characteristics of Options
on Physicals and Options on Futures

Consider a good such as the German mark and the financial instruments that are based on it. There is a futures contract on the mark, a forward contract for the mark, an option on the mark (an option on the physical), and an option on the futures contract (an option on the futures). Not all goods have so many different types of associated instruments, although many do. In this chapter we focus on the option on the futures contracts.

The structure of a futures option is very similar to an option on the physical. For both instruments, the option owner has the right to exercise, and the seller has a duty to perform upon exercise. Upon exercising a futures option, however, the call owner receives a long position in the underlying futures at the settlement price prevailing at the time of exercise. The call owner also receives a payment that equals the settlement price minus the exercise price of the futures option. (The call owner would not exercise if the futures settlement price did not exceed the exercise price.) When a call option is exercised against her, a call seller receives a short position in the underlying futures at the settlement price prevailing at the time of exercise. In addition, the short call trader pays the long trader the futures settlement price minus the exercise price.

When the owner of a futures put option exercises, he receives a short position in the underlying futures contract at the settlement price prevailing at the time of exercise. In addition, the put owner receives a payment that equals the exercise price minus the futures settlement price. (The put owner would not exercise unless the exercise price exceeded the futures settlement price.) Upon exercise, the put seller receives a long position in the underlying futures contract, and the put seller must pay the exercise price minus the settlement price.

We can clarify the exercise rights and responsibilities with an example. On February 1 a trader buys a call option on the MAR German mark futures contract. The exercise price is $.44 per mark for the German mark futures maturing in March. On February 15, the futures settlement price is $.48, and the owner of the call option decides to exercise. Upon exercise, the owner of the call receives a long position in the MAR DM futures contract. In addition, the call owner receives a payment that equals, $F_0 - E$, or $.48 - .44$. With a contract amount of 125,000 marks, the actual payment will be $5,000. The seller of a call in this situation receives a short position in the DM futures and must pay $5,000. Both traders can now offset or continue to hold their futures positions.

To illustrate the exercise of a put, consider a trader who buys a put option on the MAY wheat futures contract with an exercise price of $2.40 per bushel. On April 4, the wheat futures contract settles at $2.32, and the trader decides to exercise. The owner of the put receives a short MAY futures position and a payment of $E - F_0$, or \$2.40 - \$2.32. With the wheat futures consisting of 5,000 bushels, the actual cash flow to the put owner is \$400.00. The put seller in this situation would receive a long position in the MAY wheat futures and would pay \$400.00.

In every exercise, the option owner and seller receive a futures position. The futures position received upon exercise has no inherent gain or loss. The traders may offset the futures position or continue to hold the positions. For both the call and the put, the purchaser originally paid the option premium to the seller. This payment induced the seller to give the option owner the right to exercise as we have described. The overall profitability of the transactions depends upon the original premium and the prices that become available before expiration of the option.

Results of Futures Option Exercises

Option	Futures Results	Cash Flows
Call	Owner holds long futures position. Seller holds short futures position.	Owner receives $F_0 - E$. Seller pays $F_0 - E$.
Put	Owner holds short futures position. Seller holds long futures position.	Owner receives $E - F_0$. Seller pays $E - F_0$.

where:

F_0 = futures settlement price at time of exercise
E = exercise price of the futures option

The Market for Options on Futures

Figure 13.1 presents some illustrative quotations for futures options, which resemble the quotations for options on physicals discussed in Chapter 12. In the figure, the option quotations are divided into puts and calls and then further divided into the different contract maturities and striking prices.

While a tremendous variety of futures options have been introduced, it appears that not all will be successful. Futures options have been introduced on a number of agricultural commodities, such as wheat, soybeans, coffee, orange juice, corn, cotton, and sugar, but these have met with varying success. The most successful contracts appear to be concentrated in financial futures, with about 85 percent of trading volume in financial options on futures. For example, the

Figure 13.1
Quotations for Options on Futures

COMMODITY FUTURES OPTIONS

Thursday, October 18, 1990.

–AGRICULTURAL–

CORN (CBT) 5,000 bu.; cents per bu.

Strike	Calls–Settle			Puts–Settle		
Price	Dec-c	Mar-c	May-c	Dec-p	Mar-p	May-p
210	18	27	....	½	¾	1½
220	10	19	25	1⅝	2¼	2¼
230	3⅞	12	18	5⅝	5	5½
240	1¼	7	12½	13	9½	9½
250	½	4	8½	22⅜	16½	15½
260	⅜	2⅜	5¾	32	25	22¼

Est. vol. 5,000, Wed vol. 3,589 calls, 2,415 puts
Open interest Wed 115,992 calls, 84,921 puts

SOYBEANS (CBT) 5,000 bu.; cents per bu.

Strike	Calls–Settle			Puts–Settle		
Price	Nov-c	Jan-c	Mar-c	Nov-p	Jan-p	Mar-p
550	60¼	....	....	⅛	⅛	....
575	35¼	50¼	....	⅛	¾	1½
600	10¾	29	42	¾	4	4¾
625	¼	14¼	25¾	14¾	14	12⅞
650	⅛	6⅜	15¾	39¾	31¼	27
675	⅛	3	9½	64¾	52½	45

Est. vol. 7,500, Wed vol. 5,459 calls, 3,222 puts
Open interest Wed 72,312 calls, 37,385 puts

SOYBEAN MEAL (CBT) 100 tons; $ per ton

Strike	Calls–Settle			Puts–Settle		
Price	Dec-c	Jan-c	Mar-c	Dec-p	Jan-p	Mar-p
175	9.30	....	....	.75	....	1.25
180	5.75	8.00	11.50	1.90	2.00	2.25
185	2.75	5.25	8.50	4.00	4.25	4.25
190	1.60	3.00	6.25	7.70	7.25	6.75
195	.90	2.00	4.50	11.85	....	10.00
200	.50	1.20	3.40	16.75	....	....

Est. vol. 400, Wed vol. 846 calls, 215 puts
Open interest Wed 8,843 calls, 5,062 puts

SOYBEAN OIL (CBT) 60,000 lbs.; cents per lb.

Strike	Calls–Settle			Puts–Settle		
Price	Dec-c	Jan-c	Mar-c	Dec-p	Jan-p	Mar-p
20	2.370	....	....	.010	....	....
21	1.400	....	....	.040	....	.100
22	.500	....	....	.150	.200	.220
23	.250	.300	.300	.850	.650	.650
24	.100	.150	.150	1.700	1.500	1.250
25	.030	.100	.100	2.700	2.450	....

Est. vol. 200, Wed vol. 370 calls, 48 puts
Open interest Wed 8,135 calls, 8,328 puts

WHEAT (CBT) 5,000 bu.; cents per bu.

Strike	Calls–Settle			Puts–Settle		
Price	Dec-c	Mar-c	May-c	Dec-p	Mar-p	May-p
240	24	....	....	....	....	....
250	15	....	....	1½	2	3¾
260	8	21¼	....	4¼	4	5
270	3¾	14¾	23	10	7	8
280	1½	9¾	18	17½	11¾	17½
290	⅞	6¼	12¾	26¼	17¾	....

Est. vol. 2,000, Wed vol. 753 calls, 406 puts
Open interest Wed 41,948 calls, 10,859 puts

Strike	Calls–Settle			Puts–Settle		
Price	Dec-c	Feb-c	Apr-c	Dec-p	Feb-p	Apr-p
54	1.35	1.10	0.55	1.35	....	....
56	0.55	0.60	....	2.60	....	....
58	0.17	0.40	....	4.22	....	....
60	0.10	0.25	....	....	....	....

Est. vol. 312, Wed vol. 71 calls, 397 puts
Open interest Wed; 4,778 calls, 5,676 puts

PORK BELLIES (CME) 40,000 lbs.; cents per lb.

Strike	Calls–Settle			Puts–Settle		
Price	Feb-c	Mar-c	May-c	Feb-p	Mar-p	May-p
62	7.45	....	....	3.55	....	....
64	6.40	6.55	....	4.50	....	....
66	5.40	5.60	....	5.50	....	....
68	4.50	....	....	....	....	....
70	3.75	4.10	....	....	....	....
72	3.10	3.45	....	....	....	....

Est. vol. 13, Wed vol. 23 calls, 41 puts
Open interest Wed; 793 calls, 992 puts

–METALS–

COPPER (CMX) 25,000 lbs.; cents per lb.

Strike	Calls–Last			Puts–Last		
Price	Dec-c	Mar-c	May-c	Dec-p	Mar-p	May-p
105	9.70	8.70	8.20	0.80	4.95	6.50
110	5.95	6.10	6.10	1.95	7.20	9.10
115	3.20	4.30	4.40	4.20	10.20	12.40
120	1.60	2.85	3.05	7.55	13.60	16.00
125	0.65	1.95	2.30	11.55	17.55	20.00
130	0.30	1.35	1.75	16.15	21.70	24.30

Est. vol. 350, Wed vol. 295 calls, 541 puts
Open interest Wed 4,020 calls, 3,840 puts

GOLD (CMX) 100 troy ounces; dollars per troy ounce

Strike	Calls–Last			Puts–Last		
Price	Dec-c	Jan-c	Feb-c	Dec-p	Jan-p	Feb-p
350	25.20	31.50	32.70	2.50	4.90	6.20
360	18.10	24.40	26.00	5.10	7.70	9.30
370	11.60	18.50	20.20	8.60	11.60	13.30
380	7.20	13.70	15.70	14.10	16.70	18.60
390	4.30	10.00	11.90	22.20	22.80	24.70
400	2.50	7.30	9.00	29.20	29.90	31.60

Est. vol. 6,200, Wed vol. 10,444 calls, 1,688 puts
Open interest Wed 101,760 calls, 33,117 puts

SILVER (CMX) 5,000 troy ounces; cents per troy ounce

Strike	Calls–Last			Puts–Last		
Price	Dec-c	Mar-c	May-c	Dec-p	Mar-p	May-p
375	51.0	61.6	69.5	2.0	5.0	6.8
400	28.8	43.1	51.0	4.8	11.0	13.0
425	12.3	29.2	36.5	13.3	21.0	22.5
450	4.7	18.5	26.0	30.7	35.0	36.5
475	2.3	12.3	18.0	53.3	54.1	52.5
500	1.5	8.3	12.4	77.5	75.1	72.0

Est. vol. 3,700, Wed vol. 3,258 calls, 1,339 puts
Open interest Wed 56,787 calls, 22,383 puts

Source: *The Wall Street Journal*, October 19, 1990.

T-bond and Eurodollar futures options have been very successful, with open interest exceeding 100,000 contracts consistently. The T-note, German mark, and Eurodollar futures options all have active trading interest. Table 13.1 shows the trading volume for futures options trading more than one million contracts in the fiscal year ending September 30, 1989. (The S&P 500 missed inclusion by fewer than 1,000 contracts.)

Table 13.1
Trading Volume (000s) for Futures Options
(Year Ending September 30, 1989)

Commodity	Exchange	Calls	Puts	Total
Corn	CBT	976	580	1,556
Soybeans	CBT	1546	718	2,264
T–bond	CBT	10,576	10	10,586
T–note	CBT	572	560	1,132
Sugar	CSCE	1,271	447	1,718
Eurodollar	CME	2,670	2,694	5,364
German mark	CME	1,781	1,753	3,534
Swiss franc	CME	688	729	1,417
Japanese yen	CME	1,436	1,865	3,301
Gold	COMEX	738	581	1,319
Crude Oil	NYMEX	2,778	3,345	6,123

Source: Commodity Futures Trading Commission, *Annual Report*, 1989.

Pricing of Futures Options

In Chapter 12 we considered the famous Black–Scholes option pricing model for stocks that pay no dividends. Strictly speaking, the Black–Scholes model pertains only to **European options**, options that can be exercised only on the expiration date, but not to **American options**, options that can be exercised at any time prior to expiration. If the underlying good pays no dividend, then Black and Scholes were able to show that American and European call options have the same value. The dividend issue and the difference between American and European options are crucial to pricing futures options. As a consequence, we approach the problem in easier stages, starting with options on forward contracts.

Although futures contracts pay no dividends, the daily settlement on a futures means that there is a series of cash flows associated with a position in the futures market. For futures options, these daily settlement cash flows play the role of a continuous dividend. When there is a dividend, the Black–Scholes model does not apply exactly. Nonetheless, if the dividend rate is constant, a modified form of the Black–Scholes Model can reflect the dividend. If the dividend rate varies, there is no easy modification to the Black–Scholes model.

This means that, strictly speaking, the Black-Scholes model is not suitable for valuing futures options.

A forward contract has no daily settlement and no problem with intermittent cash flows over the life of the asset. This means that it should be possible to adjust the Black-Scholes model to price options on forward contracts. Therefore, we begin our exploration of futures option pricing by considering forward option pricing. We then consider the complications of daily settlement for determining the prices of futures options. Throughout we focus on call options for simplicity. As we will see, models like the Black-Scholes Model apply quite practically to futures options.

The Black Model for Options on Forward Contracts

In his 1976 paper, Fischer Black showed how to adjust the Black-Scholes option pricing model for options on forward contracts.[2] The value of a call option on a forward contract is:

$$C = e^{-rt} [F_{0,t} N(d_1^*) - E N(d_2^*)]$$ 13.1

where:

r = risk-free rate of interest
t = time until expiration for the forward and the option
$F_{0,t}$ = forward price for a contract expiring at time t
E = exercise price
σ = standard deviation of the forward contract's price

$$d_1^* = \frac{\ln (F/E) + .5 \sigma^2 t}{\sigma \sqrt{t}}$$

$$d_2^* = d_1^* - \sigma \sqrt{t}$$

The model of equation 13.1 is very similar to the Black-Scholes model of Chapter 12. The main differences are in the computation of d_1^* and d_2^*. First, these expressions have no interest rate term, because the forward contract requires no cash commitment. Second, the entire bracketed term is discounted by e^{-rt}. If there were no uncertainty, $N(d_1^*)$ and $N(d_2^*)$ would both equal 1.0 and equation 13.1 would simplify to:

$$C_f = e^{-rt}[F_{0,t} - E]$$ 13.2

Equation 13.2 says that the value of the option under certainty equals the present value of the exercisable proceeds. The exercisable proceeds are the cash flows realized when the option is exercised. For a call option, the proceeds from exercising are $F_0 - E$, the current forward price minus the exercise price.

In summary of the Black model, we must keep in mind that it applies to European forward options. This is a key, because restricting it to forward contracts lets us ignore the daily settlement cash flows that make futures contracts behave as though they have dividends. Also, with no dividends, we can treat the American call option as a European option, because there will be no difference in prices.

Pricing Futures Options

Because futures options are generally American, they can be exercised any time. This makes them extremely difficult to price exactly. Essentially, an American futures options consists of an infinite series of European options. The exercise of an American futures option has an exercise price equal to the explicit amount that must be paid, plus the sacrifice of the remaining European options in the series. Because the American futures option is analyzed as an infinite series of European options, there is no closed-form solution for the value of the American futures option. Instead, we must approximate the value of the American futures option.

European versus American Futures Options. The Black–Scholes' focus on European options avoids problems with dividends which give rise to early exercise—exercise before the option matures. Futures options are always subject to early exercise, whether the good on which the futures contract is written pays dividends or not. This section explains why it may be reasonable to exercise a futures option early.

For a European option on a non-dividend paying stock, early exercise never makes sense. Upon exercising, the call owner receives the intrinsic value, $S - E$. In effect, exercising a call discards the excess value of the option over and above $S - E$. In Chapter 12 we saw that the price of such a call option always equals or exceeds $S - E$. The difference, $C - (S - E)$ will normally be greater the longer the time until expiration.

If the underlying stock pays a dividend, early exercise of an option on the physical can be reasonable. When a stock pays a dividend, the value of the share drops by the amount of the dividend, approximately. In this case, value is "leaking out" of the underlying good, so it may be wise to exercise before expiration.

Similarly, it may be wise to exercise futures options before expiration. Consider a call option with an exercise price $E = \$50$ and a futures contract with a price $F = \$100$. Assume for the moment that the futures price will not change anymore, and consider whether the call owner should exercise early or wait until expiration. In this example, the call owner should exercise immediately. Upon exercise, the call owner receives $50, which can earn interest until the expiration date. In short, the benefit of early exercise on a futures option is that exercise provides an immediate payment of F - E. The incentive to exercise early is the interest that can be earned between the time of exercise and the expiration date: $e^{rt} [F - E]$.

In the example just considered, we have assumed that the futures price does not change. In that circumstance, it was clearly wise to exercise early to capture the interest on the mark-to-market payment F - E. However, in actual markets the futures price will fluctuate. That means that early exercise of a futures option discards the option's value over and above the intrinsic value F - E. Therefore, early exercise of a futures option has a benefit and a cost:

Benefit: Use of the funds F - E until expiration
Cost: Sacrifice of option value over and above intrinsic value F - E

Here we have a classic problem of trading off a cost against a benefit. We can illustrate the problem graphically.

A Graphical Approach to American Futures Options. We have already noted that the values of $N(d_1^*)$ and $N(d_2^*)$ in equation 13.1 approach 1.0 as the futures price becomes very large relative to the exercise price. If the two cumulative normal terms equal 1.0, equation 13.1 would be identical to equation 13.2. Figure 13.2 illustrates this possibility for otherwise identical European and American futures options. The horizontal axis graphs the futures price F, and it shows the exercise price for the futures option, E.

We have already observed that the minimum price that a European futures option could ever obtain is $(F - E)e^{-rt}$, because this is the value of the immediately available exercisable proceeds. In Figure 13.2, the European option attains this minimum when its price touches the line designated as $(F - E)e^{-rt}$. This point is shown as F' in Figure 13.2. This is equivalent to $N(d_1^*)$ and $N(d_2^*)$ both equaling 1.0 in equation 13.1. In economic terms, this situation arises when it is virtually certain that the option will remain in the money. In that case, the option will pay F - E at maturity. Before maturity, its price must be the present value of F - E, or $(F - E)e^{-rt}$.

The bottom curved line in the figure represents the value of the European futures option. For high futures prices, the European option value converges to the present value of the exercisable proceeds, attaining this point at F'. It converges only to the present value, because the exercisable proceeds are not available until the option is at expiration and can be exercised.

The top curved line in Figure 13.2 shows the value of an American futures option. Because an American futures option can be exercised early, it must always be worth at least as much as the corresponding European option. In the figure, the value of the American option converges to its exercisable proceeds, F - E, where the futures price reaches F*. In the graph, F* is the **critical futures price,** the lowest futures price at which the American option value equals F - E. If the futures price equals F*, the owner of the call is indifferent between exercising and continuing to hold the option. In other words, it is the futures price at which the costs and benefits of exercising are exactly equal. If the futures price exceeds F*, the trader should exercise. If the futures price is less than F*, the trader should not exercise but should either continue to hold the option or sell it. In terms of the trade-off between exercising and not exercising we discussed earlier, F* is the point of indifference for an American futures option.

We can divide the problem of pricing an American futures option into two situations, when the futures price equals or exceeds F* and when the futures price is less than F*. First, if the futures price equals or exceeds F*, the value of an American futures option is F - E, the exercisable proceeds. Second, if the futures price is less than F*, there is no direct solution and we must approximate the price of the American futures option.

Figure 13.2
Pricing of American and European Futures Options

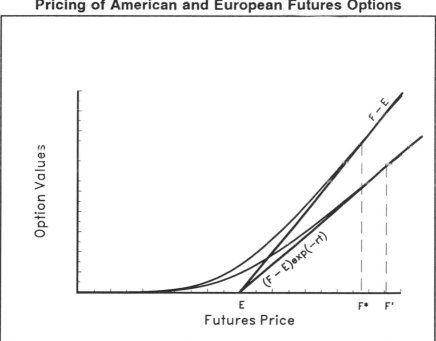

Approximating European and American Futures Option Values. The approximation techniques for the American futures option require mathematics beyond the scope of this text. However, the intuition is clear. From Figure 13.2 we see that the American futures option has a maximum value equal to F - E, which it attains when F rises to F*. If the current futures price, F, lies below the critical futures price, F*, the value of the American futures option equals the European futures option plus the value of the early exercise privilege. Approximating the value of the early exercise privilege requires some mathematical expertise. Nonetheless, we can see the results of the approximation and compare the approximate American option values with exact theoretical European option values.

Table 13.2 compares theoretical values for European and American futures options. Data in the Table are drawn from an article by Giovanni Barone-Adesi and Robert Whaley. The table assumes that a futures option expires in half a year and has an exercise price of 100. The risk-free rate of interest is 8 percent and the standard deviation of the percentage change in the futures price is .20. Table 13.2 shows theoretical prices for European and American call options for futures prices from 80 to 120. The European call price is computed from equation 13.1. The American futures call price is approximated using a quadratic technique developed by Barone-Adesi and Whaley.[3]

Table 13.2
Comparison of European and Approximate American Futures Option Call Values

r = .08   σ = .20
t = .5 years   E = 100

Futures Price	European	Approximate American
80	0.30	0.30
90	1.70	1.72
100	5.42	5.48
110	11.73	11.90
120	19.91	20.34

Source: G. Barone–Adesi and R. Whaley, "Efficient Analytic Approximation of American Option Values," *Journal of Finance*, 42:2, June 1987, pp. 301–320.

For out-of-the-money options, the values of European and American options are very close. In terms of Figure 13.2, this situation arises when futures prices are low. On the left-hand side of Figure 13.2, there is little difference between the American and European prices. As Table 13.2 shows, when the futures price exceeds the exercise price by a substantial amount, the differences between the European and American option values become larger. In Figure 13.2, these values are on the left-hand side, when the futures price is high. Notice that these are theoretical prices for both the European and American calls. Later we consider how well theoretical prices match actual market prices. For Figure 13.2 and Table 13.2 we see that European futures option prices are good approximations for American futures option prices. The approximation works best for out-of-the-money options.

Efficiency of the Futures Options Market

In this section we evaluate some of the evidence on the efficiency of the futures options market by considering two related issues. Most tests of efficiency test whether market prices match the prices of a theoretical model. A discrepancy between the market price and the theoretical price could mean either that the model is poor or that the market is inefficient. Therefore, a test of market prices against a theoretical model is a joint test of the market's efficiency and the model's ability to correctly represent the price.

Robert Whaley compared the actual market price of S&P 500 futures options with the market price. Table 13.3 presents results from his study. The table shows the difference between the market price and the theoretical price. The table classifies the differences according to time to expiration expressed in weeks. For example, t < 6 means that there were fewer than six weeks to expiration. The table also classifies the options by the extent to which they are in the money, measured as ratio of the futures price to the exercise price F/E. Accordingly, a large value of F/E indicates that an option is well in the money, with the futures price being large relative to the exercise price. The first value in the table, -0.0630, shows the average deviation of the observed option price from the model price for all of the call option transaction prices with an in-the-moneyness (F/E) less than 0.98 and time to expiration (t) less than six weeks.

Although all of the values in Table 13.3 appear to be small, there are some significant differences. In particular, the results of Table 13.3 indicate systematic differences between the market and theoretical prices for S&P 500 futures options. For call options well in-the-money (F/E ≥ 1.02), the market price tends to exceed the theoretical price. For example, for a call with more than one year until expiration and with F/E ≥ 1.02, the market price exceeds the theoretical price by 0.0702. For options out-of-the-money, the market price tends to be less than the theoretical price. For options with a long period to expiration, the model

Table 13.3
Pricing Discrepancies for S&P 500 Futures Options
Observed Market Price — Theoretical Price

Summary of average pricing errors of American futures option pricing models by the option's moneyness (F/E) and by the option's time to expiration in weeks (t) for S&P 500 futures option transactions during the period January 28, 1983 through December 30, 1983.

	Calls				Puts			
	t<6	6≤t<12	t≥12	All t	t<6	6≤t<12	t≥12	All t
F/E < 0.98	−0.0630	−0.1372	−0.0872	−0.1028	−0.1064	−0.0914	−0.1056	−0.1014
0.98 ≤ F/E <1.02	−0.1228	−0.0775	0.0073	−0.0924	−0.0816	−0.0196	0.1336	−0.0406
F/E ≥ 1.02	0.0577	0.1175	0.0702	0.0806	0.1286	0.1906	30.3060	0.1929
All F/E	−0.0757	−0.0599	−0.0120	−0.0606	−0.0191	0.0808	0.2287	0.0537

Source: R. Whaley, "Valuation of American Futures Options: Theory and Empirical Tests," *Journal of Finance,* March 1986, p. 138.

price tends to be small relative to the market price.

Whaley's results cover an early period of futures option trading, the second half of 1983. Subsequent studies appear to find more efficient pricing, as Table 13.4 summarizes. Blomeyer and Boyd found inefficient T-bond futures option pricing in early trading. However, results for both Whaley in the S&P 500 and for Blomeyer and Boyd in T-bonds may have been due to a lack of market seasoning. Some of the studies summarized in Table 13.4 compare actual prices with Black model prices. For example Jordan, McCabe and Kenyon compared soybean futures option prices with Black model prices and found an average difference of only 4/100 of a cent per bushel. With a bushel of soybeans worth about $6.00, this is only about 1/100 of a percentage difference between the model price and the actual price.

A Simplification.   Because the American futures option price can only be estimated with great computational expense and because the difference between American and European futures option prices is relatively small, we will treat futures options as though they were priced as European futures options in the remainder of this chapter. This will provide a considerable simplification of our discussion without a loss in content.

Table 13.4
Tests of Efficiency for Futures Options

Study	Key Results
Whaley (1986)	For S&P 500 futures options, market and theoretical prices are systematically different.
Jordan, McCabe, and Kenyon (1987)	For soybeans, compared the difference between actual market prices and the Black model price, with average differences being 4/100 of a cent per bushel.
Ogden and Tucker (1987)	For currencies, futures options appear to be efficiently priced.
Bailey (1987)	For gold, futures options appear to be efficiently priced.
Blomeyer and Boyd (1988)	In early trading of T-bond futures options, inefficiencies may have existed. However, inefficient prices were rare and difficult to exploit.
Wilson and Fung (1988)	For grain futures options, prices closely conformed to the Black model. In periods of high volatility, actual prices did not rise as much as Black model prices.

Price Relationships Between Options on Physicals and Options on Futures

We have seen that options on physicals, options on futures, futures, and forward contracts all trade on the same instruments in some cases. In Chapter 3 we saw the conditions under which futures and forward prices could differ. As a practical matter, however, research shows that futures and forward prices are virtually identical.

In this section we consider the pricing relationship between options on physicals and options on futures. We concentrate on call options, and we assume that the two options differ only with respect to the character of the underlying good. In other words, the two options have the same expiration and exercise price. Also, the two options are on the same underlying commodity, except one option is on the commodity itself, while the other option is on the futures on the commodity. We first consider European options. Then we analyze American options on underlying assets with no cash flows. Finally, we examine American options on underlying assets with cash flows.

European Options on Physicals and Futures

We will first consider European options and whether the call option on the physical or call option on the futures should be worth more. In Chapter 12 we saw that a call on the physical will be worth S - E at expiration. For a futures option, the exercise value of a call is F - E. However, for European futures options, exercise can occur only at expiration. At expiration, the futures basis must be zero, so $F_{t,t} = S_t$. At expiration of the futures, it must then be the case that:

$$F_{t,t} - E = S_t - E$$

For European options the exercise value for options on physicals and options on futures is the same. Further, both options afford access to the exercise value only at expiration, assuming a common expiration date. Therefore, European options on physicals and European options on futures must have the same value. This conclusion holds for both calls and puts.

American Options on Physicals and Futures When the Underlying Asset Has No Cash Flows

For American options, any difference in value between options on physicals and options on futures must stem from the early exercise privilege inherent in American options. After all, the only difference in European and American option prices comes from the early exercise privilege. We now consider options on an underlying asset that involves no cash flows, such as gold. We focus on assets without cash flows, because cash flow from the underlying good is the factor that prompts the early exercise of an American option on the physical. When the underlying asset has no cash flow, a call on the physical should not be exercised. The call will always be worth at least as much as its exercise value and may be worth more. Exercising the call discards the excess value that the option has over its intrinsic value.

From our earlier analysis, we have seen that exercising an American futures option can be rational. On the one hand, early exercise discards the excess value of the option over and above the intrinsic value or exercise value. On the other hand, early exercise of an American futures call gives immediate access to the payment F - E, which can then earn interest. Thus, as we saw, the early exercise decision for the American futures call depends on trading off this additional interest against the excess value of the call over and above the exercise value. In our discussion of Barone–Adesi and Whaley, we saw that there will be a critical futures price, F^*, at which one is indifferent about exercising the

American option. For futures prices above F*, early exercise is rational. If the futures price is below F*, the trader should not exercise.

For options on an underlying asset with no cash flows, exercising an option on the physical generates no cash flow. However, exercising a futures option can generate a cash flow even when the underlying asset itself has no cash flows. As we have seen, exercising the futures option gives a cash flow of F - E, because the futures is marked-to-market against the exercise price. Because it can generate cash flows by exercise, the American option on the futures will be worth more than the American option on the physical, when the underlying asset generates no cash flows.

Table 13.5, drawn from a paper by M. Brenner, G. Courtadon, and M. Subrahmanyam, shows the excess value that the option on the futures can have over the option on the physical in percentage terms. The table assumes a risk-free rate of 15 percent, and it assumes that the standard deviation of the percentage price change on the underlying asset is .25. The table shows the difference in value for different times to expiration and for different ratios of the physical price to the exercise price. For example, consider an option on gold with 270 days until expiration and assume that the price of gold is $360 per ounce and the exercise price is $300. The ratio of the physical good's price to the

Table 13.5
Percentage Difference in Value
for Call Options on Futures and Options on Physicals

Assumptions:

Underlying asset has no cash flows.
r = .15
σ = .25

Ratio of Physical Price to Exercise Price	Days Until Expiration				
	30	60	90	180	270
0.8	0.00	0.00	0.00	1.20	2.02
0.9	0.00	0.00	0.47	1.58	3.15
1.0	0.29	0.56	1.02	2.48	4.51
1.1	0.61	1.15	1.72	3.79	6.34
1.2	1.22	2.13	2.89	5.52	8.70

Source: M. Brenner, G. Courtadon, and M. Subrahmanyam, "Options on the Spot and Options on Futures," *Journal of Finance*, 40:5, 1985, pp. 1303-1317.

exercise price is 1.2, corresponding to the last row in the table. In this situation, the price of the option on the futures would be 8.70 percent more than that of the option on the physical.

As Table 13.5 shows, the call option on the futures is worth at least as much as the call option on the physical in every case. The difference in prices is greatest when the price of the physical is high relative to the exercise price and when expiration of the option is distant. Although not shown in Table 13.5, the relationship is just the reverse for put options. The put option on the physical is worth more than the put option on the futures.

American Options on Physicals and Futures When the Underlying Asset Has Cash Flows

We now consider options on physicals and options on futures when the underlying asset has cash flows. This case is particularly relevant to options on stock indexes and options on stock index futures. As we saw in Chapters 9 and 10, the dividend stream from stocks in a stock index is a major factor in the pricing of stock index futures.

Cash flows from the underlying good reduce its value. For example, when a stock pays a dividend, the stock price drops by approximately the amount of the dividend. These cash flows affect both the option on the physical and option on the futures. For stocks, dividends are typically quarterly. For currencies, the "dividend" is really the rate of interest and is approximately continuous. In this section, we consider only continuous cash flows that we call dividends. We begin by considering a special case: The underlying physical asset pays a continuous dividend equal to the risk-free rate of interest.

In equation 13.2 we saw that, under conditions of certainty, a futures call option would be worth the present value of $F_{0,t}$ - E. At t=0, the perfect markets Cost-of-Carry Model shows that the futures price itself will be:

$$F_{0,t} = S_0 (1 + C)$$

For financial futures, the cost-of-carry is essentially the risk-free interest rate. We are also assuming that the underlying asset pays a continuous dividend equal to the risk-free rate of interest. Therefore, the cost-of-carry is the difference in the two rates, or zero. Under this special circumstance, the futures price equals the spot price.

$$F_{0,t} = S_0 e^{rt} e^{-rt} = S_0 \qquad 13.4$$

Substituting the value of $F_{0,t}$ from equation 13.4 into equation 13.1 gives:

$$C_f = e^{-rt} [S_0 N(d_1^*) - E N(d_2^*)] \qquad 13.5$$

where:

C_f = the price of a call option on the futures

We now compare this special case for the value of a call option on the futures to the call option on the physical. With the stock paying a continuous dividend, the continuous dividend adjustment requires that we subtract the present value of the dividend from the stock price in the original Black-Scholes model:

$$C_f = e^{-rt} S_0 N(d_1^*) - e^{-rt} E N(d_2^*)$$
$$= e^{-rt} \left[S_0 N(d_1) - E N(d_2) \right] \qquad 13.6$$

The values for the call option on the futures and the call option on the physical are the same in equations 13.5 and 13.6 (the value of $d_1^* = d_1$, and $d_2^* = d_2$ in this special case).

This analysis leads to an important conclusion. If the physical asset pays a continuous dividend equal to the risk-free rate of interest, then the value of the option on the physical and the option on the futures will be the same. We can generalize this result. For an underlying asset that pays no dividend, such as gold, the option on the futures is worth more than the option on the physical. Likewise, if the dividend rate on the underlying asset is less than the interest rate, the call on the futures will be worth more than the call on the physical. The excess value of the option on the futures over the option on the physical falls as the dividend rate on the underlying asset increases. When the dividend rate on the underlying asset equals the risk-free rate, the call option on the physical and the futures have the same value. If the dividend rate on the physical asset exceeds the risk-free rate of interest, the call on the physical will be worth more than the call on the futures.

Summary

In analyzing the relationship between options on futures and options on physicals, we have focused on call options. For European call options, the value of the option on the physical and the option on the future must be the same. This conclusion holds for puts as well. For American options on underlying assets with no cash flows, the futures call option must be worth more than the call on the physical. Conversely, the futures put option must be worth less than the put on the physical.

When the underlying assets generate cash throw-offs, such as the dividends on a stock or the interest rate on a foreign currency, the analysis becomes more complex. We considered an underlying asset with a continuous cash throw-off, which we call a dividend. This specification is realistic for a foreign currency and a good approximation for a stock index. If the interest rate exceeds the dividend rate, the futures call option will be worth more than a call on the physical, and the futures put option will be worth less than a put on the physical. If the dividend rate equals the interest rate, the futures call and the call on the physical will be worth the same, as is true for the put. Finally, if the dividend rate exceeds the interest rate, the call option on the physical will be worth more than the call option on the futures. Similarly, when the dividend rate exceeds the interest rate, the put option on the futures will be worth more than the put option on the physical.

Relative Prices of Options on Physicals and Futures

Option Characteristics	Call	Put
European Options	$C_f = C_p$	$P_f = P_p$
American Option—No Dividend	$C_f > C_p$	$P_f < P_p$
American Option—Continuous Dividend		
Dividend Rate < Interest Rate	$C_f > C_p$	$P_f < P_p$
Dividend Rate = Interest Rate	$C_f = C_p$	$P_f = P_p$
Dividend Rate > Interest Rate	$C_f < C_p$	$P_f > P_p$

Where:

C_f, C_p = call on the futures and call on the physical
P_f, P_p = put on the futures and put on the physical

Put–Call Parity for Futures Options

In Chapter 12 we saw that it is possible to establish a **put–call parity** relationship between the price of a physical good and a combination of European call and put options on the good. Specifically, a long call and a short put position, plus an investment equal to the present value of the common exercise price for the two options, has the same value as the underlying good at the time the option expires. As we saw in Chapter 12, for non-dividend paying assets put–call parity asserts:

$$C - P = S_0 - Ee^{-rt} \qquad\qquad 13.7$$

where:

C = value of a call with exercise price E
P = value of a put with exercise price E
E = exercise price of both the call and put
S_0 = stock price
r = risk-free rate of interest
t = time until the options expire

A similar parity relationship holds for futures options. It is possible to duplicate a futures contract by using the same parity arguments developed in Chapter 12. For example, assume that the gold futures today is $400 per ounce. A call and a put on the futures both have an exercise price of $390. Figure 13.3

Figure 13.3
Profits and Losses on a Long Futures versus
a Portfolio of a Long Call and Short Put Option

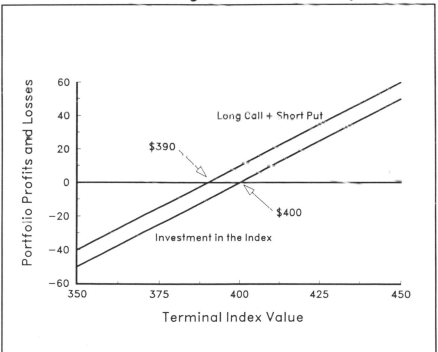

shows the profits and losses on the futures position and a combined long futures call/short futures put position at expiration. As the figure shows, the profits on the futures position are exactly $10 less than the profits on the long call/short put position, no matter what the spot price of gold is at expiration. For example, assume that the spot price of gold at expiration is $405. The futures price is also $405, because of the convergence that must occur at expiration. With a price at expiration of $405, the put option expires worthless and the call option is worth $5. Therefore, the entire long call/short put portfolio is worth $5. The futures position gives a profit equal to the current price of $405, less the original price of $400, so the futures is worth $5. This illustrates the idea that the profit on the long call/short put portfolio will always exceed the profit on the futures position by the difference between the futures price at contracting and the exercise price on the options. Notice that this entire analysis applies to values at expiration.

The long call/short put position is sure to generate a profit at expiration that equals the difference between the current futures price and the common exercise price on the option. Before expiration, at the time of contracting, the long call/short put position must be worth the present value of that certain profit. Therefore we can express the **put–call parity for futures options**:

$$C_f - P_f = (F_{0,t} - E)e^{-rt} \qquad\qquad 13.8$$

where:

C_f = futures call option with exercise price E
P_f = futures put option with exercise price E
$F_{0,t}$ = current futures price
E = common exercise price for C_f and P_f
r = risk-free rate
t = time until expiration for the futures and options

Comparing equations 13.7 and 13.8 shows the similar structure of put–call parity for options on the physicals and options on futures. For options on the physical, the long call/short put portfolio has a value equal to the current price of the stock less the present value of the exercise price. For the futures option, the long call/short put portfolio has a value equal to the present value of the difference between the futures price and the exercise price. For both parity relationships, the option portfolio on the left-hand side secures the right to the payoff on the right-hand side.

Equation 13.7 for the put-call parity relationship for options on physicals differs slightly from equation 13.8 for the put-call parity relationship for options on futures. Notice the subtle but important difference on the right-hand side of these equations. For the option on physicals of equation 13.7, the exercise price is discounted, but the stock price is not. However, for the option on futures, both the futures price and the exercise price are discounted.

In our discussion of the difference between options on physicals and options on futures, we noted that the price of European options on physicals and options on futures should be the same. Because this analysis of put-call parity focuses on European options, it should be possible to show the identity of the two put-call parity relationships. Using continuous compounding, the Cost-of-Carry Model for a perfect market is:

$$F_{0,t} = S_0 e^{rt}$$

Substituting this expression for the futures price into equation 13.8 gives:

$$C_f - P_f = (S_0 e^{rt} - E)e^{-rt} = S_0 - Ee^{-rt} \qquad 13.9$$

Equation 13.7 for options on physicals has the same structure as equation 13.8 for options on futures.

Options on Futures and Synthetic Futures

From the put-call parity relationship for options on futures, we can see how to construct futures positions by trading futures options. For simplicity, we continue to focus on European options. From Figure 13.3, we see that a long futures call/short futures put position gives the same profits and losses as a long futures position entered at the common exercise price of the futures options. This shows that we can use options to create a **synthetic futures**, a position that duplicates the profits and losses from a futures, but consists of positions in other instruments. For example, in Figure 13.3 the long call/short put gave exactly the profits and losses at expiration that a futures contract entered at a price of $390 would give. Equation 13.10 provides the basic relationship for creating synthetic futures:

Futures Call - Futures Put = Synthetic Futures   13.10

In equation 13.10, a minus sign indicates a short position, so equation 13.10 states that a long call/short put position creates a synthetic futures. Table 13.6 summarizes the rules for constructing synthetic positions. All of the rules in Table 13.6 are based on equation 13.10. As Table 13.6 shows, if we consider calls, puts, and futures, any two instruments can be used to create a position in the third. Further, any position in any instrument, long or short, can be created

Table 13.6 Rules for Creating Synthetic Instruments				
Synthetic Futures	=	Call	– Put	
Synthetic Call	=	Put	+ Futures	
Synthetic Put	=	Call	– Futures	
Synthetic Short Futures	=	Put	– Call	
Synthetic Short Call	=	– Put	– Futures	
Synthetic Short Put	=	– Call	+ Futures	

Note: A synthetic instrument has the same profit and loss characteristics as the actual instrument. However, the synthetic instrument does not necessarily have the same value as the actual instrument.

synthetically. In creating a synthetic instrument, we mimic the profits and losses from the instrument being duplicated.

Creating a synthetic instrument is not the same as creating a position that will have the same value as the instrument being synthetically replicated. In the next section, we will see the difference in value between a synthetic instrument and the instrument itself.

Risk Management with Options on Futures

Chapter 12 has already explored the basic features of speculating and hedging with options. As we have discussed in this chapter, prices of futures options behave similarly to options on physicals. Therefore, essentially similar speculative and hedging strategies are available for users of both options on physicals and options on futures. This section considers some uses of options on futures that were not directly considered in Chapter 12. We approach the subject through an extended example or case study.

Background for the Case Analysis

In this section we consider how to use options on the physical or options on futures to tailor the risk of an investment. For convenience, we focus on payoffs at option expirations, so we can ignore the difference between American and European options. Because the analysis focuses on European options, the conclusions we reach apply to both futures options and options on the physical.

We present the case analysis for a stock index, although the conclusions we reach apply to many different instruments. Consider a stock index that is currently at $100. Stocks in the index pay no dividends, and the expected return on the index is 10 percent, with a standard deviation of 20 percent. A put option on the index with an exercise price of $100 is available and costs $4. We consider three investment strategies:

Portfolio A:	Buy the index; total investment $100.
Portfolio B:	Buy the index and one-half of a put; total investment $102.
Portfolio C:	Buy the index and one put; total investment $104.

At expiration in one year, the profits and losses associated with these three portfolios depend entirely on the value of the index, because the value of the put at expiration also depends strictly on the index value. For the put, the value at expiration equals the maximum of either zero, or the exercise price minus the index value.

At expiration, the three portfolios will have profits and losses computed according to the following equations:

Portfolio A:	Index Value - $100
Portfolio B:	Index Value + .5 MAX{0, Index Value - $100} - $102
Portfolio C:	Index Value + MAX{0, Index Value - $100} - $104

The value of Portfolio A at expiration is just the index value, and the profit or loss is the value of the portfolio at expiration less the investment of $100. The terminal value of Portfolio C is the index value plus the value of the put. The profit or loss is the terminal value less the investment of $104. Portfolio B consists of the index plus one-half of a put. This gives a total investment of $102, and the terminal value of Portfolio B consists of the index value plus the value of the half put. Figure 13.4 graphs the profits and losses of these three portfolios for different terminal index values.

Portfolio Insurance

Of particular interest in Figure 13.4 is the profit and loss graph for Portfolio C, consisting of the index plus a put on the index. The worst possible loss on Portfolio C is $4. This loss occurs if the terminal index value is $100 or below. With a terminal index value of $100, the portfolio is worth $100, because the put expires worthless. This is the worst possible loss, however. For instance, if the terminal index value is $95, the put is worth $5 and the index investment is worth $95, for a total of $100. Portfolio C must always be worth at least $100.

Figure 13.4
Profits and Losses of Three Portfolios

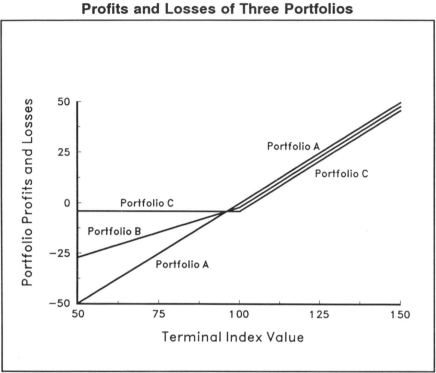

Portfolio C is an insured portfolio. In **portfolio insurance** a trader transacts to insure that the value of a portfolio cannot fall below a given amount. In the case of Portfolio C, the value cannot fall below $100. Further, this example is the classic case of portfolio insurance: buying a good at a given price and buying a put on the same good with an exercise price equal to the purchase price of the good. To create Portfolio C, a trader bought the index at $100 and bought an index put with an exercise price of $100.

In Chapter 10 we considered portfolio insurance with stock index futures. There we noted that portfolio insurance required dynamic hedging. Stock index futures were held in conjunction with a stock portfolio, and the portfolio was managed carefully to allow frequent adjustments to the futures position. In dynamic hedging, the hedger adjusts the futures position carefully to ensure that the profits and losses on the futures closely mimic the profits and losses on a put. Through dynamic hedging with futures, the trader replicates the put. Thus, dynamic hedging with futures creates a **synthetic put**.

Synthetic Puts and Dynamic Hedging

Earlier in this chapter we noted that a futures position alone could not create a synthetic put. That statement now requires qualification. In our earlier discussion of synthetic futures and options, we considered only payoffs at expiration, and we analyzed strategies in which traders created synthetic positions that would behave just like the actual instrument in the payoffs at expiration. For instance, we saw that we could create a synthetic long futures position by holding a long call and a short put. With dynamic hedging, it is possible to trade futures alone to create a synthetic put. However, it is not possible to create a futures position before expiration that can be held without modification and still replicate the put's payoffs at expiration. In short, dynamic hedging consists of trading futures to replicate the short term pricing behavior of a put. Thus, both futures and options can be used to insure a portfolio. The insurance is direct and simple with options. To insure a portfolio with futures requires dynamic hedging.

Synthetic Portfolio Insurance and Put–Call Parity

Figure 13.4, shows that the insured portfolio's profit and loss profile is exactly the profile for a call option on the stock index. This should not be surprising. Earlier we saw that a synthetic call could be created from a long position in the underlying good plus a long put. Applying the same analysis to the present context, we have:

$$\text{Synthetic Call} = \text{Put} + \text{Index}$$

From Figure 13.4, the Put + Index portfolio has the same profits and losses as a call option with an exercise price of $100.

Applying the put–call parity equation to our index example, we have:

$$\text{Call} = \text{Put} + \text{Index} - Ee^{-rt} \qquad \qquad 13.11$$

where:

$$E \; = \; \text{exercise price on the index option}$$

The put–call parity equation shows that an instrument with the same value and profits and losses as a call can be created by holding a long put, long index, and borrowing the present value of the exercise price. The portfolio on the right-hand side of equation 13.11 will have the same value and same profits and losses as the call. By contrast, the synthetic call merely has the same profits and losses as the call. At expiration, the value of the put plus index will exceed the value of the call.

Synthetic Calls and Put–Call Parity

Synthetic Call = Put + Index	A synthetic call replicates the profits and losses from the call, but it does not have the same value as the call.
Put–Call Parity: Call = Put + Index – E^{-rt}	The long put/long index/short bond portfolio duplicates the value and profits and losses of the call option.

Therefore, we now see that an insured portfolio is the long put/long index position that creates a synthetic call. From put-call parity, there is another way to create a portfolio that exactly mimics the insured portfolio's value at expiration. We can hold a long call plus invest the present value of the exercise price in the risk-free asset. From the put-call parity equation above, we see:

$$\text{Call} + E^{-rt} = \text{Put} + \text{Index} \qquad\qquad 13.12$$

The long call plus investment in the risk-free asset creates the same insured portfolio as the long index plus long put. Both positions have the same value and the same profits and losses at expiration.

This also shows why the put plus index portfolio that creates a synthetic call does not have the same value as the call that is being synthesized. The put plus index portfolio requires considerable investment to purchase the underlying index.

Tailoring Risk and Return Characteristics with Futures and Options

To this point we have not explicitly considered Portfolio B as defined above. Portfolio B consists of buying the index and buying one-half put. In essence, Portfolio B is half-insured. Expressed differently, Portfolio B consists of two equal portions: $50 in an insured portfolio, plus $50 in an outright position in the index. As Figure 13.4 shows, Portfolio B has profits and losses that fall between the totally insured and completely uninsured portfolios.

The partially insured Portfolio B has less risk than the uninsured Portfolio A, but it has more risk than the fully insured Portfolio C. Figure 13.4 shows this intermediate risk position by showing that the losses for the half-insured Portfolio B are less than the losses for the uninsured Portfolio A, but more than the losses for the fully insured Portfolio C. This example suggests that traders can use futures and options to tailor the risk characteristics of the portfolio to individual taste. With the variety of futures and option instruments, almost any feasible combination of risk and return is possible.

The one dominant lesson of modern finance concerns the risk/expected return trade-off. In well-functioning markets, finding the chance for higher returns always means accepting higher risk. In comparing the fully and partially insured portfolios with the uninsured portfolio, we have seen that portfolio insurance reduces risk. However, there must be a reduction in expected return that accompanies the reduction in risk.

Risk and Return in Insured Portfolios

We now explore the risk and expected return characteristics for Portfolios A–C. The portfolios have different probabilities of achieving given terminal values that depend on the price of the index at expiration. Likewise, the probability of achieving a given return on the portfolios depends on the index value at expiration. We explore these issues by assuming that returns on the index follow a normal distribution with a mean of 10 percent and a standard deviation of 20 percent.

Terminal Values for Portfolios A–C.   The portfolio values at expiration depend on the price of the index at expiration. For each, the terminal value is:

Portfolio A = Index
Portfolio B = Index + MAX{0, .5(100.00 − Index)}
Portfolio C = Index + MAX{0, 100.00 − Index}

We can now answer questions such as: What is the probability that Portfolio C will have a terminal value equal to or less than $100? Portfolio C will have a terminal value of at least $100 no matter what the value of the underlying index. In fact, there is a 30.85 percent probability that Portfolio C will have a terminal value of exactly $100. Portfolio C is worth $100 at expiration if the index is $100 or less at expiration, and there is a 30.85 percent chance that the index value will be $100 or less. What is the probability that Portfolio A will have a terminal value less than $90? The probability that the terminal value of portfolio A will lie below $90 is the probability that the terminal index value will fall more than 1.0 standard deviation below its expected value. Because we assume the returns on the index are normally distributed, there is a 15.87 percent chance that Portfolio A's value will be less than $90 at expiration. Table 13.7 shows some portfolio values and the probabilities that each portfolio will be equal to or less than the given terminal value at the expiration date.

In Table 13.7, the uninsured Portfolio A has the largest chance of an extremely low terminal value. For example, the chance that Portfolio A will be worth $80 or less is 6.68 percent. For Portfolio B, the chance of such an unhappy outcome is less than 1 percent, and there is no chance that Portfolio C could be worth $80 or less. (We already know that Portfolio C has to be worth at least $100.) It is interesting to note in Table 13.7 that the chance of each portfolio being worth $100 or less is the same—30.85 percent. Likewise, there is a 50 percent chance for each portfolio that the portfolio's value will be $110 or less. In fact, for terminal portfolio values at or above $100, the three portfolios have exactly the same probabilities. This makes sense, because if the terminal index value is $100.00 or more, the put option has zero value, and the remaining portion of each portfolio is the same.

Figure 13.5 graphs terminal portfolio values from $50 to $170 and shows the probability for each portfolio that the terminal portfolio value will be below or equal to the given amount. The three probability graphs differ for terminal portfolio values below $100. However, for all terminal portfolio values at or above $100, the graphs are identical. This matches the values we already saw in Table 13.7.

Concentrating only on terminal values, and neglecting the different investments required to obtain each portfolio, Figure 13.5 shows that the fully insured portfolio is the most desirable, followed by the half-insured portfolio, and then the uninsured portfolio. If we could choose one of these three portfolios

Table 13.7
Probability that the Terminal Portfolio Value Will Be Equal to or Less than a Specified Value

| | Probabilities | | |
| | --- | --- | --- |
Terminal Portfolio Value	Uninsured Portfolio A	Half–Insured Portfolio B	Fully Insured Portfolio C
50.00	0.0014	0.0000	0.0000
60.00	0.0062	0.0000	0.0000
70.00	0.0228	0.0002	0.0000
80.00	0.0668	0.0062	0.0000
90.00	0.1587	0.0668	0.0000
100.00	0.3085	0.3085	0.3085
110.00	0.5000	0.5000	0.5000
120.00	0.6915	0.6915	0.6915
130.00	0.8413	0.8413	0.8413
140.00	0.9332	0.9332	0.9332
150.00	0.9773	0.9773	0.9773
160.00	0.9938	0.9938	0.9938
170.00	0.9987	0.9987	0.9987

Figure 13.5
Probabilities that Terminal Values of Portfolios A–C
Will Be Equal to or Less than a Given Amount

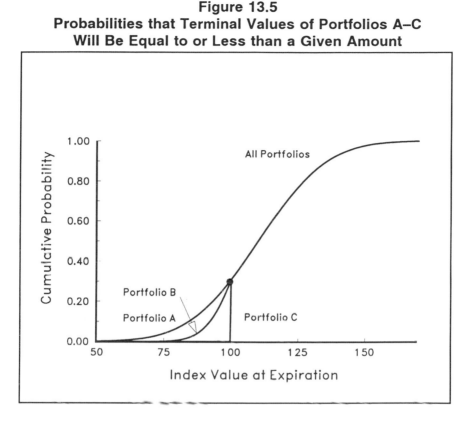

as a gift, the fully insured portfolio is the clear choice. No matter what the terminal index value is, the fully insured Portfolio C will pay at least as much as either Portfolio A or B. If the terminal index value is less than $100, the insured portfolio still pays $100, which is more than either Portfolio A or B. However, this conclusion neglects the different investment costs. Portfolio A cost only $100, while Portfolio B cost $102, and Portfolio C cost $104. We now consider the returns on each portfolio.

Returns on Portfolios A–C. Because Portfolios A–C have different costs, we need to compare the returns on each portfolio to make them more directly comparable. As we saw, Portfolio C is preferable to Portfolios A or B if we neglect cost. Once we consider cost, the answer is much less clear. Instead of having a clear choice, the investor faces the risk/expected return trade-off in portfolio insurance.

For each portfolio, we can evaluate the chance of a given return. For example, the lowest possible terminal value for the fully insured portfolio is

$100, which implies a return of $(100/104) - 1 = -0.0385$. The chance of a return on Portfolio C below -0.0385 is zero. However, the chance of Portfolio C having a return of exactly -0.0385 is 30.85 percent, the chance that Portfolio C is worth $100 at expiration.

Table 13.8 shows the probability that each portfolio will achieve a return greater than a specified return. For example, there is an 84.13 percent probability that the uninsured Portfolio A will do better than -10 percent. The half–insured Portfolio B has a 90.66 percent chance of returning at least -10 percent. For fully insured Portfolio C, there is no chance the return could be as bad as -10 percent.

So far, everything still looks good for the insured portfolios. The greater the level of insurance, it seems, the better the portfolio performs. However, we must now consider other possible returns. For example, what is the probability of no gain or a loss? For the uninsured Portfolio A, there is a 31.85 percent chance of a loss. The fully insured Portfolio C, however, stands 38.21 percent chance of a zero gain or a loss. Similarly, let us consider the chances of gaining more than 10 percent. The uninsured Portfolio has a 50 percent chance, because there is a 50 percent chance the terminal index value will exceed the expected value of $110. The insured portfolio has only a 41.29 percent chance of beating a 10 percent return.

Now we can see the risk/expected return trade-off implied by portfolio insurance strategies. Portfolio insurance protects against large losses by sacrificing the chance for large gains. Thus, portfolio insurance is aptly named.

Table 13.8
Probability of Achieving a Return
Equal to or Greater than a Specified Return

| | Probabilities | | |
Portfolio Return	Uninsured Portfolio A	Half–Insured Portfolio B	Fully Insured Portfolio C
-0.5000	0.9987	1.0000	1.0000
-0.4000	0.9938	1.0000	1.0000
-0.3000	0.9773	0.9996	1.0000
-0.2000	0.9332	0.9904	1.0000
-0.1000	0.8413	0.9066	1.0000
0.0000	0.6915	0.6554	0.6179
0.1000	0.5000	0.4562	0.4129
0.2000	0.3085	0.2676	0.2297
0.3000	0.1587	0.1292	0.1038
0.4000	0.0668	0.0505	0.0375
0.5000	0.0228	0.0158	0.0107

With any insurance contract, the insured pays the insurance premium to insure against some unpleasant event. By paying the insurance, the insured knows that the expected return on the portfolio will be less than it would be without insurance, but the insured hopes to avoid the extreme loss.

Figure 13.6 graphs the probabilities for each portfolio for the range of returns from -50 percent to 50 percent. Each point in the graph shows the probability that a portfolio will have returns greater than the return specified on the X-axis. For example, consider the returns in the range of -15 percent. There is a 100 percent chance that the fully insured Portfolio C will beat a -15 percent return. Also, Portfolio C has a 100 percent chance of beating any return up to -3.846 percent. The chance of doing better than -3.846 percent, however, is only 61.15 percent. Similarly, the half-insured Portfolio B has a very good chance of beating -15 percent. Portfolio A has the lowest chance of beating -15 percent.

As we noted from Table 13.8, however, the fortunes of the portfolios turn when we consider the probability of particularly favorable outcomes. For

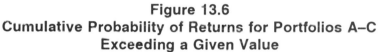

Figure 13.6
Cumulative Probability of Returns for Portfolios A–C
Exceeding a Given Value

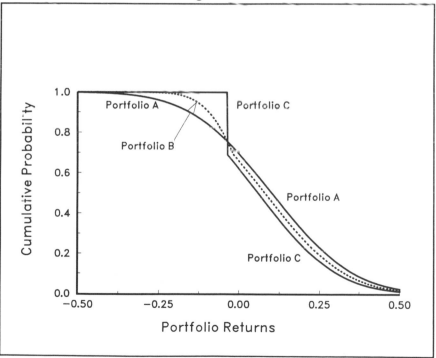

instance, the probability of exceeding a 20 percent return is 30.85 percent for Portfolio A, but only 26.76 percent for Portfolio B and only 22.97 percent for Portfolio C. Thus, the uninsured Portfolio A has the biggest chance of big gains and big losses. By comparison, the fully insured Portfolio C gives up the chance for big gains to avoid the chance of large losses. The half-insured Portfolio B occupies the middle ground.

Summary.   In this section we have seen that holding a stock index in conjunction with a put option creates an insured portfolio. By increasing the degree of insurance, the trader can avoid more and more risk. However, this risk avoidance has a price—the sacrifice of the chance for high returns. Thus, the concepts of portfolio insurance constitute one more example of the perennial trade-off between risk and expected return.

The analysis in this section focused on European options being held over a year-long horizon. We should not lose sight of the fact that the same principles apply to holding futures options on a futures contract. We have already seen that European options on physicals and options on futures have the same value. We also know that the futures price must converge to the spot price at expiration. Therefore, for the situation in this case study, we could just as easily have expressed the same ideas with futures and futures options.

Why Futures Options?

In our analysis of pricing options on futures and using options on futures to manage risk, we have seen that there is no price difference between European options on futures and options on physicals. Differences between options on futures and options on physicals do arise, however, for American options. Even for American options, price differences between options on futures and options on physicals are small, unless the price of the underlying good is quite distant from the exercise price of the options. This section considers some of the reasons for the popularity of options on futures.

Options on Futures versus Futures

Comparing options on futures with futures themselves, we see that the usefulness of options on futures stems from their special price performance characteristics. A futures position exposes a trader to a theoretically unlimited risk of gain or loss, but this is not true for the buyer of a futures option. In Chapter 12, for example, we saw that a long call position offers considerable potential for profit but that it also limits the maximum loss a trader can sustain. Other option positions have similar loss-reducing characteristics.

From our discussion of synthetic futures and option positions, we have seen that it is possible to create all futures and option positions synthetically. This might suggest that either futures or options are unnecessary. From Table 13.6, however, we see that options can create a synthetic futures position, but futures alone cannot create a synthetic option position.[4] Therefore, options provide the opportunity to create positions with payoff characteristics that the futures cannot provide. Futures options, then, have a role over and above the role played by the futures themselves.

Futures Options versus Options on Physicals

Realizing that traders can create synthetic futures positions from options alone, but that they cannot create synthetic option positions from futures alone, it may seem that options on futures are more important than the futures themselves. Options on futures, however, require the futures as the underlying instrument. As a consequence, options on futures cannot exist without the futures. We have seen that prices for options on physicals and options on futures are very similar. This price similarity suggests that options on physicals might be able to serve the function of both the futures and options on futures. As we now discuss, however, options on futures possess characteristics that are not available with options on physicals. We contrast options on futures with options on physicals to see why options on futures have become so popular.

In essence, options on futures dominate options on physicals in some markets because the futures market for some goods is much more liquid than the market for the physical good itself. Consider, for example, a commodity such as wheat. Wheat has many different grades and varieties. The different grades are held in different locations and have different uses. The different varieties grow in different parts of the country and come to harvest at different times. As a result, the character of the physical good is not conducive to supporting a new derivative instrument. It would be difficult to develop a liquid market for options on wheat itself.

Every new market requires growing liquidity to thrive. For an option contract, a liquid market for the underlying good is very important to the success of the option market. Therefore, chances for a successful option on wheat futures are probably much better than the chance for an option on wheat itself. Compared with wheat itself, the wheat futures market offers greater liquidity, a more uniform product, better price discovery mechanisms, greater ease of delivery upon exercise, and the financial backing of a clearinghouse.[5] If the physical good has desirable characteristics, options on the physical may dominate options on the futures. This appears to be the case in stock index trading. The S&P 100 option on the index itself is much more successful than any option on a stock index futures. Stock indexes do not have the poor cash market qualities that we noted for wheat.

For some goods, there are successful markets for options on physicals and options on futures. This seems to be the case for foreign currency. The Philadelphia Exchange trades options on currencies, while the CME trades options on currency futures. In currencies, futures began trading first, followed by options on the currency, followed by options on the currency futures. Even though options on currencies were established, options on currency futures were able to gain a toehold and survive. Perhaps the success of the options on currency futures is due to their being traded on the same exchange with currency futures. This trading proximity promotes trading of the futures against the option on futures, stimulating liquidity in both markets.

Another reason for preferring options on futures to options on the physical good itself is the economy and ease of exercise. To exercise an option on the good itself generally requires the entire striking price. By exercising a futures option, the owner of the option receives money and a futures position. Thus, exercise requires only the funds necessary to margin the new futures position. The exercise proceeds of the option will almost certainly cover the futures margin requirement. For traders with capital constraints, this difference can be important in extending the possibilities for leverage.

Conclusion

This chapter has explored options on futures. We began by contrasting options on futures with options on physicals. We discussed the market for options on futures and considered the factors that have made options on futures popular.

In analyzing the pricing of options on futures, we compared the options on futures with options on physicals. We found that options on futures are generally more valuable than options on the physical. However, there are some exceptions to this general rule. It is even possible for options on physicals to be worth more than the corresponding options on futures. The character of the options as American or European plays an important role in the relative pricing, as does the dividend rate on the physical asset. We considered the evidence on the efficiency of the market for options on futures. In general, the market is quite efficient, but there are some noteworthy exceptions.

Just as there is a put–call parity relationship for options on physicals, there is a put–call parity relationship for options on futures. In essence, a long futures call/short futures put simulates a long position in the futures. The futures options portfolio of a long call and short put has the same payoffs as a futures contract at expiration. Thus, the long futures call and short futures put creates a synthetic futures contract. This observation led to a general discussion of synthetic instruments.

Finally, we considered risk management techniques with options on physicals and options on futures. We developed the analysis of these risk control techniques within the framework of a case study of managing the risk of a stock index portfolio. As we showed, a fully insured portfolio consists of a long position in the underlying portfolio plus a long put on the portfolio. We showed how different degrees of portfolio insurance could be obtained by varying the proportion of the underlying portfolio covered by the put. As always, there is no free lunch; risk reduction through portfolio insurance carries a price. In portfolio insurance, the trader reduces the chance of big losses by sacrificing the chance for big returns. Thus, portfolio insurance can be useful in some circumstances, but it is not a general panacea or a strategy that every trader should pursue.

Questions and Problems

1. A holder of a call futures option exercises her option. What position does she hold after exercise? Does the owner of the futures option receive any funds when she exercises? Are there any exceptions to this rule?

2. Compare and contrast the position of a seller of a futures option and the purchaser of a futures put as a result of exercise. Be sure to state what positions the two traders hold and the cash flows that they incur.

3. Explain why the Black Model applies to forward options but does not apply exactly to futures options.

4. Consider the following data. A forward contract on wheat is priced at $4 per bushel and it expires in six months. The risk-free interest rate is 10 percent, and the standard deviation of the forward contract is 25 percent. A forward call option has an exercise price of $3.80 per bushel. Find the Black Model price for this forward option, assuming that the underlying contract amount is 5,000 bushels.

5. For the forward option in problem 4, find the value of the option if there is no uncertainty about the price of the forward contract.

6. For an option on a no-dividend stock, explain why a trader would never exercise a call option before expiration. Contrast your reasoning for the stock option to explain the circumstances that can make the early exercise of a futures call option rational.

7. Which kind of futures call option will have a higher price, a European or an American style option? Explain the conditions that create the maximum difference in value for two such options on the same underlying good with the same time to expiration and the same striking price.

8. For European call options, what is the price relationship between an option on the physical and an option on the futures? Explain.

9. For American futures options, explain the relationship between call option prices on futures and physicals when the underlying good pays a continuous dividend. In particular, explain how the pricing depends on the relationship between the dividend rate and the interest rate.

10. A futures contract on soybeans is priced at $6 per bushel and it expires in three months. The futures call on this contract has an exercise price of $5.90 and it is priced at $.50. If the interest rate for this period is 8 percent, what is the price of the futures put option?

11. The futures market just closed and you were unable to close a long position in wheat. Somehow, futures options are still trading. Explain how you would completely hedge the risk of your futures contract by trading futures options.

12. You hold a well-diversified stock portfolio and your pesky broker calls you and says: "Now is the time for you as an individual trader to get involved with portfolio insurance. Portfolio insurance is wonderful, because it lets you avoid risk by simply buying a call option on the index. Further, this is effectively costless, because the call option is fairly priced. (you get what you pay for in the options market.) With portfolio insurance, you get the upside potential, but you are protected from downside risk. With portfolio insurance, your insured portfolio can have exactly the same value at the end of the horizon as your uninsured portfolio. You can't lose!" Analyze the sales pitch for potential weaknesses.

Notes

1. Two comprehensive books covering options are: P. Ritchken, *Options: Theory, Strategy, and Applications*, Glenview, IL: Scott, Foresman and Co., 1987 and R. Jarrow and A. Rudd, *Option Pricing*, Homewood, IL: Richard

D. Irwin, Inc., 1983. See also R. Kolb, *Options: An Introduction*, Miami: Kolb Publishing Co., 1991.

2. Fischer Black, "The Pricing of Commodity Contracts," *Journal of Financial Economics*, September 1976, pp. 167-79.

3. G. Barone-Adesi and R. Whaley, "Efficient Analytic Approximation of American Option Values," *Journal of Finance*, 42:2, June 1987, pp. 301-320, also provide estimations based on other approximation methods. For the most part, these approximations are quite similar. The main contribution of the Barone-Adesi and Whaley paper was to develop a computationally superior method for approximating the values.

4. This statement requires qualification, because dynamic hedging with futures can replicate the payoffs on options. However, it is not possible to create a futures only position before expiration that will be certain to have the same payoffs at expiration as an option. With dynamic hedging, the trader continuously trades futures to simulate the option. That is quite different from the buy and hold synthetic instruments we consider.

5. See J. Sinquefield, "Understanding Options on Futures," *Mortgage Banking*, July 1982, pp. 35-40.

Appendix A

Cumulative Distribution Function
for the Standard Normal Random Variable

	.00	.01	.02	.03	.04	.05	.06	.07	.08	.09
0.0	.5000	.5040	.5080	.5120	.5160	.5199	.5239	.5279	.5319	.5359
0.1	.5398	.5438	.5478	.5517	.5557	.5596	.5636	.5675	.5714	.5753
0.2	.5793	.5832	.5871	.5910	.5948	.5987	.6026	.6064	.6103	.6141
0.3	.6179	.6217	.6255	.6293	.6331	.6368	.6406	.6443	.6480	.6517
0.4	.6554	.6591	.6628	.6664	.6700	.6736	.6772	.6808	.6844	.6879
0.5	.6915	.6950	.6985	.7019	.7054	.7088	.7123	.7157	.7190	.7224
0.6	.7257	.7291	.7324	.7357	.7389	.7422	.7454	.7486	.7517	.7549
0.7	.7580	.7611	.7642	.7673	.7704	.7734	.7764	.7794	.7823	.7852
0.8	.7881	.7910	.7939	.7967	.7995	.8023	.8051	.8078	.8106	.8133
0.9	.8159	.8186	.8212	.8238	.8264	.8289	.8315	.8340	.8365	.8389
1.0	.8413	.8438	.8461	.8485	.8508	.8531	.8554	.8577	.8599	.8621
1.1	.8643	.8665	.8686	.8708	.8729	.8749	.8770	.8790	.8810	.8830
1.2	.8849	.8869	.8888	.8907	.8925	.8944	.8962	.8980	.8997	.9015
1.3	.9032	.9049	.9066	.9082	.9099	.9115	.9131	.9147	.9162	.9177
1.4	.9192	.9207	.9222	.9236	.9251	.9265	.9279	.9292	.9306	.9319
1.5	.9332	.9345	.9357	.9370	.9382	.9394	.9406	.9418	.9429	.9441
1.6	.9452	.9463	.9474	.9484	.9495	.9505	.9515	.9525	.9535	.9545
1.7	.9554	.9564	.9573	.9582	.9591	.9599	.9608	.9616	.9625	.9633
1.8	.9641	.9649	.9656	.9664	.9671	.9678	.9686	.9693	.9699	.9706
1.9	.9713	.9719	.9726	.9732	.9738	.9744	.9750	.9756	.9761	.9767
2.0	.9772	.9778	.9783	.9788	.9793	.9798	.9803	.9808	.9812	.9817
2.1	.9821	.9826	.9830	.9834	.9838	.9842	.9846	.9850	.9854	.9857
2.2	.9861	.9864	.9868	.9871	.9875	.9878	.9881	.9884	.9887	.9890
2.3	.9893	.9896	.9898	.9901	.9904	.9906	.9909	.9911	.9913	.9916
2.4	.9918	.9920	.9922	.9925	.9927	.9929	.9931	.9932	.9934	.9936
2.5	.9938	.9940	.9941	.9943	.9945	.9946	.9948	.9949	.9951	.9952
2.6	.9953	.9955	.9956	.9957	.9959	.9960	.9961	.9962	.9963	.9964
2.7	.9965	.9966	.9967	.9968	.9969	.9970	.9971	.9972	.9973	.9974
2.8	.9974	.9975	.9976	.9977	.9977	.9978	.9979	.9979	.9980	.9981
2.9	.9981	.9982	.9982	.9983	.9984	.9984	.9985	.9985	.9986	.9986
3.0	.9987	.9987	.9987	.9988	.9988	.9989	.9989	.9989	.9990	.9990
3.1	.9990	.9991	.9991	.9991	.9992	.9992	.9992	.9992	.9993	.9993
3.2	.9993	.9993	.9994	.9994	.9994	.9994	.9994	.9995	.9995	.9995
3.3	.9995	.9995	.9995	.9996	.9996	.9996	.9996	.9996	.9996	.9997
3.4	.9997	.9997	.9997	.9997	.9997	.9997	.9997	.9997	.9997	.9998

References

Abken, P., "An Introduction to Portfolio Insurance," *Economic Review*, Federal Reserve Bank of Atlanta, 72:6, November/December 1987, pp. 2-25.

Allen, L. and T. Thurston, "Cash-Futures Arbitrage and Forward-Futures Spreads in the Treasury Bill Market," *The Journal of Futures Markets*, 8:5, October 1988, pp. 563-573.

Anderson, R. W., *The Industrial Organization of Futures Markets*, Lexington, Mass: D. C. Heath and Company, 1984.

Anderson, R. W., "Some Determinants of the Volatility of Futures Prices," *The Journal of Futures Markets*, 5:3, Fall 1985, pp. 331-348.

Anderson, R. W. and J. P. Danthine, "The Time Pattern of Hedging and the Volatility of Futures Prices," *Review of Economic Studies*, 50:2, April 1983, pp. 249-266.

Arak, M. and L. Goodman, "Treasury Bond Futures: Valuing the Delivery Options," *The Journal of Futures Markets*, 7:3, June 1987, pp. 269-286.

Bailey, F., "Emergency Action: July 1989 Soybeans," Chicago: Chicago Board of Trade, 1990.

Bailey, W., "An Empirical Investigation of the Market for Comex Gold Futures Options," *Journal of Finance*, 42:5, December 1987, pp. 1187-1194.

Barnhill, T., "Quality Option Profits, Switching Option Profits and Variation Margin Costs: An Evaluation of Their Size and Impact on Treasury Bond Futures Prices," *Journal of Financial and Quantitative Analysis*, 25:1, March 1990, pp. 65-86.

Barnhill, T. and W. Seale, "Optimal Exercise of the Switching Option in Treasury Bond Arbitrages," *The Journal of Futures Markets*, 8:5, October 1988, pp. 517-532.

Barone-Adesi, G. and R. Whaley, "Efficient Analytic Approximation of American Option Values," *Journal of Finance*, 42:2, June 1987, pp. 301-320.

Bassett, G., V. France, and S. Pliska, "The MMI Cash-Futures Spread on October 19, 1987," *The Review of Futures Markets*, 8:1, 1989, pp. 118-138.

Baxter, J., T. E. Conine, Jr., and M. Tamarkin, "On Commodity Market Risk Premiums: Additional Evidence," *The Journal of Futures Markets*, 5:1, Spring 1985, pp. 121-125.

Becketti, S. and G. Sellon, "Has Financial Market Volatility Increased?" *Economic Review*, Federal Reserve Bank of Kansas City, June 1989, pp. 17-30.

Behof, J., "GLOBEX: A Global Automated Transaction System for Futures and Options," Federal Reserve Bank of Chicago, Department of Supervision and Regulation, June 1990.

Behof, J., "Intermarket Cross-Margining for Futures and Options," Issue Summary of the Federal Reserve Bank of Chicago, May 1989.

Benninga, S. and M. Smirlock, "An Empirical Analysis of the Delivery Option, Marking to Market, and the Pricing of Treasury Bond Futures," *The Journal of Futures Markets*, 5:3, Fall 1985, pp. 361-374.

Bhattacharya, A. A., A. Ramjee, and B. Ramjee, "The Causal Relationship Between Futures Price Volatility and the Cash Price Volatility of GNMA Securities," *The Journal of Futures Markets*, 6:1, Spring 1986, pp. 29-39.

Bierman, H., "Defining and Evaluating Portfolio Insurance Strategies," *Financial Analysts Journal*, 44:3, May-June 1988, pp. 84-87.

Bierwag, G., "Measures of Duration," *Economic Inquiry*, 16:4, October 1978, pp. 497-507.

Bierwag, G. and G. Kaufman, "Coping with the Risk of Interest Rate Fluctuations: A Note," *Journal of Business*, 50:3, July 1977, pp. 364-370.

Billingsley, R. and D. Chance, "The Pricing and Performance of Stock Index Futures Spreads," *The Journal of Futures Markets*, 8:3, 1988, pp. 303-318.

Black, D. G., *Success and Failure of Futures Contracts: Theory and Empirical Evidence*, Salomon Brothers Monograph Series in Finance and Economics, Monograph 1986-1.

Black, F., "The Pricing of Commodity Contracts," *Journal of Financial Economics*, 3:1/2, September 1976, pp. 167-79.

Black, F. and R. Jones, "Simplifying Portfolio Insurance," *Journal of Portfolio Management*, 14:1, Fall 1987, pp. 48-51.

Black, F. and M. Scholes, "The Pricing of Options and Corporate Liabilities," *Journal of Political Economy*, 81:3, Part 1, 1973, pp. 637-654.

Blomeyer, E. and J. Boyd, "Empirical Tests of Boundary Conditions for Options on Treasury Bond Futures Contracts," *The Journal of Futures Markets*, 8:2, April 1988, pp. 185-198.

Blume, M., A. Mackinlay, and B. Terker, "Order Imbalances and Stock Price Movements on October 19 and 20, 1987," *Journal of Finance*, 44:4, September 1989, pp. 827-848.

Bodie, Z. and V. Rosansky, "Risk and Return in Commodity Futures," *Financial Analysts Journal*, 36:3, May-June 1980, pp. 27-39.

Bodurtha, S. and T. Quinn, "Does Patient Program Trading Really Pay?" *Financial Analysts Journal*, 46:3, May-June 1990, pp. 35-42.

Bookstaber, R. and J. Langsam, "Portfolio Insurance Trading Rules," *The Journal of Futures Markets*, 8:1, 1988, pp. 15-31.

Bowsher, M., "Repurchase Agreements," *Instruments of the Money Market*, Richmond: Federal Reserve Bank of Richmond, 1981.

Boyle, P., "The Quality Option and Timing Option in Futures Contracts," *Journal of Finance*, 44:1, March 1989, pp. 101-113.

Braga, F., L. Martin, and K. Meilke, "Cross Hedging the Italian Lira/U.S. Dollar Exchange Rate with Deutschemark Futures," *The Journal of Futures Markets*, 9:2, 1989, pp. 87-99.

Branch, B., "Testing the Unbiased Expectations Theory of Interest Rates," in G. Gay and R. Kolb, *Interest Rate Futures: Concepts and Issues*, Richmond, VA: Robert F. Dame, Inc., 1982.

Breeden, D., "Consumption Risk in Futures Markets," *Journal of Finance*, 35:2, May 1980, pp. 503-520.

Brennan, M. J., "A Theory of Price Limits in Futures Markets," *Journal of Financial Economics*, 16:2, June 1986, pp. 213-233.

Brenner, M., M. Subrahmanyam and J. Uno, "Arbitrage Opportunities in the Japanese Stock and Futures Markets," *Financial Analysts Journal*, 46:2, March-April 1990, pp. 14-24.

Brorsen, B. W., "Liquidity Costs and Scalping Returns in the Corn Futures Market," *The Journal of Futures Markets*, 9:3, June 1989, pp. 225-236.

Brorsen, B. W. and S. H. Irwin, "Futures Funds and Price Volatility," *Review of Futures Markets*, 6:2, 1987, pp. 118-135.

Capozza, D. and B. Cornell, "The Efficiency of the Treasury Bill Futures Market: An Analysis of Alternative Specifications," in G. Gay and R. Kolb, *Interest Rate Futures: Concepts and Issues*, Richmond, VA: Robert F. Dame, Inc., 1982.

Capozza, D. and B. Cornell, "Treasury Bill Pricing in the Spot and Futures Markets," in G. Gay and R. Kolb, *Interest Rate Futures: Concepts and Issues*, Richmond, VA: Robert F. Dame, Inc., 1982.

Cargill T. F. and G. C. Rausser, "Temporal Price Behavior in Commodity Futures Markets," *Journal of Finance*, 30:4, September 1975, pp. 1043-1053.

Carlton, D., "Futures Markets: Their Purpose, Their History, Their Growth, Their Successes and Failures," *The Journal of Futures Markets*, 4:3, Fall 1984, pp. 237-271.

Carter, C. A., G. C. Rausser, and A. Schmitz, "Efficient Asset Portfolios and the Theory of Normal Backwardation," *Journal of Political Economy*, 91:2, April 1983, pp. 319-331.

Castelino, M. G. and J. C. Francis, "Basis Speculation in Commodity Futures: The Maturity Effect," *The Journal of Futures Markets*, 2:2, Summer 1982, pp. 195-206.

Cavanaugh, K., "Price Dynamics in Foreign Currency Futures Markets," *Journal of International Money and Finance*, 6:3, 1987, pp. 295-314.

Chambers, D., "An Immunization Strategy for Futures Contracts on Government Securities," *The Journal of Futures Markets*, 4:2, Summer 1984, pp. 173-187.

Chambers, S. and C. Carter, "U.S. Futures Exchanges as Nonprofit Entities," *Journal of Futures Markets*, 10:1, February 1990, pp. 79-88.

Chance, D., "Futures Contract and Immunization," *Review of Research in Futures Markets*, 5:2, 1986, pp. 124-141.

Chance, D., "A Semi-Strong Form Test of the Efficiency of the Treasury Bond Futures Market," *The Journal of Futures Markets*, 5:3, Fall 1985, pp. 385-405.

Chance, D., M. Marr, and G. Thompson, "Hedging Shelf Registrations," *The Journal of Futures Markets*, 6:1, Spring 1986, pp. 11-27.

Chang, C. and J. Chang, "Forward and Futures Prices: Evidence from the Foreign Exchange Markets," *Journal of Finance*, 45:4, September 1990, pp. 1333-1336.

Chang, E., "Returns to Speculators and the Theory of Normal Backwardation," *Journal of Finance*, 40:1, March 1985, pp. 193-208.

Chang, E. and C. Kim, "Day of the Week Effects and Commodity Price Changes," *The Journal of Futures Markets*, 8:2, April 1988, pp. 229-241.

Chang, E. and R. A. Stevenson, "The Timing Performance of Small Traders," *The Journal of Futures Markets*, 5:4, Winter 1985, pp. 517-527.

Chang, J. and L. Shanker, "Hedging Effectiveness of Currency Options and Currency Futures," *The Journal of Futures Markets*, 6:2, 1986, pp. 289-305.

Chiang, R., G. Gay, and R. Kolb, "Commodity Exchange Seat Prices," *Review of Futures Markets*, 6:1, 1987, pp. 1-10.

Chiang, R., G. Gay, and R. Kolb, "Interest Rate Hedging: An Empirical Test of Alternative Strategies," *Journal of Financial Research*, 6:3, Fall 1983, pp. 187-197.

Chiang, R. and D. J. Lasser, "Tax Timing Options on Futures Contracts and the 1981 Economic Recovery Act," *The Financial Review*, 24:1, February 1989, pp. 75-92.

Chiang, T. "Empirical Analysis on the Predictors of Future Spot Rates," *Journal of Financial Research*, 9:2, Summer 1986, pp. 153-162.

Chicago Board of Trade, Commodity Trading Manual, 1989.

Chicago Mercantile Exchange, "SPAN Overview," Jul 1990.

Chicago Mercantile Exchange, "SPAN Technical Specifications," July 1990.

Chicago Mercantile Exchange, "Standard Portfolio Analysis of Risk," 1989.

Clark, P. "A Subordinated Stochastic Process Model with Finite Variance for Speculative Prices," *Econometrica*, 41, Part 1:1, January 1973, pp. 135-155.

Clark, R. and W. Ziemba, "Playing the Turn-of-the-Year Effect with Index Futures," *Operations Research*, 35:6, November-December 1987, pp. 799-813.

Commodity Futures Trading Commission, "Economic Analysis of Dual Trading on Commodity Exchanges," November 1989.

Cook, T. and B. Summers, *Instruments of the Money Market*, Richmond, VA: Federal Reserve Bank of Richmond, 1981, 5th edition.

Copeland, T. and F. Weston, *Financial Theory and Corporate Policy,* 3rd Ed. Reading, MA: Addison Wesley, 1988.

Cornell, B., "Taxes and the Pricing of Stock Index Futures: Empirical Results," *The Journal of Futures Markets*, 5:1, 1985, pp. 89-101.

Cornell, B., "The Weekly Pattern in Stock Returns: Cash versus Futures: A Note," *Journal of Finance*, 40:2, June 1985, pp. 583-588.

Cornell, B. and J. Dietrich, "The Efficiency of the Market for Foreign Exchange Under Floating Exchange Rates," *Review of Economics and Statistics*, 60:1, February 1978, pp. 111-120.

Cornell, B. and K. French, "Taxes and the Pricing of Stock Index Futures," *Journal of Finance*, 38:3, June 1983, pp. 675-694.

Cornell, B. and M. Reinganum, "Forward and Futures Prices: Evidence from the Forward Exchange Markets," *Journal of Finance*, 36:5, December 1981, pp. 1035-1045.

Cornew, R. W., "Note on Initial Margin to Net Asset Value: Average Values for the Commodity Pool Industry," *The Journal of Futures Markets*, 6:3, Fall 1986, pp. 495-501.

Cornew, R. W., D. E. Town, and L. D. Crowson, "Stable Distributions, Futures Prices, and the Measurement of Trading Performance," *The Journal of Futures Markets*, 4:4, Fall 1984, pp. 531-558.

Cox, J., J. Ingersoll, and S. Ross, "The Relation Between Forward Prices and Futures Prices," *Journal of Financial Economics*, 9:4, December 1981, pp. 321-346.

Debreu, G., *Theory of Value,* New Haven: Yale University Press, 1959.

Diamond, B. B. and Mark P. Kollar, *24-Hour Trading*, New York: John Wiley, 1989.

Dusak, K., "Futures Trading and Investor Returns: An Investigation of Commodity Market Risk Premiums," *Journal of Political Economy*, 81:6, November/December 1973, pp. 1387-1406.

Dusak-Miller, K., "The Relation Between Volatility and Maturity in Futures Contracts," in *Commodity Markets and Futures Prices*, ed. R. M. Leuthold, Chicago: Chicago Mercantile Exchange, 1979.

Dyl, E. and E. Maberly, "The Daily Distribution of Changes in the Price of Stock Index Futures," *The Journal of Futures Markets*, 6:4, Winter 1986, pp. 513-521.

Dyl, E. and E. Maberly, "The Weekly Pattern in Stock Index Futures: A Further Note," *Journal of Finance*, 41:5, December 1986, pp. 1149-1152.

Eaker, M. and D. Grant, "Cross-Hedging Foreign Currency Risk," *Journal of International Money and Finance*, 6:1, 1987, pp. 85-106.

Easterbrook, F., "Monopoly, Manipulation, and the Regulation of Futures Markets," *Journal of Business*, 59:2, Part 2, April 1986, pp. S103-S127.

Ederington, L., "The Hedging Performance of the New Futures Market," *Journal of Finance*, 34:1, March 1979, pp. 157-170.

Edwards, F., "Does Futures Trading Increase Stock Market Volatility?" *Financial Analysts Journal*, 44:1, January-February 1988b, pp. 63-69.

Edwards, F., "Futures Trading and Cash Market Volatility: Stock Index and Interest Rate Futures," *The Journal of Futures Markets*, 8:4, 1988a, pp. 421-439.

Edwards, F. R., "The Clearing Association in Futures Markets: Guarantor and Regulator," *The Journal of Futures Markets*, 3:4, Winter 1983, pp. 369-392.

Edwards, F. R. and C. Ma, "Commodity Pool Performance: Is the Information Contained in Pool Prospectuses Useful?" *The Journal of Futures Markets*, 8:5, October 1988, pp. 589-616.

Ehrhardt, M. C., J. V. Jordan and R. A. Walkling, "An Application of Arbitrage Pricing Theory to Futures Markets: Tests of Normal Backwardation," *Journal of Futures Markets*, 7:1, February 1987, pp. 21-34.

Elliot, J. and M. Echols, "Market Segmentation, Speculative Behavior, and the Term Structure of Interest Rates," *Review of Economics and Statistics*, 58:1, February 1976, pp. 40-47.

Elton, E. J., M. J. Gruber, and J. C. Rentzler, "Professionally Managed, Publicly Traded Commodity Funds," *Journal of Business*, 60:2, April 1987, pp. 175-199.

Eytan, T., G. Harpaz, and S. Krull, "The Pricing of Dollar Index Futures Contracts," *The Journal of Futures Markets*, 8:2, 1988, pp. 127-139.

Fama, E., "Efficient Capital Markets: Theory and Empirical Work," *Journal of Finance*, 25:2, May 1970, pp. 383-417.

Fama, E., "Perspectives on October 1987, or, What Did We Learn from the Crash?" in *Black Monday and the Future of Financial Markets*, Homewood, IL: Dow Jones-Irwin, 1989.

Fama, E. and K. French, "Commodity Futures Prices: Some Evidence on Forecast Power, Premiums, and the Theory of Storage," *Journal of Business*, 60:1, January 1987, pp. 55-73.

Feinstein, S. and W. Goetzmann, "The Effect of the Triple Witching Hour on Stock Market Volatility," *Economic Review*, Federal Reserve Bank of Atlanta, September/October 1988, pp. 2-18.

Fieleke, N., "The Foreign Currency Futures Market: Some Reflections on Competitiveness and Growth," *The Journal of Futures Markets*, 5:4, 1985, pp. 625-631.

Fieleke, N., "The Rise of the Foreign Currency Futures Market," *New England Economic Review*, March/April 1985, pp. 38–47.

Figlewski, S., "Explaining the Early Discounts on Stock Index Futures: The Case for Disequilibrium," *Financial Analysts Journal*, 40:4, July–August 1984, pp. 43–48.

Figlewski, S., "Futures Trading and Volatility in the GNMA Market," *Journal of Finance*, 36:2, May 1981, pp. 445–456.

Figlewski, S., "Hedging Performance and Basis Risk in Stock Index Futures," *Journal of Finance*, 39:3, July 1984, pp. 657–669.

Figlewski, S., "Hedging with Stock Index Futures: Theory and Application in a New Market," Finance Working Paper No. 139, University of California at Berkeley.

Figlewski, S. and S. Kon, "Portfolio Management with Stock Index Futures," *Financial Analysts Journal*, 38:1, January–February 1982, pp. 52–60.

Finnerty, J. E. and H. Y. Park, "Stock Index Futures: Does the Tail Wag the Dog?" *Financial Analysts Journal*, 43:2, March–April 1987, pp. 57–61.

Fischel, D., "Regulatory Conflict and Entry Regulation of New Futures Contracts," *Journal of Business*, 59:2, Part 2, April 1986, pp. S85–S102.

Fishe, R. and L. Goldberg, "The Effects of Margins on Trading in Futures Markets," *The Journal of Futures Markets*, 6:2, Summer 1986, pp. 261–271.

Fortune, P., "An Assessment of Financial Market Volatility: Bills, Bonds, and Stocks," *New England Economic Review*, November/December 1989, pp. 13–28.

France, V. G., "The Regulation of Margin Requirements: A Survey," Unpublished working paper, August 1990, University of Illinois.

Franckle, C., "The Hedging Performance of the New Futures Market: Comment," *Journal of Finance*, 35:5, December 1980, pp. 1272–1279.

French, K., "A Comparison of Futures and Forward Prices," *Journal of Financial Economics*, 12:3, November 1983, pp. 311–342.

Froewiss, K. C., "GNMA Futures: Stabilizing or Destabilizing?" *Federal Reserve Bank of San Francisco* Economic Review, Spring 1978, pp. 20–29.

Garbade, K. and W. Silber, "Cash Settlement of Futures Contracts: An Economic Analysis," *The Journal of Futures Markets*, 3:4, Winter 1983, pp. 451–472.

Garcia, P., R. M. Leuthold, and H. Zapata, "Lead-Lag Relationships Between Trading Volume and Price Variability: New Evidence," *The Journal of Futures Markets*, 6:1, Spring 1986, pp. 1–10.

Gastineau, G. and A. Madansky, "S&P 500 Stock Index Futures Evaluation Tables," *Financial Analysts Journal*, 39:6, November–December 1983, pp. 68–76.

Gay, G. and T. Kim, "An Investigation into Seasonality in the Futures Market," *The Journal of Futures Markets*, 7:2, April 1987, pp. 169–181.

Gay, G. and R. Kolb, "Immunizing Bond Portfolios with Interest Rate Futures," *Financial Management*, 11:2, Summer 1982, pp. 81–89.

Gay, G. and R. Kolb, *Interest Rate Futures: Concepts and Issues*, Richmond, VA: Robert F. Dame, Inc., 1982.

Gay, G. and R. Kolb, "Removing Bias in Duration Based Hedging Models: A Note," *The Journal of Futures Markets*, 4:2, Summer 1984, pp. 225–228.

Gay, G. and S. Manaster, "Implicit Delivery Options and Optimal Delivery Strategies for Financial Futures Contracts," *Journal of Financial Economics*, 16:1, May 1986, pp. 41–72.

Gay, G. and S. Manaster, "The Quality Option Implicit in Futures Contracts," *Journal of Financial Economics*, 13:3, September 1984, pp. 353-370.

Gemmill, G., "Hedging Crude Oil: How Many Markets Are Needed in the World?" *The Review of Futures Markets*, 7 (supplement), October 1988, pp. 556-571.

Gerety, M. S. and J. H. Mulherin, "Patterns in Intraday Stock Market Volatility: Past and Present," Working paper, Office of Economic Analysis, U.S. Securities and Exchange Commission, October 1990.

Giddy, I., "An Integrated Theory of Exchange Rate Equilibrium," in G. Gay and R. Kolb, *International Finance: Concepts and Issues*, Richmond, VA: Robert F. Dame, Inc., 1982.

Giddy, I., "Why It Doesn't Pay to Make a Habit of Forward Hedging," in G. Gay and R. Kolb, *International Finance: Concepts and Issues*, Richmond, VA: Robert F. Dame, Inc., 1982.

Glassman, D., "The Efficiency of Foreign Exchange Futures Markets in Turbulent and Non-Turbulent Periods," *The Journal of Futures Markets*, 7:3, 1987, pp. 245-267.

Gordon, J. D., "The Distribution of Daily Changes in Commodity Futures Prices," Technical Bulletin No. 1702, ERS, United States Department of Agriculture, 1985.

Gould, F., "Stock Index Futures: The Arbitrage Cycle and Portfolio Insurance," *Financial Analysts Journal*, 44:1, January-February 1988, pp. 48-62.

Government Accounting Office, "Automation Can Enhance Detection of Trade Abuses but Introduces New Risks," September 1989.

Grammatikos, T. and A. Saunders, "Stability and the Hedging Performance of Foreign Currency Futures," *The Journal of Futures Markets*, 3:3, 1983, pp. 295-305.

Grant, D., "How to Optimize with Stock Index Futures," *Journal of Portfolio Management*, 8:3, Spring 1982, pp. 32-36.

Grant, D., "A Market Index Futures Contract and Portfolio Selection," *Journal of Economics and Business*, 34:4, 1982, pp. 387-390.

Grauer, F. L. A., "Equilibrium in Commodity Futures Markets: Theory and Tests," Unpublished Ph.D. dissertation, Stanford University, 1977.

Gray, R., "Onions Revisited," *Journal of Farm Economics*, 45:3, May 1963, pp. 273-276.

Gray, R., "The Search for a Risk Premium," in A. Peck, *Selected Writings on Futures Markets*, Chicago: Chicago Board of Trade, 1977, pp. 71-82.

Greising, D., "This Time, the Feds' Case May Not Be the Pits," *Business Week*, September 24, 1990.

Greising, D., "Was the Scandal in the Pits Mostly Small Potatoes?" *Business Week*, July 23, 1990.

Grossman, S., "An Analysis of the Role of Insider Trading on Futures Markets," *Journal of Business*, 59:2, Part 2, April 1986, pp. S129-S146.

Hall, J. A., B. W. Brorsen, and S. H. Irwin, "The Distribution of Futures Prices: A Test of the Stable Paretian and Mixture of Normals Hypotheses," *Journal of Financial and Quantitative Analysis*, 24:1, March 1989, pp. 105-116.

Hansen, L. and R. Hodrick, "Forward Exchange Rates as Optimal Predictors of Future Spot Rates: An Econometric Analysis," Journal of Political Economy, 88:5, 1980, pp. 829-853.

Hardy, C. O., *Risk and Risk Bearing*, Chicago: University of Chicago Press, 1940.

Harpaz, G., S. Krull, and J. Yagil, "The Efficiency of the U.S. Dollar Index Futures Market," *The Journal of Futures Markets*, 10:5, October 1990, pp. 469-479.

Harrington, D., F. Fabozzi, and H. Fogler, *The New Stock Market*, Chicago: Probus Publishing Co., 1990.

Harris, L., "The October 1987 S&P 500 Stock-Futures Basis," *Journal of Finance*, 44:1, March 1989, p. 77-99.

Harris, L., "S&P 500 Cash Stock Price Volatilities," *Journal of Finance*, 44:5, December 1989, pp. 1155-1175.

Hartzmark, M. "The Effects of Changing Margin Levels on Futures Market Activity, the Composition of Traders in the Market, and Price Performance," *Journal of Business*, 59:2, Part 2, April 1986, pp. S147-S180.

Hartzmark, M., "Returns to Individual Traders of Futures: Aggregate Results," *Journal of Political Economy*, 95:6, December 1987, pp. 1292-1306.

Hazuka, T. B., "Consumption Betas and Backwardation in Commodity Markets," *Journal of Finance*, 39:3, July 1984, pp. 647-655.

Hegde, S., "An Empirical Analysis of Implicit Delivery Options in the Treasury Bond Futures Contract," *Journal of Banking and Finance*, 12:3, September 1988, pp. 469-492.

Hegde, S., "On the Value of the Implicit Delivery Options," *The Journal of Futures Markets*, 9:5, October 1989, pp. 421-437.

Hegde, S. and B. Branch, "An Empirical Analysis of Arbitrage Opportunities in the Treasury Bill Futures Market," *The Journal of Futures Markets*, 5:3, Fall 1985, pp. 407-424.

Hegde, S. and B. McDonald, "On the Informational Role of Treasury Bill Futures," *The Journal of Futures Markets*, 6:4, Winter 1986, pp. 629-643.

Helms, B. P., F. R. Kaen, and R. E. Rosenman, "Memory in Commodity Futures Contracts," *The Journal of Futures Markets*, 4:4, Winter 1984, pp. 559-567.

Helms, B. P. and T. F. Martell, "An Examination of the Distribution of Futures Price Changes," *Journal of Futures Markets*, 5:2, Summer 1985, pp. 259-272.

Helmuth, J., "A Report on the Systematic Downward Bias in Live Cattle Futures Prices," *Journal of Futures Markets*, 1:3, Fall 1981, pp. 347-358.

Hemler, M., "The Quality Delivery Option in Treasury Bond Futures Contracts," Ph.D. dissertation, University of Chicago, 1988.

Herbst, A. and E. Maberly, "Stock Index Futures, Expiration Day Volatility, and the Special Friday Opening: A Note," *The Journal of Futures Markets*, 10:3, 1990, 323-325.

Herbst, A., J. McCormack and E. West, "Investigation of a Lead-Lag Relationship Between Spot Stock Indices and Their Futures Contracts," *The Journal of Futures Markets*, 7:4, 1987, pp. 373-381.

Hill, J., "Program Trading, Portfolio Insurance, and the Stock Market Crash: Concepts, Applications and an Assessment," Kidder Peabody, January 1988.

Hill, J. and F. Jones, "Equity Trading, Program Trading, Portfolio Insurance, Computer Trading and All That," *Financial Analysts Journal*, 44:4, July-August 1988, pp. 29-38.

Hill, J. and T. Schneeweis, "A Note on the Hedging Effectiveness of Foreign Currency Futures," *The Journal of Futures Markets*, 1:4, Winter 1981, pp. 659-664.

Hill, J. and T. Schneeweis, "Risk Reduction Potential of Financial Futures," in G. Gay and R. Kolb, *Interest Rate Futures: A Comprehensive Introduction*, Richmond, VA: Robert F. Dame, Inc., 1982.

Hodrick, R. and S. Srivastava, "Foreign Currency Futures," *Journal of International Economics*, 22:1/2, 1987, pp. 1-24.

Houthakker, H. S., "Can Speculators Forecast Prices?" *Review of Economics and Statistics*, 39:1, 1957, pp. 143-151.

Hudson, M. A., R. M. Leuthold, and G. F. Sarassoro, "Commodity Futures Price Changes: Recent Evidence for Wheat, Soybeans, and Live Cattle," *The Journal of Futures Markets*, 7:3, June 1987, pp. 287-302.

Hunter, W. C., "Rational Margins on Futures Contracts: Initial Margins," *Review of Research in Futures Markets*, 5:2, 1986, pp. 160-173.

Irwin, S. H., and B. W. Brorsen, "Public Futures Funds," *The Journal of Futures Markets*, 5.2, Summer 1985, pp. 149-171.

Jarrow, R. and G. Oldfield, "Forward Contracts and Futures Contracts," *Journal of Financial Economics*, 9:4, December 1981, pp. 373-382.

Jarrow, R. A. and Andrew Rudd, *Option Pricing*, Homewood, IL: Richard D. Irwin, 1983.

Johnston, E. T. and J. J. McConnell, "Requiem for a Market: An Analysis of the Rise and Fall of a Financial Futures Contract," *The Review of Financial Studies*, 2:1, 1989, pp. 1-23.

Jones, C. and J. Wilson, "Is Stock Price Volatility Increasing?" *Financial Analysts Journal*, 45:6, November-December 1989, pp. 20-26.

Jordan, J., W. Seale, N. McCabe, and D. Kenyon, "Transactions Data Tests of the Black Model for Soybean Futures Options," *The Journal of Futures Markets*, 7:5, October 1987, pp. 535-554.

Junkus, J., "Weekend and Day of the Week Effects in Returns on Stock Index Futures," *The Journal of Futures Markets*, 6:3, Fall 1986, pp. 397-407.

Kahl, K., R. Rutz, and J. Sinquefield, "The Economics of Performance Margins in Futures Markets," *The Journal of Futures Markets*, 5:1, Spring 1985, pp. 103-112.

Kane, A. and A. Marcus, "The Quality Option in the Treasury Bond Futures Market: An Empirical Assessment," *Journal of Futures Markets*, 6:2, Summer 1986b, pp. 231-248.

Kane, A. and A. Marcus, "Valuation and Optimal Exercise of the Wild Card Option in the Treasury Bond Futures Market," *Journal of Finance*, 41:1, March 1986a, pp. 195-207.

Kane, E. J., "Market Incompleteness and Divergences Between Forward and Futures Interest Rates," *Journal of Finance*, 35:2, May 1980, pp. 221-234.

Kane, E. and B. Malkiel, "The Term Structure of Interest Rates: An Analysis of a Survey of Interest Rate Expectations," *Review of Economics and Statistics*, 49:3, August 1967, pp. 343-355.

Karpoff, J. M., "The Relation Between Price Changes and Trading Volume: A Survey," *Journal of Financial and Quantitative Analysis*, 22:1, March 1987, pp. 109-126.

Kawaller, I., "Hedging with Futures Contracts: Going the Extra Mile," *Journal of Cash Management*, July-August 1986, pp. 34-36.

Kawaller, I., "A Note: Debunking the Myth of the Risk-Free Return," *The Journal of Futures Markets*, 7:3, June 1987, pp. 327-331.

Kawaller, I. and T. Koch, "Cash-and-Carry Tradings and the Pricing of Treasury Bill Futures," *The Journal of Futures Markets*, 4:2, Summer 1984, pp. 115-123.

Kawaller, I. and T. Koch, "Managing Cash Flow Risk in Stock Index Futures: The Tail Hedge," *The Journal of Portfolio Management*, 15:1, Fall 1988, pp. 41-44.

Kawaller, I., P. Koch, and T. Koch, "The Relationship Between the S&P 500 Index and S&P 500 Index Futures Prices," Federal Reserve Bank of Atlanta, *Economic Review*, May/June 1988, pp. 2-9.

Kawaller, I., P. Koch, and T. Koch, "The Temporal Relationship Between S&P 500 Futures and the S&P 500 Index," *Journal of Finance*, 42:5, December 1987, pp. 1309-1329.

Kenyon, D., K. Kling, J. Jordan, W. Seale, and N. McCabe, "Factors Affecting Agricultural Futures Price Variance," *The Journal of Futures Markets*, 7:1, February 1987, pp. 73-91.

Keynes, J. M., *A Treatise on Money*, Vol. 2, 1930, London: Macmillan.

King, M. and S. Wadhwani, "Transmission of Volatility Between Stock Markets," *The Review of Financial Studies*, 3:1, 1990, pp. 5-33.

Klemkosky, R. and D. Lasser, "An Efficiency Analysis of the T-Bond Futures Market," *The Journal of Futures Markets*, 5:4, Winter 1985, pp. 607-620.

Kmenta, J., *Elements of Econometrics*, New York: Macmillan, 1971.

Kodres, L., "Tests of Unbiasedness in Foreign Exchange Futures Markets: The Effects of Price Limits," *The Review of Futures Markets*, 7:1, 1988, pp. 139-166.

Kohlhagen, S., "The Forward Rate as an Unbiased Predictor of the Future Spot Rate," *Columbia Journal of World Business*, 14:4, Winter 1979, pp. 77-85.

Kolb, R. *Investments*, Glenview, IL.: Scott Foresman, Inc., 1989, Chapters 13-15.

Kolb, R., *Options: An Introduction*, Miami: Kolb Publishing Co., 1991.

Kolb, R. and R. Chiang, "Duration, Immunization, and Hedging with Interest Rate Futures," *Journal of Financial Research*, 10:4, Autumn 1982, pp. 161-170.

Kolb, R. and R. Chiang, "Improving Hedging Performance Using Interest Rate Futures," *Financial Management*, 10:4, 1981, pp. 72-79.

Kolb, R. and G. Gay, "The Performance of Live Cattle Futures as Predictors of Subsequent Spot Prices," *Journal of Futures Markets*, 3:1, Spring 1983, pp. 55-63.

Kolb, R., G. Gay, and J. Jordan, "Are There Arbitrage Opportunities in the Treasury-Bond Futures Market?" *Journal of Futures Markets*, 2:3, Fall 1982, pp. 217-230.

Kolb, R., G. Gay, and J. Jordan, "Futures Prices and Expected Future Spot Prices," *Review of Research in Futures Markets*, 2:1, 1983, pp. 110-123.

Kolb, R. and P. T. Spiller, *The Hunt Silver Manipulation*, forthcoming from Yale University Press.

Koppenhaver, G. D., "Futures Market Regulation," *Economic Perspectives*, 11:1, January/February 1987, pp. 3-15.

Kritzman, M., "What's Wrong with Portfolio Insurance?" *Journal of Portfolio Management*, 13:1, Fall 1986, pp. 13-17.

Kyle, A., "A Theory of Futures Market Manipulations," in R. Anderson, *The Industrial Organization of Futures Markets*, Lexington, MA: D. C. Heath, 1984.

Landes, W., J. Stoffels, and J. Seifert, "An Empirical Test of a Duration-Based Hedge: The Case of Corporate Bonds," *The Journal of Futures Markets*, 5:2, Summer 1985, pp. 173-182.

Lane, M. N., "Round the Clock, Round the World," *FIA Review*, January/February 1990.

Lang, R., and R. Rasche, "A Comparison of Yields on Futures Contracts and Implied Forward Rates," in G. Gay and R. Kolb, *Interest Rate Futures: Concepts and Issues*, Richmond, VA: Robert F. Dame, Inc., 1982.

Lasser, D., "Influence of Treasury Bill Futures Trading on the Primary Sale of the Deliverable Treasury Bill," *The Journal of Futures Markets*, 22:4, November 1987, pp. 391-402.

Lasser, D., "A Measure of Ex-Ante Hedging Effectiveness for the Treasury-Bill and Treasury-Bond Futures Markets," working paper.

Lee, W., T. Maness, and D. Tuttle, "Non-Speculative Behavior and the Term Structure," *Journal of Financial and Quantitative Analysis*, 15:1, March 1980, pp. 53-83.

Leuthold, R., "The Price Performance on the Futures Market of a Nonstorable Commodity; Live Beef Cattle," *American Journal of Agricultural Economics*, 56:2, May 1974, pp. 271-279.

Leuthold, R. and W. Tomek, "Developments in the Livestock Futures Literature," in R. Leuthold and P. Dixon, *Livestock Futures Research Symposium*, Chicago: Chicago Mercantile Exchange, 1980.

Levich, R., "Are Forward Exchange Rates Unbiased Predictors of Future Spot Rates?" *Columbia Journal of World Business*, 14:4, Winter 1979, pp. 49-61.

Levich, R., "Currency Forecasters Lose Their Way," *Euromoney*, August 1983.

Levich, R., "The Efficiency of Markets for Foreign Exchange: A Review and Extension," in G. Gay and R. Kolb, *International Finance: Concepts and Issues*, Richmond, VA: Robert F. Dame, Inc., 1982, p. 406.

Levich, R., "Evaluating the Performance of the Forecasters," in R. Ensor (ed.) *The Management of Foreign Exchange Risk*, Second Edition, Euromoney Publications, 1982, pp. 121-134.

Levine, R., "The Pricing of Forward Exchange Rates," *Journal of International Money and Finance*, 8:2, 1989, pp. 163-179.

Lien, D. H. D., "Entry-Deterring Contract Specification on Futures Markets," *Journal of Futures Markets*, 10:1, February 1990, pp. 89-95.

Little, P., "Financial Futures and Immunization," *Journal of Financial Research*, 9:1, Spring 1986, pp. 1-12.

Lockwood, L. and S. Linn, "An Examination of Stock Market Return Volatility During Overnight and Intraday Periods, 1964-1989," *Journal of Finance*, 45:2, June 1990, pp. 591-601.

Loosigian, A., *Interest Rate Futures*, Princeton, NJ: Dow Jones Books, Inc., 1980.

Lukac, L. P., B. W. Brorsen, and S.H. Irwin, "Similarity of Computer Guided Technical Trading Systems," *The Journal of Futures Markets*, 8:1, February 1988, pp. 1-13.

Lukac, L. P., B. W. Brorsen, and S. H. Irwin, "A Test of Futures Market Disequilibrium Using Twelve Different Technical Trading Systems," *Applied Economics*, 20:5, May 1988, pp. 623-639.

Lukac, L. P., B. W. Brorsen, and S. H. Irwin, "The Usefulness of Historical Data in Selecting Parameters for Technical Trading Systems," *The Journal of Futures Markets*, 9:1, February 1989, pp. 55-65.

Luskin, D. L., *Portfolio Insurance: A Guide to Dynamic Hedging*, New York: J. Wiley, 1988.

Lypny, G., "Hedging Foreign Exchange Risk with Currency Futures: Portfolio Effects," *The Journal of Futures Markets*, 8:6, 1988, pp. 703-715.

Ma, C., R. Rao, and R. Sears, "Volatility, Price Resolution, and the Effectiveness of Price Limits," *Journal of Financial Services Research*, 3:3, December 1989, pp. 165-199.

Macaulay, F., *Some Theoretical Problems Suggested by the Movements of Interest Rates, Bond Yields, and Stock Prices in the United States Since 1856*, New York: Columbia University Press, 1938.

MacKinlay, A. and K. Ramaswamy, "Index-Futures Arbitrage and the Behavior of Stock Idex Futures Prices," *The Review of Financial Studies*, 1:2, Summer 1988, pp. 137-158.

Malkiel, B., "Expectations, Bond Prices, and the Term Structure of Interest Rates," *Quarterly Journal of Economics*, 76:2, May 1962, pp. 197-218.

Mann R. and R. G. Heifner, "The Distribution of Short-Run Commodity Price Movements," Technical Bulletin No. 1536, ERS, United States Department of Agriculture, 1976.

Martell, T. F. and A. S. Wolf, "Determinants of Trading Volume in Futures Markets," *The Journal of Futures Markets*, 7:3, June 1987, pp. 233-244.

Mayer, T., "SPAN-ning the Margin Problem for Commodity Options," *Futures*, December 1989.

McCulloch, J., "An Estimate of the Liquidity Premium," *Journal of Political Economy*, 83:1, Part 1, February 1975, pp. 95-119.

McCurdy, T. and I. Morgan, "Tests of the Martingale Hypothesis for Foreign Currency Futures," *International Journal of Forecasting*, 3, 1987, pp. 131-148.

McMurray, S., "Futures Pit Trader Goes to Trial," *The Wall Street Journal*, May 8, 1990.

McMurray, S., "What Went Wrong in Chicago Pits Case," *The Wall Street Journal*, July 11, 1990.

Meese, R. and K. Rogoff, "Empirical Exchange Rate Models of the Seventies: Do They Fit Out of Sample?" *Journal of International Economics*, 14, February 1983, pp. 3-24.

Meiselman, D. *The Term Structure of Interest Rates*, Englewood Cliffs, NJ: Prentice Hall, Inc. 1962.

Merrick, J., "Early Unwindings and Rollovers of Stock Index Futures Arbitrage Programs: Analysis and Implications for Predicting Expiration Day Effects," *The Journal of Futures Markets*, 9:2, 1989, pp. 101-111.

Merrick, J., "Portfolio Insurance with Stock Index Futures," *The Journal of Futures Markets*, 8:4, 1988, pp. 441-455.

Merton, R. C., "Theory of Rational Option Pricing," *Bell Journal of Economics and Management Science*, 4:1, 1973, pp. 141-183.

Miller, M., "Volatility, Episodic Volatility and Coordinated Circuit-Breakers," keynote address 2nd Annual Pacific-Basin Finance Conference, Bangkok, Thailand, June 1990.

Miller, M., B. Malkiel, M. Scholes, and J. Hawke, "Stock Index Futures and the Crash of '87," *Journal of Applied Corporate Finance*, 1:4, Winter 1989, pp. 6-17.

Miller, M. and F. Modigliani, "The Cost of Capital, Corporate Finance, and the Theory of Investment," *American Economic Review*, 48:3, June 1958, pp. 261-297.

Milonas, N. T., "Price Variability and the Maturity Effect in Futures Markets," *The Journal of Futures Markets*, 6:3, Fall 1986, pp. 443-460.

Modest, D., "On the Pricing of Stock Index Futures," *Journal of Portfolio Management*, 10:4, Summer 1984, pp. 51-57.

Modest, D., and M. Sundaresan, "The Relationship Between Spot and Futures Prices in Stock Index Futures Markets: Some Preliminary Evidence," *The Journal of Futures Markets*, 3:1, Spring 1983, pp. 15-41.

Modigliani, F. and R. Sutch, "Innovations in Interest Rate Policy," *American Economic Review*, 56:2, May 1966, pp. 178-197.

Monroe, M. and R. Cohn, "The Relative Efficiency of the Gold and Treasury Bill Futures Markets," *The Journal of Futures Markets*, 6:3, Fall 1986, pp. 477-493.

Morgan, D., *Merchants of Grain*, New York: Penguin Books, 1982.

Morgan, G. E., "Forward and Futures Pricing of Treasury Bills," *Journal of Banking and Finance*, 5:4, December 1981, pp. 483-496.

Moriarty, E. J. and P. A. Tosini, "Futures Trading and the Price Volatility of GNMA Certificates-Further Evidence," *The Journal of Futures Markets*, 5:4, Winter 1985, pp. 633-641.

Moser, J., "Circuit Breakers," *Economic Perspectives*, Federal Reserve Bank of Chicago, September/October 1990, pp. 2-13.

Murphy, J. A., "Futures Fund Performance: A Test of the Effectiveness of Technical Analysis," *The Journal of Futures Markets*, 6:2, Summer 1986, pp. 175-185.

Muth, J.F., "Rational Expectations and the Theory of Price Movements," *Econometrica*, 29:3, July 1961, pp. 315-335.

Myers, S., "A Time State-Preference Model of Security Valuation," *Journal of Financial and Quantitative Analysis*, 3:1, March 1968, pp. 1-33.

Neftci, S. N. and A. J. Policano, "Can Chartists Outperform the Market? Market Efficiency Tests for Technical Analysis," *The Journal of Futures Markets*, 4:4, Winter 1984, pp. 465–478.

Nelson, C. "Estimation of Term Premiums from Average Yield Differentials in the Term Structure of Interest Rates," *Econometrica*, 40:2, Part 1, March 1972, pp. 277–287.

O'Brien, T., "The Mechanics of Portfolio Insurance," *Journal of Portfolio Management*, 14:3, Spring 1988, pp. 40–47.

Ogden, J. and A. Tucker, "Empirical Tests of the Efficiency of the Currency Futures Options Market," *The Journal of Futures Markets*, 7:6, December 1987, pp. 695–703.

Palme, L. and J. Graham, "The Systematic Downward Bias in Live Cattle Futures: An Evaluation," *Journal of Futures Markets,* 1:3, Fall 1981, pp. 359–366.

Park, H., "Reexamination of Normal Backwardation Hypothesis in Futures Markets," *Journal of Futures Markets*, 5:4, Winter 1985, pp. 505–515.

Park, H. and A. Chen, "Differences Between Futures and Forward Prices: A Further Investigation of the Marking-to-Market Effects," *Journal of Futures Markets*, Spring 1985, 5:1, pp. 77–88.

Peters, E., "The Growing Efficiency of Index-Futures Markets," *The Journal of Portfolio Management*, 11:4, pp. 84–85.

Petzel, T., "The Time Series Behavior of Corn and Soybean Prices," Unpublished, Food Research Institute, Stanford University, 1980.

Phillips-Patrick, F. and T. Schneeweis, "The Weekend Effect for Stock Indexes and Stock Index Futures: Dividend and Interest Rate Effects," *The Journal of Futures Markets*, 8:1, 1988, pp. 115–121.

Pierog, K. and J. Stein, "New Contracts: What Makes Them Fly or Fail?" *Futures*, September 1989.

Pinsky, N. and J. Kvasnicka, "The European Monetary System," in G. Gay and R. Kolb, *International Finance: Concepts and Issues*, Richmond, VA: Robert F. Dame, Inc., 1982.

Poole, W., "Using T-Bill Futures to Gauge Interest-Rate Expectations," in G. Gay and R. Kolb, *Interest Rate Futures: Concepts and Issues*, Richmond, VA: Robert F. Dame, Inc., 1982.

Powers, M., "Does Futures Trading Reduce Price Fluctuations in the Cash Markets?" *American Economic Review*, 60:3, June 1970, pp. 460–464.

Pring, M. J., *The McGraw–Hill Handbook of Commodities and Futures*, New York: McGraw-Hill, 1985.

Puglisi, D., "Is the Futures Market for Treasury Bills Efficient?" in G. Gay and R. Kolb, *Interest Rate Futures: Concepts and Issues*, Richmond, VA: Robert F. Dame, Inc., 1982.

Purcell, W., D. Flood, and J. Plaxico, "Cash-Futures Interrelationships in Live Cattle: Causality, Variability, and Pricing Processes," in R. Leuthold and P. Dixon, *Livestock Futures Research Symposium*, Chicago: Chicago Mercantile Exchange, 1980.

Raynauld, J. and J. Tessier, "Risk Premiums in Futures Markets: An Empirical Investigation," *Journal of Futures Markets*, 4:2, Summer 1984, pp. 189-211.

Rendleman, R. and C. Carabini, "The Efficiency of the Treasury Bill Futures Market," *Journal of Finance*, 34:4, 1979, pp. 895-914.

Resnick, B., "The Relationship Between Futures Prices for U. S. Treasury Bonds," *Review of Research in Futures Markets*, 1984, 3:1, pp. 88-104.

Resnick, B. and E. Hennigar, "The Relationship Between Futures and Cash Prices for U.S. Treasury Bonds," *Review of Research in Futures Markets*, 2:3, 1983, pp. 282-299.

Richard, S. and M. Sundaresan. "A Continuous Time Equilibrium Model of Forward Prices and Futures Prices in a Multigood Economy," *Journal of Financial Economics*, 9:4, December 1981, pp. 347-371.

Ritchken, P., *Options: Theory, Strategy, and Applications*, Glenview, IL: Scott, Foresman and Co., 1987.

Rockwell, C., "Normal Backwardation, Forecasting and the Returns to Commodity Futures Traders," *Food Research Institute Studies*, 7 (supplement), 1967, pp. 107-130.

Roll, R., "The International Crash of October 1987," *Financial Analysts Journal*, 44:5, September-October 1988, pp. 19-35.

Roll, R. and B. Solnik, "On Some Parity Conditions Encounter Frequently in International Economics," *Journal of Macroeconomics*, 1:3, Summer 1979, pp. 267-283.

Rosenbaum, A., "Are Exchange Fees Worth Scrutiny of Traders?" *Futures*, July 1990.

Ross, R. L., "Financial Consequences of Trading Commodity Futures Contracts," *Illinois Agricultural Economics*, 1975, pp. 27-31.

Rubinstein, M., "Alternative Paths to Portfolio Insurance," *Financial Analysts Journal*, 41:4, July-August 1985, pp. 42-52.

Rutledge, D. J. S., "A Note on the Variability of Futures Prices," *Review of Economics and Statistics*, 58:1, February 1976, pp. 118-120.

Rutz, R. D., "The Myth and Reality of Intermarket Cross-Margining," *Intermarket*, 5:8, August 1988 pp. 18-21..

Rzepczynski, M., "Risk Premiums in Financial Futures Markets: The Case of Treasury Bond Futures," *The Journal of Futures Markets*, 7:6, December 1987, pp. 653-662.

Samuelson, P., "Asset Allocation Could Be Dangerous to Your Health," *Journal of Portfolio Management*, 16:3, Spring 1990, pp. 5-8.

Samuelson, P. "Proof that Properly Anticipated Prices Fluctuate Randomly," *Industrial Management Review*, 6:2, Spring 1965, pp. 41–49.

Santomero, A. "The Error Learning Hypothesis and the Term Structure of Interest Rates in Eurodollars," *Journal of Finance*, 30:3, June 1975, pp. 773–783.

Santoni, G., "Has Programmed Trading Made Stock Prices More Volatile?" *Review*, Federal Reserve Bank of St. Louis, May 1987, pp. 18–29.

Santoni, G., "The October Crash: Some Evidence on the Cascade Theory," *Review*, Federal Reserve Bank of St. Louis, May/June 1988, pp. 18–33.

Sargent, T. J., "Commodity Price Expectations and the Interest Rate," *Quarterly Journal of Economics*, 83:1, February 1969, pp. 127–140.

Saunders, E. and A. Mahajan, "An Empirical Examination of Composite Stock Index Futures Pricing," *The Journal of Futures Markets*, 8:2, 1988, pp. 211–228.

Savit, R., "When Random Is Not Random: An Introduction to Chaos in Market Prices," *The Journal of Futures Markets*, 8:3, June 1988, pp. 271–290.

Schap, K. and C. Flory, "Ferruzzi vs. CBOT: Who Is Right?" *Futures*, September 1989.

Schwert, G., "Stock Market Volatility," *Financial Analysts Journal*, 46:3, May/June 1990, pp. 23–34.

Schwert, G., "Stock Volatility and the Crash of '87," *The Review of Financial Studies*, 3:1, 1990, pp. 77–102.

Sharpe, W., *Investments*, Englewood Cliffs, NJ: Prentice Hall, Inc., 1981.

Silber, W. L., "Marketmaker Behavior in an Auction Market: An Analysis of Scalpers in Futures Markets," *Journal of Finance*, 39:4, September 1984, pp. 937–953.

Siler, C., "Fraud Busters," *Forbes*, February 19, 1990.

Singleton, J. and R. Grieves, "Synthetic Puts and Portfolio Insurance Strategies," *Journal of Portfolio Management*, 10:3, Spring 1984, pp. 63–69.

Sinkey, J., *Commercial Bank Financial Management*, New York: Macmillan Co., 1989.

Sinquefield, J., "Understanding Options on Futures," *Mortgage Banking*, July 1982, pp. 35–40.

Smith, C. and R. Stulz, "The Determinants of Firms' Hedging Policies," *Journal of Financial and Quantitative Analysis*, 20:4, December 1985, pp. 391–405.

So, J. C., "The Sub-Gaussian Distribution of Currency Futures: Stable Paretian or Nonstationary?" *Review of Economics and Statistics*, 69:1, February 1987, pp. 100–107.

Stevenson R. A. and R. M. Bear, "Commodity Futures: Trends or Random Walks?" *Journal of Finance*, 25:1, March 1970, pp. 65–81.

Stewart, B., "An Analysis of Speculative Trading in Grain Futures," *U.S.D.A* Technical Bulletin, No. 1001, 1949.

Stigum, M. *The Money Market*, Homewood, IL: Dow Jones-Irwin, 1983, Revised Edition.

Stoll, H., "Index Futures, Program Trading and Stock Market Procedures," *The Journal of Futures Markets*, 8:4, 1988, pp. 391-412.

Stoll, H., "The Relationship Between Put and Call Option Prices," *Journal of Finance*, 24:5, December 1969, pp. 801-824.

Stoll, H. and R. Whaley, "Expiration Day Effects of Index Options and Futures," New York University: Monograph Series in Finance and Economics, 1986.

Stoll, H. and R. Whaley, "Program Trading and Expiration Day Effects," *Financial Analysts Journal*, 43:2, March-April 1987, pp. 16-28.

Stulz, R., "Optimal Hedging Policies," *Journal of Financial and Quantitative Analysis*, 19:2, June 1984, pp. 127-140.

Swanson, P. and S. Caples, "Hedging Foreign Exchange Risk Using Forward Foreign Exchange Markets: An Extension," *Journal of International Business Studies*, 18:1, Spring 1987, pp. 75-82.

Tamarkin, R. , *The New Gatsbys: Fortunes and Misfortunes of Commodity Traders*, New York: William Morrow and Company, Inc., 1985, pp. 26, 43.

Tauchen, R. and M. Pitts, "The Price Variability-Volume Relationship on Speculative Markets," *Econometrica*, 51:2, Part 1, March 1983, pp. 485-505.

Taylor, G. and R. Leuthold, "The Influence of Futures Trading on Cash Cattle Price Variations," *Food Research Institute Studies*, 13, 1974.

Taylor, S. J., "The Behavior of Futures Prices over Time," *Applied Economics*, 17:4, August 1985, pp. 713-734

Taylor, S. J., *Modelling Financial Time Series*, New York: John Wiley, 1986.

Telser, L., "Futures Trading and the Storage of Cotton and Wheat," in A. Peck, *Selected Writings on Futures Markets*, Chicago: Chicago Board of Trade, 1977.

Telser, L., and P. Cootner, "Returns to Speculators: Telser vs. Keynes," in A. Peck, *Selected Writings on Futures Markets*, Chicago: Chicago Board of Trade, 1977.

Thomas, L., "Random Walk Profits in Currency Futures Trading," *The Journal of Futures Markets*, 6:1, 1986, pp. 109-125.

Thosar, S. and S. Trigeorgis, "Stock Volatility and Program Trading: Theory and Evidence," *Journal of Applied Corporate Finance*, Winter 1990, pp. 91-96.

Toevs, A. and D. Jacob, "Futures and Alternative Hedge Ratio Methodologies," *Journal of Portfolio Management*, 12:3, Spring 1986, pp. 60-70.

Tomek, W. G. and S. F. Querin, "Random Processes in Prices and Technical Analysis," *The Journal of Futures Markets*, 4:1, Spring 1984, pp. 15-23.

Tosini, P., "Stock Index Futures and Stock Market Activity in October 1987," *Financial Analysts Journal*, 44:1, January/February 1988, pp. 28-37.

U.S. Congress, Office of Technology Assessment, "Electronic Bulls & Bears: U.S. Securities Markets & Information Technology," OTA-CIT-469, Washington, DC, September 1990.

Venkataramanan, L., *The Theory of Futures Trading*, New York: Asia Publishing House, 1965.

Vignola, A. and C. Dale, "Is the Futures Market for Treasury Bills Efficient?" in G. Gay and R. Kolb, *Interest Rate Futures: Concepts and Issues*, Richmond, VA: Robert F. Dame, Inc., 1982.

Wang, G., E. Moriarty, R. Michalski, and J. Jordan, "Empirical Analysis of the Liquidity of the S&P 500 Index Futures Market During the October 1987 Market Break," Commodity Futures Trading Commission Staff Working Paper #88-6, February 1989.

Weiner, N., "The Hedging Rationale for a Stock Index Futures Contract," *Journal of Futures Markets*, 1:1, Spring 1981, pp. 59-76.

Westerfield, J., "How U.S. Multinationals Manage Currency Risk;" L. Jacque, "Management of Foreign Exchange Risk: A Review Article;" in G. Gay and R. Kolb, *International Finance: Concepts and Issues*, Richmond, VA: Robert F. Dame, Inc., 1982.

Whaley, R., "Valuation of American Futures Options: Theory and Empirical Tests," *Journal of Finance,* 41:1, March 1986, pp. 127-150.

Williams, J., *The Economic Function of Futures Markets*, Cambridge: Cambridge University Press, 1986.

Wilson, W., "Hedging Effectiveness of U.S. Wheat Futures Markets," *Review of Research in Futures Markets*, 3:1, 1984, pp. 64-79.

Wilson, W., "Option Price Behavior in Grain Futures Markets," *The Journal of Futures Markets*, 8:1, February 1988, pp. 47-65.

Wilson W. and H. Fung , "Information Content of Volatilities Implied by Option Premiums in Grain Futures Markets," *Journal of Futures Markets*, 10:1, February 1990, pp. 13-27.

Witt, H., T. Schroeder, and M. Hayenga, "Comparison of Analytical Approaches for Estimating Hedge Ratios for Agricultural Commodities," *The Journal of Futures Markets*, 7:2, April 1987, pp. 135-146.

Working, H. "Financial Results of Speculative Holding of Wheat," in A. Peck, *Selected Writings on Futures Markets*, Chicago: Chicago Board of Trade, 1977, pp. 79-120.

Working, H., "Hedging Reconsidered," *Journal of Farm Economics*, 35:4, November 1953, pp. 544-561.

Working, H., "Price Effects of Futures Trading," *Food Research Institute Studies*, 1, 1960.

Wright, B. and J. Williams, "A Theory of Negative Prices for Storage," *The Journal of Futures Markets*, 9:1, February 1989, pp. 1-13.

Zhu, Y. and R. Kavee, "Performance of Portfolio Insurance Strategies," *Journal of Portfolio Management*, 14:3, Spring 1988, pp. 48-54.

Name Index

Subject Index

Above full carry, 111
Abusive trading practices, 62
Academic arbitrage, 89
Accommodation trading, 62
Account executive as broker, 6
Accrued interest, 243, 279n
  option of, 357
Accuracy, in price discovery, 149-50
Agricultural commodities, future options on, 579
Agricultural contracts, 20-21
Agricultural markets, sources of information on, 36n
Alerts Window, 57
American options, 576, 581
  versus European options, 583-84
  graphical approach to, 584-85
  on physicals and futures, 590-93
  values of approximating, 586-87
Anticipatory hedge, 25, 172
Arbitrage, 89-90
  academic, 89
  cash-and-carry, 91-95, 97, 100, 105, 109, 115
  covered interest, 510
  croissant, 515-16
  cross-rate, 498-99
  and efficiency of foreign exchange futures markets, 521-22
  geographical, 497-98
  and interest rate futures, 305-8
  and pricing call options at expiration, 546-47
  profit from, 83
  reverse cash-and-carry, 93, 97, 101, 105
  and stock index futures efficiency, 446
  in Treasury-bond futures market, 349-53
Arbitrage boundaries, 102
Arbitrageur, 89
Around-the-clock trading, 53-54
Artificial price, 31-32
Asian dollars, 279n

Asked price, 99
Asset allocation, 465, 489n
Associated person (AP), 51
At the money, 557
Audit trails, 61-62
Aurora, 74n
Autocorrelation, 136
  evidence on, in futures price changes, 137
  first order, 136-37

Backwardation, 114
  normal, 118-23, 174
Balance of payments, 504
  influence of, on exchange rates, 504-5
Banker's acceptance, 144n
Bankers' Trust Company, 495
Bank immunization case, 269-72, 401-4
Basis, 77, 83-87, 205
Basis point, 283
Basis point (BP) model, 388-91, 398
Bear market, 437
  and altering beta of portfolio, 462
Bear spread, 217-20
Below full carry, 111
Beta(s), 458
  altering, of portfolio, 461-64
Bias, in market, 296
Bid-asked spread, 99
Bid price, 99
Black-Scholes Model, and pricing of futures options, 581-82
Bond(s)
  accrued interest, 243
  bond portfolio maturity strategies, 267-69
  and changing interest rates, 250
  duration, 252-54
  major money and bond market instruments, 244-47
  money market yield calculations, 243-44
  need for summary measure, 251-52
  passing of time, 247, 249
  portfolio immunization techniques, 269-76

Fixed loan rate, 373-74
  converting floating rate to, 374-76
Floating rate loan, 373-74
  converting to fixed loan rate, 374-76
Floor broker, 6, 50-51, 60
Floor trader, 60
Forced sell-off, 44
Forecasting oil prices, 151-52
  performance for different commodities,
    152-53
Foreign currencies, 21
Foreign exchange forward market,
  characteristics of, 499-503
Foreign exchange futures, 494-95
  characteristics of market, 499-503
  determinants of foreign exchange rates,
    503-7
  efficiency of market, 521-24
  foreign exchange forecasting accuracy,
    518-19
  market-based forecasts, 521
  methodology for tests of forecasting
    accuracy, 519
  tests of market-based forecasts, 520-21
  forward and futures market characteristics,
    499-503
  forward and futures prices for foreign
    exchange, 507-9
  futures price parity relationships, 509
  deviations from interest rate parity,
    514-15
  expected future exchange rates, 517-18
  foreign exchange futures prices and
    interest rate parity and cost-of-carry
    model, 510-13
  interest rate parity theorem, 509-10
  purchasing power and interest rate parity,
    517
  purchasing power parity theorem, 515-16
  geographical and cross-rate arbitrage,
    497-99
  hedging with, 528-29
  hedging import/export transactions,
    530-32
  hedging transaction exposure, 529-30
  recent studies of hedging strategies,
    534-35
  translation exposure, 532-34

price quotations, 495-97
prices and expected future exchange rates,
  517-18
speculation in, with an outright position,
  524-25
Foreign exchange futures market
  characteristics of, 499-503
  efficiency of, 521-24
Foreign exchange rates, determinants of,
  503-7
Foreign exchanges, growth of, 52
Foreign products, U.S. trading of, 55
Forward contracts
  Black model for options on, 582-83
  comparison of, with futures contracts,
    4-18
  definition of, 2
  origins of, 2-3
  value of call option on, 582
Forward market
  organization of, 6
  trading of foreign currencies in, 494
Forward prices
  for foreign exchange, 507-9
  versus futures prices, 131-34
Forward rates of interest, 256, 258-59
  and futures yield, 309-310
Freely floating currency, 507
Front running, 28-29, 62, 63
Full carry market
  concept of, 111-14
  precious metals in, 198-204
Futures, versus options futures, 608-9
Futures Commission Merchant (FCM), 51
Futures contract
  agricultural contracts, 20-21
  comparison of with forward contracts,
    4-18
  foreign currencies, 21
  indexes, 21-22
  innovation, 47
  interest-earning assets, 21
  manipulating price of, 64
  metallurgical contracts, 21
  mutual obligations of buyer and seller,
    34-35n
  standardized terms, 6-8
  success of, 47

fixed and floating loan rates, 373-76
hedging with T-bond futures, 384-87
basis point (BP) model, 388-91
conversion factor (CF) model, 388
face value naive (FVN) model, 387
market value naive (MVN) model, 387-88
price sensitivity (PS) model, 393-95
regression (RGR) model, 391-93
immunization with interest rate futures, 396-97
bank immunization case, 401-4
planning period case, 397-401
strip and stack hedges, 377-81
tailing the hedge, 381-84
Treasury-bill investment
lengthening the maturity, 372-73
shortening the maturity of, 371-72
T-bill/T-bond spread, 319-21
Treasury bond, 246-47
around-the-clock trading in, 54
Treasury bond futures, 43, 289-96, 337
cost-of-carry model for, 311
cheapest-to-deliver bond, 338-49
case of intervening coupons, 343-47
case of no intervening coupons, 339-43
and the implied repo rate, 347-49
hedging with, 384-87
review of, 338
and risk arbitrage, 349 53
seller's options in, 353
end-of-the-month option, 357
in the real market, 357-61
wildcard option, 353-56
Treasury/Eurodollar (TED) spread, 322
Treasury note, 246-47
Treasury-note futures, 297-99
Triple witching hour, 477-78
volatility associated with, 491n
Turn of the year effect, 488n

Unbiased predictor, 519
Unequal borrowing and lending rates, 433-34
and stock index futures trading, 433
Unsystematic risk, 462-63

Value Line Contract on the Kansas City Board of Trade, 442n
Value Line Index, 22
Value weighted index, 413
Variation margin, 11, 13, 41
Volatility, of futures prices, 137-40

The Wall Street Journal, 76, 77, 288, 289-90, 322, 495, 496
Wash trading, 62
Weak form of the efficient markets hypothesis, 168
Wheat
cost-of-carry model in, 211-14
hedging, 233-35
trading of contracts in, 46-47
and wheat futures, 205-11
Whipsawed, 223
Wiener process, 563
Wildcard option, 353-56
Worldwide exchanges, 18
Writer of an option, 541-42
Writing an option, 541-42

Yield concepts, 241-42
accrued interest, 243
major money and bond market instruments, 244-47
money market yield calculations, 243-44
Yield curve
liquidity premium theory on, 265, 266
with long hedge, 326
market segmentation hypothesis on, 265-66
and notes over bonds spread, 323
pure expectations theory of, 265
Yield, discount, 243
Yield to maturity, 242

Zero betas, 125
Zero exercise price call option with, and infinite time until expiration, 551-52
Zero sum game
futures market as, 362
options market as, 551